Learning to Teach Everyone's Children

EQUITY, EMPOWERMENT, AND EDUCATION THAT IS MULTICULTURAL

CARL A. GRANT
University of Wisconsin

MAUREEN D. GILLETTE
Northeastern Illinois University

THOMSON
★
WADSWORTH

Australia • Brazil • Canada • Mexico • Singapore
Spain • United Kingdom • United States

THOMSON

WADSWORTH

Learning to Teach Everyone's Children: Equity, Empowerment, and Education That Is Multicultural
Carl A. Grant and Maureen D. Gillette

Publisher: *Vicki Knight*
Acquisitions Editor: *Dan Alpert*
Development Editor: *Tangelique Williams*
Assistant Editor: *Jennifer Keever*
Editorial Assistant: *Larkin Page-Jacobs*
Technology Project Manager: *Barry Connolly*
Marketing Manager: *Terra Schultz*
Marketing Assistant: *Dory Schaeffer*
Marketing Communications Manager: *Tami Strang*
Senior Project Manager, Editorial Production: *Kimberly Adams*
Executive Art Director: *Maria Epes*

Print Buyer: *Karen Hunt*
Permissions Editor: *Sarah Harkrader*
Production Service: *Scratchgravel Publishing Services*
Photo Researcher: *Robin Sterling*
Copy Editor: *Margaret C. Tropp*
Cover Designer: *Irene Morris*
Cover Image: *Arthur Tilley and David Buffington/Getty Images*
Cover Printer: *Transcontinental Printing/Louiseville*
Compositor: *Cadmus Professional Communications*
Printer: *Transcontinental Printing/Louiseville*

Printed in Canada
1 2 3 4 5 6 7 09 08 07 06 05

For more information about our products, contact us at:
Thomson Learning Academic Resource Center
1-800-423-0563

For permission to use material from this text or product, submit a request online at **http://www.thomsonrights.com**. Any additional questions about permissions can be submitted by email to **thomsonrights@thomson.com**.

Library of Congress Control Number: 2005923115

ISBN 0-534-64467-8

Thomson Higher Education
10 Davis Drive
Belmont, CA 94002-3098
USA

Asia (including India)
Thomson Learning
5 Shenton Way
#01-01 UIC Building
Singapore 068808

Australia/New Zealand
Thomson Learning Australia
102 Dodds Street
Southbank, Victoria 3006
Australia

Canada
Thomson Nelson
1120 Birchmount Road
Toronto, Ontario M1K 5G4
Canada

UK/Europe/Middle East/Africa
Thomson Learning
High Holborn House
50–51 Bedford Row
London WC1R 4LR
United Kingdom

Latin America
Thomson Learning
Seneca, 53
Colonia Polanco
11560 Mexico
D.F. Mexico

Spain (including Portugal)
Thomson Paraninfo
Calle Magallanes, 25
28015 Madrid, Spain

DEDICATION

Throughout my life, including my professional career, I have been blessed with friends who ask the tough questions and demand thoughtful responses. I want to recognize nine individuals, most of whom I have known for a lifetime, who have been great mentors and sources of valued personal and professional support to me and to one another. It is rare, even today, to see ten Black men—who all work in the field of education and are committed to social justice in education for all children—share this type of relationship with one another.

To these friends (whom I call the "guys")—

Ernest Billups
Stan Conners
Robert Crumpton
Ernest M. Grant
William Norwood
Lonnie Phillips
Robert Saddler
James B. Wilder
Edward Wilson

—and to great friendships everywhere, I dedicate this book. Thanks, guys!

—Carl

To my parents, Tom and Lois McDonough, who together taught me almost everything I know about good teaching.

—Maureen

Contents

Chapter 2

Becoming an Effective Teacher   52

Chapter 3

The Dilemmas of Discipline and Classroom Management   94

Chapter 4

Curriculum   135

Chapter 5

Teaching, Planning, and Assessment   172

Chapter 10
Teachers' and Students' Rights and Responsibilities   372

Foreword

Learning to Teach Everyone's Children is a book about teaching and learning to teach. There are many such books on the market, commonly used in all sorts of teacher education courses and programs at universities and colleges across the country to introduce students to teaching and to the whole field of education. Many of these books have similar chapter headings and cover the same territory.

But *Learning to Teach Everyone's Children* is different from most. This book encourages you, as a person preparing to teach (or thinking about becoming a teacher), to ask yourself hard questions about teaching, learning, and schooling and to think from the beginning about equity, diversity, and empowerment.

When I first read this book, I said to myself, "At last, a book for prospective teachers that puts equity and multicultural issues at the beginning *and* throughout each of its chapters. At last, a book that connects diversity to the everyday realities of classroom life." Many other books that introduce prospective teachers to teaching and to the field of education include a separate chapter on these issues (often toward the back of the book with the other "current" issues). Many teacher education programs that prepare teachers for initial teaching certification offer a separate course that addresses these topics (often referred to as the "diversity course" and sometimes optional or set apart from the rest of the required curriculum). What message do separate chapters toward the end of the books possibly convey to prospective teachers and their instructors? What else can they convey but the message that issues of equity, access, and diversity are separate from the rest of what teachers have to deal with? What message do separate optional courses convey? What else can they convey but that worrying about equity is optional, or at least supplementary, to the real work of teaching?

This book is different. This book puts issues of equity, empowerment, and multicultural education front and center. It takes what some sometimes call a "both-and" approach to these issues. This book concentrates specifically on equity, empowerment, and multicultural issues in certain parts of the chapters, as in the vignette in Chapter 3, where a teacher candidate is challenged by her instructor to think about the racial and cultural stereotypes that seem to be influencing the management choices she makes in the classroom. But the book also integrates equity, empowerment, and multicultural issues into its discussion of all the other topics in the book, as in Chapter 11 on school finance, which raises questions about the different resources that suburban and urban schools have available to them to provide education for students. This is what the both-and approach means—*both* concentrating explicitly on equity, diversity, and multicultural issues *and* showing how these are connected and relevant to the more general topics in teaching and education.

This book asks you to take an active thinking stance about teaching and learning to teach. Such a perspective is much different from just reading the chapters in a textbook and highlighting important ideas with a colored marker. Each chapter in this book provides very helpful ways for you to actively reflect on who you are, what you believe, and what you will be up against as a multicultural teacher. Each chapter provides concrete ways for you to take the ideas to another level and make connections among theories, history, current practice, and school policies. As a teacher educator myself for many years and as a firm believer in the kind of teaching that the authors of this book are discussing, I strongly urge you to follow up on their suggestions. Really reflect on the questions they pose at the end of each chapter. Don't concentrate on what the "right answers" are supposed to be. Answer the questions for yourself. Try to connect what you have read to what you are seeing in schools or what you remember from your own school days. Do the activities that are suggested. Interview teachers, students, college instructors, and children. Keep systematic lists of the things you observe in schools. Participate in discussions with teachers and administrators at the schools you visit. Look up the electronic and other resources and the websites that are provided on each of the chapter's topics. Many of these activities and questions at the ends of the chapters give you a way to develop an active, questioning stance about what goes on in schools and classrooms. These activities ask you to be a participant, not just a passive observer, in your own process of learning to be a teacher.

The "Finding a Voice" section of each chapter, in particular, takes the big ideas the chapter deals with—educational philosophy, curriculum theory, school organization—and shows how these theories and concepts play out in real school situations. The stories and vignettes in these sections are very engaging and detailed. They present more than one side of each issue. They complicate things. They show what the dilemmas of teaching are. They encourage you to put yourself in the place of the teachers who are being described.

In a certain way, the chapter vignettes are all about empowerment. They offer profiles of teachers—most of them either student teachers or teachers who are in their first few years of teaching—who are struggling to challenge everyday school practices that are not in the best interests of children and equity. The authors of this book call this "boat rocking." In my own work with student teachers, I have called this "teaching against the grain." Both terms describe teachers who are empowered to teach in ways that are multicultural and equitable for all students even if those ways don't fit neatly with what the rest of the school is doing. Both terms describe teachers who are working both within and against the educational system that has traditionally disadvantaged certain groups of students. When teachers are empowered to teach against the grain, they work to empower their students to be lifelong learners who think critically and are not afraid to challenge the system as well.

This book has very lofty and important goals. But one of the things I like best about it is that it also provides very practical information. The authors tell you what is involved in becoming certified as a teacher, looking for a job, and being interviewed. They provide information about the average teacher's salary in different areas across the country and show how a teacher's salary compares with the salaries of other professions. They explain educational governance, pointing out how federal and state legislation influence day-to-day work in schools and classrooms. They talk about your rights as a teacher and your students' rights as learners and participants in your classroom. They make clear why working with parents and communities is so important.

This book also introduces you to learning theories, philosophies of education, and the principles behind different pedagogical approaches. The book includes big thinkers and big ideas. The concepts are handled in ways that are theoretical as well as practical. Social psychologist Kurt Lewin once said that there is nothing so practical as a good theory. This book makes it clear why this is true. In each of the chapters where theoretical frameworks and philosophies are presented, the many vignettes, examples, and cases show how these ideas are connected to the real world of schools. The theoretical perspectives give you more tools for thinking and acting effectively in the classroom. Theory and practice are perfectly blended in this book, not artificially separated as is so often the case.

Anyone who is studying to be a teacher or considering teaching as a career will find this book extremely helpful. If you are reflective and actively engaged, this book will open your mind to issues you have never thought about before and inspire you to join with others who are working to make schools more caring, more just, and more multicultural places.

Marilyn Cochran-Smith
Lynch School of Education
Boston College

Preface

Writing this book has been a challenging and humbling task! We began this effort with a vision for a different type of text. It was a challenging task because in spite of our years of experience as classroom teachers, education professors, and scholars, we knew that to craft a book that infused throughout each chapter the issues of power and education that is multicultural would take time, perseverance, and a little bit of luck. We knew that we wanted our text to communicate to teacher candidates in a caring, "plain talk" manner the importance of understanding the complexities of education in the United States from a multicultural perspective. We wanted to delve into difficult educational issues that other texts often avoid. Substantive attention to the concepts of "power" and "education that is multicultural" was difficult to locate in most education texts we examined. To accomplish our goals, we would have to be good teachers through our writing. The Greek philosopher Plato wrote, "A need or problem encourages a creative effort to meet or solve the problem." So we tried to find creative ways to give a strong voice to education that is multicultural and to make visible the multiple discourses on power embodied in past and current educational practices and policies.

Writing this book was a humbling experience because, as we tested and retested each chapter with students in our programs, practicing teachers, and "no-nonsense" colleagues, we discovered that in order to be successful, we would have to leave our egos at the door and listen well to others. We listened to some harsh critiques at times, but we believe we learned from these experiences. That is what good teachers do in order to be successful. We want you to approach the process of learning to teach everyone's children with the same attitude: Listen to others, take careful note of feedback even if it is tough to take, and learn from your experiences.

Fundamental to the task of writing this book was the challenge to write an affordable text for teacher candidates. In doing so, we would be responsive to one of the foundational tenets of culturally responsive teaching: access to high-quality educational resources for all. *Learning to Teach Everyone's Children* is an immediate reference on becoming an effective teacher for all students, on working effectively with all families, on understanding the importance of the community to schooling, and on beginning to grapple with the complexities of the role of "teacher" in a diverse nation. In keeping the cost lower than that of other texts on the market, we hope that you will keep this book throughout your journey in the teaching profession, refer to it often, and let us know what you think about it in light of your experiences.

The values of equity and justice form the cornerstone of this book. We trust that if these values were at the core of educational policy and practice in districts, schools, and classrooms, the result would be equal educational outcomes for all students. But that has not been the case, nor does the current educational land-scape appear to offer much hope that all children will receive a free public educa-tion that provides them with the knowledge, skills, and dispositions to become full, participatory members of the United States. Currently, too many students complete their K–12 education inadequately prepared for college, for the world of work, and for active participation in our democracy. Our vision is that readers of this text will enter the teaching profession with a commitment to help all stu-dents achieve high levels of academic success and develop the skills (e.g., critical thinking) and dispositions (for example, empathy, open-mindedness) to become active citizens who continually work for the betterment of society. To that end, we have woven attention to equity, social justice, and fairness for all throughout each chapter.

Learning to Teach Everyone's Children includes 12 chapters and an epilogue. We believe that together they will help you build a foundation for teaching excel-lence. Chapter 1, "The Changing Face of Teaching and Learning," will introduce you to the context of teaching in the United States today. It will also begin to explain the twin themes of the text: power and education that is multicultural and social reconstructionist.

Chapter 2, "Becoming an Effective Teacher," begins the discussion of cultur-ally relevant teaching, a concept that is important for all teachers, regardless of the student population you serve. Chapter 3, "The Dilemmas of Discipline and Classroom Management," explains the difference between discipline and class-room management. We place this chapter near the beginning of the book because we know from experience that teacher candidates have student discipline upper-most in their minds and are often perplexed or scared by the thought of keeping the attention of an entire classroom of students. We also know from working with teachers and administrators that they believe teacher preparation programs should pay more attention to discipline and classroom management.

Chapter 4, "Curriculum," addresses the ways that decisions have historically been made about who selects the curriculum, whose story is represented in the curriculum, and who controls the resources for curriculum. The chapter presents some new ideas about curriculum development and implementation. Chapter 5, "Teaching, Planning, and Assessment," emphasizes the key linkages among these three concepts. Lesson and unit planning, interdisciplinary teaching, and authen-tic assessment are included.

Chapter 6, "Teaching: The Profession," will assist you in thinking about "pro-fessional" issues such as teachers' unions, different types of certification, and career paths in the field of education. Chapter 7, "The Organizational Structure of Schooling in the United States," describes the diversity of organizational patterns used by districts, schools, and classroom teachers. You will see that some of these patterns have enhanced school success for various groups of students, whereas others have been used to marginalize some groups.

Chapters 8–11 are focused on the foundations of education. An educational philosophy is the foundation on which teachers select curriculum and instructional methodologies. Chapter 8, "Pursuing an Educational Philosophy," is written in a way that not only explains various philosophies but is designed to help you begin to sort out your basic beliefs about the purpose of education in the United States. This chapter provides tools to help you clarify and develop your own educational philosophy. Public education is a highly regulated business, and Chapter 9, "Governance of Education: Who Controls Education?" illustrates the ways in which national, state, and local governing bodies, as well as individuals, influence and control education. The legal aspects of education are addressed in Chapter 10, "Teachers' and Students' Rights and Responsibilities." Important court cases, laws, and mandates are reviewed. This chapter makes the point that while we all have rights, we also have concomitant responsibilities to our students, our society, and ourselves. The financing of our educational system is complex and, some would argue, in need of an overhaul. Chapter 11, "Educational Finance: Who Pays?" explains federal, state, and local fiscal responsibilities for education. The chapter discusses the ways in which each and every citizen contributes financially to the educational system, thereby affecting the lives and work of teachers.

Chapter 12, "We're All in This Together: Meaningful Family and Community Involvement in Schools," stresses the importance of the African proverb "It takes a village to raise a child." Student success means involving families, extended families, and communities in the educational process. To do this well, a teacher must be open to a diversity of family structures, multiple modes of communication, and alternative ways of thinking about family involvement. Finally, the "Epilogue: Ten Things You Can Do *Now* to Begin Your Professional Journey" sends you to the next phase of your teacher preparation program with some ideas about how you can prepare yourself to be the best teacher possible.

Features in the Text

Vignettes Each chapter contains stories of beginning teachers or teacher candidates who experience everyday teaching dilemmas that illustrate how diversity issues affect all aspects of teaching. These vignettes are true and come from our own experiences or those of teachers and teacher candidates with whom we work. Sometimes the vignettes continue later in the chapter, so that you can think about the dilemma and consider what you would do in each situation before you read about what actually happens.

What Parents Want One of the most difficult aspects of teaching to address is parent involvement. The "What Parents Want" boxes provide the viewpoints of parents, either through the reporting of research results on parental issues or through actual parental reflections. As you read these boxes, you can start thinking about, talking about, and developing strategies for working with parents now; then you will have these strategies available when you enter student teaching or your first job.

Finding a Voice   Each chapter ends with a short story of a teacher or teacher candidate who took action to solve a personal teaching problem. Sometimes the action meant standing up to colleagues when it was not popular. We use these stories to show you that, even as beginning teachers, you can make a difference in your classroom, school, and community.

Getting Connected   This section of each chapter provides websites, both traditional and diversity-related, to encourage you to examine resources that will help you in your profession. Often teacher candidates do not delve deeply into the Web, going only to the first site found by Google. "Getting Connected" provides resources that you might not otherwise find but that offer new perspectives on the chapter topics.

Acknowledgments

This book would not exist without the support and feedback of special people in our personal and professional lives. No one accomplishes important tasks alone. We stand on the shoulders of those who came before us and those who are now with us in order to leave something behind for those who will come after us.

Our current and former institutions offered time, resources, and support as we completed the phases of this project. Students and faculty at the University of Wisconsin–Madison's Department of Curriculum and Instruction provided major feedback, reviewed sections of chapters, and loaned materials. The support staff at UW–Madison assisted with charts, diagrams, keying in material, and photocopying.

The College of St. Rose in Albany, New York, provided a sabbatical for Maureen, and her colleagues and students at William Paterson University–New Jersey were sources of critical review and collaboration.

Our deepest gratitude goes to some outstanding graduate students, professional colleagues, and personal friends. This wonderful group of folks provided feedback on multiple drafts of the manuscript, piloted chapters in courses to get candidates' reactions, edited our work, formatted our disks, taught us valuable lessons, and provided personal support when we needed it most. Their assistance ensured that this work got to the publisher in a somewhat timely manner. Maureen owes a debt of gratitude to Nalisio Tavares, Nancy Derbyshire, Ellen Ryan, Karen Lapadura, Yolanda Dye, Leslie Agard-Jones, Djanna Hill, C. Edwards, Jennifer Harvey, and the PT4T Scholars. Carl gives a super thanks to Jennifer Austin and Chris Kruger, who lent their computer knowledge and organizational skills to this project over several years. Peter Cupery was invaluable in locating all kinds of information and in finding lost references. Tyng Gau was a great help with the section on Eastern philosophies.

Our most sincere thanks and gratitude go to Kim White, who read this text more times than anyone should have to and offered succinct and cogent critiques. Keffrelyn Brown's help on the Instructor's Manual was invaluable.

We both owe a great deal to Art Pomponio, who saw the vision, believed in the goal, and convinced us to make this text a reality.

The love and support of our families underpin our work. Their lives and experiences teach us about the complexities of power and diversity. They keep us grounded in reality, and we know they love us in spite of whatever shortcomings are found in this text. Maureen could not have written this book without the support of her talented daughter, Lisa Jarvis, and her family: Kim, Mark, and Logan Zinman; Mike, Ryan, Mick, Andy, and Rhee McDonough; Kevin, Sheri, Kyle, Kevin, and Matt McDonough; Tonya, Dave, Katie, and Gracie Lindgren; and Jeremy, Christian, and Josh Klein.

Carl is kept on task by his brothers, educators Alvin, Shelby, and Ernest Grant, and by his wonderful children and grandchildren, Carl, Alicia, Gavin, and Amaya Grant.

We would like to thank the following group of reviewers for their outstanding suggestions:

Henry C. Amoroso, Jr., University of Southern Maine
Gloria Ayot, Eastern Washington University
Barbara Bourne, University of Maryland, Baltimore County
Karen Cadiero-Kaplan, San Diego State University
Christine Channer, Utica College
Prem S. Dean, National University
Holly Hubert, College of DuPage
Allen R. Lias, Robert Morris College
Melissa Mohammad, Salisbury University
Andrew Dean Mullen, Westmont College
Illham Nasser, Trinity College
Dutchie S. Riggsby, Columbus State University
Michael H. Romanowski, Ohio Northern University
Nyna Rynberg, Lake Superior State University
Shari Saunders, University of Michigan–Ann Arbor
Olusegun Sogunro, Central Connecticut State University

Finally, sincere thanks to the marvelous team at Thomson Wadsworth. When others told us we were "too far outside of the mainstream," Dan Alpert gave us latitude, encouragement, and dinner. His vision for an affordable introductory text that dealt head-on with issues of power and diversity was refreshing, and his enthusiasm and unwavering belief in the project brought it to fruition. Tangelique Williams, Dory Schaeffer, and Beatrix Mellauner have also been helpful and supportive.

Carl A. Grant
Maureen D. Gillette

THE CHANGING FACE OF TEACHING AND LEARNING

© Zephyr Picture/Index Stock Imagery

Focus Questions

1. What are the major purposes of schooling?
2. Why and how has the public view of teaching changed over the past two decades?
3. What do you think are some of the effects of power in education?
4. What are the effects of education that is multicultural and social reconstructionist in today's classrooms?
5. How might your knowledge and disposition about important issues in education, such as the impact of ethnicity, class, gender, ability, sexuality, and power, influence your teaching?
6. What major educational policies and instructional changes await you when you begin to teach that were not so visible when you were in grades PreK–12?

VIGNETTE

Miranda's Decision: Choosing What Is Best for a Student

Miranda is a third-year teacher in a school district located in the same city where she went to college. She had known that she wanted to be a teacher since she was a young girl. She wanted to work with children and develop personal relationships in her career rather than choose a profession in which interpersonal contact was minimal. She had also always assumed that after college she would move back to her hometown and teach where she went to school. However, during her student teaching experience at the state university she became committed to the students and schools in the district where she gained her first experience teaching children. Although teaching can be more difficult and time consuming than Miranda had first anticipated, she enjoys the satisfaction she receives from watching her students grow intellectually, as well as socially and emotionally.

Today is one of those days when, at the end of the day, Miranda sits back and reflects on how challenging the day was. She rubs her forehead as she sips her soda. Her thoughts turn to the conference she had earlier in the day. She was involved in a meeting to update the individual education plan (IEP) of one of her students. Sean is a boy in her class who is autistic. He is just one of the diverse learners in the classroom. Sean loves to be in the classroom learning with his classmates, and his presence is both challenging and rewarding for the other students. He can be a distraction to the others as he is fidgety, often chewing on his pencil or shirt. He has several friends in the class, although he occasionally misinterprets social situations. He sometimes takes things too literally and has a difficult time understanding when students are just joking with him. Yet he tries very hard and is an important part of the classroom community.

Sometimes Miranda questions her own ability to relate to Sean or love him the way she does with some of her "easier" students. What he experiences on a daily basis is different from anything she has ever had to endure. She wants him to succeed and does not question her desire for him to have a positive educational experience. Yet at the same time she has 24 other students that she must also think about. It is difficult to determine just what will give Sean a positive experience and what this may mean for the other students.

Miranda looks over her notes and replays in her mind the meeting between herself, the principal of the school, the school's special education coordinator, and Sean's parents. Although she does not question that each person is focused on Sean's best interests, she is amazed at how different their opinions are. It is difficult to reach a decision that will please everyone as there are differing views on what kind of an education will best meet Sean's needs.

Sean's parents, Robert and Michelle, were the first to voice their concerns. They spoke frequently about the education each of them had received. They want Sean to have a similar experience, to have the same exposure to basic ideas that are needed to function in society. They want him to have plenty of experience in the traditional "three R's"—reading, writing, and arithmetic. However, they also want Sean to be thought of as an individual, and they question whether his needs can be met in a classroom of other students whose abilities may be different from Sean's.

Mr. Miller, the school principal, used Sean's scores on district performance tests when making his arguments for the best course of action for Sean. He pointed to Sean's below-average scores on these standardized tests and implied that they are due to Sean's autism. He, too, believes that Sean needs an individualized approach focusing on the basic skills needed to eventually pass these tests for graduation. He also believes Sean needs a different curriculum focus from what the higher-achieving students receive. Mr. Miller believes Sean should receive life skills training. He says that the best way to meet these objectives would be to pull Sean out of the regular classroom and instead have him work in a separate classroom.

Miranda and the special education coordinator, Ms. Williams, spoke together. Ms. Williams started by voicing her concerns with the views expressed up to that point in the meeting. She pointed out that what Robert and Michelle experienced in school may not meet Sean's needs in today's society. As an example, she discussed the increasing role of computers and other technology in today's society and pointed out that with the "three R's" approach Sean may miss out on other valuable experiences such as his class's weekly computer lab time. Ms. Williams continued that although it is important that Sean learn valuable life skills, making this the main focus of his education would deny Sean the challenge and reward of learning. She recounted how much Sean enjoys the science investigations Miranda facilitates in her classroom. Both teachers spoke of their desire to include Sean in the regular classroom. They want to integrate him with the other students. Miranda mentioned how much the students can learn from Sean and how much he can learn from the other students. Being in the classroom allows him to learn appropriate social cues from other students in the class. The other students are then given the opportunity to experience peer teaching and peer modeling. Most important, Miranda stressed that they want to give Sean the opportunity to change the current system and Sean's role in society rather than provide him with the skills he needs to simply fit within the existing system.

Although everyone at the meeting was respectful and listened to what the others had to say, Miranda isn't sure whether there was enough time to really change anyone's perspective. The meeting time ran out, as Miranda's students would soon be returning from their art class. It was decided that Miranda and Ms. Williams would write up an educational plan specifying what accommodations would be made for Sean. They would then send copies to everyone to sign.

Miranda sighs as she pulls herself back to the present moment. She sits in front of her computer and begins to type. She knows the decisions affecting Sean's year are not clear-cut. In the end the plan will most likely be a combination of the views expressed in the meeting. Miranda hopes that all can agree to have Sean remain in the regular classroom with resource support. He will be pulled out of the classroom on a limited basis for language needs. The main issue to resolve is how to combine the approaches in a way that will support Sean's learning. What decision do you think Miranda and her colleagues should make?

The decision facing Miranda is not uncommon in today's schools. In recent years there have been many changes in student demographics and needs that affect the nature of teaching. Teachers must often compare the needs of individual students with those of the whole class. These decisions, in turn, can be affected both by philosophies of education and by the views of other administrators, parents, and community members affected by the decisions. Power affects how the involved parties come together to make educational decisions. When reading this chapter, think back to Miranda's case and how the ideas discussed may be relevant to her experience.

Many people work to make schools successful. Parents, teachers, staff, administrators, community members, and students themselves have a vested interest in maintaining successful schools. Yet each of these players may have a different view of the purpose of schooling and what makes a successful school. In the first sections of this chapter we will look at the two major participants in schools: teachers and students. We will explore why teachers choose to teach and why students attend schools. We will then discuss the public's changing view of teaching and the changing demographics of the student population. Finally, we will analyze how these changes influence teaching and learning in the schools.

PRIMARY REASONS FOR TEACHING: A CALLING, THE LOVE OF CHILDREN, AND THE DESIRE TO HELP

Perhaps more than other professionals, teachers are asked to justify why they chose to be a member of their profession. Think back to your experience. Have you ever been asked, "Why do you want to be a teacher?" How do you answer that question? As you read this chapter, you will be asked to consider your reasons for wanting to teach children and what this may mean to your future practice as a teacher.

In writing his book *Working*,[1] Studs Terkel interviewed people about the jobs they hold and how they feel about them. People have numerous reasons for choosing a profession but for many, Terkel notes, the reason is simple: to have a job. Most teachers, however, are in a special category: They select teaching to fulfill a life goal or dream. Many teachers select the profession at an early age—during high school, middle school, or before—and hold steadfast to their dream even when friends and acquaintances say to them, "You plan to do what?!"[2] Herbert Kohl, the widely acclaimed teacher and author, had such an experience when he graduated from Harvard. Kohl reports:

> My fantasy about being an elementary school teacher maintained its strength throughout college, though I never told anybody about it until the week before graduation from Harvard. My tutor asked me what I wanted to do after graduation and in a moment of intimacy I shared my dream with him. He laughed and expressed a viewpoint I was to hear many times after that: "People don't go to Harvard to become elementary school teachers."[3]

In addition to feeling called to teach, when asked why they chose to teach, most teachers say that they love children and want to help them. Collins and Frantz interviewed more than 150 representative teachers from across the country and concluded that for most educators, teaching is a love affair. The teachers they interviewed are passionate, devoted, demanding, and generous, and many could not imagine another profession so glorious and all-consuming. Additionally, they report that "studies over the past twenty years have found that nearly seven of every ten teachers decided to become a teacher because of a desire to work with young people, and it is the chief reason cited by six of every ten teachers for staying in the profession.[4] Parker Palmer in *The Courage to Teach* believes love of students is a primary reason for teaching. Palmer says that his book is written for "teachers who refuse to harden their hearts because they love learners, learning and the teaching life."[5]

Another reason some teachers cite for becoming a teacher relates to their role in the community. Biklen points out that for decades the reason many African American women pursued teaching was to help or provide a service to the African American community. The idea started after slavery when most African Americans saw teaching heavily tied to "upliftment" of all African American people.[6] We are beginning to hear these reasons again as we talk to people of color who enter the teaching profession. As you will learn in this text, educational opportunity and outcomes have not been equal, and many historically underrepresented groups in society are looking to teaching as a way not only to give back to their community but to strengthen those communities.

Do you feel you are called to be a teacher? Are "love of children" and "wanting to help students" your reasons for wanting to become a teacher? If so, you are in good company. But what do these words mean to you? When we ask our students and other teacher candidates what it means to "love and help students," we receive stares, as though the question is a no-brainer or we are trying to trap them. We are not trying to trap them, but we do believe the question to be very substantive. Why? It is because a love of children and the desire to help students have taken on expanded meanings, challenges, and responsibilities. Classrooms have changed over the past few decades. Family structures have changed, student demographics vary widely, there is greater use of and need for multicultural education, and the explosion of technological hardware and software challenges teachers to keep up. Pressures coming from society and national leaders include increased attention to curriculum standards and students' performance on tests, growing demand for more academics at the preprimary and kindergarten level, greater concern about school violence, debates over bilingual education and biliteracy, and the use of different models of parental and community participation.

No longer are love and help defined strictly in the context of the classroom; teaching includes experiences with students outside of the school building, in students' homes, and in their communities. Additionally, no longer are love and help readily rewarded by students' and teachers' having the same cultural and socioeconomic backgrounds and experiences. Love of children and the desire to help them are regularly tested. Teachers today have to cope with a job that is complex and demanding and that includes increased responsibility for the moral instruction students receive. Students must be considered as "works in progress" with multiple interests, unique experiences and perspectives, and the enduring potential to construct and reconstruct both themselves and their social world if that potential is not to be squandered.[7] In addition, teachers should foster in students a sense of responsibility to critique the forces surrounding them in which their access to power and to enactment of social change reside.

Every teacher has a special story about what led her or him into teaching, and although the sources of influence may differ, the reasons are very much the same. What are your reasons? How do they compare with the reasons given in the previous discussion?

WHY DO STUDENTS GO TO SCHOOL? THE THREE PURPOSES OF SCHOOLING

Just as teachers have reasons for wanting to teach, there are reasons students go to school. In this section, we discuss some different ways people might answer the question "Why do students go to school?" Then we point out three common purposes of schooling. We hope that our discussion of these purposes will help you practice thinking about schooling as you begin to think about the practice of teaching and becoming a teacher. We will ask you to begin to "unpack" some of what we call your taken-for-granted notions about all aspects of schooling. By "taken for granted," we mean ideas and practices that we grew up believing in or doing and never bothered to question. Some people adopt or adapt to ways of thinking and doing things because they want to follow the crowd and not stand out, because that is the way that everyone else thinks and acts. Often we do not even realize that we have or do not have certain information and skills that we might need in certain situations. This section and this text will help you examine schooling practices in a way that "unpacks" what might be taken for granted so that the decisions you make as a teacher are conscious and purposeful.

Some say that a teacher's responsibility to citizenship in a democracy is to provide students with an education that will enable "we the people" to reflect on and articulate different points of view on problems and issues in society. A crucial question that is debated continuously during national election time and at school board meetings is, "How should the school serve the public?" This question has confronted the United States since the establishment of public schools and U.S. citizens have yet to reach a consensus on the answer. Instead, the question causes debates over the purpose of education, the curriculum to be taught, the pedagogy to be used, how schools are to be organized, which educational issues are considered of immediate importance and which are not, and who should be involved in these discussions.

Responses to questions about the role of schooling in a democracy fall mainly into one of the following three philosophical perspectives: preserving and transmitting the past cultural and social heritage; selecting and preparing students for occupational status levels; and preparing students to build a better society. Schools may do all three of these at once, but it is difficult to give equal emphasis to all three functions simultaneously. Therefore, politically charged philosophical debates over how the schools should serve the public have stemmed, in part, from conflicting views concerning which function is to be emphasized. We will briefly describe the three philosophical perspectives most often heard in answering questions about the role of school in society and some areas in which those holding different positions might disagree. For each perspective, we will discuss how it was represented in the vignette at the beginning of the chapter. You will read much more about these philosophies in Chapter Nine.

Preserving and Transmitting the Cultural Heritage

Advocates of the idea that schools should preserve and transmit the traditional cultural heritage argue that America's heritage contains a rich tradition of enduring truths and values that should be preserved and made a part of the culture of each succeeding generation. They argue that students must possess a certain fund of knowledge (e.g., great literature, history, and Western philosophy) to be considered educated and to be successful in society. Also, they assert that a democratic nation requires a certain degree of consensus and conformity on the part of the public, which can be promoted only if all children become familiar with the same heritage. Advocates of this approach to schooling suggest that it is not possible for people from many different walks of life to converse intelligently or to debate issues on a level playing field unless everyone has been equipped with the same foundational knowledge. Thus, in some schools you may find a "great books" curriculum in which every student is required to read certain texts in each grade.

Educators with a different philosophical position argue that this perspective orients students more to the past than to the present or the future, and that knowledge of and from the past, though it should be respected and appreciated for its contribution, nevertheless needs to be examined in the context of present-day understanding of the past. If not, it can mystify social and political relations, support biased thinking of the past, and impede or contribute little to solving current problems. They also argue that in a world that is being rapidly changed by technology and a global market economy, students need preparation for the future as much as they need an appreciation of the past. In addition, critics charge that the cultural heritage that is usually transmitted in schools represents the cultural heritage of only a portion of the American public. They contend that this position is Eurocentric and contributes to the marginalization of many diverse groups of Americans.

In the opening vignette, the opinion of Sean's parents most closely aligns with the cultural heritage purpose of schooling. Based on their view, they believe that Sean must possess certain basic ideas and knowledge to be successful in today's society. What they did not mention or recognize is that the knowledge they acquired in school may be thought of as limited and may not represent the American public today. Ms. Williams also pointed out that Sean needed preparation for the future rather than just an appreciation of the past.

Selecting and Preparing Students for Occupational Status Levels

Another way some believe that schools should serve the public is by certifying students for status levels in the nation's occupational structure. For example, many employment want ads require certain academic degrees and diplomas of certification for jobs. By offering these degrees and diplomas, high schools, colleges, and universities become the connection between the knowledge, skills, and general education required and the competence needed for certain kinds of jobs. Advocates of the belief that schools should serve society through the selection and preparation of students for certain economic status levels believe that, in our highly complex society, the school is the ideal instrument for such decision making. Those holding this position believe that a student's demonstrated intellectual ability should serve as the chief determinant for this decision and that standardized tests and interest inventories are the most reliable means of identifying students who have the aptitude and attitude for college study and those who may be more suited to a vocational high school. An illustration of this belief is seen in the support of tracking systems (e.g., ability grouping, advanced honors classes, college prep classes, essential math and science classes) in which high school students are advised, based on test scores and grades, to pursue a college or vocational track.

Critics of this philosophical belief argue that this purpose of schooling teaches students to seek knowledge for its practical value (e.g., its use on the job, or acceptance at a particular college) at the expense of its aesthetic value (e.g., the joy found in literature, or learning for the sake of learning). They also claim that this is basically a conservative function of schooling as it prepares citizens to fit into, rather than question and attempt to make fairer, the existing social economic structure. Students wanting to see an example of this belief portrayed in a film should rent *Norma Rae.* This film depicts a situation in which workers who had little schooling, poor working conditions, and low pay did not challenge the authority and pay structure of the factory's management, passively accepting a poor working situation as the best they could get, until they were motivated by Norma Rae's leadership. Similarly, *The Dead Poets Society* provides an example of a prep school constructed on policies and practices designed to place students in elite colleges and universities with little regard for the students' interests and needs. Finally, critics argue that by preparing students to fit into unequal occupational status levels, schools continue to perpetuate inequalities in schooling based on class, race, and gender and create an unwritten caste system of socioeconomic inequalities. By serving this purpose, schools have historically served some segments of the public on the backs of others.

As the principal in the opening vignette, Mr. Miller is responsible for the performance of the students in his school on standardized tests. Thus, it may be logical for him to use this information when considering Sean's education and future potential. He believed Sean's test scores indicated that he should receive more training in life skills to prepare him for a future job in society. Ms. Williams argued that this approach robbed Sean of the value and joy of learning. She and Miranda believed that this approach would only prepare Sean to fit into rather than question the existing social economic structure.

Preparing Students to Build a Better Society

Probably all Americans share the dream of having a better society in which to live. What is not shared is agreement as to the role the school should play in creating a better society and whose definition of "better" should prevail. Advocates of the belief that the school's role is to improve and reform society argue that in the thousands of hours children spend in school, they can just as effectively learn skills and attitudes for social reform as they can for fitting into society as it exists. Because schools are responsible for educating citizens and tomorrow's leaders, they also ask if schools do not assume this responsibility, who will? Two centuries ago Thomas Jefferson argued that an informed citizenry is needed to have a productive society. Today, Jefferson's words still speak the truth. However, what citizens must be informed about has increased exponentially in both the academic and social areas of life, and teachers are the ones who are central to students' becoming informed.

Critics of this belief assert that placing the burden of responsibility on the schools to change society is unrealistic. They further claim that students need certain skills and knowledge in order to succeed, and if the emphasis of the curriculum is shifted to focus on other skills, some students will leave school overly idealistic about the changes they would like to bring about and poorly prepared to attend college or be a productive employee. Finally, some critics point out that the idea is good but its intent can be and often is subverted, depending on who identifies the social problems to be tackled and what philosophies they bring to bear on these problems.

In the vignette, Sean's teachers felt that his educational experience should allow him to enjoy learning as a student as well as prepare him for a future occupation. However, in this preparation they wanted to give him opportunities that would allow him more choices regarding his future role in society. Their view was that an inclusive education would best meet Sean's needs. If given more time, Sean's parents and Mr. Miller could argue that this is too idealistic and Sean would be poorly prepared to be a productive employee in the future.

Other philosophical ideas about how schools should serve society do exist, but our purpose is not to be exhaustive. We want to point out that in a democracy, a single agreed-upon belief about the role of school does not exist. Nevertheless, it is important to note that schools and teachers are guided by philosophical beliefs. Teacher candidates should therefore examine their beliefs about the role of schools in society and their philosophical ideas about teaching in a democracy. When reading the opening vignette, did you seem to relate to the opinion of Sean's parents, Mr. Miller, or Sean's teachers? What experiences have you had that may have caused you to read the story in a particular way? Most of us have some taken-for-granted notions and some uncertainties about public education, such as how teachers should be trained, which instructional practices should be used to teach PreK–12 students, and how issues related to race, sexual orientation, gender, and social/occupational status should be handled or not handled in public schools. Presenting our beliefs about public education and addressing schooling issues related to race, social class, ability, sexual orientation, and gender are often not easy. This is so because many of us feel vulnerable during such discussions. We want to avoid the embarrassment that may come when others disagree with our ideas and wonder what logic we used to arrive at our beliefs. Often these same beliefs are expressed in our teaching and in our behavior at school, and are thereby imposed on our students without our fully understanding what we are doing. For this reason and others, it is crucial that teachers examine and get to know their own attitudes and thoughts about public education.

CHANGES INFLUENCING TEACHING AND LEARNING

Schools in the United States mirror the changes that are happening in society, the business market, and the technology arena. Changes in how the public views education as well as changes in the student population result in the need for educational reforms. This section will look at these two major forces influencing the changing nature of teaching and learning in public classrooms.

Recent Changes in the Public's View of Teaching

Teacher candidates will enter a profession that has been seriously engaging in reform efforts for the past two decades. The public has demanded reform because some test comparisons indicate that students in the United States lag behind students from many other developed nations and because corporate America is dissatisfied with the knowledge and skill levels of the students they hire as employees. Robert Reich, former Secretary of Labor, reported in 1990 that almost one-third of major U.S. corporations provide basic skills training for employees, spending $25 billion annually on remedial education.[8] Employers argue that students are not being prepared to meet the demands of a highly technological and global society. Societal forces such as these have led politicians and many organizations, including education associations, to call for teacher candidates to demonstrate on standardized tests that they have subject matter knowledge in areas such as math, science, and literacy before they are licensed to teach. In fact, Congress mandated in 2001 that states that require standardized tests for teacher candidates must report to the federal government the percentage of students who pass and do not pass those tests. We will explore this debate throughout this book and let you decide on your own version of the "truth."

Teacher Quality **Teacher quality** is the term that is presently used to discuss the subject matter knowledge and pedagogical knowledge and skills teachers need in order to be licensed to teach. From the 1700s to the early 1900s, teachers' quality in the United States was often associated with "morals." It would not be unusual to require a female teacher to submit to a moral code such as the following: "I promise to abstain from all dancing, immodest dressing and any other conduct unbecoming a teacher and a lady." During the 1940s and 1950s, teacher quality had a good deal to do with personality and character traits. Ryans' *Characteristics of Teachers* (1960) listed the essential qualities approved for good teaching during that time:

- Superior intellectual abilities
- Above average school achievement
- Good emotional adjustment
- Attitudes favorable to pupils
- Enjoyment of pupil relationships
- Generosity in the appraisal of the behavior and motives of other persons
- Strong interests in reading and literary matters

- Interest in music and painting
- Participation in social and community affairs
- Early experiences in caring for children and teaching[9]

Throughout the 1960s and 1970s, teacher quality was defined in relation to instructional skills. Such skills as pacing of the lesson, wait time after asking a question, and the quantity of material teachers covered were used as the barometer for determining teacher quality.[10] During this period, however, both teachers and parents of color argued that although instructional skills were important, teacher quality must also include a cultural sensitivity toward students. In a seminal publication designed to help teachers understand the content, strategies, concepts, and resources needed to teach comparative ethnic studies and to integrate ethnic content into the regular curriculum, Banks (1975) told teachers that "the teaching of ethnic studies is not only appropriate, but essential."[11] He argued that students need a global view of ethnicity in America to be effective and productive citizens in the 21st century.

The 1980s ushered in an era in which teacher quality was closely identified with subject matter knowledge. This trend continues today. National legislation known as No Child Left Behind, enacted in the opening years of this century, promises to have lasting effects on how teacher quality is defined. Part of this "highly qualified" definition includes demonstrating strong competency in the subject area of instruction, either by passing a rigorous test or by having earned a major in the subject area taught.[12] We will have more to say on this act in the next chapter. Influenced by this type of legislation, policy makers at the federal and state levels have adopted reforms in education. One focus has been on the initial licensure of teachers. In particular, many states have increased the educational and academic requirements for prospective teachers, set new standards for approval of teacher education institutions, and added requirements that teachers demonstrate evidence of subject matter knowledge or understanding of teaching and learning.[13] Teacher candidates at all grade levels at many institutions are being strongly encouraged or even required to have an academic major. In some institutions, graduates are asked to develop electronic teaching portfolios in conjunction with teaching standards. This portfolio is then used during the job search. Think of your own teacher education program. Is there an increasing emphasis on equating evidence of teacher quality with subject matter knowledge? (See Exhibit 1.1.)

As the push for subject matter knowledge intensifies, advocates for **marginalized students**—students who are neglected or oppressed because of their gender, race, class, physical or mental ability, or sexual orientation—have expanded their demands for teacher quality beyond subject matter knowledge and pedagogical content knowledge. Educational experts are now calling for teachers to exhibit skill and to better prepare themselves for teaching students of color, students living at or below the poverty line, students who have same-sex parents, students who are physically or mentally challenged, and students whose first language is not English.[14]

The Public's Perception of Teachers' Work   Another change in the public's view of teaching has to do with the public perception of teachers' work. In the past, it was commonly believed that people entered teaching because it was an

---

EXHIBIT 1.1   TEACHING QUALITY REFORM INITIATIVES

Teaching quality reform initiatives include:

- Strengthening teacher certification, licensing standards, and preparation—including alternative routes to certification—to ensure that new teachers have stronger academic content knowledge and teaching skills

- Holding entire institutions of higher education—not just schools of education within the college or university—accountable for preparing high-quality teachers with both content knowledge and teaching skills

- State efforts that improve links between colleges and elementary and secondary schools, with more time spent in K–12 settings by teacher education students and faculty and greater use of technology in the teacher education programs

- New strategies to attract, prepare, support, and retain highly competent teachers in high-poverty urban and rural areas

- Building and sustaining K–16 partnerships across all levels of the education system to ensure that the necessary teacher quality policy and practice changes take place in higher education and in the schools, with accountability for results

---

Source: Ed Funds 52 New Grants to Improve Teacher Quality, Recruitment and Preparation, www.ed.gov/PressRelease/08-2000.

"easy" job; the workday ended at three o'clock in the afternoon, and most teachers received the summer months off. Also, teaching was and sometimes still is seen as women's work, with low status and low pay. Many in society believed that a career in teaching lent itself to concurrently raising a family or supporting a husband while he attended law school or medical school.

Though some may still cling to these ideas, others now realize that teachers are professionals of both sexes who work long hours after school, in the evenings, and on weekends. The general public is also coming to realize that teachers must engage in lifelong learning if they are to keep pace with new knowledge, new technologies, and new ways of understanding what students know and are able to do. Teachers are also increasingly respected for the professional way in which they handle the additional educational responsibilities that the public gives to the schools, such as AIDS education and drug and alcohol awareness. Today we know that teachers are willing to demonstrate their dedication by braving new horizons, as did Christa McAuliffe, the teacher who lost her life aboard the *Challenger* space shuttle in 1986 in an attempt to bring the celestial community into the classroom.

Changes in Student Demographics

Student demographics—racial, ethnic, socioeconomic, academic ability, language, and social and emotional characteristics—have changed substantially in many schools in the United States. In some schools, student demographics include those from single-parent homes, those qualifying for free or reduced cost lunch, and those from lesbian and gay families.

Your first assignment might include a class that looks like this one: Out of 29 students (15 girls and 14 boys), 19 are White, 5 are African American, 3 are Latino,

1 is Asian, and 1 is biracial (Puerto Rican and African American). Two African American, one Latino, and three White students come from families who live below the poverty line ($17,000 for a family of four); another four White students are from upper-income homes. These social class distinctions are not readily visible, because most students are clad in jeans and cotton shirts or T-shirts. However, a glance at their home addresses and at the free lunch roster suggests their social class backgrounds. The students' families vary widely: only three students come from homes in which the father works and the mother stays home, six are from single-parent families (three of which live below the poverty line), and both parents of the remaining 20 students hold or have recently held jobs at least part-time. Most of the students grew up speaking English, but two students speak Spanish at home and another speaks French at home. The students' academic skills also vary widely. Eight students are two years behind grade level in reading and math, 12 students are at grade level, and the other 9 have reading and math scores one grade level more or higher. Two students are assigned a special education teacher who works with them in the class throughout the day, and four others participate in a program for the gifted.

Some teacher candidates look upon teaching students with these differences as a challenging opportunity that will require them to develop more knowledge of multicultural education. Other teacher candidates see these demographic changes as representing a problem to U.S. society, especially to the schools. How teacher candidates accept the change in student demographics will be consequential for both teachers and students. We look first at some of the diversity among the present generation of students, next we discuss how classrooms have adapted to student diversity, and finally we describe diversity within students' social support for learning.

Student Diversity   Students in today's classroom are far from homogenous. They come with ethnic and racial differences, exhibit different learning abilities and styles, and speak languages other than, or in addition to, English. They come from different social classes. They may be gay or lesbian, or may come from gay families. Although some classrooms may appear to be relatively homogeneous around one of these characteristics, teachers need to be aware of the other dimensions across which apparently homogeneous groups may actually be diverse.

ETHNIC AND RACIAL DIVERSITY   The new century brings with it a great deal of ethnic and racial diversity in the schools. By 2020 it is projected that the number of White children will decrease from 71% to 63%, Latinos will increase from 11% to 15%, Asians will increase from 5% to 8%, and African Americans will remain stable at 13% Many communities in the United States whose populations heretofore were only or predominantly of European ancestry are experiencing major increases in the number of students of color. In some major cities, especially in California and New Mexico and in Washington, DC, people of color are in the majority.

LANGUAGE DIVERSITY   According to the 2000 census, 46.9 million people in the United States speak a language other than English. This language diversity is having an inevitable impact on schools. Exhibit 1.2 indicates the number of different languages being spoken in homes that have children of school age.

EXHIBIT **1.2**   **NATIVITY BY LANGUAGE SPOKEN AT HOME BY ABILITY TO SPEAK ENGLISH FOR THE POPULATION 5 YEARS AND OVER**

	United States
Total	262,375,152
Native born	231,666,088
Speak only English	210,211,516
Speak Spanish	14,760,788
Speak other Indo-European languages	4,431,729
Speak Asian and Pacific Island languages	1,448,275
Speak other languages	813,780
Foreign born	30,709,064
Speak only English	5,212,041
Speak Spanish	13,340,264
Speak other Indo-European languages	5,586,260
Speak Asian and Pacific Island languages	5,511,790
Speak other languages	1,058,709

Source: U.S. Census Bureau, Census 2000.

Teacher candidates must now learn ways to teach children who enter school with little or no fluency in English. Proponents of bilingual education are increasingly encouraging **biliteracy.** Students who become biliterate are able not only to speak in their native language but also to read and write in it fluently. Teacher candidates are discovering that their preparation also needs to include lessons on how to develop effective strategies for communicating with parents who cannot read or write in English. For example, in the Los Angeles Unified School District they are gaining experience from sending double-sided notes home to parents. One side of the note has information in English and the other side has information printed in the parents' home language. Also, some school districts are involving teacher candidates in the programs they set up to teach English to parents and are including them in activities designed to increase parents' and community members' participation in school programs.

SOCIAL CLASS AND POVERTY   The movement to a global market economy, the downsizing of many major U.S. corporations, and the movement to a service-based economy have left an increasing number of families earning less money than previously. The term **working poor** describes "individuals who live in poverty despite working year-round at a full-time job."[15] Teacher candidates may encounter parents who work at poverty wages, and therefore cannot work hard enough or long enough to attain economic security. Also, they may have the students of parents who have intensified needs because of larger families or special

Multicultural Education Means . . . Effectively Teaching English as a New Language

Language diversity has long been present in U.S. society. One has only to visit the local school and inquire about the number of students over the years who have spoken a language other than English or who came from homes where a language other than English was spoken. In support of the importance of bilingualism and biliteracy to the United States as a nation, as well as in the global community, the National Board of Professional Teaching Standards endorses and promotes proficiency in languages other than English.

Because students in U.S. schools whose first language is not English number in the millions and that number is continuing to grow, teachers of linguistically and culturally diverse learners must provide them with English skills. These skills give them access to important subject matter and help to advance their knowledge. These skills also help students become part of the fabric of the school and contributing members of this democracy.

Teachers are aware that special challenges arise when deeply held values, beliefs, and understanding of the home culture that sustain a student's sense of identity conflict with the mainstream values and beliefs taught in the school. In such circumstances, teachers should proceed in a sensitive manner, alert to the potential for disagreements and respectful of cultural differences and differences in interpretations of historical events. For example, many Chicanos (Latinos) may have an interpretation of the battle at the Alamo that is different from that found in the elementary school social studies textbook. Teachers also understand the value of the home language and are mindful of their obligation to educate students to function productively in society. Most teachers are aware that some students come to school from families that prize formal education and, therefore, will readily take advantage of all the school offers. Other students' families may be skeptical

expenses such medical bills. In such cases, even standard wages would tend to leave the family financially destitute.[16] The number of students that live below the poverty line is rapidly increasing. According to the Children's Defense Fund (2002):

> 1 in 3 children will be poor at some time in their childhood; 1 in 5 children under three is poor now; that 1 in 16 lives in extreme poverty; that 1 in 8 has no health insurance (more than 9.2 million children nationally); that 1 in 6 is born to a mother that did not have prenatal care during the first three months of pregnancy; that 1 in 13 is born with a low birth weight, 1 in 141 dies before the first birthday.[17]

These students can be found in suburban, urban, and rural areas. If we use 100 as our index for the total number of children living at or below the poverty line, we discover that 28 live in suburban areas, 27 in rural areas, and 45 in urban areas. Also, at a time when more money is required to live and well-paid jobs are of, unfamiliar with, or in disagreement with some of the goals the teacher and the school seek to achieve. Teachers need to demonstrate a sincere understanding of these different points of view and challenges faced by students learning a new language and negotiating their way through an unfamiliar society.

In addition to mastery of their subject matter and understanding of the challenges their students face, teachers of linguistically and culturally diverse learners must understand the social, political, and historical events and problems that frame their students' learning. For example, have these students experienced emotional trauma from leaving behind friends and loved one during their immigration to the United States? Are they placed in classes where their history and cultural are not central? Were they made to feel unwanted by their ethnically different classmates? Also, teachers of English

as a new language should realize that educational policies, practices, and personnel often ignore these needs and overtly or covertly discriminate against linguistically and culturally diverse people.

Consequently, teachers must become advocates for their students, both in school and in the wider community. In school, teachers may show their advocacy and understanding of these students by helping other students to better appreciate their circumstances and by reminding them that some of their relatives may have endured similar experiences. Encouraging students to talk with their grandparents or community elders about adjusting to a new country, especially when they have experienced displacement, starvation, culture shock, or discrimination, will be enlightening. Having students read letters and stories that address these issues will also be helpful.

dwindling, an increasing number of both urban and suburban students are becoming latchkey children because their parents have to work additional hours to meet their expenses. The children of working parents and single parents often have to care for themselves after school. The lack of parental or adult supervision sometimes leads to a lack of responsibility toward homework and school attendance. Students who attend schools in communities where there is little or no poverty are more likely to do their homework, watch less television, and have fewer absences than students who attend schools where poverty is high.[18] Thus we can see how some students will "fit" the school culture and other students, because of other demands, may fall behind if not caught and encouraged early.

GAY AND LESBIAN STUDENTS AND FAMILIES   Many gay and lesbian couples are choosing to have or adopt children, and it is no longer unusual to have students in a class who are living with two mothers or two fathers. Some families may downplay this information, but others may make it available as publicly appropriate knowledge. However, many teacher candidates will teach in schools where teachers do not consider sexual orientation as part of the diversity discussion of multicultural education. Many people in our society are opposed to gay and lesbian couples and do not believe that gay and lesbian families exist. Some teachers hold these beliefs; it is possible that you may hold these beliefs. In addition, pre-service teachers may be gay or lesbian themselves, and addressing these issues may make them feel vulnerable. A question for each teacher candidate to face is, How will you work effectively with students who are gay or lesbian and with parents who are gay or lesbian? A response to this question is to treat them fairly, with respect and dignity, the same as you would any other students or parents. During the discussion of classroom philosophy, policies, and procedures, inquire about any issue that is of concern, including gay and lesbian issues. Contact and connections with community leaders also provide good opportunities to get a reading on issues that you may consider too sensitive.

Although it is estimated that 6 to 14 million children have gay or lesbian parents, even teachers who are passionately committed to issues of inclusion and social justice in elementary schools are uncertain as to what to do when encountering lesbian or gay families in their classrooms.[19] They also are unsure about how to teach about same-sex parents in typical primary grade units on "The Family" in classrooms where there are no gay or lesbian parents. These teachers will be happy to know that with the growing acknowledgment of gay and lesbian families in schools, more resource materials are becoming available to teachers. For example, two outstanding videos, *It's Elementary: Talking About Gay Issues in Schools* and *That's a Family,* produced by Debra Chasnoff and Helen Cohen of Women's Educational Media, will help you begin to learn about effective practices for addressing all types of family situations in schools. It is important for children to learn about these issues even if no one in the class has a gay or lesbian family because it will make them more tolerant and knowledgeable about different groups of people.

Inclusive Classrooms   Classrooms have had to adapt to changes in student demographics. Inclusive classrooms are one such change. Since the passage of PL 94-142, the Education for All Handicapped Children's Act, in 1975, educators have been teaching students identified as having disabilities in the same classrooms with students not labeled with disabilities. Within the last decade, this effort has greatly increased as more and more students identified as having disabilities are placed for the entire day in the "regular" classroom. This practice is often referred to as inclusion.

Inclusive education is a value-based practice that attempts to bring all students, including those with disabilities, into full membership within their local school community.[20] In this instructional model, a special education teacher works alongside the classroom teacher. They collaborate on planning and implementing the learning experiences in a way that meets the needs of all the students in the classroom. Udvari-Solner argues that inclusive education has become a major player in the reform effort to reconceptualize traditional educational practices so that they are responsive to the needs of all learners. She reports that proponents of inclusive education believe that the term *inclusion* will become obsolete as school districts across the county construct ways to make all students integral members of the school community.[21] It is important for teachers to try to erase society's stigmas about people with disabilities because exposure plus education can erase ignorance. In seeking to include Sean in the classroom, Miranda hopes that all of her students will become aware of what they can learn from students with special needs and that this interaction can positively influence the education of all involved.

Diversity in Social Support for Learning   The phrase **social supports for learning** refers to the human (e.g., parents, grandparents) and material (e.g., books) resources as well as learning activities (e.g., visit to a library) available to a student. The effectiveness of the human resources is sometimes influenced by family characteristics such as educational attainment, income level, and number of parents in the home.

Over the past two decades family characteristics have been changing, along with ideas about the impact of these characteristics on learning. Teacher candidates will find that some of their peers and teachers believe that the social supports students receive are *the* major factors affecting student learning. Their reasoning could be justified in the past based on the research on family characteristics of the 1960s and 1970s, but much of this research has since been criticized for its biases, assumptions, and faulty methodology.[22] Teacher candidates will therefore have to proceed cautiously when assessing how social supports for learning are influencing students' academic and social performance.

For example, teacher candidates will learn that the percentage of 5- to 17-year-old students who live with only their mother increased from 13% in 1976 to 22% in 2001. Conversely, the percentage of students who live with two parents decreased from 83% to 68% during the same period.[23] The poverty rate in 2001 remained relatively unchanged at about 17%, the percentage of non-poor students increased, and the percentage of near-poor students decreased.[24] At the same time, the educational attainment of children's parents increased. The percentage of 5- to 17-year-olds whose parents had at least completed high school increased from 76% in 1979 to 88% in 2001. The percentage of parents with a bachelor's degree or higher increased from 19% to 31% during the same period.[25] Additionally, from 1993 to 2001 there has been an increase in the number of students who are read to three or more times a week, told a story at least once a week, and taught letters, words, numbers, songs, or music (see Exhibit 1.3).[26] These data suggest that teacher candidates may wish to base their teaching plans and expectations for students on the idea that increasingly parents and guardians are doing more to ensure the academic success of their children.

You may be wondering if you are up to the challenge of teaching in this ever-changing multicultural society. You are the only person who can truthfully answer that. However, if so far you have interpreted what we have described as a challenge and see multiple kinds of intrinsic satisfying rewards and the opportunity for a glorious career, we believe that with hard work you can become the dynamic teacher you have always dreamed of becoming.

EXHIBIT **1.3** **PERCENTAGE OF CHILDREN AGES 3–5 NOT YET ENROLLED IN KINDERGARTEN WHO PARTICIPATED IN HOME LITERACY ACTIVITIES WITH A FAMILY MEMBER THREE OR MORE TIMES IN THE WEEK BEFORE THE SURVEY, BY SELECTED CHILD AND FAMILY CHARACTERISTICS**

Child and Family Characteristics	Read To[1]		Told a Story		Taught Letters, Words, or Numbers		Taught Songs or Music	
	1993	**2001**	**1993**	**2001**	**1993**	**2001**	**1993**	**2001**
Total	78.3	84.1	43.0	54.3	57.7	74.2	41.0	54.1
Age								
3	79.4	83.6	46.4	54.5	57.2	71.2	45.0	59.9
4	77.8	85.2	41.2	54.6	58.1	77.1	38.9	51.7
5	75.9	81.5	35.8	52.0	57.9	74.6	33.1	40.6
Race/Ethnicity[2]								
Asian/Pacific Islander	68.8	87.4	52.1	58.1	61.8	77.9	35.9	50.4
Black	65.9	76.7	39.0	51.2	62.7	77.5	48.9	53.9
White	84.8	89.4	44.3	57.9	57.2	74.8	40.2	53.4
Other[3]	75.9	86.5	48.1	61.8	56.0	78.4	31.3	57.9
Hispanic	58.2	70.7	37.7	42.3	53.9	68.2	38.7	56.6
Poverty Status[4]								
Below poverty threshold (poor)	67.5	73.7	39.1	50.7	59.6	72.4	45.2	57.0
At or above poverty threshold (nonpoor)	82.1	87.1	44.3	55.3	57.0	74.7	39.5	53.3

[1]In 1993, respondents were asked about reading frequency in one of the two versions of the survey questionnaire. The percentages presented in the table are for all of the respondents who answered three or more times on either version of the questionnaire.
[2]Black includes African American, Pacific Islander includes Native Hawaiian, and Hispanic includes Latino. Race categories exclude Hispanic origin unless specified.
[3]Other includes American Indian and Alaska Native.
[4]Data on household income from the National Household Education Surveys Program combined with information from the Bureau of the Census on income and household size are used to classify children as poor or non-poor. Children in families whose incomes are at or below the poverty threshold are classified as poor; children in families with incomes above the poverty threshold are classified as non-poor. The thresholds used to determine whether a child is poor or non-poor differ for each survey year. The weighted average poverty thresholds for various household sizes for 1991, 1993, 1995, 1996, 1999, and 2001 are shown in the Supplemental Note 1 of the Condition of Education.
Source: U.S. Department of Education, National Center for Education Statistics. (2003). *The Condition of Education 2003* (NCES 2003–067), Table 37-1.

CHANGES IN TEACHERS' WORK

Within this context of rapid changes, teachers are constantly searching for new ways to meet the academic, social, and emotional needs of all of their students. Some of these new ways include putting to use the knowledge of how power is vested in different groups and how multicultural education needs to play a role in the education of students. This section discusses how the changes in society's view of teaching and learning and merge with the changes in student population to influence changes in teachers' work.

In the early days of schooling, teachers were expected to stoke the fire, scrub the classroom floor, and teach students who ranged in grades from kindergarten through high school in a one-room schoolhouse. The profession has come a long way, and over the past few decades (including the time since you were in school) there have been a number of changes in teachers' professional responsibilities. Some teacher candidates may believe that some of the topics we discuss here are educational fads that will soon disappear. They may be correct as it is difficult to predict how long an educational topic or issue will remain at the center of attention. However, the recent changes presented here, we believe, have "legs"; that is, they will remain central to teaching for a number of years. These changes are organized into three areas: ways of teaching, standards and accountability, and increased teachers' voice.

Ways of Teaching

Teacher candidates on the campus and in schools should learn about the many ways that power manifests itself in schools and classrooms, about multicultural education, and about instructional technology in order to be successful with a large number of students. The increased inclusion of these ideas in teaching has changed the nature of instruction.

Power in Schools   **Power** is a concept that you may not think about when you think of schools. When we think of power, we picture batteries to make things go or a quality that superheroes possess. However, power is a much more complicated concept. Although power has always been present in society and its public institutions, there is more awareness of how power functions in schools. We will provide you with many examples of the ways that power operates in society, schools, and classrooms as you read through the chapters. The point we want to make here is that as a teacher, you will have a good deal of power to control what goes on in your classroom, in your school and district, and in the larger society. Often teachers hold even more power collectively when working toward a common school-related goal. Student teachers, especially when several are placed in the same school, should discuss ways of working together to accomplish identified goals. The student teachers' seminar affords a good time to plan together and to develop strategies for helping students and one another. When they work together, teachers as a group have historically been able to accomplish many needed reforms in education simply by exercising the power that they have vested in them by the public, by parents, and by virtue of their teaching license.

The history and literature of humankind are replete with stories of people and power. Since the civil rights era of the 1960s, people of different ethnic and social groups have strived to contribute to this history and literature by demanding multiple interpretations of historical events, the inclusion of literature by members of their group in the "traditional" curriculum, and the elimination of those social, political, and material differences that are inequitable. In the 1990s, understanding power in relation to education became a component of a number of educators' curricula.[27] Educators are now teaching that power in societal institutions, including schools and colleges, needs to be understood as not only existing in top-down relations (principal-to-teacher; teacher-to-students) but existing and circulating between people in all relationships.[28] Teacher candidates who acquire knowledge of how power is exercised in relationships and who understand that it is an integral part of teaching will be better able to use the policies and practices of teaching to help their students and themselves.

PAYING ATTENTION TO POWER   Many different definitions and forms of power operate in society and in schools. It is important to have an understanding of what forms power can take, how it benefits some while denying others, and the ways it may surface either visibly or invisibly. Michel Foucault, a French philosopher, wrote that although many forms of power exist in society, including legal, administrative, economic, and military power, they have one thing in common. This common strand is a reliance on methods of application and the gaining of authority by referring to scientific "truths."[29] In other words, those who have power justify their actions by claiming that data or research or proven fact (scientific truth) is the basis for what they do. Remember that at one time it was an accepted truth that the world was flat. This conclusion was based on scientific evidence of the time. Even today, scientists and astronomers are debating the "fact" that Pluto is a planet! Does this mean there are no truths? No, but you need to remember that truth for the moment, or for one person, may not represent a final answer.

Currently, scientific "truths" in education are based on standardized test scores, IQ test results, and psychological theories. Does this mean that we ignore such evidence in planning, teaching, and learning activities? It does not. But teachers need to look at this evidence in perspective, as one means of describing a student at one particular point in time. We need to remember that multiple factors influence how we measure and record data about a student. Just look back at your old report cards and standardized tests. How well do they reflect the student that you are today?

Cleo Cherryholmes, an educational theorist, claims that power should be seen as relations among individual or groups based on social, political, and material **imbalances,** or **asymmetries,** whereby some people are indulged and rewarded and others negatively sanctioned and deprived based on who they are, what they have, or what they believe or practice. In some classrooms, material asymmetries (such as a student's economic status or the presence of computers in the home) lead to placement of some students in a higher academic track than others. Cherryholmes further observes that these asymmetries are based on differences in possessions or characteristics, and power is constituted by relationships among these differences. For example, some students may have not only greater material resources (e.g., money, computers in the home) but also more "cultural capital," and therefore be indulged with more positive attention and power. Cultural capital is knowledge about how the dominant society operates. If you are a parent or have extensive experience working as a teacher's aide or classroom volunteer, you have some "cultural capital" of the classroom because you have been in a position to see things from the teacher's point of view. Students, too, can bring cultural capital. Five-year-olds whose parents could afford to send them to preschool may come to kindergarten knowing their numbers, colors, the "rules" of school like raising your hand to speak, and even how to read. In the 1950s, students came to kindergarten to learn these things. Today, if a student comes to school without knowing the "rules" of school, without knowing numbers and colors, or with little experience in working with a storybook, he or she may be viewed as "deficient" because such a student lacks the cultural capital for kindergarten. In a classroom, cultural capital can be a student's English language speaking ability or knowledge of fairy tales because they were read at home and then read at school.

Cherryholmes goes on to say, "It is redundant to refer to a power relation, because power is a relation."[30] In fact, power is present within all relations. For example, you may have a job while you attend school. There is a power dynamic between you and your boss, based on hierarchy, even if your boss is younger than you. You have a certain degree of power, which you opt to exercise in a certain way. Schools are full of power relations, and the authors of this text believe that these should be highlighted to provide you with a greater understanding of the way your own power as a teacher and the power inherent in the system of schooling in the United States can work to benefit or negatively impact all those who participate in the system.

THE CHOICE OF POWER   We choose power as a theme for this book because, in some form or fashion, power influences all events and relations, including those that take place in schools. There is, according to Nietzsche, power behind all societal events, wherever there is an "exercise of relationships." We can use an example about the practice of student teaching to examine Nietzsche's claim and to see how multiple and complex layers of power operate within society's social rituals.

During student teaching, power will emerge from such multiple relations as state regulations governing courses teacher candidates take, schools' policies and procedures, cooperating teachers' daily routines, and the student teaching sequence. Relations among these groups (e.g., schools and universities) have been ongoing for years, so they are interconnected by political and social histories, and become a network of relations that influence teacher candidates' preparation and student teaching experiences. For example, in traditional teacher preparation programs, teacher candidates across the country are required to student teach for a certain number of weeks, to have a TB test before they begin to teach, to pass several educational methods courses, and in some cases to have a certain grade point average. This network of relations is made up of the state, university, and local school districts, leading to the creation of state education regulations, school and university policies, and cooperating teachers' routines. This network of relations results in an emergence of power that affects the discourses and practices that teacher candidates use.

The educational choices and policies that educators and others make, or have to adhere to, are the effects of power that stem from a network of relations. When teacher candidates enter a classroom, they will usually find a reading, science, mathematics, and social studies curriculum. That this curriculum is offered rather than some other curriculum is an effect of power that emerges from a network of relations among the state board of education, local boards of education, principals,

Tracing Power in Education Historically

When formal schooling was introduced into ancient Greek society, it was to give the state power within social institutions. In other words, schooling was to govern the actions of the family and military through what was taught to them. Aristotle, in *Politics,* points out the influence of education on society. He states, "The superintendents of education must exercise a general control over the way in which children pass their time."[31] Aristotle is not arguing that education must totally occupy one's life, but that its presence is essential to the development of a good society and a good life for citizens. The good life and the good society are symbiotic; and in order to have the good life and the good society, one must consider the kind of education that is necessary to bring that society and life into existence and sustain it. Hence, there is no vision or version of the good life that does not imply a set of educational policies; and conversely, every educational policy has implicit in it a vision of the good life. It was early in history that states sought to invest themselves with power by monitoring education and, through education, their vision of "the good life."

When schooling was introduced into the American colonies, it was first to give the church-state commonwealths the power to promote and establish Puritan theocracy.[32] In 1816 Thomas Jefferson, like Aristotle, recognized the importance for the state to have voice in education. His reason was that education was essential to a free society. Jefferson wrote, "If a nation expects to be ignorant and free, in a state of civilization, it expects what never was and never will be."

Early U.S. states were in agreement that a primary purpose of schools is to educate students to live and participate under a democratic system of government. "Education formed a key center of efforts to convert traditional workers into modern, efficient producers imbued with appropriate middle-class zeal and to mold new arrivals into 'good Americans.'"[33] Horace Mann, the architect and icon of the common school movement (about whom you will read much more later in this book) believed that the social responsibility of the schools was as crucial to the welfare of the nation as it was to the intellectual development of students.[34]

The importance that states place on schools to educate students is seen in compulsory school attendance policies. These policies were put in place to make certain that parents enrolled their children in school and impress upon students that school attendance is to be taken seriously. According to the California school code, if students violate attendance laws the school attendance review board can direct the school district to make and file a criminal complaint against the parent or guardian.[35] Imber and Van Geel state, "Laws designed to ensure that children receive a government-approved education constitute the single greatest intrusion on the general right of parents to direct the upbringing of their children and the single greatest restriction on the general right of all Americans to spend their time in pursuits of their own choosing."[36] Beginning in 1852 in Massachusetts, states have established compulsory school attendance laws. By 1918 all states had some compulsory attendance policy. Although over the years some parents have challenged the constitutionality of attendance laws on the grounds that they usurp legally recognized parental prerogatives, state courts usually reject these challenges.[37]

teachers, community interest groups, and textbook companies. For example, during their attendance at college, students may hear for the first time about the internment of Japanese Americans during World War II and wonder why they did not learn about this in elementary, middle, or high school. Choice of curriculum content is based on a network of relations, which can sometimes be observed at school board meetings. Such observations might include the use of influence by members of different professional associations, a bloc of members on the school board, or certain community members to sway a vote to go a particular way.

Power need not always be perceived as negative, because acknowledging a network of power relations more easily leads to questioning different ideas of justice and who benefits from each. Also, understanding power as a network can facilitate recognition of the existence of multiple truths or new understandings.[38] For example, during the early 1970s, parents of students with disabilities, some members of Congress, and other interested civil rights advocates came together to create a coalition of power. This coalition promoted the passage of the previously mentioned Education for All Handicapped Children Act (PL 94-142). This legislation mandated a "free appropriate public education" for all students with disabilities and required that schools and teachers develop an individualized education plan (IEP) for each student with a disability and place all students in the least restrictive education environment.

It is often claimed that the relations that make up power are hierarchical. In fact, many relations among individuals or groups are organized hierarchically, according to social (e.g., racial, gender), political (e.g., government official, local school board president), and material (e.g., socioeconomic status, residential neighborhood) differences in which some individuals or groups are prized and rewarded much more than others.[39] Power, or its effects, can be seen within this network of relations, as in the differences and dissimilarities between students based on their possessions (e.g., having money or access to a gold card), their ability to speak standard English fluently, their knowledge (e.g., having the information and behaviors accrued from attending middle-class schools), or their personal characteristics (e.g., being male, having "cover girl" looks, being straight, not being disabled).[40]

In elementary schools where ability grouping is used or in high schools where tracking is employed, the dissimilarities between students are said to be based on students' ability or prior achievement scores. However, "abilities" such as proficiency in reading, speaking, and math are sometimes the result of a network of relations (e.g., local school board policy, school goals) that demand the selection and design of curricula and instruction strategies that accommodate the learning preferences, needs, and interests of some groups of students more than others—for example, students who are from poverty homes or students of color. Brenda Marshall also believes that power emerges as political in classrooms when teachers make interpretations about curriculum. Marshall states:

> Every interpretation is a political move. Every artistic, historical, literary, daily creation, discourse, comment, is a political act. *Beloved* is a political text. So is *Gone With the Wind*. So is *Alice in Wonderland*. So is the *Bible*. Any interpretation

of *Beloved, Gone With the Wind, Alice in Wonderland,* or the *Bible* must be political, because each interpretation involves choices that we make, but more importantly reflect choices that we don't know we make, those choices we would call common sense: what we've come to identify as ideology.[41]

POWER OPERATES BOTH VISIBLY AND INVISIBLY   Ropers-Huilman writes that power "passes through and is exercised by persons and structures at all levels in social systems."[42] The effects of power in schools, classrooms, and other societal institutions can be both visible and invisible.

Power in schools operates *visibly* through norms, expectations, and school rules that must be satisfied.[43] For example, Ms. Smith tells her first-grade class that they are to complete their assignment on community helpers before they take the field trip to the fire station. She also tells her student teacher, Thad, that she would like him to call the parents of the three students who have not returned the permission slip for the field trip. The students and Thad not only understand what they are expected to do, but also understand that Ms. Smith, in her role of teacher to both the students and Thad, can direct them to perform school-related activities and expect them to carry out her requests.

Power also operates visibly in public statements of educational goals, such as standards. For example, the national standards movement grew out of a network of relations that included actions by President George Bush, Sr., and Congress. President Bush created the National Council on Education Standards and Testing, which released a report in 1991 recommending the development of three types of national standards: content standards that identified what students should learn in each grade; performance standards that identified what levels of learning were "good enough"; and delivery standards that identified what resources schools were to provide to give students a fair chance to learn.[44] This network of relations expanded in 1992 when national standards and national assessments were endorsed by Bill Clinton during his presidential campaign. Also in 1992, professional associations representing each subject area—for example, the National Council of Teachers of English and the National Science Teachers Association—joined this network of relations as they began to develop standards. Soon states, school districts, and teacher education programs across the country were setting up committees to develop standards. Government officials, national professional associations, state departments of education, local school districts, and teacher education programs formed a network of relations from within which power emerged to make educational standards a household word.

The role that the media played in reinforcing this network of relations with stories about standards must also be acknowledged. Additionally, the criticism of public schooling by some in corporate America led to increased attention to performance accountability and standards. Educational standards became an idea that pierced the cultural, political, and economic spheres of U.S. society. Teacher candidates will find other expressions of visible power in their Student Teaching Handbook and other school of education policy documents.

Power can also operate *invisibly* through the actions (e.g., demands and expectations) of individuals, institutions, and agencies. For example, in school the general expectation is that students are "straight" and live with heterosexual parents. This is manifested each time the teacher says, "Take this paper home and have your mom and dad sign it." The power invested in societal norms (of heterosexuality as the dominant but unstated assumption about most people's identity) often silences teachers and students about the concerns of gay and lesbian people. Other demands and expectations that are the effect of invisible power are attitudes that students learn about, such as punctuality, female–male relationships, and career expectations. Also, power operates invisibly through the ways that some people and histories are valued in classrooms.

The flow of visible and invisible power can be perceived through what some educators refer to as a discourse. A discourse is a system of statements that provide rules of information and sets of practices within a social milieu.[45] Discourses can be transmitted through the media, passed down within families, or taken for granted within the workplace. A discourse does not have to be a set of true statements; but in defining what can be said and thought, a discourse comes across as true.[46] The dominant discourse in a historical period and geographical location determines what counts as true, important, or relevant, what gets spoken, and what remains unsaid.[47] For example, during Galileo's time the teachings of the Church were the dominant discourse. After writing *A Dialogue on the Two Principal Systems of the World* in 1632,[48] a paper that went against the teaching of the Church, Galileo was called to the Holy Office to face an Inquisition. After a lengthy trial, he was forced to repudiate the ideas published in the manuscript. The teachings of the Church, the dominant discourse of the time, were generated and governed by rules invested with power, and were products of history, culture, politics, economics, and language. Galileo, as well as most Christians and clergy, had been socialized by the Church's ways of thinking and behaving, and the effects of this power helped to shape how they thought and acted.

The teaching practices of Marva Collins, an African American teacher in Chicago, can be used as a more recent educational illustration of the relationship between discourse and power. Marva Collins became angry that poor children, especially African Americans, were not being educated to their fullest potential. She knew that commonly held discourses about poor African American children were based on assumptions of academic inferiority. A common discourse was to "blame the victim," or to say that the children were not achieving because of cultural deficiencies. Collins vowed to discredit this discourse by proving that she could successfully educate African American children, especially those who came from poverty-level backgrounds.

To fulfill this goal, Collins started her own school, the Westside Preparatory Academy, in which she challenged the ways of thinking of those who argued that poor African American students could not learn complex ideas. To help the students learn, Collins:

1. Openly believes in the students and encourages their belief in themselves
2. Teaches students to believe in and help each other
3. Teaches students "the classics," yet goes beyond this to offer a well-rounded, culturally relevant curriculum
4. Expects them to be able to demonstrate to any visitor that they know and understand this material at the highest academic level

5. Views students, most of who are living at or below the poverty level, without recrimination and helps them to prepare for the achievements of their professional goals and personal dreams[49]

Every single student who has graduated from Westside Preparatory is either enrolled in further schooling (high school or college) or is employed.

The Marva Collins example shows how a certain discourse about students has historically been invested with power, to the point that many believe that poor African American students cannot learn or have great difficulty learning. The example also shows that teachers can resist the effects of power portrayed in dominant discourses about students and teaching practices. Learning from the ideas of people like Marva Collins, who believes that all students have high potential, can improve the attitudes of teachers who have doubts about the academic ability of some students. This is the important part about changing attitudes.

Teachers may wish to help students understand that they too have a discourse—a "students' discourse"—and that they too have power. Students' discourses are systems of statements made up by students that are invested with values about what is acceptable behavior in their cultural milieu. Student groups—for examples, "jocks," "geeks," or "skaters"—have a discourse that informs their groups about such things as how to dress, where to eat in the school cafeteria, whom to associate with, and the kinds of grades they should seek to achieve. Students' discourses are crisscrossed with references to and from multiple media and popular culture. The student discourse does not have to be a set of true statements, but because it defines what can be said and thought, it comes across as true, especially to other students.

Keep these ideas about power in mind as you read about the second theme of this text: education that is multicultural and social reconstructionist. It is related to power and speaks directly to the examination of current school practices, including the discourses that exist in school and society about important educational issues.

Multicultural Education   Multicultural education refers to the ways in which all aspects of schooling address the needs and talents of a diverse population to ensure equity for all. It is both a philosophy and a process. As a philosophical concept, it is rooted in the principles of democracy, social justices, equity, and the affirmation of human diversity. As a process, multicultural education continually undergoes modification to meet the needs and demands of a growing society. As both a philosophy and a process, it can inform educational policies and practices.[50]

Many teachers have had a history of advocating for social justice and cultural pluralism. They see multicultural education as an essential approach for educating teacher candidates. They believe that for teacher candidates to be successful with all students, and for them to prepare the students they teach to participate in our democracy, to reform our society when needed, and to work for the elimination of poverty, racism, sexism, and homophobia, multicultural education is necessary.[51] Notice that we spoke of success for *all* students. Many teacher candidates enter their coursework believing that they do not need to pay attention to diversity issues unless they plan to teach students of color. This is not true. In order for our educational system to contribute to a more just and equitable democracy, all of us need to understand how we can play a part in this effort. Multicultural education is just as important in a suburban school as it is in an urban school. This section will examine how multicultural education has resulted from changes in society and how it can, in turn, inform teaching and learning in all classrooms.

EDUCATION THAT IS MULTICULTURAL AND SOCIAL RECONSTRUCTIONIST (EMCSR)   Along with paying attention to power in schools, our second theme is **education that is multicultural and social reconstructionist (EMCSR).** We choose this theme because it is an approach to education that uses knowledge of power relations and brings a multicultural perspective to three major changes underway in U.S. society: the changing population of the United States, which also includes differences in family structure, openness about sexuality, greater acceptance of (dis)abilities, greater religious pluralism, increased recognition of biracialism, and multiple languages; the influence of globalization, which includes, at a minimum, global communication, continued growth of multinational enterprises, the influence of global financial markets, global warming, and international attention to human rights on the political, social, and economic society; and shifting conceptions about what knowledge and whose knowledge should constitute the curriculum of schools.

We also think it is fair to tell you that our choice of themes has to do with our own conception of the purpose of school in society, the discussion that opened this chapter. We believe that there are many, many excellent schools and teachers across the United States. We know, however, that many children from all backgrounds are not receiving an education that will prepare them to be adults who contribute to the betterment of our society. There are many inequities in schools today, not only in poor, urban, or rural schools but in wealthy suburban schools too. We believe that regardless of ethnicity, social class, gender, ability, sexual orientation, language, or family structure, *all* students should be prepared to work effectively with people from all types of backgrounds, to use their well-developed skills to succeed in their chosen field, and to think critically in a way that supports their full participation in our democracy. If you ask to see the mission statement of your local school district, we believe that you will see that most schools say they are working toward these same goals. We wonder, though, how administrators and teachers are assessing the degree to which their graduates are attaining these objectives. In order to ensure that all students achieve the goal of being prepared for full participation in our democracy, we believe that it is incumbent upon teachers, administrators, parents, students, and concerned community members to examine policies and practices in schools. That is what EMCSR is all about.

The first societal shift that EMCSR addresses has to do with the dramatic change in population demographics. As mentioned previously, today there are more people of color living in California than people of European descent. Exhibit 1.4 gives the projected change between 1998 and 2008 in total graded enrollment in California public schools.

We could draw similar statistics from many locations—urban, rural, and suburban—across the country where population patterns are changing. The 2000 census figures, available on the Web, are quite telling. Differential birth rates

EXHIBIT 1.4	PROJECTED CHANGE BETWEEN 1998 AND 2008 IN TOTAL GRADED ENROLLMENT IN CALIFORNIA PUBLIC SCHOOLS	
American Indian	1,250	2%
Asian	55,610	12%
Black	−48,850	−10%
Filipino	17,202	12%
Hispanic	37,714	31%
Pacific Islander	9,083	25%
White	−385,694	−18%
Total	383,270	7%

Source: Public K–12 Enrollment Projection by Ethnicity (www.dof.ca.gov/html/demograph).

between women of color, especially Latino and Asian American women, and White women, plus a large and historic immigration from non-European countries have led to the most diverse K–12 population in history. Additionally, these people of color have become a part of U.S. society at a time when the gains from the civil rights movements and school desegregation are providing a more tolerant social and political climate.

Some teachers, however, will teach in schools where **de facto segregation** continues to exist. Students of one particular race or ethnicity will attend certain schools because of social and economic circumstances. In addition, de facto segregation may occur in individual schools. Some students, often African Americans and Latinos, will be grouped together within one classroom, and Asian American and White students will be in the other classrooms or working together within a classroom. Also, Orfield reminds us that the desegregation of African American students, which increased continuously from the 1950s to the late 1980s, has now receded to levels not seen in three decades.[52]

The second force at work in the new millennium is that the U.S. position on the world stage is changing because of the influence of globalization on the economy, environment, labor markets, politics, and culture of the United States. Also, Europe, once the sole reference point for U.S. culture, diplomacy, and economic activity, has lost its social and political monopoly. Latin American, Asia, the Middle East, and Africa now are major players. The international context for life in the United States is now global, and this requires an education that accepts and affirms cultural diversity in a manner that is even more pronounced than represented within the United States itself.[53]

The third trend has to do with the curriculum reform movement and the shifts occurring around what knowledge and whose knowledge are to be included in the curriculum. The key disciplines from which curricula have historically been drawn have shifted dramatically during the past 25 years, for the most part in directions relevant to multicultural education. The study of literature, primary grades through college, no longer simply involves a standard summary of great works, or is confined to the traditional collection of children's and adult literature. All literary works are now open to new kinds of assessments, in terms of wider cultural context, implicit assumptions about issues such as gender roles, the silence of gays and lesbians, the presence of biracial people, the portrayal of students with disabilities, and audience interaction. Literary scholarship is also more inclusive of authors who are in the early stages of their careers, authors of color, and children's literature that includes people of color as the lead characters. The purpose becomes understanding and appreciating culture, not insisting on a single aesthetic standard.[54] We must continue to work to make sure we don't think we are "done" doing this. New works are produced daily, as are the changes in demographics.

Finally, those who study and comment on social life are arguing that social change must be understood in terms of the interactions and power relations of various groups: wealthy with working-class people; women with men; regional, racial, ethnic, and religious groups with their opposite number. The past and present can no longer be understood without looking at people and events as complex and intersected by different social markers such as race, gender, and class. Social values cannot be understood simply through the ideas of those acknowledged as the most dominant or powerful thinkers; indeed, their ideas are shaped, revised, supplemented, and sometimes rejected outright by various cultural groups in the wider society. Political structures involve not only formal constitutions, but also recurrent protest and violence. The past expands, and the nature of change has been fundamentally reconceived.[55]

HOW WILL EMCSR HELP TEACHERS TEACH?   EMCSR is a philosophy and an approach to teaching that recognizes that because society is constantly changing, it is necessary to be responsive to those changes. Social reconstructionism is grounded in the belief that schools in a democracy can and should prepare citizens to work actively and collectively on problems facing society. Educational reconstruction is a philosophy that believes that social change is inevitable and that, therefore, education should serve as the agent of **cultural transformation.**

Some educators argue that there are six key elements in a reconstructiontist approach.[56] First, a reconstructionist approach to teaching fosters the idea that it is essential for teachers to connect educational philosophy to a broader social philosophy "grounded in a democratic form of life." Second, schools cannot be morally or politically neutral, but should serve as a key institution in the process of **social transformation** by using democracy "as an ideal to orient social criticism and the construction of social policy." Third, a reconstructionist approach to education sees teaching as not only concerned with the cognitive dimension, but equally concerned with a moral discourse related to the wider sociocultural context. Fourth, a reconstructionist approach to education has students participate in communal experiences so that they can learn about democratic behavior firsthand. Fifth, a reconstructionist approach to teaching believes that in order for students to construct and maintain a democratic community, they must be able to engage in open discussion in which "differences" are seen as essential and necessary, rather than deviant or a threat to society. Finally, a reconstructionist approach to education sees teachers as "transformative intellectuals" who can "help create the conditions for students to experience democratic forms of life."

The appropriateness and timeliness of Stanley's ideas on social reconstruction for teachers becomes clearer when considered alongside the four goals of reconstruction proposed by the Society for Educational Reconstruction:

1. **Cooperative power.** Educators work with others to overcome the evil effects of racism, sexism, and other forms of discrimination.
2. **Global order.** Educators work toward a world community that guarantees dignity and social justice for all.
3. **Self-transformation.** Educators work to develop skills, attitudes, and values that enhance personal growth in the context of community.
4. **Social democracy.** Educators work to increase democratic decision making and strive for a fairer distribution of the world's natural resources, wealth, and power.

EMCSR can help teachers to examine changes in educational ideas from the perspectives of equity and social justice. It gives teachers the tools to design, select, and use curriculum materials that represent multiple perspectives and to employ instructional strategies based on their students' needs, backgrounds, and learning styles. Also, it helps teachers to conceptualize classroom learning in a way that fosters personal and social growth. It additionally assists them in working effectively with parents, community members, and community agencies. Furthermore, EMCSR prepares teachers to help students to think critically about school and personal matters and to act responsibly toward these matters so that individuals and groups have not only equal opportunity but equitable outcomes in achieving the American dream. Grant and Sleeter state that the goals and objectives of EMCSR for teachers are meant to do the following:

- Promote social structural equality and cultural pluralism
- Practice democracy and fairness in the school and classroom
- Teach critical thinking skills, adapt to students' skill levels, and use students' life experiences as a starting point for analysis
- Teach students to analyze and critique social inequality and to promote equity and social justice
- Teach student social-action and empowerment skills
- Organize curriculum so that current social issues involving race, gender, class, sexuality, and ability are not marginalized
- Include curriculum concepts that will offer perspectives and experiences from different groups of Americans[57]

The EMCSR approach embodies the philosophical principles of **cultural pluralism, social structural equality** and equality of opportunity, **social justice,** and **educational equity** for all students. It offers a lens through which teachers can consider questions such as the following: What can schools do to help bring about a fairer world, or can they do anything? Do issues of poverty, discrimination, and oppression require a more vigorous solution than just promoting cross-cultural understanding and mutual respect? In the 21st century, what does it mean to be a citizen of a large democratic society in which there are major unresolved issues involving fairness and social justice?

Instructional Technology   Technology, including computers, digital video and audio equipment, hardware and software, and the World Wide Web, is changing perhaps faster than any of the other ideas discussed here. Many schools have computer labs or at least provide some opportunity for students to begin or extend their computer literacy. Teachers regularly and with an increasing level of comfort include in their assignments working on the Web or participating in chat rooms so that students and teachers can have ongoing discussions. Many school districts have set up homework help lines via technology. You may have a job interview using interactive telecommunications video.

It is estimated that about 72% of 4th graders use a computer at school at least once a week and 8th–11th graders use computers at school every day.[58] Since the mid-1980s, computer use by students at all grade levels has moved from mainly game playing and word processing to the ability to access a lot of information, communicate globally, and create multimedia projects.

Technology is also an area in which inequities exist in schools and in society. We know that poor neighborhoods and schools, many of which are populated by students of color or located in rural areas, do not have the same access to technology as do their wealthier counterparts. In such situations, discussions with other student teachers in different schools to determine the availability and quality of technology in their schools may lead to investigating why computer technology is not available, and then to organizing collaborative steps to move the school districts and community to become responsive to this technology need. Such action may not move schools to immediately run out and buy computers, but it may increase their understanding of the need for technology, which may lead to their taking action to get computers and other technological resources into the schools. Power and action are available to student teachers as well as to administrators and teachers.

The good news is that the percentage of White, Black, and Latino students in grades Pre-K through 12 who used a computer at school and at home was higher in 2001 than 1993. For example, 83.7% of Black students and 78.9% of Hispanic students in Pre-K through 12th grade used a computer at school in 2001, compared with 50.6% and 52.3%, respectively, in 1993. However, we also know that between 1993 and 2001, White students in grades Pre-K through 12 were consistently more likely than their Black and Hispanic peers to use a computer at school or at home. However, when computer use was broken down by location, 2001 computer use by Blacks and Whites was similar at school but not at home.[59]

What the technology and computer opportunities for instruction will be for your teacher candidates' cohort before retirement, we can only wonder. Nevertheless, what is becoming increasingly clear is that teacher candidates need to learn how to make technology and computers a core part of their instructional strategies because it improves the opportunities to help students. A K–12 technology report noted that in order to make effective use of educational technology, teachers will have to master a variety of tools, redesign their lesson plans around technology-enhanced resources, solve the logistical problem of how to teach a class full of students with a smaller number of computers, and take on a complex new role in the technologically transformed classroom.[60] Teacher candidates will have to consider privacy issues such as controlling access to classroom chat sites and students' records. In other words, students looking for information should be guided to sites that are appropriate for their age and in keeping with the values taught in school.

Although the Internet may link students to a wider world, their online activities need to be connected to their hands-on instructional activities. If not, students may miss the connection between what they are learning on the Internet and its impact on their lives, and the lives of people across the country and throughout the world. For example, students who use the computer to learn about the earth's ecosystems and their relation to manufacturing need to understand that when they decide to buy certain items, the purchase has implications for both the international division of labor and the earth's ecosystems. For example, manufacturing is moved from one country to another in order to avoid environmental regulations and to obtain cheaper labor. One challenge of understanding that connection is why new technology cannot, in the end, compensate for a shortage of creative, motivated, and well-trained teachers and administrators.[61]

Besides becoming technology literate, teachers will have two additional responsibilities. First, teacher candidates must learn to evaluate computer software as they do any curriculum for content, age appropriateness, relevance and interest to the student, and the types of thinking the software fosters. For example, does the software encourage thinking at different cognitive levels, include multiple perspectives, and offer culturally relevant materials? Does it address different learning styles, and is it inclusive? Second, teacher candidates must make certain that all students have an opportunity to learn computer technology and have an opportunity to keep up with the knowledge growth in this area. The concept of a **digital divide** means that availability of and access to computer technology tend to be based on the students' or school's socioeconomic status. Pre-service teachers will find that access to technology varies by schools. Teachers can bring attention to this and work for more equitable resources. One way to do this is to apply for grant money from local and national organizations to make technology more available in their schools. The degree to which all students will benefit from technology will increasingly depend on the access that students have to it. It will also depend on the skills and interest teachers show in technology, making computer use an ongoing part of their curriculum and instruction program.

Standards and Accountability

Power, EMCSR, and technology are ways of teaching that are more responsive to changes surrounding education. Teachers' work is also changing with reform efforts aimed at setting standards and making schools accountable for student performance on standardized tests. Public demands for universal academic standards, greater use of national tests, and greater accountability of teachers, principals, and students, supported by strong rewards or consequences, give rise to the professional climate that teachers are facing today.

Student Performance   Some schools convey to the teaching staff that their major focus must be on students' academic performance. Schools are told to set higher standards for students and to assess student performance with standardized tests. Students, teachers, and principals are then rewarded or punished depending on whether the standards are met. Publication of test scores in the newspaper, reassignment of teachers, and replacement of principals are some of the consequences for poor student performance. In some areas, private corporations have taken over schools whose test scores drop to a certain level. Public acclaim for a job well done and additional private monies for supplies, equipment, and field trips are some of the "perks" we have seen schools receive for raising test scores.

However, teacher candidates are questioning such reward and punishment measures. They argue that they know from being students and talking with their friends that the school and students are not the only ones responsible for student learning. They say that student learning is also influenced by previous academic preparation, learning resources, and opportunities students have and take advantage of outside of school. Some teacher candidates have anxiety about entering such a pressure-laden situation. They are fearful that they may lose their initial teaching position if the students in their classroom do not show academic growth. To ease this pressure on beginning teachers, some districts assign them mentor teachers and provide them with resource materials and staff development opportunities.

A growing number of educators, parents, and students are questioning the use of a single instrument of measurement to determine how well students are performing. They argue that teachers' judgment, students' work as demonstrated in portfolios, and scores from other standardized exams should be considered when evaluating students' performance. In Boston, Massachusetts, teachers, parents, and students boycotted standardized tests. In Scarsdale, New York, the parents voted to discontinue intensive test preparation during school hours in a show of support for the superintendent, who voiced the opinion that valuable teaching time was being wasted on practice test activities. This debate has led an increasing number of beginning teachers to investigate a district's educational approach to standards before accepting a teaching assignment. They understand that a school's instructional and assessment policy can affect their teaching and professional career.

Teacher Performance   The use of and controversy surrounding testing is not limited to students. Pre-service and in-service teachers are also increasingly tested as a way to predict and measure teacher effectiveness. Tests have long served as a gatekeeper to determine who could enter the teaching profession with a possibility to earn tenure. However, the 1970s marked the beginning of the movement toward nationwide formalized testing of teachers. By the year 2000, 41 states reported using some form of testing to ensure quality teacher education. Tests vary among the states. State agencies choose tests based on the knowledge and skills they believe teachers ought to demonstrate. However, two companies, Educational Testing Service (ETS) and National Education Systems (NES), have developed the vast majority of tests for teacher (i.e., PRAXIS, CBEST, NYSTCE). The common purposes of testing voiced by the states are to:

- Control the entry of teacher candidates into teacher training programs
- Certify successful completion of a teacher training program

Similar to the controversy surrounding student standardized tests, the National Committee on Assessment and Teacher Quality has reminded policy makers and educators at all levels that teaching quality depends on many things. Teachers must be knowledgeable about content, but good teachers are also those who can explain ideas so that all the students in their class understand them. They are also compassionate, resourceful, committed, honest, and persistent in their efforts to help the students learn.[62] How does this fit with testing? Which is more relevant to teachers' and students' success?

Increased Teachers' Voice

As a result of the changes facing teachers and their work, it is important for them to become activists and spokespersons for their own profession. Teachers' voices were often silent in the past. With a few exceptions, educational researchers, the media, and politicians often spoke about what schools needed but rarely were teachers invited or expected to participate in those discussions. This began to change about 20 years ago. Today, it is not uncommon to see the national teachers' union president or a classroom teacher give a speech during the Republican or Democratic National Convention. Educational researchers are collaborating with classroom teachers to provide a rich view of what actually happens in classrooms. Teachers are becoming activists, joining national organizations and working in grass-roots educational reform efforts. Teachers are making their presence felt both inside and outside the classroom, becoming more visible outside of school through community involvement and conducting personal classroom research or more actively participating with outside researchers. Community service learning and teacher research are two "trends" in teacher professional development today that we believe will continue long into the future.

Community Involvement and Service Learning   Community involvement and service learning are two different but equally important concepts in teaching today. Teacher candidates should know about and be involved in both efforts. Community involvement refers to any activity in which the teacher is visible in the community. Service learning is more structured and combines service to the community with academic learning so that each informs the other.

During the 1990s, the inclusion of community involvement as a part of the teacher preparation program for teacher candidates increased significantly. A growing body of research suggests that the more visible and active teachers are in the school and local community, the more these teachers understand the lives of their students and can use that information to more effectively teach the students and communicate with parents and other caregivers. Today, teachers are also establishing relationships with community organizations, agencies, and corporations and inviting them to become more active in the school programs.

Many teachers are returning to an activity of the past: making visits to students' homes. Such visits can foster positive relations with parents and other caregivers. Home visits can serve to eliminate a chasm between teachers and parents, which may be the product of a lack of communication, lack of cultural understanding, or teachers' and parents' not completely appreciating each other's role as society demands more of both parents and teachers. For example, teachers who believe that inviting parents to offer suggestions and participate in classroom activities will lead to parents' becoming overly involved in classroom routines may believe differently after meeting and talking with parents. Additionally, teachers who are feeling pressure to raise students' achievement scores, and who do not understand that learning about students' home circumstances can help them more successfully plan their instruction, may appreciate the knowledge they acquire after making a home visit. A group of veteran teachers told Carl that, at a minimum, student teachers should meet and interact with students' caretakers in some way as early in the school year as possible. They contend that the time and effort invested will bring huge dividends in teacher–student rapport and their ability to be of greater assistance to their students throughout the school year.

Some student teachers may feel hesitant about visiting certain locations within their school community. This is prudent; the "unknown" suggests caution and care. Discussing the community with the cooperating teacher, principal, school social worker, and custodial staff can provide valuable insights. Also, the first time out, invite a teacher or another student teacher to go with you or make a connection at the local high school for a student leader to accompany you.

Also included under the rubric of community involvement would be activities that place the teacher in more informal contact with parents and students. For example, many teachers regularly attend social events such as school dances, plays, and sporting events to indicate to students that their activities outside of the classroom are important to the teacher. Many teachers go even further and accept invitations to bar mitzvahs, first communions, or quinciañeras, as these are important events in the lives of students. Others volunteer at local soup kitchens and community festivals or are members of the Urban League, La Raza, or local political parties. Any time that a teacher goes beyond the normal school hours to participate in the life of students or the community, students, parents, and other community members see that teacher as committed to the community and someone with whom they can more closely identify.

Service learning differs from community involvement in that teacher candidates actually work in a specific community agency or business, such as a shelter for homeless people or a medical center. This is done in conjunction with a seminar or class in which traditional academic learning is tied to the learning that takes place in the community setting. The American Association of Colleges for Teacher Education (AACTE) notes that effective service learning addresses a genuine community need, links academic goals to the service activity, includes critical reflection on the experience, focuses on enhancing civic responsibility, and includes an evaluation of both the service and academic outcomes. AACTE further notes that service learning should be collaborative in all aspects, as opposed to the college or university's dictating requirements for teacher candidates.

An increased sense of civic responsibility, inspired by arguments that government alone cannot solve society's problems; a commitment to the idea of learning

What Parents Want

Some teacher candidates are asking, "What do parents and the general public want for their schools and teachers?" Parents have never hesitated sharing their opinions about the public school, and teacher candidates may be surprised to find that they have a strong ally in parents. Following is a summary of the most recent Gallup Polls of parents' opinions about what they want from schools.

Seventy-three percent of public school parents indicated that the focus in education should be on reforming the existing public educational system and not replacing it with private systems. Twenty-five percent opt for moving to an alternate system, and 2% don't know. Seventy-three percent also would rather improve the existing school system then be provided with educational vouchers so they can pay for private or church-related schooling.

Although parents desire improvement in schools, 62% assign the public schools in their community a grade of A or B. Another 25%

assign a C. Seventeen percent of public school parents believe that most students achieve their full potential while in school; another 80% believe that students achieve a small part of their potential. Sixty-seven percent of parents feel it is important to close the academic achievement gap between White students and Black and Hispanic students. Twenty percent feel closing the gap is somewhat important, and 11% feel it is either not too important or not at all important.

Parents identify lack of financial support/funding as the biggest problem with which schools must deal. Overcrowded schools are ranked as second. Drug abuse and lack of discipline tie for third, followed by fighting/violence/gangs. Eighty-six percent of parents believe that a zero tolerance policy should exist with regard to weapons. Eighty-five percent of parents believe there should be more instructional emphasis on drug and alcohol abuse in schools. Seventy-five percent advocate more emphasis on racial and ethnic understanding

by doing; and the desire to forge stronger links between schools and their communities have led to the recent profusion of service initiatives in teacher education programs.[63] In many teacher education programs, service learning projects occur over an extended period of time and within the context of a college course or seminar in which the new learning or experiences are discussed. Service learning fosters John Dewey's idea that it is important for students to engage in real problems with the aim of making learning meaningful.

Community involvement and service learning are both important elements of a teacher candidate's preparation. However, educational researchers such as Kathleen Densmore raise some questions about these activities that merit consideration. She argues that the goals and actions of service learning receive insufficient attention in teacher education programs. Densmore claims that the moral and

and tolerance. Sixty-five percent support more emphasis on environmental issues.

Parents support education on more than just the basics. Seventy percent of public school parents believe the primary purpose of schools is to provide a balanced education in which the basics are only one factor, compared to 28% of parents who think the basics should be the primary focus. Parents rank themselves as having the greatest effect on students' level of achievement in school. Fifty-five percent believe parents have the greatest impact, 27% believe teachers are most influential, and 15% of parents believe students are the most important factor. When asked what they thought offered the most promise for improving public schools in their community, 59% of public school parents chose qualified, competent teachers over free choice of schools, rigorous academic standards, and elimination of social promotion. In order to meet the demand for highly qualified teachers, most parents favored raising teacher salaries, allowing teachers to receive salary and pension benefits when transferring positions, and providing loans that would be forgiven when a teacher enters the profession.

Parents also responded to questions on achievement tests and computer technology. Thirty-six percent of parents believe too much emphasis is put on achievement tests, up from 19% in 1997. Twenty percent believe there is not enough emphasis on tests, and 43% believe the emphasis is about right. Seventy-five percent of public school parents believe that students in their community receive a great deal or a fair amount of computer technology instruction. Twenty-three percent believe that students receive not much computer technology instruction or none at all. Of these parents, 74% believe that technology improves instruction, 21% believe that technology does not improve instruction, and 5% don't know.

Source: Lowell C. Rose and Alec M. Gallup, *The 32nd and 33rd Annual Phi Delta Kappa/Gallup Poll of the Public's Attitudes Toward the Public Schools,* 2000, 2001.

intellectual goals of service learning need to be distinguished from the political goal. The political goal, she believes, is associated with various malfunctionings of our political and economic system. Densmore believes that social service projects are delivered to a community because they come at minimal cost to the government. The state is compelled to budget less money to an area because a social service project will provide both money and service to the area. Densmore states, "Rather than being guided by altruism as is typically implied in the enthusiastic support for service learning, volunteerism is often driven by the imperative to ease social crises."[64] She reminds educators and teacher candidates that education, in and of itself, cannot be liberating and empowering. Therefore, it is crucial that when teacher candidates undertake education projects that are a part of social action, learning about while helping out is beneficial to both teacher educators and teacher candidates because such involvement helps (1) clarify the reality of institutional inequities, (2) discern the interconnectedness among various forms of oppression, and (3) advance a notion of a citizenship that centers on collective action instead of individual charity to serve the voluntary sector.[65]

Teacher Research   Classroom teachers are becoming researchers of their own instructional practice. For decades most classroom research was conducted by university professors and other professional researchers. Now teachers and teacher candidates are conducting **teacher research,** sometimes referred to as action research, on instructional areas such as classroom discussions, gender equity, and teacher–pupil rapport.[66] Kemmis and McTaggart describe action research as a form of self-reflective inquiry undertaken by teachers in order to improve their own practices, their understanding of those practices, and the situations in which those practices are carried out. A common statement after teachers have conducted an action research project is that it gives them a feeling of "empowerment."[67] The feeling of empowerment is because this is not research that they took from textbooks or journal articles, which may or may not be applicable to their students; instead, they implemented their own research on how to better teach their students.

Many teacher candidates better understand and gain greater appreciation of the importance of educational research once they conduct a study of some instructional practice in their own classroom.[68] Action research can be a form of professional development for both teacher candidates and teachers, especially in districts where professional development opportunities are limited. As teachers' work continues to change, teacher research holds the potential for teachers to remain current in educational findings as well as to advance findings through their own research on behalf of their students.

Back to Miranda's Case: An Analysis

We opened the chapter with a vignette describing Miranda and her desire to give one of her students the best educational opportunity possible. This vignette illustrated several important ideas from this chapter. It first exemplified the debates surrounding the purposes of education. Each participant in the conference had a different view of what schooling should do for Sean. The vignette also highlighted the debate around inclusive schooling. Whereas some may question whether students with special needs can be serviced in a regular classroom, others contend that inclusive schooling is important for teaching students to work in different situations and to value the differences students bring to the classroom. Inclusive schooling can be thought of as education that is multicultural and social reconstructionist. Finally, this vignette is an example of how power functions in schools. In this case, each person in the conference was given voice and had power. Sean's educational plan would eventually be a product of how power was negotiated between his parents, his principal, and his teachers.

FINDING A VOICE

Jessica loves her student teaching placement. After only a month at Hazen Middle School, she feels as though she is fitting in, and she relates well to the students. Her cooperating teacher, Nancy Miller, started off the year by introducing Jessica as a "co-teacher," never referring to her as a student teacher or putting her in a subordinate position in the classroom. Students in her English and social studies classes turn to Jessica for help as often as they approach Ms. Miller, so Jessica feels comfortable stepping in and stepping back during lessons. The two teachers tend to co-teach lessons, bringing a diverse perspective to the material.

The diversity of students in Ms. Miller's classroom is a challenge for Jessica, but she recognizes and appreciates the opportunity she has been given. Nancy does not use homogeneous grouping in her classes but rather places students in mixed groups according to performance on assessment tests and essays (from early in the semester), personality, and "intuition." Following Nancy's example, Jessica plans her lessons to accommodate all students' needs and takes into account their special circumstances.

One of Jessica's favorite activities is the Monday morning "sharing" sessions, in which students discuss in one or two minutes what they did over the weekend. Nancy explains that she introduced this a few years ago as a way to build community in the classroom and to help students get to know each other. The students share stories about family trips to the water park, adding to their collection of compact discs, or renting rollerblades at a local park with their parents.

However, Jessica has noticed that a few students seem reluctant to take their place on the "sharing stool" and rarely contribute to this portion of the class, even though they are outgoing at other times. Manny, in particular, ignores the sharing or makes rude comments under his breath while students are talking. He is one of the students from the transitional housing program, but his family found an apartment in the same area to keep him and his two younger sisters from having to transfer to different schools. When Jessica approached Manny about his behavior during sharing, he muttered that it was "a waste of time. Why don't we just do work?"

Jessica is concerned about Manny because she believes he has the potential to be an excellent student. His in-class work is done early, and he finds the time to help his group when they are struggling with the lesson. However, he did not turn in the first major project in social studies: a realistic model of an Egyptian sarcophagus that the students had two weeks to do at home. The classroom is filled with wonderfully detailed three-dimensional representations of the coffins, but several students did not turn in anything. Although both Jessica and Nancy reminded them of the importance of the project, most students replied that they were too busy or just didn't want to do it.

The students who neglected to complete the Egypt project are often the same ones who are disruptive during the book club time on Fridays. Nancy considers reading to be of paramount importance in her classes, so she encourages her students to order from book clubs such as Troll and Scholastic. Every other Monday Nancy passes out order forms and reminds the class to bring their money by Friday.

She often gives them a few minutes to share their new purchases with the rest of the class, and many students spend their free time before the bell comparing their orders and asking who has read what books. However, some students leave their forms on their desks or wad them up and throw them on the floor. These same students are the ones who talk disruptively while Nancy collects book money or distributes orders on Fridays, and both Nancy and Jessica have issued several detentions because of it.

For one of her student teaching requirements Jessica has to observe another teacher. So, Jessica decided to see how her "problem" students behaved in other classes on the team, namely Pat Schumacher's science class. Pat had a reputation as a strict teacher, but the students seemed to love her classes. After the observation, Jessica took the opportunity to ask the veteran teacher about Manny's behavior and the other students' performance in class. Pat was surprised to learn that several students were having trouble in Jessica's classes because they were "wonderful workers" for her. The student teacher pointed out that they weren't turning in their projects, and Pat nodded thoughtfully. "I never give take-home projects in my classes, because a lot of times students don't have either the resources or the time to do it at home," she said. "I give them all the materials and time they need in class. It's not fair to expect them to spend money they really don't have on art supplies for class projects."

Jessica returned to her own classroom with a new awareness of several of her students. She reevaluated what she and Nancy had been asking of them, both for behavior and for schoolwork, and found that her assumptions had set them up to do poorly. How many times, she wondered, had she planned her lessons with her own school experience in mind, not taking into account the fact that not all children's families have disposable income? She remembered her own excitement in ordering from the book clubs, realizing now how left out some of her classmates must have felt.

Although Jessica enjoys being in Nancy Miller's classroom, she is beginning to question some of Nancy's methods and activities. She asks herself, "How can we make the classes more equitable and comfortable for *all* students?" She would like to accommodate the needs of Manny and the others, but she is unsure how to go about this or how to approach Nancy about it.

Sue is the supervisor for Jessica and eight other student teachers. Also, she is a graduate student who is studying the effects of power within social groups. What Sue is learning from her reading and research informs her work with the student teachers. For example, she believes that Jessica is reluctant to criticize any of Nancy's classroom routines because she is afraid that it will sour their rapport. She also believes that several of the other student teachers are playing the same "don't rock the boat" game. Their two major goals are to please their cooperating teacher, and therefore get a good letter of recommendation, and to keep the students under control when student teachers are lead teaching.

Frustrated with what she had been observing, Sue decided to use some of the seminar time to discuss—without overtly using the language from any of the theoretical discourses about power—the effects of power on the student teaching experience. Sue opened the discussion in the seminar by asking, "Is it important for student teachers to have a voice in the triad relation (cooperating teacher, student teacher, and university supervisor)?" "Yes," claimed the seminar participants in almost perfect unison. Sue then asked, "Why?" The "why" question did not elicit a unison response. Randy said, "So we can get to do some of the things we want to do—for example, teaching a unit we developed, observing other teachers teach." Trina chimed in, "So we can negotiate with you about the kind of lesson plans we need to have when you come out to observe and the best time for you to come." The purpose of "voice," Sue was noting as the student teachers gave answers, had more to do with the student teachers' having agency to do for themselves and minimizing bumps in the student teaching experience. Their comments were not taking into account the importance of having a voice in order to affect others, especially the students.

Next, Sue asked, "Can the nature of the triad relation influence the voice of any of the triad members?" "Yes," claimed everyone. "How?" asked Sue, looking at Jessica. "Jessica," said Sue, "you and your cooperating teacher have excellent rapport. How has the nature of that relation influenced your voice?" Jessica responded, "It has allowed me to start this experience being treated as a co-teacher, instead of a student teacher." Sue then asked, "Has the relation silenced or muted your voice in any way?" At first, Jessica was surprised with the question and hesitantly responded, "I don't think so." Sue then asked the class, "If you are immediately and positively accepted into a group, can that acceptance influence your voice about the group?" Before the other students could begin to respond, Jessica said, "I get it. You believe that I am soft on the way I view the actions of my cooperating teacher—that I accept Nancy's methods and curriculum ideas without question." Sue smiled and said, "You do get it. Has your voice been muted or silenced because of your relation with Nancy? And if so, how and where?"

The next morning when Jessica saw Nancy, she said to her, "Can we have lunch together in the classroom today instead of going to the teacher lounge? I want to talk with you about some ideas I have for my lead teaching week. My ideas include making some changes in the way we do a few things. OK?"

SUMMING UP

In this chapter we began with a discussion of why teachers and students go to school. We started by discussing reasons why teachers enter the profession, including a sense of calling, the love of children, and the desire to help. We then turned to the reasons why students attend schools. The three purposes of schooling were outlined: preserving and transmitting cultural heritage, selecting and preparing students for occupational status levels, and preparing students to build a better society. We provided a critique of each purpose, related it back to the opening vignette, and concluded the section by noting that schools are not guided by any one philosophical belief alone.

We next turned to the changes influencing teaching and learning. Since the late 1950s and early 1960s, teaching has been changing. Some of the changes include the way the public thinks about teaching. Years ago, teaching was believed to be an easy job and "women's work." Presently for most people, teaching is a profession whose members work long hours, are engaged in lifelong learning, and are increasingly responsible for educating students to deal with life's social and health problems as well as preparing them academically for life in a technological, global world.

Classrooms across the United States are becoming increasingly diverse in several ways. The population of students of color is increasing while the population of White students is decreasing. As the century begins, one-third of the U.S. population is nonwhite and 31.8 million people communicate in 329 languages other than English. Eighty-five percent of the entering workforce will be women and people of color, and it is projected that citizens of color will soon become the majority in 50 U.S. cities. Language diversity is having an inevitable impact on school. In some areas of the country bilingual education is a popular tool for educating non-English speakers. In other parts of the country bilingual education is very controversial, and 26 states have passed English Only legislation. Over the past decade, inclusive classrooms, in which teachers are teaching students identified as having disabilities in the same classrooms as students not labeled with disabilities, have become commonplace.

We then addressed ways in which teachers' work is changing as a result of these changes in the public's view of teaching and student demographics. Different ways to understand the purpose and function of power have been developing for the past few decades. The idea that power exists for the parties involved in all relationships is causing teachers to learn about how power functions in the classroom and how power influences educational policies and practices. We began the discussion of this theme by defining power, particularly highlighting that it exists in all relations, and then discussing its role in schooling. We then discussed that power is not neutral and how it operates both visibly and invisibly in schools.

Next we discussed the second theme of the book, education that is multicultural and social reconstructionist (EMCSR). We explained that the dramatic changes in population demographics, the influence of globalism, the need to better understand how school policies and practices affect certain groups of students, and changes in curriculum content have caused us to choose EMCSR as a thinking and language tool to help examine and influence schooling practices. We discussed the goals and objectives of EMCSR, explaining how it will help teachers.

We then discussed instructional technology as a third major change in the way teachers approach teaching. We pointed out that technology is an area in which inequities exist in schools and societies, as poor neighborhoods and schools may not have the same access to technology as wealthier districts. We also noted that teacher candidates will need to learn how to make technology and computers a core part of their instructional strategies because it improves their opportunities to help students.

The public demand for academic standards, with a strong emphasis on students,' teachers,' and principals' accountability, is the professional climate that teacher candidates are entering. Although educators accept the importance of standards and accountability, a growing number of educators and others are questioning the use of a single instrument to determine how well students are performing.

As the nature of teaching changes, teachers are becoming activists, making their presence felt both inside and outside of the classroom through community involvement and teacher research. Community involvement and service learning projects are additional hands-on ways teachers are learning more about the communities in which they teach. Community involvement includes teachers' inviting local businesses, agencies, and community residents to participate with the school in the education of students. Teacher research, or action research, has gained momentum as a form of inquiry undertaken by teachers. It serves to improve teachers' own instructional practices, their understanding of those practices, and the situations in which those practices take place.

KEY TERMS

biliteracy
cultural pluralism
cultural transformation
de facto segregation
digital divide
education that is multicultural and
   social reconstructionist (EMCSR)
educational equity
imbalances (asymmetries)
inclusive education
marginalized students

power
service learning
social justice
social structural equality
social supports for learning
social transformation
student demographics
teacher quality
teacher research
working poor

QUESTIONS FOR REFLECTION

1. How would you explain the ways in which schools serve the public? Do you see your own schooling as tending toward any one or a combination of the three purposes we have described?
2. Some educators believe that only active participation in your campus classes and schools will begin to prepare you for your first teaching assignment. What other learning experiences can you have in the school community or conducting action research that will help to prepare you?
3. What meaningful experiences have you had with adults and children who come from a different race, class, and language background than your own?
4. Think of an interaction you have recently observed in an educational setting. How was power invested in words and actions in this interaction? Can you think of a way in which power was productive and not negative from your perspective?
5. Why is EMCSR important to classrooms in suburban, rural, and urban areas?
6. Some educators define teacher quality mainly as knowing subject matter. Others define teacher quality as also including being able to explain ideas

so that different students can understand them, and having compassion, commitment, honesty, resourcefulness, and persistence. Which notion or notions of teacher quality would you prefer to guide your teaching?

ACTIVITIES

1. Interview 10 college students (not enrolled in the school of education) about the purpose of schooling. Do the purposes described by these 10 adults match the purposes described in this chapter? How are they different? Which purpose is seen as the most dominant? What are these students' backgrounds—educational, racial, gender, socioeconomic, and so on? In what ways might student background, multicultural issues, and power issues be connected?
2. Select three ideas that you have learned from your liberal arts and science courses—for example, in one of your sociology classes you may have learned about how census information is collected and used—and discuss how they will help you in teaching.
3. Gather demographic information (e.g., ethnic breakdown, income levels) on the communities where your college or university places teacher candidates for their field experiences. Select two schools within a community that have different ethnic backgrounds and income levels, and find out how the teachers in the two schools are preparing students to become successful in a highly technological world.
4. Observe in a classroom for two or three hours or longer and note the effects of power and the inclusion of EMCSR.
5. Sit in on several site-based management team meetings at your school, or a departmental meeting at the university, or a school board meeting in your community. Identify and analyze which points of view about teacher quality are being voiced.

GETTING CONNECTED

Getting Connected will be a section in each chapter of this book. We will provide you with online resources to help in your journey to become an effective teacher. We remind you, however, that the Web is constantly changing as websites are updated and come and go. Most of the online resources that we provide are general sites. This will give you more opportunities for selection. Also, since you are starting out on a journey that is filled with a good deal of adventure, it may be smart to work out how you can personally connect with others so you can check in with your peers for support and help. Your instructor, of course, is there to give support.

We, too, wish to offer our services. We invite you to e-mail or write us. This is an open invitation as you tackle each chapter in the book. For some chapters, we will also include names and e-mail addresses of colleagues who are specialists in particular areas under discussion. These colleagues for the most part will be members of our editorial board and as such will be very familiar with the contents of this book as well as the area under discussion.

Author e-mails:

Carl A. Grant: grant@education.wisc.edu
Maureen D. Gillette   m-gillette@neiu.edu

Following are websites for assistance with the concepts of power and education that is multicultural and social reconstructionist:

http://www.aauw.org	The American Association of University Women is a national organization that promotes education and equity for all women and girls.
http://www.glsen.org	The Gay, Lesbian, and Straight Education Network informs educators and students about issues, available resources, local chapters, and news and events affecting GLSEN.
http://www.rethinkingschools.org	Rethinking Schools is an urban education journal dedicated to helping teachers work more successfully with the current educational problems and issues they are facing.
http://www.nameorg.org	The National Association for Multicultural Education (NAME) is an organization of educators PreK–College committed to a philosophy of inclusion that embraces the basic tenets of democracy and cultural pluralism.

SUGGESTED RESOURCES

Parker J. Palmer. *The Courage to Teach.* San Francisco: Jossey-Bass, 1998.
This book for beginning and experienced teachers reminds them that they chose teaching because they care deeply about their students and about their subject. Palmer takes the reader on a journey into the inner and outer landscape of a teacher's life, discussing both the pain and joy of teaching.
Carl A. Grant and Christine E. Sleeter. *Turning On Learning: Five Approaches to Multicultural Teaching Plans for Race, Class, Gender, and Disability,* 3rd ed. New York: Wiley, 2003.
This book discusses five approaches to multicultural education and then shows how the theories of multicultural education are included in lesson plans. The design of the

book is to present a "before" multicultural plan and an "after" multicultural plan, immediately followed by a discussion of the changes made between the two plans. Also included in the book are action research activities.

Eugene Garcia. *Student Cultural Diversity: Understanding and Meeting the Challenge*. Boston: Houghton Mifflin, 1999.

This book discusses the social, cognitive, and communicative roots of diversity. It explores how children learn to think and communicate within their home, community, and social environments. The discussion takes into account the relationship between home and school and addresses linguistically diverse students.

American Educational Research Association, American Psychological Association and National Council on Measurement in Education. *Standards for Educational and Psychological Testing*. Washington, DC: AERA, 1999.

This book discusses the construction of tests, fairness in testing, and testing applications. It argues for the sound and ethical use of tests and offers a basis for evaluating the quality of testing practices.

G. E. Burnaford, J. Fisher, and D. Hobson, eds. *Teachers Doing Research: The Power of Action Through Inquiry*. Mahwah, NJ: Erlbaum, 2001.

Mills, G. E. (2003). *Action Research. A Guide for the Teacher Researcher*. Upper Saddle River, NJ: Prentice Hall.

These two books provide guidance and important knowledge for students interested in doing action research or better understanding what this idea is all about.

NOTES

1. Studs Terkel, *Working* (New York: Pantheon Books, 1972).
2. Dan C. Lortie, "Observations on Teaching as Work," in *Handbook of Research on Teaching*, 2nd ed., ed. Robert M. Travers (Chicago: Rand McNally, 1973), 487.
3. Herbert Kohl, *Growing Minds: On Becoming a Teacher* (New York: Harper and Row, 1984), 5.
4. Catherine Collins and Frantz Douglas, *Teachers Talking out of School* (Boston: Little, Brown, 1993), 15.
5. Parker J. Palmer, *The Courage to Teach* (San Francisco: Jossey-Bass, 1998).
6. D. Biklen, *Parents, Educators and Inclusive Education* (Lanham, MD: Scarecrow Press, 2002).
7. Lou Anne Johnson, *My Posse Don't Do Homework* (New York: St. Martin's Press, 1992), 22.
8. Robert Reich (1990), quoted in Donna Shaw, "Helping At-Risk Students," *Curriculum Administrator* 35, no. 9 (1999): 30.
9. D. G. Ryans, *Characteristics of Teachers* (Washington, DC: American Council on Education, 1960), 366.
10. J. Brophy and T. L. Good, "Teacher Behavior and Student Achievement," in *Handbook of Research on Teaching*, ed. M. C. Wittrock (New York: Macmillan, 1986), 328–375.
11. James A. Banks, *Teaching Strategies for Ethnic Studies* (Boston: Allyn and Bacon, 1975), xi–xii.
12. Rod Page, *Meeting the Highly Qualified Teachers Challenge* (Washington, DC: U.S. Department of Education, Office of Postsecondary Education, 2002).
13. Committee on Assessment and Teacher Quality, *Tests and Teacher Quality: Interim Report* (Washington. DC: National Academy Press, 2000), 4.

14. G. Pritchy Smith, *Common Sense About Uncommon Knowledge: The Knowledge Bases for Diversity* (Washington, DC: American Association of Colleges for Teacher Education, 1998).
15. Bradley R. Schiller, *The Economics of Poverty and Discrimination* (Englewood Cliffs, NJ: Prentice Hall, 1995), 98.
16. Ibid., 90.
17. "Children's Defense Fund Reports Latest U.S. Child Poverty," www.childrens-defense.org, p. 1.
18. Laura Lippman, Shelley Burns, and Edith McArthur, *Urban Schools: The Challenge of Location and Poverty* (Executive Summary) (Washington, DC: U.S. Department of Education, Office of Educational Research and Improvement, National Center for Education Statistics, 1996), 8.
19. Pat Hulsebosch, Mari E. Koerner, and Daniel P. Ryan, "Supporting Students/Responding to Gay and Lesbian Parents in Queering Elementary Education," in *Advancing the Dialogue About Sexualities and Schooling,* ed. William J. Letts and James T. Sears (Lanham, MD: Rowman and Littlefield, 1999).
20. Alice Udvari-Solner, "Inclusive Education," in *Dictionary of Multicultural Education,* ed. Carl A. Grant and Gloria Ladson-Billings (Phoenix, AZ: Oryx, 1997), 141.
21. Ibid., 143.
22. Tommie J. Hamner and Pauline H. Turner, *Parenting in Contemporary Society,* 3rd ed. (Boston: Allyn and Bacon, 1996), 152.
23. U.S. Department of Education, National Center for Education Statistics, *The Condition of Education 2003* (NCES 2003–067).
24. Ibid.
25. Ibid.
26. Ibid., Table 37-1.
27. David Blades, *Procedures of Power and Curriculum Change* (New York: Peter Lang, 1997); Thomas S. Popkewitz, *Changing Patterns of Power: Social Regulation and Teacher Education* (Albany: State University of New York Press, 1993).
28. Thomas S. Popkewitz, *Struggling for the Soul: The Politics of Schooling and the Construction of the Teacher* (New York: Teachers College Press, 1998).
29. Alec McHoul and Wendy Grace, *A Foucault Primer: Discourse, Power and the Subject* (New York: New York University Press, 1993).
30. Cleo Cherryholmes, *Power and Criticism* (New York: Teachers College Press, 1988), 35.
31. Aristotle, *The Politics,* trans. Ernest Barker (Oxford, UK: Oxford University Press, 1995), 295.
32. F. Cordasco, *A Brief History of Education* (Totowa, NJ: Littlefield, Adams, 1970).
33. Peter Stearns, "Multiculturalism and the American Educational Tradition," in *Campus and Classroom: Making Schooling Multicultural,* 2nd ed., ed. Carl A. Grant and Mary L. Gomez (Upper Saddle River, NJ: Merrill Prentice Hall, 2001).
34. Lawrence A. Cremin, *Popular Education and Its Discontents* (New York: Harper and Row, 1989).
35. California Codes: Education Code Section 48291.
36. Michael Imber and Tyll Van Geel, *Education Law,* 2nd ed. (Mahwah, NJ: Erlbaum, 2000).
37. Ibid.
38. Michel Foucault, *The Foucault Reader,* ed. Paul Rabinow (New York: Pantheon Books, 1984), 194.
39. C. H. Cherryholmes, *Power and Criticism: Poststructural Investigations in Education* (New York: Teachers College Press, 1988), 5.

40. Ibid.

41. Brenda K. Marshall, *Teaching the Postmodern: Fiction and Theory* (New York: Routledge, 1992), 192.

42. Becky Roper-Huilman, *Feminist Teaching in Theory and Practice: Situating Power and Knowledge in Postructural Classrooms* (New York: Teachers College Press, 1998).

43. Cherryholmes, *Power and Criticism.*

44. National Council on Education Standards and Testing, *Raising Standards in American Education* (Washington, DC: U.S. Government Printing Office, 1991).

45. Marshall, *Teaching the Postmodern,* 99.

46. Robin Usher and Richard Edwards, *Postmodernism and Education* (London: Routledge, 1994), 90.

47. Cherryholmes, *Power and Criticism,* 35.

48. Carl Chase, *Galileo: The World Book* (Chicago: Field Enterprises Educational Corporation, 1970), 9–11.

49. Marva Collins, *Marva Collins' Way* (New York: St. Martin's Press, 1990).

50. James A. Banks, *Multiethnic Education* (Boston: Allyn and Bacon, 1988); Donna M. Gollnick and Philip C. Chinn, *Multicultural Education in a Pluralistic Society* (Upper Saddle River, NJ: Merrill, 1988).

51. Christine I. Bennett, *Multicultural Education: Theory and Practice* (Boston: Allyn and Bacon, 1995); Duane E. Campbell, *Choosing Democracy: A Practical Guide to Multicultural Education* (Englewood Cliff, NJ: Merrill, 1996); Carl A. Grant and Christine E. Sleeter, *Turning On Learning: Five Approaches to Multicultural Teaching Plans for Race, Class, Gender, and Disability,* 3rd ed. (New York: Wiley, 2003); Sonia Nieto, *Affirming Diversity: The Sociopolitical Context of Multicultural Education* (New York: Longman, 1992).

52. G. Orfield and C. Lee, *Brown at 50: King's dream or Plessey's nightmare?* (Cambridge, MA: Harvard University, The Civil Rights Project, January 2004).

53. Stearns, "Multiculturalism and the American Educational Tradition."

54. Ibid.

55. Ibid., 23.

56. William B. Stanley, *Curriculum for Utopia: Social Reconstructionism and Critical Pedagogy in the Postmodern Era* (Albany: SUNY Press, 1992).

57. Grant and Sleeter, *Turning On Learning.*

58. John Wirt, Tom Snyder, Jennifer Sable, Susan P. Choy, Yupin Bae, Janis Stennett, Allison Gruner, and Marianne Perie, *The Condition of Education* (NCES 98-013) (Washington, DC: U.S. Department of Education, National Center for Education Statistics, 1998), 38.

59. U.S. Department of Education, National Center for Educational Statistics, *Digest of Educational Statistics, 2002,* prepared February 2003.

60. President's Committee of Advisors on Science and Technology: Panel on Educational Technology, *Report to the President on the Use of Technology to Strengthen K–12 Education in the United States* (Washington, DC: Author, 1997), 47.

61. Barnaby Feder, "The Internet and Schools: A Vision and the Reality," *New York Times,* 17 May 2000, A21.

62. Committee on Assessment and Teacher Quality, *Tests and Teacher Quality* (Interim Report) (Washington, DC: National Academy Press, 2000).

63. Kathleen Densmore, "Service Learning and Multicultural Education: Suspect or Transformative?" in *Integrating Service Learning and Multicultural Education in Colleges and Universities,* ed. Carolyn O'Grady (Mahwah, NJ: Erlbaum, 2000), 45–58.

64. Ibid., 50.

65. Ibid., 57.

66. Kenneth M. Zeichner, (1997, October). "Action Research as a Tool for Educational and Social Reconstruction" (paper presented at the annual meeting of the Brazilian National Association of Postgraduate Education and Educational Research (ANPED), Caxambu, Brazil, October 1997), 10–11.

67. S. Kemmis and R. McTaggart, *The Action Research Planner* (Geelong, Victoria, BC: Deakin University Press, 1982).

68. Ibid.

BECOMING AN EFFECTIVE TEACHER

CHAPTER

2

© Think Stock LLC/Index Stock Imagery

FOCUS QUESTIONS

1. What are skills, knowledge bases, and dispositions of an effective teacher?
2. Do exceptionally smart people make the best teachers?
3. Are teachers of color more effective with students of color?
4. How has technology changed teaching and learning?
5. What skills do you think you will need to work with students, other teachers, administrators, parents, and community members?
6. Why are good teachers always learning?

BECOMING AN EFFECTIVE TEACHER

It was a warm day in September as Ms. McDonough opened the door to her classroom on the first day of school. She had studied the roster of her third-grade class, made name tags for their desks, and was trying to guess who was who as they filed into the room. It wasn't hard to guess which student was David Wang. A smiling Asian American boy took his seat in the front row. Ms. Mac (as the children called her) began to call the roll. When she reached the name of David Wang, she pronounced it exactly the way it was spelled. The class rolled with laughter and David turned pink. Ms. Mac was puzzled. Finally, as David sat in silence, one of the other boys said, "You say Wong, not Wang."

Ms. Mac thanked the student and was now embarrassed herself. How could she have been so stupid? She knew better than to assume that students' names are pronounced a certain way. Her usual technique was to ask students to introduce themselves so that she could hear them pronounce their names. No teacher had ever pronounced her name correctly, and she was particularly aware of how awful it felt to have the teacher mispronounce your name, sometimes for the entire year!

The next day, as she sipped her coffee while the kids were at recess, she thought about the incident. It was the first time she had an Asian American child in her class, and she found herself—even though she hated to admit it—with stereotypes. She was not surprised to see David's name on the list of children who went to math enrichment. She was not surprised that he appeared to be so quiet. She was surprised, though, when she saw him playing football with the other boys, pretending to be Donovan McNabb. She was also surprised to find that his best friend was an African American boy in the class. They had a lot in common, more than she would have expected. Her stereotypes were subtle and they might not have surfaced had David not been in her class. In fact, she realized that she did not even know David's ethnic background. He could be Chinese American, Japanese American, or something else. Ms. Mac was upset with herself. She was beginning to realize just how little she really knew, despite having taken a course in multicultural teaching.

Becoming an excellent teacher is a lifelong process that begins with your pre-service coursework and continues throughout your career. Excellent teachers typically do not see themselves as outstanding or different from the norm. Often this is because teaching is still a rather isolated act and teachers may not get an opportunity to see their colleagues at work. Now is the time for you to begin close observation of many different teachers in all types of schools. This chapter will assist you in knowing what to look for and ask about as you begin your analysis of teaching as a profession.

FOCUS ON EFFECTIVE TEACHERS

Think about your favorite teachers, the ones who taught you the most. What characteristics did they possess that made them able to teach you in such a memorable way? Much educational research has focused on what make teachers effective, and this effort continues today. Thirty years ago, when this body of research was just beginning to be developed, the results that were disseminated throughout the educational community were very general. Researchers had only begun to go into classrooms to see exactly what it was about certain teachers that caused the students in their classrooms to score higher on standardized tests or other measures of academic success. More recently, those who study teaching have begun to ask more complex questions about what it takes to be a successful teacher for children who are not experiencing academic success or who are bored or disaffected from school. This is particularly true of children of color and children in urban and rural areas that are characterized by high levels of poverty and by middle- and upper-class students in schools that are increasingly characterized by intense violence. The focus of this chapter is on the characteristics that describe those teachers who are effective for all children, regardless of academic ability, ethnicity, socioeconomic status, family structure, and ability to speak English. We examine the types of knowledge, skills, and dispositions that are necessary to becoming an effective teacher regardless of where you teach. We analyze how the effects of power, the result of the many relations we discussed in the first chapter, influence effective teachers.

THE KNOWLEDGE BASE OF EFFECTIVE TEACHERS

Excellent teachers have a wealth of knowledge about many things. Some teacher education programs select teacher candidates who have a degree in a content discipline such as art, history, or chemistry rather than education. Although it is true that teachers must have a solid academic background, content knowledge is only one aspect of the knowledge base that effective teachers exhibit in the classroom. We will discuss the role of subject matter knowledge in this section, but we also address several other types of knowledge that are essential to becoming an outstanding, culturally responsive teacher.

Culturally Responsive Teaching

We use the term **culturally responsive teacher** to mean any teacher who knows how to build the type of educational environment (classroom climate, curriculum, instructional design, management system, and family/community relationships) that leads to academic, social, and personal growth for all students. Some teacher candidates hear the term *culturally responsive teacher* and immediately assume that it applies only to teachers who work with students of color. Nothing could be further from the truth. Many scholars and researchers have described various characteristics of culturally responsive teachers. Gloria Ladson-Billings,[1] Jacqueline Jordan-Irvine and Beverly Armento,[2] Geneva Gay,[3] and Joyce King[4] are a few of the more prominent scholars who have described the type of teacher who can reach all students and who works toward a more just and equitable society through classroom practices and community advocacy. We have synthesized their ideas here. We begin with a short list of key ideas and will then discuss these characteristics in more depth throughout the chapter. Culturally responsive teachers:

- Believe that all students can achieve and succeed in life and hold high expectations for all learners.
- Build a "community of learners" in the classroom through personal connections to each student and encourages collaboration between students.
- Build connections outward from the classroom community to families, the school community, and the community at large.
- Are not afraid to be learners themselves. While they bring a strong content knowledge and a passion for teaching and for subject matter, they are always growing and learning, especially from the students.
- Vary instructional methods to meet the needs of the learners, beginning from where each student is in terms of knowledge and skills and moving them forward.
- Know that students bring a wealth of experiences, skills, and knowledge to school and use those to teach students more effectively, encouraging shared knowledge construction and responsibility for self and others.
- Are willing to be introspective and reflective about themselves and their teaching. They constantly monitor their beliefs and actions for bias and prejudice and will not tolerate manifestations of such from students. They are not afraid to teach students about the "isms."

We elaborate on this list by starting where every good teacher must begin—with yourself!

Knowledge of Yourself: Self-Understanding and Self-Acceptance

One key characteristic of excellent teachers is their knowledge of themselves. In interviews with practicing teachers and teacher candidates who were close to finishing their programs, we observed that many were aware of or coming to recognize the significance of self-understanding and self-acceptance. Marge, a graduating teacher candidate, told us:

> The most important thing that I learned during my teacher preparation program was not the history of education, or about students' and teachers' legal rights, or how to plan and teach a successful science lesson—a subject I really dread—or where to locate multicultural materials. The most important thing that I learned was about myself; my personal strengths and weaknesses, my understanding of

people (kids and adults) and how I believe that will affect my teaching, especially if I get a teaching job somewhere that is very different from where I grew up.

In the 1950s, Arthur Jersild conducted research on the relation between self-understanding and education. He asked, what does helping students mean in a distinctly intimate, personal way in the teacher's own life? He concluded, "The teacher's understanding and acceptance of himself [sic] is the most important requirement in any effort he [sic] makes to help students to know themselves and to gain healthy attitudes of self-acceptance."[5]

Recently, researchers who study excellent teachers have written about the significance of self-understanding. The ability to critically analyze yourself and your own experiences is crucial to understanding your students. Teachers are becoming aware that the classroom is a site of struggle that is influenced by multiple and often contradictory discourses. One such discourse is embodied in the way a teacher may see the world in contrast to how some students view the world. Martin Haberman, another education scholar, posited that "to some degree, all of us are socialized to regard our culture group(s) as superior to others. Our group may be based on race, religion, language, gender, class, or all of the above."[6] This statement suggests that becoming an excellent teacher requires you to consider how beliefs about your own cultural group and those of others may affect the way you approach the teaching/learning process. It explains how a teacher's membership in a particular cultural group underlies a way of thinking that can dominate classroom discourse.

A teacher must be aware of his or her values and beliefs and understand the implications of those beliefs in the classroom. For example, when Native American children attended public boarding schools in the 1950s and 1960s, they were forbidden to speak their native language and punished for any infraction of that rule. Their teachers believed that the English language was superior to other languages and did not attempt to recognize, promote, or value bilingualism. Many teachers today understand that English is the language of influence in the world, yet they believe that students who enter schools in the United States should not be immersed in English to the exclusion of their native language. It is true that English is the language of power and that all students in our schools should be fluent in reading, speaking, and writing English—but not at the expense or denigration of students' first language. Here is an example of the effect of power we discussed in Chapter 1 and how and why some native speakers have spent a lifetime trying to overcome the effects of such power relations on their self-knowledge and self-image. Testimonials by Native American adults who experienced the denigration of their native language confirm feelings of humiliation, inferiority, and shame about themselves and their language. Though the teachers may have intended no harm, and even have believed that they were acting in the best interest of the children, the damage was significant. In addition to the personal damage such practices inflicted on the self-esteem of Native peoples, many Native languages are extinct or on the verge of being wiped out because so few people can speak or teach them. Many Native Americans are working to restore their language because it is an intimate part of their culture and a testimony to their equality with other groups.

Understanding oneself also includes understanding how one's human and social characteristics (e.g., ethnicity, class, gender, disability) influence teaching. Lisa Delpit, a noted researcher on urban schools, observed, "One of the most difficult tasks as human beings is communicating meaning across our individual differences, a task confounded immeasurably as we attempt to communicate across social lines, ethnic lines, cultural lines, or lines of unequal power."[7] Research on how a teacher's ethnicity affects students is more available than research on other teacher characteristics, such as gender or socioeconomic status. **Teacher narratives,** or personal stories, are meaningful in helping White teachers understand how their backgrounds can present barriers in the education of students of color. Similarly, narratives written by teachers of different ethnic groups of color are meaningful in helping teachers of another ethnic group understand how different students of color learn. As you read teacher narratives, see if you can locate how power or the presence or absence of education that is multicultural influences the attitudes and behaviors of those involved. Gaining this awareness will be useful as you seek voice during your field experiences and in your first assignment as a beginning teacher.

Research on the impact of characteristics such as social class is increasing. Lois Weiner's work is one example.[8] She argues that a teacher's performance in the classroom can be affected by his or her socioeconomic background. Weiner believes that teacher candidates from working-class homes are more susceptible to institutional pressures to conform than are candidates from high-status homes. She contends that because many young White working-class women are the first members of their family to attend college, they will find a home in the teaching profession, which has historically been seen as a job for women moving up from working-class backgrounds. Weiner found that for the most part teachers such as these were apt to comply with the educational system rather than challenge practices that may reproduce unequal outcomes or be considered ineffective. They tend to passively accept the status quo.

We recently did an in-service program for elementary teachers from seven schools in a single district. Over lunch, we listened to the third-grade teachers from several schools talk about having computers in their classroom. Finally, one young teacher spoke up and said that she did not have a computer in her classroom and that the entire school had one computer lab where she took her class once a week. She wondered out loud why the third-grade teachers in the magnet schools each had four state-of-the-art computers in their classroom when she had none. She explained that her students came from poor neighborhoods with no computers at home and she was concerned that they would fall so far behind their peers in the magnet schools in terms of technology that they might never catch up. All the other teachers looked rather perplexed, as if there were no answer for her question. The conversation went on and when lunch was over, we asked the teacher with no computers what she was doing about the situation. She regretted that there was nothing that she could do besides ask for computers, which she had already done. She hoped the district would get her some computers soon. The perplexed teachers did not acknowledge that financial resources affect educational opportunity. The fact that they felt perplexed and remained silent may be an indication that they did not want their privileges disrupted. They might have feared that if they spoke up for their colleague and her students, they would lose privileges that they received simply because they taught in the magnet school. Similarly, the beginning teacher's decision to wait and hope the district would get her some computers indicated that she did not understand that effective teachers must be proactive and willing to engage in struggle.

Teacher candidates who attended school in the 1980s or 1990s witnessed movements by people of color, feminists, gay and lesbian people, and people with disabilities to become accepted as groups within the mainstream culture and as individuals apart from their groups. Self-acceptance, whether as a member of a group or as an individual, has become a milestone in the lives of many individuals. Self-acceptance allows a person to reject peer pressure and the adoption of norms that mask or hide one's true persona. Implicitly and explicitly some argued that although relations between groups and individuals are important, one group or individual does not have to adhere to the social dictates of another. In society for example, the rise of hip-hop and rap music is an example of "new" ways of determining one's self-acceptance. In education, Beverly Tatum points out in *Why Are All of the Black Kids Sitting Together in the Cafeteria?*[9] that what looks like hostile or separatist behavior by adolescents may simply be a sign of their growing self-acceptance. Self-acceptance and a strong identity help us to feel comfortable "in our own skin" and better able to deal with the world around us. A teacher who has a strong sense of identity will be not be threatened by the flow of power between teacher and students. That teacher will be able to encourage students to examine how the effects of power often shape how they develop a sense of their own self-worth and that of others. A strong self-concept as a learner is an essential component for personal and intellectual growth for both teacher and student.

Psychologists and educators like Tatum argue that self-acceptance and self-understanding are especially important to teachers because of the changes taking place in education today. For example, as debates over curriculum, instruction, standards, and testing intensify, teachers who question themselves or who do not feel confident enough to take a well-thought-out stance on educational issues may find it difficult to engage in the debate because they may be uncomfortable expressing their ideas. Teachers with a strong sense of self will be able to contribute to the improvement of their school. For example, a first-year teacher we know, Noah, is one of three Jewish teachers at Jefferson Middle School. He had just been appointed to his first school committee, the activity and events committee, when he learned the plans for events related to the winter holidays. Several committee members were advocating a traditional activity, the staging of the Christmas story, and having the school choir sing traditional carols at the local mall. Noah spoke up, asking the group to consider how Jewish and Muslim beliefs would be taken into account. The committee members were surprised by Noah's comments. Two members got defensive and argued that events such as the ones described were a tradition at Jefferson. Finally, another committee member asked Noah what he thought should be done.

As a first-year teacher, Noah's ability to question a tradition at Jefferson School is due in part to his own self-acceptance and self-understanding. How do you think

Noah's ability to have a voice on this issue came about? When we discussed Noah's case in class, some students said that it was because he was Jewish and he was annoyed that his culture and religion were taking a backseat to the dominant group. Others said that it was because he had good rapport with the other committee members and was not afraid to speak up. Some argued that he was a person who was concerned about fair play and it had nothing to do with his being Jewish. These reasons and others that the students suggested are based on their conceptions of relations among groups and individuals that are shaped by the effects of power in society and manifested within what they have developed as taken-for-granted reasons for events. It is interesting to note that during this class discussion, some students could not understand the ideas of others (e.g., that Noah was motivated by his concern for equity and fairness to all groups, and not because of his religion). Such ideas seemed off target or strange to them. What we see as "normal" others may think is crazy based on their conceptions of individuals and groups. All this was evident within the activity and events committee at Noah's school. Educational issues are discussed in schools on a daily basis: inclusion, ability grouping, and the manner in which free lunch tokens are handed out in class. A strong self-understanding will assist a teacher in being cautious but not afraid to question policies and practices that are unfair to some students or that privilege some and ignore others. Good teachers have the ability to be a "boat rocker" when necessary without losing valued collegial and administrative support.

We believe that teachers should be "boat rockers," or active advocates. They should speak up in a professional, well-thought-out way to rectify unequal or unfair situations in schools. It often happens that privilege, benefits, and advantages enjoyed by some people—for example, staff who work in wealthy school districts—become a taken-for-granted way of doing business. For example, school districts often have a great deal of flexibility in the distribution of resources among their schools. When resources are consistently distributed in an inequitable way, some students are penalized. Pointing this out and working to rectify such inequities is the responsibility of all concerned citizens. In schools, it is often teachers who are in the best position to see the unfairness of policies and procedures. Altering such practices may necessitate working with the administration, the parents, the teacher's union, and the students. It takes self-confidence and self-understanding to speak up in order to serve the needs of students and of teachers.

In conclusion, understanding of self directly relates to how "love and helping students" gets played out in the classroom between teacher and students. Like Ms. Mac, it is all right to admit that our beliefs may be stereotypic, prejudiced, or uninformed. The first step is to uncover our deeply held beliefs, to consider how we got those beliefs and what implications they may have for our work in schools. Haberman notes that this soul searching is a lengthy process, and he suggests several questions for you to answer for yourself as you embark on the road to self-analysis:

- Which are the superior people(s), and what are their attitudes? Which are the "inferior" people(s), and what are their attributes?
- How did I learn or come to believe these things? Who taught them to me? When and under what conditions? How much a daily part of my life are these beliefs?

- In what ways do I benefit or suffer from my prejudices?
- How might my beliefs affect the many issues surrounding what I believe about schools, children, and how they learn best?
- What plan can I lay out to address any stereotypes and prejudices that I may have? How can I check them? Unlearn them? Counteract them? Get beyond them?[10]

If a prospective teacher does not consider these questions honestly, he or she may be unable to effectively educate all students, work well with parents and other caregivers, or become an integral part of the school community. The results of self-analysis can then be related to the most important question you will face in teaching: What type of teacher do I wish to become? This is the beginning of your educational philosophy and the subject of the next section.

Knowledge About Why You Are Teaching: A Well-Developed Philosophy of Education

One question we often hear from students who are beginning a teacher education program is, "Why do I have to begin developing an educational philosophy now?" Your **educational philosophy** is your belief system about the purposes of education as well as what constitutes an effective education. Our students argue that they will do a better job of developing their educational philosophy once they are actually teaching in the schools. However, we believe it is essential to begin exploring your educational philosophy before you enter the schools. The fact is that you already have an educational philosophy whether you know it or not. You have developed certain ideas about how schools should be run, about how teachers should teach, and about how students learn best. You have developed these ideas, either consciously or unconsciously, by observing in schools for more than a dozen years as a student. "Unpacking" your deeply held assumptions provides you with a way to examine your taken-for-granted views about teaching and learning, school policies and procedures, parents, students, and a wealth of other educational issues.

It is not unusual for teacher educators to ask teacher candidates to focus on teaching philosophy. In fact, we devote an entire chapter in this text to helping you begin to shape your philosophy of education. For decades, prospective teachers have been asked to respond to questions such as:

What is education?
What is the nature of the learner?
What is the nature of subject matter?
What is the nature of the learning process?
What is the role of school in society?

These questions often result in dualistic responses. For example, education can be viewed as training for the world of work or as developing the understanding necessary to become a lifelong learner and to be able to make judgments through reason. The learner can be seen as active and full of knowledge and experiences that make him or her willing and eager to learn, or as an empty vessel with few important experiences to contribute to the process of schooling, a blank slate waiting to be filled. Similarly, the nature of subject matter has been viewed both as a collection of specific information and as broad ideas and concepts.

Many prospective teachers discover that responses such as these are too narrow and too linear. They understand that they need to consider the world as a place where either/or, good/bad, black/white answers often do not take into account the complexity of living in today's world or the multiple perspectives that exist about issues and events. Questions about conceptions of knowledge, diversity, culture, and learning are topics for discussion that intersect with ideas about what constitutes the curriculum and what characterizes excellent teaching. They realize that it is essential to consider the possibility of myriad meanings and perspectives, and the complexity that richer responses engender. As teacher candidates look at and listen to their classmates, they can see that although the class may be mostly White and female in many mainstream institutions, predominantly African American in historically Black colleges, or Latino or Native American in institutions that target specific ethnic groups, each person comes with different backgrounds and experiences.

Developing an educational philosophy leads to the awareness that questions and concepts are not neutral or fixed and must continually be tested through practice. They need to be modified as teacher candidates, supervisors, cooperating teachers, and university faculty engage and reflect on the obligations and responsibilities of teaching.

Knowledge of Curricular Content: A Strong Subject Matter Base

How much do you know? Are there one or two curricular content areas in which you have a strong subject matter base? Did you try to avoid certain subjects as you selected high school or college courses? A common argument among civic leaders, politicians, and many educators is that in order for teacher candidates and teachers to successfully prepare students to be active citizens, they should have in-depth knowledge of the humanities and sciences. This argument has been especially strong during times of national crisis. For example, when the Russians launched *Sputnik* in 1957, a panic set in among the public that the United States would fall behind the former Soviet Union in science and technology, putting our nation at risk. The federal government immediately appropriated a significant amount of funding for the development of new math and science curricula and for teacher training in these areas.

Such crises have not been the only catalysts for a focus on the liberal arts and sciences as precursors to teacher education. As you will read in subsequent chapters, in the late 19th century the United States was moving from an agriculture-based society to an industry-based society. John Dewey, perhaps the most influential American educator in the recent past, called for teacher candidates to develop a firm grounding in the liberal arts and sciences. Dewey believed that this knowledge improves teachers' level of scholarship and helps them to present subject matter effectively because they have a firm grasp of the structure and concepts embedded in the content, enabling them to break it down for students.

Within the past two decades, educators have steadfastly urged teachers to acquire in-depth content knowledge. *A Nation at Risk*, a study released in 1983 by the National Commission on Excellence in Education,[11] reflected this trend. The ideas in *A Nation at Risk* were supported by two other influential reports that followed in 1986: *Tomorrow's Teachers* from the Holmes Group,[12] an organization of deans of schools of education; and *A Nation Prepared: Teachers for the 21st Century* by the Carnegie Foundation,[13] a "blue-ribbon panel" of educators, politicians, and businesspeople who studied education. Both reports argued for teacher candidates to be grounded in the humanities and sciences. Both of the 1986 reports recommended the elimination of undergraduate teacher education programs, instead suggesting that teacher education be a post-baccalaureate program and that teacher candidates hold a bachelor's degree in an academic discipline in addition to a degree in education. Many state departments of education have adopted this suggestion and require that teachers have a content major along with their education coursework.

President George W. Bush was successful in promoting legislation, passed in 2001, that has come to be known as the No Child Left Behind Act (NCLB). We will discuss various aspects of NCLB throughout the text, but here we address the section that requires each state to define what it considers to be a "highly qualified teacher." Although the states have the right to determine the criteria on their own, the website of the federal government provides the context in which the states will create a definition. Under Title I, a "highly qualified teacher" is one who:

- Holds a minimum of a bachelor's degree
- Has obtained full state certification or licensure
- Has demonstrated subject area competence in each of the academic subjects in which the teacher teachers
- As a new elementary teacher (after 2002–2003), has passed a rigorous state test that demonstrates competence in subject matter and teaching skills in reading, writing, mathematics, and the other areas of the basic elementary school curriculum
- As a new middle or high school subject matter teacher (after 2002–2003), has completed an academic major, a graduate degree, or coursework equivalent to an undergraduate major in the subject(s) that he or she teaches and has passed a rigorous state test in that academic subject

It is clear that in the 21st century there is a continued emphasis on liberal arts education for teachers. Most educators and parents would agree, though, that there is more to knowing content than just accumulating credit hours. B. O. Smith, another influential educator, cautioned in the 1970s that when considering the role of liberal arts training in teacher education, it is essential to ask some hard questions. "We need to know what the liberal arts can contribute to teacher education—what they can and cannot do. We need to know their strengths and weaknesses as disciplines. And we need to know also what changes should be made in the purposes for which they are used and the ways they are taught."[14]

Attention to a liberal education for all teachers continues to be at the forefront of discussions today. Almost every state has adopted learning standards or frameworks that describe the content knowledge that K–12 students must know before receiving a high school diploma. Politicians argue quite convincingly that if teachers are to teach to the new curricular standards, they must be educated broadly in those curricular areas. Even secondary teachers must know more than simply their own content. As you will learn in the chapter on school organization, many middle schools and high schools are adopting team or house approaches to teaching. Teachers in secondary education must not only know their content well, they must be able to show students how their content connects to other curricular areas. The idea of thematic or connected teaching is important throughout K–12 education.

Today, along with raising questions about the contributions of certain subject areas, traditional sources of knowledge are also being questioned. Some scholars are taking issue with the notion that knowledge is objective and fact based. Instead, they argue that knowledge is constructed by individuals based on a particular view of the world—that is, a particular body of knowledge, with its underlying facts, is based on the ideas of some to the exclusion of others. Certain conceptions or viewpoints about what constitutes acceptable knowledge are debated, shaped, and promulgated by those who have power. Scholars also argue that there is no one grand narrative that tells all about humankind, nor is there one national narrative that gives the historical truth about the United States.[15] For example, the idea of "manifest destiny"—a national narrative—has long been discussed in social studies texts as the rationale used by the U.S. government to take control of land occupied or owned by others. Often this view is presented as if it were the only logical course for the United States to take at the time. However, the idea of "manifest destiny" is challenged by others as an imperialist concept used to justify the removal or massacre of American Indians and Mexicans from land that they were occupying in order to legitimate U.S. expansion.[16]

There are a multiplicity of perspectives that inform us about ourselves, our country, and the rest of the world. Teacher candidates will have to determine where they stand in these debates. This decision will affect what gets taught as well as how the curriculum is taught. For example, if you use a historical knowledge base that places a European or Western perspective at the center of historical events, your responses to student queries will be very different than if you include Asian, African, and Latin American perspectives in your core curriculum. Similarly, if you use knowledge that draws on feminist thinking, you will design a curriculum that is different from one that takes a patriarchal view of knowledge. Finally, an understanding of the source of the knowledge is critical to understanding the relationship between power and knowledge as it is played out in the classroom. Connelly, Clandinin, and He tell us:

> Teacher knowledge and knowing affects every aspect of the teaching act. It affects teachers' relationships with students; teachers' interpretations of subject matter and its importance in students' lives; teachers' treatment of ideas whether as fixed textbook givens or as matters of inquiry and reflection; teachers' curriculum planning and evaluation of student progress; and so on. In short, it has . . . become commonplace to believe that what teachers know and how they express their knowledge is central to student learning.[17]

Examples of Connelly, Clandinin, and He's statement can be observed in many classrooms, especially during the teaching of science and math at the middle school level. For example, science and math methods courses often stress how to teach the subject matter knowledge more than the subject matter itself. Therefore, some teachers have to scramble to learn the content knowledge that they are to teach. Mary, for example, is considered a wonderful teacher by many in her community. Her colleagues like and respect her, and many parents request having their children placed in her classroom. Mary's classroom always epitomizes a caring learning environment, and her bulletin boards, exhibits, and learning centers reflect attentiveness. Mary has excellent rapport with students, who like and respect her. Mary's weakness as a teacher, however, is that she dislikes and rarely teaches science. The science that she does do is by means of textbook, teacher's guide, and worksheets. Mary is self-conscious about her lack of attention to teaching science, and she sometimes acts defensively about this. Students with high potential in science and who demonstrate an eagerness to do science activities are not encouraged by Mary to pursue science. Instead, she encourages them to do more reading, writing, and social studies. Her students rarely do well in the school science fair. In sum, Mary's lack of knowledge and interest in science dictates her relationship with students because it causes her to avoid teaching the subject except from the textbook, to divert students' interest to other areas, and to feel somewhat uncomfortable when discussing science concepts with students unless she is referring to an activity covered in the science teaching guide. Mary has the power to increase her knowledge and become an effective teacher in science, but she does not. Her refusal to improve herself and her teaching in this area has a direct impact on her students. Her actions serve to disempower students because they are being cheated out of subject matter that is essential to a good education and may affect their future educational opportunities.

Mary is acting in an unethical way. As a prospective teacher, it is your responsibility to acquire a broad-based liberal arts background and depth in your specific major or content specialty. It is not possible to become an expert on the entire K–12 curriculum, but you must be willing to commit yourself to learning how to learn and to the often difficult task of preparing lessons that are based on solid content, taught from a variety of perspectives, and connected to your students in meaningful ways. This is the topic of the next section.

Knowledge About Teaching: Pedagogical Content Knowledge

Pedagogical content knowledge is a teacher's knowledge of the organization and presentation of subject matter in a way that makes it understandable to and applicable by others. You might say that good teaching is a skill and you would be correct, but knowledge about good teaching includes an understanding of the organization and presentation of subject matter in a way that makes it understandable to and applicable by others.

There is unanimity among educators that effective teachers must know their subject matter. But to be able to *teach* that subject matter, a teacher must also know what makes a topic difficult or easy and be able to "unpack" the conceptual underpinnings of a subject. John Dewey said that teachers must be able to "psychologize" the subject matter for students.[18] Dewey meant that the teacher has to consider the nature of the subject matter, its application to the real world, and its connection to the students. Good teachers take apart concepts, place them in a real-world context, and problematize them by developing inquiry-based lessons rather than lectures. In other words, an effective teacher must know how to turn kids on to learning. In 1970, an educator named Charles Silberman wrote:

> Teachers need more than a knowledge of subject matter and a little practice teaching experience before they enter the classroom. They need knowledge about knowledge, about the ramifications of the subjects or subjects they teach, about how those relate to other subjects and to knowledge—and life—in general. They need insights into their purposes as a teacher—why they are teaching what they are teaching, and how these purposes relate to the institutional setting of the school and to the value of the local community and the society at large. . . . Most important, perhaps they need to know that they need to know these things—they need to understand the kinds of questions their teaching will raise and to have some sense of where to turn for further understanding.[19]

As a prospective teacher, you'll need to take responsibility not only for knowing your subject matter but also for being able to present your subject matter in a way that connects the content to the existing knowledge and experience of students. Gloria Ladson-Billings is one of many education scholars who draw on the work of Russian psychologist Lev Vygotsky, using the term *scaffolding* to describe a type of teaching in which the teacher constructs the learning process in a specific way. The teacher strives to take students from where they are, building on their own personal knowledge base and skill bank, and increase their knowledge and skills by connecting it to what they already know and are able to do.[20] This may seem like common sense to you. Of course a teacher would begin by finding out what the students know and using that information to design effective lessons! But you would be surprised how many teachers do not take the time to find out what students know and are able to do. Some teachers assume that all students have a specific knowledge base and just begin teaching at a place where they think the students should be able to catch on.

Effective teaching is more than transmitting facts and figures. It is presenting subject matter in such a way that students not only understand the material but see the meaning in knowing it for their life beyond school. Excellent teachers begin gathering information about their students' current interests, background knowledge, and skill levels before the school year even begins. They use this information to connect the new knowledge to what the students bring to the learning situation. They have a repertoire of teaching strategies and a well-thought-out plan for each lesson, yet are flexible enough to change direction mid-lesson if the selected content or teaching methodology does not appear to be effective with the students or if they decide to take advantage of a "teachable moment" in the classroom. A teacher with outstanding pedagogical content knowledge makes teaching look easy and fun to the students. He or she is like a symphony conductor who can bring together musicians who play many different instruments to produce a concert in which each individual plays an important role yet the overall music is cohesive and pleasing to the ear. Many factors can enhance the symphony, and one of the latest is technology. This is the subject of our next section.

Knowledge About Technology: Are Virtual Teachers the Wave of the Future?

Technology is changing the way that teaching and learning occur in schools and classrooms. Teachers who have in-depth knowledge about technology will be able to assist students in using technology to learn. Equally important is the ability to critically analyze technology and its applications to education. Teachers must be prepared with knowledge about how technology can enhance learning. To do this, teachers must be well versed in the mechanics of hardware as well as the content of software, Internet sites, and their applications to teaching and learning.

As a teacher, you should know how to design assignments that integrate technology, lessons that can be more individualized, and units that are more modular so that students can work alone or in small groups to accomplish tasks. You will also need to know how to design projects based on technology. In our technological world, students can have their questions answered by people who are currently working in the field of interest, and you will need to know how to facilitate this process. For example, if a student does not understand the results of a science experiment, he or she may decide to e-mail a scientist whose work relates to the topic of the experiment. Many teachers already communicate daily with parents through web pages, e-mail, and other interactive mechanisms. Unfortunately, access to technology in communities, homes, and schools is unequal. One of the biggest advantages for teachers who have advanced technological knowledge is that they will be able to conceptualize ways to make the situation more equitable. For example, some schools in large urban areas, as well as in isolated rural areas, are making laptops available to students and their families through loans, leases, and other creative means. In this way, the school district and the teachers facilitate access to technology.

All of these things require that teachers know the hardware and software capabilities to maximize teaching and learning. Interestingly, a recent survey indicated that only one-third of current teachers in the United States believe they received training that prepared them to incorporate technology skills into classroom instruction in their teacher preparation program.[21] It is scary for prospective teachers to realize that their students may know much more about technology than they do, and it is always difficult to admit that we do not know everything that we should know. But it is the responsibility of teachers as professionals to work hard to enhance their content knowledge, especially as it relates to technology and the issues that surround technology in schools. We have seen web pages set up and operated by middle schools and high school students. Students serve as web masters, keeping the information current and relevant to students interests. The websites contain everything from student gossip to concerns about teachers, best buys for CDs and cell phones, and comments on school policy. We have seen other students send plays and teach lessons to peers across the country using ITV equipment. The students operate the equipment and create material in a way that is creative and professional. When we see these things, we wonder how the knowledge and skills of the students are being utilized within the curriculum.

One group that can help teacher candidates learn about technology is the International Society for Technology in Education (ISTE). ISTE publishes technology standards for teaching that span your teaching career. You will find its website in the Getting Connected section of this chapter.

Will computers, online teaching, and other forms of technology replace teachers? We don't think so. If we are to foster a caring, literate, and action-oriented citizenry, students will need face-to-face contact with their teachers. But technology has changed and will continue to change the landscape of learning. Already students can be connected to their counterparts in other states and countries, engaging in science experiments and reading texts together and comparing results and interpretations. With a computer, students can take trips to places they may never be able to visit in person. Are you prepared to be their tour guide?

Knowledge About How Students Learn and Grow: Educational Psychology

Your teacher education program most likely requires courses in educational psychology where you will gain a solid grounding in the psychology of learners as well as in the psychology of teaching. You will need to understand how students develop physically, socially, and cognitively. You will also need to understand how individuals develop conceptions of themselves and how this applies to the learning process. Educational psychologists look at human growth and development as a continuous process that begins at the moment of birth. We not only grow and change physically at different rates, but our conceptions of ourselves and of others develop in a unique way as we interact with our world. Who we are culturally, our background, may be based on many possible factors—an ethnic group, a social class, a gender, a religious affiliation—as we interact with others whose backgrounds are as uniquely shaped.

Psychologists suggest that our physical and cognitive development are affected by our environment, not only the physical features (e.g., pollution, geography) but cultural and historical events as well (e.g., discrimination, poverty, war). The interaction of the individual with his or her physical and cultural environment influences the development of personal characteristics and ways of viewing the world. For example, asthma is one of the most rapidly growing childhood afflictions. It particularly affects children growing up in poor urban areas where large refuse incinerators, traffic, infestation of cockroaches and rats, and societal violence create pollution and stress, conditions under which asthma symptoms increase. Anyone who has experienced asthma knows the debilitating effect it can have on health and, as a result, on learning. Regardless of how intelligent and talented, children cannot reach their potential if they are struggling to breathe, dependent on medication, losing sleep, and missing school. Your knowledge of child development combined with your knowledge of societal issues and the way you have learned to view how inequities are shaped and structured will enable you to work effectively with children in a given situation.

Identity development is also a key topic in many educational psychology courses. It is usually here that teacher candidates learn about the significance of developing a positive self-identity. As we have already discussed, you will need to develop a positive identity for yourself as a teacher. Your role as a teacher will require you to understand students' conceptions of themselves as well as their view of themselves as learners. Our identity is shaped by membership in groups (e.g., ethnic, gender, social class) but we are also individuals with unique experiences that may be different from those of other members of our groups.

Some teacher candidates have told us that they wish to be "colorblind" in the classroom. They believe that not seeing a student's ethnicity is the only fair way to treat everyone equally. We argue that teachers should not be colorblind, but they should not fall prey to stereotypes associated with color either. An excellent teacher is one who sees color and knows its meaning in society. He or she holds high expectations for all students and does not prejudge by ethnicity. Remember the opening vignette in this chapter. Ms. Mac needed to see David's culture and understand its impact while balancing that with his individual characteristics in order to develop a whole picture of David as a person and a learner.

Your understanding about the development of students will inform your understanding of why certain decisions you make in teaching seem to "work" or "not work" and the implications of those decisions for you and for the students. Educational psychology can assist you in these understandings. For example, educators today report that by the late elementary grades many students appear disaffected from school and that the reasons for this disaffection may differ by gender. Your understanding of identity development in students may lead you to clues about why they feel the way they do. You may draw on the work of people such as Carol Gilligan,[22] Lawrence Kohlberg,[23] Mary Pipher,[24] and Dan Kindlon and Michael Thompson[25] to understand how and why males and females develop differently. You can combine this with work on gender equity in schools, such as that by Myra and David Sadker[26] or the research reported in a study sponsored by the American Association of University Women. The latter book, *Gender Gaps*,[27] will assist you in building an understanding of why some students may feel disaffected from school. Books such as *Why Are All the Black Kids Sitting Together in the Cafeteria? And Other Conversations About Race*, by Beverly Tatum, may be used in your courses to address racial identity development and the differences between how and why African American and White youth develop their identities. Many researchers are beginning to focus on the integration and interaction of ethnicity, gender, class, and sexual orientation in the complex process of identity development. For example, Kevin Kumashiro's edited book *Troubling Intersections of Race and Sexuality: Queer Students of Color and Anti-racist, Anti-heterosexist Education*[28] may be used as a tool to understand how the intersections of race and sexuality affect the daily lives of straight and gay students and teachers, and how the negative discourses about gays and lesbian are contested.

In conclusion, knowing your students is as essential as knowing yourself. The educational psychology courses that you take in your teacher preparation program will assist you in understanding how children and young adults develop conceptions of who they are in the world and how those ideas affect learning. These courses should also contribute to your understanding of how various classroom practices affect students' self-concepts as people and as learners.

Knowledge About the Community: Connecting Students to the World Outside of School

How well do you know the community where you want to teach? This is a key question because, as a teacher, you serve not only the school population but the entire community as well. It is incumbent upon teachers to become active members of the community in which they teach. In fact, Gloria Ladson-Billings, in her book *The Dreamkeepers: Successful Teachers for African-American Children*, described teachers with a positive self-identity as those who saw themselves as a part of the community and who saw teaching as giving back to the community. Excellent teachers foster this sense of giving back to the community among students.

It is easy to teach in the traditional way about the community in which the school is located. For decades, primary-grade students have been learning about the fire station, the police station, the post office, and the library. Often real community members and real community events are missing from the ways in which teachers address community in the classroom. But the prerequisite to being able to connect the community to the curriculum in a meaningful manner is an indepth knowledge of the community and its components.

If your teacher preparation program is in a large urban area, you may be thinking, "These people are crazy. I'm not living in this urban community, it's dangerous." That may be true, but consider that the children you will teach do live in that neighborhood that you consider to be dangerous. Every community has varied neighborhoods and it certainly is desirable, whenever possible, for you to live in the community where you teach. It is very difficult to build a knowledge base about a community without actual experience in the setting. If you do live a distance away from where your field experiences take you, do not just drive in and out each day. Spend time in the community. Go to events that take place there. Stop for gas or coffee in the morning. Eat in local restaurants. Talk to the people you meet. Attend worship services and meetings in the community. Read the daily community paper. Find out what's going on and about the people who are contributing to the community.

The fire station, the police station, and the post office are all places that children should be aware of, but most students have been exposed to these agencies and the "community helpers" that work in them by first grade. Recently, we were in a fifth-grade classroom in a large urban area where a student teacher was trying to elicit from the students prior knowledge about how community services function. You may remember that fifth-grade social studies typically has to do with United States history and the development of our democratic values. The goal of this particular lesson was to build the idea that local government provides services to the people and, in turn, people pay taxes and have a responsibility to obey rules. The students were rather unresponsive and the student teacher was getting frustrated as she began to list on the board all of the services provided for the people. "Come on," she prodded. "When someone has a heart attack or when your house is being robbed, you call 911 and what happens?" "Nothing," said a voice from the back of the room. The other students laughed, "Yeah, nothing." The student teacher was red-faced with anger and asked what they meant by "nothing." One female raised her hand and explained that the police and the fire department are not quick to respond to calls in her neighborhood. They arrive so slowly, she added, that it's sometimes too late. "But that can't be true," the student teacher replied. Again, the students laughed. "Cops don't care about us," said a male in the middle of the room.

After the lesson, the student teacher looked at us in dismay. She asked us if we thought that what they were telling her was the truth. We both affirmed that it was and asked her if she had read the paper recently to see that the Latino community had filed a lawsuit against the city for discrimination in emergency response procedures. She said that she had not.

We did not tell you this story to stress you out, but to stress to you that even if you are doing a short field experience in a community with which you are unfamiliar, you need to build your knowledge base about that community if you are to teach effectively. We know that the student teacher we observed lost credibility with the students that day. The students had factual examples of the effects of power within a working-class community. Students are less likely to respect a student teacher if they feel there is no effort to understand them as individuals and as a group of people who are trying to live life in circumstances that are, at times, difficult. As a result, the teacher is not as effective as he or she could be and the students may feel disrespected. We certainly do not want that to happen to you or to your students. Had the student teacher known about the issues facing the community in which she was teaching, she could have drawn on this information, making the students' knowledge base part of the "official" curriculum. Successful teachers know that children come to school, even in kindergarten, with a wealth of knowledge. It may not be the textbook knowledge that teachers assume they know, and it may not be the same knowledge base that the teacher had when he or she went to school. But when teachers include the knowledge and experiences of the students as part of the school curriculum, learning become meaningful. Without knowledge of the community, a teacher's ability to make connections between the curriculum and the students is limited.

Another reason to build your knowledge base about the community is so that you can draw on community resources by including places and people that rarely get addressed in the curriculum. Do you know your local soup kitchen and the volunteers who work there? How about the emergency medical clinic and its staff? Do you know which houses of worship are in the neighborhood and who the rabbi, pastor, or imam may be? Are your students involved in scouts, Boys and Girls Clubs, the YMCA/YWCA, the Police Athletic League, or other groups in the community? Are proprietors of local businesses graduates of the school to which you are assigned? The extent to which you are involved in the community and use community resources, including parents and other caregivers, will speak volumes about your commitment to the school and to the students.

THE SKILLS OF EFFECTIVE TEACHERS

We stated earlier in this chapter that having a strong knowledge base is an essential characteristic of excellent teachers. It is not enough, however, to simply know a lot. You probably had teachers or professors who clearly had in-depth subject matter knowledge but who could not deliver that knowledge in a way that fosters student learning. The science of teaching may lie in the content, but the art of teaching is in the delivery of that content. Grossman links knowledge and skills, but sees skills as a set of procedures:

> Skilled performance includes knowing what to do, when to do it, and how to do it. In other words, being skilled at something involves knowing a set of procedures, knowing when to apply those procedures, and being proficient at executing those procedures.[29]

Good teachers are able to teach in varied ways, to communicate effectively with students, to manage the classroom successfully, and to use technology as a tool for more advanced learning. These are the skills of teaching that will be addressed in this section.

Pedagogical Skills: The Ability to Put It All Together

You may remember a teacher who seemed to have eyes in the back of his or her head. That teacher was able to do many things at once: deliver the content, keep the classroom running smoothly, and attend to the needs of individual students as the lesson progressed. As a student, you knew that you could not get away with anything in that teacher's class! The classroom ran like a well-oiled machine, yet each student felt that he or she got a degree of individual attention every day. How did that teacher accomplish this? Why is it that some teachers seem to attain a smoothly run classroom in the first two years while it takes others longer? The answer to these questions revolves around the idea of pedagogical skills.

Pedagogical skill, or the ability to successfully implement teaching strategies in order to meet the educational and social needs of students, is a key factor in effective teaching. Pedagogical skill requires that teachers have not only a knowledge base that is derived from multiple funds of knowledge (for example, traditional text and the students' neighborhood experiences) and the ability to take that knowledge apart, but the skill to make it accessible to students. In the previous section we addressed pedagogical content, or knowing about a wide variety of excellent teaching strategies. This section focuses on the skill of knowing how to implement those strategies.

Translating content into effective units and lessons day after day is very difficult. It is a process that requires a knowledge base built from multiple perspectives, a stance toward teaching as an inquiry-based act, the ability to continually gather and use data to improve your practice, and a knowledge of the social conditions of the students and the world. You will find that some content lends itself to small-group work whereas other material is appropriate to individual or large-group lessons. You will need to be able to create and implement lessons that address the variety of learning styles and the wide span of ability levels that will characterize your students.

A prerequisite for pedagogical skill is pedagogical content knowledge. Earlier we defined this as an understanding of the organization and presentation of subject matter in a way that makes it understandable to and applicable by others. This means that an effective teacher must ensure that she or he has an in-depth understanding of the content for each lesson, from multiple perspectives, so that the content can be broken down for students. The skilled teacher can then begin the planning process. A successful lesson does not happen by accident. Excellent teachers do not "wing it"; they begin the school year by spending numerous hours understanding the "big picture" for each part of the curriculum with the entire year in mind. Once the teacher has an understanding of where the students are expected to be by the end of the year in each subject area, he or she can then break the content into manageable units of study. Although good teachers certainly maintain flexibility, they have curricular goals for the year and are constantly monitoring and adjusting their plans. A plan for the year is like a road map. There may be one destination but many possible routes. If you do not know your destination, you might wander aimlessly. Once a teacher has the big picture, and breaks it down further into units of study, she or he can begin to plan on a much smaller scale. This is where pedagogical skill is visible on a daily basis.

In the planning process, teachers typically develop content, skill, and attitudinal goals for the students. As they begin to think through their daily lessons, they select a method for teaching the content and skills. Typically, teachers prefer methods that are in line with their underlying philosophy. They begin to put structure to the lesson, envisioning in their heads how this lesson might go. They anticipate potential problems. They know what materials need to be gathered and what tasks need to be done before the start of the lesson. Once the lesson design is complete and the teacher is prepared, the art of teaching becomes obvious as you watch an excellent teacher implement his or her well-thought-out plans. Because of this intense preparation and the clear road map in the back of the teacher's mind, the teacher is now free to let his or her personality and love of the subject come through. Spontaneity, flexibility, and enthusiasm characterize excellent teachers. They do not look as though they have spent so much time in planning. You may not see a written lesson plan! But don't be fooled. Teachers with well-developed pedagogical skills make teaching look easy *because* they have used their expertise to plan thoroughly.

We often hear people say that they were born to be a teacher. Someone may have told you that you are a natural for the classroom. Although this may be true, remember that just liking children and adolescents and being able to get along with them well is not enough. You need to apply skill to your lessons in order to help students learn. More important, you need to learn every day from your own teaching. We talk about this in the next section.

Reflective Skills: The Ability to Analyze and Act on Teacher-Generated Data

The notion of the teacher as a reflective practitioner has become popular in the past two decades. The term **reflective practitioner** means different things to different people. To us, it means a teacher who not only thinks about what is happening in the classroom, but researches his or her classroom practice in order to make changes that will result in a more democratic, ethical, and student-centered classroom where learning takes place every minute of the day. The willingness or mind-set necessary to becoming a reflective teacher will be addressed in the next section, but here we wish to examine the skill aspect of being reflective.

Some teachers erroneously believe that if they spend enough time thinking about their teaching, they are being reflective. In the Chapter 3 vignette, you will read about a student teacher who was experiencing anxiety over the unequal way in which she was writing students' names on the board and placing check marks after them. She thought and thought about her problem; however, she did little about it. Teachers who are truly reflective in their practice use their research skills to assist them in gathering data and making changes when necessary in order to bring their classroom practices into line with democratic ideals (e.g., student participation; exchange of ideas; equality and equity in treatment of all members of the class, including the teacher). The teacher-as-researcher model is appropriate to reflective practice. Increasingly, teacher candidates are learning how to gather information about the classroom environment, about the students, and about themselves in order to enhance their professional skills and effectiveness in the classroom.

Becoming a reflective teacher involves many skills: identifying issues or problems, researching the professional literature related to the issue, gathering classroom data, developing implementation plans for altering current practice, and assessing actions through a variety of means. For example, in the section on content knowledge we presented the example of Mary, a teacher who was weak in science and always gave short shrift to the subject in her classroom. If Mary were a reflective teacher, she would stop being defensive about her lack of knowledge in this area, admit that she had a deficiency, and begin the task of educating herself about science. Perhaps she would enroll in some courses to build her content base. She might commit herself to planning and teaching at least four science lessons per week, researching each topic completely before planning her lessons. She would also need to gather some classroom data. By audiotaping each class, Mary could assess her interactions with the students and her own teaching of the content. She might also design a questionnaire to assess student attitudes about science to ascertain the degree to which her own negative attitudes have been communicated to the students. Mary could ask colleagues who she knows to be strong teachers of science if she could observe their teaching to gain ideas and content.

There are many possible steps that Mary could take. The point is that reflective teachers take action and then assess the results of their work. As Mary implements a change, she might keep a journal to record her feelings, ideas, and reactions. This will help her track her progress and identify further areas for study.

In some ways, the skills of reflective teaching are similar to those used by other social science researchers. Reflective teaching is one of the hallmarks of an excellent teacher.

Communication and Collaboration Skills: The Ability to Build Relationships

Later you will read about the one-room schoolhouse of the past. The teacher was free to select curriculum and design lessons to meet the needs of his or her learners. Often there was not even an administrator nearby. Once a month, a principal or superintendent from afar might visit as he or she made the rounds to many one-room schools to ensure that things were running smoothly. Those days are long gone. Today, classroom teachers have to work collaboratively with many other professionals, such as team members, special education teachers, teacher aides, and parents. They work on school and district-wide committees, team-teach, job-share, and spend nonclassroom time in graduate school or in communities of action researchers who are working on improving their practice.

Perhaps the most important people with whom excellent teachers build relationships are students and their parents or caregivers. Research clearly indicates that the most effective teachers are those who build positive relationships with the students, seek to get to know the students, and allow the students to get to know them through learning activities that are relevant to both teacher and students.

Management Skills: The Ability to Arrange Successful Learning Environments

A teacher can be reflective, know his or her content, design exciting lessons, and have meaningful and appropriate relationships with parents, colleagues, and students. But if he or she cannot foster an environment that leads to learning, the purposes of schooling will not be achieved.

We will address classroom management and discipline in Chapter 3, so we will not repeat that material here, except to remind you that excellent teachers have several common characteristics. Most important, they get to know their students well, they genuinely care about each and every one of them, and they use their knowledge of and caring for the students as the basis for creating an atmosphere for learning. Teachers who make the biggest difference with students provide structure with flexibility, freedom within parameters, and options for projects and assignments. These teachers involve the students in learning but set clear goals for academic achievement. They create a safe classroom environment where students' ideas, opinions, and knowledge bases are woven into the very fabric of the classroom within lessons and decisions about policies, rules, and regulations.

Developing such a classroom involves skill in planning and managing such a learning environment. You may not achieve this type of learning environment in your first year or two of teaching, but if you work at knowing your students, planning effectively, knowing your curriculum, and learning from your experiences, you will surely get there.

Technological Skills: The Ability to Use Technology as a Teaching/Learning Tool

We told you in the section on teacher knowledge that you would have to know the ins and outs of hardware and software if you are to be effective in the classroom. There is also a certain amount of skill involved in using technology in the classroom to reap the greatest benefits. Every school district usually has at least one technology expert who can assist teachers with using computers, digital cameras, and other technology applications in the classroom. But a teacher who knows the technology and is skilled at using it will make the most of what is available to enhance learning. We know that currently drill-and-practice computer programs and computer learning games constitute much of what is called technology education. However, more and more students are learning word processing, searching for information through the Internet and World Wide Web, using hypermedia systems, and developing computer-based projects or presentations that reflect high levels of learning. As a teacher, you must be a model for students by using technology to teach the curriculum, designing assignments that require them to use technology, and constantly learning new technological applications that you can bring to the classroom.

We have discussed the content base that is necessary for teaching today. The skill level required of excellent teachers is constantly increasing. If we are to prepare students to access all the opportunities available to them, to analyze these opportunities in terms of our democratic values, and to make responsible choices in their careers and personal lives, our own skills as teachers must be honed.

The third important characteristic of outstanding teachers, combined with knowledge and skills, is attitude. There was a popular television commercial that claimed, "Attitude is everything." Although we clearly do not think that attitude is *everything* in effective teaching, the dispositions that you display will speak volumes to students, families, and the community.

THE ATTITUDES AND DISPOSITIONS OF EFFECTIVE TEACHERS

Do you believe that all children are capable of high-quality learning and achievement? Do you believe in holding high expectations for all students regardless of their life circumstances? Do you trust all students? Do you believe that all parents want what is best for their children, even if they may not be sure how to help them achieve success? Do you believe that as a teacher you have the power to make a difference in the lives of students? Are you willing to teach any students regardless of ethnicity, gender, sexual orientation, cultural practices, and socioeconomic status? Do you believe that teachers are role models for students? Do you think of teaching as a job or as a career? When you look out at a class of students, where do you see them in ten years? We want you to consider these questions as you think about your attitude toward teaching and toward becoming a teacher.

The final chapter of Martin Haberman's book *Star Teachers of Children of Poverty* is titled "Only Decent People Can Be Prepared to Teach."[30] Some of our students feel that this is a harsh statement, but Haberman believes in being blunt. He does not believe that everyone who wants to be a teacher should be allowed to teach just because they want to. What does Haberman consider to be the characteristics of decent people? He lists 12, although he adds that there are probably many more. Read through Haberman's list and see what you think about them. Haberman says that "star" teachers:

- Tend to be nonjudgmental. As they interact with children and adults in schools, their first thought is not to decide the goodness or badness of things but to understand events and communications.
- Are not moralistic. They don't believe that teaching is preaching.
- Are not easily shocked by horrific events. They tend to ask, "What can I do about this?" and if they think they can help, they do; otherwise, they get on with their work and their lives.
- Not only listen, they hear. They not only hear, but they seek to understand. They regard listening to children, parents, or anyone involved in the school community as a potential source of useful information.
- Recognize that they have feelings of hate, prejudice, and bias and strive to overcome them.
- Do not see themselves as saviors who have come to save their schools. They really do not expect their school to change much.
- Do not see themselves as being alone. They network.
- See themselves as "winning" even though they know their total influence on their students is much less than that of the total society, neighborhood, and gang.
- Enjoy their interactions with children and youth so much that they are willing to put up with the irrational demands of the school system.
- Think their primary impact on students is that they have made them more humane and less frustrated, or raised their self-esteem.
- Derive all types of satisfactions and meet all kinds of needs by teaching children and youth. The one exception is power. They meet no power needs whatever by functioning as teachers. [31]

What do you think of Haberman's list? We don't present his list to say that you must exhibit all of these qualities or that no other qualities are necessary. But we do want you to examine your reasons for going into teaching. Your attitude about teaching and why you are in the profession will be evident to the students who know a committed teacher when they see one!

The Reflective Teacher: Open-Mindedness, Wholeheartedness, and Responsibility

John Dewey noted that content knowledge and pedagogical expertise are not enough if a teacher does not have the attitude to work at becoming an effective teacher. It is the difference between a teacher who teaches the same way for

20 years and a teacher who teaches for 20 years but makes each year different and increasingly better because he or she continues to learn from practice and from the students, their parents, and the community. Systematic inquiry into one's own practice is hard work. Dewey believed that teachers need to have three characteristics in order to connect knowledge and skill: open-mindedness, wholeheartedness, and responsibility.

Dewey defines *open-mindedness* as "freedom from prejudice, partisanship, and such other habits as close the mind and make it unwilling to consider new problems and to entertain new ideas."[32] Here Dewey refers to a teacher's willingness to examine him- or herself, to admit mistakes and learn from them, and to work at always becoming more effective. Like Ms. Mac in the opening vignette, an open-minded teacher is one who does not get defensive when faced with an uncomfortable situation. An open-minded teacher is willing to learn from teaching and to explore alternatives, continually taking in new information and evaluating it in light of personal teaching goals, the role of schooling in our democracy, and beliefs about equity, justice, and fairness for all.

Dewey says that teachers exhibit *wholeheartedness* when they are so interested in something that they throw themselves totally into it with "a whole heart." Excellent teachers are wholehearted about teaching. In other words, they are so excited by learning about teaching, by turning students on to learning, and by continually challenging themselves to do better that it seems as if teaching well is a mission and not a job. Dewey said that when a person is absorbed by what he or she is doing, questions occur continually and new ideas spring up spontaneously. They change and they challenge ideas that are not fair to all students. Researching teaching and finding colleagues who are interested in talking about teaching and learning come naturally to teachers who are wholehearted. The most exciting characteristic of a person who teaches with his or her whole heart is that the enthusiasm is spread to the students, who then want to learn for the sake of learning.

Dewey's describes responsibility as *intellectual responsibility*. This term means two things: the desire to learn new things and the willingness to become absorbed in the task. It also means that an effective teacher holds him- or herself accountable for teaching in an educationally stimulating and exciting way. Inherent in this description is that the teacher implements practices that are educationally and ethically defensible.

Implementing personal change in the classroom means that teachers take risks. This is not always easy because teachers are holding their teaching up for scrutiny. They are admitting that their work can always be improved. A key element in the process of becoming a reflective teacher is the willingness to engage in the process. Once a teacher is willing to take the risk to examine and alter teaching practices, the skills involved become important.

Dewey believed strongly in democratic teaching. By this he meant that excellent teachers are those whose "actions and attitudes ensure that all children participate and succeed" and whose classrooms "are strengthened, not divided, by diversity.[33] Ken Zeichner describes the characteristics of powerful teaching in multicultural contexts. These characteristics are important for teachers who work with students of color and students who are not native English speakers, but they can be applied to all teachers because all teachers, it has been argued since the time of Thomas Jefferson and Horace Mann, are expected to prepare all students to be active citizens in our democracy. Educational researcher Zeichner enumerated these characteristics:

- Teachers have a clear sense of their own ethnic and cultural identities.
- High expectations for the success of all students are communicated to the students.
- Teachers are personally committed to achieving equity for all students and believe that they are capable of making a difference in students' learning.
- Teachers have developed a personal bond with their students and cease seeing students as "the other."
- Students are provided with an academically challenging curriculum that includes attention to the development of higher-order cognitive skills.
- Instruction focuses on the creation of meaning about content by students in an interactive and collaborative learning environment.
- The curriculum is inclusive of the contributions and perspectives of the different ethnocultural groups that make up society.
- Scaffolding is provided by teachers that links the academically challenging and inclusive curriculum to the cultural resources that students bring to school.
- Teachers explicitly teach students the culture of the school and seek to maintain students' sense of ethnocultural pride and identity.
- Parents and community members are encouraged to become involved in students' education and are given a significant voice in making important school decisions related to programs (i.e., staffing, resources).[34]

Hopefully, you have been lucky enough to have had a teacher or two who believed in you, held you to high expectations, treated you fairly, stood up for you when it was needed, knew you as a person, and increased your knowledge and skills. We know that you are on your way to becoming such a teacher. Now is the time for you to begin to develop the knowledge, skills, and attitudes necessary to reach that goal!

An Ethic of Caring: Creating Relationships and Learning Communities

In 1984, educational philosopher Nel Noddings published a book titled *Caring: A Feminine Approach to Ethics and Moral Education*.[35] This text was the catalyst for a dialogue among critical educators about the idea that effective teachers should possess an **ethic of caring.** A teacher who operates from an ethic of caring is one who can step out of his or her own perspective and consider not only the perspective of others (students, support staff, parents) but also the other person's needs, motivations, and expectations. Sonia Nieto, in her book *The Light in Their Eyes: Creating Multicultural Learning Communities*,[36] writes that creating communities of learners assumes that teachers care for and about their students. This does not mean that the teacher holds a sentimental "these poor students" type of attitude, which is characteristic of a teacher who has lowered expectations for students based on environment, socioeconomic status, or home situation. That attitude does not signify real caring. Nieto points out that caring teachers hold students to high expectations, place rigorous demands on them, provide support systems to meet high standards, and have respect for their identities and their families.[37]

Noddings would agree with Nieto because she states that an ethic of caring is a tough and practical ethic that recognizes that there is a significant relationship between what she calls the "one caring" and the "cared-for." Within this relationship, the "one caring" does not give up or sacrifice him- or herself when moving toward the "cared-for." The one caring desires "the well-being of the cared-for and acts, or abstains from acting, to promote that well-being."[38] This is where the ethic of caring interfaces with the concepts of the reflective teaching and teacher power. A teacher cannot act in a way that promotes the well-being of students without having understood the students' perspectives and having chosen to act from among alternative actions with the best interest of the student in mind. Reflective teachers do not use the power vested in the role of "teacher" to hold students back. They care for the students in a way that empowers them, even if it means being tough or strict or unbending at times. Reflective teaching, like acting out an ethic of caring, assumes purposeful action based on thoughtful consideration of what it means to educate a student for full participation in a diverse society. Thus, teachers who are reflective, who approach their work from an ethic of caring, know that teaching students means teaching the whole student, not just preparing them academically, but interpersonally and personally as well.

Nel Noddings makes an important point when she says that no rigid set of rules or prescriptions for action can describe an ethic of caring. Creating a community of learners based on an ethic of caring may look very different depending on the teacher. An excellent and informative book that illustrates this point is Miles Corwin's story of highly gifted students of color at Crenshaw High in Los Angeles. In *And Still We Rise: The Trials and Triumphs of Twelve Gifted Inner-City High School Students,*[39] Corwin describes two teachers, one African American and one White, who work with the students profiled in the book. These teachers, as well as the counselor to the gifted program, can all be described as having an ethic of caring, yet they take very different approaches to working with the students and have different opinions on how best to prepare them for life after high school. It can be argued that one of the teachers struggled throughout the year to maintain her ethic of caring, but all of the students in the text described these three educators as caring adults in their lives. So, students themselves may differ in how they describe the characteristics of caring teachers because these perceptions are based on their prior knowledge and experience. Research tells us that students respect a teacher, regardless of ethnicity, gender, or sexual orientation, if that teacher demonstrates respect and care for the students.

In discussing an ethic of caring, we cannot give you a definition or a "bag of tricks" for developing this aspect of effective teaching. We do agree with Haberman that just "loving kids" is not enough to be effective or to ensure that you will teach from an ethic of caring. You must consider your reasons for wanting to teach in light of the fact that sometimes students will be angry, cantankerous, obstinate, and disrespectful. Do you have the commitment to continue to be the "one caring" even when it seems that the "cared-for" does not want you around?

BACK TO MS. MAC'S DILEMMA

Ms. Mac immediately began a plan of action. She knew from her multicultural course at the university that in order to be the best teacher possible for David, she would need to understand his culture and how he viewed his own ethnicity. Additionally, she wondered how his culture affected him. But she would also need to get to know him as an individual, and she would need to examine and correct any further stereotypes about David. It made her shudder to think what might have happened had she acted on them. What if she assumed that David would be good in science, placed him as a group leader for tomorrow's experiment, and it turned out that he did not know as much as she assumed he did? David might be embarrassed again. She certainly did not want that to happen.

Ms. Mac knew that feeling bad about her own lack of knowledge and her blunder on the first day of class was something she had to get over. Everybody makes mistakes and she knew that the only way to really make changes was to face your blunders and your ignorance and make a plan to correct them. She had seen teachers she knew get very defensive when parents accused them of bias or when she told them that a remark they made was inappropriate. She did not want to be defensive; she wanted to learn from this experience. She had already planned a getting-to-know-you activity for the afternoon, and now she decided to switch the focus to an activity in which she would trace each child's silhouette. They would then cut out words that described them from magazines to paste on their silhouette. Having tried this with seventh graders, she knew it revealed a lot about how each child viewed him- or herself. She would also participate, having the kids trace her head and make a silhouette. They'd love that! This would be the first step in really getting to know all the kids. She knew that you can't teach kids whom you don't know.

As the recess bell rang, Ms. Mac vowed to spend the weekend catching up on home visit appointments with the parents. She had fallen behind, and not meeting David and his parents before school began led to the first day disaster. She had already met with five families, but with her own daughter starting third grade she had gotten away from her initial plan to meet as many families as possible before school began. As she rose from her chair, she thought about the work that lay ahead of her to maximize success for all of her students. She smiled and thought, "That's what good teaching is all about."

We think Ms. Mac is most likely an effective teacher. What qualities did you think about as you read her story? We hope that you were able to connect the ideas presented in this chapter with Ms. Mac's experience. Culturally relevant teachers make mistakes just like everyone else, but what separates good teachers from mediocre teachers is their willingness to examine themselves and work to do better. You may have felt defensive or you may recognize defensiveness in some of your colleagues when a professor, mentor, or friend points out areas that need attention in your words or actions. You will need to develop ways to move beyond feelings of hurt or defensiveness, especially when you are trying as hard as you can, and consider objectively what you can learn from such feedback. When you can do that, you will be on your way toward being an excellent teacher for everybody's children.

FINDING A VOICE

It was a beautiful January evening when Steve Johnson walked into his first graduate class. He was halfway through his third year of teaching and had just found out that he had been awarded tenure in his district. Attaining a master's degree was the next goal for him, and he was excited at the prospect of reacquainting himself with academic life. He planned on taking one course each semester and as many as he could handle in the summer sessions. Not only would his master's degree increase his effectiveness in his sixth-grade classroom, it would move him up on the salary schedule, and that would be nice. His advisor at Middletown University had suggested he begin with a course on curriculum development. As the professor walked in and passed out the syllabus, Steve's attention turned to the work ahead.

When class ended, Steve stopped by the bookstore to get the texts. Things seemed a bit fuzzy to him as the professor talked about the kids "being" the curriculum. He always incorporated the kids' interests into his lessons, but this guy seemed to be operating from a whole new perspective. Steve did not expect to be so challenged on the first night. He felt he was a good teacher; the principal had given him excellent evaluations each year.

His only problem was the other teachers in his building. He would never say so in public, but many of his colleagues at the middle school were burned out. When he began eating lunch with the children and going out to chat with them before school, some of the teachers made snide comments about his dedication. When he began the chess club, encouraging the kids to come in before school to play, someone called the union about the fact that he was getting to school at 7:00 A.M. with no other adults around. He hated to think that it was another teacher, but who else knew that the club was so popular? Steve was one of the few teachers in the building who hung the students' work out in the hall, put stickers and smiley faces on their math homework, and called parents on a regular basis to give brief progress updates. When he and his teammate held a summer picnic for the incoming sixth graders, a couple of the seventh-grade teachers commented that they hoped the picnic would not become an expected practice for everyone. Steve knew that all of these extra activities paid off for him when it came to incorporating the kids' interests into his lessons and to maintaining discipline—he had few behavior problems because of his frequent contact with parents in settings like the picnic. He didn't worry too much about his colleagues' opinions because his teammate was his educational soul mate, and he really did not socialize with the rest of the staff. Was this graduate course going to make a difference in his teaching? He wasn't sure.

By the fourth week of the curriculum class, Steve was beginning to think about his lessons and units differently. The professor had shown the class how to use old 16-millimeter film to make movies. They also learned the technique of claymation the old-fashioned way, with old 8-millimeter projectors. All of the students had seen or used video cameras, but the original way of making movies and cartoons, frame by frame, would be perfect for Steve's upcoming science unit on motion and location. What better way to learn about the way the eye and brain work together to see motion and determine location? The kids could make movies and learn the basics the old-fashioned way and then use QuickTime to learn how to do it in "high-tech" style. The best part was that he could tie all this to the math, science, and technology standards and use the textbook as a supplement. Now he was beginning to see what the professor meant by "making the kids the curriculum." If they chose their topics and designed and produced a film by hand, they would cover several standards and later move on to working with the video camera they have come to take for granted. This unit could provide a base for working them into designing a digital video about a social issue in the community, thereby covering the language arts and social studies standards too. He grabbed a pen and began to sketch out his unit plan.

Steve had a difficult time locating an 8- and a 16-millimeter projector, but his trips to the school district warehouse turned up two projectors in relatively good shape. He also unearthed several old movie reels and bleached out the original movie to reveal clear film that could be written on with permanent markers. Steve decided to introduce the unit on motion and location by making a class film himself. He began with the introduction, "Mr. Johnson's Class," carefully printing six frames of each letter. The concept of motion would be clear to the students when they unrolled the film and noted that each letter has to be written six times in order for the eye to catch it as it moves through the projector. He followed the title with some curlicues, making them swirl in and out through a series of lines, beginning with short strokes, each written six times, and then increasing each spiral until he knew the movement would come to life on the film. This was followed by the name of each student in the class. Steve chuckled as he pictured the kids' faces as they watched the film. He could drill home the science concepts of motion and location while teaching them the technological base for filmmaking.

Steve's unit was a huge success. The class got so into making film the "old-fashioned way," as they liked to say, that they had not even mentioned video yet. Steve got a graduate student from the university to assist him for the science period as the students worked on their movies. They asked if they could set their films to music and, after a discussion of the criteria for appropriate music (no put-downs, no swear words, etc.), Steve agreed. Formal lessons on the concepts in the textbook motion and location unit were held three times a week, always relating to some aspect of moviemaking. The first quiz, on which every student scored at least 86%, told him they were learning more than just filmmaking. The First Annual Mr. Johnson Film Festival took place the Friday before spring break. The class had designed criteria for judging the films, developed the rubrics and descriptors for evaluation, and agreed to provide each other with feedback (another idea from Steve's curriculum course).

Steve was having so much fun with his unit that he did not notice the stares from several teachers as they walked past his kids working in the hallway. Some students had laid out their film on sheets to keep the strips clean and the sprockets from tearing as they worked. Doors slammed nearby as the students set up or cleaned up their area. In the faculty room, one teacher asked what the students were doing and remarked that she did not see the academic relevance of filmmaking. Steve was often oblivious to his colleagues' reactions, but this time their disapproving looks were upsetting to him. Finally, the librarian stopped by to compliment Steve on the project. "I haven't seen kids this involved in something in quite a few years. You sure have brought a breath of fresh air to this school," Mrs. Beck said. "Don't worry about what the others are saying about you; keep up the great projects."

Steve reflected on the librarian's comments after the kids went home. A requirement for his graduate course had sparked this project, but once he jumped in, tied it to science, and saw the kids take off, he knew that his teaching would be changed forever. Whenever other teachers made remarks about his eating lunch with the kids, starting the chess club, or any of the other things Steve did, he sloughed it off. After all, he was doing what was best for the students. He decided that he needed to apply this thinking more to his teaching as well. This project was in the best interest of the students; they were achieving academically, they were getting along, they were totally turned on to school, and they were proud of their accomplishments. What more could he ask for? The stage had been set for the next phase, the community-based videos. He thought to himself, "I'm teaching for the kids, so I know I'm doing the right thing."

The next week the principal announced that Mrs. Worthy, the school secretary, would be retiring after 25 years at the school. The PTA would be having a retirement party in two weeks on a Friday afternoon. Each class in the middle school was to prepare a card for Mrs. Worthy to be presented at the party. When Steve told his class, they insisted on making Mrs. Worthy a movie. The enthusiasm was high, and after the science unit, there was no talking the kids out of this! So, Steve set up the movie center in the corner of the room complete with a very long piece of film, the markers, and some sheets. The class brainstormed the text and motion designs for the film. They decided to set the film to Whitney Houston's recording of "The Greatest Love of All," Mrs. Worthy's favorite song. Each student took responsibility for a section and worked on it during their free time. For two weeks, the kids worked on the film and the day before the party, held a debut in the classroom. Even Steve was impressed with the film, because the kids had really put time into letting Mrs. Worthy know how much they appreciated her work at the school.

As the middle school students assembled in the gym, Steve's class wheeled the projector into the back corner. Steve told the PTA president that his class would be presenting a film and she suggested that his class be the final presentation of the party. The seventh and eighth grades each presented Mrs. Worthy with a card and some students added artwork, songs, and poems. The other sixth grade presented their card and then the PTA president called Steve's class up to the front. Steve remained seated. After all, it was the students' gift. The kids wheeled the projector onto the floor and pulled down the screen. The other students looked on in amazement as Jamal, one of Steve's students, went to the microphone and thanked Mrs. Worthy on behalf of Steve's class. Michelle turned on the projector. As the message and visual images skipped across the screen to the music, ooohs and aaaahs rose up from the other students. Shouts of "Cool!" and "How did you do that?" came from the gym floor. As Steve sat back feeling very proud of his class, he noticed that the other teachers were looking at him with disdain.

After the party, several of the parents stopped to tell Steve what a great idea the film was. Students from other classes surrounded the projector to ask Steve's class how they made the film. The other teachers gathered up their classes, hurrying them out of the gym. When school was out for the day, two eighth-grade teachers stopped by Steve's room. Mrs. Bigley, the eighth-grade science and math teacher, spoke. "Look, Steve, several of the faculty feel that you have gone overboard. Some people feel that you are making us look bad if we don't want to do the type of projects that you do. Also, have you considered, that you're making students expect too much, which could be detrimental in the rest of their academic career? Also, hand-on projects are nice now and then but learning/memorizing the material should be the larger focus. We attributed your enthusiasm to the fact that you were a new teacher but now you have tenure and you are doing even more than before. We don't want to be held to your standard. I mean, I like you, Steve, but I think it's fair to tell you that some people are suggesting that maybe you would be happier at another school. Have you thought about a transfer?"

Steve replied that he had not considered a transfer. He lived in the neighborhood and did not want to move from the area where he taught. He was stunned. He looked at his colleagues and began packing his bookbag for the evening. Mrs. Bigley and the other eighth-grade teacher turned to go, and as they were about to leave, Mrs. Bigley said, "I know you think that you are doing the right thing, but these kids will come to expect that kind of project every year. Don't you understand? Some of us don't feel comfortable teaching your way."

Steve rode home in disbelief. His colleagues were asking him to teach in a way that was nonthreatening to them and not in the best interest of the students. He replayed the events of the past few months in his head as he ate dinner. He began to see clearly that some of the remarks, looks, and whispers in the hall were indications that the discontent among other teachers had been brewing for quite a while. After tossing and turning until two in the morning, Steve decided to speak to the principal the next day. He began to think that maybe he should transfer to another school. He decided to discuss the situation with his principal, Dr. Compton. Steve trusted her. She had been the principal who hired him and she would have some good advice.

Dr. Compton liked Steve and tried to encourage his innovation. She was not surprised, though, to hear Steve's story. In her career as a teacher and an administrator, she had occasionally seen teachers who viewed teaching as a nine-to-three job and who felt threatened by teachers who really were committed to the students.

She had tried to reward Steve's creativity by sending him to conferences, supporting his graduate work, and letting him know on a personal level that he was an outstanding teacher. However, she knew that she had avoided talking to him about how dominant ways of doing things in a school could influence the school culture. New teachers, like new principals, can be influenced to excel by outstanding colleagues or to lose their idealism and become less that they are capable of by teachers who are cynical or burned out. She knew that Steve was doing some soul searching, trying to understand clearly what was happening and why it was happening.

Dr. Compton began by reminding Steve of all he had accomplished in three years of teaching. She noted that Steve had taken several students who came from elementary school with a reputation for being disruptive into his classroom and they had really turned around. She told him that they were achieving at grade level, due in no small measure to their involvement in the chess club. It was because of his extra effort, she reminded him, that the chess club had as many female as male members and that the school received the glowing story in the local paper for winning the regional chess competition. She advised Steve to go through his desk and reread the many notes he had received from parents thanking him for all he had done for their children. "Take the night off," she suggested, "and remember why you went into teaching in the first place." Finally, she said, I will support whatever you want to do, but once you have reviewed your situation, I believe you will conclude that you have won this struggle. You have successfully resisted accepting what others want you to do and you have given many students and parents who had very little visibility a dynamic presence in the school. I am the one who has failed by being silent and not taking a stance to disrupt the pressure on you and some others to conform.

Steve left Dr. Compton's office feeling confident that she knew that he was a good teacher and that she was going to help. He decided, at that moment, to continue to do what he knew was best—to put the students first. It might not be easy if his colleagues continued to be so unprofessional in their remarks and behavior, but he was not in teaching for them. Before he headed home, he took a strip of film and wrote "Kids First" down the cells. He hung it up on the file cabinet next to his desk so he could look at it every day, reminding himself that sometimes being an excellent teacher is not easy—but it's worth it.

Sometimes gaining a voice means convincing yourself to trust yourself. You will come across many teachers in your career who do not have the characteristics that are described in this chapter. Many people, both inside and outside of schools, have criticized our beliefs in equity and multicultural education. It has sometimes been difficult for us to hear stories and see examples of students who get less than they deserve. But we have come to realize that excellent teaching—teaching from a multicultural perspective and teaching in a manner that empowers us as teachers and empowers our students—is what gives us hope for the future. When we see students excel, we know that there will be many exceptional teachers out there to support you. It will be important to be your own person as a teacher, to maintain your own identity, and to be true to yourself and your students. In this way, teaching will be the joyful, exciting experience for you that it is for us.

SUMMING UP

This chapter has described the knowledge, skills, and attitudes necessary to become an excellent teacher. You will need a vast knowledge base, a repertoire of skills, and most important, the attitude to succeed. But you are not in this alone. Your knowledge, skills, and dispositions develop from a wide range of sources, not the least of which is the students. You may feel overwhelmed at the prospect of learning all you need to know about the practical aspects of teaching (lesson and unit planning, classroom management, assessment, technology), the theoretical foundations of teaching (educational psychology, philosophy of education, multicultural concepts), the knowledge base in content and pedagogy, and reflective practice. But remember, your college program and your clinical teachers in the schools are there to assist you. You need to take advantage of all that your college and community have to offer. Most important, the most effective teachers you will have are the students! Look, listen, and learn from them—they hold the key to your future success.

KEY TERMS

culturally responsive teacher
educational philosophy
ethic of caring
pedagogical content knowledge

pedagogical skill
reflective practitioner
teacher narratives

QUESTIONS FOR REFLECTION

1. Do you agree that knowledge of yourself is one of the most important knowledge bases for excellent teaching? Why or why not? How well do you think you know yourself now? List your strengths and areas where you still need to do some work.
2. Why is each type of knowledge discussed in this chapter important for excellent teaching?
3. What is the difference between pedagogical knowledge and pedagogical skill?
4. What is the role of educational psychology in the teacher education program?
5. What attitudes do you think are necessary for successful teaching?
6. Why do you think the attitudes you just described are necessary?
7. After reading this chapter, what are some steps that you can take to increase your chances of becoming an outstanding teacher?

ACTIVITIES

1. Begin to keep a reflective journal. This does not mean you sit down every day and do a chronology of your experiences. Although you do write down events and information that seem significant to you, "reflective" means that your journal is a place where you think critically about those things. For example, if you are in a school as part of your course, you are probably engaged in observing in the school. Record your observations, but also write about what you see as the strengths, weaknesses, pros, cons, and reasons for what you see. If you read an article or chapter for your class, do not just use your journal to restate what the article says. Use your critical thinking skills to analyze the article.

2. Which of the knowledge, skills, and dispositions discussed in this chapter do you feel you currently possess? Which ones might you need to specifically address as you go through your teacher education program? Make a plan for how you will address these.

3. Does your state have K–12 curriculum standards or frameworks? If so, obtain a copy of the standards that you will be expected to teach children in math, science, technology, English, language arts, social studies, health, and career development. What content will you need to know in order to teach at your level? Where are your strengths now? What will you need to learn or "brush up" on? How will you go about doing this?

4. What do you currently know about the community in which you hope to teach? Make a list. Then begin to really look at that community. Drive or take a bus through all of the neighborhoods. What different types of businesses are there? What community services are in the neighborhood? Aside from the traditional ones (e.g., firefighters, letter carriers, police officers), who are the workers in the community?

5. Rent several movies about teachers and examine past and current television shows to get an idea about the range of views the media present to the public as "good teaching." Some suggestions from television are *Welcome Back Kotter, The Education of Max Bickford, Boston Public*, and various episodes of *Little House on the Prairie*. Some suggestions from the movies are *To Sir With Love, Fast Times at Ridgemont High, Dead Poets Society, Music of the Heart, Stand by Me*, and *Stand and Deliver*. Compare and contrast what you watched with other class members. What do you see in those pieces that represents the characteristics of a "good" teacher? How do the concepts of teacher power and student power manifest themselves in each show? Do you see the ethnicity, socioeconomic status, gender, sexual orientation, and language of the teachers and students playing a role? Describe.

6. If you plan to teach PreK–12, find someone who is studying to be a special education teacher. If you are studying special education, find a partner who hopes to teach PreK–12. Compare notes on what you feel are the most important characteristics of a good teacher and discuss why. Discuss how special education and PreK–12 teachers can work together to serve all students effectively.

GETTING CONNECTED

The Office of Educational Research and Improvement (OERI) was, until 2002, a branch of the Department of Education at the federal level. OERI funds several centers for effective teaching and learning across the country. In 2002, President George W. Bush signed the Education Sciences Reform Act that established a new organization, the Institute of Education Sciences. Although this reorganization changes some aspects of the research centers, there are currently 12 such centers that produce a wealth of important research about teaching and learning. Following are the addresses and websites for the centers that are related to K–12 education. Additionally, we have provided some other sites related to topics covered in this chapter. They will provide you with the latest research and information on important topics in effective education.

National Center for Improving Student Learning and Achievement in Mathematics and Science, Wisconsin Center for Educational Research
School of Education
1025 Johnson Street
Madison, WI 53706
http://www.wcer.wisc.edu

Provides the latest research on effective strategies for teaching mathematics and science.

National Research Center for English Learning and Achievement (CELA)
State University at New York–Albany
School of Education
1400 Washington Avenue
Albany, NY 12222
http://www.cela.albany.edu

Provides the latest research on effective K–12 strategies for teaching reading and language arts.

Center for Research on Education, Diversity, and Excellence
University of California–Santa Cruz
1156 High Street
Santa Cruz, CA
http://www.crede.ucsc.edu

Provides the latest research, books, and materials on diversity issues in education. Researchers focus on "improving the education of students whose ability to reach their potential is challenged by language or cultural barriers, race, geographic location, or poverty."

Center for Research on the Education of Students Placed At Risk
Howard University
2900 Van Ness Street NW
Washington, DC 20008

CRESPAR provides the latest research, development, and evaluation information on transforming schools to better serve students who are considered to be at risk for school failure.

Johns Hopkins University
Center for Social Organization
of Schools
3003 North Charles Street,
Suite 200
Baltimore, MD 21218
http://crespar.law.howard.edu
http://www.scov.csos.jhu.edu

International Society for
Technology in Education (ISTE)
e-mail: iste@iste.org
website: http://www.iste.org

ISTE is a nonprofit organization dedicated to the improvement of education
through the use of computer-based
technology in the curriculum. ISTE
directs the National Educational Standard for Teachers project and supports
many other technology-related initiatives and resources.

National Center for Early
Development and Learning
UNC–Chapel –Hill
CB #185
http://www.ncedl.org

This national research project on early
childhood education provides information and resources related to what
states are doing to improve and provide
early childhood education.

National Center for the Study of
Teaching and Policy
University of Washington
College of Education
203C Miller Hall
Seattle, WA 98195
http://www.ctpweb.org

This center is really a consortium of five
universities that investigate the relationship between excellent teaching
and policy making at the state, national,
and local levels.

National Coalition for Sex Equity
in Education
http://www.ncsee.org

Provides information, teaching ideas,
and resources for ensuring gender
equity in teaching.

National Research Center on the
Gifted and Talented
University of Connecticut
Storrs, CT 06269
http://www.gifted.uconn.edu

NRC/GT conducts and disseminates
research for educators, parents, and
policy makers related to identifying,
nurturing, and developing talent poten-
tials in diverse students. NRC/GT has
nationwide partners all working to
identify strategies to promote "high
expectations, rigorous standards, and
greater student engagement with subject matter" for all learners.

SUGGESTED RESOURCES

Ayers, W. *To Teach: The Journey of a Teacher.* New York: Teachers College Press, 1993.

Codell, E. R. *Educating Esme: Diary of a Teacher's First Year.* New York: Algonquin Books of Chapel Hill, 2001.

Comer, J. *Waiting for a Miracle: Why Schools Can't Solve Our Problems and How We Can.* New York: Penguin Putnam, 1997.

Corbett, D., Wilson, B., and Williams, B. *Effort and Excellence in Urban Classrooms: Expecting and Getting Success With All Students.* New York: Teachers College Press, 2002.

Corwin, M. *And Still We Rise: The Trials and Triumphs of Twelve Gifted Inner-City High School Students.* New York: Morrow, 1997.

Haberman, M. *Star Teachers of Children of Poverty.* Bloomington, IN: Kappa Delta Pi, 1995.

Irvine, J. J. *Educating Teachers for Diversity: Seeing With a Cultural Eye.* New York: Teachers College Press, 2003.

Johnson, L. *The Girls in the Back of the Class.* New York: St. Martin's Press, 1995.

Johnson, L. *My Posse Don't Do Homework.* New York: St. Martin's Press, 1992.

Kohl, H. *I Won't Learn From You: And Other Thoughts on Creative Maladjustment.* New York: New Press, 1991, 1994.

Ladson-Billings, G. *The Dreamkeepers: Successful Teachers of African-American Children.* San Francisco: Jossey-Bass, 1994.

Meier, D. *The Power of Their Ideas: Lessons for America From a Small School in Harlem.* Boston: Beacon Press, 1995.

Palmer, P. *The Courage to Teach: Exploring the Inner Landscape of a Teacher's Life.* San Francisco: Jossey-Bass, 1998.

Rose, M. *Possible Lives: The Promise of Public Education in America.* New York: Penguin Books, 1995.

Smith, G. P. *Common Sense About Uncommon Knowledge: The Knowledge Bases for Diversity.* Washington, DC: AACTE, 1998.

Weiner, L. *Urban Teaching: The Essentials.* New York: Teachers College Press, 1999.

Wilson, B. L., and Corbett, H. D. *Listening to Urban Kids.* Albany: SUNY Press, 2001.

NOTES

1. G. Ladson-Billings, *The Dreamkeepers: Successful Teachers of African-American Children* (San Francisco: Jossey-Bass, 1994).

2. J. Jordon-Irvine and B. Armento, *Culturally Responsive Teaching: Lesson Planning for Elementary and Middle Grades* (New York: McGraw Hill, 2001).

3. G. Gay, *At the Essence of Learning: Multicultural Education* (Bloomington, IN: Kappa Delta Pi, 1994).

4. J. King, Ideology, "Identity, and the Miseducation of Teachers," *Journal of Negro Education* 60, no. 2 (1991): 133–146.

5. A. Jersild, *When Teachers Face Themselves* (New York: Teachers College Press, 1955), 30.

6. M. Haberman, *Star Teachers of Children of Poverty* (Bloomington, IN: Kappa Delta Pi, 1995).

7. L. Delpit, *Other People's Children: Cultural Conflict in the Classroom* (New York: New Press, 1996), 66.

8. L. Weiner, *Preparing Teachers for Urban Schools* (New York: Teachers College Press, 1993).

9. B. Tatum, *Why Are All the Black Kids Sitting Together in the Cafeteria? And Other Conversations About Race* (New York: Basic Books, 1997).

10. Haberman, *Star Teachers*.

11. National Commission on Excellence in Education, *A Nation at Risk: The Imperative for Educational Reform* (Washington, DC: Author, 1983).

12. The Holmes Group, *Tomorrow's Teachers* (East Lansing, MI: Author, 1986).

13. Carnegie Forum on Education and the Economy, *A Nation Prepared: Teachers for the 21st Century* (New York: Author, 1986).

14. B. O. Smith, "The Liberal Arts and Teacher Education," in *The Liberal Arts and Teacher Education*, ed. D. Bigelow (Lincoln: University of Nebraska Press, 1971), 111.

15. P. Slattery, *Curriculum Development in the Postmodern Era* (New York: Garland Publishing, 1995).

16. H. Zinn, *A People's History of the United States: 1492–present* (New York: Perennial, 2003).

17. M. Connelly, J. D. Clandinin, and M. F. He, "Teachers' Personal Practical Knowledge on the Professional Knowledge Landscape," *Teaching and Teacher Education* 13 (1997): 666.

18. J. Dewey, *The Child and the Curriculum* (Chicago: University of Chicago Press, 1902).

19. C. E. Silberman, *Crisis in the Classroom: The Remaking of American Education* (New York: Random House, 1970), 489–490.

20. Ladson-Billings, *The Dreamkeepers*.

21. U.S. Department of Education, *Teachers' Tools for the 21st Century: A Report on Teachers' Use of Technology* (ED 444 599) (Washington, DC: Author, 2000).

22. C. Gilligan, *In a Different Voice: Psychological Theory and Women's Development* (Cambridge, MA: Harvard University Press, 1982).

23. L. Kohlberg, *Child Psychology and Childhood Education: A Cognitive Developmental View* (UK: Longman Group, 1987).

24. M. Pipher, *Reviving Ophelia* (New York: Ballantine Books, 1994).

25. D. Kindlon and M. Thompson, *Raising Cain: Protecting the Emotional Life of Boys* (New York: Ballantine Books, 2000).

26. D. Sadker and M. Sadker, *Failing at Fairness: How Our Schools Cheat Girls* (New York: Scribner, 1995).

27. American Association of University Women, *Gender Gaps: Where Our Schools Still Fail Our Children* (New York: Marlowe, 1999).

28. K. K Kumashiro, ed., *Troubling Intersections of Race and Sexuality: Queer Students of Color and Anti-racist, Anti-heterosexist Education* (Boulder, CO: Rowman and Littlefield, 2002).

29. P. L. Grossman, *The Making of a Teacher: Teacher Knowledge and Teacher Education* (New York: Teachers College Press, 1990), 37.

30. Haberman, *Star Teachers*, Chapter 6.

31. Ibid., 93–94.

32. J. Dewey, *How We Think: A Restatement of the Relationship of Reflection Thinking to the Educative Process* (Chicago: Henry Regnery, 1933).

33. North Central Regional Educational Laboratory, *The Essentials of Democratic Teaching* (2003), available at www.ncrel.org

34. K. Zeichener, *Educating Teachers for Cultural Diversity* (East Lansing, MI: National Center for Research on Teacher Learning, 1993), 23.

35. N. Noddings, *Caring: A Feminine Approach to Ethics and Moral Education,* 2nd ed. (Berkeley: University of California Press, 2003).

36. S. Nieto, *The Light in Their Eyes: Creating Multicultural Learning Communities* (New York: Teachers College Press, 1999).

37. Ibid., 100.

38. Noddings, *Caring,* 24.

39. M. Corwin, *And Still We Rise: The Trials and Triumphs of Twelve Gifted Inner-City High School Students* (New York: Morrow, 1997).

THE DILEMMAS OF DISCIPLINE AND CLASSROOM MANAGEMENT

Courtesy of Bill Lisenby

FOCUS QUESTIONS

1. What is the difference between classroom management and discipline?
2. How does history, or the way things have traditionally been done in schools, influence today's school practices in regard to discipline and classroom management?
3. How might a teacher inadvertently show bias in discipline and management policies and procedures?
4. Who are some of the leading proponents of specific discipline and management strategies today and how do they differ?
5. What steps can teachers and administrators take to prevent school violence?

Carol's Discipline Dilemma[1]

Carol, a 27-year-old White female, was student teaching in her local elementary school. She was placed in a second-grade classroom of 22 students, 9 girls and 13 boys. Five of the students were African American, 1 was biracial, 1 was American Indian, 1 was a Latino, and 14 were White. The class was socioeconomically diverse, consisting of sons and daughters of physicians, lawyers, and local politicians as well as a number of students whose parents were unemployed or receiving state or federal economic assistance. Academically, the class was heterogeneous, with a wide range of academic abilities present.

Carol's cooperating teacher attempted to foster a caring environment in the classroom; however, she used a form of assertive discipline[2] that involved extrinsic rewards and public accountability. Assertive discipline is a program designed by Lee and Marlene Canter in which teachers place students' names on the board for rule infractions with additional check marks for continued misbehavior (you will read more about assertive discipline later in this chapter). Although Carol's cooperating teacher, Felicia, gave her permission to adapt classroom practices according to her own personal style, Carol attempted to maintain consistency by using Felicia's system of discipline.

As Carol began to assume more of the teaching duties in the classroom, she became uncomfortable with the assertive discipline approach. She discussed her dilemma with her college supervisor, Lori, who asked Carol to explain how she was using the check marks to deal with rule infractions. Carol said, "Well, we have an elaborate simulated money system. We give each student five dollars a day and then for every check, they lose a dollar. One of our students, Hope [American Indian female], is on her way to receiving her last check. They get a timeout in the principal's office if they lose all five dollars. But I notice that I'm so inconsistent. Like some days, I'll just barely give one or two checks, and today I said to myself, 'I'm just giving them checks, I'm sick of talking.'"

Lori asked how she felt about this and Carol added, "Well, I guess I'd rather be consistent. The bad part is that I've been noticing that sometimes I'll let the better kids by. I'll give them a look or something, whereas I'll give a kid who already has two or three checks another check. I really hate that about myself."

When Lori questioned Carol about what she meant by "better" kids, Carol continued, "Better behaved, but a lot of times those are the better students academically. It's mainly those girls, Kitty, Diane, and the two Lauras [all White females]. I really want to change what I'm doing, but I don't know why I don't. It just happens that these four girls are smart and pretty well behaved, although not always. I give checks all the time to the other girls: Sherry, Val, Felicia, and Hope [all females of color]."

Lori asked Carol to think about what she was doing from a multicultural perspective. Carol said, "What bothers me is that three of those girls that I always give checks to are Black and one is American Indian, and three out of the four are from low socioeconomic backgrounds. The other four girls are all White and upper middle class. . . . I hate to say it but the four girls who I give checks to are, well, academically and behavior-wise, really low. The idea that they are Black or American Indian may be a factor in their academic performance and social behavior, but it's not why I give checks. I don't think I look at them and say, 'You're Black so you are at the bottom.' But they work together because they are all in the same reading and math groups. They play together at recess and after school. When I brought this whole issue up in seminar, Professor Stevens said that I have stereotypes. I am really confused with this discipline system and how I am supposed to be fair."

DISCIPLINE AND MANAGEMENT: A DILEMMA FOR TEACHERS

How can Carol solve her dilemma? In this chapter, we will consider some answers to this question, and we will return to Carol's dilemma at the end to analyze her situation. First we draw a distinction between "classroom management" and "discipline," defining them in terms of your work as a teacher. A historical discussion of how societal beliefs and pressures have influenced teachers' decisions in relation to classroom management and discipline will follow. We will then examine management and discipline in light of today's educational concerns by examining some popular classroom discipline programs and their implications for teaching and learning in schools. Finally, we will discuss school violence, an issue that is on the minds of educators and the public today.

We have chosen to place classroom management and discipline toward the beginning of the text for several reasons. First, we know that as someone preparing for the classroom, you are concerned about learning how to manage your classroom, including acquiring the knowledge to respond to inappropriate classroom behaviors and strategies for maintaining an effective learning environment. These are all part of becoming an effective teacher. The teachers and student teachers we met with as we researched this book told us that classroom management and discipline were rarely addressed directly in their teacher preparation programs. They insisted that readers of this text would need to be aware of these important issues. These teachers even went so far as to list the most common discipline and management problems they face daily (see Exhibit 3.1). Second, many school administrators have told us that the ability to manage the classroom is one of their top priorities in hiring a new teacher. Third, *classroom management* and *discipline* are often misunderstood terms. For us, they represent practical concepts that can be used to illustrate how the themes of power and education that is multicultural manifest themselves in the classroom. It is important for you to understand the difference between them before you consider how you will address these concepts in the classroom.

EXHIBIT **3.1**   **Most Common Discipline and Management Problems Faced by Teachers**

In-Class Discipline Problems	Out-of-Class Discipline Problems
Talking without permission	Pushing, shoving, and hitting in the hallways
Doing work for another class	Fighting on school grounds
Passing notes	Name-calling
Disrespecting others, name-calling	Threatening and intimidating others
Throwing objects around the room	Selling drugs, cigarettes, or alcohol
Excessive tardiness or absence	Possession of weapons
Failure to bring needed materials to class	Swearing
Not doing class work or homework	Leaving school grounds without permission
Constantly walking around the room	Defacing or damaging school property
Stealing the property of others	Disrespecting hall or playground monitors
Not following directions	Not allowing others to play games
Constantly leaving to go to the bathroom	Smoking or inappropriate behavior in the restrooms
Cheating on exams	Gang or clique activity
Using inappropriate language	Kissing, hugging, fondling in the hallways
Talking back to the teacher	Talking back to administration or staff
Tattling	Stealing school property
Fighting in class (verbal and physical)	Forging parent's/guardian's signature
Refusing to work	Under the influence of drugs or alcohol
Bothering other students, hair pulling, poking	Not sharing playground equipment

Classroom Management and Discipline: What's the Difference?

The terms *classroom management* and *discipline* are often used interchangeably. In reality, though related, they are two different concepts. Teachers and administrators often speak of classroom control as "management" and control of individuals as "discipline." A teacher who is described by parents or the principal as having "good discipline" is typically one whose classroom is relatively quiet and orderly and whose students are well behaved. We will discuss issues of control and order from our perspectives of power and education that is multicultural as we address classroom management and discipline.

Classroom Management: Creating an Environment for Learning

The commonsense notion of **classroom management** refers to the teacher's ability to arrange the learning environment, the physical setup of the classroom (e.g., desk arrangement), the learning activities, and the learners themselves in ways that foster the smooth flow of learning activities as well as daily routines (e.g., moving children to the gym, taking attendance, and collecting lunch money). Included within classroom management is the teacher's responsibility for planning and managing routines and activities for a classroom of between 25 and 35 students from around 9:00 A.M. until about 3:00 P.M. Within these hours, the students may move between teachers or classrooms for different academic subjects or requirements (e.g., physical education class). The teacher not only is responsible for smooth transitions between lessons that occur in one classroom, but may also be responsible for activities in more than one school setting. Additionally, classroom management involves ways to ensure that students know and accept their responsibilities (e.g., where to place completed assignments). Most important, classroom management includes the ways in which the teacher plans and executes daily lessons.

Some teacher candidates may think that achieving a smooth flow of activities is the hallmark of good classroom management. We argue that classroom management is much more than achieving a smooth and orderly flow. In fact, some teachers with excellent classroom management skills have classrooms that may seem disorganized to the causal observer. We will explain.

Classroom management is born out of a relationship between the students, the teacher, and the instructional environment. Teachers, because of their role, are vested with certain institutional responsibilities, with a certain authority that is granted by virtue of the fact that the teacher is "in charge" of a classroom. It is up to the teacher to determine how this responsibility is put into practice. For example, in a teacher-centered or tightly controlled classroom, the flow of power from teacher to student is rigidly controlled. Within this type of classroom, teachers tend to exercise tight authority in most daily activities. Students have little input into how the day is structured, how the subjects are organized, or how the material is taught. Students in these classrooms often do not just go along with the teacher. They look for ways to resist this control, often in the form of misbehavior or renegotiation of what is taking place.

Teachers who strive for a more democratic, or student-centered, classroom, are invested with the same institutional power but choose to use it in a different way. The flow of power between teacher and students and among students in the class reflects an effort to share roles and responsibilities in the classroom. Teachers provide opportunities for students to make curricular decisions, establish codes of conduct, and be "the teacher" in appropriate situations. These classrooms are characterized by the camaraderie between members and a sense of community. Students know that their voice matters and they willingly participate more often in classroom life, even knowing that their ideas may not always be implemented.

Examples of two different teachers may help illustrate these different styles of classroom management, one teacher-centered and one student-centered. Consider how the flow of power works in each one.

Amanda Mathews is a fourth-grade teacher who believes that students can make substantive decisions about curriculum and follow through with those decisions. She begins class each morning with a class meeting. Early in the year, she discussed different learning styles with the students and they identified themselves as either learners who need structure or learners who need flexibility. With the help of a practicum student and a student teacher from a nearby university, the adults in the classroom assist the students at morning meeting in planning their day. The fourth graders ask for either a time schedule (a daily schedule with 45-minute time blocks penciled in) or a task schedule (a daily schedule with only recess, lunch, and specials for the day filled in) depending on their learning style. They fill in a schedule for themselves for the day. Prior to ending the class meeting, the students share their plans for the day. Sometimes, if more than one student is working on a topic—long division, for example—they may choose to schedule a group work session and ask the teacher to join them. For example, a student with a task schedule may choose to work on reading for the entire morning, whereas a student who believes she need more structure will schedule her day in 45-minute subject blocks of math, reading, social studies, and science. Students then pick up their individual work folders from a hanging file and move around the classroom or go to the library, gathering books and materials they need for their work. They are free to alter their schedule if they are involved in a project and do not want to stop at the time they scheduled for themselves.

Amanda uses her "teacher power" to establish the minimum number of minutes a student must spend on each subject area during the week. She also uses her authority to monitor the students' activities and to call them for small-group and large-group lessons when necessary. At the end of every day, the class meeting reconvenes and students compare their daily charts so that if, for example, a student has not done any math by Tuesday afternoon, she knows that she must spend a big block of time doing math each day for the rest of the week. Each afternoon, Amanda and her student teacher review the students' work folders and make plans to guide any students who may not be attending to certain academic areas. They keep running notes on students' progress in a huge binder with a section for each student. Amanda writes quarterly narrative reports to the parents for each of the 23 students in her class. Although this is time consuming, she believes it provides parents with a better picture of what their children are accomplishing.

Gary Beach, a middle school teacher, could not function in a classroom like Amanda's (nor she in his!). His classroom is highly teacher-centered. The first thing Gary does when he enters the classroom in the morning is write the daily schedule on the board. The schedule rarely varies because Gary believes that students need predictability and structure. Next, Gary writes a daily sentence on the board that contains many errors in spelling, grammar, and punctuation because the students know that the first task of the day is to write the sentence correctly as soon as they take their seats. The class then corrects the sentence together. After the daily sentence lesson, Gary begins his block schedule with his homeroom. He does the same thing every day, unless a school assembly or other unusual circumstance arises. Gary plans his weekly lessons according to the textbooks chosen by the district. He typically proceeds in the order that the text provides because he believes this offers the most comprehensive coverage of the curriculum standards. Gary often jokes and talks informally with his students between classes but they rarely get up from their desks. Gary learned about cooperative learning in his teacher preparation program but really does not feel comfortable with a lot of student movement in the class. Gary collects student work at the end of each subject period and tries to grade it promptly and return it to students the next day. He always remembers to record students' grades each day so that he is prepared to determine grades on report cards each quarter.

Neither Amanda nor Gary has many discipline problems and both teachers have classrooms with consistently high standardized test scores. Both teachers are well liked by the students and the parents would say that they are excellent classroom managers. But each views the power vested in the teacher's role differently. Amanda gives students wide latitude and readily accepts their input on important curricular decisions. Gary controls all of the curricular decisions and most of the scheduling decisions. What is different about Amanda and Gary is the messages students receive in each classroom about the role of the teacher and the role of the student. In Amanda's class, power is shared by teacher and students, although the teacher does not abdicate her professional responsibility to ensure that the students are learning the curriculum. Gary's class is a good example of power that is vested in the teacher with students having no voice in curricular decisions.

Management of the classroom, as you can see, focuses on the teaching/learning process and the relationships between and among administrators, teachers, and students in creating a school environment that is conducive to learning. Teacher candidates often think that once they have the schedule and routines down, they will know how to react to the myriad situations that arise in schools. They may also believe that once they have an established approach to working with students, be it teacher-centered or student-centered, the students' behavior will be predictable and manageable on a day-to-day basis. However, the very nature of the flow of human relationships and power within them implies that they will never be static, predictable, or manageable the same way every day. Understanding this unpredictability is also an important part of classroom management. One way to think about this is to ask yourself if you think or react to similar situations in the same way. Do you expect people to treat you the same way after getting to know you as they did when they first met you? Do certain people, events, places, and activities inspire new and creative responses from you? You most likely answered these questions in a way that illustrates that your behavior is not static. As an individual, you and your responses are unique. It is to these individual situations that most educators refer when they discuss discipline.

You could argue that discipline has the same focus as management, and to some extent this is true. Good discipline is about relationships between people, situations, and environments. You may recall our mentioning that in tightly controlled environments students may openly resist teacher control. This usually manifests itself in the form of misbehavior. So, when administrators and teachers talk about classroom discipline, they are usually referring to the never-ending issue of getting individual students, and sometimes the entire class, to behave in a manner desired by the teacher.

Discipline: Fostering Individual and Collective Responsibility

As defined by *The American Heritage Dictionary* (1997), **discipline** is "training expected to produce a specific character or pattern of behavior, especially training that produces moral or mental improvement." This definition is in line with the beliefs of many educators that the ultimate goal of an educational system is to foster individuals who are capable of directing their own academic and personal growth through self-discipline. Yet the fact that "training" is mentioned suggests that rewards that come from a source outside oneself, or **extrinsic rewards** (e.g., stickers, candy, or skip-one-homework coupons), and sanctions that come from an outside source, or **extrinsic punishments** (e.g., after-school detention, in-school suspension), are used to promote a learning environment that is free of disruptions by individual students.

The use of extrinsic motivators to assist in the production of internal motivation is a topic of debate among education professionals. Many teachers do not believe in systems of extrinsic rewards and punishment, opting instead for an approach that fosters **intrinsic rewards**—a student's sense of satisfaction that comes from learning new material, successfully completing a difficult book, or doing well on an exam. These teachers strive to make the classroom an exciting place full of hands-on activities that fully involve students in the conception, design, and evaluation of projects. This approach is meant to maximize the time students stay "on task" and are not engaged in inappropriate behaviors. Other teachers argue that society itself is based on systems of rewards (e.g., paychecks, prizes, winning a game) and punishments (e.g., getting fired from one's job, losing a game) and that rewarding students for academic achievement and proper behavior and punishing them for inappropriate actions is no different from what they will encounter in life after school.

The manner in which a teacher chooses to approach discipline, just like classroom management, says much about how he or she views power. Inherent in the disciplinary techniques that the teacher uses are clues to how she or he understands the flow of power in the classroom, the teacher–student relationship. In some classrooms, the teacher is very autocratic, an absolute dictator. This type of teacher makes and enforces all of the rules and consequences. When students engage in inappropriate behavior, it is often an attempt to change the power dynamic—that is, to resist the teacher's dominance and to gain back some power for themselves. We have probably all been in classrooms where the teacher and the students engage in a struggle for power. It is not a pretty sight, and no one is helped, teacher or student.

Other teachers strive for a democratic classroom where power is shared. Because the teacher is the adult in the classroom, he or she will always be the authority figure. However, it is possible to foster a sense of community in the classroom with a shared sense of group responsibility for creating and maintaining an effective learning environment. In such a classroom, the teacher and the students jointly make the rules and decide on the consequences. The teacher fosters a concern for the academic and social success of each student. The classroom *ethos*, or spirit, embodies the idea of collective responsibility—"We're all in this together."

Most student teachers fear the day when, left alone in the classroom for the first time, several of the students begin to misbehave. You know now that the relationship you develop with your students and your ability to control the class will be a crucial element in how others evaluate your teaching skill.

DISCIPLINE AND MANAGEMENT: WHAT'S THE PAST GOT TO DO WITH IT?

Today, classroom discipline and management are "hot topics" in education, but that was not always the case. The current debates over systems of discipline and classroom management schemes have their roots in the early 20th century. In this section, you will see that many of the practices that exist in schools today can be traced to the beginning of schooling in the United States. Although this historical review of classroom management is not meant to be exhaustive, it will provide you with an understanding of the development of educational philosophies in this country so that you can focus on your own philosophy.

Colonial Schools: Spare the Rod?

When formal schooling began in the United States, it was closely tied to the Protestant religious beliefs of such groups as Lutherans, Calvinists, and Presbyterians. The prevailing Protestant philosophy about the role and nature of children dictated policy and practice related to the ways in which children were treated in the classroom. The Puritans, one of the most conservative Protestant groups to come to the United States, established sects in what are now the New England states. This group believed in strict religious discipline and a strong connection between church and state. The Puritans believed that all humans, including children, had an inherently evil nature. Elementary school–aged students were seen as lacking the maturity to make proper decisions and, thus, unable to choose a path of righteous behavior. Therefore, children had to be instilled with a fear of God's retribution in order to do the right thing. Instilling the fear of God in children typically occurred through physical punishment.[3] In 1699, a famous Puritan, Cotton Mather, wrote *A Family Well-Ordered*, parts of which addressed the purpose of school and the behavior of children. Historians have stated that Mather argued "if parents wanted their children to fear God, the home must be ruled with absolute authority, children must be kept in subjugation, and the parents' word must be law."[4] In Puritan philosophy, good teaching practices were synonymous with strict discipline, which included scare tactics and an emphasis on obedience to the unquestioned authority of the teacher or parent.

It is not difficult to envision what those early colonial schools were like, given the view of children prevalent at the time. Desks were in straight rows. Students did not speak unless they were spoken to by the teacher. Rote memorization of biblical verse constituted the curriculum. The teacher was the ultimate authority, making and enforcing the rules. Further, **corporal punishment**—physical consequences such as spanking or asking students to kneel in the corner wearing a dunce cap—was not only an option, but the norm. Schoolmasters typically kept a bundle of switches in a holder next to their desk and whipping posts were commonplace in the schoolyard.

> The ability to impose some sort of order on a poorly taught and, in consequence, an unruly school, was another of the prerequisites for a schoolmaster. . . . The greatest waste of time came from the individual methods of instruction universally followed in teaching. Children came forward to the teacher's desk and recited individually to the master or dame. . . . Hearing lessons, assigning new tasks, setting copies, making quill pens, dictating sums, and keeping order completely absorbed the teacher's time.[5]

This passage from the writings of historian Ellwood Cubberly speaks to both discipline and management. Children were disciplined through external punishment and coerced into the behavior desired by the teacher and demanded by society. Management of the classroom and the students, the curriculum, room arrangement, teaching methods, and assessment strategies all supported the belief that children needed to be controlled, by force if necessary, to ensure their salvation.

Not every religious group believed that such harsh treatment of children was necessary. In particular, the Quakers advocated a more humane approach to discipline and a curriculum geared toward teaching for understanding as opposed to rote memorization. Pacifism is embedded in the Quaker philosophy and manifested in the educational environment. There are still Quaker schools in the United States today that emphasize a caring, conflict-free learning environment.

The 1800s: Changing Times, Changing Attitudes

Changing social, political, geographical, economic, and intellectual forces began to have an impact on the colonies. The period between 1779 and 1865 saw the development of an American character that showed signs of deviating from that of the White Anglo-Saxon Protestant settlers. For example, there was a marked increase in the number of immigrants from Ireland. This group was not so willing to adopt Standard English and forgo their Catholic religion in order to fit into society. New immigrants such as those from Ireland challenged the status quo. Prevailing views about children and educational practices were beginning to change accordingly.

Three key issues had the greatest impact on the type of education that leaders saw as appropriate, and thus the type of discipline and management systems used in the schools. First, the idea of people as inherently evil was called into question. Second, debates arose over what type of knowledge was of most worth and how knowledge should be organized and used. The third issue centered on the needs of our developing nation and the type of educational system that would produce adults who would participate in the democratic process and improve our society.[6] The importance of an educated citizenry was becoming clear to our "Founding Fathers," men such as Benjamin Franklin and Thomas Jefferson. For example, in

1779, when Thomas Jefferson was governor of Virginia, he authored a Bill for the More General Diffusion of Knowledge in which he argued for a system of free, public education for all children to foster an enlightened citizenry. Although this bill did not pass the Virginia legislature, the seeds of public education for all were firmly planted in the minds of many influential people. This was an important change in thinking from colonial times. No longer was the education of children to be entrusted to home and church, nor was the curriculum to be based on the Bible.

As key politicians and educators began to speak out about these educational issues and as the school-age population grew and became more diverse, changes resulted that you would recognize today: students divided by age, graded curriculum, secular (nonreligious) textbooks, and new schools subjects such as science and physical education. In particular, the educational system was coming to be seen as one means to foster free thinking boys (girls were typically not taught academic subjects at the time), creative minds that could contribute to the economic, political, social, and cultural growth of the United States. Free thinkers are not developed through rote memorization and recitations but through study, research, and debate. In other words, a growing emphasis was being placed on active as opposed to passive learning, on utilitarian as opposed to religious curriculum, and on students who could think critically as opposed to those who would unquestioningly follow the dictates of religion.

Horace Mann and the Debate Over Discipline

Into the social milieu of the early 1800s came one of the most famous educators in the United States, Horace Mann (1796–1837). In 1837, Mann was appointed secretary of the State Board of Education in Massachusetts and he became the champion of the Common School idea, or schooling for the masses. Mann's work will be detailed later in this text. For now, it is important to know that Mann rejected the idea that the child was inherently evil. He believed that children were innocent and capable of learning without fear of retribution. In his *Seventh Annual Report* (1843), he stated:

> A teacher who cannot rule by love must rule by fear. A teacher who cannot supply material for the activity of his pupils' minds by his talent, must put down that activity by force. A teacher who cannot answer all of the questions and solve all of the doubts of a scholar as they arise, must assume an awful and mysterious air, and must expound in oracles, which themselves need more explanation than the original difficulty.[7]

Not everyone agreed with Mann. Many experts continued to cling to Puritan beliefs, and corporal punishment remained a dominant practice. In fact, Mann's ideas directly conflicted with those of the Boston Association of Masters of the Public Schools, a group of 31 Boston teachers. A prime example of the clash of educational philosophies that existed at the time is found in beliefs about the practice of **emulation.** The idea was that the teacher would focus on a student who did something right. This student was publicly rewarded or given special privileges that were not accorded to the rest of the students. It was expected that the others would emulate, or copy, the behavior or performance of the rewarded students. For example, in the early days of the common school, students were often seated by performance, with the best students seated toward the front of the room. When a student exhibited exceptionally outstanding behavior or did exceedingly well on a recitation, that student's seat, and thus his class rank, would be moved up. Techniques such as spelling bees and speed recitations were common, and teachers passed out tokens or tickets to students to represent the number of "opponents" they had beaten in the game.[8]

The Boston Masters approved of emulation because they believed that competition fostered hard work, an idea that was consistent with our growing capitalist economic system. Mann, on the other hand, disapproved of such methods. He believed that such competition destroyed the community spirit that was necessary for learning in a classroom. Mann opined that such tactics would encourage students to become materialistic and aggressive rather than cooperative.[9] This disagreement between the Boston Masters and Horace Mann demonstrates the changing attitudes of the time.

Colonial and Postcolonial Schooling: Diversity and Power

Colonial and postcolonial schooling, the periods covered in the previous sections, can be used to illustrate the ways in which diversity and power became intertwined in American education. The colonists established a system of organizing and operating schools that was based on the notion that the language and culture of Protestant European males was superior to those of other people. Their discourses and ways of viewing the world were used as the benchmark for judging others. Differences in the education and treatment of males and females flowed from these beliefs. For example, it was taken for granted that males needed math, science, and the language arts because they were expected to be successful in a world that was increasingly being shaped by commerce and business. Females were destined for the world of homemaking; if they received any education at all, it was one that prepared them for running a household.

As an increasing number of immigrants who were not White, Protestant, or from England entered the United States, the dominant standards of language, behavior, and social status were upheld by the White Anglo-Saxon Protestant majority and used as the measuring stick for judging anyone who was "different." Disciplinary techniques and classroom organization and management became tools by which to assimilate those who were different into the mainstream. For example, emulation quickly taught students their place in society. Sitting by rank solidified the notion that those who succeeded in and maintained the status quo would move up in the world, whereas those who did not behave or achieve as expected would be sent to the back of the classroom where they would remain second-class citizens.

Notions of power help us to understand how this happened. Rules for behavior and codes of conduct were not written down as "rules"; that is, when new immigrants entered the country, they were not handed a book with all of society's regulations written down for them. In this socialization process, the belief systems, language, and social expectations of the dominant group were simply taken for granted. This is similar to asking why something happens in a certain way and being told, "That's the way we always do it." Most people did not stop to ask if using corporal punishment or practicing emulation in school was good or bad; it just seemed to work, because students appeared to conform to the standard way of behaving.

Many current practices related to controlling students' behavior have their roots in colonial and postcolonial schooling; assumptions about what works, still taken for granted, have remained in place. For example, emulation can commonly be seen in elementary schools today in such games as Around the World and spelling bees, or when the teacher is attempting to get the class settled down and ready for instruction. He or she may say, "I like the way Omar is sitting, with his eyes on me. And I really like the way Stephanie has placed her paper and pencil on her desk as I asked you all to do." Today Omar and Stephanie may not be rewarded by having their seats moved to the front of the class, but they are used as explicit examples of how the rest of the class is expected to behave. What might be the positive and negative consequences of emulation techniques?

The 1900s: John Dewey and Progressivism Versus the Status Quo

The end of the 1800s ushered in a new philosophical era referred to as **progressivism.** Progressivism is a belief system that emphasizes learning through experimentation—a nonauthoritarian, learner-centered approach to teaching and learning. Society was rapidly changing by 1900 because of the rise of industrialism, the accumulation of scientific knowledge that led to new ways of thinking, and demographic shifts as new waves of southern and eastern European immigrants, from Russia, Poland, Greece, and Rumania, entered the United States in record numbers.

John Dewey (1859–1952) is perhaps the best known of the group of educational reformers who came to be known as progressivists. Although Dewey's ideas were on the "fringe" of educational thinking, and many question if his ideas have ever really been implemented in schools, his thinking has had a lasting impact on debates about the role of the school in society. Dewey believed that the purpose of schools should be to prepare students for life in our ever-changing democracy. Dewey saw that schools were totally unprepared to handle the demographic, social, and economic changes that were occurring in the United States.[10] He and other progressivists were opposed to the strict authoritarian methods that characterized most public schools. Dewey argued that children learn best by "doing." He favored an approach to teaching and learning that emulated the scientific method of experimentation, actively engaging students in hands-on activities and fostering the ability to think critically about issues and problems that were of practical and personal importance to students. You will read much more about Dewey and the progressive movement later in this text. For now, we will look at the influence of progressivism on practices of discipline and classroom management.

School as a Microcosm of the Community   Dewey believed that school is a social institution, education a social process. He also held that the school and classroom should represent the best of community life, where children participate in a democratic order and have full responsibility for their roles in the classroom society. For Dewey, education represented the best means for fostering the type of individuals who can reconstruct society for the better. He was highly critical of standardized curriculum and teacher-directed instruction. He believed that curriculum emanates from the interests of the students and that effective classroom management can be seen as a direct correlate of the excitement generated when students are working on projects of genuine interest. Knowledge of subject matter, the ability to closely observe children, an understanding of their physiological and social growth, and the ability to use this knowledge to facilitate learning were key characteristics of effective teachers for Dewey. In an 1897 critique of the prevailing practices of the time, Dewey wrote:

> Much of present education fails because it neglects this fundamental principle of school as a form of community life . . . that the best and deepest moral training is precisely that which one gets through having to enter into proper relations with others in a unity of work and thought. The present educational systems so far as they destroy or neglect this unity, render it difficult or impossible to get any genuine, regular moral training. . . . The teacher is not in the school to impose certain ideas or to form certain habits in the child, but is there as a member of the community to select the influences which shall affect the child and to assist him in properly responding to these influences . . . the discipline of the school should proceed from the life of the school as a whole and not directly from the teacher.[11]

Dewey and the Chicago Laboratory School   For progressivists, learning is a reward in and of itself. Dewey believed that the combination of practical and theoretical knowledge in a community environment was the best way to develop individual moral character in the context of concern for the total community. In this view, there is no need for extrinsic rewards and punishments. Dewey attempted to implement his philosophy through the development of a laboratory school at the University of Chicago that he began and ran from 1896 until 1904. It was not unusual to visit the lab school and find children working together to plant gardens, take care of animals, or sew clothing, taking the process from refining the raw material to make cloth and thread to the finished article of clothing. These practical activities engaged children's hands and minds in a way that built the foundations of many content areas (e.g., mathematics, science, reading, and writing), illustrating the progressive idea that when students' minds were occupied in meaningful activities, their behavior was "on task." Most educators of the time disagreed with Dewey. You will now read about one of them, Colonel Richard Henry Pratt.

Standard-Bearer of the Dominant Society: Colonel Richard Henry Pratt   There were many jobs for factory workers in the early 1900s, jobs necessary to meet the production needs of our industrialized society. There were also clear distinctions between workers and management. Many people believed that the purpose of schools, despite more egalitarian rhetoric, was to train factory workers who were not free thinkers but who would work on assembly lines hour after hour without complaint. This type of training hearkened back to controlled, strictly disciplined teaching. One of the harshest examples of this occurred between 1897 and 1930 in Carlisle, Pennsylvania, where Colonel Richard Henry Pratt established the Pratt Institute for the education of American Indian children.

Many White Americans saw American Indians as a "problem" in the late 1800s. As settlers moved west, they desired land that was occupied by indigenous peoples. The U.S. government had already acquired prime pieces of property, such as the Black Hills of South Dakota, through illegal treaties with American Indians. Colonel Pratt subscribed to a prevailing belief of the dominant society in the 1900s: If the Indians could only be led to "civilization," they could become contributing members of American society. In an effort to assimilate American Indians into mainstream White middle-class society, Pratt struck a deal with the skeptical leader of the Brulee Sioux and began removing Indian children from the Dakota Territory to his boarding school in Carlisle.

Once at boarding school, the children had their hair cut and were given uniforms to replace their tribal clothing. The Sioux were then assigned Anglo names to replace those given to them by their kin group, or *oyate*. A system of regimented daily routines was implemented as the school attempted to prepare American Indian children for factory work in the industrialized society. Desks were in rows. The curriculum consisted of basic subjects in the morning and manual labor job training in the afternoon. The students, ranging in age from kindergarten through high school, were taught values consistent with an industrialized nation: hard work, ambition to succeed at all costs, and responsibility only to the individual. Children who outwardly resisted the school program or who defied the rules were harshly disciplined. Corporal punishment, including isolation in solitary confinement, was used to enforce the rules and regulations.

Colonel Pratt's ideas were so popular that they were used to enforce the American government's assimilation policy for Indians. By 1889, there were 25 Indian boarding schools similar to Carlisle in 13 states across the county. Pratt's boarding schools remained in place until the 1930s (others existed until much later) when the government revised its policies and sent the children back to their reservations. Unfortunately, the majority of the children who spent years at boarding schools suffered emotional as well as physical damage. They were a group caught between two cultures, unable to speak their native Sioux language and communicate with family and not accepted by White society as equals.

Using discipline and management to prepare students for life as workers in factories was quite common. Although Colonel Pratt appeared to be well meaning, he worked to destroy the Indian values and cultural beliefs that the children brought to school in favor of those of the dominant society. He believed that his ways of thinking and believing were superior to those of American Indians. He did not even consider that American Indians had cultural values, beliefs, and practices of their own. The prevailing belief that American Indians were "savages" who needed to be tamed, together with an industrialized society's need for workers, drove Pratt and others like him to implement discipline and management polices that privileged one set of values over another. Colonel Pratt and the Carlisle Indian School represent an extreme case of the power relationships associated with discipline and management policies, but the idea of using school policies to prepare children for industrial jobs was prevalent in the 1900s despite the ideas of the progressivists.

To learn more about Colonel Pratt and the education of American Indian children during this time, see the PBS video *In the White Man's Image.*[12]

You can see that in the 1900s, the debates between educators who believed in more progressive, child-centered discipline and management styles and those who believed in more authoritarian, teacher-centered styles had their roots in differing conceptions of the role of schools in our democratic society. The arguments between the social reformers and those who sought to prepare students for a specific role in society have raged throughout the development of schooling in the United States. These differing philosophies are still being played out in various forms in schools and classroom today. The next section will describe two ways of thinking about discipline and management that are popular in education today. Can you detect their "roots"?

MAKING CONNECTIONS: PAST TO PRESENT

Many discipline and management "programs" have appeared over the past 50 years. You may be asked about any of the names that appear in Exhibit 3.2 when you are being interviewed for a teaching position. All of them have contributed to our thinking about discipline and management in education. The strategies for management and discipline proposed by these educators have taken many different forms as teacher training and professional development options: workshops, online courses, videotaped training, lectures, and lengthy "how-to" manuals. Some strategies are attempts to systematize approaches to dealing with children's behavior; others rely on more generalized aspects of schooling such as teacher–student relationships and interactions with parents. For example, some books on discipline present sample scripts for parents and teachers to follow in conversing with children about their behavior. Spend some time reading and thinking critically about the ideas of each of these people as part of your preparation for the classroom and the job market. What aspects of each can you attribute to the historical development of discipline and management beliefs and strategies presented in this chapter?

Most of the current theories about discipline and management have philosophical orientations that date back to the beginning of schooling in the United States and represent conflicting beliefs about the nature of children, the role of the teacher, and the role of schools in our society. Two opposing views on classroom discipline and management will be described here: that of popular educational theorists Lee and Marlene Canter, whose work on assertive discipline represents one viewpoint, and Alfie Kohn, whose ideas about building classroom community are quite different from those of the Canters. We have chosen these two theories not only because they represent opposite ends of the spectrum, but also because they are very popular with teachers and administrators today. As you read each one, consider what aspects of each are rooted in the history that has been presented in this chapter.

EXHIBIT 3.2 PROPONENTS OF SPECIFIC DISCIPLINE AND MANAGEMENT THEORIES

Author	Description	Major Work(s)
William Glasser	A psychiatrist, Glasser became famous for his new approach to dealing with adults, known as "reality therapy." Later, he applied these ideas to school situations. *Key concepts*: class meetings, behavior choices, students' needs, quality teaching, quality learning.	*Schools Without Failure* (1969); *Control Theory in the Classroom* (1986); *The Quality School: Managing Students Without Coercion* (1992)
Jacob Kounin	Kounin, an educational psychologist, videotaped many teachers to determine successful strategies for engaging students in academic work to prevent inappropriate behavior. *Key concepts*: with-it-ness, momentum, smoothness, group alerting, overlapping, satiation, fun with challenge.	*Discipline and Group Management in Classrooms* (1970/1977)
Haim Ginott	A psychologist, Ginott honed in on communication skills as a key to positive classroom discipline. He distinguished between "congruent communication" between teachers and students to address the situation and behavior and "noncongruent communication" in which the teacher focuses on the person or characteristics of the person. *Key concepts*: sane messages, "I" messages versus "you" messages, inviting cooperation, laconic language.	*Teacher and Child* (1971)
Thomas Gordon	Gordon, a psychologist, became famous for his Parent Effectiveness Training (PET) and later applied his ideas to teaching with his Teacher Effectiveness Training (TET). *Key concepts*: the behavior window, who owns the problem?, modify the environment, "I" messages, shift gears, no-lose conflict resolution.	*Discipline That Works: Promoting Self-Discipline in Children* (1989)
Lee and Marlene Canter	Described in this chapter.	*Assertive Discipline: Positive Behavior Management for Today's Classroom* (1992)
Fredric Jones	A psychologist, Jones observed many classroom teachers in developing his positive classroom management/discipline model. He notes that a teacher's nonverbal behavior is key to keeping students on task. *Key concepts*: classroom structure, body language, incentives, efficient help.	*Positive Classroom Discipline: Instructor's Guide* (1987)
Richard Curwin and Allen Mendler	Curwin, a former teacher, and Mendler, a psychologist, first gained fame with *Taking Charge in the Classroom* (1983). Their work focuses on the small percentage of students whose behavior is extremely disruptive or negative by building students' dignity and helping them to become successful classroom participants. *Key concepts*: dignity, sense of hope, classroom social contract, behaviorally at-risk, prevention dimension, consequences (logical, conventional, instructional, and generic).	*Discipline With Dignity* (1988)
Barbara Coloroso	Coloroso, a former teacher, gained attention with a series titled *Kids Are Worth It!* She believes that children can develop inner discipline, or self-discipline, with the assistance of adults. *Key concepts*: school and teacher types; brick wall, jellyfish, backbone, the three cons, six-step problem-solving strategy, RSVP, natural consequences and reasonable consequences.	*Kids Are Worth It!* (1994); *Winning at Teaching* (1990); *Discipline: Creating a Positive School Climate* (1990)

(continued)

EXHIBIT **3.2**   CONTINUED

Author	Description	Major Work(s)
Linda Albert	Albert, a former classroom teacher, has appeared on talk shows and has written popular magazine columns to assist teachers and parents with her cooperative discipline model. Her work is based on the idea that students act in particular ways in order to meet personal needs. *Key concepts*: hands-on, hands-off, and hands-joined styles; AGMs, or attention-getting mechanisms; I-can level; students' need to feel they are capable, connected contributors; classroom code of conduct.	*Coping With Kids and School* (1985); *Cooperative Discipline* (1996); *Cooperative Discipline: Implementation Guide* (1996)
Alfie Kohn	Described in this chapter.	*Beyond Discipline: From Compliance to Community* (1996); *What to Look For in Classrooms* (1998)

The Canters: Assertive Discipline

Lee and Marlene Canter began writing books and offering workshops on **assertive discipline** in the 1970s. It is difficult to say whether their work is the result of any actual research because it is rare to find a citation in their texts. They often preface their advice on managing students' behavior with phrases such as "In many classrooms we have seen . . ." or "Many teachers tell us. . . ." The description of the Canter system presented here is based on the book *Lee Canter's Assertive Discipline: Positive Behavior Management for Today's Classroom* (1992).

The Canters believe that the teacher should be in charge of the classroom. They state that teachers have the right and the responsibility to establish rules for the classroom, to set the limits for acceptable and unacceptable student behavior, to teach students to follow the rules, and to ask parents and administrators to assist them in this process.[13] Students have the right, say the Canters, to know the rules and limits, to be taught to obey the rules, and to receive positive recognition for following the rules and limits.[14] The Canters state that many teachers feel powerless to control students' behavior because of their own perceptions that if children receive poor parenting, live in poverty, or have emotional problems or special needs that are shaped by circumstances beyond the teacher's control, it is almost impossible to get them to behave properly.[15] The Canters advise teachers that these are not excuses for poor behavior and that teachers must believe that if a student is not behaving, it is because he or she *chooses* not to or because he or she *does not know how* to behave.

Assertive Discipline   The Canters recommend an assertive style of teaching in which the teacher selects the rules and expectations, conveys them "clearly, confidently and consistently to the students," and is prepared to back up his or her words with actions at all times. There should be a limited number of rules, and they should refer to actions that are observable by the teacher (e.g., no yelling or screaming, no profanity). The rules should apply at all times throughout the day and should be targeted at behavior only, not at academic or homework issues. There should also be clear negative consequences for rule infractions that involve punishments that the students do not like but that do not humiliate or physically harm them (e.g., timeout, staying after class, writing in a behavior log). The Canters suggest that the teacher get input from the students but that the ultimate decision about classroom rules and consequences is the responsibility of the teacher. A teacher should set an atmosphere of "warmth and support" as students learn to obey the rules. In this way, the students will learn to trust and respect the teacher who has set these firm limits and sticks to them.[16]

Rewards and Consequences   Along with developing the rules and teaching them to the students, the teacher must develop a system of positive rewards and negative consequences. In the past, the Canters suggested public means of punishment, such as names on the board with check marks for further infractions, a system similar to the one that our student teacher questioned in the opening vignette. However, the most recent edition of the Canters' text focuses first on positive reinforcement. Praise is recommended as "the number one choice" for shaping students' behavior. Positive rewards can be given to individuals or provided to the entire class if everyone follows all of the rules for a designated period of time. It is recommended that the teacher use special privileges to reward those individual students who follow the rules on a regular basis. The Canters recommend "catching students being good" and offering such rewards as being line leader, classroom monitor, or paper corrector for the teacher. Students who follow the rules can also take part in special activities. The Canters suggest that these students be allowed to tutor younger pupils, read a special book, or work on a fun activity.[17]

The class-wide reward program can be used simultaneously with individual rewards and is a system whereby all of the students work toward a positive reward for the entire class. For example, points can be awarded or marbles placed in a jar each time the teacher notes that the class is cooperative and well-behaved. A certain number of points or a jar full of marbles can earn popcorn parties, movies, extra PE time, or an opportunity to listen to the radio in class. The Canters note that peer pressure is a powerful tool in shaping the behavior of individual students as they work toward a class reward.[18]

The Canters advise that involving parents and administrators in the rules–consequences–rewards system is essential. They suggest sending notes and making phone calls to parents when the students are exhibiting good behavior as a proactive means of enlisting the assistance of parents should the teacher require their attention for undesirable behavior.

Can you trace the "roots" of the Canters' work? Their teacher-centered model draws many of its main tenets from the colonial days of schooling. Appropriate classroom behavior is not generally seen as a function of a well-planned lesson; a positive relationship between the teacher, students, and parents; or the students' intrinsic desire to learn and be a part of the classroom community. Instead, the use of explicit rewards and punishments to shape behavior is based in the belief that students are incapable of making appropriate choices on their own because of circumstances beyond the teacher's control, such as poor parenting, biological disorders such as the inability to pay attention or attention deficit disorder, and just plain stubbornness. You will need to know about the Canters' assertive discipline model because many school districts across the country use the model or a variation of it.

Alfie Kohn: Classroom as Community

Alfie Kohn presents a view at the opposite end of the spectrum from Lee and Marlene Canter. In fact, in his book *Beyond Discipline: From Compliance to Community* (1996), Kohn is highly critical of the Canters as well as proponents of other discipline programs. Kohn's work, like that of the Canters, is based not on specific research but on a philosophical orientation to schooling. Kohn's focus is on creating community in the classroom and on a theoretical framework called **constructivism**—the idea that students construct their own new knowledge by interacting with materials, the teacher, and their peers. Both constructivism (which you will learn more about later in this text) and the notion of **classroom as community** have their roots in progressivist theory.

Constructivism   Constructivists believe that students come to school with a wealth of knowledge and use this base to build, or "construct," new and more complex understandings. The role of the teacher is to find out "where the students are" by investigating their knowledge bases and understandings and to use this information to plan ways of presenting new information in meaningful ways. Hands-on experiments and inquiry-oriented projects are two popular ways that teachers plan lessons to actively involve students in constructing new knowledge. This process of constructing meaning is an active one, and Kohn believes that it cannot occur unless "the learner has substantial power to make decisions."[19]

Kohn suggests that the terms *discipline* and *management* are inappropriate for application to a classroom in which the teacher is attempting to foster a sense of community. He also notes that teachers often "blame the victim"—that is, the students—rather than taking the responsibility to find out what students know and are able to do and using this information to develop innovative lessons. Kohn argues that, as educators, "our first question should be, 'What do children need?'—followed immediately by 'How can we meet those needs?'—and that from this point of departure we will end up in a very different place than if we had begun by asking, 'How do I get children to do what I want?' Reminiscent of the work of Dewey, Kohn notes that a 'right behavior' focus does not help children become good people."[20]

Kohn notes that a discussion of curriculum is often absent from many discipline programs and suggests that "a huge proportion of unwelcome behaviors can be traced to a problem with what children are being asked to learn."[21] If the work that is given to students is too hard, too easy, too boring, or irrelevant, it is logical that students might misbehave. Kohn makes a clear connection between the curriculum, the structure of the task students are asked to complete in relation to the curriculum, and the students' behavior.

No External Punishments, No External Rewards   Kohn is harsh in his criticism of a system of punishments and rewards. He argues that teachers who rely on punishment to coerce students to do what they want often end up returning to the same ineffective strategies time and again. These teachers typically do not solve problems, they only generate new ones, and the new problems are often worse than the original ones.[22] Kohn claims that punishments are a misuse of teacher power; rather than foster the ability to reason and cooperate, they warp a student's value system. Teachers who rely on punishment foster a relationship in which the teacher is the enforcer, thus undercutting the development of a caring, respectful relationship. Finally, Kohn suggests that punishment "actually impedes the process of ethical development" because it focuses the student on figuring out what the teacher wants and what will happen if the student does not comply with the teacher. Instead, Kohn suggests that a student should be figuring out what type of person she or he is to become and relating that to the type of community that should be created in the classroom.[23]

Reward, in Kohn's view, is equally harmful. He cites a litany of research that suggests that public praise and extrinsic motivators (e.g., stickers, free time, popcorn parties) actually lead students to do less than they are capable of, to be less generous and less cooperative than students who work hard and cooperate because they simply want to behave this way. He argues that the use of peer pressure makes students "unwitting accomplices of the teacher" and does nothing to foster a "caring alliance, a connection (between student and teacher) based on warmth and respect."[24]

If a teacher should not rely on a system of punishments and rewards, what should a teacher do? Kohn suggests that what students truly need is "the chance to make real decisions about what happens in the classroom. Some of these decisions concern the academic part of their education—what to learn, how and why."[25] Teachers must listen to students and get to know them as people. Kohn is a firm believer in classroom meetings in which students discuss the business of the classroom community, academic and social. A class meeting is a place for sharing personal and academic achievements and information (e.g., the death of a friend, winning a chess tournament). It is also a venue for collaboration between teacher and students in making key decisions and planning for and reflecting on both the classroom as it exists and the classroom that teacher and students want.[26]

Kohn acknowledges that developing the classroom community can be a difficult and lengthy process that requires patience on the part of the teacher. Students need time to change, and teachers need time to evaluate the quality and quantity of the effectiveness of the new practice. The implementation of most new classroom ideas will require patience on the part of both teachers and students. The result, however, will be a classroom in which mutual respect exists among all members of the community and power is more equally shared through negotiation, collaborative decision making, and cooperation.

The ideas of John Dewey are evident in the writings of Alfie Kohn. Kohn's emphasis on the classroom and school as communities of learning, on child-centered as opposed to teacher-centered classrooms, and on the teacher's planning and implementing relevant lessons that emanate from the interests and needs of the students can all be traced to ideas expressed by Dewey (as well as other progressivists). Kohn, like Dewey, believes that students must be given responsibility for participating in the design and management of classroom life if they are to be able to operationalize these skills and internalize democratic values in their own lives. The idea that students set learning goals, design classroom rules and procedures, and participate in solving problems that arise in the classroom can be found in the work of both men. Both believe that when students are able to practice democratic values such as justice, equity, and fairness, they learn to become caring, contributing members of society.

SCHOOL VIOLENCE: CHALLENGES TO THE SCHOOL COMMUNITY

Most school districts across the country do not have any serious problems with violence, but we have witnessed an increasing number of incidents of physical and sexual violence, including rape and murder, in schools over the past 10 years. Despite the rise of violent incidents since 1999, then President Clinton's Secretary of Education Riley reminded parents and teachers after the tragic shootings at Columbine High School in Colorado that 90% of our schools are violence-free and only 1% of homicides involving school-age children (ages 5–19) occurred in or around schools. Teachers must be aware, however, that violence of one type or another may occur in school each day. Educators must take an active part in creating school environments that prevent violent situations. Violent acts are acts of power, and they occur for many reasons. We begin with a definition of violence and then describe its various forms.

One broad definition of **violence** is any "threat to inflict, or actual infliction of physical or emotional injury or discomfort upon another person's body, feelings, or possessions."[27] Verbal violence, in the form of name-calling, verbal harassment, spreading rumors, teasing, taunting, threatening, and other nonphysical acts is much more prevalent in schools than one might imagine. Sixty percent of public school students reported that they had been the recipient of some type of verbal insult in the past year.[28] Sometimes, however, nonphysical violence can also occur in a nonverbal way. For example, isolation, in which a group of students intentionally excludes one person and refuses to speak to her or him, is a form of violence. Isolation, as well as verbal violence, is often based on perceived differences or prejudice based on skin color, socioeconomic status, lifestyle, speech patterns, clothing, or other visible variables that people use as identity markers.

Sexual violence is any act based on gender or sexual orientation that causes physical or emotional harm. This includes any unwanted kissing, touching, or groping of genitals or breasts, as well as rape and other forms of sexual assault. The Equal Employment Opportunity Commission of the federal government uses the term **sexual harassment** and defines it in the following way:

> Sexual harassment is unwelcome sexual advances, requests for sexual favors, and other verbal or physical contact of a sexual nature. It usually occurs when one person has formal (supervisory) power over another, but it can also occur when

one person has informal power (i.e., size, perceived popularity, tenure) over another. Sexual harassment often occurs when: 1) submitting to the conduct is made either explicitly of implicitly as a term of an individual's employment or educational program; 2) submission to or rejection of such conduct by an individual is used as the basis for employment or educational decisions affecting such individual; 3) such conduct has the purpose or effect of unreasonably interfering with an individual's work or academic performance or creating an intimidating, hostile, or offensive working or educational environment.[29]

Sexual violence has been reported as early as preschool and has included incidents of sexual contact between teachers and students. Sexual violence can be physical, as in sexual assault, or verbal, such as whistling and crude noises, but we have placed it as a separate category to underscore its importance. Research tells us that teachers and school officials often ignore sexual harassment among students even when girls are being harassed by boys right in front of them.[30] More than one-half of the students surveyed in an Ohio study reported that they would be uncomfortable reporting sexual harassment to a teacher or other school officials (see Exhibit 3.3).[31]

Physical violence is any form of contact between individuals that is unwanted, threatens personal safety, or causes harm to the individual. This includes poking, hitting, slapping, tripping, robbery, and fighting with or without weapons. Most people think of weapons as guns, knives, and brass knuckles, but students have made weapons out of rulers, protractors, and other items typically used in classrooms for learning. Although most students report never having first-hand experience with weapons, 44% reported that they have pushed, kicked, slapped, or grabbed another student.[32] Physical violence is often seen as different from vandalism or extortion, yet stealing or damaging the property of others or threatening someone in a menacing way has the effect of compromising people's personal safety. You will read in Chapter 7 about the Harvey Milk School in New

---

EXHIBIT **3.3**   **SEXUAL HARASSMENT SURVEY**

Percentage of student responding positively to the question: Have you ever had the following events happen to you in school, that you found offensive?

39%	Students brushing up against you in a sexual way
48%	Suggestive looks or leering
30%	People touching you sexually when you did not want them to
69%	Name-calling
34%	Fondling
37%	Sexual threats
35%	Other behavior of a sexual nature that you found offensive

Source: Results from an Ohio survey of 6,173 students in grades 9–12 in seven School-to-Work Regions. Vocational Sex Equity, *Ohio Survey Results on Equity Issues.* Columbus: Ohio Department of Education, 1998.

York City, which serves gay and lesbian youth and supporters. This school began as a safe haven for gay and lesbian students from typical schools, who were taunted, beaten up, and had their property destroyed on a regular basis because of their sexual orientation.

What causes some students to be violent? A complete discussion of that question is complex and beyond the scope of this chapter. We will, however, offer some thoughts on this topic and we hope that you will take time to discuss this issue with your instructor, your peers, and the teachers in the schools where you observe and teach.

Many educators and politicians focus on societal institutions, particularly the family, when discussing reasons for violence. They suggest that lack of parental supervision, increased exposure to violence in the media, and peer pressure are all significant factors in the propensity for a student to commit violent acts. Additionally, the rise of technology and a focus on individual achievement and the accumulation of material wealth are factors that social analysts believe serve to isolate students and deemphasize personal relationships. These are all viable explanations; many students bring frustration, isolation, depression, and anger that have their roots in home and community into the school. Teachers and administrators cannot, however, control what goes on in a student's home or in the community. They do have control over what goes on inside the school and the classroom. We would like to examine some factors that you, as a teacher, will have a degree of control over, thus enabling you to affect students in a positive way.

Many studies and theories, including some of these mentioned in Exhibit 3.2, tell us that students who are disruptive or violent in school may also be reacting to a school setting in which they feel oppressed, lack involvement, or are themselves the victims of violence. Herb Kohl, in *I Won't Learn From You and Other Thoughts on Creative Maladjustment*,[33] describes high school students who deliberately disrupt class as exhibiting a form of resistance to authoritarian teachers who tightly control the curriculum and the class. While using their personal power to resist the unfairness of their lack of involvement in the curriculum, they also compromise their own education. Similarly, Vivian Gussin Paley's *You Can't Say You Can't Play*[34] addresses the responsibility of early childhood educators to create classrooms in which all children participate and are not isolated by others.

One of the worst examples of school violence occurred in 1999 with the shootings at Columbine High School in Littleton, Colorado. This tragedy provided us with a picture of students who, despite enjoying the privileges of upper-middle-class suburban life, were filled with hatred for students of color, athletes, and others who had made fun of them and excluded them from the "mainstream" student life. In this instance, the feelings of exclusion and powerlessness in the school community were at the heart of the choice of the self-proclaimed "Trench Coat Mafia" to exercise the ultimate power over others—that of life or death. The school principal stated several times during television interviews that he did not know this "Trench Coat Mafia" existed in his school, and many teachers were in complete shock that such violence could occur in their suburban high school. In 2005 a similar shooting took place on the Red Lake (Minnesota) Indian Reservation. A male teen, reportedly teased and isolated by his peers, killed several classmates, a teacher, and a guard. His reported style of dress and attraction to neo-Nazi websites suggested a level of disaffection from school similar to the Columbine shooters.

These incidents are extreme, yet some form of violence occurs daily in many classrooms. Students are called names by their classmates and the teacher looks the other way rather than address the specifics of the name-calling. Students get the message that name-calling is not acceptable, but often they do not understand why using terms like "faggot," for example, is wrong. Two students may fight and both be suspended, yet without a discussion of the implications of their violent acts the behavior is likely to continue. Bored students disrupt a lesson by throwing objects at each other and the teacher, with little concern for the loss of their own education. Sometimes teachers are unwilling or unable to see the connection between the ways that they choose to use their classroom power and the behavior and attitudes of the students. We are not, by any means, placing all of the blame for school shootings such the one at Columbine High School or other violent incidents on school faculty and administrators. We are simply suggesting that there is a close connection between students' sense of community and belongingness in school and their behavior. Teachers and administrators who rule with an iron fist, who refuse to smile until December, and who create lessons and units without regard for students' interest and input can quickly end up with a school full of angry and disaffected students. When punishments are doled out in schools and classrooms without regard for the underlying causes of the misconduct, and when these practices are taken for granted and repeated without an analysis of their effectiveness, a climate of violence exists. When poor students do not receive the same high-quality education that their suburban counterparts enjoy, or when the teachers of poor children do not hold high expectations for their success, the students and their parents become increasingly frustrated. A climate of violence can exist. In these situations, the rights of both teachers and students are often violated in a constant cycle of misbehavior, punishment, miseducation, and lack of involvement.

How can teachers and administrators prevent school and classroom violence? They must take control of those aspects of schooling over which they have control. We currently have some evidence that the following characteristics are important in creating violence-free schools and classrooms:

1. A positive school climate exists where "nurturance, inclusiveness, and a feeling of community are evident."
2. The school principal is an active, visible participant in school and community activities.
3. Teachers address incidents of verbal, physical, and sexual violence directly. Teachers are not afraid to discuss students' differing opinions, even on the most controversial topics such as racism, sexism, homophobia, and human differences.
4. Strategies for conflict resolution that focus on problem solving, mediation, negotiation, and collaboration are taught and utilized consistently.
5. The school is seen as a community center, open to parents and other community members.

6. Positive male and female role models of all ethnic backgrounds are included in all school activities. An effort is made to reach out to fathers, grandfathers, and other significant males who practice nonviolent problem-solving strategies.
7. The curriculum and instructional practices are multicultural and inclusive and ensure that all students can achieve to high standards.
8. Decision-making power is shared with parents, students, and community members regarding school and classroom policies and procedures.[35]

Finally, we would like to mention a movement that has a long historical tradition but has recently been revived based on the concerns of teachers, administrators, teacher educators, and community members: character education. **Character education** has been described by Evelyn Holt Otten, who based her definition on the work of educator and scholar Kevin Ryan, as a "holistic approach that connects the moral dimension of education to the social and civic realms of students' lives."[36] Although you will find many different ways that character education is taught in the schools, in its most relevant form it draws on our democratic principles of citizenship to help K–12 students learn to evaluate information, consider opposing viewpoints, and demonstrate fairness, empathy, and respect for others. Some teachers use a prepared curriculum, but the most effective teachers use actual classroom and community events to assist students in developing the characteristics of open-mindedness and responsible decision making that Dewey values and that you read about in Chapter 2. Proponents of character education believe that if we foster these democratic principles in students, they will be better able to understand and affirm differences in their peers and to ameliorate their differences in a nonviolent manner.

The Getting Connected feature at the end of this chapter contains some useful Web resources for dealing with violence in schools, establishing conflict-free classrooms, and helping students develop the capacity for respect and affirmation of peers. Check them out!

Today's Classroom: Where Do You Stand?

Most of the well-known theorists mentioned in this chapter are White males with a background in psychology who have little practical experience in the classroom. Few of these educational theorists place their ideas in a context of actual classroom events, nor do they address the dynamics of individual students' culture in the classroom. What impact, if any, might this have on their views, and should an awareness of their background have any bearing on how teachers interpret and use their ideas? The monocultural background or particular experience of a researcher does not mean that the educational research and theory should be discounted. However, as a professional, you should critically analyze the latest theories and suggestions for classroom practice, placing the advice of others in the context of your own community and the school in which you work.

Most good teachers are not wedded to a particular discipline program. They strive to develop a management style that is clear to the students yet flexible enough to meet the needs of a wide variety of learners. As you learned in Chapter 2,

Haberman's research reveals that those teachers who are "stars" are not overly concerned with discipline and management issues.[37] Effective teachers realize that children sometimes misbehave and can even act downright awful! These teachers *expect* to have to deal with inappropriate behavior and view planning classroom management strategies as part of the job. Haberman's "star" teachers concentrate on building rapport and effective relationships with students and their parents in order to maximize opportunities for positive interactions. Their classrooms are communities of learners in which students and the teacher care about each other's success. Most important, effective teachers clearly understand the relationship between the curriculum, the instructional strategies, and student engagement. In other words, teachers with "good" classrooms are those who have high expectations for behavior and academic achievement, who are firm but fair in their dealings with students, and who carefully plan units and lessons that are relevant, interesting, and challenging for all. Students in these classrooms do not have time to behave inappropriately—they are too busy learning!

Many prospective teachers ask for a course on discipline and classroom management. Although such a course can provide you with some practical tips for dealing with problems and dilemmas in the classroom, *how* you choose to work with students in regard to discipline and management is intimately connected to *what* you believe about the nature of the child and the role of students in society.

Just as early colonial schools were influenced by Puritan philosophy about the "evil" nature of children, your classroom practice will be based, in part, on what it is *you* believe about how and why children act the way they do in school. There is no recipe book for effective discipline, and each lesson you plan may call for flexibility in your management of the class. It will be up to you to bring your personal philosophy of teaching to bear on the discipline and management decision that you make.

BACK TO CAROL'S DILEMMA

At the end of her student teaching semester, we asked Carol how she had resolved her discipline dilemma over the unfair way she saw herself giving out check marks, focusing on the girls of color and ignoring the middle-class White girls she knew were also misbehaving. As you will recall, she reported that discipline was one of the hardest things about student teaching. Carol told us that although she hadn't really thought much more about the check mark system, she did begin to consider the children's point of view. She said that she spent more time talking to the children to find out what was wrong and began to deal with them individually, not using the check marks and names on the board as much by the end of the semester.

This answer was a bit problematic for us. To her credit, Carol recognized that her actions impinged unfairly on the females of color, but we were dismayed to learn that she took no specific action to document, confirm, or negate her suspicions about the impact of her actions. She did not analyze her practices in any way, neglecting to examine the consequences of her decision to use assertive discipline procedures despite her feelings of uneasiness.

We can examine Carol's dilemma and her actions on two levels. First is the micro (or classroom) level. Second is the macro level, projecting the consequences of her action (or inaction) onto the lives of the children outside of school and onto their futures.

Carol was attempting to implement a practice that is common in many classrooms today. Children's names are placed on the board for such reasons as misbehavior or incomplete homework. Often a pattern develops, as in Carol's case, in which the same children's names are placed on the board day after day. What consequences might this have? At the level of the classroom, Carol's actions can be viewed in several ways: the implications for students whose names were consistently placed on the board, the implications for students whose names were not consistently placed on the board, and the possible the effects of her actions on the social relationships among the two groups of females.

Children whose names are continually placed on the board rarely improve their demeanor over the course of the year. Instead, they often live up to the teacher's low expectations. They begin to see themselves as "bad," or less able than their classmates, because they never seem to meet the teacher's expectations for "proper" behavior, for completing assignments on time, or for bringing in their homework. Their classmates, too, begin to ascribe these negative characteristics to this group of students. At the same time, their classmates come to view themselves as "good" or superior because they have successfully internalized the teacher's rules or are able to complete assigned tasks within allotted time frames. As Carol noted, once this pattern is established, the teacher often continues to punish those children who have established a relationship as "bad" or "incapable" while overlooking undesirable behaviors in those children who have established themselves as "good." No attempt is made to seek alternative explanations for why students may be exhibiting certain behaviors. Some teachers even discredit the parents of children who do not seem to fit into the school program, stating that "the apple doesn't fall far from the tree."[38] It is up to Carol to examine herself. Because of her background and experiences, Carol may in fact hold racist, sexist, and classist notions about the students and their parents. At the least, she is operating with stereotypes about them. As the semester closed, Carol did not face up to her own role in perpetuating the inequities she recognized. She was engaged in racist and classist behavior.

As noted, this cycle can have detrimental effects on the social relationships in the classroom. In Carol's room, these second-grade females had already segregated themselves by race and social class based on the ability groups that Carol's cooperating teacher used in the class. The nonwhite females whose names regularly appeared on the board worked and played together. Carol correctly noted that these four girls, who came from families whose income was at the low end of the socioeconomic scale, were below grade level academically. The had been placed in the "low group." The four White girls whose inappropriate behavior Carol admittedly overlooked came from families in the upper-level income brackets and were academically at or above grade level, constituting the "high group."

Let's consider the effects of these patterns on the children's lives as they progress through school and face the grim realities of racism, sexism, and classism outside of the classroom. Evidence indicates that once a child is labeled as behaviorally or academically different from what is considered normal for a particular grade level, this label follows a child through school.[39] Compounding this problem is evidence related to the relationship between a teacher's expectation and a student's academic performance. Decades ago, it was documented that children tend to behave and to perform academically according to the teacher's expectations.[40]

Given the situation in Carol's classroom, it is likely that the female students of color whose names continually appeared on the board will carry negative labels about themselves in their heads as they move through the grades. They may consider themselves failures and even vocalize such ideas by saying, "I am such a loser" or "I cannot do this math, I'm dumb." These labels may manifest themselves year after year if a teacher does not stop to examine what is behind the label or what factors are affecting a student's behavior and academic performance.

For the students in Carol's class, it is a grim projection. Currently, females of color are more likely to drop out of high school and college and be unemployed between the ages of 20 and 35 than are White females or males. Those women of color who do hold full-time jobs often occupy minimum wage positions and earn lower weekly salaries than their male or White female counterparts.[41] *All* students, but especially female students of color, must be provided with positive educational experiences and early academic success if the cycle of undereducation and underemployment is to be broken.

In addition, the social relations in Carol's classroom are being cemented by the cooperating teachers' instructional management strategy of academic grouping that places children of like background together for much of the day. When a teacher groups students according to ability, often students of color are placed in the "low" group, as was the case in Carol's classroom. In a situation such as this, the children are rarely afforded the opportunity to work with other classmates. Opportunities to learn about and appreciate the talents and abilities, the uniqueness and similarities among all class members are lost. When the peer group is limited by ability grouping or tracking, students miss the opportunity to debate issues with others who may have different opinions and experiences, or to listen to and consider other perspectives. In short, the degree to which students are able to become open-minded, critical thinkers is in jeopardy.

FINDING A VOICE

Thomas Jefferson Middle School is a suburban middle school with a new principal, Ms. Hopkins. Recently promoted, she opened the school year eager to implement some innovative programs at Jefferson. Students at the school are assigned to teams of four teachers and are grouped heterogeneously (i.e., mixed ability) for the entire day. They stay with a homeroom teacher for a reading/language arts block in the morning and then rotate among the other three teachers in a block scheduling plan (120-minute periods) for the remainder of the day. By the end of the week, the team covers the core subjects of mathematics, technology, science, and social studies. Students also take classes in a non-English language and once a week have a period that the school staff term "specials," in which the teachers teach courses not typically found in schools. Some of the selections include karate, rollerblading, first aid, and double-dutch jump rope.

A school policy put into place by Ms. Hopkins and the assistant principal prevents students who have not completed their homework for the week in the core subjects from attending the special courses. Ms. Hopkins implemented this policy because several influential parents who met with her when she accepted the principalship expressed concern that many teachers required too little homework and some teachers were unlikely to correct the homework they did assign. As a new principal, Ms. Hopkins wanted to be sensitive to parental concerns, and the "no homework, no specials" policy seemed like a good way to reinforce the importance of homework.

Mr. Davidson, a member of the sixth-grade team, was becoming increasingly concerned as the winter holidays approached. Several sixth graders rarely participated in the weekly special courses because they failed to complete one or more homework assignments. In fact, three students, Simone, Oscar, and Kevin, had yet to attend a single special course. Mr. D., as the students called him, did not understand why they did not do their homework. They seemed like nice enough kids, but their lack of preparedness disrupted his class. He hated to see the three students in the homework room each week during specials. Mr. Davidson decided to do a little investigation.

Right before the winter break, Mr. Davidson volunteered to be the teacher in charge of the homework room during the special period. Predictably, along with a few others sat Simone, Oscar, and Kevin. Mr. Davidson did not have much trouble getting them to complete their assignments. They seemed to know how to do the work, and when they asked to work together in a group, he took the opportunity to talk informally with them. "You three really know how to work together," he said. "It makes me wonder why you don't do this at home so that you can attend specials." Simone, Oscar, and Kevin looked at each other, seeming unsure what to say. Finally, Oscar spoke up.

"It's my fault, Mr. D. Only Simone and Kevin know this, but my family got evicted from our apartment because my dad lost his job and we couldn't pay the rent. We've been living at the homeless shelter on Fifth Street since the end of September. It's so noisy in there that I can't concentrate. All the people at the shelter live in one big room, with only sheets hanging as dividers. I don't really have any place to do my homework even if it is quiet because there's always someone around. Simone and Kevin have been doing their homework, and offered to do mine, but I don't want to cheat. So instead, they've been not handing in a couple of assignments a week so that they can keep me company in here. Besides, the courses I'm really interested in cost money. I mean, I'd love to learn to rollerblade, but man, those things cost over a hundred bucks and I can't ask my parents for money for stuff like that."

Simone chimed in, "Mr. D., Oscar isn't the only one with problems getting homework done. My mom works the 3 to 11 shift, and I've got to get dinner for my sisters, help them with their homework, get them a bath and put them to bed before my mom gets home. I don't even start my homework until 10:00. I really want to go to college, Mr. D., but sometimes I don't know if I'll make it. A lot of the other kids have computers at home, and some teachers get mad if you turn in your work all written out. Sometimes they yell at me. But I can't go to the computer lab after school, and if I stay up until midnight doing homework, I'm too tired to get up and get here by 7:30 to type it up before school starts."

Mr. Davidson was silent. Simone and Oscar's words had caught him completely off guard. He knew there was a homeless shelter in town, but he never considered that any of his students might live there. He was also feeling like a complete fool for not realizing that many of the "specials" required the students to bring materials from home that they would have to buy. He had assumed that because he taught in the suburbs, most of the families were pretty well off. He looked at Oscar, "Hey, Oscar, thanks for explaining all of this to me. Don't worry, I won't tell anyone about your situation." In the back of his mind, Mr. Davidson was already trying to figure out a way to bring this to the attention of the administration and faculty without breaking Oscar's confidence.

When winter break rolled around, Mr. Davidson finally did what he had been promising himself, he volunteered at the local soup kitchen. While he was there, he saw not only Oscar but four other students from Jefferson as well. He wondered if the problem of money and quiet space for homework was greater than he imagined.

When school resumed, Mr. Davidson met with Ms. Hopkins and related his experience at the soup kitchen. He told Ms. Hopkins that he was beginning to question the "no homework, no specials" policy. Also, he wanted to revisit the type of special courses that were offered. She suggested that he address the faculty with his concerns at the next meeting.

Mr. Davidson told his story to the faculty. At first some of the teachers rolled their eyes upward as if to say that the issues he was raising were not that big a deal. When Mr. Davidson told of his experiences at the soup kitchen, however, the teachers became silent. Most of them had never considered the fact that students at Jefferson used social services. Mr. Davidson acknowledged that it was important for middle school students to get some opportunities for independent practice and that it was disruptive to the class when students did not complete their out-of-class assignments. But he expressed his concerns about the homework policy. He proposed that there might be other ways to help students get their homework completed, given what he was learning about the living conditions of some of the students. He continued by raising the issue of offering special courses that required the students to have costly materials or to spend money to complete the special course.

All of the teachers agreed that this was an important issue, but some were more interested than others. Ms. Hopkins stated that she never really considered the possible scope of reasons why students do not complete homework and reiterated that she was only responding to parental concerns. She said that she was willing to entertain alternative proposals if a committee of teachers was willing to work on the issue and get back to her. Mr. Davidson and five teachers volunteered.

The committee met several times before they agreed on possible solutions to the problems raised by Mr. Davidson. Mr. Davidson convinced the committee to join him in volunteering at the soup kitchen, which he was now doing twice a month. They gave the following list of suggestions to Ms. Hopkins, who asked them to present it to the faculty at the March meeting:

1. No special courses should be offered that cost more that $10 per semester unless the materials are provided for the students. The offerings could be expanded by asking students about the types of special courses that could be offered within the $10 guideline.
2. Students could be recruited to teach special courses in which they have expertise. (Here Mr. Davidson was thinking of students like Simone, who might be able to offer a course in cooking based on meals that she prepares for her sisters).
3. A before-school, after-school, and Saturday homework club should be held at Jefferson, open to anyone who wants a quiet place to do homework or to get some extra help.
4. The policy of "no homework, no specials" should be suspended. Attendance at special courses is important and it sends the wrong message if they are used as a punishment.
5. A permanent committee of teachers and administrators should be formed to provide the faculty with several types of data that would inform future decisions. For example, the committee could begin to examine other school policies (e.g., attendance, tardiness, dress code) to ensure that they are not impacting unfairly on any particular group of students.
6. A list of organizations in the community that need regular volunteers should be developed and circulated among teachers to encourage community participation. Service learning courses should be developed for credit so that students can learn more about their community.

The faculty debated the suggestions, some with more vigor than others. The homework club and suspension of the "no homework, no specials" policy were implemented immediately. A permanent committee was established and a survey was developed to obtain new ideas for inexpensive special courses. The idea of students teaching special courses and that of service learning were somewhat controversial and continued to be debated.

Mr. Davidson is clearly a teacher who "found" his voice. His principal and many of the faculty were supportive of his idea, but many were not. This is often the case with a school faculty, and Mr. Davidson was not discouraged. Because he had facts to back up his views and because he had volunteered at the food pantry himself, he was able to speak with authority. All institutional policy changes may not be so easy, but Mr. Davidson's leadership role will most likely continue.

SUMMING UP

In this chapter, we have discussed the topics of discipline and management from the perspective of power and through stories and vignettes that bring issues of ethnicity, social class, and gender to the forefront of the discussion. The subtle and not-so-subtle differences between discipline and classroom management were discussed. We discussed classroom management as focusing on the teaching–learning process that evolves from the relationship between the teacher, the

Multicultural Education Means a Just and Equitable Classroom

Many students ask us, "What do classroom management and discipline look like from a multicultural perspective?" We think it means:

- Creating a community of learners within the school and the classroom where mutual respect between adults and students and collective responsibility for academic, personal, and social success are fostered.
- Ensuring that students, parents, and staff are full participants in the development of school policies and procedures.
- The school community (the grounds, the school, and each classroom) is free from verbal, physical, and emotional abuse, and such instances, should they occur, are dealt with in an appropriate, fair, and effective manner that advances the learning community.
- Teachers, administrators, and staff examine their beliefs and actions on a regular basis to ensure that policies, procedures, and practices are just and equitable.
- Teachers focus on making the curriculum and the learning activities relevant, challenging, and hands-on, as opposed to doling out punitive rewards and punishments designed to coerce students into doing boring or irrelevant tasks.

students, and the material. We hope that you have begun to consider how you will set up a classroom environment that is conducive to learning. We described discipline as being intertwined with management but as focusing on the way in which a teacher chooses to deal with individual and group behavior. We distinguished between extrinsic motivation (from the outside) and intrinsic motivation (from within) in terms of rewards and punishments.

We have looked briefly at discipline and management issues from a historical perspective to help you understand that today's school practices have a history and that they are the result of the philosophical perspectives of those who implement them. For example, you were able to see how the practice of isolating or calling negative public attention to students who misbehave or forget their homework has its roots in colonial schooling and developed from a philosophy or belief system that characterized children as inherently prone to poor behavior.

The stories of Carol in the opening vignette and Mr. Davidson in Finding a Voice demonstrate the impact of socioeconomic status, ethnicity, and gender on the classroom. We made the point that a responsible teacher examines his or her actions to ensure that policies and procedures are implemented equitably, and changes those practices when necessary. Some teachers feel guilty if they find that their classroom actions are biased or unfair. The way to get over feelings of guilt is to take action. You need to work to change what you do so that you are always striving to be an excellent teacher for all students. Some of the key tenets of equitable classroom management are summarized in the box "Multicultural Education Means a Just and Equitable Classroom."

What Parents Want

Natesha is the mother of Ashanti, a high school student. She works two jobs and attends college part-time to ensure a good life for herself and Ashanti. When asked how she wants her local public school teacher to address discipline and classroom management, Natesha replied:

> What do parents want in terms of classroom management and discipline? What I want, and I think that most parents would agree, is more communication between parents, teachers, and administrators. Most schools stress that they have an open door policy but from my experiences with the schools my daughter has attended, this is not true. In order to maintain classroom management, schools need to decrease class size, allowing for a closer connection between home and school. The teacher has more time to spend with parents if he or she has fewer students. We, as parents and teachers, can gain more control and have more supervision of our children through smaller class sizes. When teachers deal with fewer students each day, there are fewer interruptions and there is more time for teacher–student interactions.
>
> I am also in favor of having more than one teacher or adult in the classroom. We need to provide more teacher assistants, school counselors, and specialists in certain areas such as reading, math, technology, and speech. These specialists can provide one-on-one assessments of students so that teachers can detect and respond to a child's learning difficulties or personal problems. Students who have trouble learning often act up in school.
>
> Teachers should consider having an open circle discussion at least once a week, beginning in kindergarten. This would be a time for students to discuss feelings, classroom issues, or just express themselves. This is one way that teachers can maintain a positive classroom.
>
> School violence is increasing and we all need to work together as a community to provide children and parents with an awareness of safety issues. If we provide more public safety programs and get the community involved in the schools, we can reduce school violence. I know that in some schools, security guards have been hired and are necessary to maintain safe schools. If this is the case, we should be sure that security guards are in uniform, are well trained to work with children, and are actively patrolling the school during the day.
>
> Finally, classroom discipline problems can be reduced by teaching subjects that are relevant to the students. For example, as a parent I want my daughter to be computer literate. Technology education is of great interest to all students and instruction should begin in kindergarten. I want my Board of Education to include subjects that prepare my child for the future and interest her in school. I want my child to have access to computer labs and I would like to see her using technology on a daily basis. Interest in topics like technology would keep students interested and motivated to learn new things. When the curriculum teaches students things that they like and will use in the future, they pay attention!

School violence is a topic that is on the minds of many teacher candidates as well as everyone who cares about schooling today. We discussed physical, verbal, and sexual violence and presented some characteristics of schools in which violence is minimal or nonexistent. Clearly, teachers and administrators have a lot of control over the school and classroom environment and over the way that students, parents, and community members are involved in the life of the school. When all members of the school community feel valued, connected, and involved, the result is a climate of nonviolence.

The Canter–Kohn comparison examined the work of two more recent proponents of differing discipline philosophies in order to demonstrate that even today, despite years of educational research, experts do not agree on the best classroom practice. We hope that you see that it is not possible for a professor or a cooperating teacher to give you a "bag of tricks" to help you with discipline and management issues. You will have to find your way through the dilemmas of discipline policies and management practices by uncovering your own beliefs about the nature of students, the role of the teacher, and how these beliefs relate to the type of discipline and management strategies that you implement in the classroom. Any strategy or technique that you read about or see in the classroom will have to match your belief system in order for you to make it "work" for you; as you probably already know, what "works" for one teacher may or may not be successful for another. You will also need to discuss expectations for discipline and management with the parents and caregivers of your students (see the box "What Parents Want"). It may seem frustrating at times as you deal with the dilemmas of discipline and classroom management, but your hard work in building relationships with students, parents, and other community members will eventually pay off in your classroom and you will become one of those teachers that others refer to as "star" teachers!

KEY TERMS

assertive discipline

character education

classroom as community

classroom management

constructivism

corporal punishment

discipline

emulation

extrinsic punishment

extrinsic reward

intrinsic rewards

physical violence

progressivism

sexual harassment

violence

QUESTIONS FOR REFLECTION

1. How would you explain the difference between discipline and classroom management in your own words?
2. How did Protestant religious beliefs, especially those of the Puritans, affect discipline and management practices in colonial schools? Give one example of how those practices may still be visible in schools today.

3. One of the stated goals of schooling in the United States is to prepare students to be effective, participating citizens in the country's democracy as well as the world. What type of classroom management and discipline practices would facilitate this goal today, given what you see as the needs of our global, technologically oriented society?

4. Compare the characteristics of a teacher-centered discipline and management style, such as that described by the Canters, with those of a student-centered discipline and management style, such as that described by Alfie Kohn. What are the main philosophical differences? Which aspects of the two approaches might you embrace and which would you avoid?

5. How were discipline and management handled when you were in elementary, middle, and high school? What are the historical roots of those practices? What were the implications of those practices for you?

6. If you were Mr. D. in the "Finding a Voice" section, how would you have reacted to the information shared by Oscar, Simone, and Kevin? What might be the implications of speaking out for a nontenured versus a tenured teacher? Would tenure matter to you in deciding whether or not to speak out? Why or why not?

ACTIVITIES

1. Make a scale model of your ideal classroom setup for effective management. How will student desks and the teacher's desk be arranged? Will you even have desks? Why or why not? What other furniture will be in the room and why? Will you have "areas" or centers? Why or why not? If so, where will they be and how will students use them? Bring your model to class and share your ideal classroom with your colleagues. Attach a one- to two-page paper that explains the rationale for your model. What does the type of room arrangement you prefer tell about your philosophy of classroom management?

2. If you are unable to implement your ideal classroom setup, given the reality in your field placement, how will you adjust?

3. Read and analyze Tracey Kidder's book *Among Schoolchildren.* Most prospective teachers believe that the teacher described in the book, Chris, is a good teacher. Do a critical analysis of her practices. Make a list of Chris's discipline and management strategies. You may need to distinguish between specific practices that she uses for individual children, for the entire class, and for various groups (e.g., the "low" group, the boys vs. the girls). What might be the implications of Chris's actions for the students in each case? What are the implications for how the class might come to view individual students (e.g., Clarence, Judith)? Chris spends a lot of time *thinking* about her teaching. Make a list of every change she makes as a result of her thinking. Does Chris make deliberate and systematic changes to improve her practice? Why or why not?

4. Read *Assertive Discipline* (1992) and *Beyond Discipline: From Compliance to Community* (1996). Consider the philosophical underpinnings of the practical ideas presented in the books—that is, the authors' views about the nature of the child, the role of the curriculum, and the role of the school in society. Then, using the books, develop a set of interview questions that

you can use with an experienced teacher. Interview the teacher and try to uncover his or her philosophy about discipline without asking directly. Later, observe the classroom as the teacher interacts with the students. To what degree do the teacher's stated beliefs match his or her actual practice?

5. Go to Exhibit 3.2 and select a theorist whose model of classroom discipline or management has become popular. Read a book or several articles by that theorist. The work of many of these educators has been translated into videos, teacher workshops, or training manuals for teachers, which you may also find in the library. Select one theorist and do the following:
   a. Research the person's educational background. Describe her or his training and classroom experience.
   b. Summarize the main points of her or his philosophy and its concomitant applications to the classroom.
   c. What fundamental beliefs about the role of the school in society, the nature of students, the role of the curriculum, and the role of the teacher does the theorist reflect?
   d. Compare and contrast the model and philosophy with your own.
   e. If you are currently student teaching, answer the following question: What aspects of this theorist's approach would or would not work for you in your current context? Why would or would not they work?

6. Locate two teachers, one whose classroom represents a teacher-centered style as described by the Canters and one whose classroom represents a student-centered style as described by Alfie Kohn. Observe each classroom for at least a day. What are the characteristics of each classroom? What are the implications of the teacher's style for the students? If you were a student in the classroom, how would you feel at the end of the day?

7. Interview three principals at different levels of schooling (e.g., elementary, middle school, high school) about how decisions and policies related to discipline are made in that building. To what extent are parents, students and teachers involved in decisions and policy making? What factors affect differences between buildings?

8. Many teachers and students perceive school violence as affecting their school experience. Brainstorm a list of what can be done about school violence and discuss your ideas with your classmates and with teachers you know.

GETTING CONNECTED

Following are resources for creating a nonviolent community culture in schools:

National School Safety Center
141 Suesenberg Drive, Suite 11
Westlake, CA 91362
Phone: 805-373-9977
Fax: 805-373-9277
E-mail: info@nssc1.org
Web: http://www.nssc1.org

NSSC advocates for the prevention of school violence. It provides resources, strategies, and information on promising programs. Information on training sessions, seminars, and resources for parents and educators is available.

Center for the Prevention of
School Violence
North Carolina State University
20 Enterprise Street, Suite 2
Phone: 800-299-6054 or
919-515-9397
Fax: 919-515-9561
Web: http://www.ncsu.edu/cpsv

The CPSV is a clearinghouse for
information on school violence. It
provides research, develops programs
on violence prevention, and maintains
a resource library.

Girls Incorporated National
Headquarters
120 Wall Street, Third Floor
New York, NY 10005
Phone: 212-509-2000
Fax: 212-509-8708
Web: http://www.girlsinc.org

Girls Incorporated is a national youth
organization dedicated to helping every
girl become strong, smart, and risk-
taking. GI develops youth programs
addressing such topics as math and
science education, media literacy,
adolescent health, substance abuse
prevention, and sports participation.

U.S. Department of Justice
website
http://www.usdoj.gov/kidspage

This website includes a page titled
"Hateful Acts Hurt Kids." The goal of
this page is to prevent physical and
emotional violence through discussion,
problem-solving skills, and actions that
can make a difference.

Conflict Resolution Education
Network (CREnet)
1527 New Hampshire
Avenue, NW
Washington, DC 20036
Phone: 202-667-9700
Fax: 202-667-8629
E-mail: nidr@crenet.org
Web: http://www.crenet.org

CREnet is a national clearinghouse for
information and resources in the field
of conflict resolution education. The
website contains a wealth of resources
on conflict resolution.

U.S. Department of Education
www.ed.gov/offices/OSERS/
OSEP/earlywrn.html

Guidebook containing strategies for the
prevention of school violence.

National School Boards Association
http://www.keepschoolssafe.org

Ten-point safety plan for schools.

National Institute for Dispute
Resolution (NIDR)
1726 M Street, NW, Suite 500
Washington, DC 20036-4502
(202) 466-4764
fax: (202) 466-4769

The National Institute for Dispute
Resolution is a national center of
expertise and resources on consensus
building and dispute resolution. NIDR
sponsors the Conflict Resolution
Education Network, a clearinghouse

E-mail: nidr@nidr.org

for information, resources, technical assistance, and training in the field of conflict resolution and education.

Anti-Defamation League
http://www.adl.org

The Anti-Defamation League is a national organization with local affiliates. They offer programs for professional development and for K–12 students in character education, anti-bullying, equity and affirmative action, standards-based curriculum, and safe and drug-free schools.

Character Education
Partnership (CEP)
1025 Connecticut Avenue,
NW, Suite 1011
Washington, DC 20036
http://www.character.org

CEP is a nonpartisan coalition of organizations and individuals interested in developing moral character and civic participation in youth. It offers programs for staff development, K–12 school support, community programs, and information dissemination.

NOTES

1. The events and people described in this vignette are real. Pseudonyms are used to protect the identity of the people involved.
2. Assertive discipline is a program developed by Lee Canter and described in books that he has written with Marlene Canter, *Assertive Discipline: A Take Charge Approach for Today's Educator* (1976) and *Assertive Discipline: Positive Behavior Management for Today's Classroom* (1992). Both books are published by Lee Canter and Associates, Santa Monica, CA.
3. R. F. Butts and L. A. Cremin, *A History of Education in American Culture* (New York: Holt, Rinehart and Winston, 1953).
4. Ibid., 68–69.
5. E. P. Cubberly, *Public Education in the United States* (Cambridge, MA: Riverside Press, 1919), 36–37.
6. Butts and Cremin, *History of Education*.
7. H. Mann, *Seventh Annual Report of the Board of Education; Together With the Seventh Annual Report of the Secretary of the Board* (1843), 127–128.
8. R. L. Church, *Education in the United States* (New York: Macmillan, 1976).
9. Ibid., 102–103.
10. R. D. Archambault, ed., Introduction to *John Dewey: On Education* (Chicago: University of Chicago Press, 1964).
11. J. Dewey, "My Pedagogic Creed," in *John Dewey: On Education*, ed. R. D. Archambault (Chicago: University of Chicago Press, 1897), 431–432.
12. *In the White Man's Image* (PBS Video, 1992).
13. Canter and Canter, *Assertive Discipline: Positive Behavior Management*.

14. Ibid., 11–12.
15. Ibid., 18–19.
16. Ibid., 36–37.
17. Ibid., 62–69.
18. Ibid., 71–72.
19. A. Kohn, *Beyond Discipline: From Compliance to Community* (Alexandria, VA: Association for Supervision and Curriculum Development, 1996).
20. Ibid., xv.
21. Ibid., 18.
22. Ibid, 26–27.
23. Ibid., 27–28.
24. Ibid, 35–36.
25. Ibid., 82–83.
26. Ibid, 88.
27. C. Remboldt, *Violence in Schools: The Enabling Factor* (Center City, MN: Hazelden Information and Educational Services, 1998).
28. Metropolitan Life, *The Metropolitan Life Survey of the American Teacher 1999* (New York: Author, 1999).
29. Equal Educational Opportunity Commission, *Policy Guidance on Current Issues of Sexual Harassment* (N-915-050) (Washington, DC: Author, March 19, 1990).
30. L. Phillips, *The Girls Report: What We Know and Need to Know About Growing Up Female* (New York: National Council for Research on Women, 1998).
31. "Vocational Sex Equity," *Ohio Survey Results on Equity Issues* (Columbus: Ohio Department of Education, 1998).
32. Ibid., 69.
33. H. Kohl, *I Won't Learn From You and Other Thoughts on Creative Maladjustment* (New York: New Press, 1994).
34. V. Paley, *You Can't Say You Can't Play* (Cambridge, MA: Harvard University Press, 1985).
35. D. Walker, "School Violence Prevention," in *School Safety: A Collaborative Effort,* The ERIC Review (Washington, DC: U.S. Department of Education, 2000).
36. E. Otten, *Character Education* (ERIC Clearinghouse for Social Studies/Social Science Education, 2000).
37. M. Haberman, *Star Teachers of Children of Poverty* (Bloomington, IN: Kappa Delta Pi, 1995).
38. T. Kidder, *Among Schoolchildren* (New York: Avon Books, 1989).
39. This phenomenon has been documented by a number of educational researchers. Seminal studies include those by Jeannie Oakes (*Keeping Track,* 1985) and John Goodlad (*A Place Called School,* 1981).
40. R. Rosenthal and L. Jacobson, *Pygmalion in the Classroom: Teacher Expectation and Pupils' Intellectual Development* (New York: Holt, Rinehart and Winston, 1986).
41. U.S. Department of Education, *The Condition of Education, 1996* (Washington, DC: Office of Educational Research and Improvement, 1996).

CURRICULUM

Courtesy of Bill Lisenby

FOCUS QUESTIONS

1. What is curriculum, if it is not the books and experiences provided by the school?
2. Does the hidden curriculum or the overt curriculum have the greater influence on students?
3. How do power and knowledge play a role in curriculum debates?
4. How can the way a curriculum is organized affect teaching and student learning?
5. What curriculum concerns do teacher educators have about teacher candidates?

VIGNETTE

CURRICULUM AND TURKEY: MARCY, MRS. PLATT, AND JOANNA

MRS. PLATT: *Come in, Marcy. Did you have a happy Thanksgiving? Joanna will be ready as soon as she finishes talking on the phone to her grandmother.*

MARCY: *Thanks, Mrs. Platt. Yes, I had a really nice Thanksgiving. Please tell Jo to take her time. I'm early anyway. Mrs. Platt, I hope you all had a happy Thanksgiving.*

MRS. PLATT: *Yes, Marcy, this was a pretty good Thanksgiving weekend— no family crises and everyone seems to be getting along, even the twins.*

MARCY: *Mrs. Platt, did you have an opportunity to look over Jo's education books? She told me that you wanted to see what the university is teaching its teacher candidates.*

MRS. PLATT: *Right, Marcy, I am especially interested in what you are learning about curriculum and standards. Everyone is talking about standards these days. There are content and performance standards for students and standards for teachers set by the National Board for Professional Teaching Standards.[1] The information that the university is giving you on standards looks pretty much like what we are receiving at my school. What we hear at school is that standards are not meant to hamper teachers' teaching, but are designed to help bring about a better educational system.*

MARCY: *You're right, Mrs. Platt, that's what we are learning in our classes. Also, we are told that almost every state, professional organization, and school district has developed its own sets of standards in each subject area.*

MRS. PLATT: *Marcy, what I did find different is what you are learning about curriculum. What you are learning seems much more timely and proactive than what I studied at State U. 20 years ago. Also from what I can see in your text, discussions of curriculum are much more in keeping with current times than our discussion at school about curriculum. Much of our focus is on the "basics"—math, science, technology, writing, and reading. Joanna showed me a definition of curriculum that she likes, written by a Professor Popkewitz. I don't disagree with him, but he certainly is introducing a different way of thinking about curriculum.*

MARCY: *I like his definition, too, but not everyone in our class agrees with Popkewitz. Some students say he's into "power" too much and others say that our discussion of curriculum is paying too much attention to multicultural education. However, the great thing about all of this disagreement is that our classes are not boring; they are pretty lively.*

JOANNA: *Come on, Marcy, let's hit the road. You can tell me what my mom said to you about curriculum while I am eating my last and final turkey sandwich of the weekend. 'Bye, Dad, 'bye, Mom. I'll call you when I get there.*

CURRICULUM: DOES IT MEAN WHAT YOU THINK IT MEANS?

Do you remember when you first heard the word *curriculum*? You probably do not as it's not a catchy word that sticks in your mind. In fact, Harold Rugg, one of the founders of the present-day field of curriculum, once said that curriculum is "an ugly, awkward, academic word."[2] When we tried to remember, Maureen recalls it wasn't until she was in college, during the teacher preparation sequence, and Carl recalls it was in junior high. We both agree that when we heard the word *curriculum,* it did not come to us as a "prophetic thought." In other words, we had no idea at the time that we were destined to become professors with a specialty in curriculum and instruction. We begin this chapter by asking, "What is curriculum?"

Definitions of Curriculum

In the *Handbook of Research on Curriculum,*[3] Philip W. Jackson provides readers with three definitions of **curriculum** taken from textbooks that span almost 50 years. He notes that these definitions are representative of definitions you will find in most textbooks:

> Curriculum is all of the experiences children have under the guidance of teachers. (Caswell and Campbell, 1935)
> Curriculum encompasses all learning opportunities provided by school. (Saylor and Alexander, 1974)
> Curriculum [is] a plan for all experiences which the learner encounters under the direction of the school. (Oliva, 1982)

Jackson goes on to explain that these definitions of curriculum are not identical. One discusses "learning opportunities," and the other two "experiences"; one describes curriculum as a plan or program, and the other two do not. Nevertheless, they are not worlds apart. Jackson argues that all three limit the term *curriculum* to what takes place in school or under the supervision of teachers. Each of the three contends that curriculum includes *all* of the "experiences" or "learning opportunities" that the school offers, not just those associated with the teaching of certain subjects or the use of special teaching methods such as lecturing or recitation.[4]

Many teachers that we talk with see curriculum in much the same way as Jackson but stress that it is a relationship between themselves, what they are teaching, and the students. It is fairly common for teachers such as Joyce Kilmer, a fourth-grade teacher, to observe: "Curriculum is the experiences *I* plan for *my* students." Thus teachers take ownership of the curriculum and speak of the relationship between themselves, what they are teaching, and the students, when they share in the responsibility for determining what will be taught and how it will be taught in their classes.

Who Owns the Curriculum?

The question of curriculum ownership and the question of the relationship between subject matter, teacher, and students emerge early in a teacher's education. "How much say does a teacher have in the curriculum?" is one of the popular questions asked of principals and curriculum coordinators when teacher candidates visit schools. We agree with Joyce. She does have a major say and responsibility, along with students, for the curriculum in her classroom. However,

Joyce's responsibility for curriculum needs to be understood within a larger context and in a legal sense. Joyce is legally permitted to teach at her school because she is an employee of the school district, and the school district is an educational agency of the state. It is the state—the governor, the legislature, and the state board of education—that has the ultimate responsibility for the education of children who live in the state, including the curriculum. (The governance structure will be discussed in Chapter 9.)

The 50 states of the United States receive responsibility for the education of students from the U.S. Constitution. If you read the Constitution you will find that it does not refer directly to education or delegate power to the federal government for participation in educational areas. Nevertheless, the 10th Amendment provides direction in this area: "The powers not delegated to the United States by the Constitution, nor prohibited by it to the States, are reserved to the States respectively, or to the people." With these words, the states became responsible for education, and teachers hired by the state are obligated to teach the curriculum mandated by the state. For example, each of the 50 states mandates teaching the history of that state, and teachers hired by the state are responsible for teaching the history curriculum mandated by the state.

So, although Joyce has a major say in what she teaches and how she teaches, it is the state that has the legal responsibility for curriculum. And, as many teacher candidates point out and as newspapers and television tell us daily, although a state may have the legal responsibility for education, curriculum is always an area in which there is much debate. Local boards of education, the federal government, special interest groups, textbook publishers, teachers, and students all demand a say in curriculum because the curriculum presents ways of thinking and notions of truth that shape the way we think.

Thomas Popkewitz, whom Mrs. Platt referred to at the beginning of this chapter, reminds us of the significance of curriculum in his definition of it:

> I view curriculum as a particular, historically formed knowledge that inscribes rules and standards by which we "reason" about the world and our "self" as a productive member of that world. The rules for "telling the truth" in curriculum, however, are not only the construction of objects for our scrutiny and observation. Curriculum is a disciplining technology that directs how the individual is to act, feel, talk, and "see" the world and "self." As such, curriculum is a form of social regulation.[5]

Implicit in the definitions of curriculum offered here by Popkewitz and earlier by Philip Jackson and in the questions raised by teacher candidates are discussions of power relationships. The power under discussion is not something that one owns or holds. Power is not perceived here as in the days of King Arthur and Merlin, when people conducted their behavior in ways that suggested that power was sovereign-owned—in other words, in the hands of kings, queens, and nobles. Nor is power located solely in the hands of present-day bureaucrats or administrators (e.g., superintendents, principals) or in policies and mandates of bureaucracies (e.g., standards, goals).[6] If it were, the discussion would be of sovereign-owned power and mainly center on who or what is included in schools' policies and practices, and it would be about notions of power that deal with control.

Our discussion of power recognizes that it comes from the public and personal knowledge of experts, which includes teachers. Popkewitz argues that expert knowledge shapes our thinking about much in our daily life—for example, the kind of diet and program that best contributes to personal health, our mind as having stages of development, and the students in our schools.[7] This knowledge is not a form of power that prevents bureaucrats, teachers, and Sally and Joe Public from doing the things they wish to do, but instead gives direction to the things they do. Popkewitz explains that although such thinking (e.g., about students) comes to be assumed as natural, it is not natural; it is built from expert systems of knowledge. The power of such expert knowledge is that it is not simply knowledge. It is "the knowledge" that is assumed to be true, or valued enough to learn over other "truths." Expert knowledge is a way of thinking that fashions how we participate as active, responsible individuals. It influences what we don't question because it is assumed to be true, versus what we do end up questioning in light of this "truth." This fusion of public and personal knowledge that influences our choices and possibilities can be thought of as the effect of power.

We continue this discussion of classroom curriculum by considering it from several perspectives. We will look at standards, overt and covert knowledge "that inscribes rules and standards by which we 'reason' about the world and our 'self,'"[8] curriculum as a major source of educational debate, and student teaching. Finally, we will consider the organization, scope, sequence, and continuity of curriculum and its focus within teacher preparation.

Curriculum Standards

Any discussion of curriculum today has to first consider standards, and consider if the standards are a form of social regulation. The educational reform efforts of the 1980s encouraged the development of curriculum standards in most, if not all, subject areas. Standards, however, are not a new idea in education. In 1909, E. L. Thorndike developed handwriting standards that were used to determine students' penmanship performance.[9] Thorndike's notion of a standard, as a scale calibrated on the basis of a large sample of students' handwriting and used to judge students' handwriting performance, is somewhat different from ours today. Nevertheless, the standards of 1909 and of today both consider content and performance, and remove the need for teachers to guess or make inferences from their own observations about what students need to know.

Standards are not the curriculum. Instead, standards are statements that define what the public feels students should know and be able to do, and they are not supposed to impede the teaching of the state or local curriculum. What the public believes students should know is often based on what politicians and the media portray as "problems" with the educational system. Much of the time, this includes a political/ideological agenda on the part of the politician that is then transmitted through the mass media to the public. Often educators and educational policy makers are kept out of this debate, or portrayed as "in opposition to" the politician, and thus as resistant to change. States and many local school districts across the nation have developed academic content and performance standards. In many of these states, the legislature has voted that schools must adopt such standards. Sometimes standards, especially those developed by national organizations and associations, are referred to as "national standards." Calling them national standards does not mean that they are federal standards, but that they can be applied to learning in any state and they have been developed by parents, teachers, members of the business community from across the country, and professional educators other than teachers.[10]

Content standards specify what students should know and be able to do. They are broad descriptions of the knowledge in an academic area. For example, students in Wisconsin will use numbers effectively for various purposes such as counting, measuring, estimating, and problem solving. Performance standards specify the ways in which students will show that they are meeting a content standard. Performance standards specify or detail the type of demonstration needed to provide evidence of a student's achievement. Here are the Wisconsin performance standards that demonstrate achievement of the previously specified mathematics content standard for grades 4, 8, and 12:

For fourth-grade mathematics:
In problem-solving situations involving whole numbers, students will select and efficiently use appropriate computational procedures such as:

- Recalling the basic facts of additions, subtraction, multiplication, and division
- Using mental math (e.g., $37 + 25$, 40×77)
- Estimation
- Selecting and applying algorithms for addition, subtraction, multiplication, and division
- Using a calculator

For eight-grade mathematics:
Students will perform and explain operations on rational numbers (add, subtract, multiply, divide, raise to power, extract a root, take opposites and reciprocals, determine absolute value).

For twelfth-grade mathematics:
Students will compare real numbers using order relations and transitivity ($>$, $<$), ordinal scales, ratios, proportions, percents, rates of change.[11]

Many national professional associations advocate standards and have developed them for their K–12 curriculum area (see Exhibit 4.1). These organizations argue that students should have the opportunity and resources to learn the standard. They recommend having high expectations for students and that students come prepared to learn. Also, they claim neither teachers nor students should think that having standards will hamper the teaching and learning process. For example, the National Council of Teachers of English and the International Reading Association (NCTE/IRA) address these points—opportunity, resources, preparedness, and facilitation of the learning—when they state:

The vision guiding these standards is that all students must have the opportunities and resources to develop the language skills they need to pursue life's goals and to participate fully as informed, productive members of society. These standards assume that literacy growth begins before children enter schools as they

EXHIBIT 4.1   NCTE/IRA STANDARDS FOR THE ENGLISH LANGUAGE ARTS

1. Students read a wide range of print and non-print texts to build an understanding of texts, of themselves, and of the cultures of the United States and the world; to acquire new information; to respond to the needs and demands of society and the workplace; and for personal fulfillment. Among these texts are fiction and nonfiction, classic and contemporary works.

2. Students read a wide range of literature from many periods in many genres to build an understanding of the many dimensions (e.g., philosophical, ethical, aesthetic) of human experience.

3. Students apply a wide range of strategies to comprehend, interpret, evaluate, and appreciate texts. They draw on their prior experience, their interactions with other readers and writers, their knowledge of word meaning and other texts, their word identification strategies, and their understanding of textual features (e.g., sound–letter correspondence, sentence structure, context, graphics).

4. Students adjust their use of spoken, written, and visual language (e.g., conventions, style, vocabulary) to communicate effectively with a variety of audiences and for different purposes.

5. Students employ a wide range of strategies as they write and use different writing process elements appropriately to communicate with different audiences for a variety of purposes.

6. Students apply knowledge of language structure, language conventions (e.g., spelling and punctuation), media techniques, figurative language, and genre to create, critique, and discuss print and non-print texts.

7. Students conduct research on issues and interests by generating ideas and questions, and by posing problems. They gather, evaluate, and synthesize data from a variety of sources (e.g., print and non-print texts, artifacts, people) to communicate their discoveries in ways that suit their purpose and audience.

8. Students use a variety of technological and informational resources (e.g., libraries, databases, computer networks, video) to gather and synthesize information and to create and communicate knowledge.

9. Students develop an understanding of and respect for diversity in language use, patterns, and dialects across cultures, ethnic groups, geographic regions, and social roles.

10. Students whose first language is not English make use of their first language to develop competency in the English language arts and to develop understanding of content across the curriculum.

11. Students participate as knowledgeable, reflective, creative, and critical members of a variety of literacy communities.

12. Students use spoken, written, and visual language to accomplish their own purposes (e.g., for learning, enjoyment, persuasion, and the exchange of information).

experience and experiment with literacy activities—reading and writing, and associating spoken words with their graphic representations. Recognizing this fact, these standards encourage the development of curriculum and instruction that makes productive use of emerging literacy ability that children bring to school. Furthermore, the standards provide ample room for the innovation and creativity essential to teaching and learning. They are not prescriptions for particular curriculum or instruction.[12]

Although standards are developed at different levels of government (national, state, and local) and by professional organizations, teachers have to be mindful of the standards advocated by their school district. For example, the California Department of Education argues that the primary focus of the teacher's efforts is his or her commitment to ensuring that all students will meet the district's academic content and performance standards.[13]

Committees that develop standards argue that "standards are not marching orders . . . but a trumpet call to action."[14] Standards do greatly influence the way teachers think about what they are going to teach and how they are going to teach it. For example, in the NCTE/IRA Standards for the English Language Arts (see Exhibit 4.1), Standard 9 deals with "understanding of and respect for diversity in language use," and Standard 10 deals with students whose first language is not English and the use of their native language to develop proficiency in English language arts.[15]

Popkewitz's notion of "curriculum as a form of social regulation" is seen in these standards because although educators are being asked to prepare students to live in a global society, none of the 12 standards advocates a maintenance program that would encourage non-English-speaking students to keep their native language. These standards do not clearly advocate students' being fluent in any language other than English, nor do they advocate bilingualism.

Although most educators who develop content and performance standards argue that these standards are not the curriculum, standards do suggest the learning experience and opportunities that students should have under the guidance of the teachers. The performance standards in particular imply behaviors and attitudes that are necessary for success in life after school. Performance standards are found in the ways teachers organize and carry out the daily routines of the class. Depending on how a district implements the interpretation of standards, and to what extent the standards form a prescriptive curriculum, the teachers may be very limited in what and how they teach. Additionally, for many teachers, the standards have become the fusion of teachers' public, professional, and personal knowledge that disciplines their choices and possibilities, and must therefore be thought of as the effects of power.[16]

The Overt Curriculum

What goes on in the school and classroom, or the curriculum, some educators argue, should be defined along two dimensions: the overt dimension and the covert or hidden dimension. The overt curriculum is the open, or public, dimension and includes current and historical interpretations, learning experiences, and learning outcomes. The experiences and outcomes are planned by school officials (e.g., teachers, curriculum coordinators). They are openly discussed, consciously planned, usually written down, and presented through the instructional process. Textbooks, learning kits, curriculum guides, lesson plans, school plays, and concerts are examples of the overt curriculum. To some, the important content of the overt curriculum in K–12 classrooms is the "basics"—reading, writing, and arithmetic. Others may describe the overt curriculum as the academic subjects: science, history, math, reading, and writing. One purpose of the overt curriculum is to provide students with science, history, mathematics, and literary knowledge. Another purpose is to provide students with the knowledge that "society wants them to have." Some examples of this latter knowledge is information on cleaning up the environment and leading a healthy life without drug abuse.

The Overt Curriculum and Social Responsibility

If society deems that students should know about something, and the school should teach it, then it is placed in the overt curriculum. The overt curriculum was charged with this social responsibility centuries ago. Benjamin Franklin was one of the forefathers of the idea that the overt curriculum should be society's messenger. Franklin argued that the United States should welcome immigrants from Europe, and he charged the public schools, through both the overt and the hidden curricula, with the responsibility to teach students to become good American citizens. Franklin and other civic leaders made a charge to schools that to "Americanize" immigrants is an enactment of power that comes out of their position and status. It is not an idea of power by which teachers are controlled, but of how curriculum and instruction should be carried out in the classroom to control and shape the populace through what is learned.

Franklin was not the first to argue that the American school curriculum should have an *educating* purpose. During early colonial times (1600s), schools were established for religious reasons. In New England, for example, the curriculum was developed to preserve the ways of thinking and notions of truth advocated by Puritan faith. By near mid-century (1642) the General Court of Massachusetts enacted laws that required every town of 50 families to employ a teacher of reading and writing, and the community or families were required to pay the teacher's salary. Reading and writing were for the most part designed around religious ideas, as the students' curriculum was catechism and extracts from the Bible. In order to organize what the students were learning, as well as what the teachers were to teach, the *New England Primer* was published in 1690. The *Primer* was heavily religious in content. Republished for more than 200 years, it became one of the early and long-lasting examples of an overt curriculum designed to influence certain ways of thinking.

After the 1750s, as the country pushed westward and the colonists came to accept that more than an understanding of and faith in religion was necessary for the development of a young country, the school curriculum changed to include history, mathematics, geography, and English grammar. In 1783 Noah Webster, of Webster's Dictionary, called by some "schoolmaster to America," published his *Grammatical Institute of the English Language*. It sold some 75 million copies and placed the study of English grammar at the forefront of the school curriculum. However, religion as subject matter that should be included in the schools' curriculum maintained its prominence with the passage of the Northwest Ordinances of 1785 and 1787. The Ordinance of 1785 made possible the sale of public lands with the stipulation that the 16th section in each township would be set aside for educational purposes. The Ordinance of 1787 argued for a school curriculum that included religion, morality, and knowledge because they were believed to be necessary for good government and the happiness of humankind (See Chapter 9 for further discussion of the Northwest Ordinance.)

In the 1800s the focus in education became making the curriculum available to the students. This problem occurred because many developing towns and communities could not afford to raise a school or pay a teacher's salary. The U.S. Office of Education claims that during the 1800s, many citizens attended school for only about 82 days throughout their lifetime. It was not until the 1870s that education in the United States began to expand significantly. Schools were influenced by the Industrial Revolution and were organized based on a "factory model." School districts were organized to serve the educational needs of the surrounding area. It was at this time that the curriculum changed to reading, spelling, writing, and grammar. The "three Rs" were seen as essential for young people to live and function in a society that was becoming increasingly modern thanks to technology advances such as the invention of the telephone in 1876, transatlantic steamship service, and greater exporting of manufactured goods and cotton.

Today, although much of the curriculum still deals with the basics and technology, responsibility is also being placed on schools to include in the curriculum information that formerly was discussed in the home or place of worship. For example, sex education, conflict resolution, acceptance of differences in others, and information about drugs can often be found in the classroom. This curriculum information represents different ideologies and philosophies, such as conservative or liberal. Therefore, teachers' knowledge of the different ways of thinking and notions of power will help them to better understand curriculum and the decisions that surround curriculum implementation. Clearly visible in the overt curriculum are rules and standards to which students must adhere, and expectations of achievement assigned by those in control. Therefore, it is important for teacher candidates to understand that the curriculum they use is a form of discourse that helps to develop and promote a certain kind of society and school by teaching students certain ways of thinking and notions of "truth."

The Hidden Curriculum

According to Jules Henry, the **hidden curriculum** is the "processes—the noise—by which the overt curriculum is transmitted.

> It is not primarily the message (let us say, the arithmetic or the spelling) that constitutes the most important subject matter to be learned, but the noise! The most significant cultural learnings . . . are communicated as noise.[17]

In addition to the progress students make in school in reading, writing, arithmetic, and technology, they are also learning and modifying attitudes, motives, and values in relationship to the experiences they have in the classroom. For example, female and male students may come to believe, after being instructed with materials that are gender biased, that certain careers are more suited for certain people because of their gender. These nonacademic outcomes of formal education are sometimes of greater consequence to the students' well-being than is learning the subject matter, and are the result of the hidden curriculum.[18]

The hidden curriculum works in concert with the overt curriculum. Both curricula instill ways of thinking and notions of truth. The hidden curriculum includes the many attitudes and behaviors that students learn in school that may not be visible but, instead, are subtle. Aronowitz and Giroux explain that the hidden curriculum operates within the dominant school culture. The dominant school culture, they argue, not only legitimizes the interests and values of dominant groups but also functions to marginalize and disconfirm knowledge forms and experiences that are important to subordinate and oppressed groups. This is observable in the way school curricula highlight the history and contributions of the dominant culture and omit or treat superficially the histories of Asian Americans, Latinos, women, and people with disabilities.[19] This omission or superficial treatment may not be recognized by students, but affects them nonetheless.

The message, or noise, as Jules Henry describes it, is an authoritative expression of power, because it comes from people and materials that students trust and rely on. It comes from textbooks, school administrators, teachers, and other students.

The hidden curriculum also influences teachers. Because the hidden messages help shape the norms in schools, they provide teachers with ways of thinking for assessing student behavior and attitudes. When teachers see student behavior or attitudes that are in conflict with the normalized standards of conduct, they communicate their displeasure through such responses as "a look" or statement of rebuke.

Four notions of truth, ways of thinking, and unstated implications that students acquire from the hidden curriculum discourses are appraisals of self-worth, social roles, middle-class perspectives, and attitudes and behavior required for work.

Appraisals of Self-Worth   After many classroom observations, Philip Jackson discovered that students are evaluated both by teachers and by fellow students.[20] Students learn about their own personal worth based on how peers and authority figures define them. For example, if during class Ms. Jones discourages the use of Maria's native language in favor of an English-only approach, and other students in the class hear the teacher's preference for the English-only approach, it could lead to students' "putting down" class members whose native language is not English. Similarly, if Mr. Wilson does not permit students to use race, gender, and class stereotypes but allows negative remarks about gays and lesbians to go unchallenged, the students may come to believe that Mr. Wilson dislikes gay and lesbian people. Thus, students who are gay or who come from homes with gay parents may believe that Mr. Wilson holds a grudge against them.

Social Roles   After years in classrooms, being judged both publicly and privately by dominant group standards that have by and large ignored them, marginalized students learn to appraise their own value in accordance with the ways of thinking and notions of truth of those who have marginalized them. From this appraisal of their self-worth, students take on social roles. Do you remember which students in your school were the "popular students," the "rebels," or the "loners"? How did you learn to perceive these students this way? Could it have been the way the teachers treated them or the way the students treated them? Students learn their social roles through interactions with peers and others, and they learn which behaviors, dress, language, and attitudes are appropriate to these roles in their peer society and society at large.

Recently, while giving a lecture at a local community college, Carl witnessed the influence of peer society as well as the larger society on the social roles of students. Most of the approximately 100 students at the lecture were from classes studying the state and federal government. When Carl asked, "How many students plan to pursue a career in government at the local, state, or federal level?" only three students responded in the affirmative. When he asked if the reason why so few were interested in a career in government was because of the way they see government officials and elected politicians being investigated by the media and special prosecutors, several students laughed spontaneously. When he said, "Oh, I wouldn't let the media and special prosecutors stand in my way," several students laughed again. Then one male said, "You don't get it, Professor Grant. Most of us are really just a bunch of red-neck farmers. Farming isn't what it used to be, and the future doesn't look as good as it did during our fathers' time. Many of us are here to get a little more education, and some of us have not really figured out what we are going to do. But we don't think—do you think?—they would let us in the government. Working in government or running for office seems like it's for people with money, not us."

Many of these college students believed that their family occupation and way of life assigned them to a social role designed by others. They believed it would be difficult for them to escape from their present role and move into a higher socioeconomic status. They did not seem angry about the ways of thinking and notions of truths (poor farm boys and girls do not go into government) that were shaping their destiny, nor did they seem to be resisting the ways of thinking that constructed this knowledge and that led to a notion of power that qualified or disqualified them for certain ways of life. In fact, they were conforming to the dominant discourse, which told them that they were not rich enough to change perspectives and careers.

Middle-Class Perspectives   Students beginning school are entering a well-established culture complete with linguistic codes, behavioral expectations, and assumptions about the nature of teaching and learning. Most of these communicative and behavioral codes reflect the values, power dynamics, and knowledge base of mainstream middle- or upper-class cultures.[21] Students entering school may come from families occupying different social positions. Nevertheless, for the most part, children in schools learn the ways of thinking, notions of truth, knowledge, behavior, and values of the middle class. For example, students are taught history from a European American middle-class perspective, without much debate and discussion. The acquisition of the Southwest from Mexico receives very little debate. It is portrayed as a heroic achievement in the name of liberty and Manifest Destiny. Few students are taught, as Howard Zinn argues, that the Southwest was acquired from Mexico through trickery and force[22] and that the concept of Manifest Destiny itself masked illegal land stealing by European Americans from Native American and Mexican people. From lessons that omit or only minimally include other groups' perspectives and contributions, and are not debated, students learn to accept notions of truth and interpret events from the perspective of the European American middle class and consequently to believe that other Americans have contributed very little of importance to the United States. This may lower the expectations that individuals in these groups have for themselves, and thus this is an effect of power working against these people.

Attitudes and Behavior Required for Work   Closely akin to the teaching of middle-class values is the teaching of the behaviors and attitudes valued for work. In several studies of student socialization, it has been found that school is designed to prepare students for occupations in impersonal, bureaucratic types of organizations. Cusick's study explains this well:

> The school demanded that students (1) accept a limited role, which requires only part of their faculties for a set number of hours each day, (2) promised them future-oriented rewards in return, and (3) provided a not-unpleasant environment where they were free to exercise other faculties in search of other rewards as long as that activity did not interfere with the organization.[23]

In recent years the United States has moved from an industrial economy to a high-tech and service economy. Advance placement courses, honors classes, inclusive classes, and programs designed to help students having difficulty finishing school all teach students the attitudes and behaviors they will need to be professionally successful in our highly technological society. On the other hand, models of classroom management and discipline that are too controlling, classroom groupings (e.g., ability groups) indicating to students that they are inferior, and curriculum that does not take the students' life experiences into account are preparing students for a lifetime job career at the low end of the service industry.

In addition, what is increasingly missing from discussions of attitudes and behaviors for work is attention to **family work.** By this we mean that some may decide not to enter the professional workforce, but instead choose to care for their children or others. Such decisions greatly aid the family and often others in the neighborhood, and should be respected. A mother recently told Carl that she had taken off for a year to make certain that her son, who was a sophomore in high school and very active in sports and other school events, was getting the help, support, and supervision he needed. Help and support included providing transportation to events for her son and many other students. Her family work brought peace of mind to many other parents who knew that their children were being supervised by a responsible adult.

The overt and the hidden curriculum are constantly in operation in each and every class. Together they provide students with ways of thinking that give credence to the truths that students come to accept and the actions that students decide to take. These "truths" and ways of acting often remain a part of students' behavior for years to come.

CURRICULUM: A MAJOR SOURCE OF EDUCATIONAL DEBATE

Some of the more contested debates throughout the history of education in this country have been over curriculum issues. These debates have usually centered on what knowledge and whose knowledge should be included in the K–12 curriculum.

The "What Knowledge" Debate

This section begins with the age-old educational question, "What knowledge is of most worth?" The so-called Scopes Monkey Trial in Dayton, Tennessee, is an example of a debate over what knowledge should be included in the school curriculum. In 1925, John Scopes, a high school science teacher, was put on trial for teaching evolutionary theory, even though it was included in the state-approved science textbook. The theory of evolution was at odds with the belief of many at the time who supported only the teaching of biblical creationism in the schools. In 1925, the state of Tennessee had declared it unlawful to teach any theory that denied the story of the Earth's creation as presented in the Bible. After listening to arguments presented by two of the nation's leading political figures and orators, prosecutor William Jennings Bryan and defense attorney Clarence Darrow, the jury found Scopes guilty.

This trial, although ostensibly about a high school teacher's curriculum, had much to say about the social and cultural significance of the way of life in the United States. "It marked a watershed in intellectual history; before *Scopes*, religious faith was the common, if not universal, premise of American thought; after *Scopes*, scientific skepticism prevailed."[24] The intense debates caused people to question their fundamental beliefs about human existence.

Another major debate related to "what knowledge" took place in 1969 when a high school English teacher assigned his senior class an article "The Young and the Old" that appeared in the *Atlantic Monthly*. The article provided a discussion related to "dissent, protest, radicalism, and revolt" and repeatedly included reference to the word *motherfucker*. The word was not artificially placed in the article but was used to help the author develop his thesis. In the discussion of the article, the teacher explained why the author had chosen this word. He also provided an alternative assignment for any student who found the assignment personally distasteful. The teacher was called before the school committee and asked to defend his use of the word in the classroom. When he refused, he was suspended. A lower court upheld the suspension; however, the teacher filed suit against the verdict in the U.S. Court of Appeal and the decision was overturned.

More recently, especially since the publication of *A Nation at Risk* in 1983,[25] "what knowledge" has been debated within the context of the argument for a return to the "basics"—that is, including more science and technology subject matter for all K–12 students, as opposed to a course selection that includes an array of classes in the social sciences and humanities. There are numerous other examples of the "what knowledge" debate in the educational literature; it is also fairly commonplace to find a "what knowledge" debate in newspapers and magazines.

The "Whose Knowledge" Debate

The "whose knowledge" debate is sometimes referred to as the canon debate. This debate causes teacher candidates to examine the primacy of Western European history and culture over non-Western history and culture. This debate is of concern to all student teachers, even those who believe that education that is multicultural is of only minimal importance to them because they plan to teach in a socially homogeneous area and they believe that they have learned enough about multiculturalism.

Since the civil rights movement of the 1960s, the "what knowledge" debate has received competition from the "whose knowledge" debate. People of color, feminists, gays and lesbians, and individuals classified with disabilities are groups that have argued that they are not included in the curriculum. They demand inclusion. William Pinar reminds us that "Curriculum is one highly significant form of representation, and arguments over curriculum are also arguments over who we are as Americans, including how we wish to represent ourselves to our children."[26]

Two newspaper articles from the 1990s, "History According to Whom?" by Carol Gluck and "Historical Blindness" by John Patrick Diggins, are examples of this debate. These articles, each representing different questions (who should be included in U.S. history instructional materials and teaching, and how they should be included) on the National History Standards, appeared on the same op-ed page of the *New York Times*. Gluck, who believes that U.S. history needs to become more inclusive and representative, writes:

> Standing before a classroom of African-American children in downtown Baltimore or a multi-ethnic melange in Los Angles has for years impelled teachers to expand their explorations of American history. The same is true of world history. The 21st century demands an understanding of America-in-the-world. Schools across the U.S. have been incorporating Asia, Latin America and the rest of the "non-west" into their history classes for well over a decade. . . . Exploring the paths that connect the past to the present world is not politically but historically correct. . . . The principle of public debate is itself an American value. So is the expansiveness that manages, through social conflict, to enlarge our definition of America, acknowledge the bad with the good and recognize parts of the past that earlier versions of American history ignored. . . . Unless Americans want a ministry of education to dictate "official knowledge," we had better welcome the continuing debate and more important, get on with the real job of improving the schools.[27]

Gluck's antagonist, Diggins, has problems with the "expanded explorations of American history" because he believes in the great man version of history. He argues:

> Lincoln understood something that . . . the curriculum reformers denigrate: the study of history cannot be separated from the study of outstanding leaders.

"What! Think these places would satisfy an Alexander, a Caesar or a Napoleon?" Lincoln asked in reference to routine political offices, "Never! Towering genius disdains a beaten path."

In the thoughts and actions of towering figures can be found much of the meaning of history—what Max Weber called "charismatic authorities." These are exceptional, event-making historical agents who challenge conventions, figures like Harriet Beecher Stowe and the Rev. Dr. Martin Luther King Jr. In dismissing the "great-man theory," the new social history is engaging in what Weber called the "castration of democracy at the expense of grasping the dynamics of leadership." And if we tell students to study history "from bottom up," will they also understand what Hegel meant when he observed about Napoleon that truth resides in power?

Let us not be deceived by the cult of multiculturalism that is behind the new standards. The genuine multiculturalists were actually the Western intellectuals of the late 19th century, historians like Weber and Henry Adams, who studied Samoa, China, India, and the Islamic world as well as medieval and ancient Judaism. The ideas of these dead white men are still alive today with insights into the origins of institutions and social customs.[28]

The Canon Debate

This debate over "whose knowledge" on many campuses and in the media is often referred to as the canon debate. Paul Lauter defines *canon* as "the set of literary works, the grouping of significant philosophical, political, and religious texts, the particular accounts of history generally accorded cultural weight in society."[29] Lauter notes that "defining what is 'central' and what is 'marginal,' a basic function of canonization, will itself decide who studies, who teaches, and who has power in determining priorities in American colleges"[30] and schools. It is from such canonization that notions of truths and ways of thinking are formed and become central to the overt and hidden curriculum.

For years "the" canon was considered, and is still considered by many, to be Western literary work—mainly European male authors who address the human condition as described in the masterpieces, classics, or greats books by such authors as Shakespeare and James. A literary canon has also been in place for years in the United States. This canon includes the work of predominantly European American male authors, such as Hemingway and Hawthorne, who are generally found in basic American literature college courses and textbooks and are ordinarily discussed in traditional volumes of literary history, bibliography, or criticism.[31] Since the social movements of the 1960s and 1970s, especially with the establishment of ethnic studies courses and women's studies, the traditional Western (European) and American literary canon has been under attack to change and include the works of many more authors of color and women. Although there is now more inclusion of authors of color and female writers, literary work still remains predominantly European or European American and male.

As teachers or teacher candidates, you will find it difficult to escape the "whose knowledge" or canon debate because it is becoming an increasingly important and hotly contested issue to consider throughout the K–12 school years. Also, how to celebrate traditional holidays (such as Columbus Day, Halloween, Thanksgiving, and Christmas) is a source of major debate in some school districts. Similarly, how to celebrate (including how much attention to give to) Black History Month, Women's History Month, and Cinco de Mayo is a source of debate at some local and state school board meetings and in teachers' lounges. The outcome of the "whose knowledge" debate will determine the notions of truths that K–12 students learn or do not learn.

Student Teaching and the "Whose Knowledge" Debate

At a recent meeting Maureen held with the university supervisors responsible for working with student teachers, the "whose knowledge" debate surfaced. The meeting began with supervisors' sharing ideas and curriculum materials they were using in their student teachers' seminars. Shortly, the discussion moved to how to overcome the resistance of the student teachers toward multicultural education generally and, specifically, the inclusion of more than just a token consideration of multicultural education in the writing of lesson plans. Several supervisors pointed out that a common reaction of the student teachers was that "they have enough multicultural education and they just want to teach." Some student teachers argued that they saw multicultural education as a "minority thing," and a good number of these student teachers contended that they were not planning to teach in a school with any significant number of "minorities." Maureen pointed out to the supervisors how important multicultural education is in any educational setting, regardless of the demographics of the students. Whether or not the students in a classroom differ by race, they will differ by gender, social class, religious orientation, and other cultural markers. She encouraged her supervisors to discuss with their student teachers how multicultural education helps students to function in a multicultural society.

CURRICULUM ORGANIZATION

Over the past two decades, curriculum organization has received major attention. How curriculum is organized often leads to how power/knowledge relationships between school people and other status groups in society are addressed. John Goodlad identifies four levels of curriculum organization: societal, institutional, instructional, and ideological.[32]

Societal Level

The societal level involves the determination of curriculum goals and subjects the students will study at the national or state level. Politicians, special committees, representatives from different professional associations, and academic specialists determine the goals, organization, and content to be studied in school. For example, the *Curriculum Standards for Social Studies: Expectations of Excellence* was prepared by a national committee of members representing the National Council for Social Studies.[33]

The resurgence of curriculum organization at the societal level began with the 1983 report *A Nation at Risk,* which stated, "If an unfriendly foreign power had attempted to impose on America the mediocre educational performance that exists today, we might well have viewed it as an act of war."[34] With this declaration, the report constructed ways of thinking about education in the United States that caused many Americans to become concerned about the education system, and this concern led to the federal and state governments' taking a greater role in K–12 education and the preparation of teachers. Both Presidents Bush Sr. and Clinton responded to the reform effort brought on by *A Nation at Risk* by setting curriculum goals and encouraging the federal and the state governments to become more involved in curriculum organization. President Bush offered America 2000, which, besides organizing educational goals at the societal level, encouraged states to take a more active (rather than passive) leadership role in education. Similarly, President Clinton's Goal 2000, which determined educational goals at the societal level, also encouraged greater leadership at the national level. (See Chapter 9 for further discussion of presidential influence on education.) In 1991, Congress established the National Council on Educational Standards and Testing (NCEST), and in 1992 NCEST recommended voluntary national standards and national achievement tests in key content subject areas.[35] Standards, it was argued, would become the means by which the national goals would be met and would serve to put the United States on track to respond to criticisms voiced in *A Nation at Risk.* The involvement of the federal government in setting standards for education continues through the No Child Left Behind Act implemented under President G. W. Bush.

Textbook publishers are another group that organizes curriculum at the societal level and plays a major role in deciding on the notions of truths and ways of thinking that students are to learn or not learn. This has especially been the case regarding knowledge about women and people of color, whose history and contributions have typically been left out of textbooks. In some cases, textbooks have become the sole or major instructional resource, dictating the curriculum for a state, school district, or school. In 1955, L. J. Cronbach observed, "Only the teacher, and perhaps a blackboard and writing materials, are found as universally as the textbook in our classroom."[36] Michael Apple more recently underscored the central importance of the textbook operating at the societal level when he observed that "it is the textbook which establishes so much of the material conditions for teaching and learning in classrooms in many countries throughout the world, and it is the textbook that often defines what is elite and legitimate culture to pass on."[37]

Publishing textbooks is a huge business in the United States. Sometimes decisions about what is included in the textbook are about money as well as ideology. Textbook publishers may be unwilling to include controversial or multicultural content if they believe that teachers, school districts, or states will not purchase a particular text based on content. Thus, what goes into textbooks has become hotly contested, as it sometimes has more to do with private enterprise than with the public good.

An example of textbook curriculum organization at the societal level and the controversy that sometimes surrounds it occurred in California during the early 1990s. The debate in California was over the approval of a new series of social studies textbooks. It has been described as a debate between the multiculturalists, who advocate a social studies curriculum that is much more inclusive of the different groups that make up California and have contributed to its history, and the traditionalists, who argue that the United States is a melting pot, a land of immigrants where all peoples can be assimilated into society. This debate in California was played out in the newspapers, on television, and on the cover of weekly publications such as the *New York Times* Sunday Magazine.[38] This battle in California over the control and design of textbooks shows how groups within society can advocate certain ways of thinking and particular notions of truth, and how having these ways of thinking in place promotes particular forms of knowledge. These forms of knowledge control, to a great degree, the curriculum information students receive.[39]

Talking about textbooks at the societal level and the presence of power in curriculum organization, Apple writes:

> Texts are not simply "delivery systems" of "facts." They are at once the results of political, economic, and cultural activities, battles, and compromises. They are conceived, designed, and authored by real people with real interests. They are published within the political and economic constraints of markets, resources, and power. And what texts mean and how they are used is fought over by communities with distinctly different commitments and by teachers and students as well.[40]

The typical classroom teacher may feel that she or he is on the margin of most textbook debates, especially when they become the focus of national attention. However, it is the teacher and students who put textbooks to work. How they choose to use textbooks and the information presented becomes the "final" word in the textbook debate.

Institutional Level

Curriculum organization at the institutional level takes place when curriculum goals and content are set at the school, school district, or college and university level. This curriculum organization is usually along subject matter disciplines (e.g., mathematics, music, art). Educators who work at this level usually argue that because they teach the students, they are in a better position to understand their needs and therefore should be in charge of curriculum organization.

Curriculum organization at the institutional level also invites its share of controversy because different groups (e.g., ethnic, women, political) demand to have their interests represented, and sometimes the demands of the different groups lead to a canon debate war on college campuses and in K–12 education. For example, in some colleges of education and K–12 school districts there is debate between advocates of the phonetic approach and the whole language approach to teaching reading. The debates on college campuses are often hard to resolve because college professors argue on the grounds of academic freedom that they should make the curriculum decisions for the students they teach. **Academic freedom** refers to the right to speak freely and pursue academic inquiry without social constraints.

In order to avoid or reduce the number of curriculum debates at the K–12 level, school administrators are increasingly inviting representatives from business, civic groups, and the school community, including parents, to serve as advisors to curriculum committees. Some schools are also giving students a greater voice in curriculum planning. Teachers are discussing with students their curricular interests, goals, learning difficulties, or learning preferences. In some school districts and schools, students serve on the curriculum committee. Students can often offer suggestions that take into account community resources that teachers may not be aware of because of their unfamiliarity with the community or student culture.

Instructional Level

Curriculum organization at the instructional level has the teacher planning the curriculum and teaching the students. The classroom teacher carries the responsibility for what will be taught and how it will be taught within the guidelines of the local board of education and state statutes on education (see Chapter 9, "Governance of Education"). Most teacher candidates look forward to the day when they can design and teach their own curriculum unit to a class of students. This act gives teacher candidates a feeling of professionalism—or perhaps more correctly, a feeling that they have arrived. Carl remembers, as if it were yesterday, the first lesson he taught when he prepared the curriculum. Carl recalls:

> It was a science lesson on the digestive system. I scheduled the lesson for the first hour after lunch, on a day when the lunch menu was hamburger, fries, green salad, and a soft drink. I wanted this day because I believed engaging students in tracing the passage of food that they really like through their body would motivate them. Along with printed material that explained the purpose, function, and operation of the digestive system I had the hamburger and fries meal from the lunchroom, a student who wanted (and could easily consume) another meal, and a life-size model of the human body. The student and the model allowed me to show, chalk-talk, and demonstrate what happens to the food from the moment of the first bite and first swallow through its absorption by the body to its coming out as waste.
>
> The students got caught up in the lesson more than I imagined and in ways that I had not planned on. A few developed upset stomachs; a few took the idea of the waste material and had too much fun with it (need I say more?); and a very few asked why I did not bring more meals to the class. However, all the students were excited about the idea that they were learning to trace food through their body, and all did very well learning the material.

Allowing teachers to have the responsibility that Carl had for organizing the curriculum has not been without its critics. Some curriculum experts have wanted to teacher-proof curriculum, by giving teachers strict direction on what to teach and how to teach it. Some members of special interest groups do not want classroom teachers having the power to decide what to teach and how to teach. Finally, some critics argue that teachers are not academically prepared to teach high-level content. As educators, we must ask these critics how else is the power vested, if not with teachers? Who else are we trusting with our children's education, if not trained professionals?

In spite of the educational critics and the governance structure in place at schools, it is at the instructional level of curriculum organization that teachers can, if they choose, exert the most power and influence over the curriculum. When teachers enter their classrooms, the curriculum is in their hands.

Ideological Level

Curriculum organized based on an ideology involves designing the content and goals of curriculum around important ideas from learning theorists and subject matter experts. An example of this comes from the 1950s. After the Soviet Union launched *Sputnik* in 1957, many people blamed the public schools for the United States's tumble into second place in space exploration. Schools, said the critics, were no longer focusing on the basics skills and academic disciplines, and students in the United States were far behind students in many other countries. These criticisms led in 1958 to congressional passage of the National Defense Education Act (NDEA), which provided federal monies to improve the quality of education, especially in mathematics and science.

In order to decide how to improve K–12 curriculum and instruction in science, a two-week meeting was held at Woods Hole on Cape Cod in 1959. The meeting was attended by 35 scientists, scholars, and educators. At the Woods Hole conference, which led to Jerome Bruner's book *The Process of Education*,[41] these experts discussed and critiqued curriculum projects and developed an ideological concept for how subject matter should be taught in the schools. National attention soon focused on how curriculum is designed and organized—the structure of curriculum. "To learn structure," Bruner argued, "in short, is to learn how things are related."[42] For example, a structured curriculum is used to teach K–1 about social relationships by teaching them about neighborhood and community helpers. K–1 students first learn about the members of their family and their roles, next they learn about their neighbors and neighborhood helpers, then about the local community and community helpers, then city and city helpers, and so on. Structure in curriculum planning and organization became the instructional ideology that guided teaching in PreK–12 classrooms. Students were to study science and other subjects as if they were aspiring scholars.

Another example of ideological curriculum organization is founded on President Johnson's War on Poverty in the 1960s. In that context, two ideological concepts influenced curriculum goals and content. The first was a belief in the power of education. Johnson believed that education could make a difference in the lives of the poor. Lawrence A. Cremin explains this point:

> Lyndon B. Johnson's legislative program is an unparalleled example of the power of the President to influence the nature and purposes of American popular education. President Johnson himself has remarked that he would like to go down in history

---

as the President who provided every American child with "all of the education, of the highest quality, which his or her ambition demands and his or her mind can absorb"; and he has more than demonstrated in his proposals to the Eighty-ninth Congress that this is no idle aspiration.[43]

The second ideological concept that guided President Johnson's educational war was compensatory education. Compensatory education, in the form of projects such as Head Start and Follow-Through, was the educational idea used to help overcome the lack of learning opportunities for poor children and many children of color. Over the decades Head Start has continued to be an important ideological concept to improve the education of poor children. President George H. W. Bush argued that Head Start programs were important to successfully completing his first goal of America 2000: "All children in America will start school ready to learn."[44]

Finally, understanding the levels of curriculum organization (societal, institutional, instructional, and ideological) helps to better comprehend its purpose and politics. Being aware of the ways of thinking that are giving direction to the level of curriculum organization is also vital, for education in any form and at any level cannot be assumed to be neutral. Michael Apple reminds us:

> It is naive to think of the school curriculum as neutral knowledge. Rather, what counts as legitimate knowledge is the result of complex power relations and struggles among identifiable class, race, gender/sex, and religious groups. Thus, education and power are terms of an indissoluble couplet. It is at times of social upheaval that this relationship between education and power becomes visible. Such a relationship was and continues to be made manifest in the struggles by women, people of color, and others to have their history and knowledge included in the curriculum.[45]

Teacher candidates are a part of this power and knowledge struggle that operates at the different levels of curriculum organization. This was evident in two major questions, with follow-up questions, that Maureen proposed to a group of student teachers:

> As teacher-candidates or first-year teachers, would you like the responsibility for deciding on the curriculum goals and content of the curriculum for your students? If so, why? What responsibility would you be willing to accept for curriculum development?
>
> Should ethnic studies and women's studies be included in the humanities and infused into courses and field experiences in the teacher education sequence? If so, to what extent? In all lesson and unit plans or just some lessons, perhaps social studies?

COMMONPLACES IN CURRICULUM ORGANIZATION

According to Schwab, the commonplaces—the points in curriculum planning that receive the most attention—are students, teacher, curriculum, and milieu (environment, instructional context).[46] The commonplaces are where a teacher candidate's ways of thinking, the students' ways of thinking, and other (e.g., societal, institutional, instructional, ideological) ways of thinking come together. None of the stakeholders at this meeting come representing a neutral position; therefore, working out the "indissoluble couplet," or the relationship between knowledge and power that each stakeholder brings, is an essential task of the teacher candidate preparing the curriculum to teach.

A teacher, Jenny Lore, preparing a science lesson on simple machines to students in the sixth-grade class in a rural area of Georgia, would consider several factors. Important considerations would include the reading level of the students, the students' prior academic and experiential knowledge of the subject, and the students' ability to maintain self-control while working with science materials. Jenny needs to examine how the hidden curriculum that Henry and Aronowitz and Giroux speak of is operating in the class and how it may be influencing her teaching.

Jenny also needs to examine how she has been socialized to think about these students. The systems of reasoning used to assess what the students bring to the classroom is what helps to determine whether these students are taught in a way that prepares them for the University of Georgia, Harvard, or the local vocational technical college, or to end their pursuit of education upon completing high school.

Additionally, Jenny needs to assess her understanding of the concept to be taught, and needs to seek information for areas that are unclear. She has students observe simple machines in work and play situations in order to give the students real-life examples.

Jenny considers the curriculum from multiple perspectives, and prepares lesson plans that are engaging, gender responsive, and take into account the needs of all the students. All experiments are tried out before being presented to the class, and instruction includes varied approaches to the different learning styles of the students and culturally responsive activities. Students are evaluated authentically and participate in the evaluation of their learning, including placing materials in their portfolios.

In this assessment of the curriculum, Jenny is on notice to determine if the curriculum has been "dumbed down," which implicitly carries with it an idea of low expectations for the rural Georgia students. If so, Calhoun Lee, who completes his PreK–12 education in this school district with an *A* average, more than likely will face "academic shock" when he attends the University of Georgia and encounters students whose education was based on teacher expectations that their work would be of the caliber expected for success at Georgia or Harvard.

Finally, Jenny takes into account the milieu—the conditions or circumstances that would affect instruction and student learning. For example, she discovers a construction site near the school where many students can observe simple machines in operation on their journey to and from school. She makes a record of other simple machines in use in their rural community. Also, she assesses the opportunities and conditions for learning within the milieu to determine how to enrich the strengths and improve the learning opportunities for students. For example, if Jenny discovers that most of the students have never been to Atlanta or visited the University of Georgia in Athens, she may arrange a field trip in order to expose the students to the broader Georgia community and to allow them to see firsthand how their region of the state contributes to the total Georgia community. Visits to a college campus or a business in a large city allow students to learn firsthand that they would be welcome and successful in that environment.

SCOPE, CONTINUITY, SEQUENCE, AND INTEGRATION

When textbook publishers and curriculum developers, including teachers, prepare instructional materials (e.g., science, history) for K–12 classrooms, the organization of the curriculum usually takes into account the following common elements: scope, continuity, sequence, and integration. The *scope* of the curriculum refers to its breadth: the range of concepts and topics presented to middle school students studying the human body, or the array of U.S. history courses students are required to complete to earn a degree in history. *Continuity* in curriculum organization means providing students with repeated opportunities to learn or review the same skills or concepts, and *sequence* allows students to build on preceding lessons (the skills and concepts) and to push the learning to greater depth.

In a science class in a school district in one of the wealthier areas outside Detroit, we (Carl and Maureen) observed Janice Carey, a teacher candidate, demonstrate scope, continuity, and sequence in teaching a science lesson. Janice was teaching a unit on the circulatory system and wanted the students to understand its two parts, pulmonary and systemic circulation.

She presented the scope of the subject matter when she began the lesson by showing a film that identified and discussed the various organs that make up the circulatory system, including their function. Using a plastic model of the body, she pointed out the organs of the circulatory system. She provided continuity when she gave the students multiple opportunities to learn the material by (1) conducting a Q&A session on the names and functions of the circulatory system; (2) stopping the film partway through and asking the students to predict how they might describe the circulatory system; (3) having the students draw and label the organs that make up the circulatory system; and (4) having the students explain the circulatory system to their classmates using the plastic model. Janice employed the concept of sequence when she asked the students to work in small groups to write and act out a skit that demonstrated the functions of the circulatory system. She ended the lesson by having the students write a short essay on the circulatory system and bring it to her for feedback. Once evaluations and needed corrections were made, each student placed the essay in his or her science portfolio. Finally, Janice promised the students that after they acted out their skits, she would do one demonstrating how the circulatory and respiratory systems worked together to carry oxygen throughout the body.

In discussions of curriculum you will also encounter the term **curriculum integration.** For many teachers this means bringing together or infusing the teaching of several subject matters, such as science, mathematics, social studies, and language arts. Often this type of curriculum integration is used when teaching a unit. An interdisciplinary unit focuses on learning a concept through the integration of several subject areas. A somewhat less discussed but nevertheless very important notion of the integration of curriculum is bringing together all of the elements the teacher is teaching—concepts, skill, and values—so that they are mutually reinforcing.[47] Janice brought together her lesson by asking each of four cooperative groups to write a skit on the circulatory system, describe and explain the function of each of the organs that make up the system, and identify and explain the organs of the circulatory system using the plastic model. Janice also planned a follow-up lesson in which each student would write an essay on his or her willingness or reluctance to donate organs if the occasion arose.

After class, we complimented Janice on her lesson. We then asked her to explain how she thought about it and what she thought about the students. We explained to her that if she told us about her way of teaching, we would be better able to discuss how power is ever present in the teaching and learning in her class-room. For example, "What kind of expectations do you have of your students, and what are their achievement levels?" Janice explained that the information she received when assigned to student teach at the school included data that pointed out that most of the students at this school are expected to go on to college; of the 24 students in her class, she believes that at least 8 students will attend one of the elite U.S. colleges, 8 students will attend some state college in the region, and the other 8 students will probably attend a college in the Detroit area. We asked her how receiving these data affected her teaching. Janice said, "I came in having high expectations for all the students. It pushes me to prepare my lessons very carefully. In fact, most times I overprepare. I don't expect discipline to be a prob-lem, and I expect students to do what they are asked."

The school's way of thinking about the students was passed on to Janice, who accepted it and planned her teaching around it. Janice's way of thinking about her students is one effect of power that teacher candidates must understand. It is not a form of power that stopped Janice from working with her students, but more an enactment of power that says to her, "You should teach these students a particular way, which is not only as college-bound students, but as students who are on their way to prestigious and elite colleges." As we prepared to leave Janice, Maureen asked, "Do you think you would approach your teaching the same way if you were placed in the central city of Detroit?" Janice shifted her glance between the two of us and responded, "I have wondered about that myself."

CURRICULUM AND TEACHER PREPARATION

Since the publication of *A Nation at Risk* in 1983, there have been major efforts to reform the teacher education curriculum—that is, what should be taught, and where within K–12 schools it should be taught. The report stated, "The teacher-preparation curriculum is weighted heavily with courses in education methods at the expense of courses in subjects to be taught."[48] With this fiery statement came others, including "not enough of the academically able students are being attracted to teaching" and "too many teachers are being drawn from the bottom quarter of graduating high school and college students."[49]

The Holmes Group, an organization made up of 100 leading universities, and the Carnegie Foundation, a nonprofit corporation chartered by an act of Congress in 1906 that uses income from an endowment to support activities for the advancement of teaching, set about to change teacher education in the United States. The Holmes Group argued that "good teaching is defined by a compound of knowledge of four elements: (1) a broad general and liberal education, (2) the subject matter of the teaching field, (3) pedagogy and educational literature, and (4) reflective practical experience."[50] Therefore, Holmes and Carnegie argued for the elimination of undergraduate degree programs in education and recommended that the teacher education program be extended so that teacher candidates would receive a bachelor's degree in a discipline, preferably liberal arts, and obtain a master's degree in teaching after completing a B.A. Some colleges and universities (e.g., Duke, Texas, and Oregon) did eliminate their undergraduate teacher education program, and others made minor program changes.

Arguably, however, the most significant change was in efforts by colleges of education to reach out to school districts and establish professional development schools (PDSs; also known as partner schools, professional development academies, professional development centers, centers for teaching and learning, teaching schools, or induction schools). Reaching out to school districts is accomplished in a variety of ways, including inviting teachers to teach or co-teach classes with professors, having teacher advisory committees that counsel the teacher education program, having teachers supervise teacher candidates, and showcasing the work and commitment of teachers to the teacher education program. According to Ismat Abadal-Haqq, "Collaboration is a hallmark of professional development schools. They are partnerships that generally include one or more colleges or universities, and, in some cases, one or more teachers' unions."[51] This partnership offers the promises of having K–12 teachers and university faculties working more closely together than in the past to prepare the teacher candidate. There are about 600 PDSs, and Abadal-Haqq's research suggests that they share a common set of goals and principles:

- Preparation of pre-service teachers and other school-based educators
- Professional development of practicing teachers and other school-based educators
- Exemplary practice designed to maximize student achievement
- Sustained, applied inquiry designed to improve student and educator development[52]

PDSs have been compared to teaching hospitals with their attention to practice-oriented inquiry. In 1967, Robert J. Schaefer proposed a similar idea about practice-oriented inquiry as it is related to the role of schools in professional development. Schaefer wrote:

> We can no longer afford to conceive of the school simply as distribution centers for dispensing cultural orientations, and knowledge developed by other social units. . . . It must also be a center of inquiry—a producer as well as a transmitter of knowledge. . . . Educational literature unduly concentrates . . . on the problem of recruiting "good" teachers to the relative neglect of analysis of the nurturing

qualities of the institutions for which recruits are sought. . . . [We] have the economic resources and manpower . . . , and the preliminary knowledge to make that vision [of the school as a center of inquiry] a reality.[53]

Today, Schaefer's idea in the form of professional development schools has led to changes in the where and how of the curriculum for teacher candidates. Curriculum concepts are being discussed in schools immediately after teacher candidates have implemented them. Abadal-Haqq notes, "Coursework is more likely to be site based, collaboratively developed and taught by school–college faculty teams, and linked to both professional development of inservice teachers and school needs and priorities."[54] Instead of portfolio assessment, community participation, or classroom management being discussed on the university campus after reading about them, these topics are discussed in the schools where teacher candidates, cooperating teachers, university supervisors, and professors can immediately participate in a critique and analysis of the teaching concept or method.

According to the educational literature, professional development schools are a great idea, but schools are not neutral sites. As we learned from Jenny and Janice, schools are influenced by power that is articulated in ways of thinking that qualify and disqualify students from certain opportunities. Much of the literature on professional development schools ignores this point of view and casts them as neutral sites. Teacher candidates must assess how power and how education that is multicultural are present in their schools.

Learning about how power and EMCSR operate in schools through curriculum and the many different experiences students engage in is an ongoing education. Mrs. Platt, Marcy, and Joanna, whom you met at the beginning of the chapter, were just in the process of developing their understanding of curriculum and standards as they are discussed by teacher educators. Learning about how power may be invested in curriculum and may be played out in a school setting is something Marcy and Joanna will discover when they read the following story by Professor Gomez.

FINDING A VOICE

It was a sunny spring day in Boston and Professor Gomez, in her introduction to education class, was discussing the teacher's power to make curriculum decisions and the importance of providing students with a multicultural curriculum. A student raised his hand and said, "All this stuff about multicultural curriculum is great but I don't want any parents down my back when I'm teaching. Not everyone agrees with providing students material that presents multiple perspectives. What happens if a parent complains to the school board or my principal about what I'm teaching? Sometimes it's just easier to go with the textbook."

Professor Gomez smiled as she began her reply. "You know how I'm always giving you a hard time about the rationale section of your unit plans? I know you are sick of hearing me tell you that you have to be well versed on why you are teaching the content you select and why you are using the methodology you choose. Well, let me tell you a story about what happened to one of my former students a few years ago. It will show you that if you know what you are doing and why you are doing it, you will be able to speak as a professional to anyone who questions your decisions in the classroom. Not everyone will agree with every decision you make, but the ability to explain yourself clearly and to show your principal, the parents, or whoever asks how what you are doing fits into the curriculum will serve you well." She began the story.

My home phone rang at 7:30 P.M. and I heard a rather frantic voice on the other end. "Dr. G., I think I'm in big trouble and I need your help!" It was Tanesha, an African American fifth-grade teacher in a local magnet school. Tanesha had completed her master's degree in elementary education in our program and was in her second year of teaching at the magnet school.

"What is happening, Tanesha? You can't be in that much trouble!" On the verge of tears, Tanesha explained that she had developed a mini-unit on the Million Man March, the 1996 gathering of African American men in Washington, D.C., for the purpose of recommitting to their families and to their communities. The march was presented in the media as controversial because its organizer, the minister Louis Farrakhan, had been accused of making anti-White and anti-Semitic remarks in the past. The fact that the march included only men was also a point of criticism from some women's groups.

Tanesha began the conversation with a statement that made me feel somewhat guilty: "I swear, Dr. G., I was teaching social studies just like you taught me to do!" She explained that she had spent the entire week before the march clipping articles about it and about Louis Farrakhan from a wide variety of publications and by a variety of authors. Tanesha had the students read various articles in cooperative groups, comparing and contrasting differing views. They held a debate about whether the march should take place based on their readings. Tanesha had the students look at copies of Louis Farrakhan's prior remarks and read transcripts of interviews with him about why he organized the march. They learned about perspective by assessing who wrote certain articles and discussed the ways in which who the author was may have influenced his or her views. Tanesha also connected the march to the fifth graders' study of the Constitution as they discussed our basic freedoms, including the freedoms of speech and assembly. A culminating event in the mini-unit was having the class watch the march, listening to various speakers throughout the day and discussing such topics as the predictions of violence in comparison to the calm that prevailed throughout the march. Finally, the day after the march, the students wrote culminating essays discussing their own opinions of the march.

At the end of the school day on that final day of the unit, Tanesha was called to the office of Mr. McGee, the principal. Tanesha and Mr. McGee did not always see eye to eye. Tanesha wondered what the problem could be. Mr. McGee told Tanesha that Mr. Watson, the father of one of the students in her class, was very upset that she had allowed the students to watch the Million Man March. He said that Farrakhan was a racist and he did not believe that the march was of any value. He strongly felt that the only reason Tanesha had allowed the students to watch the march was because she agreed with Farrakhan and she was trying to influence the students to agree with her views.

Tanesha explained her rationale for the unit and her activities to the principal. She went and got work samples to show Mr. McGee because she had been so impressed by how the kids got "into" the lessons. Their final essays were, for the most part, thoughtful, accurate, and well written. Many students were even passionate about their opinion, and they wrote more than they had written all year. Tanesha was proud of their efforts.

Mr. McGee insisted that the two of them meet with Mr. Watson so that Tanesha could tell him why she chose the topic. Tanesha agreed, but she was worried. She had never dealt with an angry parent before, let alone one who was basically accusing her of trying to brainwash the students.

I asked Tanesha how she saw the unit fitting into the curriculum. She stated that the social studies standards of the state as well as those of the National Council for Social Studies called for students to be aware of current events from social, political, and economic perspectives. She also reminded me that the fifth-grade curriculum related to American history covered the constitutional issues she had mentioned earlier. I suggested that she had a strong rationale for her decision to teach about the Million Man March. Now she just needed to calm down, organize her thoughts, and remember not to let Mr. Watson drag her into an argument. Yes, parents had the right to disagree, but the teacher also has a professional right to make well-informed curriculum decisions. I asked Tanesha if she wanted me to be there. She declined the offer, saying that she had to learn to handle these situations on her own.

Professor Gomez's class was dying to hear how the story ended. Several students cringed at the thought that they could find themselves in such a predicament.

The next night, I called Tanesha to see how the conference went. She was excited, talking a mile a minute. "Oh, Dr. G., you should have been there. I remembered what you told us about the standards. Last night I pulled out my copies of the Learning Standards for Social Studies from NCSS and the state standards for social studies. I used different colored Post-It notes to mark the pages that dealt with teaching current events, the Constitution, and the Bill of Rights. I also noted the critical thinking skills sections. This morning I organized some more work samples and placed Tommy Watson's work on the top of the pile. It worked out because he had done some great writing. When Mr. Watson came in, Mr. McGee asked him to start by explaining why he was upset. He was a little nasty, but not too bad. I listened and it was hard, but I didn't say a word. Then it was my turn. I showed him my lesson plan book with the activities for the week outlined so that he could see I was organized. Then I hit him with the part about how all of the things that we did met the standards. At the end, I showed him Tommy's work and said what a wonderful job he did. I acknowledged that not all of us agree on what content is important to teach, but the way I had the activities laid out, he could see that I was not promoting one way of thinking. Dr. G., you should have seen his face. There was *nothing* he could say. You would have been so proud of me!"

I told Tanesha that I have always been proud of her and I knew she could handle this situation like the professional that she was. I resisted the urge to say, "I told you so" about having a strong rationale for everything you do in the classroom. I just complimented Tanesha on a job well done and told her that I was going to use her story with my current social studies methods class because they were complaining that the standards were too restrictive. Some teachers use the standards as an excuse for not developing innovative lessons. Tanesha used the standards to her advantage to really turn on learning for the students.

The curriculum, often more so than students or teachers, receives the most attention in education. This is so because many people (e.g., educators, various interest groups, politicians, and the local school districts) believe that the curriculum plays the major role in transmitting the culture, student achievement, and establishing codes of conduct for students to live by. This degree of influence sometimes causes people to forget that a school's curriculum should be designed primarily for, or at least center on, the students at the local school. Teachers, in spite of the debates surrounding curriculum, have to ask, "What curriculum and curriculum organization is best for my students?" Teachers, during their career, will experience numerous curriculum debates, receive suggestions to use a particular curriculum, and hear suggestions about how to teach their curriculum. Tanesha had such an experience during her student teaching. Some may feel bad for Tanesha because of the experience she had, but we believe that Tanesha will be a much more successful teacher because she had the experience and she knew how to explain what she taught and why she taught it. Important to successful teaching is knowing the curriculum and teaching a curriculum in the way that best satisfies the academic and social needs of the students.

SUMMING UP

Marcy, Joanna, Tanesha, and the other voices that have contributed to this chapter have clearly come to understand that over the years, the definitions of curriculum, although varied, have centered on what takes place: experiences and learning opportunities in school or under the supervision of teachers. However, more recently, curriculum scholars are arguing that curriculum is knowledge that inscribes rules and standards. These rules and standards are used to develop ways of thinking and notions of truth that are used to view the world.

Two types of curriculum operate in school: the overt and the hidden curriculum. The overt curriculum is the visible or public curriculum. It is what is presented, for example, in lesson plans and textbooks. The hidden curriculum is the attitudes and behaviors that students learn in schools, which may not be directly intended or anticipated by the teacher. Both curricula have a very powerful influence on students.

In schools a major location for the enactment of power is in the curriculum. One expression of this power is seen in the "what knowledge" debate. This debate often contested whether the sciences or social sciences were more important for students to know. Another expression of this power is seen in the "whose knowledge" debate, or the canon debate. This debate is usually over an inclusive curriculum, as opposed to token representation in the curriculum of non-Western literary works and works by people of color and women.

Curriculum is usually organized to influence one of four levels: societal, institutional, instructional, and ideological. In planning and writing curriculum, the emphasis is usually on one or more of the following areas: students, teachers, curriculum, and milieu. Schwab refers to these locations as "commonplaces."[55] Teachers writing curriculum and textbook publishers usually take into account scope, continuity, sequence, and integration. The scope is the breadth or range of concepts and topics; continuity is providing students with many and varied opportunities to learn what is being taught; sequence allows students to build on previous lessons and take the skills and concepts they have learned to a greater depth; and integration of curriculum is bringing together all of the concepts, skills, and values that a teacher is teaching so that they may mutually reinforce one another.

Finally, teacher educators have deemed it important to place teacher candidates in school settings, such as professional development schools (PDSs), where they will have numerous opportunities to develop curriculum collaboratively with students and teachers and to see the curriculum put into practice. Also, by working in PDSs teacher candidates have the opportunity to see firsthand the enactment of power expressed through the many ways curriculum is organized and taught to the different students within the school.

KEY TERMS

academic freedom   family work
curriculum   hidden curriculum
curriculum integration

QUESTIONS FOR REFLECTION

1. In a one-page essay explain how Popkewitz's definition of curriculum differs from the definitions offered by Saylor and Alexander (1974) and Oliva (1982)[56] presented at the beginning of this chapter.
2. Do you think the focus on content standards will make U.S. education more effective? If so why? If not, why not?
3. Describe and discuss the differences between the overt and the hidden curriculum.
4. In a two-page essay discuss why there is often debate regarding "what knowledge" and "whose knowledge" should be taught in schools.
5. Explain what Apple means when he says that "texts are not simply 'delivery systems' of 'facts.' They are at once the results of political, economic, and cultural activities, battles, and compromises."[57]
6. How is what Marcy and Joanna are learning about curriculum different from what Mrs. Platt learned when she was at State?

7. Discuss the issues in the canon debate that took place on your campus during the 1990s. If you learn that no such debate took place on your campus, why do you believe this was so?
8. Examine a curriculum guide in your favorite subject area and describe the scope, continuity, and sequence of one concept over three grade levels.

ACTIVITIES

1. Locate a textbook publisher's teacher's guide for your favorite subject (e.g., reading, science, math). Then select a concept (e.g., photosynthesis, community helpers) and trace how the publisher presents the scope, continuity, sequence, and integration of the concept.
2. Get the K–12 standards for your favorite subject area online or from the school district where you are attending school. Also write to the Department of Public Instruction of your state for that same set of standards. Examine both sets of standards in relation to the educational goals set forth by Presidents Bush and Clinton. Prepare a short paper that discusses (a) how the state and local standards compare and (b) which educational goals will be met by the standards you selected.
3. Observe in a classroom and record the number of times you see evidence of the hidden curriculum. Also record the context in which you see the curriculum operating. If possible, film yourself teaching a lesson and record this information on yourself.
4. Collect samples of the overt curriculum from three grade levels and analyze them to determine what ways of thinking and notions of truth are present.
5. Take a trip to the library and select newspapers from 10 different locations. Try to include urban and rural areas and big and small cities. First, copy or summarize the articles on curriculum; second, examine the articles to see if the topics are the same or similar. Are the articles about what knowledge or whose knowledge is important? Discuss the ways of thinking or notions of truth presented in the articles.
6. This chapter discusses Schwab's commonplaces in curriculum planning: students, teachers, curriculum, and milieu. Take a concept from your favorite subject area and write a lesson plan that covers Schwab's commonplaces.[58] Share and discuss the plan with three other students.

GETTING CONNECTED

Key Questions to Ask About the K–12 Social Studies Program

As you work to plan and strengthen social studies instruction in your schools, consider the key questions listed below. Be sure to add your own.

1. Is the K–12 program (or this specific course) designed with clear purpose(s) to ensure important, cumulative learning?
2. Is sufficient instructional time available to accomplish the purpose(s)?

3. Within the K–12 curriculum, is enough coverage provided to establish the context for several in-depth studies of highly significant issues, topics, or events? Has an appropriate balance been established between coverage (to ensure sufficient context for comprehension) and depth (to ensure interest and meaning)?

4. Does the content include a balance among the past and present and the application of imagination to the future, so that students recognize the link between social studies learning and real life and its improvement?

5. Is there appropriate attention to a balance of local, national, and international content and recognition of the interrelationship among these contexts?

6. Is the content based on history, geography, and the social sciences (e.g., psychology, sociology, economics, anthropology, political science) as well as integration with other natural allies such as literature, the arts, science, composition, and speech?

7. Are a variety of materials available (e.g., textbooks, visuals, related fact and fiction, news sources, primary sources)?

8. Are a variety of strategies implicit (e.g., cooperative learning, discussions, simulations, research projects, community service)?

9. Are a variety of types of evaluations possible (e.g., projects, service, exhibitions, portfolio collections)?

10. Do classroom and school climate model democracy and promote participatory citizenship?

11. Do the social studies professionals recognize social studies as the cornerstone of preparation for each student to assume with competence the office of citizen?

12. Will each student gain knowledge of her or his heritage and develop a hopeful and powerful vision of his or her own personal importance to the improvement of the common good within the immediate local community and beyond?

13. Is each student encouraged to make a positive contribution in her or his current and future spheres of influence—the classroom, the school, the community, the nation, and the world?

SUGGESTED RESOURCES

Banks, James. *Teaching Strategies for Ethnic Studies,* 6th ed. Boston: Allyn and Bacon, 1997.

Berger, Pam. *Internet for Active Learners: Curriculum-Based Strategies for K–12.* Chicago: American Library Association, 1998.

Grant, Carl A., and Christine E. Sleeter. *Turning On Learning: Five Approaches to Multicultural Teaching Plans for Race, Class, Gender, and Disability,* 3rd ed. New York: Wiley, 2003.

McLaren, Peter. *Life in Schools: An Introduction to Critical Pedagogy in the Foundations of Education,* 3rd ed. New York: Addison Wesley Longman, 1998.

Pangrazi, Robert P. *Lesson Plans for Classroom Teachers: Fifth and Sixth Grades.* Boston: Allyn and Bacon, 1997.

Passe, Jeff. *Elementary School Curriculum,* 2nd ed. Boston: McGraw-Hill, 1999.

Perie, Marianne, David P. Baker, and Sharon Bobbitt. *Time Spent Teaching Core Academic Subjects in Elementary Schools: Comparisons Across Community, School, Teacher, and Student Characteristics.* Washington, DC: U.S. Department of Education, Office of Educational Research and Improvement, 1997. For sale by the U.S. Government Printing Office, Superintendent of Documents.

Reinhartz, Judy, and Don M. Beach. *Teaching and Learning in the Elementary School: Focus on Curriculum.* Upper Saddle River, NJ: Merrill, 1996.

NOTES

1. National Board for Professional Teaching Standards, *Toward High and Rigorous Standards for the Teaching Profession: A Summary*, 2nd ed. (Detroit: NBSTS, 1991).
2. Harold Rugg, *American Life and the School Curriculum: Next Steps Toward Schools of Living* (Boston: Ginn, 1936), 18.
3. P. W. Jackson, ed., *Handbook of Research on Curriculum* (New York: Macmillan, 1992).
4. Ibid., 5.
5. Thomas Popkewitz, "The Production of Reason and Power: Curriculum History and Intellectual Traditions," *Journal of Curriculum Studies* 29, no. 2 (1997): 132.
6. Michael Foucault, *The Foucault* Reader, ed. Paul Rabinow (New York: Pantheon Books, 1984); Thomas Popkewitz, *Struggling for the Soul: The Politics of Schooling and the Construction of the Teacher* (New York: Teachers College Press, 1998).
7. Popkewitz, *Struggling for the Soul.*
8. Popkewitz, "Production of Reason and Power," 132.
9. Charles Judd, Glenn Holmes, and Ward Reeder, "History of Education," in *The Lincoln Library of Essential Information,* ed. Clyde Park (Buffalo, NY: Frontier Press, 1963), 1615–1698.
10. National Center on Education and the Economy, *For Our Children: A Parent's Guide to New Standards* (Washington, DC: Author, 1998), 1.
11. State of Wisconsin Department of Public Instruction, *Questions and Answers About Academic Standards and the High School Graduation Test* (Madison, WI: Author, 1997).
12. National Council of Teachers of English and International Reading Association (NCTE/IRA), *Standards for the English Language Arts* (Newark, DE: Author, 1996), viii.
13. California Department of Education, *Standards, Students and Success* (Sacramento, CA: Author, 1997), 7.
14. T. K. Rabb, "The National History Standards Wars," *History Matters!* 7, no. 4 (December 1994): 1.
15. NCTE/IRA, *Standards for the English Language Arts.*
16. Popkewitz, *Struggling for the Soul.*
17. Jules Henry, *Golden Rule Days: American Schoolrooms in Culture Against Man* (New York: Vintage, 1963), 290.
18. P. Jackson, "Introduction," in *The Unstudied Curriculum: Its Impact on Children,* ed. Norman V. Overly (Washington, DC: Association for Supervision and Curriculum Development, 1970).
19. S. Aronowitz and H. Giroux, *Education Under Siege* (New York: Bergin and Garvey, 1985), 147.
20. Jackson, "Introduction."

21. Toni Griego-Jones, "Reconstructing Bilingual Education From a Multicultural Perspective," in *Making Schooling Multicultural: Campus and Classroom,* ed. Carl A. Grant and Mary Louise Gomez (Englewood Cliffs, NJ: Merrill, 1996), 112–129.

22. Howard Zinn, *A People's History of the Untied States: 1492–Present,* rev. and updated (New York: Harper Perennial, 2003).

23. Philip A. Cusick, *Inside High School* (New York: Holt, Rinehart and Winston, 1973), 220–221.

24. Edward W. Knappman, "John Thomas Scopes Trial," in *American Trials of the 20th Century,* ed. Edward W. Knappman (Detroit: Visible Ink Press, 1994), 93.

25. National Commission on Excellence in Education, *A Nation at Risk: The Imperative for Educational Reform* (Washington, DC: U.S. Department of Education, 1983).

26. William F. Pinar, *Notes on Understanding Curriculum as a Racial Text* (Albany: State University of New York Press, 1993), 60.

27. Carol Gluck, "History According to Whom?" *New York Times,* 19 November 1994, op-ed, Y15.

28. John Patrick Diggins, "Historical Blindness," *New York Times,* 19 November 1994, op-ed, Y15.

29. Paul Lauter, *Canons and Contexts* (New York: Oxford University Press, 1991), ix.

30. Ibid.

31. Ibid., 23.

32. John I. Goodlad and Maurice Richter, *The Development of a Conceptual System for Dealing With Problems of Curriculum and Instruction* (Los Angeles: University of California, Institute for Development of Educational Activities, 1966); John I. Goodlad, "The Scope of the Curriculum Field in Curriculum Inquiry," in *The Study of Curriculum Practice,* ed. John Goodlad and Associates (New York: McGraw-Hill, 1979), 17–42.

33. National Council for Social Studies, *Curriculum Standards for Social Studies: Expectations of Excellence* (Dubuque, IA: Author, 1990), 4–5, 12–13.

34. National Commission on Excellence in Education, *A Nation at Risk,* 5.

35. National Council on Education Standard and Testing, *Raising Standards in American Education* (Washington, DC: Government Printing Office, 1991).

36. Lee Cronbach, "The Text Material Study," in *Text Materials in Modern Education,* ed. Lee J. Cronbach (Urbana: University of Illinois Press, 1955), 3.

37. Michael Apple and Linda Christian-Smith, "The Politics of the Textbook," in *The Politics of the Textbook,* ed. Michael Apple and Linda Christian-Smith (New York: Routledge, 1991), 2.

38. Robert Reinhold, "Class Struggle," *New York Times Magazine,* 29 September 1991, 26–29, 46–52.

39. Popkewitz, *Struggling for the Soul.*

40. Apple and Christian-Smith, "Politics of the Textbook," 2.

41. Jerome Bruner, *The Process of Education* (Cambridge, MA: Harvard University Press, 1960).

42. Ibid., 7.

43. Lawrence A. Cremin, *The Genius of American Education* (New York: Vantage, 1965), 98.

44. Mark Pitsch, "President's 1993 Budget Will Include $600 Million Increase for Head Start," *Education Week,* January 1992, 1, 26–27.

45. Michael W. Apple, "The Process and Ideology of Valuing in Educational Settings," in *Curriculum and Evaluation,* ed. Arno A. Bellack and Herbert M. Kliebard (Berkeley, CA: McCutchan, 1977), 2.

46. Joseph Schwab, "The Practical 3: Translation Into Curriculum," *School Review* 81, no. 4 (1973), 501–522.
47. John I. Goodlad and Zhixin Su, "Organization of the Curriculum," in *Handbook of Research on Curriculum,* ed. Philip W. Jackson (New York: Macmillan, 1992).
48. National Commission on Excellence in Education, *A Nation at Risk,* 22.
49. Ibid.
50. Holmes Group, *Tomorrow's Teachers: A Report of the Holmes Group* (East Lansing, MI: Author, 1986).
51. Ismat Abadal-Haqq, *Professional Development Schools: Weighing the Evidence* (Thousand Oaks, CA: Corwin Press, 1998), 6.
52. Ibid.
53. Robert Schaefer, *The School as a Center of Inquiry* (New York: Harper and Row, 1967), 22.
54. Abadal-Haqq, *Professional Development Schools,* 14.
55. Schwab, "The Practical 3."
56. Galen Saylor and William Alexander, "Planning Curriculum for School," in *Handbook of Research on Curriculum,* ed. Philip W. Jackson (New York: Macmillan, 1974), 4; Peter Oliva, "Developing the Curriculum," in *Handbook of Research on Curriculum,* ed. Philip W. Jackson (New York: Macmillan, 1982), 4.
57. Apple, "Process and Ideology."
58. Schwab, "The Practical 3."

TEACHING, PLANNING, AND ASSESSMENT

Courtesy of Bill Lisenby

FOCUS QUESTIONS

1. Does history play a role in why teachers teach as they do?
2. Which forms of instruction best engage students in their lessons?
3. Can a teacher be a good teacher and not write lesson plans?
4. What is "authentic" about authentic assessment?

VIGNETTE

TEACH AS I SAY, NOT AS I TEACH

CHAD: *You know, Molly, I'm confused. For the past three years, the "teaching" that we have had at this university has been exactly like when I was in elementary, middle, and high school: being lectured to or told how to complete written assignments. Even here in the school of education, much of the teaching is professor-dominated discussion, and almost all of their evaluations consist of paper-and-pencil or multiple-choice assessment. But then lots of our assigned readings are about different ways of teaching and assessing students and some of this material criticizes the lecture method and large-group tests. Why don't they practice what they preach? How do they expect us to teach students once we have our own classrooms if we never see the good stuff?*
MOLLY: *Isn't that the truth! They preach to us about best practices of teaching and assessing, but when do they model it? When we were at the elementary and middle schools observing, the instruction was*

> *mostly teacher discussion with the whole class. Also, I am confused*
> *about lesson plans. Some teachers have lesson plans, but I was really*
> *surprised at how many didn't. Our instructors make us write plans for*
> *the lessons we teach, but then they sometimes don't seem to have plans*
> *other than their syllabus.*

Many educators and students agree with Chad and Molly's observations about instruction from kindergarten through college. But *why* do large group assessment and the lecture method dominate our way of teaching? How can teachers make their lessons more instructionally engaging for students? More educators are recognizing that power relationships affect what it is possible to do in teaching. A teacher's choices within teaching, planning, and assessment are often shaped by the overt and hidden curriculum they receive through Pre-K to college, life experiences, their race, class, gender, ability, and sexuality, and existing policies and practices. Educators are coming to understand that, because of their position, they can influence opportunities in students' lives. In this chapter, we will answer Chad and Molly's questions about teaching, planning, and assessment.

TEACHING

Teachers' ways of teaching can make learning exciting or dull, relevant or irrelevant. Teachers, therefore, become gatekeepers to the career dreams and opportunities of students. As gatekeepers and as selectors of ways of teaching, teachers enact power. This power plays a large role in shaping the lives of their students, as illustrated in the following example.

Marge Smith, a fifth-grade teacher, demonstrates the gatekeeping function and the importance of different ways of teaching science. First, Marge decides to thoroughly integrate science into her teaching. She does this by using interdisciplinary units, setting up a science center in the classroom, and encouraging students' parents to schedule visits to science events during their family outings. Second, Marge decides to teach science concepts by using a hands-on experiment and inquiry approach. In the first instance, Marge is opening up the gate of opportunity by regularly teaching science and holding her students to high expectations. Marge knows that many middle school teachers avoid teaching science; however, she also knows that knowledge of science is important to students' future academic success.

In her way of teaching, Marge differs from the way we still see science too often taught at the middle school. In many elementary and middle schools, the learning of science is passive; for example, students read a chapter and answer questions on a worksheet. When Marge teaches science, every student has the opportunity to be a scientist—reading, researching, conducting experiments, taking notes, and collecting data. Marge's way of teaching science may prepare students for future academic opportunities that are influenced by the knowledge and love of science they are acquiring. Her way of teaching may both encourage and prepare students to take other science courses and will arm them with the knowledge of science they need to be successful on academic tests. She helps empower them with more life choices in careers later on.

Our discussion of teaching continues with some history. Learning about how schools came to be organized as they are is one important step in understanding teaching. Once this history is understood, teachers like Marge can use this knowledge to inform their ideas of best practices and what types of teaching is needed to meet the needs of today's students.

Instruction 1890–2000

Once students like Chad and Molly understand our nation's educational history, they may learn several reasons why some educators teach in ways that may not be the most engaging for students. One reason has to do with educating large numbers of students. Joseph Lanchester and Andrew Bell were the originators of one such method, the **monitorial method.** In a monitorial school, a headmaster teaches the brightest students. As student teachers or monitors, these students teach small groups of other students. Monitorial schools were started in England in the 1800s as a way of teaching large groups of students cheaply. Teaching in this manner allows a headmaster to teach several hundred students. In 1806, a monitorial school was opened in New York and this way of teaching soon became popular with educators in many other U.S. cities.

In the mid-1800s, another method of educating students was introduced into the United States. During a trip to Europe, Horace Mann, secretary of the State Board of Education for Massachusetts, visited Prussian schools that used an instructional plan adopted during medieval times called the **graded system.**[1] The graded system allows students who are of the same age or who start an academic program at the same time to be taught together. Impressed by the potential efficiency of the system, Mann encouraged James Philbrick, a school administrator for Boston Quincy Grammar School, to try it. By the latter half of the 19th century, the graded system had become the established pattern for schools in the United States. Proponents of the graded system offered several points in its favor: (1) it lowers the cost of instruction because fewer teachers are needed; (2) instruction can be more effective because there is a better opportunity for chalk and talk; (3) it facilitates good discipline because all the pupils are under the control and instruction of the teacher; and (4) it affords a better means of encouraging students because there is constant competition among them.[2]

By the 1890s most schools in the United States had adopted the graded system and established a nine-month school year. Under the graded plan, teachers had their own classrooms and taught between 40 and 48 students. Each classroom usually had 48 desks bolted to the floor. The desks faced the front of the room, where the teacher's desk and the blackboard were located. Instruction included having students recite passages from textbooks, work at their desks, and listen to their classmates and teacher during whole-group instruction. Teachers expected uniformity in students' work and behavior. Students were told what to do and how to do it—when to sit, stand, turn their heads, and hang their coats.[3] Finkelstein describes instruction during the 1820s–1880s as follows:

> The teacher assigned lessons, asked questions and created standards of achievement to compel students to assimilate knowledge and practice skills in a particular fashion. It was a fashion dictated by the textbooks usually—and often with dogmatic determination.[4]

According to Finkelstein, there were three types of teachers in the elementary schools during that time. The "intellectual overseer" assigned work, punished errors, and had students memorize subject matter. The "drillmaster" led students in unison through lessons requiring them to repeat content aloud. The "interpreter of culture" clarified ideas and explained content to students. Finkelstein reports that she found an "interpreter of culture" only a few times in her survey of the era.[5]

Those in charge of education in the 1800s designed a system to educate greater numbers of students. Nevertheless, the decisions these educators made favored those who could learn in certain ways (e.g., teacher-centered rather than student-centered instruction). The design of the educational system and the curriculum, very significant to the growth and development of the country as we now know it, need to be understood for their strengths and weaknesses and how decisions were made to develop and implement such a system and curriculum. Understanding this history is important because much of what we do in education today (lecture method, nine-month school calendar) is influenced by the decision-making actions of yesterday.

As the 20th century approached, some K–8 teachers began to experiment with other teaching practices. These practices included greater student participation through small-group work, project activities, increased student expression, the use of different student grouping patterns, interdisciplinary teaching including two or more subjects, more involvement with the community through field trips, and more freedom for students to move about the classroom.[6] The teachers trying out these teaching practices believed they would provide better learning opportunities for their students and enhance their achievement.

This change in teaching practices did not take place to the same extent at the high school level. Teacher-centered instruction continued to dominate in most high schools, although some loosening up on formal methods of recitation did occur, along with somewhat more student discussion, reports, and debates. Also, although movable furniture was being placed in some high school classrooms, the classroom space was still arranged much as it had been. Student desks, although no longer bolted to the floor, nevertheless continued to face the teacher's desk at the front of the room.

By the 1940s, alternatives to the earlier teaching practices of lecture, uniformity, efficiency, and control were known to teachers. Ideas about small-group work, project activities, increased student involvement, and interdisciplinary teaching practices were becoming increasingly familiar to and understood by many educators. These alternative ways of teaching were gaining respectability from educators. However, the extent to which teachers adopted them in their classroom practices was small, and continues to be small even today. Many teachers today still lecture, do some grouping, and make a point of making efficiency and control their number one mission.[7]

Those continuing to use rigid discipline and efficiency-based classrooms ignore a good deal of what educators have discovered about learning dating as far back as Socrates. What many educators have discovered is that students should be at the center of teaching. For example, teachers should take students' background and knowledge into account. Being at the center of instruction is one way that students' power, and their motivation and preferred ways of engaging with ideas and materials, can be channeled directly toward their learning. Placing students at the center of instruction is also an expression of teachers' power, for it indicates that teachers are relying more on their ways of teaching and the curriculum to promote classroom discipline instead of relying on the authority they receive from their status as teacher. This, in turn, allows students to share some of this power.

We have previously referred to how ideas about learning date back to the time of Socrates. In one of Plato's writings about Socrates, *Meno*, there is a dialogue between Socrates and Meno about teaching Anytus. In his dialogue with Meno, Socrates understands that Anytus is a slave and therefore has very few rights and is expected to obey. Socrates nevertheless sees his authority in his teaching relationship with Anytus as being an outcome not of state-mandated decrees but of his ability to help Anytus learn. Rather than telling Anytus what he should know, Socrates helps Anytus to construct his own understanding by asking questions to further his already acquired knowledge.

Using what they have observed in some classrooms, Chad and Molly will have to make a decision about how they wish to teach. They may use practices with which they are familiar through their own experience or they may adopt methods that are more responsive to student needs. However, they are unlike the traveler in Robert Frost's poem "The Road Not Taken," who stands at a fork in the road deciding which unfamiliar path to take. Unlike that traveler, they have personal knowledge gleaned from their journey from kindergarten though college about the practices on each road. Also, they have professional knowledge gained from what they are learning about the shortcomings of chalk and talk and rigid control of students in their teacher education classes. Like Frost's traveler, will Chad and Molly take the road less traveled, or will they follow the crowd? Chad will probably see this question as a no-brainer. "Take the road less traveled," he will say. Molly, however, knows that it is easier said than done because, she explains, "Once in the school, following the other teachers often becomes the thing to do." Which road will you take on your teaching journey?

Connecting Teaching and Curriculum: Instructional Engagement

Teachers who choose the "road less traveled" recognize that central to effective instruction is the development of a tight relationship between the teaching and the curriculum. To develop such a connection, teachers need to make the curriculum as instructionally engaging as possible. A research study by Strong, Silver, and Robinson reported that "students who are engaged in their work are energized by four goals: success, curiosity, originality and satisfying relationships."[8] *Success* is the need for mastery; *curiosity* is the need for understanding; *originality* is the need for self-expression; and *satisfying relationships* is the need for involvement with others.[9] These researchers also discovered that students who are engaged persist, despite challenges and obstacles, and they take visible delight in successfully completing their work. Additionally, Strong, Silver, and Robinson believe that students who are engaged want work that will enhance their relationships with people they care about.[10]

There are several ways to foster student engagement and reach the goals described by Strong, Silver, and Robinson. These include using culturally relevant teaching, having a culturally responsive classroom climate, fostering student involvement and leadership, being gender responsive, and focusing on an achievement goal approach.

Culturally Relevant Teaching   **Culturally relevant** teaching occurs when the curriculum content is related to the students' background and the teacher's instruction takes advantage of this connection. Culturally relevant teaching enhances instructional engagement because it uses the culture of the students during instruction. It is effective in both monoracial and multiracial classrooms, as well as classrooms where students speak a language other than English, have disabilities, or have not had the advantage of the kinds of social experiences that prepare them for school. (See Exhibit 5.1.)

Gloria Ladson-Billings explains that culturally relevant teaching is engaging to African American students because using their culture in instruction helps to maintain that culture and transcend the negative effects of the dominant culture.[11] Geneva Gay tells teachers that culturally relevant teaching is engaging because it is comprehensive and inclusive. She explains, "Fragmented and isolated units, courses, and bits of information about ethnic groups interspersed sporadically into the school curriculum and instructional program will not do the job. . . . Nor will additive approaches, wherein school curriculum remains basically the same, and ethnic content becomes an appendage."[12] For example, if a teacher is teaching poetry, she should use similar poetry written by members of different ethnic groups both in the United States and abroad. This approach not only teaches students that individuals from different groups have written poetry; it also enriches the concept of poetry by enabling students to explore various poetic forms as well as study those elements that are common to poems from diverse ethnic groups.

Sleeter and Grant point out that in culturally relevant teaching, the contributions and perspectives of the groups that a teacher uses should depict each group as it depicts itself and show those aspects of the group's culture that are important to them.[13] Sleeter and Grant explain this point with the following example: "Teachers wishing to include American Indians in the curriculum sometimes choose Sacajawea as a heroine to discuss; but from many American Indian perspectives, Sequoya would be a preferable historical figure. Sacajawea served dominant group interests by leading Lewis and Clark west, whereas Sequoya served the interests of the Cherokee by developing an alphabet for encoding the Cherokee language."[14]

EXHIBIT 5.1	FOUR CONDITIONS NECESSARY FOR CULTURALLY RESPONSIVE TEACHING		

1. Establish Inclusion	2. Develop Positive Attitude	3. Enhance Meaning	4. Engender Competence
Norms: • Emphasize the human purpose of what is being learned and its relationship to the students' experience. • Share the ownership of knowing with all students. • Collaborate and cooperate. The class assumes a hopeful view of people and their capacity to change. • Treat all students equitably. Invite them to point out behaviors or practices that discriminate.	*Norms:* • Relate teaching and learning activities to students' experience or previous knowledge. • Encourage students to make choices in content and assessment methods based on their experiences, values, needs, and strengths.	*Norms:* • Provide challenging learning experience involving higher-order thinking and critical inquiry. Address relevant, real-world issues in an action-oriented manner. • Encourage discussion of relevant experiences. Incorporate student dialect into classroom dialogue.	*Norms:* • Connect the assessment process to the students' world, frames of reference, and values • Include multiple ways to represent knowledge and skills and allow for attainment of outcomes at different points in time. • Encourage self-assessment.
Procedures: Collaborative learning approaches; cooperative learning; writing groups; peer teaching; multidimensional sharing; focus groups; reframing.	*Procedures:* Clear learning goals; problem-solving goals; fair and clear criteria of evaluation; relevant learning models; learning contracts; approaches based on multiple intelligences theory; pedagogical flexibility based on style; experiential learning.	*Procedures:* Critical questioning; guided reciprocal peer questioning posing problems; decision making; investigation of definitions; historical investigations; experimental inquiry; invention; art; simulations; case study methods.	*Procedures:* Feedback; contextualized assessment; authentic assessment tasks; portfolios and process-folios; tests and testing formats critiqued for bias; self-assessment.
Structures: Ground rules; learning communities; cooperative base groups.	*Structures:* Culturally responsive teacher/student/parent conferences.	*Structures:* Projects; problem-posing model.	*Structures:* Narrative evaluations; credit/no credit systems; contracts for grades.

Source: Based on R. J. Wlodkowski and M. B. Ginsberg, "Diversity and Motivation: Culturally Responsive Teaching," *Educational Leadership* 53, no. 1 (September 1995): 20.

Culturally Responsive Classrooms The **culturally responsive classroom** is one in which teachers and students strive to create a caring social-emotional climate that serves individual and group needs of all members of the learning community. Whereas the term *culturally relevant teaching* is used to describe a way of presenting curriculum and instruction, the term *culturally responsive classroom* is used in relation to classroom climate. John Withall believes that the climate of the classroom influences (1) the private world of the student; (2) the "esprit de corps" of the class; (3) the sense of purpose and relevance to group and individual goals and activities; (4) the ability to look at problems objectively; and (5) the student–teacher and student–student rapport.[15] Anne Dodd supports Withall's observations and claims that instructional engagement demands a classroom environment in which every student comes to believe, "I count, I care, and I can.'"[16]

Addressing the content of the lesson and instructional engagement, Wlodkowski and Ginsberg argue that a climate that supports instructional engagement helps to relate the content of the lesson to the students' backgrounds.[17] They describe four motivational conditions important to establishing a classroom that promotes student engagement and is culturally responsive to the students:

> *Establishing inclusion*—creating a caring learning community, where respect is established between teacher and student and students to students
> *Developing attitude*—teacher and students deciding upon learning experiences that both believe are important to students' achievement and life circumstances
> *Enhancing meaning*—providing challenging, relevant learning experiences that teach students how to have greater control over their life circumstances
> *Engendering competence*—understanding that all students are academically curious and should be expected to learn[18]

Wlodkowski and Ginsberg argue that these four conditions work together as they influence teachers and students, and they occur in a moment as well as over a period of time.[19]

One of Carl's students restated Wlodkowski and Ginsberg's four conditions as follows: "The belief that every student can learn and treating them so leads to positive relationships between teachers and students, which in turn fosters a classroom climate where students look forward to challenging learning experiences which help them to have control over their life circumstances." However, a colleague of Carl's visiting the class stated, "That sounds good, but what do you do when one of your students has lost her academic curiosity through years of poor schooling? How do you rebuild that academic curiosity?"

The challenge that such a student brings is awesome, and each teacher will have his or her share of highly motivated and unmotivated students. Nevertheless, teachers who implement Wlodkowski and Ginsberg's ideas are off to a good start in connecting with the student because they are developing a caring classroom, which is important to reestablishing a student's interest in school. Also, as this student observes the use of relevant learning experiences and notes that they are received favorably by the other students, the stage will be set for the teacher to reach out to her—through short chats in which the teacher works on keeping the student from skipping school and on discovering her social and academic interests in order to gradually reignite her academic curiosity. The teacher should enlist the help of other students, caregivers, classroom friends, and other staff members, especially if the teacher has several other challenging students or a very large class. Other teachers are familiar with challenging students and several other students, if not more, will know about the circumstances of these students. Having such a challenge is all a part of teaching.

Both culturally relevant teaching and culturally responsive classrooms help students use their energy and determination to foster instructional engagement instead of having to focus on figuring out how they should behave in the classroom. This allows them to share in the power dynamics of the classroom as well. These two instructional ideas fit within the framework of education that is multicultural and social reconstructionist (EMCSR), celebrating and accepting diversity and appreciating multiple perspectives or interpretations.

Student Involvement, Leadership, and Engagement   Since the 1940s, some teachers have been using teaching practices that promote students' active participation in the instructional process. Ana Maria Andrade and Delia Hakim claim that student involvement and leadership are essential to their becoming instructionally engaged. They say that by involving their first-grade students in instruction and allowing them to make decisions about it, "We now see learning through a much more powerful lens, viewing the whole child in relation to his or her prior knowledge and dominant language and culture. The more we look, the more we see."[20]

Working with middle school students, Wasserstein identifies five maxims that teachers can use to help students become engaged:

1. All students need to see the link between routine drill-and-practice and more complex work.
2. Students need to tinker with real-world problems, and they need opportunities to construct knowledge.
3. The basics should not be an end in themselves but a means to an end.
4. Teachers need to nurture a strong self-image by allowing students to develop an internal locus of control, and to be aware of their strengths and weaknesses.
5. Self-esteem is enhanced when students accomplish something they thought impossible, something beyond them.[21]

Instructional Engagement and Gender-Responsive Classes   Increasingly, teachers are being asked to examine how their teaching engages their female students. Developing gender equity is a basic instructional concern. This is especially true in the areas of science and mathematics, subjects in which it was previously assumed that males excelled over females.

An early response to the gender equity problem was to teach girls to act more like boys—for example, to encourage girls to be more aggressive, tough, and competitive. However, this approach of having girls act like boys has not met with much success, and it points to the way people think that boys/men do things the "right" way, the "normal" way, whereas girls/women do things in opposition to the "norm." This dynamic is played out in the larger society in the ways that we choose our leaders, pay men more than women, and so on. Ann Pollina suggests that teachers should let a *feminist approach* to math and science inform their pedagogy.[22] By a feminist approach, Pollina means that teachers should encourage all students to question ways of doing things that favor the type of work and notions of success that make male views and roles the "norm." Although specifically focused on math and science instruction, Pollina's suggestions can make instruction more gender responsive to students in all areas:

1. Connect mathematics, science, and technology to the real world.
2. Choose metaphors carefully or have students develop their own in order that they do not only take into account boys' life experiences.
3. Foster true collaboration; pulling desks into a circle does not ensure a collaborative, noncompetitive experience.
4. Encourage girls to act as experts. Only when a student group is responsible for verifying its own logic and when students critique their own work and that of their peers do they begin to see themselves as scientists.
5. Give girls the opportunity to be in control of technology.
6. Portray technology as a way to solve problems as well as a plaything.
7. Capitalize on students' verbal strengths. For example, Pollina's calculus students keep journals in which they reflect on their experiences in the course, comment on their progress, and set goals for themselves. Two possible journal questions:
    a. You died while doing your physics homework. Write your physics obituary.
    b. You are a spider on the wall of your room observing you doing your mathematics homework. What do you see?
8. Experiment with testing and evaluation. Assessment methods must reflect the research suggesting that girls do not think in linear right/wrong categories.
9. Give frequent feedback, and keep expectations high. Because girls still may not expect to do well in mathematics and science, they tend to need more encouragement than do boys.[23]

Today a feminist approach not only focuses on increasing the success of female students, it encourages teachers to utilize practices that meet the needs of all students in a variety of subject areas. For example, teachers are encouraged to use collaborative methods rather than assuming that competition is the best motivator in a classroom. In this way, feminist approaches may meet the needs of male and female students alike.

Instructional Engagement and the Achievement Goal Approach

Rachel Collopy and Theresa Green argue that the instructional goals that students pursue greatly influence the quality of their learning. They contend that students' pursuit of their goals should be defined by their quest for knowledge and not be determined by students' ability.[24] Teacher candidates observe that when students become interested in an educational idea, they became motivated to learn about it. In many instances this joy of learning causes students to exceed the learning expectations teachers have of them, bringing forth the students' true learning capabilities. Also, Collopy and Green believe that report cards should reflect progress and mastery rather than emphasizing comparative performance with letter grades.[25]

From these several ways of fostering student engagement, teachers will come to believe that students will be more encouraged to learn if they see a relationship between what they are studying and their life experiences.

Finally, instruction as introduced in this section and curriculum as discussed in Chapter 4 need to be connected. Dewey explains the idea of a seamless web between curriculum and instruction when he claims that curriculum should not be seen as fixed and outside of students' background and experiences, but should be seen as seamless.[26] Dewey encourages us to:

> Abandon the notion of subject matter [curriculum] as something fixed and ready-made in itself, outside the child's experience; cease thinking of the child's experience as also something hard and fast; see it as something fluent, embryonic, vital; and we realize that the child and the curriculum are simply two limits which define a single process.[27]

Connecting this point to instruction, Dewey claims that just as there is a difference between learning about the land from a map and learning firsthand from the journey itself, there is also a difference, for example, between learning about fractions from a text and learning about fractions through experimentation under the patient guidance of the teacher. The latter learning experience should be connected with, and derived from, the student's experience, and thus be more meaningful.[28]

Having a close connection between a culturally relevant curriculum and instruction gives students a greater understanding of and appreciation for the learning experience. It will also make curriculum less of an oppressive form of social regulation for students who are not members of the dominant group and will allow marginalized students to choose academic excellence and still identify with their own culture.[29]

PLANNING

Planning is critical to developing a seamless web between teaching and curriculum and to having instruction engage students. Some teachers believe that only by planning can they meet the challenges and responsibilities of the multicultural, multilingual population in their classrooms, as well as of students with differing abilities. Students, teachers say, come with different needs and dreams. Having a curriculum that meets those needs and dreams as well as prepares students to critique the social injustices and inequalities that govern their life chances requires planning what to teach and how to teach it.

Teachers have different ideas about planning. We have collected four different sets of teachers' opinions about writing lesson plans. First are those teachers who view lesson planning as an essential framework for practically all classroom instruction. To them, lesson plans that take into account pedagogical strategies to individualize the lesson to different students are a must. Second are the teachers who find writing lesson plans too time-consuming and following a lesson plan too constraining. These teachers argue that they plan, but much of the planning stays in their head. Having mental plans allows them to respond to students based on daily occurrences in the class. Third are teachers who see planning as mechanical and void of any real teacher input. A number of these teachers rely on ideas from their subject matter textbook teaching guides. These teachers often put just the dates, times, and textbook page numbers in their plan books. They claim that preparing lesson plans is busywork. The fourth, very populous group of teachers are those who claim that writing lesson plans is something that teachers do when they first begin to teach but that can be put it aside once they become comfortable with teaching.

Chad and Molly's observations illustrate some of these lesson-planning ideas. While observing in a school, Chad and Molly discovered that the teacher each observed had different ideas about lesson planning. This caused them to become concerned about what they should know and do about lesson planning. Ms. Johnson, a teacher with 10 years of experience, told Chad, "For the last seven years, I have been teaching fourth grade. I know these students and I know the curriculum, so it's not necessary for me to write out any plans. Besides, when I used to write plans, I never used them. The students always did something that made me change what I was going to do." In contrast, Mrs. Wilson, a teacher with 12 years of experience, told Molly, "For the last six years I have been doing a lot of planning. I usually spend Sunday night getting ready for the week. I write out fairly comprehensive plans for every subject that I teach. The reason I started to write plans is that the students are different than they used to be. Today's sixth-grade students are much worldlier than sixth-grade students years ago. Also, my life experiences are so different from those of a good number of the students. Students are more active, come from many different backgrounds, ask more questions, want to be more involved, and some even will challenge you if you seem unsure about the answer. You have to be prepared for them; otherwise you will have a lot of tough days."

Confused about planning, Chad and Molly decided to find out how planning is addressed at their college. They discovered that their professors have different views about experienced teachers writing lesson plans. The professors' answers for the most part paralleled the responses given by the four groups of teachers described above. If, for their student teaching experience, Chad and/or Molly are placed with a teacher who does not plan, it will be up to them and their university supervisor to negotiate with the cooperating teacher to receive help with planning.

Discussions over "to write lesson plans or not to write lesson plans" will continue. Ultimately, each teacher makes his or her own decision about what to do. We believe that the diversity among students, the necessity for students to develop basic literacy in all subject areas, the importance of student engagement in instruction, the call for students to have a voice, and the reality that much of the curriculum in school today needs to be examined with regard to social justice and equity issues are all reasons that make careful planning a requirement before teaching.

Levels of Planning

Teachers who write plans usually find three types of plans helpful: long-range, medium-range, and short-range. For most teachers these types of plans are not separate and distinct. In fact, often they are used in conjunction with one another.

Long-Range Plans   Long-range planning allows the teacher to investigate the concepts and practices of a curriculum area to determine students' needs and how students can best be instructionally engaged. Also, long-range planning provides time to get the community, businesspeople, and parents involved and to determine how one subject area best interfaces with other subjects—for example, math with history and music. Mrs. Wilson provides an example of long-range planning.

Mrs. Wilson has discovered that many of the graduates from her school, Kennedy Middle, are not doing well in math when they move into high school. In fact, she has learned that an increasing number of Kennedy's graduates are not enrolling in regular high school math courses, but instead are opting to take basic math or general math classes. Taking the basic math or general math courses, Mrs. Wilson knows, may affect the students' chances of going on to college and attending the college of their choice. She fears that the students' failure in math may cause them serious career and personal problems. Also, Mrs. Wilson is concerned because the National Council of Teachers of Mathematics (NCTM), as part of the education reform effort proposed by both Presidents G. H. W. Bush and Clinton, is stressing mathematical literacy. NCTM has identified five new mathematical literacy goals that need to be given major consideration: (1) that students learn to value mathematics, (2) that students become confident in their ability to do mathematics, (3) that students become mathematical problem solvers, (4) that students learn to communicate mathematically, and (5) that students learn to reason mathematically.[30]

Because students are falling behind in math as well as avoiding it, and new goals for math literacy are in place to prepare students for the 21st century, Mrs. Wilson decides she needs to develop some long-range plans. These will start Kennedy's students on their way to achieving the math goals.

To help the students value math, Mrs. Wilson wants them to learn that math is much more than addition and subtraction. She wants students to know the importance of math in conducting business such as shopping and banking and in making decisions related to health care, politics, defense, technology, and leisure. Also, she would like students to have varied experiences related to the cultural and scientific applications of mathematics in both the Western and the non-Western world. First, she enlists three parent volunteers from different ethnic groups to contact museums and art galleries in the city to see if any math-related exhibits are planned for the year. She encourages these parents also to contact museums and art galleries located in the ethnic communities. Then she asks two other parents to contact some architectural firms to invite members of the firm to discuss math and architecture. These parents are asked to invite a female architect and an architect of color, if possible. Finally, Mrs. Wilson asks some parents to identify businesspeople and local university faculty in the social sciences, the physical and life sciences, and the humanities to discuss the role of mathematics in their fields.

Mrs. Wilson and the parent volunteers develop an information kit on the school to send to the consultants. The kit includes information about the purpose of the math curriculum for the year and a copy of the NCTM goals to help the consultants keep them in mind as they prepare their presentations. Also in the information kit are suggestions for and questions about the consultants' presentations.

Mrs. Wilson believes that allowing students and parents to participate in long-range planning will increase the students' appreciation and understanding of math and their confidence in their mathematical ability. For example, Heriberto is a student who claims to hate math. However, he is now, after the presentations, becoming more comfortable with it thanks to a furniture maker invited to speak to the class, who befriended Heriberto. Now Heriberto spends several hours twice a week after school helping her. He helps to measure wood, cuts out different geometric designs, and puts tools away according to their mathematical size. Having this experience is helping him become more knowledgeable about math and more confident in his mathematical ability.

Mrs. Wilson believes that helping students see how math is used in many different fields will provide them with many opportunities to become mathematical problem solvers and increase their ability to communicate and reason mathematically. Mrs. Wilson and the students will continue to shape their long-range plans until the curriculum and instruction become a seamless web.

Medium-Range Plans   Teachers often consider a medium-range plan a *unit plan*. A **unit plan** is a set of learning objectives, activities, experiences, materials, and resources concerned with a topic or problem. It is much more specific than a long-range plan. Most units last from two to six weeks, but the length and scope can vary depending on the subject matter, topic or theme, grade level, students, and individual teachers.

Unit plans can take several directions: subject matter, experience, interdisciplinary, and resource. For example, Mrs. Wilson learns from the architects' presentation that a number of the students are interested in shapes and symbols, how they are used in architecture and in other areas in society. She then plans a *subject matter* unit on geometric ideas and shapes. She asks the art teacher, Ms. Richards, to develop an *experience* unit on geometric shapes, especially polygons. The activities in this unit will include having students identify and draw international traffic signs and symbols and having them write and perform a skit about geometric shapes.

An *interdisciplinary* unit focuses on learning a concept through the integration of several subject areas. For example, Mrs. Wilson and the students plan a combined social studies and science unit that includes students' using beakers of different sizes and shapes, as well as prisms and wedges. Mrs. Wilson asks the librarian, Ms. Nieto, if she would help identify some fiction and nonfiction books that address geometric signs and symbols in the literature and culture of different groups, and periods of architectural design that showcase structures such as geometric signs and symbols.

The *resource* unit is another type of unit plan. Rather than an outline of a plan to be implemented, the resource unit is usually a collection of ideas and materials related to the concept being studied. Many teachers collect materials within varying resource categories to free themselves from reliance on textbooks or prepackaged curricula as primary sources of knowledge. For example, Ms. Nieto and the consultants that Mrs. Wilson invites from the business world and university will provide her with a number of materials for her resource unit.

EXHIBIT 5.2   **A SAMPLE FORMAT: SHORT-RANGE DAILY PLAN**

Subject: Grade:

Lesson Topic:

 I. Daily objective (What do I want students to learn, and why do I want them to learn it?)

II. Concepts to be treated

   A.

   B.

   C. (etc.)

III. Procedures and activities (What will I do to meet objectives?)

   A.

   B.

   C.

   D. (etc.)

IV. Materials and resources (What materials do I need to collect in advance?)

   A.

   B.

   C.

   D. (etc.)

V. Assessment

   A. Teacher (How did I . . .?)

     1.

     2.

     3.

     4. (etc.)

   B. Students (How did they . . .?)

     1.

     2.

     3.

     4. (etc.)

Short-Range Plans   Individual lesson plans that cover one to ten school days are often considered short-range plans or daily lesson plans. They vary from a brief outline to detailed descriptions collected within loose-leaf binders or traditional plan books. Some include the time and day of instruction. Many daily lesson plans list a specific curriculum area, objectives, activities, resources, and assessments (see Exhibit 5.2). They are designed to fit the interests, achievement levels, and learning styles of the different students in the class. Increasingly, students are taking a more active role in lesson planning. They are offering ideas about content, learning activities, and assessment. One way teachers include students in planning is to start a unit with a KWL chart. Students chart what they know about a topic (K), what they want to learn (W), and at the end of the unit what they did learn (L). Lesson plans often serve as a reflective tool, encouraging teachers to clarify their instructional objectives and the means for attaining them. Also, they allow teachers to examine how they are putting their teaching philosophy, educational theory, and mandates (standards) into practice.

In conclusion, regardless of the range of a plan, it is merely a *guide* for action. No matter how appropriate and meaningful they appear to be, plans are not complete until they meet students' needs and are instructionally engaging. Through planning, teachers and students can determine how best to approach a subject so that both their knowledge and their interests are better served. Also, from planning with students, teachers can ascertain how and where in the curriculum to encourage students' voices, especially those of students who have made contributions to the lesson. Finally, it is at the planning level that power, which usually operates in favor of teachers' knowledge and authority, can be enacted in a way that encourages both teachers and students to learn. For example, students can be asked about their backgrounds, and their knowledge of people and resources in the community can be used in the lessons being planned. The teacher will not know all that the students know and experience, and the teacher's open acknowledgment and use of students' experiences will contribute to a fluid circulation of power among teacher and students.

Regardless of whether the same subject matter is taught and the knowledge and disposition of the students seem the same, the lesson plans need to be changed each year to be instructionally engaging and to meet the particular needs of that year's students. Finally, the challenge to most teachers making long-range, medium-range, and short-range plans is making them multicultural and instructionally engaging and situating both teachers and students as learners.

Planning and Education That Is Multicultural and Social Reconstructionist

Carl Grant and Christine Sleeter suggest using an EMCSR (education that is multicultural and social reconstructionist) framework when planning lessons.[31] This framework offers suggestions in many areas that need to be considered when planning for teaching: curriculum materials and multiple perspectives, instructional strategies, language diversity, grouping of students, visuals, role models, home and community relations, celebration of diversity and equal opportunity, practice of democracy, analysis of inequality, and encouragement of social action. Although paying attention to 11 areas of planning is a very challenging task, such attention can eliminate many classroom discipline problems and help to make students' learning instructionally engaging. We begin with the first of these areas, curriculum materials and multiple perspectives.

Curriculum Materials and Multiple Perspectives   Historically, schools have tended to teach children to seek *the* right answer rather than consider different points of view. For example, for years U.S. schools have taught that Davy Crockett was killed as he fought off charging Mexican soldiers at the Alamo. Now, however, this view is being challenged; other notions of truth and new perspectives are being offered. One perspective, from the diary of a Mexican officer, José Enrique de la Pena, present at the Alamo during its siege, alleges that Davy Crockett was killed by Mexican soldiers along with six other survivors after the fall of the Alamo.[32] A perspective from a Mexican officer telling even a slightly different tale about the Alamo offers students another way to think about an event in history, to consider how events are reported historically and today by the mass media, and to think about other events as not given because they are written one way in a textbook.

Teachers can decide whether to teach one perspective or multiple perspectives about such events as Davy Crockett at the Alamo. How a teacher decides what and how to teach is influenced by multiple factors. Many teachers were taught about such an event with that one right narrative stressed. What a school board states should be taught also strongly influences what texts and materials are available to the teacher. We have discussed power throughout this text and how it circulates and invests decisions made by teachers, school boards, and others differently. When teachers begin to acknowledge and put to use multiple perspectives, they may be challenging how power has usually worked. Teaching one perspective about the Alamo and teaching multiple perspectives are both socially regulating. Teaching is not a neutral act. All actions within a classroom are socially regulating in that teachers socialize students. A perspective on a historical event is passed down from generation to generation and thereby influences the way youth come to accept or interpret an event. The determination of perspectives is an expression of power, and thus socially regulating.

A multiple perspectives approach also includes using materials in lesson plans that represent different discourses and do not promote stereotypes or exoticize the diverse groups that make up the United States. Gathering materials that represent diverse groups when they are not included in existing materials calls for teachers to take the initiative, inviting groups, as Mrs. Wilson did, to participate in gathering resources and ideas for lessons.

Understanding the concept of multiple perspectives also involves examining the idea of *privilege*. Privilege and issues of whose interests are being served are taboo topics in most K–12 curriculum discussions. Privilege may be discussed in association with such issues as environmental degradation. An example of an environmental question would be asking which countries are using fuel at such a capacity that the planet Earth is being endangered. Economic, political, or gender privilege is not often discussed. Teachers have a choice to openly include in their lessons discussions of economic, political, and gender privilege and power so that students can learn how they are situated in life circumstances. An example would be discussing how women are hired to perform similar jobs but earn less than men doing the same job. Teachers also have a choice to exclude discussions of privilege and power in the overt curriculum. However, when this happens, privilege in its varied manifestations (e.g., gender, race) becomes a part of the hidden curriculum, where its message is learned by the student without the benefit of teacher–student critical analysis. If the student is feeling the effects of the power that comes from others' having privilege, not discussing it or using materials promoting this privilege implicates the teacher in this dynamic, possibly making it more difficult for the student to trust and learn from that teacher.

Finally, plans that include multiple perspectives lead students to develop flexible thinking and the expectation that other valid viewpoints exist besides their own or the one "in the book." With multiple perspectives comes a truer picture. This also allows for better problem solving when needed.

Instructional Strategies   In the first section of this chapter, we argued that instructional engagement is an important instructional strategy. Here, we want to offer another suggestion for making instruction engaging. Chimerine, Panton, and Russo believe that teachers should use strategies that consider students' use of out-of-school time. These strategies include learning about (1) students' options for how to spend time, (2) their ability to make intelligent and constructive choices among those options, and (3) the direct and indirect effects of those choices upon academic achievement.[33] A teacher's knowledge of the availability and quality of after-school programs at the school, local Boys and Girls Clubs, programs at the YMCA or YWCA, organized sport teams, local library book or computer clubs, or other programs is useful information for developing lesson plans that engage students, especially those students who are losing their academic curiosity. Discovering students' interest and level of participation in after-school opportunities can be informative about how to instructionally engage students, and to assess how students transfer what they learn in the classroom to out-of-school activities. Finally, putting into practice the strategies suggested by Chimerine, Panton and Russo will help teachers to select curriculum and design instructional strategies that take into consideration student lifestyles outside of school. This communicates to students that teachers are not just concerned about their 8 A.M. to 3 P.M. welfare.

Language Diversity   Language diversity is found in more than 46% of the nation's schools; in central cities and urban fringe and large towns, about 60% of the schools have language diverse students.[34] More than 27% of schools have difficulty filling bilingual and ESL teaching positions, increasing the responsibility for each teacher to be sensitive to language diversity.[35] When some students cannot receive the full benefit of instruction because schools have not been able to hire bilingual or ESL teachers, schools work in favor of the students who have teachers who can speak their language. This power differential, between students who have teachers who speak their language and those who do not, will influence career opportunities and life choices if it is not corrected.

Lesson planning needs to take into account the language concerns and needs of the students. Teachers should consult those in charge when they see students being shortchanged in their opportunity to learn English and to continue learning about their native language as well.

Grouping Students   Flexible grouping and small-group activities help students address their own academic needs and get to know one another. Flexible grouping means using a variety of homogeneous and heterogeneous groups. Depending on the objective, teachers may assign groups, randomly pick students, or let students choose their own groups. The groups should be organized so that one or two students are not privileged because of their personality or role in the group. Students should receive an explanation of the responsibilities and privileges that go with their roles. Students have to be taught to work across differences. Grouping should consider placing students with different academic skills, races, genders, and social class status together in hopes of forging a greater understanding and appreciation of diversity among all student groups. The forging of diversity in groups can lessen tension between students of different ethnicities and social classes. This becomes essential because as classes discuss power and privilege issues in society, students will be less inclined to personalize or to verbally attack one another.

Visuals   It has been said that "A picture is worth a thousand words." The credibility of this statement is less important than the fact that pictures do convey significant messages to students. Some visuals tell students what historians, textbook authors, or community leaders think about the worth of the groups students belong to. These visual messages in textbooks or trade books or in the art or photographs displayed in the classroom and school need to be responsive to race, class, gender, and disability concerns. For example, teachers should ask: What do the visuals in textbooks and other instructional materials convey to the students? What do the pictures in the classrooms and halls say about the school to parents when they enter? Whose pictures are mostly displayed—males or females, poor or middle-class people? Is the student work displayed representative of all students? Is there respect for languages other than English? Do the visuals convey the school's dedication to *all* the students enrolled and reflect its preparation of students to live in a global society, appreciating different ways of thinking? The multicultural representation in the visuals displayed through a school is a testimony to how the people who govern the school exercise power. Decisions about whose pictures or which pictures to display are usually made by administrators and teachers. In many schools, the decisions made by teachers and administrators tend to favor pictures of White males and a few White females. In many schools, it is by and large sports participants (particularly male) whose pictures and awards are on display, rather than scholars, musicians, artists, and others. This also sends a message to students of power and privilege.

Finally, the overwhelming number of visuals observed in school settings often portrays a European American or Western civilization message. Such representation, by omission, conveys a message that Americans of color and non-Western civilizations are not important. Because many visuals used in schools are purchased, teachers can choose to accept the status quo or to use the political muscle they have been developing since the 1960s to demand greater diversity in the instructional visuals.

Role Models   Claire Graue, a first-year fifth-grade teacher at Martin Luther King Middle School, surveyed her students to find out who their role models are. Claire had originally thought that her class of 25 African American students would mostly identify sports and entertainment stars. She was surprised that sports and entertainment stars represented only 18% of their top three choices. Discussing these results with Richard Bent, a 10-year veteran at King, Claire learned that the survey results for sports and entertainment stars are nevertheless higher than he believes they should be. Richard told Claire, "Seven years ago the school underwent a major reform: changed its name, implemented a multicultural curriculum, and brought in a new principal, Ms. Wilder, who encouraged four teachers to transfer, encouraged five other teachers to enroll in literacy classes at the university, launched a very active parent/community participation program, and got students involved in the reform effort."

"The reform effort," Richard continued, "was designed to help students achieve academically and learn to better manage their life circumstances and opportunities. In order for this to happen, students had to become realistic about their life goals." Richard continued to tell Claire about how the program affected students and parents who became actively involved in coaching their children in their career choices and goals. Richard said, "Near the end of the second year of the reform, the students' achievement improved, and students' career goals and role models became more realistic. The students' role models were fashioned less by sports and entertainment stars and more by people they met or read about in the career information they received. Also, many students developed a much more favorable respect for the job their parents were doing for them, and increasingly identified them among their role models."

As Claire left Richard to return to class, she had a new sense of discovery about her students and herself. What Richard had implicitly told her was that her students are intelligent and just as capable as any other students of achieving their life dreams. She needed to help them by instructionally engaging and challenging them, and holding them to high expectations. What Richard had made her see is that she needs to examine her own beliefs about the students she is teaching. Why did she decide to teach, and why did she take this position in an urban area? "Wow," thought Claire, "I need a *re-education* about myself and my students. Richard's comments are making me question my beliefs about African American boys and girls, their dreams and expectations. More important, he is causing me to wonder if I have what it takes to change my beliefs and become a good teacher."

Home and Community Relations   Lesson planning should consider how parents and community members can assist the teacher with teaching. Planning with parents and community members can include sharing curriculum ideas with parents and inviting their suggestions. Also, attention needs to be given to the students' home language so that students' work and other information sent home is in a language parents can read. Necessary to developing parent/community–teacher relations is learning about the community where the school is located: the community's history, housing patterns, and leaders. Visiting organizations, associations, and religious institutions and regularly reading community newspapers and neighborhood bulletins can also inform teachers about the community.

The extent to which teachers and parents work together is often a reflection of how groups rise above notions of prejudice and mistrust. For years in many areas there have been tensions between communities of color and those who govern the school system. These tensions are founded upon racial and economic prejudices that were set in place during the early days of this country (e.g., slavery, black codes, people from the other side of the tracks) and continue today (e.g., at-risk students, segregated schools). These attitudes are enactments of power that come out of legacies of social class, language, cultural, and racial dominance. Sara Lawrence-Lightfoot's *The Essential Conversation: What Parents and Teachers Can Learn From Each Other* addresses these issues. The book provides an enlightening discussion of the exchange that take places between parents and teachers more than 100 million times a year across the country within a race, class, gender, culture, and language context. It discusses numerous ideas, such as parent anxiety and institutional barriers (e.g., time of meetings), that will be useful to teachers preparing to foster more effective home–school relations.

Celebration of Diversity and Equal Opportunity   Many school policies and practices since the 1950s have made reference to equal opportunity, equity, and multicultural education. Although there has been progress, much is left to be achieved in the area of social justice. Planning should provide opportunities for students to discuss both historical and contemporary issues of racism, sexism, classism, heterosexism, and ablism in school and society. Concepts and issues discussed in the class should be examined for bias, and the extent to which notions of truth and ways of thinking of different social groups are presented should be examined.

Some teachers believe that younger students should not be involved in discussions of equity and equal opportunity. These teachers argue that young students are not mature enough and that the focus should be on their seeing the beauty in the world. These teachers forget that in the early days of the civil rights movement, young students were the foot soldiers. In many cases, they dealt with racism, stereotypes, and prejudice much better than adults. From 9 A.M. to 3 P.M., many PreK–12 students were leaders in making classrooms diverse and in demanding equal educational opportunities. A teacher's decision to promote diversity and equal opportunity in his or her classroom is more like the decision that confronts Claire. It is a decision of choice, to engage in self-reflection and re-education, more than a question of whether a teacher's students are old enough to learn about diversity.

Practice of Democracy   Planning should provide opportunities in the school and classrooms for students to develop decision-making skills that will prepare them to accept the privileges and responsibilities of the democratic way of life. Learning the rules and procedures for voting and participating in class and school elections are essential preparation. However, practicing democracy also includes teaching students how to seek the information necessary to make informed decisions. Additionally, it includes voicing ideas, respecting diverse points of view, and offering alternative points of view. Power, students are told, is shared through democratic action. Therefore, it is imperative that students have many opportunities to practice democracy in the classroom, and be taught politics and how power is enacted in democratic settings.

For some, this discussion refers to ideas and activities that should be left to those who teach social studies, but teachers of every discipline should work at practicing democracy in their field. In science and mathematics, practicing democracy is, for example, enabling female students to have a presence and a voice in the high-level classes. Achieving such presence and voice begins early in the grades as girls are given the assistance and/or opportunities to become a part of the track that leads to placement in the high-level mathematics and science classes.

Analysis of Social Inequality   Analysis is located very high on the critical thinking ladder. Similarly, resolving issues of equity and social justice is central to making democracy work for all people in the United States. Lesson plans, therefore, should include activities in which students have to analyze social issues. Some of these activities should address general societal issues and provide a connection between these broader social issues and students' life circumstances. For example, both female and male students should examine gender-related issues such as the *glass ceiling* concept to discover why and how it exists. Students can discuss with role models problems of inequity they have experienced. They can also investigate the careers they are seeking to ascertain whether inequities exist.

To increase instructional engagement, students should be encouraged to suggest topics for analysis, along with developing the criteria that will be used to assess the analysis. It is important for students to learn about social issues that may not appear to affect them directly, because they will be better prepared to recognize societal problems and take action with the affected group to help alleviate some of these inequities for the greater good. This is key because in some cases, some individuals or groups may not recognize that they are being systematically marginalized or oppressed because of the way that privilege works. Other individuals who have had a similar experience may recognize it sooner and should help the oppressed individual to take action in a way that he/she feels comfortable doing.

Encouraging Social Action   Vital to making a democracy work is that people know they are free to take social action. Learning about the many forms of social action starts at home. When students are very young and, for example, lobby for a particular meal, protest going to sleep, complain they need water, or want to hear another bedtime story, they are engaging in a form of social action. In school, social action takes many different forms, including writing letters of protest, engaging in community service, and producing and distributing literature (see also the discussion of teachers' and students' rights and responsibilities in Chapter 10).

Lesson planning should include activities that teach students social action skills. Teaching the concept and purpose of social action and providing opportunities to practice these actions increase students' ability to deal with events later on in their lives. Some classroom teachers do not include social action activities in their lessons because they believe that social action activities inadvertently teach students to be disruptive in the classroom. Central to teaching social action skills is teaching students when and how to use them, and the responsibility that they assume when they use them.

In conclusion, there is no formula for determining how much multicultural detail is necessary for a "good plan." However, reviewing lesson plans against this Grant and Sleeter framework provides one way to ascertain the extent to which the plans are responsive to multicultural education.

Procedures for Planning

When developing plans, whether long-, medium-, or short-range ones, many teachers adhere to the following four guidelines:

1. List purposes and objectives. The purpose enables the teacher to answer the invariable student question, "Why do we want to learn this?"
2. List the procedures to be followed and learning experiences for students. This part of the plan should answer the questions "How will I meet my purpose?" or "What do I expect the students to do?" and "What materials and resources will I require to meet the purpose?"
3. Specify the means for assessing the outcome and procedures for answering the question "Did we meet the purpose?"
4. Specify procedures for follow-up work and activities. Follow-up work should include supplementary, enrichment, or collateral ideas, materials, and resources that can aid in accommodating individual needs. For example, your plan should include the reminder that two of your students, Alice and Rudolfo, have information from their personal experiences that will enrich the lesson and make it more student-friendly.

A plan should answer the following questions for the teacher: (1) What should students learn? (2) Why should students learn this? (3) How will I meet my purpose, and what do I expect the students to do? (4)What materials and resources are needed? Once a teacher has the answers to these four question, it is time to consider two other questions that the following section on assessment of instruction will help us with: (5) How will I know if the plan worked for each student and for me? (6) What will we (teacher candidate, teacher, and students) do next?

ASSESSMENT OF INSTRUCTION

The educational reform that started in the 1980s with *A Nation at Risk* and continued into the 21st century with No Child Left Behind paid particular attention to student evaluation. Concerned educators and social critics argued that students' test scores were moving in reverse and that far too many poorly prepared students were receiving social promotions and not being evaluated on their academic performance. Many business leaders agreed with these claims. They complained that too many of their employees, despite a high school diploma, did not have basic (sixth-grade level) reading and math skills.

Mary Shafer and Sherian Foster support this assertion and extend the discussion to the changing needs of business and industry: "The biggest industry and the smallest of businesses, even the service professions, need people with mathematical and scientific understanding and skills vastly different from those needed as little as a decade ago. . . . No longer is shopkeeper math or a little general biology sufficient to meet the demands of living and working in a technology-driven information age."[36] Shafer and Foster contend that, along with a change in what students are taught in the subject matter areas, there also needs to be a change in assessment.

> As school mathematics and science change to meet contemporary needs, assessment must also change. No longer is it sufficient for students to memorize and recite isolated facts, execute memorized algorithms to do paper-and-pencil calculations, or carry out prescribed laboratory routines. No longer is it appropriate to test only these skills.[37]

Traditional forms of student evaluation, such as standardized tests, do not tell teachers if students can really perform. Selecting one answer among several on a multiple-choice test does not provide an authentic statement about students' ability to perform.

To know if students can at least perform at a basic skills level in such areas as reading and math, many states turned to minimum competency tests. Carl and Maureen recall visiting several schools to investigate teachers' thinking about minimum competency tests. What they discovered was that teachers were very busy teaching the material on the tests, sometimes called "teaching to the test." Teachers were under undue pressure to make certain that their students achieved at least at a minimum basic level. The information from tests became the school curriculum. What Carl and Maureen discovered, others have discovered as well and have argued for additional changes in the ways students are assessed.

Curriculum, instruction, learning, and assessment, politicians and others argue, need to be inextricably linked. Good performance assessment mirrors good instruction, and both should engage students in critical thinking in every lesson, unit, and activity throughout the school year. Many educators refer to this notion of relating curriculum content standards, instruction, and assessment as **alignment.**

What is needed to determine how well students are faring in this new instruction and assessment climate is a type of assessment that will tell how well students are performing an academic skill (e.g., addition) or how well students understand a concept (e.g., polygons). The National Council of Teachers of Mathematics eloquently captured the direction that educators want assessment to move when they described shifts in the world of assessment

- Away from basing inferences on single-source evidence and toward basing inferences on multiple and balanced sources of evidence
- Away from reliance on comparing students' performance with that of other students and toward reliance on comparing students' performance with established criteria
- Away from relying on outside sources of evidence and toward a balance between these sources and evidence compiled by teachers

- Away from a preponderance of assessment items that are short, skill-focused, single-answer, and decontextualized toward a greater use of tasks that are context-based, open to multiple approaches and in some cases to multiple solutions, and complex in the responses they demand[38]

This new direction in assessment became known as performance assessment or authentic assessment.

Authentic Assessment

Some teachers see authentic assessment as judging students' real learning on the basis of the quality of their performance or product that is an outcome of their work on real (authentic) learning tasks. C. D. Ryan explains, "Authentic assessment is the process of gathering evidence and documenting a student's learning and growth in an authentic context."[39] Authentic assessment is applicable in all areas of instruction as it involves gathering a variety of examples of student work.

Newmann, Secada, and Wehlage suggest that for a math and social studies task to be authentic, the following seven standards within three criteria need to be adhered to:

CONSTRUCTION OF KNOWLEDGE

1. Organization of information
2. Consideration of alternatives

DISCIPLINED INQUIRY

3. Disciplinary content
4. Disciplinary process
5. Elaborated written communication

VALUE BEYOND SCHOOL

6. Problem connected to the world
7. Audience beyond the school[40]

The following example takes into account Newmann, Secada, and Wehlage's suggestions.

Mrs. Wilson and her student Maria examined the mathematical information (evidence) Maria used to determine the number of yards of material that were needed to make a dress worn by a woman from the community to Lincoln's presidential inauguration in 1861(the dress was on display at the local museum). Mrs. Wilson and Maria discussed the math concepts and skills Maria could use to find a solution to her problem. They also planned to inquire at the library to see if the librarian knew how to get an old sewing catalog that could provide the information Maria was seeking. Mrs. Wilson and Maria discussed her knowledge of measurement and reviewed how Maria had put this knowledge into practice in her daily life. They also discussed Maria's mathematical progress since the beginning of the school year. This assessment procedure allowed Maria to see firsthand what was taking place and to participate in the process, and thereby gain a sense of efficacy, especially when her results were good.

In authentic assessment, attention is on the growth of the student (Maria) and not on comparing her to other classmates. Maria and her teacher decided that she should write an essay discussing the historical information and math concepts pertinent to her problem, and include the essay in her portfolio. For example, because the dress on display had a bustle and Maria was interested in discovering how many yards of material were needed to make an average size bustle in the 1860s, she prepared a short essay on the size of women's bustles. Authentic assessments encourage a closer working relationship between teacher and student. Also, authentic assessment does not privilege some data and marginalize other data. Observing a student do math problems on the computer is just as important as the score on an achievement test in determining the student's strengths and weaknesses in math.

Ellen Kronowitz adds that authentic assessment addresses the process and continuum of learning and pays attention to the demonstration of knowledge, skills, and attitudes.[41] According to Kronowitz, Mrs. Wilson would need to be sensitive to Maria's attitude about this project. She could have asked herself whether Maria was working on this project because of her own interest in it, or only because she, Mrs. Wilson, was interested in it.

Some teachers may contend that authentic assessment is too labor intensive, especially in large classes. What we hear from teachers who use authentic assessment is that at first it is a bit of a challenge, but as the teacher and students engage in the process it becomes much easier. These teachers argue that the rewards to both the teacher and students make the effort worthwhile.

Portfolio Assessment

Authentic assessment is often associated with the use of portfolios. Paulson, Paulson, and Meyer describe a portfolio as "a purposeful collection of student work that exhibits the students' efforts, progress, and achievements in one or more areas. The collection must include students' participation in establishing the criteria for selection and the criteria for judging merit or the *rubric*, selecting content and evidence of student self-reflection."[42] One idea behind portfolio assessment is that it should be an act of learning for both teacher and student. An example of portfolio assessment would be Mrs. Wilson's helping Maria to organize her work into a portfolio that includes a statement of purpose, an outline of the contents, criteria for selection, and criteria of evaluation. Included in Maria's portfolio would be materials that feature both longitudinal and multidimensional work and material that illustrates that Maria examines issues from multiple perspectives. Also included would be materials that show Maria engages in self-reflection.

Portfolios can be and are often different from one another. They do not come from a "cookie cutter" design. However, Barton and Collins do believe that the following seven characteristics are important to portfolios:

1. The presentation of the concept or idea should come out of many different sources and teachers should have opportunities to evaluate a variety of specific evidence—for example, *artifacts* (e.g., student papers), *reproductions*

(e.g., special projects produced outside of the classroom or school), *attentions* (e.g., observational notes taken during an oral presentation), and *productions* (e.g., documents students prepare for the portfolio)—to determine the student's competency.
2. They are authentic; instruction and evidence in portfolio are directly linked.
3. They are a dynamic form of assessment. They capture student growth and change over time.
4. They explicitly define the purpose of instruction so that students are clear before they begin developing evidence for their portfolio.
5. They promote integration. The portfolio evidence the students compile must establish a correspondence between academic coursework and their life experience.
6. They are each a unique creation because students determine the evidence to be included and complete a self-evaluation reflection.
7. They are multi-purposed in that teachers can assess their instruction using the same evidence they use to evaluate the student.[43]

Exhibition Assessment

Exhibitions are presentations of the results of learning in a particular area. They may vary from school to school, but they are occasions such as science fairs in which students demonstrate comprehensive and cumulative knowledge and understanding through the use of several different disciplines. Theodore Sizer, chairman of the Coalition of Essential Schools, popularized exhibitions as a form of assessment. The sixth "Common Principle" of the Coalition discusses exhibitions:

> The diploma should be awarded on a successful final demonstration of mastery for graduation—an Exhibition. This Exhibition by the student should demonstrate his or her knowledge of the school's curriculum.

Exhibitions may be conducted by both faculty members and school district officials. Performance assessment of portfolios, students' essays, science experiments, and classroom debates, according to Johnson, are checkpoints that enable students and teachers to assess students' work as it builds toward a cumulating activity, the exhibition.[45]

Several students in Mrs. Wilson's class, including Maria, may prepare exhibitions. Maria's exhibition may include the following elements: a dress with a bustle modeled on a mannequin that she made with Mrs. Wilson's help; essays on Lincoln's presidential inauguration, Mexican American life in the United States in the 1860s, and women's clothes during the 1860s; reports containing mathematical information on the amount of material needed to make dresses and other clothes worn during that time; and design sketches of the dress Maria made in pencil and color. Maria will exhibit her essays, reports, and sketches on poster board with appropriate labels and titles. School officials, parents, and other students invited to the exhibitions will have a scoring rubric to assess Maria's and the other students' work.

Exhibitions are one of many forms of authentic assessment. Movement toward authentic assessment has continued to grow as state departments of education, politicians, local boards of education, parents, and teachers recognize that it has academic and social promise for students. Teachers know that testing students with a Friday or six-week quiz does not provide them or the students with an accurate picture of learning and teaching. Also, because different curriculum models (e.g., interdisciplinary) are being used, tests that consider only one subject area (e.g., spelling or science) are inappropriate. Parents and education officials see authentic assessment as a way to restore confidence in schools. They can examine students' portfolios and attend an exhibition, receiving both a long-range and short-range view of the students' progress. By reading teachers' feedback on essays or examining scoring rubrics, parents and education officials can get an indication of teacher–pupil rapport and how teachers are preparing students to live on our culturally and socioeconomically diverse planet. Also, by examining rubrics, checklists, and anecdotal comments within portfolios, students' exhibitions, and other documents, parents can acquire substantive data about how their child is being judged, the learning opportunities they are receiving at school, and the career goal opportunities they are being steered toward.

Finally, how well teachers and education officials actively support authentic assessment will serve as an indicator of their willingness to pursue better and more equitable assessment procedures for all children, regardless of how varied their needs and backgrounds may be. This is especially relevant in this time when politicians and the business community are pushing "quick-fix" standardized paper-and-pencil tests to assess students and teachers over these other, more reliable assessment methods.

FINDING A VOICE

Kathy O'Brien hurried into the school building. She had a meeting scheduled with Mr. Shaw, her principal, in 10 minutes. Kathy had scheduled the meeting to see if Mr. Shaw would allow her to attend a workshop at her alma mater on authentic assessment and portfolios. Kathy was in her second year of teaching, but she was not comfortable using portfolio and authentic assessment. For some reason, while in college, she had tuned out the discussion in her methods classes on authentic assessment and portfolios and had avoided using either during her student teaching. Now she was floundering, and Mayfield School District's board of education and superintendent Harold Austin were very big on authentic assessment and portfolios.

Kathy had learned from her alumni newsletter that the school of education was sponsoring a two-weekend session on *All You Want to Know About A.A &P.* and her former advisor, Dr. Joanna Faulkner, was in charge. When Kathy called Joanna to learn more about the workshop, she was pleasantly surprised that Joanna remembered her from her language arts methods class. Joanna's cordiality encouraged Kathy to explain her A.A.&P. problem. Joanna was both empathetic and annoyed with Kathy. She was empathetic because she understood how Kathy was feeling, but annoyed because she remembered how Kathy had circumnavigated dealing with A.A.&P. while a teacher candidate, in spite of being told several times that many school districts were moving toward authentic assessment and portfolio use. Joanna promised Kathy that if she attended the workshop, she would give her extra time and attention.

After stopping by the teachers' lounge to put her macaroni salad lunch in the fridge, Kathy entered the school office. Mrs. Blake, the school secretary, looked up from the paper she was reading and said, "Mr. Shaw is ready to meet with you. You can go in." As Kathy moved toward the door of Mr. Shaw's office, her mind was racing a mile a minute. She was thinking, "How can I tell him that need the next two Friday afternoons off to attend a workshop on A.A.&P.?" I used all my personal days when I went to help my mom move. I can't lie and say I'm sick, since that would not work. Also, if I say I don't know anything about A.A.&P., he'll probably fire me. I told them I had used A.A.&P. when I interviewed for my teaching position."

"Hello, Kathy, come on in. Have a seat," said Richard Shaw. "Do you need coffee? Or are you a diet soda person in the morning? I'm a big coffee drinker—decaf, however. You know, Kathy," continued Mr. Shaw, "I was planning to stop by your room, so I'm glad you scheduled this meeting. Let me hear what's on your mind and then I'll tell you why I want to see you."

Although Kathy was anxious and wanted to get on with what was on her mind, she heard herself say, "Oh, please continue, Mr. Shaw."

"Kathy," he continued, "we need someone to attend a workshop on authentic assessment and portfolio use at Lincoln College. Since Lincoln is your alma mater, I thought I would give you the opportunity. Lisa Horton, who teaches fourth grade, has already consented to go. The two of you would make a great team. Your major responsibility will be to report what you learn to the faculty. What do you think?"

Kathy was flabbergasted. She thought maybe the good fairy did exist. She smiled at Mr. Shaw and said, "Of course, I will go. Lisa and I will make a good team. We will make certain that we learn a lot and bring it all back to the staff."

"Good," said Mr. Shaw. "Mrs. Blake has all of the details. She will arrange a sub for your class for the next two Fridays. I suggest that you take off midmorning to avoid the highway traffic that starts early on Friday afternoon. There is no need to come in, work half a day, and then race down the highway. Also, Friday and Saturday will be long days for you according to the program. Now, Kathy, what did you want to see me about? I hope I can help you."

Relieved, Kathy smiled and said, "Mr. Shaw, I would like to take my class to the youth concert, and I need to know the school's rules about students riding in private cars. Several of the parents have volunteered to be drivers."

"Kathy," said Mr. Shaw, "that's an easy one. Mrs. Blake has permission slips for parents to sign for such events."

After a bit more chitchat, Kathy left Mr. Shaw's office. As she proceeded down the hall to her class, she asked herself, "Should I feel dishonest for not telling the truth? Maybe I should a little bit, but there are many other things I should feel good about: I recognized my problem with authentic assessment and portfolio

---

use, I called Dr. Faulkner to learn about the workshop, and I made the appointment to see Mr. Shaw. That I didn't have to beg for time off is no one's business but my own." Nevertheless, Kathy heard an inner voice say, "If you put me in such a situation again, I am going to give you a few sleepless nights."

Most teacher candidates believe they will never be anything but awe-inspiring teachers. They believe that their love and desire to help will serve as the motivation to make them successful teachers. But Langston Hughes, in the poem "A Dream Deferred," reminds us that not all dreams become reality. Sometimes a dream, Hughes contends, "just sags, like a heavy load."[46] For some, teaching becomes the "heavy load" that Hughes suggests.

Why do some teachers allow their teaching dream to "sag, like a heavy load?" The answer, as Chad and Molly discovered at the beginning of the chapter, is complicated, because both personal and institutional factors must be taken into account. For example, as we learn from Larry Cuban,[47] some teachers adopt and hold fast to ways of teaching that are student-centered and culturally responsive, in spite of institutional factors (e.g., class size, negative comments from fellow teachers). However, we also learn from Cuban that there is a history of teachers' falling into line, unwilling to challenge the status quo and more willing to accept business as usual. What causes one teacher to take the road less traveled and others to take the one more traveled? Perhaps it has as much to do with personal choice as institutional factors. Studies of teachers acknowledge that a teacher does have agency, or the power to make important decisions about her or his teaching. So the answer is often personal and particular to each teacher. Instruction should be carried out by teachers who believe in their students' academic abilities and social success and who possess ways of thinking that encourage them to make instructional choices that best meet the needs and interests of their students.

SUMMING UP

The desire of every teacher candidate is to become a dynamic teacher. Becoming a dynamic teacher involves deciding how to instructionally engage each and every student in the classroom. Planning that takes into account students' backgrounds and needs is essential, along with having students participate in deciding what will be taught and how. Assessment is meant to be a tool that informs students and teachers about the learning experiences and opportunities needed. It is more than a form of judgment.

Power is expressed in every teaching, planning, and assessment act. An acknowledgment of the presence of power helps teachers realize that nothing in teaching is neutral. Education that is multicultural and social reconstructionist offers suggestions for teaching, planning, and assessment that can help teachers not only acknowledge power within their teaching but also use this acknowledgment to become the dynamic teachers they wish to be, meeting the needs of all students in their classrooms.

KEY TERMS

alignment   graded system
culturally relevant teaching   monitorial method
culturally responsive classroom   unit plan

QUESTIONS FOR REFLECTION

1. Why has instruction in kindergarten through college remained mostly the same for decades?
2. Why and how should lesson plans be revised each year?
3. Why are an increasing number of educators arguing that instruction should be connected to students' backgrounds and interests?
4. Why is the instructional approach of teaching girls to act like boys unsuccessful?
5. Why do Shafer and Foster argue that, with a change in what students are taught in the subject matter areas, there must also be a change in assessment?
6. What are some advantages and disadvantages of portfolio and exhibition assessment for teachers, students, parents, and education officials?
7. What are some of the issues in trying to make lesson plans that align with the EMCSR (education that is multicultural and social resconstructionist) framework in your teaching context and discipline area?

ACTIVITIES

1. Interview two or three instructors and collect data on how the teacher education program has changed over the past 10 years. During the interview, ask about changes in program entrance assessments, curriculum, location of field experiences, and increased participation with the schools.
2. Keep a record of the different instructional methods you experience over one week in your college classes. Write a brief statement on why you like or dislike each instructional method.
3. Make a record of the different teaching methods you observe during your visits to grades kindergarten through high school. Which ones seem to have the students most engaged?
4. Discuss with your cooperating teacher his or her approach to lesson planning. Is the teacher's reasoning based more on personal convenience or professional responsibility?
5. Discover if any of the teachers and students in the school where you are observing use performance assessment. If so, discuss with these teachers why they use it. Ask if you may examine one of their scoring rubrics for portfolios or exhibitions. Also, interview several students to determine their role in the assessment procedure and the extent to which they like it. What are some of the advantages and disadvantages of using portfolio and exhibition assessment?

GETTING CONNECTED

National Center on Education
and the Economy
E-mail: info@ncee.org
Website: http://www.ncee.org

The National Education Goals Panel
1255 22nd Street, NW, Suite 502
Washington, DC 20037
Phone: 202-724-0015
Fax: 202-632-0957
E-mail: NEGP@goalline.org

Standards for our schools: What we
need to do now!

SUGGESTED RESOURCES

Grant, Carl A., and Mary Louise Gomez, *Making Schooling Multicultural: Campus and Classroom.* Englewood Cliffs, NJ: Merrill, 1996.
Kumashiro, Kevin. *Against Common Sense: Teaching and Learning Toward Social Justice.* New York: Routledge Falmer, 2004.
Lawrence-Lightfoot, Sara. *The Essential Conversation: What Parents and Teachers Can Learn From Each Other.* New York: Random House, 2003.
Leistyna, Pepi. *Presence of Mind: Education and the Politics of Deception.* Boulder, CO: Westview Press, 1999.
Mitchell, Ruth. *Testing for Learning: How New Approaches to Evaluation Can Improve American Schools.* New York: Free Press, 1992.

NOTES

1. Barbara Finkelstein, "Governing the Young: Teacher Behavior in American Primary Schools" (Ph.D. diss., Columbia University, 1970).
2. Ibid., 1.
3. Larry Cuban, *How Teachers Taught* (New York: Longman, 1984).
4. Finkelstein, "Governing the Young," 19.
5. Ibid.
6. Cuban, *How Teachers Taught*, 138.
7. Ibid., 137.
8. R. Strong, H. F. Silver, and A. Robinson, "What Do Students Want (and What Really Motivates Them)?" *Educational Leadership* 53, no. 1 (September 1995):
8.
9. Ibid., 9.
10. Ibid., 11.

11. Gloria Ladson-Billings, *The Dreamkeepers: Successful Teachers of African American Children* (San Francisco: Jossey-Bass, 1994), 17.

12. Geneva Gay, "Organizing and Designing Culturally Pluralistic Curriculum," *Educational Leadership* 33 (1975): 176–183.

13. Christine E. Sleeter and Carl A. Grant, *Making Choices for Multicultural Education* (Upper Saddle River, NJ: Merrill, 1999), 166.

14. Ibid., 166.

15. John Withall, "The Development of a Technique for Measuring the Social-Emotional Climate of the Classroom," *Journal of Experimental Education* 17 (1949): 347–361.

16. Ann Dodd, "Engaging Students: What I Learned Along the Way," *Educational Leadership* 53, no. 1 (September 1995): 65–69.

17. R. J. Wlodkowski and M. B. Ginsberg, "A Framework for Culturally Responsive Teaching," *Educational Leadership* 53, no. 1 (September 1995): 17.

18. Ibid., 19.

19. Ibid., 19.

20. Ibid., 24.

21. Paulette Wasserstein, "What Middle Schoolers Say About Their Schoolwork," *Educational Leadership* 53, no. 1 (September 1995): 41–43.

22. Ann Pollina, "Gender Balance: Lessons From Girls in Science and Mathematics," *Educational Leadership* 53, no. 1 (September 1995): 30–33.

23. Ibid., 31–32.

24. Rachel Collopy and Theresa Green, "Using Motivational Theory With At-Risk Children," *Educational Leadership* 53, no. 1 (September 1995): 37.

25. Ibid., 38.

26. John Dewey, "The Child and the Curriculum," in *Curriculum and Evaluation*, ed. Arno A. Bellack and Herbert M. Kliebard (Berkeley, CA: McCutchan, 1977).

27. Ibid., 35.

28. Ibid.

29. Ladson-Billings, *The Dreamkeepers*, 17.

30. National Council of Teachers of Mathematics, *Curriculum and Evaluation Standards for School Mathematics* (Reston, VA: Author, 1989), 5.

31. Carl A. Grant and Christine E. Sleeter, *Turning On Learning: Five Approaches to Race, Class, Gender, and Disability*, 2nd ed. (Upper Saddle River, NJ: Merrill, 1998).

32. Rick Lyman, "Mexican's Memoir of an Alamo Rage," *New York Times*, 18 November 1998, A14.

33. C. B. Chimerine, K. L. Panton, and A. W. W. Russo, *The Other 91 Percent: Strategies to Improve the Quality of Out-of-School Experiences of Chapter 1 Students* (Washington, DC: U.S. Department of Education, 1993), iii.

34. U.S. Department of Education, National Center for Education Statistics, *The Condition of Education 1997* (NCES 97-388), Thomas Smith, Beth Aronstamm, Yupin Bae, Susan P. Choy, and Nabeel Alsatar (Washington, DC: U.S. Government Printing Office, 1997).

35. Ibid.

36. Mary Shafer and Sherian Foster, "The Changing Face of Assessment," *Principled Practice in Mathematics and Science Education* 1, no. 2 (Madison: Wisconsin Center for Educational Research, Fall 1997): 1.

37. Ibid.

38. Mark Driscoll and Deborah Bryant, *Learning About Assessment, Learning Through Assessment* (Washington, DC: National Academy Press, 1998), 1–2.

39. Concetta D. Ryan, *Authentic Assessment* (Westminster, CA: Teacher Created Materials, 1994).

40. Fred M. Newmann, Walter G. Secada, and Gary G. Wehlage, *A Guide to Authentic Instruction and Assessment: Vision, Standards and Scoring* (Madison: Wisconsin Center for Educational Research, 1995), 15.

41. Ellen L. Kronowitz, *Your First Year of Teaching and Beyond*, 3rd ed. (New York: Longman, 1999).

42. F. Paulson, L. Paulson, and C. Meyer, "What Makes a Portfolio, a Portfolio?" *Educational Leadership* 48, no. 5 (1991): 60.

43. James Barton and Angelo Collins, "Starting Out: Designing Your Portfolio," in *Portfolio Assessment: A Handbook for Educators*, ed. James Barton and Angelo Collins (Menlo Park, CA: Addison-Wesley, 1997), 2.

44. Theodore Sizer, *Horace's Schools* (Boston: Houghton Mifflin, 1965), 208.

45. Bill Johnson, *Performance Assessment Handbook: Performance and Exhibitions* (Princeton, NJ: Eye on Education, 1996).

46. Langston Hughes, "Harlem (A Dream Deferred)," in *The Compact Bedford Introduction to Literature*, ed. Michael Meyer (Boston: Bedford Books of St. Martin Press, 1994), 1227–1228.

47. Cuban, *How Teachers Taught*.

TEACHING: THE PROFESSION

FOCUS QUESTIONS

1. Why is there so much debate over teachers being regarded as professionals?
2. What is the purpose of teacher licensure, and how do licenses and certifications differ?
3. What is the role of the placement and career services office in helping teacher candidates obtain a job?
4. How do teachers' salaries compare with those of other professionals?
5. How do teacher associations and organizations influence the work and professionalism of teachers?
6. How do teachers influence relations with others (groups and individuals) through the professionalization of teaching?

THE DEBATE OVER PROFESSIONALISM IS AN ANNOYANCE AT TIMES

Mr. Lockwood said, "At the close of our last Introduction to Education class meeting, Susan, you raised a significant question, one that has special implications for all of you. As I recall, you asked, 'Is teaching a profession?' I would argue yes, and add that the term *professionalism* has taken on different meanings over the years. Additionally, these meanings, or interpretations of what constitutes a profession, especially the teaching profession, have not included teachers' perspectives. More important than what I think is, what do you think, Susan?"

"Yes, it is a profession," responded Susan. "But it annoys me that there is so much debate about teachers being professionals and that teachers make so much less than people in comparable professions."

"Yeah, I know it's a profession," claimed Brenda. "Both my mother and father are teachers, and that's what I have learned from them. But I had to find a new roommate because my old roommate was constantly giving me grief about becoming a teacher, and life is too short to constantly debate that issue."

Shawn asked, "Mr. Lockwood, is one of the reasons that there is debate over teaching being considered a profession because teachers are mostly women?"

Shirley said, "Yes, Shawn, that's what a few of the readings say, but the *real* reason is you men are control freaks and have problems with women as equals. You always want something for nothing, or you want to pay less than you should. Much of what you read does not directly tackle the problem of professionalism and teacher salaries. Much of it is about what teachers are not doing and about poor student achievement."

Susan said, "What are the teachers' unions and other education organizations doing to make teaching equal to all the other professions, and to get teachers more money?"

Dick asked, "Will standards, national board certification, and membership in professional organizations and associations improve teacher status, salaries, and benefits, or do membership fees mainly go to support political candidates?"

Mr. Lockwood responded, "Shawn, I agree with Shirley's answer to your question. The feminization of teaching included the idea that teachers, because they were mostly women, were not the 'breadwinners' of the family and therefore could be paid less than men, who were regarded as the breadwinners. And Susan and Dick, we will answer your questions about teachers' unions, standards, certification, professional organizations, and more in this very class!"

The discussion in Mr. Lockwood's class typifies often heard statements of concern, along with questions that teacher candidates have about their profession. This chapter seeks to outline the many debates that are considered when discussing teaching as a profession.

TEACHERS AS PROFESSIONALS

The authors of this text, like most teachers, believe that teaching is a profession. In fact, most teacher candidates and teachers we know do not spend time or lose sleep over the question "Is teaching a profession, or is it not?" Nevertheless, there has been a debate for decades about whether or not teachers are professionals. The position within the debate that teachers are not professionals is rooted in ways of thinking that minimize the power teachers have to affect education for teachers and students and to affect policies and procedures that govern their profession. It was argued, and still is, that professionals such as doctors and lawyers have a body of specialized knowledge grounded in the sciences that is unique to their profession and that teachers do not have such a codified body of knowledge. Critics of the idea of teachers as professionals argue that teachers have borrowed heavily from other disciplines for their body of knowledge, including psychology, and do not have their own "knowledge base."

Christopher Lucas claims that a **profession** must meet the following criteria:

1. The members perform a unique, definite, and important social service, one that those outside the profession are unable to supply or generate on their own.
2. Those practicing the profession possess specialized knowledge inaccessible to those not trained and they are able to demonstrate that knowledge with expertise.
3. A period of preparation—a training program—is indispensable for successful performance.
4. Members of the profession enjoy broad autonomy, direction, and independence of action in determining the substance of their work.
5. Members assume personal responsibility for judgments made and acts performed in the exercise of their duties.
6. Attention is given to service, more so than economic gains.
7. There is a comprehensive and authoritative self-governing organization to which the members give their allegiance and support. This governing organization is empowered to define and pass judgment on what constitutes acceptable or "best" practice.
8. The profession has a regulative code of ethics governing entry into the field, along with standards and procedures for penalizing those found in violation of its tenets and precepts.[1]

How many of these criteria do you believe that the students in Mr. Lockwood's class will argue that teaching meets?

Placed in a historical context, the journey to professionalization for teachers is much more than just an interesting story. It is a commentary on how the role of teachers as professionals is kept uncertain and out of the control of teachers. In the early days of this country, teachers were not provided a high level of professional training. Society's major concern was not professionalization for teachers. Instead, it was getting individuals to "teach" children the basics and in some areas, the Bible. Ease of access meant that many would be permitted to enter teaching. At the same time, ease of access curtailed the need to offer higher rewards to teachers. This practice contrasts sharply with the increasingly rigorous training required for doctors and lawyers. As we have previously noted, the principal expectations for teachers were moral conduct and having a bit more knowledge about the basics than the students they were teaching. Lucas argues that teachers were expected to know "little more than a brief review of the common branches of learning to be taught."[2] Those in charge of schooling were not concerned with promoting breadth or depth of knowledge in the minds of those preparing to teach. The goal of teacher training was to make certain that teacher candidates gained minimal acquaintance with a limited, highly circumscribed curriculum and that they acquired the practical competence needed to convey its substance to schoolchildren.[3] Along with the lack of professional training, teachers were denied a voice in the bureaucratic structure of schooling where policy decisions were made about the educational requirements and training of teachers. The muting of teachers' voices undermined their contribution to efforts toward achieving professional status.

The recent educational reform effort demands that teacher candidates demonstrate their preparedness to receive a license through the establishment of curriculum and performance standards, along with different certification levels such as National Board Certification. Such reform efforts are lending credence to the claim that teaching has its own knowledge base and therefore meets the criteria for being classified as a profession. This chapter brings together much of the information that is of concern to teacher candidates as they think about teaching as a profession. We begin with teacher licensure and certification.

TEACHER LICENSING AND CERTIFICATION

Lifelong learning is a term that describes the continuum of teacher learning from a candidate's preparation program through his or her entire career. The concept of lifelong learning is central to the professionalization of teachers. Over the decades teachers have increasingly engaged in updating their subject matter knowledge and instructional skills. Once you finish your initial coursework and become a certified teacher, you are not finished learning your craft. Teachers participate in myriad types of learning, ranging from workshops and training that takes place through schools' staff development programs to university coursework, degree programs, and sabbatical leaves.

Traditional License

Licensing systems are used by many professions to select individuals into their field and prevent those considered incompetent from practicing in the field.[4] Setting the standards of licensure for most professions is the state's responsibility. Some states issue more than 900 licenses in professions such as electrical, law, cosmetology, and medicine. According to Benjamin Shimber in 1977, the U.S. Department of Health, Education, and Welfare defined licensure as "the process by which an agency of government grants permission to persons to engage in a given profession or occupation by certifying that those licensed have attained the minimal degree of competency necessary to ensure that the public health, safety, and welfare will be reasonably well protected."[5]

A teacher license is conferred when a teacher candidate demonstrates minimum standards of competence. Earning the license is a major step in the journey toward excellence. However, the nature of the journey is particular to each state. Forty-two states require that teacher candidates take a licensure test as part of the process to receive the teaching license, although each state has different exams.[6] In many states, candidates take the Praxis exam; in New York, they take a test called the New York State Teacher Certification Exam (NYSTCE). Some states require tests of academic content; others require a test of content plus a test of pedagogy. More often than not, the tests contain a writing section to ensure that the prospective teacher is competent in structure, grammar, and usage. Each state sets its own cutoff scores for passing the tests. Teacher education programs are required to report their passing rates on required tests to their state education department, which then reports the scores to the U.S. Department of Education. Passing cutoff scores vary widely from state to state, as do the resulting failure rates.[7] The result of using different cutoff scores is that teacher candidates who earned their license in one state and who are working in their first teaching job with candidates who earned their license from another state may have been assessed for the license by different criteria. In some states, cutoff scores have been raised in order for the state to say, "Our teachers are the best qualified." Just as the standardized, fill-in-the-bubble tests that students have to take are not a sure-fire method of assessing knowledge and skill, attaining a high score on a test is not a certainty that a teacher candidate will be a successful teacher. Similarly, a low passing score does not indicate a teacher's potential quality of teaching practice.

The way that licensure tests are used to assess teacher candidates varies among state and educational programs. Some use scores on the tests as one criterion for admission to the teacher education program. Others use scores on the test as a prerequisite for student teaching or a condition of graduation. Some states use scores for the initial licensure of teachers and require that teacher candidates take multiple tests. Assuming that teacher tests are a given, what do you think is the fairest way to use them: as an initial gatekeeper to determine who enters the teacher education program, as a gatekeeper just before student teaching, or as a gatekeeper to determine who can receive the license?

Tests are only one aspect of the teacher licensing process. Most professions set and enforce standards in three ways: (1) professional accreditation of preparation programs; (2) state responsibility for issuing licenses to applicants; and (3) state certification of practitioners. The process of accreditation is one of peer review, meaning that in higher education, teams of professors, teachers, and university administrators visit a campus to certify that a program is meeting its stated outcomes. The accreditation of teacher education programs is carried out voluntarily by higher education institutions through one of two outside agencies approved by the U.S. Department of Education: the National Council for the

Accreditation of Teacher Education (NCATE) or the Teacher Education Accrediting Council (TEAC). Most institutions also participate in regional accreditation organizations. Of the approximately 1,367 institutions that prepare teachers, all but 38 are nationally or regionally accredited. In addition to accreditation by an outside agency, in most states the Department of Education conducts periodic evaluations of the teacher education programs within the state. Most colleges and universities also conduct in-house evaluations of their programs. In all of these forms of peer review, teacher candidates, cooperating teachers, and university faculty are often interviewed for their perspectives on the program. These occasions provide an opportunity for teacher candidates to constructively critique their program and have a voice in the evaluation, enabling teacher candidates to see that power is not static and that their voice can influence institutional norms and procedures. Critiques by teacher candidates often lead to improvement in the program, especially when problems are "hidden" from faculty members who not aware of the difficulties teacher candidates are experiencing.

Alternative Teacher Certification

An alternate route to teaching is any entryway into teaching other than a traditional teacher education program typically found at a college or university. Approximately 40 states plus the District of Columbia provide alternative routes to entering teaching, though only 8 states reported they had some type of alternative teacher certification program in 1983.

The idea of alternative certification has a long history. During the 19th century it was fairly common for each school district to hire and certify its own teachers, and many large urban school districts set up their own normal schools.[8] Feistritzer and Chester note:

> The term "alternative certification" has been used to refer to every avenue to becoming licensed to teach, from emergency certification to very sophisticated and well designed programs that address the professional preparation needs of the growing population of individuals who already have at least a baccalaureate degree and considerable life experience and want to become teachers.[9]

Or as Zeichner and Schulte put it:

> Alternative teacher certification programs refer to any alternative to the 4-year or 5-year undergraduate teacher education program including both those programs that have reduced standards and those that hold teachers to the same standards as college and university based undergraduate teacher education.[10]

It is estimated that approximately 125,000 teachers have been licensed using an alternative route.[11] This number represents about 7.5% of the teachers certified during the period 1983–1993.[12]

Although routes to certification vary greatly, most include an entrance requirement for content expertise and experience in the field. Many states require that alternate route candidates hold a bachelor's degree and pass the same standardized test that traditionally prepared candidates are required to take (e.g., Praxis,

NYSTCE). Some programs range from requiring full teacher certification for entrants who have already completed a four-year undergraduate degree to offering 8 to 12 weeks of instruction prior to granting a teaching license. Some states also provide individually tailored programs based on reviews of the candidate's academic and professional background.

There are several reasons for alternative certification. In the past, the United States relied almost exclusively on high school students who attended college and entered the teacher preparation program for the quality and quantity of teachers. Alternative certification is appealing to those entering much later in their lives and later in their academic careers. These "career changers" are seeking a faster route to the classroom. Programs such as Troops to Teachers are designed to attract professionals from other fields (for example, from the U.S. armed forces) to make a career change to teaching. Other programs, such as the New York City Teaching Fellows and Teach for America, are designed to attract graduates from the nation's leading universities into teaching in high-needs urban and rural areas for at least two years. Such programs have been developed to respond to the teacher shortage, which has been cited a reason for the need for alternative certification. Perhaps the most controversial alternate program is the American Board for Certification of Teacher Excellence (ABCTE). In this program, candidates are simply required to pass a multiple-choice exam via computer in order to attain a teaching credential. To date, ABCTE's program has been approved only in Pennsylvania, Florida, and Idaho.

In a study of alternative teacher certification programs, Zeichner and Schulte concluded that alternative certification programs are here to stay. They found that because of the severe teacher shortage in urban and outlying rural schools across the United States and a continuing shortage of qualified teachers in mathematics, science, bilingual education, and special education, traditional teacher education programs in the 1,300 plus colleges and universities that prepare teachers will not be able to address the problems by themselves.[13] It is important for us to point out that these data stand in contrast to the evidence about who is entering teaching through traditional routes. Most candidates in college- and university-based teacher education programs are White females from suburban and rural areas. In general, they desire to teach close to where they grew up. Although the statistics indicate that there is a teacher shortage, they also tell us that many of the candidates who complete teacher certification programs never teach. One reason is that they are not able to get jobs in suburban schools and they do not want to teach in urban or very rural areas. Additionally, the difficulty of completing an undergraduate degree in mathematics, science, or a language other than English in addition to teacher certification courses leads candidates into other fields or into alternative programs.

We currently have little data on how alternatively certified teachers fare in the first years of teaching, how long they actually stay in the classroom, or their impact on student learning. What we do know is that poor children, those in high-needs districts, are most likely to be taught by a teacher who was certified through alternate means. We need much more information on the impact of alternative certification before judgments can be made about alternative versus traditional teacher preparation.

Would Susan, Shawn, and Shirley argue that alternative certification such as Teach for America is a plus or a minus in their argument that teachers are professionals? Many professionals are willing to relocate to accept a position in their field. Are you willing to relocate to obtain a teaching job?

National Certification

Licensing is different from certification because a license is conferred when minimum standards of competence are demonstrated. *Certification* is a professional recognition of higher standards of accomplishment and is generally associated with advanced study and practice.

The National Board for Professional Teaching Standards was created in 1987 for the purpose of developing nationwide standards for advanced teacher certification. This independent organization is governed by a 63-member board of directors, of whom 42 are classroom teachers. The board sets up procedures for establishing a voluntary national system of board certification, which includes a review process designed to identify and reward exceptional elementary and secondary teachers.[14] Board members believe that having a voice and a comprehensive and authoritative self-governing organization empowered to define and pass judgment on what constitutes acceptable or best practice is essential for teaching to be seen as a profession. The board believes that its most immediate goals are to "establish high and rigorous standards for what accomplished teachers should know and be able to do" by forging "a national professional consensus," to "reliably identify teachers who meet these standards," and to "communicate what accomplished teaching looks like."[15]

The National Board argues that certification assessment activities will enhance the culture of teaching, "making it possible for teachers to advance in responsibility, status, and compensation without leaving the classroom."[16] Teachers are encouraged to search for new knowledge and better practices through a study regimen that includes collaboration and reflection with peers and others.[17] The fee of $2,300 for teachers seeking board certification is often subsidized by the federal and state governments and the local school board. Paying the fee is one way the government encourages teachers to seek National Board certification; some districts also pay a bonus of up to $10,000 for teachers who obtain certification. The National Board is developing standards and assessment in more than 30 certification fields according to subjects taught and the developmental level of the students. To be eligible for National Board certification, teachers must have the following: (1) a baccalaureate degree; (2) a minimum of three years' teaching experience at the early childhood, elementary, middle, or secondary level; and (3) a valid state teaching license for each of those three years, or where a license is not required, teachers must be teaching in schools recognized and approved by the state.[18] In 2003–2004, the following certificates were available:

6.1. Early Childhood/Generalist (students ages 3–8)
6.2. Middle Childhood/Generalist (ages 7–12)

6.3. Early and Middle Childhood/Art (ages 3–12)
6.4. Early Adolescence through Young Adulthood/Art (ages14–18+)
6.5. Early and Middle Childhood/Physical Education
6.6. Early Adolescence through Young Adulthood/Physical Education
6.7. Early and Middle Childhood/English as a New Language
6.8. Early Adolescence through Young Adulthood/English as a New Language
6.9. Early and Middle Childhood/Literacy—Reading Language Arts
6.10. Early Adolescence/English Language Arts (ages 11–15)
6.11. Adolescence and Young Adulthood/English Language Arts (ages 14–18+)
6.12. Early Adolescence/Science
6.13. Adolescence and Young Adulthood/Science
6.14. Early Adolescence/Mathematics
6.15. Adolescence and Young Adulthood/Mathematics
6.16. Early Adolescence/Social Studies—History
6.17. Adolescence and Young Adulthood/Social Studies—History
6.18. Early Childhood through Young Adulthood/Exceptional Needs (ages 3–18+)
6.19. Early Adolescence through Young Adulthood/Career and Technical Education
6.20. Early Childhood through Young Adulthood/Library Media
6.21. Early and Middle Childhood/Music
6.22. Early Adolescence through Young Adulthood/Music
6.23. Early Childhood through Young Adulthood/School Counseling
6.24. Early Adolescence through Young Adulthood/World Languages Other than English

Teachers who pursue National Board certification are increasing their status as professionals by demonstrating that they possess the specialized knowledge, skills, and dispositions that characterize master teachers. The route to achieving National Board certification is a difficult one, but it is an important step in being a professional who is a lifelong learner.

SEARCHING FOR A TEACHING POSITION

Getting your first teaching position is a dream fulfilled, and an excellent culmination to your long journey to become a teacher. As noted in Chapter 1, many teacher candidates have anticipated this event since their preteen years and they have particularly looked forward to securing that first job for the last four years of their education. The first position a teacher candidate receives can greatly influence a career in teaching. This is especially so because 29% of beginning teachers leave the profession after only three years and 39% have left teaching after five years.[19] Teachers cite "job dissatisfaction and the desire to pursue a better job, another career, or to improve career opportunities in or out of education" as reasons for leaving teaching.[20]

Teachers who depart because of job dissatisfaction most often link their departure to low salaries, although this is not the main reason they leave the profession. The significant factors that lead many new teachers to leave are lack of support from school administrators, lack of student motivation, discipline problems, and lack of teacher influence in school governance.[21] The amount of support that a new teacher gets from colleagues and administrators is key to whether or not the teacher leaves. It is therefore important that time and attention be put into the search for the first teaching position in order to optimize getting the best situation available. The search can start with your visit to the placement and career services office on your campus.

Placement and Career Services Office

Most colleges and universities have established a **placement and career services office**. Students and alumni of the university are eligible to register for these services. Initially, the placement bureau in most schools of education was established to bring together teacher candidates and prospective employers. The current mission of the education placement and career services office is to enhance the job search and career management skills of graduates of the school of education. A teacher candidate can expect to receive help in the preparation of employment credentials and resumes, including electronic and paper portfolios. Teacher candidates have opportunities to participate in discussions of job search strategies and skills and to receive overall advice on career planning. Many placement and career services offices hold workshops to prepare candidates for the different phases of job searching. Workshops such as the following are held on campus to get candidates ready for the recruitment season:

> Portfolios for Teachers
> Resume/Cover Letter Writing for Education
> Job Search and Resume Writing for Industry and Nonprofit Sector Jobs
> The Education Job Search
> The Educational Employment Interview

Some teacher candidates may wonder whether the electronic or paper portfolio is the better way to go. The jury is still out on which is better; both have advantages and disadvantages. However, many teacher preparation programs, including some alternate routes to teaching, are requiring that student teachers develop electronic portfolios because faculty believe that they are one way to demonstrate technology competence as well as teaching competence.

You will need to keep in mind that there are different types of portfolios for different purposes. You may be required to create a portfolio during your teacher preparation program with your professors assessing your work periodically, or you may be required to complete one portfolio at the end of your program to demonstrate that you have met the outcomes of your program. These types of developmental and cumulative portfolios are often organized by program outcomes and contain many, many artifacts that demonstrate your growth as a beginning professional. For example, you may be asked to compare the first lesson plan you ever wrote with one that you successfully taught during student teaching or internship. You may be asked to include a reflective essay that analyzes your progress over time in lesson development. These types of portfolios are not what you would take to a job interview. The interview committee typically wants to see only your best work, and although you want to demonstrate your ability to be reflective, the committee will not have time to wade through the numerous artifacts that demonstrate your competence in multiple areas. Your interview portfolio should be a document (paper or electronic) that all members of the interview committee—principals, teachers, and parents—will understand. Your career services advisor or the faculty in your program will be able to assist you in creating an interview portfolio from the larger, more comprehensive program portfolio that you create.

A candidate's employment credential, the dossier that is sent by career services, may include demographic information, a course summary page, and letters of reference. These items may be stored at the placement office. Most universities will charge a yearly processing fee if the candidate remains actively on the job market and requests to have credentials mailed to prospective employers. Although forms and procedures may differ from school district to school district, there is sufficient uniformity in practice to make using the services of the placement and career services office a workable process.

When to Use a Letter of Inquiry

If for some reason the placement and career services office is unable to provide information on the school districts in which the teacher candidate is interested, a *letter of inquiry* may be sent to the Personnel Office or Office of Human Resources in the school district of interest. Such a letter of inquiry may seek to discover if a teaching position is available or to inform the office of the teacher candidate's interest in the event of a vacancy. Before writing the letter, obtain the name of the director of the office to which the letter is to be sent. Using a personal name instead of "To Whom It May Concern" or "Superintendent of Schools" demonstrates a teacher candidate's professionalism. The name of the existing administrator as well as any other pertinent information can usually be obtained through a state's School Directory. Using such resources is the first sign that a teacher is willing to do research and to use resources in her or his professional pursuits.

When seeking a position, there is no magic number regarding how many applications or letters of inquiry to complete. Decisions should be guided by considering how scarce or abundant the opportunities are in the location of interest. If job opportunities are scarce, it may be wise to broaden the geographical area of the search. Teacher candidates who understand and teach according to the precepts outlined in this text will be comfortable and ready to work in all school districts.

Personal Interview

In this age of electronic communication, many prospective employers may "see" teacher candidates before conducting a personal interview. Classroom videos and electronic portfolios allow a search and screening committee to evaluate a candidate before the actual in-person interview. The credentials and resume package from the placement and career services office provides much useful information. Nevertheless, most search and screening committees, including the building principal, want to meet candidates personally. A personal interview enables them to determine a teacher candidate's ability to express him- or herself personally and to hear candidates express their educational philosophy and values. During the interview, candidates can be asked follow-up questions and are available to offer clarifications about anything in the dossier that may not be clear.

Following are several hints useful for the interview: getting off to a good start, knowing when to shut up, knowing when to speak up, and knowing what to wear.

Off to a Good Start   How do you relax, when your heart is pumping and your knees feel weak? You have to tell yourself that you are the greatest, based on your knowledge, personality, preparation, and experiences. Remind yourself that you are standing at the threshold of your long desired dream, suck it up, relax, and get on with it. We know this is easier said than done! Do your homework on the district where you have the interview. Go on the district website and look at the school report card. Talk with people in the community who may have children in the school. Do they use a certain whole-school reform model? How are the test scores as compared to other schools in the district? Is a specific system of classroom management used?

Arrive at the school a few minutes early for your interview. This gives you an opportunity to look around the school and notice the environment. What is on the walls? How does this make you feel? When you meet the secretary and the interview team, be cordial and polite. Make your initial responses to questions comprehensive, but to the point. Avoid brownnosing or kissing up regardless of how excited you are about the job. Let the *real* you shine through. Remember that the people interviewing you are human; they too have anxieties and may feel uncomfortable being on the search and screening committee. Their goal is to do the best job possible. Therefore, if you can help make them comfortable, you will increase your chances of being offered the teaching position.

Know When to Listen   An interview has three important phases. The first phase is when the search and screening committee is quizzing the candidate. At this time the candidate should let the committee determine the direction and set the pace of the interview. The committee is probably asking a set of prepared questions. These questions are asked of every candidate who applies for the position. The purpose of this procedure is to ensure fairness for each candidate. Responses to questions should be as clear and precise as possible, and should take into account practice as well as theory. For example, you may be asked, "Please explain your philosophy of discipline and classroom management." Your response needs to address what you plan to do to maintain an orderly classroom and establish control and rapport with the students. Included in this response may be ideas from the discipline and management theories of, for example, Alfie Kohn or Jacob Kounin. To claim that philosophically you believe in self-discipline and you will encourage students to get to know you by calling you by your first name may lead the search and screening committee to believe that you are not ready for the real world of teaching. Although your response may not adequately capture all that you actually intend to do, it is wiser to describe your intended practice than to get caught up in verbal exchanges that are difficult for the search and screening committee to believe without seeing you teach. Use your portfolio to demonstrate how you would implement various techniques that you describe. For example, if you are describing how you would manage the classroom, show the committee photos of how your class was arranged during student teaching and describe how you used the arrangement to develop self-discipline and clear management strategies.

It is important to look directly at the person who asks you a question. However, if your response is somewhat long or complex, looking at other committee members is recommended. Have your portfolio labeled so that as you answer questions and move your eyes from person to person, you don't have to spend a lot of time looking for the example you want. Many principals have told us that when a candidate answers the questions in a straightforward manner and uses clear portfolio examples to demonstrate that he or she has actually implemented some of the strategies being discussed, it often leads to that candidate's getting the job.

Ask Good Questions   The second phase of the interview is the time when the job candidate is encouraged to ask questions about the job. The nature of the questions asked informs the committee about your interest in the job and how you think about teaching. Questions could include the following:

1. Tell me why teachers like to teach here.
2. Do any of the teachers live in the community?
3. Please give me a brief history of the school.
4. What expectations do parents and community members have for the teachers and the school?
5. What is the nature of parent–school relations?
6. What is the average class size?
7. Is there a set curriculum that I will be expected to follow in each subject?
8. Are there additional responsibilities other than classroom teaching, such as teaching in after-school programs?
9. To what extent are teachers involved in school governance?
10. If I am offered the position, where can I locate information on a salary schedule, health benefits, and other personnel data?

Interview Reflection   Once the interview is over and after you have had time to "come down" and relax, take a few minutes to reflect on the experience. Some questions you might ask yourself are the following:

1. Did I give clear responses to the questions? If not to some, what could I have said to respond better?
2. How were my actions? Did I seem arrogant, or did I come across as if I would be a good colleague? Did I include knowledge of both theory and practice in my responses?
3. Do I have additional questions about the position?
4. Did the search and screening committee seem to include people I will enjoy working with and can learn from?
5. Did I learn anything from the interview that I can carry into the next one, if I don't get the assignment?

It is important to understand how power and multicultural education work through the hiring process in school districts. You may not get a job you want for several reasons, and you need to be aware of the possibility that you may have to go on several interviews before getting a job and that the job you are offered may not be your first choice. For example, if you are a female candidate who desires to teach in kindergarten, the district may prefer an equally qualified male candidate because there are so few men teaching in the lower grades. If you are a female high school biology candidate, you may have an advantage if the rest of the high school science faculty are men. If you are a White candidate, you may lose a job to a candidate of color in a district that has a predominantly White faculty and is attempting to build a teaching staff that mirrors the demographics of the community and the United States. If you speak only English, you may lose a job to a candidate who is bilingual, especially when the school community is bilingual. You should take some time to explore how you feel about the myriad factors that enter into a district's decision about whom to hire. We have seen some of our teacher candidates develop bitter feelings about losing a job to a candidate who had a different gender, ethnicity, or linguistic background. They immediately assume that the successful candidate was "less qualified" but got the job simply because of the external characteristic. It is important to understand that districts have a responsibility to serve the community, to present various role models to the students, and to select from a pool of qualified candidates the teacher who meets the needs of the district at the time of hiring. Most teachers have three, four, or five interviews before successfully landing a position.

Knowing What to Wear   The days have long passed when most teachers wore heels and skirts or ties and jackets. It is not unusual to see some teachers in jeans when they are doing a messy project or when the school is having "school spirit" day and jeans and a school sweatshirt are the norm. During your student teaching, you probably adapted your dress to parallel that of other teachers at the school. However, dressing more formally is a wise thing to do for the interview. First impressions are important. Businesslike attire shows that this interview is very special for you. After you receive the assignment, you may wish to continue with more formal attire for the first few weeks as you meet and greet your new colleagues and students' parents. Here we are saying that a successful entrance into most groups or communities is conditioned by ways of thinking that often have a history established through the effects of power relations. This is especially important to our discussion of teachers as professionals and how they are invested with a sense of power, to be known as professionals, to take part in school governance, and to have good relations with community members.

Our discussion about knowing what to wear considers how teachers as professionals will be viewed upon entrance into a new school community, simply through attire. Of course, conduct, language, and communication used are just as important. We want readers to be aware of how power circulates and how they are affected by it on those first days, making those first impressions, when they enter a new school community. When we discuss dress with our candidates, we often rankle some in our classes. We believe that it sends a positive and important message to students when teachers "dress up" rather than "dress down" to teach students each day. You are sending them the message that they are important and you have respect for them based on your outward appearance. It is not an exaggeration to say that most of the best teachers we know (there are some exceptions!) dress in the classroom in clothing that is not formal but is considered to be "business casual." Of course, norms of dress vary from community to community. You can conduct your own informal survey of students on this matter. Ask elementary, middle, and high school students about the teachers for whom they have the most respect and get them to explain their rationale. Ask them about how those teachers dress on a daily basis. You will be able to develop your own conclusions about this issue!

TEACHERS' SALARIES

Most teacher candidates want to know what their approximate starting salary will be. Some are curious about how their salary compares with others in different fields. We answer these questions by discussing the following: (1) dollar amounts; (2) comparison with other occupations and professions; (3) relationship of salaries to different positions and years of experience in the teaching profession.

Dollar Amounts

According to the American Federation of Teachers, the estimated average annual teaching salary in 2001–2002 was $44,367[22]; the estimated average salary in 1998 was $39,347.[23] Exhibit 6.1 shows the 10-year trend in annual salaries since 1993. The 2.7% gain in the average teacher salary in 2001–2002 was the first time that salary growth had exceeded inflation by one percentage point since 1987–1988. In fact, teacher salaries accounted for a much smaller proportion of total education spending in 2002 than they did 40 years ago. In 1964–1965, the average percentage of education expenditures allocated to teacher salaries was 53.4%. In 2001–2002, teacher salaries made up just 37.1% of education spending.[24]

Average beginning salaries for teachers are usually higher in medium and larger school systems than in smaller school systems. Also, dollar amounts vary according to geographical area. However, the northeast states typically have the highest salaries, followed by western, middle, and southeastern states. The estimated average beginning salary for classroom teachers across the country for 2001–2002 was $30,719. North Dakota's $20,988 was the lowest, and Alaska's $36,035 was the highest.[25] Exhibit 6.2 gives the average beginning salary for teachers by state and region.

Teacher salaries influence some who may wish to teach. They argue that the pay does not match the responsibility. Salaries also influence society's perception of teachers as "working class" or "middle class." Some years ago, Dan Lortie argued that teachers' salaries help to define their middle-class standing. Teaching

| EXHIBIT 6.1 | TEN-YEAR TREND IN AVERAGE ANNUAL SALARIES FOR PUBLIC SCHOOL CLASSROOM TEACHERS, 1993–2003 |

School Year	Elementary	Secondary	All
1992–1993	34,350	35,880	35,029
1993–1994	35,233	36,566	35,737
1994–1995	36,088	37,523	36,675
1995–1996	37,138	38,397	37,642
1996–1997	38,039	39,184	38,443
1997–1998	39,008	39,945	39,351
1998–1999	40,097	41,303	40,550
1999–2000	41,326	42,571	41,827
2000–2001	42,937	44,028	43,400
2001–2002	44,308	45,246	44,683
2002–2003	45,658	46,119	45,822

Source: American Federation of Teachers, *Survey and Analysis of Teacher Salary Trends 2002* (Washington, DC: Author, 2002), available at http://www.aft.org//research/survey/national.html.

is seen as a white-collar occupation because of the educational level required to be certified. These two factors have helped teachers garner a certain amount of community respect.[26] Lortie believed that because of these advantages (white-collar instead of blue-collar, a bit more money in the pay envelope, and four years of college), teaching became an important route into the middle class for many lower-class and working-class people. Teaching provided the way for students from blue-collar homes to become white-collar.[27]

However, the prestige associated with teaching, including the salary levels of teachers, has been limited to a certain extent by the ambivalent feelings of society toward teachers. On one hand, society places the same high expectations on teachers as on other professionals. They are expected to be lifelong learners, to continue professional study in order to increase their competence, to participate in civic and recreational activities, and to be good role models. On the other hand, society is not sure whether to recognize teachers as professionals. Some members of society believe that almost anyone with a college education can walk into the classroom and teach. Some teachers contribute to this way of thinking when they tell teacher candidates to forget what they have learned in methods classes. Rather than considering early field experiences and student teaching as supervised experiences in which candidates learn to blend theory and practice, they undermine the profession. Although it may seem that all you need to learn about teaching you learn in student teaching, we want to point out that without guided preparation you could not be successful in student teaching!

Teachers in this country were not historically provided a high level of professional training. Some, it is argued, preferred to get teachers by easing access

EXHIBIT 6.2 AVERAGE AND BEGINNING TEACHER SALARIES, BY STATE AND REGION

New England	Average	Beginner	Southeast	Average	Beginner
Connecticut	$52,376	$34,551	Georgia	$43,933	$33,283
Rhode Island	51,619	30,272	North Carolina	42,118	29,359
Massachusetts	48,732	32,746	Virginia	41,752	31,238
New Hampshire	39,915	25,611	South Carolina	39,923	27,268
Vermont	39,771	25,229	Florida	39,275	30,096
Maine	37,300	24,054	Tennessee	38,515	28,857
Mid-East	**Average**	**Beginner**	Kentucky	37,951	26,813
New York	$51,020	$34,577	Alabama	37,206	29,938
DC	51,000	31,982	West Virginia	36,775	25,633
Pennsylvania	50,599	31,866	Louisiana	36,328	28,229
New Jersey	50,115	35,311	Arkansas	36,026	27,565
Delaware	49,011	25,493	Mississippi	33,295	24,567
Maryland	48,251	31,828	**Rocky Mountains**	**Average**	**Beginner**
Great Lakes	**Average**	**Beginner**	Colorado	$40,659	$28,001
Michigan	$52,497	$32,649	Idaho	39,194	25,316
Illinois	49,679	31,761	Utah	38,153	28,806
Indiana	44,609	28,440	Wyoming	37,853	26,773
Ohio	44,266	29,953	Montana	34,379	22,344
Minnesota	42,175	29,998	**Far West**	**Average**	**Beginner**
Wisconsin	41,056	27,379	California	$54,348	$34,180
Plains	**Average**	**Beginner**	Alaska	49,028	36,035
Iowa	$38,230	$27,553	Oregon	46,033	31,026
Kansas	37,059	26,596	Nevada	44,621	28,734
Nebraska	36,236	26,010	Hawaii	44,306	31,340
Missouri	36,053	27,554	Washington	43,470	28,348
North Dakota	32,468	20,988	**U.S. Average**	**$44,367**	**$25,735**
South Dakota	31,383	23,938			
Southwest	**Average**	**Beginner**			
Texas	$39,230	$30,938			
Arizona	38,510	27,648			
New Mexico	36,716	27,579			
Oklahoma	32,870	27,547			

Source: American Federation of Teachers, *Annual Survey of State Departments of Education.*

rather than offering higher rewards, a practice that contrasts sharply with the increasingly rigorous training required of doctors and lawyers. Teachers' relatively low level of professional training, the proliferation of alternate routes to teaching that are solely dependent on passing a test to be certified, and teachers' relative lack of power within the firmly established bureaucratic structure of schooling are factors contributing to the continued confusion regarding their professional status.

If teachers are to receive the salaries necessary to maintain a standard of living appropriate to an important and respected profession, they will have to be perceived in a more positive and professional manner. The work of national, state, and local teacher associations and organizations to help the public recognize and accept the professional status of teachers is paramount. Equally significant, if not more so, in encouraging the public to accept and respect teachers as professionals is the effort of each classroom teacher and teacher candidate as she or he communicates with students, parents, and community members.

Comparison With Other Professions

Although our purpose for using power as a theme of this text has more to do with helping teachers to help students, the effects of power on some (e.g., beginning teachers) more than others is profoundly clear when teachers' salaries are compared with those in comparable professions. Decades of data indicate that the situation is not greatly improving.

The ability to attract high-quality teacher candidates depends on the salary and benefits package. Although teachers have made some small gains over the years, they continue to be paid less than those in other professions requiring a similar educational background and training.[28] The ambivalent attitude of the public toward teachers as professionals is seen when the average salary of public school teachers is compared with salaries in other white-collar professions. Salaries in other white-collar occupations remain high in comparison to those of teachers—ranging from twice as much for a full professor at a public university to 7% more for an assistant professor (see Exhibit 6.3). It is important to keep in mind that there are some differences in the amount of education required to do each job listed in Exhibit 6.3. For example, lawyers must earn an advanced degree and pass the bar exam in order to practice law. The educational requirements for teachers, on the other hand, vary from state to state. Some states require that teachers have a master's degree in order to achieve full certification. Others simply require that teachers document the completion of professional development hours that can be fulfilled through a wide variety of activities.

The information presented in Exhibit 6.3 is quite conclusive.[29] For example, the mean teacher salary in 2002 was $44,367; the mean salary of an assistant, or beginning-level, university professor was $47,476; the mean salary of an Accountant III was $54,503; the mean salary of a computer Systems Analyst III was $74,543; the mean salary of an Engineer IV was $76,298; the mean salary of an attorney was $87,978; and the mean salary of a full professor was $89,631.

EXHIBIT 6.3 **TRENDS IN TEACHER SALARIES COMPARED TO THE AVERAGE ANNUAL SALARIES OF SELECTED WHITE-COLLAR OCCUPATIONS**

	Mean Teacher Salary	Accountant III	Buyer/Contract Specialist III	Attorney III	Computer Systems Analyst III	Engineer IV	Full Prof. Public Doctoral	Asst. Prof. Public Comprehensive
2002	$44,367	$54,503	$59,981	$87,978	$74,543	$76,298	$89,631	$47,476
2001	43,187	52,664	57,928	82,712	71,155	74,920	84,007	45,147
2000	41,731	52,323	57,035	77,150	66,849	72,427	82,535	43,362
1999	40,475	49,257	57,392	69,104	66,782	68,294	78,830	41,940
1998	39,360	45,919	54,625	71,530	63,072	64,489	75,150	40,760
1996	37,594	42,172	46,592	66,560	57,772	60,684	69,760	39,000
1994	35,764	39,884	44,616	64,532	54,548	56,368	64,860	37,220
1992	34,027	37,648	41,392	65,884	53,300	53,404	61,950	35,730
1990	31,347	35,489	38,385	59,087	47,958	49,365	57,520	32,730
1988	28,071	33,028	36,040	55,407	45,093	46,680	51,080	28,380
1986	25,260	31,143	33,580	50,119	41,548	42,667	45,600	26,000
1984	21,974	28,721	30,610	44,743	38,057	39,005	39,800	23,000
1982	18,945	25,673	27,424	39,649	NA	34,443	35,700	20,800
1980	16,100	21,299	22,904	33,034	NA	28,486	30,100	17,800
1978	14,207	18,115	19,590	27,738	NA	23,972	26,400	15,900
1976	12,591	15,428	17,122	24,205	NA	20,749	24,200	14,600
1974	10,778	13,285	14,659	21,082	NA	17,929	21,600	13,100
1972	9,705	11,879	13,117	18,392	NA	16,159	19,800	11,800
1970	8,635	10,686	11,665	16,884	NA	14,695	18,100	10,800
1968	7,423	9,367	10,260	15,283	NA	13,095	16,100	9,500
1966	6,485	8,328	9,252	14,052	NA	11,784	14,100	8,300
1964	5,995	7,908	NA	12,816	NA	11,016	12,500	7,700
1962	$5,515	$7,416	NA	$11,844	NA	$10,248	NA	NA

Source: American Federation of Teachers, Department of Research, *2002 Salary Survey,* Table II-5, available at http://www.aft.org//research/survey/tables/tableII-5.html.

BENEFITS

Teachers receive numerous benefits from the state and school districts where they are employed. Benefits usually include health insurance, dental insurance, group life insurance, tenure, tax-sheltered annuity programs, retirement funds, leaves of absence, and sabbatical leaves. However, benefits in some school districts may differ from those in other school districts. Teachers' unions, which you will read about later in this chapter, have played an important role in ensuring that teachers receive the benefits accorded other professionals. It is wise to seek information about benefits and about the teachers' union when applying for a teaching position.

SIGNING THE CONTRACT

Affixing your signature to the teaching contract makes it a legal document. The board of education that offers the contract and the teacher who signs that contract have entered into a legal commitment. The contract normally states the terms of service, the nature of the assignment, the salary, and the method of payment. Contracts are not easily broken unless both parties agree, or where state law indicates differently. In some cases, when one party wants to get out of the contract, party A will not allow party B to break the contract, or party A will insist on some financial remuneration. For years, teachers in most states, unlike many other professionals, have been able to break their contract without agreement from the board of education, especially if they do it before a certain date—typically, July 1 or August 1. Recently, in part because of teacher shortages, states are becoming much less lenient. The breaking of a contact is considered in some circles something that *professionals* do not do. It is viewed as unethical. Teachers who ignore returning to their assignment or living up to the provisions of the contract may lose their state teaching license for a year.

During contract discussions, the school district may ask for the following documents: official transcript of college training, certificate of health, birth certificate, and state license to teach. Teacher candidates may wish to consider the following suggestions before signing a contract:

1. Check out as many as possible or at least several teaching opportunities where you are qualified to teach.
2. Review as many contracts and positions as possible, but do not sign a contact until you have completed your homework. For example, the school board in the adjacent town may offer you a contract. Your review of the contracts, including salary schedule and health benefits package, may lead you to discover that, all things considered, both districts offer basically the same to their beginning teachers, with the exception that the dental plan in one district is far superior to the other district's plan. A dental plan may or may not influence your decision of which job to accept. Nevertheless, it is better to know about which benefits will or will not be yours.
3. Know the deadline date by which the contract must be returned.
4. Once you have signed the contract and it has been accepted, remove your name from other job opportunities.

TEACHING OPPORTUNITIES

Some teacher candidates begin their preparation program with the intention of seeking employment in a parochial, independent, or private school system. Others hope to get the necessary background to do home schooling with their children.

Sometimes these candidates are silent about their future ambitions. They are concerned that they will be viewed as "different" by their peers. We have found that when this silence prevails, all teacher candidates are denied the opportunity to learn different perspectives from one another on the different, varied values and purposes of education. The silences are the effects of power within the class that privilege some students more than others. It is important to remember that although you may desire a specific teaching opportunity, you never know what life will hold and you may find yourself teaching in a private or home setting. Learn all that you can from your colleagues!

CAREER OPPORTUNITIES IN EDUCATION

There are numerous employment opportunities within the field of education other than classroom teaching. Earning a teaching license can be seen as the first step on the career ladder in the field of education. There are also many opportunities outside of education for teacher candidates who have earned their licenses.

Substitute Teaching

Substitute teaching allows one to practice the craft of teaching at different times in different places. It provides a way for teachers to work in a school district if they have not been able to obtain a permanent position. Sometimes substitute teaching can lead to being first in line when a teaching position becomes available. Subbing is also a way to learn about the schools in a district. You may have already tried your hand at substitute teaching and realize how difficult it is! The benefits are that you rarely have the daily amount of work that a classroom teacher faces, but the drawback is that you do not have your own class of students. Subs also do not enjoy the pay and benefits of full-time teachers. Excellent substitute teachers are very difficult to find and you may find yourself, if your circumstances warrant, enjoying the life of a substitute teacher.

Administration

Teachers are the largest group of professionals within the field of education, and they are important to the successful education of students. Administrators, beginning with the superintendent of schools, play a major role in influencing the policy and practice that make instructional success for teachers possible. It is rare that a teacher candidate says, "I want to teach so that I can eventually become a superintendent." Such an idea usually comes after teaching successfully for several years, working in various administrative positions, and earning an administration license by taking courses and participating in experiences (e.g., internships) needed to meet the qualifications. Although this discussion may seem a little far removed at this point in your career, it is important because, even if you never choose to become an administrator, you will be working with them.

Superintendent of Schools The chief administrator totally in charge of the operation of the school system is the superintendent, who is directly responsible to the board of education. The local board of education hires the superintendent and can fire that superintendent. The superintendent is similar to the CEO of a corporation and, in fact, many school districts have budgets and an employee roster larger than those of many companies. The superintendent presides over the budget, works with the building and district administrators to ensure that the district meets its goals, and is responsible for personnel, staff development, and parent–community relations. The turnover of superintendents is high; the tenure of a superintendent with a school district is often three to five years. Academic and social success or failure of students and the school district is laid at the doorstep of the superintendent.

Currently there is a striking absence of women and persons of color in superintendent positions; approximately 4% of superintendents are women or persons of color. On average, female superintendents are younger than male superintendents, although most were older when they received their first administrative position. They are more likely than their male counterparts to be Democrats. They have usually spent more time teaching before entering administration. As superintendents, women use educational research much more than men to resolve problems; in their leadership styles, they place a higher value on enabling and empowering those they work with.[30] Superintendents of color, especially African Americans, are most often located in urban areas or areas where the population is largely African American. They began to rise to the superintendency in the 1980s in locations where the school system was facing major financial problems. Nancy Amez wrote at the time, "Even a cursory observation can lead one to the conclusion that when big systems went bankrupt and when they became overwhelmingly black, black men and women were recruited."[31]

The reasons why women and people of color make up such a low percentage of superintendents, it can be argued, have to do with the effects of political power relations that exist throughout the educational and social systems of this country. Simply stated, these systems have worked to privilege mostly White, male, middle-class people who are invested not only with more material resources to achieve better educational and financial opportunities, but also are invested with "cultural capital." Having cultural capital means having access to privileged positions because of the cultural and language background within which individuals or groups exist and feel at ease. Currently, White middle-class men have the educational and professional opportunities to become administrators and to rise within educational systems because of their privileged ease of access to the language, dispositions, and credentials perceived as necessary for the all-responsible superintendent of a school district.

As an example of how cultural capital works, until Tiger Woods entered the golf scene, there were few people of color on the professional golf circuit. Tiger generated interest in golf among youth of color and started a foundation dedicated to teaching inner-city youth the game of golf. Golf has been a sport of the privileged because it is expensive and many public and private courses have historically barred persons of color from playing. Knowledge about and skill in golf were forms of social capital that were restricted to certain people. Golf, for a long time, was known as a "good old boys" sport, meaning that it was primarily played by wealthy White men. Power in a community rested with the wealthy males, and much business was done (and continues to take place) on the golf course. It has happened that the town "fathers" have selected the superintendent because he was in the correct social circle, belonged to the same golf club, and went to the same church. Although we like to think that this type of thing is from an age long past, there are many communities where women and persons of color have difficulty gaining membership in some golf clubs or, in the case of women, are excluded from playing golf at certain times or entering certain areas of the club. It is interesting to see that many school organizations now sponsor golf outings, and access to formerly restricted sports such as golf is becoming more inclusive.

School Principal   The principal is the administrative and instructional leader of the school. She or he is a person who should possess a thorough knowledge and understanding of how children from different cultures and backgrounds grow, develop, and learn. After teaching for several years, it is not uncommon for a teacher to consider becoming a principal. For some teachers, this administrative position is viewed as the next best way, outside of being a classroom teacher, to influence the education of students.

Teacher candidates will observe that the majority of the principal's time is devoted to supervision and interaction with staff, interaction with students, and discipline or student management. Next after those three areas the principal allocates time to parent/community and local business contacts, facilities management, curriculum and instruction, and student evaluation and placement. Safety and security issues and staff development are not ignored by the principal, but in most schools the principal has to prioritize all of the things for which he or she has responsibility and often these items end up coming last. Each principal must weigh those factors that affect his or her school community and make decisions accordingly.[32]

The average salary of principals is more than $35,000 higher than the average salary of teachers.[33] Exhibit 6.4 lists 2003–2004 average annual salaries for teachers, principals, and superintendents working in the school system.

Pupil Personnel and Guidance Services

Traditionally, teachers have been responsible for counseling and guiding students in schools. They are still responsible for many of these activities. However, with the recent accelerated rate of social change, the responsibilities of guidance counselors and pupil personnel (i.e., the school psychologist, the school social worker, the school health care worker) have expanded into both developmental and preventive services. These positions are staffed by full-time professionals.

The earliest form of student guidance focused on vocational counseling. Now, the role of the school counselor has been more broadly defined to include counseling in education and personal adjustment as well as in vocational areas.

EXHIBIT 6.4   **AVERAGE SALARIES PAID PERSONNEL IN SELECTED PROFESSIONAL POSITIONS IN ALL REPORTING SCHOOL SYSTEMS, 2003–2004**

Position	Average Annual Salary
Superintendents (contract salary)	$125,609
Assistant superintendents	100,808
Subject area supervisors	67,098
Principals:	
Elementary school	75,144
Middle school	80,060
High school	86,160
Assistant principals:	
Elementary school	62,213
Middle school	66,360
High school	70,495
Classroom teachers	45,646

Source: National Association of Elementary School Principals.

In addition to helping each student realize his or her maximum personal, educational, and vocational potential, counselors also help the teaching staff and parents better understand each student and the characteristics that contribute to his or her uniqueness. The counselor may run a support group for children whose parents are divorced, do individual counseling and assist the teacher in developing a plan for an individual student who is experiencing difficulty, and offer a workshop for parents on course selection for middle school students. The school counselor, along with the psychologist, interprets test results, analyzes the information on students' records, and helps teachers interpret information about students from outside agencies. Particularly at the small school district level, counselors also help students to deal with crises and other stressful situations (e.g., death of a family member, denial of their favorite choices for college, global issues such as war) and to learn to cope with their problems. In larger school districts, they are often aided in this regard by the school psychologist.

Although the school psychologist performs somewhat similar functions to those of the guidance counselor, he or she works with a more restricted group of students. This clientele represents students who are recognized as exceptional in the sense that they are gifted or have cognitive, emotional, or physical problems. Specifically, the school psychologist administers a battery of tests and develops case studies of exceptional students, often on an individualized basis. The school psychologist may observe the child in the classroom and consults with teachers regarding students' programmatic opportunities. The psychologist keeps the staff advised of any professional literature that might be pertinent in their daily contact with students.

The school social worker, like the other personnel specialists, helps each student realize his or her personal and educational potential. Unlike the school counselor or psychologist, who usually functions within the confines of the school, the social worker goes out into the community and into the individual homes of students. The social worker, in a cooperative effort with parents, attempts to improve school and home situations for students.

School health services are usually provided by a school nurse and in some larger districts perhaps by a school doctor. In addition to identifying those children with hearing or sight loss or those with common childhood diseases, the school nurse aids teachers in planning and implementing health instruction in their classroom. Two areas presently demanding school nurses' attention are drug education and sex education. Nurses are usually responsible for the total health care program of students in their school(s). Some school districts are fortunate enough to have occupational and physical therapists who work with students who have physical disabilities and who need therapy during the day. They, along with the special education teacher, help the classroom teacher in adapting the physical environment to meet the needs of students with physical disabilities.

To consider the different perspectives of the school personnel we have just described, we offer the example of a meeting about a student—let's call him Carlos—in which representatives of the pupil personnel and guidance services, teachers, and a school psychologist meet with Carlos's parents. If a teacher candidate were present, she could observe the flow and the effects of power as each person addresses the needs of the student from his or her perspective. The process for determining whether a special education placement is the "least restrictive environment" for a student who is not experiencing success in the classroom begins when the classroom teacher, after having worked with the student for a number of months, determines that the student's problems are not typical. If, in response to the teacher's concerns, the school psychologist had administered tests and the "team" had come together and decided that special education services seemed necessary, then a meeting would have to be held at which school and administrative personnel were present. If Carlos's parents disagreed, not wanting their son to be considered "different" from his peers, they would come to the meeting and state these concerns. They might also address the major concern that Carlos speaks two languages, with Spanish as his first language and English his second. Were tests conducted in both languages? Was the teacher doing everything in the classroom to consider not only Carlos's needs but the needs of other non–native English speakers? These are questions that Carlos's parents could raise and demand to be addressed before their son is placed in the special education system—a system within, but apart from, the regular education system.

If the school psychologist did not test Carlos in Spanish as well as in English, what would her perspective be? She might note that it is not part of her job to translate tests. Whose job would that be? If the teacher did not use techniques that were especially useful in addressing non–native English speaking learners, then what would his perspective be? He might note that teaching with techniques that are considered the domain of ESL teachers is not part of his job. He might also point out that the only way to get some extra help is to label Carlos so that he can get more individualized attention from either ESL or special education teachers.

Carlos's parents may want Carlos to get more individualized attention but not to be separated from his peers. They might raise questions about whether Carlos will be in the classroom at all times, using his peers to learn new material as much as his "special" teachers.

Noting these different perspectives can help teacher candidates to see the questions that may be raised with the different positions that school psychologists, teachers, parents, and students may take when addressing concerns for students. The relations of power have historically privileged the "experts" in schools—the psychologists, social workers, teachers, and administrators—who use the language of schooling when meeting parents to communicate concerns about students. The effect is a refusal to acknowledge the position of parents, who are bound to know their children better than teachers and other school personnel. Yet they do not always bring the language or jargon of schooling, and other cultural capital, to the meetings with school personnel.

Perhaps parents should also be considered part of the school "personnel," in that their knowledge about their children offers as much to the process of addressing student concerns as does expert knowledge from the intelligence and other standardized tests through which some school personnel come to know students.

A question that Mr. Lockwood could ask his Introduction to Education students is whether professionalization of teachers would exclude further consideration of parents' knowledge and expertise. Professionals often get the credential that allows them the position of saying they know best, leaving others at a deficit if they don't have the same "professional" status.

Librarian and Technology/Media Specialist

The rapid technological growth of our society has resulted in an abundance of information for students to learn. The development and maintenance of school computer labs and media systems can facilitate this learning by delivering information through varied modalities. A career as a librarian or as a technology/media specialist provides a challenge to a person who is interested in enabling students to "both adjust to and influence the changing society in which they live." Sometimes, these are two different positions because a school librarian typically has an advanced degree in library science. Other times, depending on the state and the certification areas, the librarian and the technology/media specialist is one staff member.

The traditional forms of library instruction are still a vital part of the technology and media programs. The librarian orients students to the school library, helps them to develop good study habits and acceptable library behavior, encourages them to read, and teaches them to use the computer, related technologies, and available materials independently. Librarians and technology/media specialists evaluate, select, order, and organize technological and print materials and equipment. In doing this, the staff members usually works in cooperation with the teachers and building administrators so that the school's computer and media services will be coordinated with the instructional program being used. The technology/media specialist may also provide staff development programs in the evaluation, selection, and use of equipment and materials as well as being responsible for the care and upkeep of the technology in the building.

Specialized Teachers

Educational research has provided vast amounts of evidence that early success in reading is the foundation for academic success for all students. A number of specialized teacher roles facilitate a focus on literacy in schools. The reading teacher is typically a classroom teacher who has an advanced degree in the teaching of reading. Some districts are also sending classroom teachers for specialized training in specific reading programs, such as Reading Recovery. These teachers are often designated as "reading coaches" or "literacy coaches" because they may not have an advanced degree in the teaching of reading but are trained in a specific type of reading instruction.

An experienced teacher may be tapped by the school district to serve as a new teacher "coach" or mentor teacher. Mentor teachers are typically teachers who are recognized as outstanding by the district and provided with released time to assist beginning or struggling teachers in the classroom. For example, a teacher may be in danger of not attaining tenure because he or she is having difficulty with classroom management or assessment. The district may send in a mentor or coach for a year to try to provide the struggling teacher with support to improve.

Paraprofessionals

At the same time that you will be expected to meet the individual needs of students in your classroom, you may be faced with a large class size and increasing involvement in various nonteaching activities. A common complaint of teachers is that they spend so much time on noninstructional tasks. It is no wonder that teacher effectiveness is not always at its peak when teachers are responsible for so many nonteaching duties and so many children with individual problems. In this context, **paraprofessionals,** sometimes termed "teacher aides," take on a very important role in schools.

School aides provide a wealth of talent and resources to enrich the total educational program. Whether working in the school library, organizing a school newspaper, providing clerical assistance, accompanying a special needs student to the physical therapist, or tutoring individuals, paraprofessionals can help to make student achievement a reality in a school. In effect, they give teachers time to teach and reteach a concept if needed, to consult with colleagues and students, and to plan effectively. Some aides bring specific skills, such as being bilingual, that help the school in unique ways.

Effective leadership on the part of teachers often determines the effectiveness of paraprofessionals. Teachers need to have a well-defined purpose, specific directions, and training sessions for teacher aides and volunteers. School aides and others who assist in the classroom must be aware of the professional and legal standards associated with their work. Ideally, their skills should complement the work of the teacher to whom they are assigned. The need for open communication cannot be overemphasized, because proper channels of communication can help ensure their effectiveness.

The salaries and qualifications of school aides vary considerably. In some areas, the salaries vary according to the skills required and the duties aides are expected to perform. In some districts, aide positions require a two-year program of preparation at the community or junior college level. Under the No Child Left Behind Act, all paraprofessionals who support instruction in Title I schools (high-needs schools) must meet certain academic requirements; they must have at least an associate degree or two years of college or meet a standard of quality set by formal state or local assessment.

Paraprofessionals are dedicated, competent people who can provide essential services to a school's operation. It would be almost impossible for many schools to operate effectively were it not for the paraprofessionals.

Volunteer Personnel

Many people enjoy volunteering to work in schools. Volunteers may include people from various backgrounds and from different age groups; they may be college students, retired persons, parents, businesspeople, or government workers. The essential characteristics for volunteers include time and a willingness to share it, an affirmative attitude toward young people, an interest in the community's progress, and a concern for making education more effective for all students. Volunteers can fill many roles in a school—tutor, reading buddy, guest speaker, mentor—but volunteers should receive instruction on their roles and duties, and their work should be supervised.

Comprehensive planning is vital to developing a successful volunteer program. Planning should include introducing the program to the community, identifying goals and specific tasks, and establishing an evaluation procedure for measuring progress. Community members are more likely to become involved in and to better understand the educational process that occurs in the schools when there has been adequate planning and they have had a role in the planning.

Although excellent training can enhance their success, many volunteers also attribute their success to the very fact that their work is voluntary. PreK–12 students are often impressed that people will give up their time, without remuneration, in order to help them improve scholastically. Programs in which the elderly offer their experience and skills have been particularly beneficial for both the students and the volunteers. Too often students stereotype the elderly as being somewhat passive, inactive, and uninteresting. Inviting elderly people into the classroom as volunteers can help improve students' attitudes not only toward them, but also toward the aging process itself.

In summary, teachers have the responsibility to meet the varied educational needs of students, and aides and volunteers can help this to become a reality. When adults other than the teacher share in classroom experiences, learning is no longer narrowly defined as what occurs within the classroom or within the school but is broadened to include what takes place in the community. Furthermore, when children interact with a number of adults, they are more likely to make friends with at least one of these individuals; the overall effect may be to help personalize and humanize the school experience.

Nonteaching School Personnel

Nonteaching personnel include the school secretary, the school custodian, the security guard, and the school bus drivers. These people are very helpful to the classroom teacher and to the students, and it is important for teachers to develop good working relationships with them.

The school secretary (or a member of the secretarial staff) is often the first person to greet visitors to the school. He or she often provides that important first impression to students, parents, and staff about the school. Besides being responsible for public contact, the secretary provides clerical assistance to the principal and a variety of invaluable services to the classroom teacher. For example, the secretary maintains files on supply companies, orders classroom materials, keeps records of who enters the building and for what purpose, and distributes supplies. Because the secretary's duties are not only varied but also relate to so many people in the school, it is important that his or her time is respected and that he or she is treated as a valuable member of the educational team.

The major responsibilities of the school custodian are to maintain the physical plant of the school and care for school property. However, this is really an inadequate explanation of the influence the custodian often has with both students and teachers. Many adults fondly remember their school custodians with a smile because, in addition to maintaining the physical plant, they often served as unofficial counselors, good listeners, and wonderful friends. To teachers, custodians and security guards often convey the impression that they are in complete control of the school, and they can be very helpful in making classrooms attractive and safe places to learn.

You may wonder what role the school bus driver plays in a teacher's life. You won't have to ask that question the first time one of the students in your class gets in trouble on the bus. What happens on the way to school often affects how a student's day will go, and if you work with the bus driver to help him or her understand the unique needs of your students, everyone's day will go better!

A wise teacher never fails to thank the nonteaching staff and regularly indicates how much the staff member is appreciated. You never know when that staff member will make your day!

TEACHER SUPPLY AND DEMAND

In the 1990s, there was a sharp rise in the number of individuals studying to be teachers. Over the past 15 years, the number of teacher candidates finishing programs has jumped 49%. The average undergraduate who is studying to become a teacher (80% of teacher candidates) is a young White female. Ten percent of the teacher candidates are African American, 6% are of Latino origin, 3% are Asian/Pacific Islanders, and 2% are American Indian/Alaskan Native.[34]

Recent efforts to reduce class size, enrollment increases, teacher retirement, and general attrition are the reasons for a demand for teachers. It is estimated that about 210, 000 new teachers per year will be needed for the next 10 years. *New teachers*, an often-used term, does not necessarily mean teachers who have just completed their teacher preparation programs. The 210,000 new teachers will include teachers who have taken a leave from teaching and decide to return (approximately 33%) and individuals who received their teacher license earlier but did not begin their teaching career (approximately 24%). The remaining approximately 42% will be those who have just completed their college programs.[35]

Especially in some urban areas, as well as in some suburbs, there is rapid teacher turnover. For example, in Washington, D.C., students have a 1 in 6 chance of getting a teacher who is new to their school or new to the profession. Approximately 50% of the new teachers within an urban district leave after three years.[36] Such supply and demand data indicate both the problems that beginning teachers are facing and the unfairness of the educational system to many students who are in need of a quality education. Reasons for such turnover include inadequate salaries, poor working conditions, teacher transfers to less stressful positions, lack of mentors, and inadequate teacher preparation.

This situation again allows us to remind you that although some argue that there is a teacher shortage, we would argue that the shortage exists only in certain areas. Wealthy suburban districts are not experiencing teacher shortages across the board. We encourage you to consider moving to take a teaching position that some might consider a challenge. There are jobs available if you are willing to relocate to take a position in an area different from the area where you grew up.

PROFESSIONAL ASSOCIATIONS AND ORGANIZATIONS

Teachers have taken on an increasingly active role in the efforts to achieve recognition of their professional status. Teacher associations and professional organizations are active in demanding full professional status, with all associated rights and privileges. They communicate members' interests to school boards and legislators in a more effective manner than any one individual teacher can and thus have become important agents for dealing with teacher concerns. These organizations, in addition to looking after the interests of teachers in areas such as salary, benefits, and grievance procedures, also provide moral supports. The two major national teacher organizations in the United States are the **National Education Association (NEA)** and the **American Federation of Teachers (AFT).** Before exploring these organizations in more detail, we will briefly review the history and growth of teacher organizations in the United States.

Early in this country's history, teachers who had legitimate complaints about their financial status or working conditions had little recourse but to confront the town leaders and hope for the best. In some cases, their demands were met, but more likely they were at the mercy of local school boards. Teachers were expected to be meek and modest and not to rock the boat. Further, they were often viewed as undeserving of higher salaries. Eventually teachers realized that group petitions got a readier response from school boards than did individual requests from teachers. There was strength in numbers, and teachers began to organize.

Teacher associations were few in number during the early 19th century and were primarily county or city organizations, 30 teacher associations were established at the state level between 1840 and 1861. During the same period, in 1857, the first national teachers' organization, the National Teachers Association, was established. Membership in this group remained relatively low until the 1870s, when it merged with the National Association of School Superintendents and the American Normal School Association to form the National Educational Association. In 1906, the "al" was dropped from "Educational," and the organization became the National Education Association (NEA). In that same year, the NEA was chartered by an act of Congress, and the charter was officially adopted at the association's annual meeting in 1907.

Many teachers, however, continued to feel the need for an organization focused primarily on teacher interests and concerns. Therefore, the first national "union" of teachers, the American Federation of Teachers, affiliated with the American Federation of Labor, was established on May 9, 1916. Membership in both major organizations was relatively low until they attempted to meet the challenge of teaching problems head on. In the 1930s, motivated by low salaries and reduced job opportunities, teachers started to join in greater numbers.

After World War II, teachers became more activist. Faced with rising inflation, teachers felt the need for more money in the 1940s and 1950s, and consequently, carried out more than 100 strike threats from 1942 through 1959. Although most of these strikes were over salaries, other goals included recognition of teacher groups as bargaining agents, stronger school personnel policies, and bigger school budgets. In 1947, even though several states had legislation providing for minimum salary levels, the average teacher's salary was only around $2,380. During the 1960s and 1970s, teacher activism continued to increase, as a result of five major factors: long-standing economic injustice to teachers, the growth in size and bureaucratization of the schools, changes in and among teacher organizations, the growing availability of the mechanisms for activism, and the changing social climate.

Teachers have traditionally had little control over their profession. Legislators determined licensure procedures and school boards determined working conditions. Both of these bodies have thus served as major influences on what is defined as quality education. Today teachers have more formal training than ever before. In addition, there has been an increase in teacher specialization, and specialized roles such as librarians, counselors, and special education personnel are increasingly prevalent. As specialization and level of education increase, aspirations to a more professional status also increase. Teachers feel that a rise in their professional status should be reflected in the degree of control they have over decisions that affect them and their classrooms.

Teachers want not only more power to control their profession but also more remuneration. They care about issues such as class size, the work hours in a day and week, and the type of professional development offered. Teachers feel that their salaries and working conditions should be comparable to those of other occupations requiring a bachelor's degree for licensure. For example, teachers are unhappy that engineers and nurses often outearn them. As salary is one index of professional status, teachers are increasingly demanding their share. It is a joke among teachers that teaching is the only profession in which you cannot go to the restroom anytime you like because you cannot leave your students alone in the classroom.

Both the National Education Association and the American Federation of Teachers have been playing an important role in improving conditions for teachers. Although historically these two teacher organizations have competed for members and power, most recently they are attempting to work together. Next, we discuss each major organization in terms of its purposes, membership, organization pattern, and services to members.

The National Education Association (NEA)

The National Education Association (NEA) is the oldest and largest organization devoted to public education in the United States. It was founded in 1857 in Philadelphia and now has its headquarters in Washington, D.C. The objectives of the National Education Association were first documented in the original NEA congressional charter in 1906 and have remained unchanged since then. Its purposes are "to elevate the character and advance the interests of the profession of teaching and to promote the cause of popular education in the United States." Although these same objectives have been proclaimed throughout the 20th century, and now in the 21st century, it is only recently that the NEA, like its counterpart, the American Federation of Teachers, has become an active vehicle for promoting its stated objectives. According to the NEA, there are 2.6 million members who serve at every level of education, from preschool to university graduate programs.[37]

Membership in the National Education Association tends to be concentrated in rural and suburban areas more than in large metropolitan areas. Membership is "open to all persons actively engaged in the profession of teaching or in other educational work or to persons interested in advancing the cause of public education who shall agree to subscribe to the goals and objectives of the association and to abide by its Constitution and By-laws." Eighty percent of the membership consists of classroom teachers. Although the NEA has never excluded any educator from membership on the basis of race, before 1954, when many southern states had a dual school system, they also had two separate affiliates in NEA. In the 1960s, this dualism started to change, and by 1966, the American Teachers Association, a national organization of African American educators, merged with NEA.

In 1978, NEA had affiliated organizations in each state as well as in some territories, and it had some 10,000 local affiliates. The total membership at that time was 1,698,736. Presently there are 2.7 million members working in schools and colleges, and annual membership dues represent the bulk of the association's income.

To meet the needs of educators working in a variety of positions—classroom teachers, supervisors, and administrators—NEA offers diverse programs in areas of professional development and economic and personal welfare for teachers. Six goal areas, three support systems, and three administrative services comprise the program structure of NEA. The six goal areas are human and civil rights in education, leadership in solving social problems, an independent united teaching organization, professional excellence, economic and professional security for all educators, and significant legislative support for public education. The goal area of professional excellence, for example, includes the following four broad objectives:

- To make pre-service and in-service teacher education relevant to the practice of teaching as measured by association policies
- To stimulate educational research that is responsive to the problems of classroom teachers
- To provide information that will enable association and affiliate leaders to influence developing public policies on education
- To provide information systems that support individual members in their professional practices

Actions directed toward these objectives include, for example, dissemination of information about NEA to members through *Today's Education*, the official publication of NEA, and through other publications, such as the *NEA Research Bulletin*.

The NEA support system includes the departments of research and communications, and UniServe. The research division of NEA, established in 1922, publishes research studies on the status of the teaching profession and on various aspects of U.S. education. The UniServe support system establishes special funds to help teachers in various ways. For example, the DuShane Emergency Fund provides for legal services and interest-free loans to teachers whose civil or human rights have been violated. The communications support division provides members with information upon request.

The three administrative services of NEA are business and finance, which houses the huge data-processing and record-keeping systems of the organization; employee relations, which serves as the personnel office for NEA; and special services, which deals with such matters as insurance, legal services, and educational travel plans.

The American Federation of Teachers (AFT)

The objectives of the American Federation of Teachers (AFT), as outlined in its 1977 constitution, include the following:

- To bring teacher associations into relations of mutual assistance and cooperation
- To obtain for teachers and other educational workers all of the rights to which they are entitled
- To improve standards for teachers by promoting better preparation, encouraging relevant in-service training, and securing the working conditions essential to the best performance of professional service

- To promote educational programs and conditions in American schools, as will enable their students to equip themselves better to take their places in the economic, social, and political life of the community
- To promote the welfare of children by providing progressively better education opportunities for all
- To fight all forms of bias in education

The AFT has tended to be more union-oriented in philosophy than the NEA. It has introduced collective bargaining methods into salary negotiations with local boards and has backed its demands with demonstrations and strikes. The current mission statement of the AFT states the following:

> The mission of the American Federation of Teachers, AFL-CIO, is to improve the lives of our members and their families, to give voice to their legitimate professional, economic, and social aspirations, to strengthen the institutions in which we work, to improve the quality of the services we provide, to bring together all members to assist and support one another and to promote democracy, human rights and freedom in our union, in our nation and throughout the world.[38]

Since its formation in 1916 and the days when John Dewey held the first membership card for this teachers' union, AFT membership has grown to more than 1 million members in 2001. These members are organized into more than 2,000 locals, which comprise the most important units of the AFT. The membership ranks of the AFT are drawn primarily from medium-sized or large cities, such as New York, Chicago, Washington, and Detroit, in part because large cities with large working populations have traditionally been union-oriented. A major breakthrough in membership followed an incident in New York City in 1960–1961, when the United Federation of Teachers, an affiliate of AFT, was selected to represent New York City teachers in contract negotiations, thus defeating the Teacher's Bargaining Organization, which was supported by NEA. This victory gave the AFT a new beginning; the victory in one large city heightened the appeal of AFT to urban teachers and they began to more actively recruit members. Similar victories soon followed in other large cities.

The American Federation of Teachers is teacher-oriented. Although administrators were not originally banned from joining the union, few actually did, and many teachers dropped their membership once they were promoted to an administrative position. In 1966, the AFT amended its constitution and now prohibits superintendents and other administrative personnel from joining the federation. In addition to teachers, locals also admit other educational workers, including librarians, school nurses, counselors, and paraprofessionals. Local unions establish their own membership dues following the guidelines in the AFT constitution. In addition to membership dues, additional funds for support at the national level are obtained from other AFL-CIO unions as well as from the AFL-CIO itself.

After 1954, the AFT expelled certain locals that had discriminatory membership policies. It also started Freedom Schools in the early 1960s, providing instructional services for children in districts that had opted to close their public schools rather than desegregate.

The AFT produces a number of publications, including *American Educator, American Teacher, Inside AFT,* and *AFT on Campus.* Like NEA, AFT is concerned with major educational issues, defending academic freedom, and striving for greater participation by teachers in educational decision making.

Possible Merger

Although NEA and AFT have developed from two different historical positions, today their differences are less apparent. Talk of a merger between the two professional groups has surfaced over the years. In the past, the major obstacles to merger were AFT's union affiliation and NEA's policy of membership for administrators. The strike, which was once an area of strong disagreement between the two organizations, is now used by other organizations. And most recently, in addition to its increased union-oriented activities, NEA has experienced a shift in power from administrators to classroom teachers.

Mergers most likely will occur at the local level before a national merger becomes a possibility. Whether such a merger would be a good thing still remains an open question. On the one hand, teacher activism has been greatly stimulated by the competition between these two organizations. On the other hand, improvement of working conditions, increased monetary rewards, and protection of personal freedom perhaps will occur more rapidly if the two organizations merge.

Still another significant point to consider is the danger that one strong professional organization for teachers could exist mainly for the benefit of its members, rather than for students. This danger needs to be addressed by both teacher organizations in the context of any potential merger. There is also the question of teachers' commitment to these organizations. Although many teachers join professional organizations, they are often unwilling to give their time and effort to participate actively. They remain passive, joining only because they are expected to or for basic survival in the sense that the organization will defend them and lobby for them.

Teacher candidates must determine whether they will become active or passive members of a professional association. At the local level, will you meet your representative, read newsletters, familiarize yourself with the issues that concern you, attend meetings, and volunteer your services to the association? At the state level, will you familiarize yourself with the educational issues and support legislative campaigns? At the national level, will you read the professional journals, use the information and resources of either NEA or AFT, attend annual meetings, and take advantage of the special services available such as consultants in the area of salary and negotiations? For most teacher candidates and many experienced ones, the main question does not concern merger but one's level of involvement in these organizations.

SUBJECT MATTER AND GRADE LEVEL ORGANIZATIONS

Any discussion of teacher involvement must also include attention to those organizations that are specifically concerned with various subjects matters, such as the National Council of Teachers of English and the National Council for the Social

Studies (NCSS), or with levels of schooling, such as the National Middle School Association and the National Association for the Education of Young Children (NAEYC). Other professional organizations serving teacher interests include umbrella organizations, such as the American Alliance for Health, Physical Education, and Recreation, and comprehensive ones, such as the Association for Supervision and Curriculum Development (ASCD). Each of these organizations offers unique services in its own area, and they all hold regional and/or national conferences, offer professional development activities such as in-service training, and provide teachers with a variety of publications ranging from newsletters to practical classroom suggestions to journals and monographs related to research findings. A brief look at two organizations, the National Council of Teachers of Mathematics and the National Council for the Social Studies, illustrates the functions and purposes of these organizations.

Founded in 1920, the National Council of Teachers of Mathematics (NCTM) has pursued its goals "to assist in promoting the interests of mathematics . . . and to vitalize and coordinate the work of local organizations of teachers of mathematics." It describes itself as "a professional organization of teachers . . . individually and collectively dedicated to the improvement of classroom instruction in mathematics at all levels. . . . [The] Council is a forum for the discussion of new developments, a means of sharing innovative classroom experiences and evaluating trends in the teaching of Mathematics."[39]

Since 1974, NCTM has been one of the largest professional organizations for subject matter teachers, counting upward of 52,000 members. Its publications include *Teaching Children Mathematics,* which features articles for preservice and in-service elementary school teachers and teacher educators; *Mathematics Teaching in the Middle School,* a monthly journal for middle school teachers; and the secondary school companion, *Mathematics Teachers,* aimed at high school, two-year college, and teacher education instructors. NCTM also publishes *The Journal for Research in Mathematical Education,* which includes comprehensive reports of empirical and major research studies and articles about current research in mathematics education; and numerous general publications on topics ranging from teaching methods and study techniques to tests and contests, computer-assisted instruction to do-it yourself teaching aids, and bibliographies. Other council activities include an annual national meeting each spring, regional meetings throughout the year, committees, panels, commissions, information resources, and insurance and travel programs. The council maintains a teacher learning center in its headquarters in Reston, Virginia, which includes a library, displays of instructional aids, work and meeting areas, and catalog files.

The National Council for the Social Studies, founded in 1921, is the largest association in the United States devoted solely to social studies education. NCSS provides leadership, service, and support for all social studies educators K–college in strengthening and advocating social studies education. Its membership is nationwide, with more than 110 affiliated state, local, and regional councils and associated groups. NCSS was one of the first organizations to bring to educators concepts and strategies for teaching ethnic studies.[40]

All of these professional organizations and associations offer important benefits to their membership. The question that most teachers face is to what extent they will be active.

FINDING A VOICE

Ann hung up the phone, screaming to Dawn, her roommate, "I got it. I got the second-grade teaching position at Softwind Elementary. This is just what I want! It's great and I am so happy!"

Dawn smiled and responded, "Great, I am very pleased for you." Dawn then walked into her bedroom leaving Ann to continue the celebration alone.

It troubled Ann that Dawn had "bugged out." This was so unlike her. Ann and Dawn had been sharing the same apartment for the past three years, and had become great friends, closer than most sisters. Ann knew that Dawn was not jealous; that was not her style. Besides, she had been accepted into law school. In fact, they both had been accepted into law school. Dawn had insisted that Ann take the Law School Admissions Test (LSAT) with her. She convinced Ann that she would be much more comfortable taking the test if Ann were taking it too; she even told Ann that was what she wanted as a birthday present. She paid for the cost of the exam and would always say to Ann, "If you don't get the teaching assignment you want, why not come to law school with me." Although Dawn knew that Ann wanted to teach, she did not think much of teaching. She would say to Ann, "As smart as you are, you can be anything you want. So why teach?"

Ann knocked on Dawn's bedroom door asking, "Are you asleep? If not, let's talk."

She heard Dawn mumble, "Come on in."

Ann entered and tossed her a can of Diet Coke. The Coke was Ann's way of saying, "Wake up! We need to talk." Ann asked, "What's eating you? Aren't you happy for me? I got the assignment I want. And you got the law school you wanted. We both should be happy."

Dawn begin to sip the Coke and said, "I want you to go to law school, too. We both have been accepted at the same school. In fact, you received your letter of acceptance much earlier than I did. You were accepted in the first cut. I was accepted as a second choice. In other words, what I am saying is that anyone can teach, but not everyone gets accepted into law school. Being a lawyer is being a professional. Being a teacher is, well, you know. . . . I am not trying to be mean. You know I care about you."

Ann stared at Dawn and said, "I thought we knew one another. I guess you don't know me and I certainly don't know you! 'Professional,' you say? Who makes one occupation a profession and another occupation a job? All of the nights you and I have sat up talking about women's rights and criticizing institutions, including our university, for their power trips on people who do not have the tools to respond, and you make such a statement to me?! What system of reason makes one thing less than the next thing? You really don't get it, do you?"

Ann continued, "To me, and every teacher who teaches, we are professionals! The sooner that people in society get that, the sooner we can begin to resolve the education problems facing this country. I've got to go now. I promised some of my students in the class where I'm student teaching that I would come and watch their softball tournament."

As Ann was about to open the door to leave, she heard Dawn say, "Ann! Can I come with you? Maybe I ought to take time to learn about a profession before I criticize it."

Ann looked up, smiled, and said, "Maybe there is hope for you yet! Come on, girl!"

SUMMING UP

In this chapter we have discussed teaching as a profession. Included in that discussion were teacher licensure and certification. We pointed out the difference between license and certification, looked at alternative routes to certification, and discussed the rise and importance of national certification for teachers. We offered suggestions for searching for a teaching position, discussing the role of the placement and career services office, the letter of inquiry, and the job interview. We compared the salary and benefits beginning teachers can expect to receive with those in other professions, and traced teacher salaries over past decades. We also considered health and other personal benefits, such as health insurance and tax-sheltered annuity plans. We discussed prudence and professionalism with regard to signing the contract.

Opportunities in education other than teaching include administrative positions such as principal and superintendent. We also discussed the role of volunteer personnel and others who work with the classroom teacher. We examined the supply and demand for teachers, including the different concepts of a "new teacher." We pointed out that the number of persons who take a teaching position immediately after receiving their teacher licenses is comparatively small, and discussed why teachers often leave the profession after teaching only a few years. Finally, we discussed professional associations and organizations. We examined the history and goals of the National Education Association (NEA) and the American Federation of Teachers (AFT), and also looked at subject matter and grade level organizations such the National Council of Teachers of Mathematics (NCTM) and the National Association for the Education of Young Children (NAEYC).

KEY TERMS

American Federation of Teachers
certification
letter of inquiry
licensing
National Education Association

paraprofessional
placement and career services office
profession

QUESTIONS FOR REFLECTION

1. What are your feelings and attitudes about teachers who have used an alternative route to receiving their license in comparison with those who have traveled the traditional route?
2. Compare the benefits of using the placement and career services office to seek a teaching position with doing it on your own.
3. What do you think John Dewey, the first holder of a membership card in the AFT, would say about the role of teacher associations in helping teachers achieve professional status?
4. Consider your legal responsibility when you sign a teaching contract. What do you imagine would be the consequences of breaking a teaching contract?
5. How important do you believe it is for teachers to join a teacher association and their subject matter organization?

ACTIVITIES

1. Compare and contrast the data on teachers' salaries and benefits to salaries of professionals in other areas over the past 10 years.
2. Go to the Teach for America website and download information on the program. Compare the pros and cons of your program with the Teach for America program. Ask members of your class if they think such alternative programs influence teacher professionalism.
3. Compare and contrast teachers' beginning salaries and cost of living in cities, towns, and rural areas in four different geographical regions of the United States. Use newspapers and websites from the four different locations to ascertain the cost of food, housing, clothes, and social life.
4. Visit the local office of the NEA or AFT in your area to ascertain which educational issues they are working on. Examine their position on these issues and compare them to your own positions on these issues. Would you be willing to work within these organizations on these issues?

GETTING CONNECTED

National Council for the Social Studies (NCSS)

Information on the history and purpose of the organization, including professional development activities, standards and positions statements, awards and grants for teachers, and resources and lesson plan for social studies teachers.

National Middle School Association
http://www.nsmsa.org

Information about the history and purpose of NMSA, including

	research reports, discussions of urban issues, and a list of publications.
National Association for the Education of Young Children (NAEYC) http://www.naeyc.org	Information on the philosophy and history of the NAEYC. Current focus of attention, publications and research reports.
National Education Association (NEA) http://www.nea.org	
American Federation of Teachers (AFT) www.aft.org//research/survey/ national.html	The Department of Research for the AFT provides a host of research data about teachers, including state comparison, trends in teacher salaries, and beginning teacher salaries.
National Council for the Accreditation of Teacher Education (NCATE) http://www.ncate.org	NCATE was the sole accrediting body for teacher education for many years. NCATE has established six standards that teacher preparation programs must meet to be accredited. The website provides much useful information and a list of currently accredited institutions.
Teacher Education Accrediting Council (TEAC) http://www.teac.org	TEAC was approved as a second national teacher education accrediting agency in 1997. The website describes the accreditation procedures and has a list of accredited institutions.

SUGGESTED RESOURCES

Campbell, Elizabeth. *The Ethical Teacher.* Maidenhead, UK: Open University Press, 2003.

Goodlad, John I., and Timothy J. McMannon. *The Teaching Career.* New York: Teacher College Press, 2004.

Haberman, Martin. *Star Teachers of Children in Poverty.* West Lafayette, IN: Kappa Delta Pi, 1995.

Ladson-Billings, Gloria. *Crossing Over to Canaan: The Journey of New Teachers in Diverse Classrooms.* San Francisco: Jossey-Bass, 2001.

Lantieri, Linda, ed. *Schools With Spirit: Nurturing the Inner Lives of Children and Teachers.* Boston: Beacon Press, 2001.

Macedo, Stephen. *Diversity and Distrust: Civic Education in a Multicultural Democracy.* Cambridge, MA: Harvard University Press, 2000.

Meier, Deborah. *The Power of Their Ideas: Lessons for America From a Small School in Harlem.* Boston: Beacon Press, 1995.

Moore Johnson, Susan. *Finders and Keepers: Helping New Teachers Survive and Thrive in Our Schools.* San Francisco: Jossey-Bass, 2004.

Nieto, Sonia. *What Keeps Teachers Going?* New York: Teachers College Press, 2003.

Palmer, Parker J. *The Courage to Teach: Exploring the Inner Landscape of a Teacher's Life.* San Francisco: Jossey-Bass, 1998.

Wardle, Francis, and Marta I. Cruz-Janzen. *Meeting the Needs of Multiracial Children in Schools.* Boston: Pearson Education, 2004.

NOTES

1. Christopher J. Lucas, *Teacher Education in America* (New York: St Martin's Press, 1997), 134–135.
2. Ibid., 100.
3. Ibid., 100.
4. *Testing Teacher Candidates: The Role of Licensure Tests in Improving Teacher Quality* (Washington, DC: National Academies Press, 2001).
5. Benjamin Shimber, *Occupational Licensing: A Public Perspective* (Princeton, NJ: Center for Occupational and Professional Assessment, 1982), 7.
6. National Association of State Directors of Teacher Education and Certification, *The NASDTEC Manual 2000: Manual on the Preparation and Certification of Education Personnel* (Denver: National Education Commission of the States, 2000).
7. *Testing Teacher Candidates.*
8. M. Haberman, "Proposal for Recruiting Minority Teachers: Promising Practices and Attractive Detours," *Journal of Teacher Education* 39, no. 4 (1986): 38–44.
9. C. Emily Feistritzer and David T. Chester, *Alternative Teacher Certification: A State-by-State Analysis 2000* (Washington, DC: National Center for Education Information, 2000).
10. Kenneth M. Zeichner and Ann K. Schulte, "What We Know and Don't Know From Peer-Reviewed Research About Alternative Teacher Certification Programs," *Journal of Teacher Education* 52, no. 4 (2001): 266–282.
11. Ibid., 5.
12. J. Shen, "Has the Alternative Certification Policy Materialized Its Promise?" *Educational Evaluation and Policy Analysis* 19 (1997): 276–283.
13. Zeichner and Schulte, "What We Know."
14. Ibid.; Lucas, *Teacher Education,* 202; www.nbpts.org
15. The Southeast Center for Teaching Quality, *National Board for Professional Teaching Standards,* Issue No. 3, July 2001, 1–2, Available at http://www.teachingquality.org
16. Ibid., 7.
17. Ibid., 7.
18. Ibid., 7.
19. Richard M. Ingersoll, *A Different Approach to Solving the Teacher Shortage Problem,* Teacher Quality Policy Briefs No. 3 (Seattle: University of Washington, Center for the Study of Teaching and Policy, 2001), 1–2.
20. Ibid., 6.
21. Ibid., 6.
22. American Federation of Teachers, *Survey and Analysis of Teacher Salary Trends 2002* (Washington, DC: Author, 2002), available at http://www.aft.org//research/survey/national.html

23. American Federation of Teachers, *Survey and Analysis of Teacher Salary Trends 1998* (Washington, DC: Author, 1998), available at http://www.aft.org//research/survey/national.html

24. American Federation of Teachers, *Teacher Salary Trends 2002.*

25. American Federation of Teachers, *Annual Survey of State Departments of Education* (Washington, DC: Author, 2002).

26. Dan Lortie, *School Teacher: A Sociological Study* (Chicago: University of Chicago Press, 1975).

27. Ibid., 35.

28. American Federation of Teachers, *Teacher Salary Trends 2002,* 29.

29. Ibid.

30. William M. Konnert and John J. Augenstein, *The School Superintendency: Leading Education Into the 21st Century* (Lancaster, PA: Technomic Publication, 1995), 34–35.

31. Nancy Amez, "Black Public Policy," *Journal of Black Studies* 16, no. 4 (1986): 397–408.

32. James L. Doud and Edward P. Keller, *A Ten-Year Study: The K–8 Principal in 1998* (Alexandria, VA: National Association of Elementary School Principals, 1998), 10.

33. American Federation of Teachers, *Teacher Salary Trends 2002,* 31.

34. C. Emily Feistritzer, *The Making of a Teacher* (Washington, DC: Center for Education Information, 1999), 1, 46.

35. Feistritzer and Chester, *Alternative Teacher Certification,* 9.

36. Jay Mathews, "School Survey 2001," *Washington Post,* 29 March 2001, B1.

37. National Education Association, *National Education Association FAQ* (Washington, DC: Author, 2001), available at http://www.nea.org/aboutnea/faq.html

38. American Federation of Teachers, *American Federation of Teachers Mission Statement* (Washington, DC: Author, 2000), available at http://www.aft.org/about/

39. National Council of Teachers of Mathematics, http://www.nctm.org

40. James A. Banks, ed., *Teaching Ethnic Studies: Concepts and Strategies* (Washington, DC: National Council for the Social Studies, 1973).

THE ORGANIZATIONAL STRUCTURES OF SCHOOLING IN THE UNITED STATES

© AbleStock/Index Stock Imagery

FOCUS QUESTIONS

1. How does the organizational structure of a district affect the instruction of students?
2. Why are some school districts more segregated by ethnicity and social class today than they were in the 1950s?
3. What are the key elements that teachers, administrators, and school board members consider when making school organization decisions?
4. What is the role of parents, students, and community members in decisions about school organization?
5. What factors are important for a teacher to consider in deciding how students will be

grouped for instruction? What are the pros and cons of heterogeneous grouping versus homogeneous grouping?

6. What is the difference between bilingual education, English as a second-language program, and two-way immersion programs?

What factors affect a district's approach to English language learners?

7. What are some recent reform efforts that have affected the organization of schools and classrooms? How has each movement challenged the status quo in public schooling?

VIGNETTE

MRS. FOWLER'S STORY

We begin this chapter with a vignette that is a compilation of an experience in Maureen's teaching career and an incident that occurred in a wealthy New York school district. Our story will begin the discussion not only of organizational structures in districts, schools, and classrooms but also of the power of parents and community members to effect change in their local school system.

Mrs. Fowler was angry as she picked up the phone to begin calling the other parents and caregivers of students in her son Angelo's class. There were two more weeks of summer vacation before the first day of school and, in her capacity as a room parent, she had just received Angelo's class roster. She was shocked to see that there were to be 30 students in Angelo's fifth-grade class. When she checked, she found out that the local school board had decided to eliminate a fifth grade because of budget cuts. An additional teacher was needed in the fourth grade, so rather than hire a new teacher, a fifth-grade teacher was moved to fourth and those fifth graders were placed in other classrooms. By dividing up the 24 students in the fifth class and sending 6 children to each of the remaining classrooms, the board had saved a considerable amount of money in teacher salary and benefits. The Fowlers, as well as many people in the community, had been on vacation when the board voted on the issue. Mrs. Fowler knew that a class size of 30 was within the contractual limits that the board had set with the teachers' union, yet she felt it was far too many students for effective learning to occur. She intended to do something about this situation.

The Shelby Valley Board of Education was having the last meeting of the summer the next evening and Mrs. Fowler spent the night on the phone, rallying support for smaller class sizes and the hiring of a new fifth-grade teacher. Several others volunteered to phone parents with children in other grades to encourage them to appear before the board so that they would not have to face this situation in the future. She worked especially closely with five of the other parents who had children going into fifth grade. Mrs. Rodriguez, an attorney and a parent of a soon-to-be-fifth-grader, was very helpful in knowing how to find research data on class size on the Internet. Not everyone would be able to speak before the board but they needed to gather appropriate evidence and present an organized argument against increasing class sizes. They divided up the work, making plans to review the research on class size as well as locate any court cases or legal precedents that had arisen in the past. The group agreed to meet for lunch the next day and compare notes in preparation for the board meeting.

Mrs. Fowler then called the secretary of the school board to secure a spot on the meeting agenda. When the secretary told Mrs. Fowler that the agenda had been set and that there was no available time to address the issue, Mrs. Fowler was both annoyed and determined. She argued that there would be a huge number of parents attending the meeting and suggested that it might not help public relations if television reporters interviewed angry parents who were not allowed to speak at the meeting. The secretary reminded Mrs. Fowler that there is a section of the meeting for "open forum" and said she would alert the board president that Mrs. Fowler would address the group.

The final phone call of the evening was to Mr. Romano, another room parent. Mrs. Fowler asked him to organize a 24-hour phone calling campaign to school board members about the issue. If nothing else, Mrs. Fowler figured that the board needed to be held accountable to the parents for this decision and a barrage of phone calls couldn't hurt.

The next evening, the board members were a bit nervous as the 7:30 meeting time approached. A buzz rose from the contingent of 175 parents, caregivers, and community members who sat in the audience. Board meetings were usually fairly calm and this looked like trouble. When the open forum began, there was only a half-hour left in the official board meeting. Mrs. Fowler rose to speak.

The conclusion of this story appears at the end of this chapter, which discusses school organization. Although educators often complain that today's parents are not involved in education, the type of direct involvement that the parents in this story were demanding is not exactly what they have in mind! Yet parents are an important constituency in decisions about school and classroom organization.

Teachers and administrators grapple with many organizational issues in attempting to create effective learning environments. Class size, the issue that caused a parental uproar in the Shelby Valley School District, is one of them. In this chapter, we will examine various organizational patterns that are common in schools, as well as the factors that influence decisions about how districts, schools, classrooms, and students are organized to maximize the chances that the goals of education in a democracy will be achieved.

The Organization of Schooling: What Does It Mean?

By organizational patterns of schooling, we mean the ways in which educators and state and local boards of education (sometimes called school boards) determine what types of schools, classrooms, and options for grouping students will optimize learning for the students in their state and district. For example, should a district have a middle school or a junior high? Should alternative schools, such as magnet schools or charter schools, be available? Should students be grouped by age or ability?

Organizational patterns in schools are not the result of decisions made by educators alone. As you will see, power relationships are also integral to the process of deciding how districts, schools, and classrooms are organized. Parents, students, and community members have a voice in the development of school structures and available options for the district. This chapter will describe various organizational patterns and analyze the many factors that have influenced how these have developed over time and continue to change.

Control of Schools and Decision Making: Power in Action

The U.S. Constitution does not specifically delegate powers related to education to the federal government, so each individual state is responsible for designing policies that govern schooling. Thus, despite the similarities in schooling across the country, each state has its own set of rules and regulations for governing all aspects of education. For example, you are most likely going to apply for teacher certification in the state where you are now attending college. If you decide to move, you will have to apply for certification in your new state and you may have to complete some additional requirements even if your state has a reciprocity agreement with your new state's education department. Yet, despite state control of schools, the national government has taken an increasingly active role in determining educational funding, curriculum, and policy for schools in the United States. Although many implementation decisions are left to local schools districts, federal as well as state governmental policies and societal trends have an impact on how local educators determine what arrangements best suit the needs of the community.

We are sure that you have heard about the one-room schoolhouse. You may even have seen old TV programs such as *Little House on the Prairie,* in which Laura Ingalls Wilder was the schoolmarm for a class of children ranging in grade from kindergarten through high school. Before the Industrial Revolution in the United States, country schools like Laura Ingalls Wilder's served a wide geographic area. In 1647, Massachusetts passed an act that required each town of at least 50 families to have a school. These "district schools," as they were called, were entirely controlled by the local townspeople. By 1850, district schools could be found across the country.[1] On the one hand, such community control of schools, or a **decentralized school system,** ensures that the people who fund schools through their tax dollars have primary say in the hiring of teachers, selection of the curriculum, and the policies and procedures implemented in the schools. On the other hand, a totally decentralized system runs the risk of becoming out of touch with core knowledge and skills that all students may need for the future. This became a concern in the 1800s. Many community members became uneasy as populations in cities and towns grew. The spread of industrialization brought an increased need for workers with strong basic skills. As a result, the notion of creating a **centralized school system,** with many schools under the control of one central board, was gaining support.

The First State Superintendent and the Rise of School Boards

Today, it seems normal to us that the governor and state legislature in each state greatly influence educational policy and practice. It is also taken for granted that the regulations and policies set by the governor, state legislature, and state boards of education are influenced and enforced by the state school board and the state superintendent or commissioner of education. The department of education in each state is typically responsible for supporting both the schools and the state board of education in the determination and implementation of regulations. This organizational framework was not established, however, until the early 1800s, when Massachusetts again took the lead in educational innovation by creating the first school board.

Decentralized control—that is, control of schools by the local people—was unsettling to many people in Massachusetts in the early 1800s. There were concerns that a two-tier system was forming, with good schools for the rich and weak schools and teachers for the poor. People worried that only those towns populated by wealthy people would eventually have schools and that our country would be back in a situation where poor people had no chance of social advancement through education. A move was afoot to centralize, or coordinate at a higher level, the individual school districts that had formed. In 1837, Massachusetts created the first state school board and appointed Horace Mann, whom you read about in Chapter 4, as the secretary, or head, of the board.[2] Thus, the first centralized bureaucracy in education was created. It did not take long for the idea to spread.

Today, states are divided up into school districts, each typically run by a local school board, sometimes called the board of education, that sets local policy in accordance with state regulations. Some districts encompass an entire city, some cities have more than one district within its boundaries, and some districts cross city boundaries. Each board sets the budget; negotiates the contracts for teachers, administrators, and school staff; approves the hiring and firing of district employees; determines school district policies; addresses local concerns; and deals with the entire scope of issues facing their district. This local board determines the organizational patterns that affect the teacher's role; however, the federal government also exerts influence over educational decisions that affect how schools are organized.

The federal government has been involved in schools since the passage of the Land Ordinance by the Congress of the Confederation. This ordinance called for public lands in the Northwest Territory to be laid out into six-mile square townships. Each township was to be subdivided into 36 lots, one square mile each, with one section of land being reserved for the maintenance and endowment of schools. This ordinance was the first legislation to establish a policy of governmental involvement and support for education.

Federal spending and federal pressure on schools began after the Soviet Union launched a space satellite, *Sputnik,* in 1957. Fearing that the then USSR was going to win the "space race," the U.S. federal government began pouring money into the development of math and science curricula. The 1960s brought further federal influence when President Lyndon Johnson, as part of his War on Poverty, signed the Elementary and Secondary Education Act (ESEA). ESEA provided more federal dollars for schools accompanied by increased accountability for states. Another significant step in federal involvement occurred in 1979, when President Jimmy Carter, acknowledging the importance of federal support for education, created the Department of Education. The department is headed by the secretary of education, who is appointed by the president. Although the Department of Education cannot directly tell states what to do, there are many ways in which it influences schools. The department supports educational research and provides funding, often in the form of competitive grants, to school districts that are working to solve educational problems, such as student underachievement or racial segregation in schools, through innovative programs. Most recently, President George W. Bush championed education legislation that was passed in 2001, familiarly called the No Child Left Behind (NCLB) Act. NCLB has significantly increased accountability to the federal government, with dollars to states tied to student performance on standardized exams among other accountability measures. Several organizational patterns, such as magnet schools, charter schools, and vouchers, which you will read about in this chapter, have been influenced by federal support.

Discussions and debates about school organization issues continue today. They are fundamentally about who will exert influence over or control schools. Of course, underpinning most educational issues are implications about who holds power. We will return to such debates in the chapter on school governance. For now, let's examine some organizational patterns and consider how issues of power and multiculturalism affect the decisions that policy makers, teachers, administrators, parents, and other community members make about how schools should be run.

ORGANIZING THE SCHOOL YEAR: MEETING THE NEEDS OF SOCIETY

One of the responsibilities of local school boards is to set the school calendar. This may seem like an easy task but it is very complex. The department of education in each state regulates the mandatory number of days that school must be in session. It is typically in the range of 180–190 days of school per academic year. Local school boards use this number to determine exactly what days school will be in session, how many days will be devoted to teacher professional development activities, when school vacations will occur, and policies and procedures for emergencies. Teacher contracts specify how many days the teachers must be in attendance, policies for teacher absence due to illness and personal business, and procedures for special professional development activities such as visiting other schools for the purpose of observing new programs.

The school calendar has become a topic of controversy for students and teachers in some districts. For example, major vacations from school have historically been based on Christian holidays: Christmas and Easter. Teachers who may be

Jewish, for example, have been forced to take personal leave days, often by special request, to participate in services during the high holy days of Rosh Hashanah and Yom Kippur. Teachers who are Christian do not lose personal leave time for holy day services.

School boards are often under pressure from community members to celebrate holidays that have local significance. For example, in Illinois Casimir Pulaski's birthday is a state holiday. Chicago is home to the largest population of Polish Americans in the United States and there was political pressure to honor Pulaski, a Revolutionary War hero. At the time that Pulaski Day was declared a state holiday, many people in Illinois did not know who Pulaski was or anything about his contributions to our nation. As a state holiday, there is typically no school on Pulaski Day. Illinois, like most states, has a waiver policy whereby any local school board can petition the state for a waiver from any required action. Many districts outside of Chicago have applied for a waiver in order to hold school on Pulaski Day.

The school district of Paterson, New Jersey, is another example of a system that is responding to the needs of its students and families. In the late 1990s, Paterson became the first school district to close school on two Muslim holidays, Eid El Fitr (celebrating the end of Ramadan) and Eid-Ul-Adha (celebrating the end of the Hajj, the traditional period of pilgrimage to Mecca), because of the large number of Muslim students in the district.

As you can see, even such a seemingly simple task as setting the school calendar is subject to political struggles and power relationships. Let's take a look at two different models for the school calendar: the traditional, or agrarian, model and a more recent, year-round school model. Both respond to the needs of our society.

The Agrarian Model

You probably know the story of the first Europeans who landed at Plymouth Rock in what is now Massachusetts. They were met by members of the Wampanoag tribe of Cape Cod. As European settlers and Native Americans mingled across the country, their farming expertise was also shared. Tribes in the East and Midwest had become expert farmers, given the climate and geography of their region. Settlers quickly adopted the farming techniques of the Native Americans, and our nation developed an agrarian economy and lifestyle. Although different crops were grown across the country, the planting and harvesting seasons were similar. A pattern of schooling developed whereby those who attended school, especially boys, followed an agricultural calendar. They were needed to assist with farming chores more at some times of the year than others. Eventually, a pattern developed that roughly mirrored the September to June schedule that continues to dominate schooling in the United States.

Year-Round Schools

There are some exceptions to the September to June attendance pattern. Overcrowded schools, weather that is extremely cold or hot causing budgetary concerns for heating or air conditioning, and the need for flexibility are some of the factors that have caused some school districts to operate on a year-round pattern. A more educationally based rationale for year-round schools is a growing concern that the typical two- to three-month summer break disrupts the learning process for too long a period of time. Some educators have argued that shorter, more frequent breaks offer opportunities for continuity of learning and less of the review and repetition that often characterizes the curriculum during the month of September.

There are several models of year-round school, but one of the most popular is the 45–15 model, or nine weeks in school and three weeks of vacation. In this model, teachers work the same number of days as in the traditional, agrarian model, but their time off comes in three-week intervals that occur at different points in the year rather than in one lengthy summer vacation. Students also attend school for the same number of days as those in the traditional model; however, the gap between June and September is nonexistent. Proponents of this model argue that it promotes continuous learning and is better for students.

Organizing a District: Choices, Choices, Choices

The way in which a community and a school district allocate public school students to school buildings has become quite complex since the early days of schooling when all children within a certain geographic distance attended the one-room schoolhouse. One of the most controversial issues in the current debates on educational reform involves plans that offer parents and other child guardians a choice in determining what school their children will attend.

Neighborhood Schools: Building Community in the Local Area

During colonial times, as we have seen, schools were formed when communities had the requisite 50 families residing within their borders. The idea of community or **neighborhood schools**—schools that serve families in the immediate geographic area—is still most popular today. You will hear young couples and families who are first-time homebuyers say that the local school is a top priority in selecting a neighborhood in which to purchase a home.

Neighborhood schools have many positive attributes. Many people believe that neighborhood schools contribute to the stability of a community. Students attend school and play together in close geographic proximity. Parents and teachers become familiar with each other and are active in school and community events. When teachers also live in the community in which the school is located, students see them outside of school, increasing the connections between families and school personnel.

There are some drawbacks to neighborhood schools. For one, they have exacerbated segregation by ethnicity and income level. In fact, the United States is currently grappling with what has been called *resegregation,*[3] or second-generation segregation. This means that, as in the early 1900s, schools have become racially imbalanced, containing an overwhelming population of one ethnic group, because people in the United States do not generally live in ethnically mixed neighborhoods. Wealthy communities continue to be predominantly White, and economically disadvantaged cities continue to be populated largely by people of color.

Resegregation is also the result of a legacy of prejudice and discrimination on the part of many Americans. In the 1950s, a phenomenon known as **White flight** occurred when middle-class White families fled urban areas that were increasingly becoming populated with people of color. Additionally, when a family of color would move into an all-White suburban area, many White homeowners, fueled by ignorance, fear, and sometimes unscrupulous real estate agents, quickly moved to another all-White area. Some home titles carried specifications that the house could not be sold to a person of color. At the same time, the government was funding massive housing projects serving low-income Whites and large numbers of people of color in urban areas. Those with resources (property and money) used their power and influence to affect educational opportunity and outcomes not only for their own children but for the children of others.

The results of these patterns can now be seen across the United States where many schools serve an almost homogeneous population of students because neighborhoods are segregated. Inequitable conditions often develop whereby schools located in poor neighborhoods, which may serve students of color with a minority of White students, lack materials and services that schools in wealthier neighborhoods take for granted. Researchers such as Gary Orfield of the Civil Rights Project at Harvard University have found that progress toward desegregation after 1960 had been seriously eroded by 2001. White students, regardless of social class, were by far the most segregated group. Orfield points out that 50 years after the *Brown v. Board of Education* decision was handed down, patterns of segregation have not only reappeared, they have accelerated and been exacerbated by social class. Segregation is most prominent in larger, urban areas; more suburban schools have diverse populations. The problem is that within any given district, segregation by ethnicity and class is increasing rapidly. This increase in segregation has brought with it an increase in the achievement gap between students of color and their White counterparts.[4]

Many teacher candidates we know enter the profession with little background knowledge about segregation and its effects on communities and in schools. We recommend that you read *The Education of a WASP* by Lois Stalvey[5] to get a first-person account of the impact of such policies and practices in the 1950s and 1960s.

Neighborhood schools thus have advantages and disadvantages. Educators who grapple with this issue ask themselves how the disadvantages might be remedied without exacerbating segregation. One response to this dilemma has been the creation of options for students within the public school system: magnet schools, thematic or centric schools, and charter schools.

Magnet Schools: Building Community Around a Theme

Magnet schools are public schools within a district that attract students from the entire district because of some unique characteristic that makes these schools distinct from traditional schools. The concept of magnet schools was a response to the segregation that began to occur in Northern states in the 1940s and 1950s when Whites left urban areas and moved to the suburbs. The idea for magnet schools rose to prominence in the 1970s as a way to draw a diverse population of students into one building. The programs offered by the schools feature special curricula—for example, a focus on the integration of computer technology. It was hoped that the features of the school would encourage White parents to send their children to magnets located in areas populated by people of color.

Magnet schools have three characteristics. They are created for the purpose of desegregation, in that students are admitted according to a specific formula that ensures racial balance. They are also in some way innovative so as to be different from the traditional educational system. Finally, they enroll students voluntarily from the entire district, not just within the boundaries of the neighborhood in which the school is geographically located.[6]

Magnet schools often enroll a portion of their population from the surrounding neighborhood, but a large percentage of the students who attend magnets come from other geographic areas within the district. One of the advantages of this system is that children from all backgrounds come together to learn and socialize. In the many parts of our society that are still segregated, this offers students an opportunity that they do not see modeled by adults. They learn about the talents, abilities, and cultures of a wider variety of people and, in many ways, are much better prepared for the world of work and higher education than students who attend schools with little diversity.

Magnet schools also have their drawbacks. It is often difficult for those students who come from neighborhoods at a distance. They spend more time traveling to and from school, they may be unable to socialize on the weekend with school friends if they lack transportation to neighborhoods around the city, and their families may be unable to attend important school functions in the evenings and on weekends because of work schedules and transportation.

Many school districts began venturing into the magnet school arena with federal grant money. This money provides resources for specialized teacher training in developing thematic curricula or in implementing specific programs, for equipment such as state-of-the-art computers and new books, and for staffing needs that can provide smaller class sizes or more teacher support. These resources may not be available to other schools in the district that are not the recipients of special grant money.

Centric Schools: Shifting the Lens Through Which Students View the World

Some teachers and community members are concerned that children are getting a one-sided view of the world in traditional public schools, a view that is skewed toward the canon, or curriculum, of the Western tradition. They believe that traditional schooling is failing to adequately serve the academic and social needs of some students and that it does not prepare all students with the knowledge and skills they need to be successful in our diverse nation and world. They have developed schools, within the public school system, that address the needs of a target population. These schools have a curriculum and other support services that, while meeting state mandates, focus on the special interests or needs of the students at that school. In other words, the core, or *center*, of instruction is focused on the students attending the school. The following are some examples.

African American Immersion (or Afrocentric) Schools

After years of struggling with models developed in response to court-ordered desegregation in Milwaukee, Wisconsin, unequal educational outcomes continued to be evident in 1990 and racial segregation still existed in the Milwaukee public schools. The district tried busing students and had developed magnet schools, but there remained a significant gap between the academic achievement of African American and White students, and the number of African American students suspended and expelled from school was two to three times higher than the rate for White students.[7] An increasing number of African American parents believed that the schools were not meeting the social and academic needs of their children. They began to take action to begin their own schools.

Other, unintended effects of desegregation were detrimental to the Black community. Busing had all but destroyed neighborhood schools that were at one time, along with the church, the centerpieces of African American communities. Faltz and Leake,[8] who studied desegregation in Milwaukee, reported that Black youth were alienated from their home communities and that parents and other community members were unable to participate in school activities. These detrimental effects, coupled with a lack of expected outcomes in academic achievement, caused educators and concerned citizens to seek alternatives to forced desegregation.

One response to these conditions was to create two African American immersion schools (AAIS) in Milwaukee. In the AAIS model, the curriculum (or the concepts, content, perspectives, and themes chosen) and the instruction place African and African American history, culture, and ways of knowing and seeing the world at the center of instruction. The entire school experience is designed to match the strengths, experiences, perspectives, and learning styles of the students. More cooperative learning activities are implemented, mentors and community role models are involved in the school, and a specific effort is made to make the school a welcoming place for parents, grandparents, and others so that a community atmosphere is developed. The school environment reflects African and African American history and culture. The traditional Eurocentric curriculum is replaced by a multicultural curriculum that removes Europe from the center of instruction and presents content from multiple perspectives with a specific focus on the history of Africa and African Americans. A sense of community is fostered by having teachers stay with the same group of students for two or more years, a concept called "looping" that you will read more about in this chapter.

The AAIS school in Milwaukee is coeducational and open to any student who wishes to attend. Because it is a neighborhood school concept located in a predominantly African American neighborhood, the students are African American. Teachers are chosen for an AAIS school because of their commitment to the school and their experience in the community and in teaching. Because AAIS schools emphasize community building, a value in the African American culture, there is a strong home–school–community connection and teachers are required to do 18 home visits per year. Students are involved in community service activities, and parents are actively involved in the educational process.[9]

Today, Milwaukee has become a leader in experimentation with charter schools and voucher programs that you will read about later in this chapter. A more recently designed school, the Khamit Institute, is a Milwaukee charter school based on Khamitic principles. This school follows the model of an immersion program but focuses on Africa and the African Diaspora. When parents and other community members become this significantly involved in the education of children in the community, they are exercising a form of power that is built on a foundation of self-determination. It is the community that determines what is best for its children.

Harvey Milk School for Gay and Lesbian Youth   Gay and lesbian adults often characterize their high school experience as miserable at best, and at worst, life-threatening. Many suffered verbal and physical abuse as students, and this remains the situation today. We all know that it is almost impossible to learn in an environment where a student does not feel safe and affirmed. In response to the violence and isolation that are often experienced by gay teens, concerned educators and community activists have begun a number of secondary schools that are designed to serve gay and lesbian teens, although any student is welcome to enroll. Harvey Milk High School in New York City is one example. Named after a gay politician and activist who was murdered in San Francisco, Harvey Milk High School first opened in the mid-1980s as an alternative school that provided a safe learning environment for gay, lesbian, and straight adolescents. In the fall of 2003, Harvey Milk opened as a full-fledged high school serving about 100 students. Despite some controversy as this opening was more widely publicized than the opening as an alternative school, the New York City public schools invested $3.2 million in the expansion of Harvey Milk.

The educators who began Harvey Milk were concerned that gay youth in traditional schools were often demoralized and had developed a sense of shame about themselves because of the harassment and physical violence they were experiencing. Suicide, substance abuse, and school dropout rates among gay teens in traditional schools were (and continue to be) extremely high. Additionally, gay students were often alienated from their families if they found little or no support for their sexual orientation at home. The curriculum at Harvey Milk addresses these issues along with the traditional academics taught in all New York high schools; 90% of Harvey Milk's students graduate and 60% go on to college. In addition to the traditional academic curriculum, students have support for acquiring a strong self-identity and for developing strategies for dealing with homophobia in the general society. Students can attend support groups, discussion groups that focus on specific issues related to being gay in a predominantly straight society, and family counseling sessions.

One organization that can help you find out more about gay and lesbian issues in education is the Gay, Lesbian, and Straight Education Network (GLSEN).

Many states and regions have local GLSEN chapters. Check out the GLSEN website, listed in the Getting Connected section of this chapter.

The Rock Point Community School and Rough Rock Demonstration School
You read about Colonel Pratt in Chapter 3. He was the former army officer who, in 1879, instituted boarding schools for Indian children, taking them from their homes and relocating them to Pennsylvania in an effort to assimilate them into mainstream White society as manual laborers. Debates over Indian education and the assimilation policies of the federal government continued for many years. Teresa McCarty, referencing research done in the Latino community,[10] stated that "one of the defining characteristics of colonial schools for Indigenous children was its intentional disregard for the community 'funds of knowledge' children bring to school."[11] In the 1960s, Indian people as well as some government supporters, pushed for self-determination, or letting tribal governments control Indian affairs. Education is a key process for any people, and Indians are no exception. The state of Indian education in the United States was dismal.

In 1969, the U.S. Senate published the results of their investigation into the state of Indian education in a report titled *Indian Education: A National Tragedy, a National Challenge*. In the preface to the report, Senator Edward Kennedy noted that dropout rates for Indians were twice the national average, that Indians were two to three years behind their White peers in academic achievement, and that most teachers of Indian children preferred not to teach Indians. This report led to passage of the Indian Education Act (1972), which provides funding for programs for Indian education. These programs required parent involvement and promoted the idea of community schools.[12]

Indian people began to take control of the education of their people. The Coalition of Indian Controlled School Boards was formed in 1971. In 1967, the Rock Point Community School was established on the Navajo reservation in Arizona. Rock Point is a two-way bilingual school, which you will read about in the next section. What makes Rock Point different from the typical two-way program that serves a diverse mix of children is that all of its students are Navajo. The majority of students at Rock Point enter school speaking only Navajo, and they first learn to read and write in Navajo. It was initially difficult to find certified teachers who were fluent in Navajo. The school hired uncertified teachers and then used community resources to establish on-site coursework so that the teachers could become certified. This "grow your own teachers" approach has ensured that the school will have teachers who truly want to teach Navajo children and who will stay in the community once they have obtained their teaching certification. The students are transitioned to English, and achievement tests indicate that the students outperform other Navajo students in reading and mathematics.[13] Other indications of success at Rock Point are the stable corps of teachers and administrators, the high degree of community involvement, and the low rates of student absenteeism.[14]

Near Rock Point are several Indian-controlled schools, all with an emphasis on Indian self-determination through the preservation of their language and culture. The story of the first school to have a Navajo governing board and a curriculum centered on Navajo language and culture, Rough Rock Demonstration School, is told in a well-researched book by Teresa McCarty.[15] Rough Rock and Rock Point are case studies that illustrate the power relationships between the dominant culture and taken-for-granted ways of doing things and the rights of groups that share specific characteristics to shape their own destiny. McCarty's book describes the struggle as well as the success and satisfaction that comes from self-determination. As the Navajo people at Rough Rock took control of the governance, the curriculum, the hiring of teachers, and all aspects of their school from the Bureau of Indian Affairs (BIA), they embarked on an empowering and complex journey to decide for themselves how best to educate their children.

The School as a Stable Entity When Students Have No Permanent Home   The pros and cons of separate schools are now being discussed for the fastest growing youth population in the United States, children who are homeless. In 2001, 39% of the total population of people who were homeless were school-age children. Currently, well over 1 million children in the United States do not have a stable place to live. In 2001, Congress reauthorized the McKinney-Vento Act, a piece of legislation that now works in concert with No Child Left Behind to provide protections for students who are homeless.

Children who live in shelters or who live on the streets are often stigmatized in school. Such students tend to change schools often because in many cities families are not allowed to stay in one shelter for more than 30 days. If a family has reached the maximum stay length and does not have a stable place to live, they may move to another shelter in the same town or to a new town altogether. For students who are homeless, life in school can be difficult. They are often subjected to teasing by their peer group because of their clothing, they may find it difficult to make friends because of their transiency, or they may be embarrassed to have classmates discover that they do not have a stable place to live. McKinney-Vento attempted to address this situation by mandating that homeless students have the right to attend their school of origin for the duration of their homelessness. As a result, debates began over how best to ensure educational stability for children who are homeless.

Administrators in some large districts that serve many, many homeless students have discussed the idea of a separate school for students who are homeless. Although McKinney-Vento states that students may not be segregated or stigmatized on the basis of homelessness, some educators argue that such a school, where children could attend no matter where their shelter is located, would provide stable faculty, a consistent curriculum, and a more supportive environment in which to learn. Many advocates for the homeless are against such an idea, arguing that it is the responsibility of the neighborhood school to welcome the student and ensure that he or she learns.

Despite positive results for students who are "segregated" in **immersion or centric schools,** these models continue to be controversial. Many people claim to have a philosophical disagreement with separating students in this way. They argue that the "real world" is not set up in segregated groups and that the students who are served by these schools have to learn to get along in their real world. Supporters of such schools respond by saying that if traditional schooling produced academic achievement and positive self-esteem for the populations served by centric schools, there would be no need for them. If you begin to examine who is making each argument, you will also begin to see how power and privilege enter these discussions.

Two-Way Bilingual Schools: Se Hablamos Inglés y Español

School districts in the United States have historically chosen different ways to deal with children who enter the district with limited proficiency in the English language. In the past, public schools were actually taught in languages other than English, such as German or French. As English became the socially accepted language for all citizens, different programs emerged to teach English to children. The English as a second language (ESL) approach is one in which the teacher only teaches in English. The teacher typically does not have to speak another language to be certified to teach in this model. It would not be unusual to find a teacher in a self-contained classroom with 12 students who speak nine different languages among them, all learning English. Bilingual programs take a different approach. The teacher is proficient in the target language and teachers in both languages, with the native language used as a base from which to learn English. Both ESL and bilingual programs are most often "pullout," in that students spend a portion of their day with the ESL or bilingual teacher with the goal of learning English and being placed in the English-speaking classroom as quickly as possible. Neither ESL nor bilingual programs emphasize maintenance of the native language. Although many bilingual teachers might argue this point, the fact remains that once the student leaves the ESL or bilingual classroom or teacher, there is no emphasis on using the native language in school or society. One approach, however, does foster dual language proficiency: the two-way, or dual-immersion, model.

It is important today to be able to communicate in more than one language. In the United States, English is the dominant language, the language of power. All children should leave school with strong skills in reading, writing, and speaking English. But the value of understanding another culture through its language increases students' knowledge base, challenges their critical thinking skills through gaining cultural competence in the structure of another language, and fosters self-esteem as students gain fluency and use their new knowledge and skills to learn more about others. Additionally, those who are concerned about the place of the United States in a global society and economy agree that the ability to speak a language in addition to English is an asset. **Two-way bilingual schools** are designed to meet these goals.

Donna Christian, a researcher who specializes in language issues in education, defines two-way bilingual programs as those that "integrate language minority and language majority students and provide instruction in, and through, two languages. One is the native language of the language minority students (called the *target* language), and the second is English. These programs provide content area instruction and language development in both languages."[16] Christian reports that there are typically three goals for two-way bilingual programs, with balanced attention to each of the following:

1. Students will develop high levels of proficiency in their first language and in a second language.
2. Students will perform at or above grade level in academic areas in both languages.
3. Students will demonstrate positive cross-cultural attitudes and behaviors and high levels of self-esteem.[17]

In 1995, there were 182 two-way bilingual schools in the United States. Most of these (167) provide instruction in Spanish and English; however, there are two-way bilingual schools with instruction in Korean, French, Navajo, Cantonese, Chinese, Arabic, Japanese, Russian, and Portuguese.[18] Most students enter a two-way program as monolingual in either of the two languages, although some may know a bit of the second language. In these programs, curriculum content, such as math, social studies, science, and reading, is taught in both languages. This is a shift in perspective from the idea that we teach a "foreign" language in school. Teachers do not see themselves as instructors of Korean, but rather as science teachers who are teaching subject matter in Korean.

There are two primary models for the allocation of language instruction as the students strengthen their skills in the primary language and begin to learn a second language. In the 50–50 model, students are taught half the time in English and half the time in the target language. In the 90–10 model, 90% percent of instruction is in the target language and 10% is in English in the primary years. As the students advance in grade, the amount of English is gradually increased until the time allotment is 50% in each language. This typically occurs in the upper elementary grades. The model used in any school depends on many factors, such as the number of students who speak a particular language and their degree of fluency in their native language.

When students complete the program in a two-way school, they are fluent speakers, readers, and writers in both languages. Children who enter school unable to speak English are not seen as a "problem" to their teachers. On the contrary, they become a resource in the educational process as they bring knowledge that their English-only peers need in order to be successful. Successful two-way programs utilize team teaching, with one teacher who is bilingual and one who is monolingual in English, and cooperative learning activities that are project oriented so that teams of students, which include speakers of both English and the target language, work together and share knowledge and expertise.

Charter Schools: Choice Within Public Education

Charter schools are schools that operate within a public school district but do not have to conform to all of the rules and regulations of a traditional public school. Joe Nathan, a charter school proponent, has outlined the characteristics of the charter school idea.[19] The charter concept:

- Allows the creation of new public schools or the conversion of existing ones
- Stipulates that the schools generally be nonsectarian and prohibits admissions testing

- Requires that these schools be responsible for improved student achievement
- Waives most state rules and regulations, along with local contract provisions, in exchange for explicit responsibility for results
- Permits several public bodies—such as state and local schools boards, universities, and city governments—to authorize creation of charter schools
- Permits educators and families to select these schools, rather than being assigned to them
- Requires that average per-pupil funding follow students to these schools, along with other appropriate funds such as Title 1 and special and compensatory educational funds

A charter, then, is a license to operate a school within a particular school district but apart from the rules and regulations that govern traditional schools in the district. Any person or group can apply for a charter in a school district whose state legislature has agreed to allow charter schools. This means that in a system that allows charters, even private corporations can enter the public domain. Minnesota passed the first charter school law in the United States in 1991; today, 28 states and the District of Columbia have such laws. As of 1998 there were approximately 800 charter schools across the country,[20] and the number is growing rapidly. Charter schools are being run by teachers, universities, private corporations, and individual citizens. Most often, a local school board awards a charter to a sponsoring person or group for a specific length of time. The application process is quite cumbersome, with applicants being asked to outline the curriculum, detail the budget, and provide the necessary building specifications for space and safety.[21] Some charter schools are in actual school buildings, but this is not mandatory. There are charter schools in former factories, shopping malls, and museums.

Charter schools usually operate around a theme or focus, or they may target a specific population of students. Some examples of thematic areas are technology, back to basics, multicultural education, and performing arts. In a thematic charter, the traditional curriculum is built around themes or infused with technology. There are also centric charter schools. For example, Detroit has two charter schools with Afrocentric themes, and Arizona has more than one school that focuses on Native American students. Carl is currently researching a charter school that was designed to serve students who are former abusers of alcohol or other controlled substances.

In the past, if a group of parents or educators was dissatisfied with the public school, they could decide to open their own school but would receive no financial assistance from state or local school agencies. Parents paid tuition or teachers sought grants to keep the schools running. The key difference between these efforts and charter schools is that charter schools are public schools. Charter schools receive the same per-pupil funding as the public schools within the district in which they are located. Typically, they have teachers who meet the qualifications of the public school system and a board that makes decisions about the operations of the school.

Charter schools are not without their problems. Researchers are only now beginning to publish initial results of studies on charter schools. It is not surprising that these results are mixed, with proponents of charter schools extolling their virtues and detractors citing examples of charter school failures. There are several issues to consider.

Proponents of charter schools believe that parents deserve options for their children and will be more fully involved in schools that they have selected. They argue that wealthy parents have always had options in that they can afford to send their children to private schools, which have smaller class sizes, more resources, and better skilled teachers. Proponents of charter schools argue that the charter concept gives all parents that same option. Many supporters of charter schools believe that public schools have developed into massive bureaucracies in which teachers are not free to innovate. They argue that a more "market-driven" system of competition will result in positive changes in all schools.

Critics of charter schools are concerned that charters will further stratify students by ethnicity and social class. Even if parents in low socioeconomic areas have choices available, they may not be able to afford transportation, uniforms, and extracurricular activities that are often found in specialized schools. Critics charge that charter schools foster a competitive atmosphere in the district and when schools compete for the "best and brightest" students, it is the students with the most aggressive, educationally savvy parents who will end up in the best schools. They note that often charter schools can be selective and can refuse to admit students who have disabilities or behavior problems.[22] Finally, critics argue that research has shown that in places like Milwaukee, the non-charter schools are more innovative and have better test results than the charter schools.[23]

To find out more about charter schools, check out the Getting Connected section at the end of this chapter.

ORGANIZING STUDENTS FOR INSTRUCTION: CONSIDERING AGE

One of the most interesting aspects of education is the decision about how to group children for instruction. At first glance, it appears easy: preschool, kindergarten, elementary school, junior high, and high school. In reality, there are many different arrangements for grouping children across the United States, and each carries with it philosophical underpinnings that determine how children will be organized for instruction. Not all school districts include children of all ages. Some districts serve only elementary students, some serve only high school students, and some serve all ages.

Decisions about when children should begin formal schooling, how long they should stay in school, and how they should be grouped for instruction while they are in school are influenced in part by the social goals of schooling. As the number of students enrolled in schools grew, the idea that students should learn and socialize with others of their same age gained popularity. Today, the vast majority of schools use an age-based graded system. Departments of education in each state also offer teacher certifications by age and grade. See the box "Graded Systems

Graded Systems and Your Teacher Certification

It is important for you to consider organizational patterns in light of your teacher certification. Some states certify elementary teachers for grades K–5, K–6, and K–8. Some do not include kindergarten certification without specific coursework related to early childhood education, and some states only certify elementary teachers through grade 8 provided the teacher documents additional coursework that focuses on adolescent development and content mastery. The same variations exist for those interested in secondary school teaching. Some states require a bachelor's degree in the content area in which the teacher candidate will be certified (e.g., social studies, mathematics, science, English) and will certify a teacher for junior high (grades 7–9) and high schools (grades 10–12). Some states may only certify a candidate for one or the other.

Your state department of education should have a website that contains certification information. Check it out!

and Your Teacher Certification" for suggestions on how to find out about the types of teacher certification in your state. This section will examine the various types of student grouping that can be found across the United States.

The Graded System: Grouping Students by Age

The transition from a one-room schoolhouse where students ranged in age from 5 to 15 to the stringently graded system that we have today was a gradual one. As we noted in Chapter 4, discipline in the multi-age one-room schoolhouse of the 1700s and early 1800s was harsh. Teachers most often controlled the class by calling individuals to the front to recite memorized text while the others sat silently at their desks. As the school-age population grew, it became more difficult for teachers to manage such a wide range of ages and abilities. By 1850, many communities had two rooms or buildings and students were divided up according to general age guidelines, younger students in one room or building and older students in another.[24] Because the system was completely decentralized, the curriculum was not standardized but depended entirely on the teacher and the materials available.

This situation was not acceptable to many educational reformers in the early 1800s. When Horace Mann became superintendent of the Massachusetts schools, he set out to accomplish the three goals of the common school movement: (1) access to a free (tax-supported) education for all White children in the United States; (2) the development of a system of teacher training that ensured that every classroom had a teacher who met stringent training standards; and (3) the creation of a state-controlled system of education that included standardized curriculum and a system of grading so that students progressed through stages that were clearly marked, typically by age.[25]

For quite some time, a two-level system was most common in the United States. This took two different forms: either the 8–4 model, with grades K–8 in one setting and grades 9–12 in another, or the 6–6 plan of having K–6 in one building and 7–12 in another. These patterns can still be found in many communities, although they are becoming rarer. As urban centers grew in the 1950s, the 6–3–3 plan gained popularity. In this model, there were K–6 elementary schools, a three-year junior high, and three years of high school. Today, many variations of these models exist in districts across the country. Let's take a look at some of the options for organizing students by age and grade.

Kindergarten and Pre-Kindergarten: Off to a Good Start   In 1840, German educator Friedrich Froebel coined the term *Kindergarten*. It means "children's garden," or to Froebel, a place where young children can grow socially and intellectually. Froebel was the first to promote the idea that very young children, ages 4 to 6, could benefit from organized play and group activity. His ideas caught on in the United States and in 1873, the first kindergarten began in the St. Louis, Missouri, public schools.[26] Kindergartens sprang up across the country, where the most popular pattern was a half-day program for children who were 5 years old. Although compulsory education laws began in the 1860s, kindergarten was not mandatory in many states until the 1900s. Even as late as the 1980s, some school districts did not require kindergarten.

The idea of a pre-kindergarten educational experience for younger children was less popular until more recent times. Although nursery schools existed, they mainly served the middle class, and before the 1960s, only a very small proportion of the 4-year-old population attended a nursery school. Two factors significantly influenced the number of children who attended some type of pre-kindergarten program. The first occurred in the 1960s when President Lyndon B. Johnson declared a War on Poverty. Under the Elementary and Secondary Education Act, part of his comprehensive package of programs to eliminate the gap between rich and poor in the United States, Congress provided federal funding for Project Head Start. **Head Start** is a preschool program that is still in existence for children who live at or below the poverty line, especially those living in urban centers and impoverished rural areas. The idea behind Head Start was to ensure that children whose families might not have money for books, toys, crayons, and other learning materials typically found in middle- and upper-class homes would receive pre-kindergarten instruction that would put them on par with their more affluent counterparts.

A second factor that has influenced the growth of early childhood education has been the steady rise in the number of women working outside of the home since the 1930s. During World War II, women replaced men in work sites across the country. Child care outside the home became a necessity. Even though relatives or an in-home nanny often assumed child care responsibilities during this time, and most women returned to the home when the men returned from war, the notion that women might work outside the home was beginning to take hold. During the 1960s, more and more families depended on two working parents or were headed by a single working mother. Since then, the number of preschools, day care centers, and nursery schools that offer some level of academic preparation has steadily risen. By the late 1990s, the importance of early childhood education in promoting lifelong learning and school success had become taken for granted. Several states have passed laws that provide free, universal pre-kindergarten for all children.

It is very common to find nursery schools and pre-kindergarten programs that divide children by age, having separate rooms or programs for 3-year-olds, 4-year-olds, and 5-year-olds. On the other hand, some early childhood programs, such as those that use the **Montessori method,** group children in mixed-age settings. Maria Montessori, an Italian physician and educational philosopher, believed that young children should be able to explore many types of activities using materials that have been specially constructed to be child-sized. A typical Montessori school is, in once sense, highly individualized. Learning areas such as mathematics, language arts, and practical life (e.g., a sink for washing dishes, a table where children use a dull knife to make their own snacks of crackers and peanut butter) are set up and children choose what they will work on during the day. The teachers monitor and record choices and student progress. A teacher may guide a child who perhaps has not chosen to work with mathematics materials for a week, but in general, the child moves from learning environment to learning environment based on personal preference. Montessori believed that children, even at a very young age, were perfectly capable of selecting a balanced range of intellectual stimulation. Teachers provide resources and guidance, designing small- and large-group activities as needed.

The Montessori philosophy is a perfect example of a highly structured, child-centered learning environment that appears to be very unstructured. It is difficult for some early childhood educators in the United States, many of whom have designed kindergartens to emulate later grades by introducing 5-year-olds to sitting at desks and doing worksheets, to trust that very young children can select challenging learning activities on their own. The Montessori philosophy has gained popularity in the United Sates, though, and Montessori schools, the majority of which are private schools, can be found in most areas.

Another option for preschool education that comes from Europe is an approach that is known to early educators as **Reggio Emilia.** Reggio Emilia is a town in Italy that was almost destroyed by World War II. The lesson that its citizens took from the aftermath of the war was the importance of investing in children. A community preschool began with a specific philosophy that focused on the development and needs of the child in a setting where respect for the child is paramount. Teachers act simultaneously as teachers and researchers, building relationships with the children that help them to understand how each child learns and grows. Art is a key medium through which children's learning is documented. The concept of community, inside and outside of school, is of prime importance. Children are not "hurried" to learn academic subjects, but allowed to explore, create, and learn at their own pace. The role of the teacher as researcher emphasizes the importance of gathering and using evidence from children to make sound educational decisions. Even at a young age, children are given choices and their ideas are taken seriously as they grow into maturing young people. The Reggio philosophy, which can be implemented in existing classrooms, is making its way into early childhood education practices in the United States.

Head Start, the Montessori method, and the Reggio Emilia approach represent the different philosophies of preschool education that can be found in the United States today. Some parents and teachers emphasize academics, whereas others prefer that preschool education provide children with time for exploration and socialization, believing that academics will follow. This difference of opinion can be found in the educational literature as well. Some scholars of color argue that middle- and upper-class parents, whose homes are often filled with books and other language-enriching materials, can afford the "luxury" of allowing children to explore, play, and create. These scholars argue that often parents who live at or below the poverty level do not have the time or the means to provide a print-rich environment at home, instead choosing to spend time talking and storytelling with their children. As a result, they believe that preschools should focus on preparing children from historically disadvantaged backgrounds with the knowledge, skills, and dispositions that will put them on a par with their suburban counterparts when they begin kindergarten. Lisa Delpit has made this argument in her book *Other People's Children: Cultural Conflict in the Classroom,* in which she provides an in-depth discussion of this issue.[27]

It's Elementary: Patterns for Ages 6–12   The traditional organization of elementary schools developed from the K–8 pattern. This pattern predominated in public and private schools until the early 1900s, when the idea for a junior high school took shape. Today, many different elementary arrangements can be found across the United States. For example, some districts now include a pre-kindergarten program within the elementary school. A configuration of kindergarten through grade 5 in one building has also become a popular pattern as junior highs and middle schools, which will be addressed below, were formed.

PRIMARY SCHOOLS   Primary schools are schools that typically serve students in pre-kindergarten or kindergarten through grade 3. Some school districts have decided to emphasize early childhood education by creating a separate learning environment for young children. This could be a wing of a school building devoted to the primary grades or it could be an entire building set aside for these early learners. Educators who place special emphasis on primary education realize that students must get off to a good start if they are to be successful lifelong learners. The focus on primary education comes from a belief that young children have unique needs, interests, and talents.

One organization that can assist you with excellent books and materials for considering issues and practices in early childhood education is the National Association for the Education of the Young Child (NAEYC). Check the Getting Connected section at the end of this chapter for a description of this organization and information on how to get catalogs and materials.

THE TRADITIONAL ELEMENTARY   The K–5 school is the most popular elementary school arrangement in the United States. Since the advent of the junior high or middle school, which you will read about in the next section, most districts have at least one elementary building in the K–5 (or K–6) arrangement. The elementary school is seen as the foundation for the advanced learning that takes place in grades 6–12 (or 7–12). If you examine the learning standards for any state, you will see that all of the content and skills that are to be mastered by high school graduation are introduced in elementary school. Additionally, elementary school teachers are expected to foster those skills needed to participate in our democracy: the ability to think critically, to solve problems by choosing wisely from a range of carefully considered alternatives, to get along with a wide variety of peers and adults, and to be involved in the community. You can see that society places a heavy burden on the elementary school teacher!

Middle School Versus Junior High: What's the Difference?   Secondary education became a focus of educational reformers in the late 1800s. There were debates over the type of curriculum appropriate for high school students (practical education in agriculture and manual labor or a classics education in literature, Latin, mathematics, and science). These debates led to additional discussions over the length of the secondary school program. The traditional eight years in elementary school and four years in high school appeared inadequate to prepare students, still mainly young White males, for the world of work. The curriculum and the self-contained classroom seemed too oriented toward nurturing students when advocates of change desired a focus on independence and preparation for careers. One response to this debate was the creation of a junior high, which would transition students from the elementary curriculum to more specific preparation in high school.

The **junior high school** was designed to resemble the "factory model" of traditional high schools. It is characterized by compartmentalization of subjects into 45- or 50-minute periods with individual teachers in self-contained classrooms instructing students who are typically grouped by ability. Students move from class to class by a system of bells that signal the beginning and ending of periods. Groups of teachers may belong to content area departments such as mathematics, science, social studies, and English language arts. Each department usually has a leader, or chair, who is in charge of departmental business and may also observe new teachers for the purpose of providing feedback as they learn to teach.

There is some controversy over where the first junior high school was established. In 1909, the Columbus, Ohio, Board of Education established a separate building for the seventh and eighth grades. In 1910, the superintendent in Berkeley, California, not only created a similar physical arrangement but also, for the first time, made curricular alterations that addressed the academic transition to high school.[28] The idea of the junior high, taking early adolescents away from the more nurturing environment of elementary schools to facilitate a transition to the more serious study of high school, caught on rather quickly. By 1950, 90% of city school districts had established junior highs.[29] But by the late 1960s, philosophical concerns began to surface about the junior high. Educational psychologists and some teachers and parents believed that although 12- to 14-year-olds did not need the intense nurturing of the primary years, they were not psychologically and emotionally ready for the impersonal nature of compartmentalized subjects and six teachers a day. They sought a more supportive environment for students to make the transition to high school. In a 1963 speech, William Alexander promoted the creation of a middle school that would serve three to five grades, including grades 6 and 7, as opposed to the predominant junior high pattern that served grades 7–9.[30] The middle school concept is a popular one today and the number of middle schools across the country continues to increase.

Middle schools are designed to recognize the uniqueness of the growth stage spanning the transition from childhood to adolescence. They are characterized by an interdisciplinary team approach to teaching, integrated curriculum, block scheduling (two or more continuous class periods), and learning activities that emphasize critical thinking, team problem solving, and the development of research skills. The middle school concept fosters closer relationships between teachers and students because a team of teachers works with the same group of students throughout the year. In some middle schools, teachers act as mentors or advisors to individual students, but at a minimum, the entire teacher team is responsible for the academic and social success of the students assigned to that team.

As you begin to visit schools as an observer and a participant rather than a student, you may see that some schools that carry the title *middle school* are really run more like junior highs. Exhibit 7.1 compares middle schools to junior highs. Which arrangement do you think is more effective for young adolescents? Why?

One group that can help you think about middle school issues is the National Middle School Association. Their website information appears in the Getting Connected section at the end of this chapter.

High School: Preparing for the Future   It was noted earlier that during the colonial period all students, kindergarten through age 17, attended the community school or one-room schoolhouse. Most students at this time did not attend school for the entire 12 years. Prior to the common school movement, schooling was intended for the sons of the wealthy. Females attended school for a number of years, but since colleges did not admit women, parents saw no point in putting priority on advanced education for their daughters. Lower- and middle-class males and females typically dropped out of school after the eighth grade to work on farms, in factories, or in some other type of employment to assist their economically struggling families. This meant that secondary education began as an institution to serve the sons of the wealthy.

The first secondary school, the Latin Grammar School, was opened in 1635 in Boston. Here the classics—Greek, Latin, English grammar and prose—were taught in a manner that prepared students for scholarly study in college and later jobs as financiers, physicians, and businessmen. The idea of secondary education grew in popularity among the rich. In 1751, another form of secondary school began: the academy. Benjamin Franklin was a staunch proponent of the academy idea because he believed that schooling should address broader educational needs and include students who may not attend college. The academies were focused

EXHIBIT **7.1**   **WHAT IS THE DIFFERENCE BETWEEN A MIDDLE SCHOOL AND A JUNIOR HIGH?**

Middle School Emphasizes	Junior High Emphasizes
A student-centered program	A subject-centered program
Learning how to learn	Learning a body of information
Creative exploration and discovery	Mastery of concepts and skills
Development of self-esteem and belief in oneself	Competition with others
Student self-direction in a reassuring climate	Adherence to the teacher-made lesson plan
Student responsibility for learning	Teacher responsibility for student learning
Student independence and democratic participation in classroom decisions	Teacher control
Flexible scheduling	The six/seven-period day
Student input into scheduling	Administrator and teacher scheduling
Variable grouping and cooperative learning	Traditional classroom learning
Team teaching, parents and others as instructional aides	One teacher for a class
Authentic learning and portfolio assessment	Textbook approach, direct instruction, lecture

Source: *The Middle School in Grosse Pointe,* an informational brochure prepared by the Grosse Point, Michigan, Public Schools.

more on preparation for the world of work and moral training, although they provided students with a background in the classics. Academies served both males and females but were still private schools and remained the domain of the upper classes.

Boston English School, which was opened in 1821, is regarded as the first public high school in the United States. Boston English was unusual at the time, not only because it was a public school, but also because its curriculum excluded study in Greek and Latin. Many historians believe that the popularity of public secondary schooling that began to dominate urban education in the mid-1800s was a result of middle-class attempts to ensure that their children had the same opportunities as upper-class families. Students who enrolled in academies like Boston English had to be at least 12 years of age. They were divided into three classes, by age, and studied a progressively complex curriculum that included mathematics, history, geography, reading and grammar, arts and sciences, philosophy, and Christianity. Also included in the curriculum were courses on morals, practical applications of mathematics skills (for example, navigation and surveying), and bookkeeping.[31]

The organizational structure of high schools has remained fairly stable since the early 1900s. This is most likely due to the work of the Committee of Ten on Secondary School Studies. The Committee of Ten was a group established in 1892 by the National Education Association to study secondary schools and to outline procedures for effective secondary education. The committee recommended that high schools should contain grades 7–12 and should prepare students who were not college bound in a manner similar to those who were going to college. They recommended that the curriculum be arranged in a logical order, or sequentially, and that credits called **Carnegie units** be awarded to courses that met certain criteria for content and for time spent studying the particular subject matter. For example, a student taking ninth-grade mathematics that meets five times per week for the semester and contains content deemed appropriate for ninth grade (sequentially following the seventh- and eighth-grade courses) would receive one Carnegie unit for the course. In most cases today, students are required to complete at least 14 Carnegie units to graduate from high school.[32]

The work of the Committee of Ten has had a lasting impact on the organizational structure of high schools in the United States. Students continue to be grouped by grades and often **tracked**, or grouped by ability for instruction. These groupings are typically based on standardized test scores and the teacher's perceptions about students' academic ability and potential for going to college. Courses are arranged sequentially so, for example, students who did not take Algebra I in the sophomore year cannot enroll in Algebra II in the junior year. Most colleges continue to have admissions criteria that require a certain number of college preparatory course units, referring to the Carnegie system of assigning units to certain courses.

Chances are that if you enter a typical high school today, you will find many of the same features that have been characteristic of high schools since the recommendations of the Committee of Ten were implemented in the early 1900s. But this does not mean all high schools have remained the same. Various reform efforts have been instituted since the 1960s that have changed the organizational structure in secondary schools. These reforms were instituted by educators and concerned citizens who believed that sorting and grouping students by age and ability (grading and tracking), standardizing the curriculum to the point that opportunities for certain students to go on to higher education were being eliminated by their course selection, and dividing class periods into 50-minute segments in a building controlled by bells were not the most effective way to educate adolescents. Additionally, many reformers believed that the top-down decision-making model, in which administrators made policy and curriculum decisions and passed them down to teachers to implement was not democratic, nor did it foster an investment in the system on the part of the teachers. This "factory model" of education was influenced by the needs of our increasingly industrialized society in the 1900s and eventually came to be seen as the antithesis of democratic schooling. In many schools, tracking separated students by ethnicity and social class, with wealthier White students populating the college preparatory tracks and poor students and students of color being assigned to courses that prepared them for manual labor positions. Students were given little say in the organization and operation of schools.

In 1983, the White House issued a call for educational reform with the publication of *A Nation at Risk*. This report was like a bombshell to the public and especially to politicians and educators. It proclaimed that our educational system was being "eroded by a rising tide of mediocrity" that was serious enough to threaten the economic foundation of our nation. This report will be discussed at many points in our text but suffice to say here, these scare tactics elicited an era of educational reform that has served to alter some of the entrenched organizational patterns in secondary schools.

One such reform effort began in 1984 when Theodore Sizer started the **Coalition of Essential Schools** (CES) at Brown University in Rhode Island. The CES is currently part of a larger movement that today is called Whole School Reform (WSR). What makes this particular reform effort unique is that there is not one model approach that all schools are to follow. Each school in the Coalition must adhere to the principles outlined in Exhibit 7.2 and, in doing so, can create a school that meets the individual needs of the student population it serves.

One such school that we will use to demonstrate how some secondary schools have broken from the predominant factory model is Central Park East (CPE) Secondary School in Harlem. It is described by CPE's former principal, Deborah Meier, in her book *The Power of Their Ideas: Lessons for America From a Small School in Harlem.* CPE serves a diverse student population made up primarily of students of color. The school is characterized by small classes in which teachers are not responsible for more than 40 students throughout the year. Looping, a practice in which teachers keep the same students for two or more years, is used to promote a sense of community and to ensure that teachers are able to closely guide and document student progress. At CPE, teachers have responsibility for making policy and curriculum decisions as well as decisions on hiring and evaluating colleagues. To the greatest extent possible, students participate in all aspects of school life, including governance decisions such as policy and curriculum.

Central Park East Secondary School is responsible for the same state and local mandates that any other public high school must meet. Their students are successful on standardized measures of achievement such as the ACT or the SAT, and meet other college entrance requirements. Their day, however, looks very different from that of the traditional high school schedule. Classes are interdisciplinary and held in two-hour blocks. Students spend two hours in Humanities (art, music, literature) and in Math/Science. They have a one-hour Advisory period in which they meet with their core teachers. Students have foreign language and required community service periods during the week. The day is flexible as the teachers and students determine needs, so it is possible to have an entire day devoted to math and science with the rest of the week arranged accordingly. Students spend time in seminars, in work groups, in independent work, and in tutorials and coaching sessions. In this way, not only do students learn how to work independently, but they also learn how to collaborate with teachers and classmates. Older students (grades 11 and 12) are able to spend a portion of their day doing externships and can select from a wider body of one-hour courses.

Assessment at CPE is not usually done through paper-and-pencil exams. Students must develop projects related to their studies and present exhibitions in which they explain and defend their work. Each student must complete a portfolio as a graduation requirement. The teachers have designed criteria for the

EXHIBIT 7.2   **NINE COMMON PRINCIPLES OF THE COALITION OF ESSENTIAL SCHOOLS**

1. The school should focus on helping adolescents learn to use their minds well. Schools should not attempt to be "comprehensive" if such a claim is made at the expense of the school's central intellectual purpose.

2. The school's goals should be simple: each student should master a number of essential skills and be competent in certain areas of knowledge. Although, these skills and areas will, to varying degrees, reflect the traditional academic disciplines, the program's design should be shaped by the intellectual and imaginative powers and competencies that students need, rather than by conventional "subjects." The aphorism "less is more" should dominate: curricular decisions are to be directed towards students' attempt to gain mastery rather than by the teachers' effort to cover content.

3. The school's goals should apply to all students, but the means to these goals will vary as these student themselves vary. School practice should be tailor-made to meet the needs of every group of adolescents.

4. Teaching and learning should be personalized to the maximum feasible extent. No teacher should have direct responsibility for more than eighty students; decisions about the course of study, the use of students' and teachers' time, and the choice of teaching materials and specific pedagogies must be placed in the hands of the principal and staff.

5. The governing metaphor of the school should be student as worker, rather than the more familiar metaphor of teacher as deliverer of instructional services. Accordingly, a prominent pedagogy will be coaching, to provoke students to learn how to learn and thus to teach themselves.

6. Students embarking on secondary school studies are those who show competence in language and elementary mathematics. Students of traditional high school age who do not yet have appropriate levels of competence to start secondary school studies will be provided with intensive remedial work so that they can quickly meet those standards. The diploma should be awarded on a successful final demonstration of mastery for graduation—an Exhibition. This Exhibition by the student of his or her grasp of the central skills and knowledge of the school's program may be jointly administered by the faculty and higher authorities. Because the diploma is awarded when earned, the schools' program proceeds with no strict age grading and with no system of credits earned by time spent in class. The emphasis is on the student's demonstration that they can do important things.

7. The tone of the school should explicitly and self-consciously stress the values of unanxious expectation ("I won't threaten you, but I expect much of you"), of trust (unless it is abused), and of decency (the values of fairness, generosity, and tolerance). Incentives appropriate to the school's students and teachers should be emphasized, and parents should be treated as essential collaborators.

8. The principal and teachers should perceive themselves first as generalists (teacher and scholars in general education) and next as specialists (experts in a particular discipline). Staff should expect multiple obligations (teacher–counselor–manager) and a sense of commitment to the entire school.

9. Administrative and budget targets should include substantial time for collective planning by teachers, competitive salaries for staff, and an ultimate per-pupil cost not more than 10 percent higher than that at traditional schools. Administrative plans may have to show the phased reduction or elimination of some services now provided for students in many traditional comprehensive secondary schools.

Source: T. R. Sizer, *Horace's School* (New York: Houghton Mifflin, 1992).

development and defense of the portfolio that address students' learning in the core subjects. Each student must present an oral defense of his or her portfolio before a committee of teachers, other adults, and a classmate.

CPE students are highly successful after graduation, as Meier reports in her book. Despite the fact that the school enrolls a typical cross section of students from New York City, many of whom live in poverty, they succeed in college and post–high school careers. Using CES principles and documenting similar results, Eliot Levine describes the Metropolitan Regional Career and Technical High School (the MET) in his book *One Kid at a Time: Big Lessons From a Small School*.[33] The MET has an ethnically and socioeconomically diverse student body, yet every student in its first graduating class was accepted into college. Impressively, the MET has one-third the dropout rate, one-third the absentee rate, and one-eighteenth the rate of disciplinary suspensions of other high schools in the state of Rhode Island where it is located.[34]

CPE is just one example of the type of innovation that is currently underway in secondary education. The Coalition of Essential Schools at Brown University can help you find out more about other unique organizational patterns in schools today. Look for their website in the Getting Connected section at the end of this chapter.

The Ungraded School: Learning Across the Ages

Some schools do not divide students by age into grades, but educate students of all ages together. Of course, most ungraded schools are private schools that typically have significantly fewer students than most public schools.

The Albany Free School, in Albany, New York, is an example of an ungraded school. The book *Making It Up as We Go Along* by Chris Mercogliano, the director of the school, describes the origins and operations of the Free School. Serving about 50 students and employing eight teachers, the Free School enrolls children who would range from preschool to eighth grade. The students are not assigned to classrooms by grade. Although they sometimes meet in small groups with children who are close to their same age, much of the day is spent in large group projects in which students of differing ages work together.

The children at the Free School meet as a large group with their teachers each morning. In a democratic fashion, they collaborate on creating the learning that will take place that day. Teachers keep anecdotal records detailing the children's progress and write up a narrative report several times a year that details each student's academic, social, and physical progress. It is not unusual at the Free School to find children assisting cooks in the kitchen as they prepare lunch, to see older students tutoring younger children, and to see children using everything from primary documents to traditional textbooks in lessons and projects.

Many of the practices of the Free School have been documented by educational researchers as excellent strategies to ensure that all students achieve to their highest potential. It is easy to say that such a school is naturally located in the private sector and that its practices cannot be replicated in public schools. The question is, what aspects of the Free School can be implemented in public education? You read about some of them in the description of Central Park East. We will now address some of the organizational dilemmas that occur within schools and buildings that foster or prevent such innovation.

Organizing Students by Ability: Whose Needs Are Served?

Decisions about how best to group students for instruction have plagued educators since the inception of schooling in the United States. Much research has been done on **heterogeneous grouping,** or grouping children of mixed ability together, as well as on **homogeneous grouping,** or grouping children with similar characteristics together. Each type of grouping has pros and cons, which we will describe in this section.

Homogeneous Grouping: Keeping on Track

Homogeneous grouping is used in many schools today; in fact, homogeneous grouping is often used within a heterogeneously organized classroom or school. Other words that you may hear educators use to describe homogeneous grouping are **ability grouping** and **tracking.** Jeannie Oakes, an educational researcher who has spent her career investigating the issue of grouping students, defines ability grouping or tracking as the routine sorting of all students into homogeneous groups and classes of "high," "average," and "low" students (or any of the creative euphemisms in vogue, such as "advanced," "accelerated," "opportunity," "basic," "sharp," "vista," etc.). Such sorting typically begins early in elementary school, sometimes even in kindergarten, and continues throughout the grades.

Schools have grouped students by ability in many different ways. For example, you may recall from your own schooling that there were programs or special classrooms for students labeled as "gifted and talented," "learning disabled," "bilingual," or "English as a second language (ESL)." Junior high and high school programs are famous for tracking. Courses are labeled and students often take "honors," "remedial," or general-level classes, especially in the areas of mathematics, science, and English.

Many educators approve of ability grouping. One argument that you may hear in support of ability grouping, or tracking, is that students with like characteristics will learn better together. Some elementary and secondary teachers will argue that they are not trained in special education methods or bilingual education and those students who have special needs belong in separate classes. Today, large numbers of students are being labeled as having attention deficit disorder (ADD) or attention deficit hyperactive disorder (ADHD). These students have problems paying attention and often cause a disturbance in class. Some teachers will argue that such children should be isolated from the typical classroom so that their behavior does not prevent the majority of students from receiving an education. Some administrators also say that organizational factors such as time blocks, student scheduling, and special courses in music, physical education, and art make homogeneous grouping an efficient way to manage large numbers of students.

The results of Oakes's research, published first in her book *Keeping Track: How Schools Structure Inequality* (reprinted in 1995), have brought to light some serious questions about these arguments. Oakes found that students are often sorted based on *teacher's perceptions* of students' abilities. Further, she documented that the use and interpretation of IQ scores to label children as mentally retarded, learning disabled, and ADD vary from state to state, and sometimes from district to district. Some studies have found that many children who are characterized as ADD or ADHD have been "diagnosed" without proper medical procedures and could also be classified as gifted. As Oakes looked into who was placed in the "low" group, she found that they were most often students of color and students who came from poverty-level backgrounds. Those labeled as "high" or placed in classes for "gifted and talented" were often students whose parents were upper- or upper-middle class. Sometimes parents who are well versed in the operations of school can advocate for the placement of their children in advantageous positions. Parents who are not aware of the implications of having their children placed in a particular grouping, or who may not have sufficient experience or background in the educational system to be outspoken advocates for their children, are often at a disadvantage in a system that labels children by certain characteristics.

Two other very serious consequences of ability grouping should be addressed. First, Oakes, as well as other researchers, found that the quality of teaching, the qualifications of the teacher, and the level of teacher expectations were very different in the "high" track courses and the "low" track courses. Teachers of students perceived to be high ability were more likely to hold degrees with full certification in the area of instruction, to use more innovative techniques, and to have higher expectations for student performance than teachers of the "low" group. Moreover, the curriculum in high-track courses is what some educators call "high-status knowledge." Students learn information and critical thinking skills that will enable them to do well on those measures of progress, such as the SAT, that will help them gain access to more high-status knowledge (at a good college) and eventually to a high-paying career. In other words, being in the "top" group can provide students with the necessary tools for future success. In the low group, teaching was found to be boring, the curriculum typically did not go beyond the basic knowledge level, and the use of worksheets and rote memorization was common.[35] These students did not have access to the type of high-status knowledge being taught in the top group. This means that "low" group students have restricted access to higher education or more prestigious colleges. Strict use of ability grouping can sort and select students for future careers in a way that is similar to the early days of common schooling, when immigrant children were educated for jobs in factories and the children of the wealthy were prepared to be the factory owners.

Second, researchers have documented that children of color, especially African American boys, are overrepresented in special education and in the "low" track and groups. Gary Orfield and Daniel J. Logen confirmed Oakes's research in *Racial Inequality in Special Education*. These researchers compiled data that showed that African American students were twice a likely as their White counterparts to be labeled as emotionally disturbed. They, along with Latino students, were substantially more likely to be pulled out of the classroom for part of the day while White students were placed in inclusive classrooms where they interacted with their peer group without interruption. Finally, Orfield found that although African Americans made up 17% of his study population, they made up only 8% of those classified as gifted. White students made up 63% of the population but 76% of those deemed gifted. Orfield and his team of researchers were most concerned that characterizations of children as "emotionally disturbed" or "gifted" often relied on subjective measures on the part of teachers and administrators rather than objective measures.[36]

Students who receive a label early in their school career rarely lose that label as they progress through the system. Eventually, their achievement becomes a self-fulfilling prophecy if they believe that they cannot achieve to the level of their counterparts in the "high" group. Educators who are concerned about the consequences of ability grouping advocate the use of flexible mixed-ability groups, or heterogeneous grouping.

Heterogeneous Grouping: In the Mix

Imagine the teacher in the one-room schoolhouse trying to instruct 20 or 30 students of differing ages and abilities. In this setting, it became common to see peer tutoring, older students helping younger students, and younger students learning the curriculum that their older classmates were mastering. It was also common to see all of the students work together on a project such as a concert or a play. Today, this much variation is rarely seen, as you learned in the previous section. Many educators, though, are firm believers in purposefully placing students of mixed ability levels in the same classroom, using heterogeneous grouping to enhance learning. Additionally, groups of non-educators such as the National Association for the Advancement of Colored People (NAACP), the American Civil Liberties Union (ACLU), and the National Governor's Board have published statements against the use of ability groups or tracking because of the research that indicates that ability grouping has a particularly adverse effect on the education of poor students and students of color.

Advocates of heterogeneous grouping argue that society comprises many different types of people and that educating students to function effectively in society requires opportunities for a diversity of students to learn together. The student who is not strong in mathematics may be a wonderful poet, and the student who is not artistically talented may be able to solve complex quantitative problems. Building learning environments in which project-oriented teaching fosters the use of many different talents and abilities results in achievement for all students without labeling any student.

It is not always easy to teach in a classroom where the range of students' talents and abilities is wide, but policies on the education of all students to meet high standards have become commonplace across the country. They have become a part of state mandates. For example, in New York the Board of Regents mandated that *all* students, including those with special needs, must pass Regents or "high" level exams before they will be allowed to graduate from high school. Inclusion—the practice of including students with special needs in regular classrooms—is another example of asking teachers to hold high expectations for all students. Inclusion is one response that attempts to address the underachievement of students placed in segregated special education classrooms where education is often limited to training for menial jobs.

Advocates of heterogeneous classrooms and schools believe that grouping children of mixed ability together, holding high expectations for all students, and expecting that children will respect and appreciate a wide variety of talents and abilities among their peers is consistent with the democratic values of our country and the purposes of schooling in a democracy.

ORGANIZATIONAL PATTERNS WITHIN THE SCHOOL BUILDING

Each school building is unique. As you observe in schools, try to find the characteristics that make each building you enter different from another school. You will be pleased to know that teachers and administrators often have a considerable amount of latitude in deciding many of the organizational patterns that occur within buildings. Although such decisions often have to be approved by the school board, board members listen to teachers and administrators who have done their research as they build a rationale for implementing innovations within schools.

Team Teaching: Doing It Better, Together

Team teaching is an arrangement in which two or more teachers plan for, teach, and evaluate a specific group of students together. The traditional teaching pattern that developed in the United States is that of the self-contained classroom. In this setup, one teacher teaches a class of between 20 and 30 students. The concept of team teaching is an acknowledgment that sometimes teaching can be a lonely and isolating experience. With teaming, the children benefit from having more than one adult in the classroom and teachers benefit from having a partner/colleague with whom to work. Though it is far more difficult to plan, teach, and evaluate together, it is truly rewarding when two colleagues develop a successful collaborative relationship.

Teacher education and teaching are placing more emphasis on teachers working together. As a teacher, you may have a colleague in special education, a paraprofessional or teacher's aide, or another subject area teacher in your classroom. By the term *team teaching* we do not mean turn teaching, in which two teachers taking turns being in front of the room or one teacher teaches while the other is doing planning in another room. We mean two professionals actually teaching simultaneously or working with individuals or small groups simultaneously so that all students benefit from the knowledge and skills of both teachers. You will need to consider how two professionals can effectively plan, teach, and evaluate together. For example, the two-way bilingual schools that you read about in this chapter often utilize team teaching. Two teachers, one fluent in the target language and one monolingual in English, teach together. One recent study of teachers in two-way schools reported that teachers unanimously agreed that working together, although challenging, had many benefits for the students and for the teachers. The teachers reported that lesson and unit planning was more fun, that learning together, and sharing successes and failures, was supportive and rewarding. Team teaching and planning made it easier to move away from dull textbooks and to create innovative, interdisciplinary units. Monolingual teachers enhanced their skills in the target language and increased their understanding of students who were learning English. Perhaps most interesting was the finding that as teachers shared perspectives about the students, more positive feelings about all students were generated.[37]

When you are in the clinical or field component of your teacher education program, you will not be an official team member, but you will be required to work on a team with your cooperating teacher, and perhaps with other professionals in the school. What do you see as key components in being able to work together successfully with your cooperating teacher?

Looping: Two Years Are Better Than One

Looping is a term used to describe the practice of a teacher's retaining the same class two (or more) years in a row. For example, a teacher may teach second grade followed by third grade with the same group of students. He or she would then "loop" back to second and begin the process again. As you might imagine, this can have some very positive results for students, although it may not be for everyone.

As you begin to talk to teachers about their profession, you will probably hear them lament the lack of quality teaching time available. Schools are continually asked to include more and more material in the curriculum as well as ensure that students have experiences in physical education, music, art, and a number of other options such as computer literacy and languages other than English. Looping allows a teacher to document a student's growth over a two-year period, taking a more developmental approach to teaching and learning. Teachers who loop do not have to spend the first month of school determining where each child is and reviewing rules and regulations. Looping provides an opportunity for the teacher to pick right up where he or she left off the previous June, thereby gaining a solid month of instructional time. Additionally, the parents and child guardians get to know the teacher well, and over two or more years they can develop a more substantial relationship.

Occasionally, it is not wise for a teacher to retain a particular student for more that one year. When this happens, the student does not get looped and is assigned to a different teacher the second year.

Multi-Age Grouping: Learning From Mixed-Aged Peers

Recalling the benefits of the one-room schoolhouse, many educators are advocating **multi-age grouping,** in which "children are flexibly grouped according to performance level, not age, and proceed through the levels at their own rates."[38]

Multi-age classrooms typically utilize subject integration and thematic, project-oriented teaching. A multi-age classroom is not the same as a **combination classroom,** in which two age groups are combined for one year.[39] In a multi-age classroom, children of several ages are placed in the same school or classroom for two or more years. Instruction is done through individualization and groupings that change depending on the subject taught and the talents and abilities of the students.

Proponents of multi-age programs believe that because students grow and learn at a pace that does not always match their chronological age, graded classrooms may not meet the developmental needs of many learners. Multi-age programs address the problems of retaining, or flunking, students because progress is made on an individual and not a group, grade-related basis. Collaborative learning is promoted as students of different ages help each other with projects. The benefits of having the same teacher for multiple years were enumerated in the section on looping, and the same arguments are used to advocate for multi-age programs. Most significantly, say proponents, multi-age programs are not locked into the type of rigid, sequential curriculum that is characteristic of graded programs.[40]

There are some potential disadvantages to multi-age programs. At times there may be only a few children of a certain age group, and friendship patterns, although varied, may be limited. Additionally, critics point to the additional time and effort it takes for teachers to plan curriculum projects, conference about student projects, and develop instructional strategies for a wide range of ages and abilities.[41] Clearly, being a teacher in a multi-age program is challenging.

The House or Team Approach: We're All in This Together

Many of today's junior high and high schools are overcrowded and impersonal. In many areas, a high school may serve more than 2,000 students. It is easy for a student to get lost in the crowd and as dropout rates increase, parents and educators have been searching for ways to foster a more personalized approach to education, especially for older students. Some have chosen an approach that breaks up large schools into smaller, more personalized *houses*, or clusters of between 90 and 120 students with a team of three to five teachers. Theodore Sizer, whose Coalition of Essential Schools movement you read about earlier in this chapter, includes such houses as a key element in Essential Schools. In this model, houses are like mini-schools within the larger school where a sense of community is created. Looping is a common characteristic of the house model, with students remaining in the same house throughout their high school years and receiving academic instruction, academic counseling, and personal and social support from a team of teachers and other school staff who get to know "their" students on an individual level. Teachers are able to plan together, interdisciplinary teaching is fostered, and parents and guardians get to know their child's teachers in a more significant way than typically happens in a large high school where students may have a different teacher for every subject, every year.

Currently more than 200 schools in 23 states subscribe to the Essential Schools model of houses,[42] and the model continues to grow in popularity.

Compare this model to the "factory" model of high school discussed earlier. What does the rising popularity of the house model say about our changing theories and priorities in education and in society?

Privatization: Inside and Outside the Public Domain

We would like to end this chapter by making you aware of some options that have been expanding in recent years and are beginning to blur the lines between public and private education in the United States. We discussed charter schools earlier in this chapter. In one sense, charter schools are privately run public schools because they operate according to their own policies, procedures, curriculum, and budget. Yet the state and district must approve the charter, and they are responsible for paying the charter school the per-pupil expenditure cost for each student enrolled. Thus, the vast majority of charter schools are still considered to be a part of a local public system.

You may know that since the inception of schooling, there have been private schools where parents may choose to pay tuition so that their child can attend. Some of these private schools are religiously affiliated. For example, the Catholic Church established private school systems in most communities in the early 1600s. Jewish congregations have established Hebrew schools, and in many communities there are now Muslim schools. Other sectarian and nonsectarian private schools may emphasize a specific area such as academics or sports. Parents who elect to send their child to a private school pay tuition in addition to the school taxes or property taxes that support local public schools. The debate over school vouchers is about parents' ability to choose to send their child to a private school with public funds.

Vouchers are "chits" or credits to parents, typically ranging from $2,500 to $5,000 depending on the district, that are then used to send children to a private school. Different states have different rules (some states have no voucher program at all), but in some states parents may use them to send their children to religiously affiliated schools. This was not always the case. In June 2002, the United States Supreme Court, in the Cleveland, Ohio, case of *Zelman v. Simmons-Harris,* upheld the parents' right to send their child to a religious school if certain conditions were met.

Proponents of vouchers say that all parents should have the same right to choose that wealthy parents now have by virtue of having the financial resources to send their children to whatever school they wish. Opponents of vouchers argue that vouchers undermine public schools, a bedrock of our democracy. They contend that voucher programs violate separation of church and state, and that economically disadvantaged families will not be able to use vouchers because most private schools' tuition and related costs total more than any voucher is worth. Some voucher programs are privately funded. This means that individuals and private foundations offer students a voucher for a portion of private school tuition.

Some public schools, including charter schools, have been contracted out to private corporations and are, in effect, private schools. The Edison Project, a for-profit educational company, is one example. Edison takes over public schools that are experiencing problems, such as in Philadelphia, but they are in operation to make a profit.

What are the implications of the increasing privatization of schools? Many privatization efforts are based on the idea that, as in our capitalist-based economy, competition in the form of a free-market educational system will force all schools to be better. Critics charge that it is not democratic to apply the free-market philosophy to schools. They argue that our democracy depends on an educated citizenry, and they raise questions about the ethics of replicating a "have" and "have not" system with our children as the powerless participants in this experiment. In fact, President George W. Bush's support for the No Child Left Behind legislation includes a voucher-like stipulation that if the test scores of a school do not meet the required standard, families may leave the school and go to another public school that does meet the standard. In a market-based system, those with the financial resources or political savvy have the power to choose and those without will be left behind. Who will be left to advocate for and teach in the schools populated by students whose parents lack the money or the political capital to choose? Critics suggest that a different approach might be for politicians and school leaders to use available resources to provide the necessary materials and environment for all children to succeed and to entice the most talented teachers into the schools where test scores are the lowest.

Finally, we would like to discuss the growing movement toward **home schooling.** Home schooling means that students are schooled at home for the majority of the day (most districts allow students to spend part of the day in the public school for sports or specific courses). Estimates of the actual number of students being home schooled in the United States vary, but research indicates that it is somewhere between 1 and 2 million students in grades K–12. Parents may choose to home school their children for many reasons. Some do not like the quality of education in their local school, some do not agree with the curriculum, and some prefer to add a religious emphasis to their child's education. Each state has rules about how and what a parent must teach when children are home schooled. Home school curricula vary depending on the philosophy of the parents and the reason for home schooling. On one end of the spectrum is "unschooling," a totally unstructured curriculum that emanates from the interests and desires of the child. On the other are tightly prescribed and usually commercially made curricula, sometimes with a religious focus. The "business" of home schooling has become quite big and a check of the Internet will reveal numerous websites where parents can purchase materials, get ideas, and exchange information. Most home schooling families counter the argument that the student misses out on socialization, with the formation of a home school collaborative. Here students from home school families get together for part of the week for activities, field trips, or lessons. In a home school situation, parents make direct decisions about the nature and content of the educational experience.

BACK TO MRS. FOWLER'S STORY

Recall the story that opened this chapter, in which the parents in the Shelby Valley School District chose Mrs. Fowler to speak before the school board about their displeasure with the decision to close one fifth-grade classroom. This action by the board had increased the size of the four remaining classes to 30.

Mrs. Fowler was a bit nervous as she began to speak. She had prepared her remarks carefully, with the assistance of the lawyer in the group and the research data gathered the previous day. She began by reviewing research on class size that clearly indicates that the smaller the class, the greater the student achievement. She told the board that this finding was particularly true in districts with high numbers of low-income and ethnically diverse students. She reminded the board that the district was growing more diverse each year and if they were not proactive in addressing this diversity through small class sizes and more individualized attention, they might begin to see the students of color and the students from low-income families falling behind academically. Mrs. Fowler added that the research indicated that smaller class size allowed teachers to be more innovative and to give more personalized attention to all students, thus making teaching and learning more effective for everyone. She acknowledged that much of the class size research had been conducted in the primary grades, but she emphasized that student success in the intermediate grades is crucial to ensure ongoing success and avoid having students drop out of school. She concluded her remarks by saying that though fifth graders may be seen by some as older, more mature, and in need of a transition to the junior high, they are still only 11 years old and their academic and social success depends on continued nurturing and personalized attention. "After all," she asked, "isn't that what we are all about here?"

The board members, knowing that the open forum is not a time for response and discussion, sat quietly as several other parents spoke in response to Mrs. Fowler. All of the speakers advocated smaller class sizes, and Mrs. Rodriguez questioned the board's wisdom and motives in making such a decision when many families were on vacation. She concluded by remarking that the shared decision-making process did not appear to be very shared!

At the conclusion of the meeting the board moved into executive session, in which they meet alone to discuss issues. Several board members began by complaining about the annoying phone calls that had been non-stop all day. The chair of the board, Dr. Williams, asked board members for their reactions to the parents' remarks, and a discussion ensued about class size. Ms. Denton, the mother of five elementary school children, finally brought the discussion to a close by saying that the money they appeared to be saving by combining the fifth-grade classes did not appear to be worth the bad public relations that had resulted from the quick decision by the board. She agreed that she wanted smaller class sizes for her children and wondered if there were other places in the budget to make reductions if they reinstated the fifth grade and hired a new teacher. She suggested that the board vote on the issue, and she called the question.

As Dr. Williams counted the hands that reluctantly went up around the table, he saw that the vote was unanimous to reinstate the fifth grade. He was not sure if the board was voting based on reconsideration of the facts or because the parents had put such pressure on the members that they were not willing to go against their will. Regardless, he sighed as he realized that the money for the new teacher's salary and benefits would have to be carved out of the budget somehow, and that would be an item for next month's agenda.

FINDING A VOICE

Julie Medina had been teaching nine years in a private school when she decided to pursue a Ph.D. in education. It had been two years since she had completed her master's degree and she missed the challenge of thinking about educational issues in the university context and balancing that with her experiences in the classroom. She realized that it would be a financial commitment to obtain another degree, so she decided to begin her studies on a part-time basis and look for a teaching position in a public school where the salary increase could help pay tuition. It was early July when she received a call from an elementary school principal asking if she would come in for an interview. He told her that there were two third-grade teaching positions open in his building and that he was impressed by her credentials.

As Julie left the interview a few days later, she was pretty confident that she had done a good job. Although it was intimidating to sit before two principals, three teachers, a teacher's aide, and two parents, she spoke with confidence about her classroom management strategies, curriculum units she had designed, and assessment instruments she had experimented with over the years. Julie used stories from her own experience, pulling several items from her portfolio as concrete examples of what she was describing. She liked the principal and the two teachers on the interview committee. All of them seemed to have the same educational philosophy as she, and Julie felt that she would fit in well at the school. She was very pleased when, two days later, she was offered one of the positions at a salary almost $10,000 a year higher than her private school job. She quickly called her advisor at the university and enrolled in the first course in her program, School and Society, figuring that she could handle one graduate course per semester as she began teaching in a new school.

The end of August was hectic as Julie prepared her room for the third graders. She was somewhat surprised when the second-grade teachers walked in one day and handed her a list of students' names divided into three groups. She recognized the names from her class roster and asked about the way in which the names were grouped. The second-grade team leader told her that those were to be Julie's reading groups. Not long after that, the third-grade team leader arrived with the other new third-grade teacher in tow and announced that it was time to decide who would teach which math group. Julie questioned what was happening. Ms. Bolton, a 30-year veteran teacher in the district, told her that although the third grades were primarily self-contained classrooms, the students were grouped homogeneously for math from 12:30 to 1:30 P.M. each day. Ms. Bolton continued by stating that since she had seniority, she was claiming the "high" math group. Mr. Silver, the other new teacher, looked toward the floor. Julie broke the uncomfortable silence by saying that she would take the "low" math group and Mr. Silver could have the "middle" or average group if he preferred. Everyone agreed and the other teachers left Julie's room.

As Julie continued to hang up beginning-of-the-year decorations, she was still reeling from the surprise. She had no idea that the district used ability grouping so extensively. She decided to disregard the reading groups and do some informal assessments and formal testing on the students during the first two weeks. She just did not feel comfortable placing students in groups based on someone else's opinions of their capabilities. There did not seem to be anything she could do about the math groups and she looked forward to working with the so-called "low" kids. Julie had struggled with mathematics throughout school, and she took great pleasure in helping kids understand and achieve in mathematics.

Julie had a busy September. She began her graduate course and decided to do the assigned research paper on ability grouping because it seemed to be such a common practice in her new district. Her third graders turned out to be a wonderful yet challenging class, as the students represented a wide range of abilities. Julie had decided not to use ability groups in reading. Her informal reading inventories indicated that all of her children were capable of comprehending text. Their basic word attack skills were good, and most of them seemed to enjoy writing in weekly dialogue journals where they wrote stories and Julie responded back, building a teacher–student dialogue and allowing her to get a weekly, individual look at their informal writing progress. She began the year by allowing the students to select from three different chapter books, and they selected their books based on interest rather than the level of difficulty of the text. Although some of the former "low group" students struggled with the vocabulary in their chosen books, the peer interaction and Julie's individual assistance resulted in a high degree of success. She was most proud of the fact that several students told her that they had never been allowed to read chapter books before, and Julie sensed their pride as they quickly realized their capabilities. She developed a list of individual projects for each book, and the students could select from the list. Each student was required to complete two projects, and they could do more if they desired. Julie complemented the heterogeneously organized reading groups with lots of cooperative group activities in social studies and science. Occasionally she would group those who struggled with reading together so she could offer extra help in the content areas but all in all, Julie was pleased with the progress of all the students. Julie kept track of how the groups were organized, taking notes on who worked well together and who had trouble during the activities. In general, the children were getting along with each other, the "top" kids were challenged, and the so-called "low" kids were making steady progress. The year seemed to be off to a good start.

Toward the end of October, Julie began to get phone calls from the mothers of some of the girls in her class. Several of the girls were apparently quite unhappy. Their mothers told Julie that friendship patterns that had existed since kindergarten were crumbling and their daughters were coming home crying that former friends were playing with different children on the playground and eating with different friends in the cafeteria. Julie began to diagram the former friendship patterns as told to her by the parents. She went out to recess with the students and watched who played with whom and compared it to the information provided by the mothers. She ate lunch with the students two days a week and observed who sat with whom, listening carefully to stories of who stayed overnight at whose house on the weekend. Julie was beginning to form an opinion about what might be occurring. She decided to investigate further.

Julie's research on ability grouping was adding to her classroom investigation. She was finding that once students were "labeled" by ability, they almost never lost that label throughout school. It seemed that "once a low group member, always a low member" was usually true. Julie went to the kindergarten teachers with her class list and asked if the children had been grouped in kindergarten. She was shocked to hear the kindergarten teacher go through her class list and label each student. Julie realized that the children in her class had been in the same ability groups since kindergarten! She could not believe that what she was reading about in the education journals was actually happening in her school. She was even more distressed because she realized that the comments by the children that frustrated her as she tried to challenge them to do more difficult work were most likely the result of inflexible grouping patterns. She grew anxious hearing the former "low" group kids tell her that they couldn't read certain books or write long stories because they were "too dumb." The research finding that by the end of first grade, children in classrooms with inflexible ability groups had internalized perceptions about their own ability as well as that of others was borne out in her classroom. The former "low" group students often characterized themselves negatively, and the former "high" group members certainly had a positive, if not inflated, view of themselves as learners. This made sense to her because she remembered her surprise as members of the former "high" group complained that they did not want to work with certain children who Julie now realized had been characterized as "low" before.

Julie hypothesized that when she broke up the ability groups for reading, she also broke up the social groups in her classroom. In other words, since the children spent at least 90 minutes in reading activities each morning, they logically became friends with those children with whom they spent so much instructional time. They went to recess and lunch with their "reading buddies" and social patterns began to form that continued over the years. When Julie broke up the groups and children began working with others because of her use of flexible groups, social patterns among the girls began to change. Some of the girls were able to successfully enlarge their circle of friends, but others had difficulty negotiating new friendships and suffered from hurt feelings as they watched their former "best" friends play with other children.

As Julie typed up her research paper, she used her classroom data as a backdrop for reporting the research she found. She began to extrapolate the effects of inflexible ability groups into the future. If teacher after teacher kept children grouped by ability year after year, what might be the results? Julie hypothesized that these friendship patterns could have multiple implications. If the "low" group children stayed together, internalizing the image of themselves as incapable, would they drop out of school? Abuse alcohol and drugs? Be more susceptible to getting into trouble? Would the "high" group students logically see themselves as college material? Julie imagined all sorts of possibilities.

Clearly Julie felt that her work was cut out for her. Her action research project for the second semester would be to examine the effects of self-perception as a learner on student achievement. She vowed that no student in her classroom would see him- or herself as incapable of learning. She began to develop more specific strategies for addressing the social relationships in her classroom and for continuing her instruction through the use of flexible groups. Julie wanted her classroom to be community-oriented, and she knew that she would never achieve that goal until all of the students could see the talents and abilities of their classmates. In this way, everyone would achieve at a higher level. The most difficult task would be addressing the entire issue of ability grouping from a school-wide perspective. As a nontenured teacher, Julie would have to spend quite some time thinking about how to approach the topic with her colleagues.

Julie was exhausted as the winter break approached. As she sat through her last graduate class of the semester, she should have been listening to the professor but found herself reflecting on the past few months. She had rarely taken such an analytical approach to her teaching practice but she felt such satisfaction at having used educational research as well as her classroom experiences to make sense of a serious issue in her teaching. As class ended, she picked up her research paper from the professor's desk and thanked him for a good class. On the way to her car, she opened up to the last page to check her grade. As the "A" jumped off the page, Julie smiled. "I guess Dr. Donovan thought that I did a good job of connecting research to practice too!"

School organizational issues are complex. The key question that should drive all educational decisions, "What is best for students?" often gets lost as factors such as finance, convenience, and legal issues play a role in how districts, schools, and classrooms operate. Exciting innovations are taking place in education today, and teachers can and should be intimately involved in debates about how schools and classrooms are organized. Some teachers, like Julie, find a voice by taking action in their own classrooms. Some find a voice by speaking out to a larger audience. The key is to remember that schools are organized for the purpose of educating children in a democracy. Those who make organizational decisions about schools must keep the central question of what is best for students at the forefront of discussions about school organization.

Summing Up

Most prospective teachers do not think too much about school organizational issues during their pre-service training. Some assume that there is little they can do about the school calendar, how schools are organized in a district, which students are at a particular grade level, and how students are grouped for instruction. In fact, a teacher can exercise a great deal of control over organizational factors as they affect his or her job. For example, teachers may not be able to change the school calendar that is set by the school board, but they can control what is done with the allotted time in the classroom. A wise teacher uses the school calendar to his or her advantage in maximizing instructional time, which results in greater academic achievement for the students.

It is also possible for teachers to work with administrators, parents, and community members on shared decision-making teams that have a great deal of influence on organizational decisions. Teachers can rally support from parents and community members for those arrangements that they feel best meet the needs of the students in the district.

Perhaps the most important thing to remember is that the organizational decisions that teachers make on a daily basis can have a lasting effect on students' academic and social achievement. The decisions that a teacher makes about how to schedule the day, how to group students for instruction, and how to work effectively with colleagues and parents have a direct impact on students. The degree of enthusiasm a teacher has for innovation, reform, and continual growth as a professional often makes the difference between a teacher who "burns out" of teaching and one who becomes a star teacher.

KEY TERMS

ability grouping
Carnegie unit
centralized school system
charter schools
Coalition of Essential Schools
combination classroom
decentralized school system
Head Start
heterogeneous grouping
home schooling
homogeneous grouping
immersion or centric schools
junior high school

looping
magnet schools
middle school
Montessori method
multi-age grouping
neighborhood schools
Reggio Emilia
team teaching
tracking
two-way bilingual schools
vouchers
White flight

QUESTIONS FOR REFLECTION

1. If you had to choose between sending your child to a neighborhood school or sending your child to a magnet school, which would you choose? Why?
2. Separating specific groups of students (e.g., African American students, gay and lesbian students) is a controversial topic. What do you see as the pros

and cons of providing separate schools for specific groups of students whose educational and social needs are not being met in traditional schools?

3. Researchers are now beginning to study charter schools in an in-depth way. What are the factors that should be considered in evaluating the effectiveness of charter schools?

4. Given what research tells us about the negative results of ability grouping on students, what strategies can teachers use to ensure that all students receive "high-status" knowledge that prepares them to advance their education beyond high school?

5. Looping, the practice of teacher and students staying together for two or more years, is gaining in popularity in the United States. If you had to convince your local school board to adopt a looping policy, what would you say?

6. What federal influences in education have you experienced or have been most evident in your local schools (e.g., Head Start, No Child Left Behind)?

7. What is the philosophical difference between a middle school and a junior high? From what historical trends does each idea emanate?

8. What factors might explain the overrepresentation of males of color in special education?

ACTIVITIES

1. Visit a school in your area that is designated as a junior high or one that is designated as a middle school. Does it meet the criteria for that designation? Interview teachers in the building about the factors that make the school either a junior high or a middle school. How do the teachers see their role? How would they describe the curriculum? How are students organized for instruction?

2. Visit a magnet school. Find out how and why students are selected for attendance at the school. How is the theme of the school manifested in the school environment, organization, and curriculum? If possible, interview students to find out why they attend the magnet school.

3. Research the history of kindergarten from its beginning in Europe to its current status in the United States. Identify the debates about the purpose and objectives of kindergarten.

4. Interview a school board member in your area about his or her role. Why did that person want to be on the school board? What issues does the board member feel are most important today? How are decisions in the district made? Ask any other questions that you may have about the important role of school boards in the community.

5. Find out if there is a high school in your area that utilizes the principles of Sizer's Coalition of Essential Schools. If so, visit the school to observe its organization and operation.

6. Get out your middle school or high school yearbook. Note which students were in the lower tracked classes and which were in the advanced placement, college preparatory, or high-track classes. Did those students remain in those tracks for their entire school career? See if you can find out what several students from each track are doing now. If possible, interview them about their school experiences, their perceptions of themselves as learners,

and their experiences after high school. Compare them to your own. What conclusions can you draw about tracking?

7. Obtain an application for a charter school. Several applications can be obtained from the websites of state education departments in states that allow charter schools (e.g., Minnesota, Massachusetts, Utah, Arizona, Florida). Examine the types of information that groups wanting to start a charter school must provide. How easy is it to obtain a charter?

GETTING CONNECTED

The Coalition of Essential Schools http://www.essentialschools.org	A reform organization of innovative schools around the country. CES was founded by Theodore Sizer.
The National Middle School Association 2600 Corporate Exchange Drive, Suite 370 Columbus, OH 43231-1672 http://www.nmsa.org 1-800-528-NMSA Fax: 614-895-4750	An organization dedicated to the education, development, and growth of young adolescents. Publishes the *Middle School Journal* and *Research in Middle Level Education Quarterly*.
National Association for the Education of the Young Child (NAEYC) 16th Street, NW Washington, DC 20036 1-800-424-2460 http://www.naeyc.org/naeyc	Organization dedicated to excellence in the education of PreK–3 students. Catalog of excellent educational 1509 books and materials is available.
U.S. Charter Schools http://www.uscharterschools.org	This site on charter schools is sponsored by WestEd, a nonprofit research, development, and service agency headquartered in San Francisco with 16 offices nationwide. The site contains information on current charter schools, charter school legislation, and other issues related to charter schools.
Rethinking Schools 1-800-669-4192 http://www.rethinkingschools.org	Rethinking Schools is an organization dedicated to equity, school reform for more humane schools, and a critical analysis of school practices. Excellent newspaper and publications on critical school issues.

Association for Childhood
Education International
11501 Georgia Ave., Suite 315
Wheaton, MD 20902
1-800-423-3563
http://www.udel.edu/bateman/acei

ACEI is an organization that promotes quality education from preprimary through early adolescence (middle school). ACEI has several publications that would be of interest to future preschool and elementary teachers.

Association for Persons with Severe
Disabilities (TASH)
http://www.tash.org

TASH is an organization that provides support and resources for working with severe disabilities in the classroom. They hold an annual conference and publish a journal.

The Gay, Lesbian, and Straight
Educators Network (GLSEN)
121 W. 27th St., Suite 804
New York, NY 10012-2317
(212) 995-8585
http://www.glsen.org

The only national organization working to end anti-gay bias in schools. Has videos and publications.

National Association for Bilingual
Education
1220 L Street, NW, Suite 605
Washington, DC 20005-4018
(202) 898-1829
http://www.nabe.org

NABE provides teachers with resource related to bilingual education. An excellent source of information about topics related to language and culture in the schools and about bilingual schools.

National Coalition for the Homeless
1012 14th Street, NW, Suite 600
Washington, DC 20005
http://nch.ari.net

These two sites provide a wealth of information and resources on the issue of homelessness in the United States, including up-to-date references on the status of children who are homeless.

National Law Center of
Homelessness and Poverty
918 F Street, NW, Suite 412
Washington, DC 20004
http://www.nlchp.org

SUGGESTED RESOURCES

Books on Charter Schools and Alternative Schools

Barr, Robert D., and W. Parrett. *How to Create Alternative, Magnet, and Charter Schools That Work*. Bloomington, IN: National Educational Service, 1997.

Meier, Deborah. *The Power of Their Ideas: Lessons for America From a Small School in Harlem.* Boston: Beacon Press, 1995.

Sarason, Seymour. *Charter Schools: Another Flawed Educational Reform?* New York: Teachers College Press, 1998.

Books on Tracking and Ability Grouping

Oakes, Jeannie. *Keeping Track: How Schools Structure Inequality.* New Haven, CT: Yale University Press, 1995.

Wheelock, Anne. *Crossing the Tracks: How "Untracking" Can Save America's Schools.* New York: New Press, 1992.

NOTES

1. R. L. Church, *Education in the United States* (New York: Free Press, 1976).
2. Ibid.
3. G. Orfield and J. Yun, *Resegregation in American Schools* (Cambridge, MA: Harvard University, The Civil Rights Projects, 1999), available at http://www.law.harvard.edu
4. G. Orfield, "Schools More Separate," in *Rethinking School Reform: Views From the Classroom,* ed. L. Christensen and S. Karp (Milwaukee, WI: Rethinking Schools, 2003).
5. L. Stalvey, *The Education of a WASP* (Madison: University of Wisconsin Press, 1989).
6. C. A. Grant and G. Ladson-Billings, *Dictionary of Multicultural Education* (Phoenix, AZ: Onyx Press, 1997).
7. C. J. Faltz and D. O. Leake, "The All-Black School: Inherently Unequal or a Culture-Based Alternative?" in *Beyond Desegregation: The Politics of Quality in African-American Schooling,* ed. M. J. Shujaa (Thousand Oaks, CA: Corwin Press, 1996).
8. Ibid.
9. Ibid., 246–247.
10. N. Gonzalez, L. Moll, M. Floyd-Tenery, A. Rivera, P. Rendon, R. Gonzalez, and C. Amanti, "Funds of Knowledge for Teaching in Latino Households," *Urban Education* 29 (1995): 443–470.
11. T. L. McCarty, *A Place to Be Navajo: Rough Rock and the Struggle for Self-Determination in Indigenous Schooling* (Mahwah, NJ: Erlbaum, 2002), 21.
12. J. Reyhner and J. Eder, "A History of Indian Education," in *Teaching American Indian Students,* ed. J. Reyhner (Norman: University of Oklahoma Press, 1992).
13. J. Reyhner, "Bilingual Education," in *Teaching American Indian Students,* ed. J. Reyhner (Norman: University of Oklahoma Press, 1992).
14. Ibid., 69.
15. McCarty, *A Place to Be Navajo.*
16. D. Christian, *Two-Way Bilingual Education: Students Learning Through Two Languages* (Washington, DC: National Center for Research on Cultural Diversity and Second Language Learning, 1994), 2.
17. Ibid.

18. D. Christian and A. Whitcher, *Directory of Two-Way Bilingual Programs in the United States,* rev. ed. (Washington, DC: National Center for Research on Cultural Diversity and Second Language Learning, 1995).

19. J. Nathan, "Heat and Light in the Charter School Movement," *Phi Delta Kappan,* March 1998.

20. B. V. Manno, C. E. Finn, L. A. Bierlein, and G. Vanourek, "How Charter Schools Are Different," *Phi Delta Kappan,* March 1998.

21. Ibid., 490.

22. J. R. McKinney, "Charter Schools: A New Barrier for Children With Disabilities," *Phi Delta Kappan,* March 1998.

23. Public Policy Forum, *Research Brief* 89, no. 9 (Milwaukee, WI: Author, 2001).

24. R. F. Butts and L. A. Cremin, *A History of American Education* (New York: Holt, Rinehart and Winston, 1953).

25. Ibid., 55–56.

26. Ibid., 416–417.

27. L. Delpit, *Other People's Children: Cultural Conflict in the Classroom* (New York: New Press, 1995).

28. Ibid., 421–422.

29. Ibid., 586.

30. C. K. McEwin, T. S. Dickinson, and D. M. Jenkins, *America's Middle Schools: Practices and Progress. A 25-Year Perspective* (Columbus, OH: National Middle School Association, 1996).

31. Butts and Cremin, *History of American Education.*

32. R. L. Church, *Education in the United States* (New York: Macmillan, 1976).

33. E. Levine, *One Kid at a Time: Big Lessons From a Small School* (New York: Teachers College Press, 2002).

34. Ibid., xix.

35. J. Oakes and M. Lipton, *Teaching to Change the World* (Boston: McGraw-Hill, 1999).

36. D. J. Logen and G. Orfield, eds., *Racial Inequality in Special Education* (Cambridge, MA: Harvard University Press, 2002).

37. M. Calderon, "Dual Language Programs and Team-Teachers' Professional Development" (paper presented at the annual meeting of the American Educational Research Association, San Francisco, 1995).

38. B. D. Day and T. Yarbrough, "Revisiting the Multi-Age Classroom: An Old Concept for a New Millennium," *Bulletin* 64, no. 4 (Summer 1998).

39. Ibid., 38.

40. Ibid., 39.

41. Ibid., 40.

42. T. Sizer, *Horace's School* (New York: Houghton Mifflin, 1992).

PURSUING AN EDUCATIONAL PHILOSOPHY

© Scholastic Studio 10/Index Stock Imagery

FOCUS QUESTIONS

1. How has philosophy served humankind?
2. How has philosophy influenced education?
3. Why do today's teachers need to be aware of the different philosophies, such as Western, Far Eastern, and Indian philosophies?
4. What role did philosophy play in the development of the educational system in the United States?
5. How do educational philosophies influences teaching?
6. Why should teacher candidates develop an educational philosophy?

VIGNETTE

GETTING STARTED ON MY EDUCATIONAL PHILOSOPHY

The students' verbal and nonverbal communication revealed confusion and frustration as Tom explained the requirement for writing the "philosophy paper" in his Introduction to Education class. Questions such as the following interrupted Tom as he was explaining the assignment: "How many pages? What percentage of the course grade is the paper? How should references and other resources be used?" Tom remained relaxed and patient with the class. The scene was "déjà vu" of what he had experienced over the past 10 years of teaching the Intro class.

The reason behind most of the students' questions, he knew, was anxiety. The anxiety was over being asked to write a paper that reflects their own ideas and to support those ideas with data from the educational philosophy literature. Tom was empathetic and gave time and attention to each question. He learned over the years that the "philosophy paper" was the first paper many students were asked to write that demanded their ideas and beliefs along with supporting literature. Also, the word "philosophy" increased the tension. The assignment was a big step up from reading a few chapters and regurgitating the information or doing a project that mainly demanded pulling information off the Internet or from some library books. None of the students had taken a philosophy class. They were at the mercy of everything good and bad that they had heard about philosophy. Most believed that the study of philosophy was old, and not relevant to today's classrooms.

Brad asked, "How can such questions as 'What is the essence of life?' be relevant to what teachers need to do when facing a group of squirming and possibly low-achieving elementary and middle school students on Monday morning?"

Sarah and several other students wanted to know why there was a need to do a philosophy paper now, so early in the teacher preparation program. Sarah said, "I believe that I will be able to do a better job writing about my philosophy of education after I have taught school for a while."

Tom replied, "Yes, your philosophy would have a more real-world quality about it if you had taught for a while. But," he added, "it is also important that teacher candidates compose their philosophies outside of the pressure to conform to the existing practices promoted by a school."

Mark called out, "I don't know where to begin. What suggestions do you have for getting started?"

Tom replied by holding up a copy of "What Is Your EP?" (Exhibit 8.1). "Here is a questionnaire, 'What Is Your Educational Philosophy?' Please complete and score it according to the directions, and an educational philosophy that is consistent with the responses you give to the questions will be revealed. The educational philosophies the survey identifies are perennialism, essentialism, experimentalism, reconstructionism, existentialism, and postmodernism."

Sarah, Mark, and the other students each took a questionnaire and began to complete it. There was some complaining about the wording of the questions, and for some of the questions they agreed with more than one response. Tom told them it was just an indicator to get them started, and they were not wedded to their responses. Of the 30 students in the class, the score from the EP questionnaire indicated that 5 were essentialists, 3 were perennialists, 14 were experimentalists, 4 were reconstructionists, and 4 were existentialists. Tom asked them to group themselves according to their philosophies and to begin to compare ideas.

EXHIBIT **8.1**   **WHAT IS YOUR EP?**

Instructions

Please check the answer under each item that best reflects your thinking. You may want to check more than one answer for any one of the questions.

1. What is the essence of education?

   A. The essence of education is reason and intuition.

   B. The essence of education is growth.

   C. The essence of education is social action.

   D. The essence of education is knowledge and skills.

   E. The essence of education is choice.

   F. The essence of education is to question rationality.

2. What is the nature of the learner?

   A. The learner is an experiencing organism.

   B. The learner is a unique, free choosing, and responsible creature made up of intellect and emotion.

   C. The learner is a rational and intuitive being.

   D. The learner is a storehouse for knowledge and skills that, once acquired, can later be applied and used.

   E. The learner is an experiencing member of social collectivities.

   F. The learner is a self-controlled, flexible, active pursuer of meaning, with a preference for the temporary over the permanent, and comfortable with multiple realities.

3. How should education provide for the needs of people?

   A. The students need a passionate encounter with the perennial problems of life: the agony and joy of love, reality of choice, anguish of freedom, consequences of actions, and the inevitability of death.

   B. Education should help people identify with and contribute to social groups, and should equip people with the knowledge and skills needed to make society a more humane place.

   C. Education provides for the needs of people when it inculcates the child with certain essential skills and knowledge that all should possess.

   D. The one distinguishing characteristic of humanity is intelligence. Education should concentrate on meeting the intellectual needs of students.

   E. Since the needs of people are variable, education should concentrate on developing the individual differences in students.

   F. Education should help people to realize there is no such thing as objectivity; it should de-center the subject, questioned modern rationality, and illuminate the systems of reasons that keep in place structures and authority.

4. What should be the environment of education?

   A. Education should have an environment in which the student adjusts to the material and social world as it really exists.

   B. The environment of education should be life itself—where students can experience living, not prepare for it.

   C. The environment of education should be one that encourages the growth of free, creative individuality, not adjustment to group thinking or the public norms.

EXHIBIT **8.1**   **CONTINUED**

D. Education is not a true replica of life; rather, it is an artificial environment in which the children should be developing their intellectual potentialities and preparing for the future.

E. The environment of education should encourage creativity and decision making; it should also include sensitivity to others and the skills for taking social action.

F. The environment of education should encourage multiple interpretations, question modern rationality and modern versions of truth, and encourage individuals to be relaxed, flexible, and comfortable with multiple realities.

5. What should be the goal of education?

A. Growth, through the reconstruction of experience, is the nature, and should be the open-ended goal, of education.

B. The only type of goal to which education should lead is the goal of truth, which is absolute, universal, and unchanging.

C. The primary concern of education should be with the development of the uniqueness of individual students.

D. The goal of education should be the preparation of citizens to construct a more just society.

E. The goal of education should be to provide a framework of knowledge for the student against which new truths can be gathered and assimilated.

F. The goal of education should be to prepare individuals to appreciate multiple interpretations and realities and to de-construct modern rationality.

6. What should be the concern of the school?

A. The school should concern itself with humanity's distinguishing characteristic, the mind, and concentrate on developing rationality.

B. The school should provide an education for the "whole child," centering its attention on all the needs and interests of the child.

C. The school should be concerned with society as a whole, the local community, and how life can be improved for social groups.

D. The school should educate the child to attain the basic knowledge necessary to understand the real world outside.

E. The school should provide each student with assistance in his journey toward self-realization.

F. The school should be concerned with preparing each student to have an open mind about notions of truths, to be comfortable with multiple realities, and to express themselves openly.

7. What should be the atmosphere of the school?

A. The school should provide for group thinking in a democratic atmosphere that fosters cooperation rather than competition.

B. The school should foster an atmosphere of collective action in tackling current human problems.

C. The atmosphere of the school should be one of authentic freedom in which a student is allowed to find his or her own truth and ultimate fulfillment through nonconforming choice making.

D. The school should surround its students with "great books" and foster individuality in an atmosphere of intellectualism and creative thinking.

(continued)

EXHIBIT **8.1** **CONTINUED**

   E. The school should retain an atmosphere of mental discipline, yet incorporate innovative techniques that introduce students to a perceptual examination of the realities about them.

   F. The atmosphere of the school should be one in which students are not pressured by old loyalties and modern affiliations, are able to freely express themselves, and are not hampered by traditional norms, general rules and regulations, and hegemonic systems of thought.

8. How should appropriate learning occur?

   A. Appropriate learning occurs as students freely engages in choosing among alternatives while weighing personal responsibilities and the possible consequences of their actions.

   B. Appropriate learning takes place through the experience of problem-solving projects by which the child is led from practical issues to theoretical principles (concrete-to-abstract).

   C. Appropriate learning takes place as certain basic readings acquaint students with the world's permanencies, inculcating them in theoretical principles that they will later apply in life (abstract-to-concrete).

   D. Appropriate learning takes place when students examine and act upon problems that affect themselves and other people.

   E. Appropriate learning occurs when hard effort has been extended to absorb and master the prescribed subject matter.

   F. Appropriate learning occurs as students examine multiple interpretations and realities, de-center subjects, and are not confined to traditional norms and regulations.

9. What should be the role of the teacher?

   A. The teacher should lead the students toward an awareness of social problems, and guide students as they analyze problems and learn to act on them.

   B. The teacher should discipline pupils intellectually through a study of the great works in literature where the universal concerns of humanity have best been expressed.

   C. The teacher should present principles and values and the reasons for them, encouraging students to examine them in order to choose for themselves whether or not to accept them.

   D. The teacher should guide and advise students, but the children's own interests should determine what they learn, not authority or the subject matter of the textbooks.

   E. The teacher, the responsible authority, should mediate between the adult world and the world of the child because immature students cannot comprehend the nature and demands of adulthood by themselves.

   F. The teacher should teach students how to expose knowledge claims that are presented as authoritative and structured. They should guide students to question structural and positivist meanings and standards, challenge biases, and shed light on the social construction of meanings.

10. What should the curriculum include?

   A. The curriculum should include only that which has survived the test of time and combines the symbols and ideas of literature, history, and mathematics with the sciences of the physical world.

   B. The curriculum should concentrate on teaching students how to manage change through problem-solving activities in the social studies, empirical sciences, and vocational technology.

EXHIBIT **8.1** CONTINUED

C. The curriculum should concentrate on intellectual subject matter and include English, language, history, mathematics, natural sciences, the fine arts, and also philosophy.

D. The curriculum should concentrate on the humanities, history, literature, philosophy, and art—where greater depth into human nature and human conflict with the world are revealed.

E. The curriculum should be organized around real social problems of concern to the students as well as others in society, and should include content and skills that bear on those problems.

F. The curriculum should be open, plural, and global; provide multiple interpretations of events; and encourage students to create texts that consider their background and experiences and that are interactive.

11. What should be the preferred teaching method?

A. Projects should be the preferred method whereby the students can be guided through problem-solving experiences.

B. Lectures, readings, and discussions should be the preferred methods of training the intellect.

C. Demonstrations should be the preferred method for teaching knowledge and skills.

D. Socratic dialogue (drawing responses from a questioning conversation) should be the preferred method for finding the self.

E. Multiple discussion formats should change according to questions and subject matter; experimental methods should use performance and exercises that de-stabilize roles of teacher and students.

Scoring the Test

This test is self-scoring. Circle the answer you selected for each of the questions checked on the test. Total the number of circles below each column.

	Peren-nialism	Essen-tialism	Experi-mentalism	Reconstruc-tionism	Existen-tialism	Post-modernism
1.	A	D	B	C	E	F
2.	C	D	A	E	B	F
3.	D	C	E	B	A	F
4.	D	A	B	E	C	F
5.	B	E	A	D	C	F
6.	A	C	B	C	D	F
7.	D	E	A	B	C	F
8.	C	E	B	D	A	F
9.	B	E	D	A	C	F
10.	A	C	B	E	D	F
11.	D	B	A	A	C	E

Source: Based on "What Is Your EP: A Test Which Identifies Your Educational Philosophy" by Patricia D. Jersin, in *Clearing House* Vol. 46, January 1972, pp. 274–278, modified by Grant and Gillette.

> Immediately, the students wanted to know what each philosophy meant in general and what each philosophy meant about the kind of teacher they would be. Tom smiled and said, "This assignment will help you to discover more about the kind of teacher you are now, and the kind of teacher you want to become. Also, you now know which classmates are in your philosophy group and which classmates are in other groups. I encourage you to discuss your philosophy with both groups of students. Evaluate the similarities and differences."

We will return to Tom, Sarah, Mark, and the other students in the Introduction to Education class later in the chapter. First, however, we discuss why it is essential that teacher candidates seek to know their philosophy of education.

PHILOSOPHY: WHAT IS IT?

To many, *philosophy* means "love of wisdom." It is an activity, a way of thinking logically about questions that concern humankind. Some say philosophy is a hunt for knowledge about questions that are as profound as the following: "What is the meaning of life?" "What is truth?" "What is happiness?" "What is right and what is wrong?" Also, philosophy is considered a hunt for knowledge about questions that deal with our daily behavior and activities: "What are my prejudices?" "Why do I believe as I do?" Additionally, philosophy can be concerned with questions about politics, religion, science, art, and education. It can be an analytical tool to help professionals such as scientists, politicians, and teachers consider questions about which they desire knowledge. Furthermore, it can be a vehicle that teacher candidates use to identify and develop those qualities that will help them to become dynamic teachers.

Is Philosophy a Part of the Sciences or the Humanities?

Philosophy at times may seem like a science, in that there is a pursuit of "truth," and a philosopher has the excitement of participating in an investigation in the way that a scientist does. On the other hand, philosophy may seem to be connected to the humanities, in that the classics of philosophy do not become dated. For example, if teacher candidates wish to learn physics or chemistry, as opposed to history, they do not read Newton or Faraday; whereas in the humanities, they read Homer and Shakespeare not merely to learn about the quaint things that people thought about in the past, but also to understand the present. And the same is true of philosophy. Confucius and Plato are not read simply in a spirit of antiquarian curiosity. So philosophy seems to combine being a discipline in pursuit of "truth," in which things are discovered as in a science, with being, like literature, a human discipline in which great works don't age.[1]

Be it science or humanities, once teacher candidates have developed their philosophy of education, they claim that is personally, intellectually, and socially rewarding.

The Value of Philosophy

The difficulty of gaining an understanding of philosophy, though a slippery slope to traverse, is often exaggerated—especially in light of the value gained from developing a philosophy and having a philosophy to deal with the big and small questions in life. Philosophy is of value, in part, because it:

1. Helps to bring new interpretation and new syntheses to existing concepts and procedures; and helps in analyzing, refining, and modifying existing concepts and procedures.
2. Acts as a clearinghouse not only for evaluating traditional knowledge, but for analyzing and clarifying problems as yet unsolved, problems whose nature are still unclear and whose solution is not yet seen obviously to belong to one of the established disciplines. It can help the scientist, the theologian, the historian, or the educationist to see their way more clearly, to ask the right questions, to avoid pursuing false trails and being misled into error by confused concepts or faulty argument.
3. Offers a source of ethical guidance; it is useful in helping to make practical decisions about right and wrong, and what one ought to do. It can help to explain the meaning of terms like "good" and "ought"; it can point to alternative choices within a situation and suggest the probable consequences of choosing one choice over another; it can thus ensure that when making a moral decision, it is based on good evidence and sound reasoning.
4. Induces valuable habits of mind like tolerance, impartiality, and suspension of judgment; it protects against precipitancy of both assent and dissent; it encourages a resolute aversion to all forms of intellectuals shoddiness. It brings, too, a serenity which springs from insights into and acceptance of the situation as it is. [2]

In other words, the value of a philosophy of education is that it can help one interpret and analyze existing beliefs. It can help in interpreting and clarifying unresolved questions, as well as distinguishing between right and wrong. Last, it may help develop intelligent and serene ways of thinking and acting.

The value to humankind of philosophy—that is, a search for wisdom and knowledge—has been appreciated since the early history of civilization. This hunt for knowledge has been undertaken by societies all over the world. Western society, Far Eastern society, and Indian society, for example, have all actively engaged in philosophical thought. Western philosophy is associated with European and North American societies. Far Eastern philosophy includes ideas and thought associated with Asian and African societies. Indian philosophy is mostly associated with India. The philosophies of these three regions are not meant to be representative of all philosophies, but to offer an idea of the different philosophies that influence educational philosophy at present.

The search for knowledge has produced many favorable results for humankind. It has provided a better understanding of the actions of men and women and how the universe functions. No longer do people think the world is flat, or that everything is made of water, or air, or that all things are numbers. However, the search for knowledge during ancient times for the most part neglected seeking knowledge about the diversity of humankind. This neglect, which has been carried over into today's society, instituted ways of thinking that for decades muted philosophical thoughts and actions about social justice in societal institutions, including schools.

Who Are Philosophers and What Do They Do?

Philosophers in ancient Greece were individuals who asked questions about anything and everything. Philosophers taught their students "to question and to question." In their quest for knowledge, some philosophers would argue and debate, and some would use deductive reasoning—reasoning that moves from a known principle to an unknown, from general to specific ideas. Arthur Conan Doyle's Sherlock Holmes is a literary figure famous for his "power of deduction." Inductive reasoning, in contrast, draws a general rule from particular facts, moving from specifics to general conclusions.

Present-day philosophers continue pretty much in the same tradition. They ask questions, argue and debate, and use both inductive and deductive reasoning. However, today many Western philosophers have moved away from discussing the perennial problems and issues of morality and truth inspired by the work of Socrates and Plato. Instead, they have moved to cultural commentary or to the offering of interpretations that attempt to explain, for example, the United States, England, or France, *to itself*, at a particular historical moment.[3] These philosophers have become concerned with power, provocation, and personality, instead of grounding knowledge, regulating instruction, and promoting tradition. Also, some of them use postmodern, poststructural, feminist, and multicultural reasoning to examine issues. They are more interested in offering ideas to people who get caught up in the whirlwinds of social crisis, the crossfire of ideological arguments, and the storms of race, class, gender, sexuality, and ability conflicts.[4]

Philosophers who are particularly interested in education ask questions that deal with such issues as school and society, the purpose of education, the role of government in education, and how to achieve equality in education. Also, they ask questions such as "What is philosophy of education?" and debate the connection between "philosophy" and "philosophy of education." Philosophers who consider themselves feminist often ask questions regarding the education of women and girls and questions that challenge the patriarchal discourses in discussions of philosophy. Similarly, philosophers interested in antiracist pedagogy and policies consider questions that challenge racist discourses in discussions of philosophy.

EARLY HISTORY

Western Philosophy

Ancient Greece, during the sixth century B.C.E., marks the beginning of Western philosophy. Thales, a Greek politician and astronomer, is credited with starting philosophy. He was searching for the unity of things in the world. He wondered if at the beginning of the world everything was made of water or air. Greeks, unlike Egyptians and Babylonians of ancient time, were not satisfied with religious and mythical answers to questions about life; they sought "scientific" answers. For example, Pythagoras, whom we all know from our geometry classes, sought mathematical truths to questions that puzzled him. He used deductive reasoning to solve geometry problems. Starting with a self-evident axiom, Pythagoras would proceed step by step to a logical conclusion. What many of us may not know from our geometry classes is that, according to some ancient sources, Themistoclea, a priestess of Delphi, contributed significantly to Pythagoras' ethical doctrines.[5] Very early philosophical thought was not a search for a better understanding of humankind. Rather, it was the search for what made up the materials of the earth and answers to problems associated with counting.

Later Greek philosophers are credited with greatly contributing to Western thought and raising questions that advanced humankind. In particular, Socrates, Plato, and Aristotle, who lived in ancient Greece, played a fundamental role in shaping much of Western thinking, including ideas on education that lasted for centuries, some to the present day. Who was Socrates, and what legacy did he leave that can be found in classrooms today?

Socrates   Socrates (470–399 B.C.E.) is perhaps the best-known philosopher, because he died defending his philosophical beliefs. Philosophy to Socrates was a way of life. He would walk about Athens, raising questions about anything and everything. Because he was considered the wisest man in Greece and had a charismatic personality, he attracted a following of young men. Males were the focus of Socrates' attention because in Greek society it was the males who were expected to enter the workplace and carry out the duties and responsibilities of citizenship. Socrates referred to himself as "the gadfly" and used a method known as the **Socratic dialogue** to encourage his students to debate ideas. Through such debates his students learned how wisdom could expose false claims, and how difficult it is to answer philosophical questions. In Chicago, Paideia schools were organized based on the principles of a classical curriculum from the Great Books and the Socratic method, with teachers and students engaging in Socratic dialogue as they discussed concepts and issues.

Socrates claimed that he knew nothing, although he believed that moral wisdom lay in oneself and that what makes a man sin is lack of knowledge. "Knowledge is virtue and the cause of evil is ignorance," argued Socrates. His contributions to philosophy and education are several, but he is mainly known for the dialectic method of questions and answers (Socratic dialogue) and for changing the focus of philosophical questions from the nature of the physical world to human morality and politics.

Maria, in Tom's class, asked some of her classmates, "What would Socrates say to the local school board about their advocacy for the passage of legislation that permits gambling because they have been promised that a certain percentage of the revenue will be used to fund schools? This is a philosophical dilemma that citizens face: the ethics of using revenue from gambling to support the education of children." How do you think Socrates would respond to this issue?

Plato   If you ever hear your professors refer to the university as the Academy, it is an idea that came from one of Socrates' disciples, Plato (427–347 B.C.E.). Plato is credited with starting the first university, the Academy. *The Republic*, one of Plato's most famous works, outlines a plan for a "perfect" society ruled by a philosopher-king. Plato believed the well-being of society depended on cultivating human beings, who are ultimately good. He stressed the importance of the surrounding environment in influencing the moral growth of students. Plato, unlike many philosophers, gave some thought to the education of women. Although he believed that they should be "educated" for the home, he nevertheless believed that women, like men, should possess the knowledge and behavior consistent with "temperance and justice." Such beliefs during Plato's time were unusual. His contributions to teaching include the *Dialogues*. His dialogues are noted for the way the main character, Socrates, engages other characters in a hunt for truth—Socratic dialogue. A big question for Plato was "What is knowledge?" In contemporary times that question has changed to "What are the multiple knowledges?" and "Whose knowledge is valued more?" The search for knowledge in some form or fashion continues to haunt philosophers today just as it did in the past.

Aristotle   Aristotle (384–322 B.C.E.) was a student of Plato at the Academy. Like Plato, Aristotle founded a university, the Lyceum. Aristotle believed that citizens should be taught to comply with the rules and regulations of government. He emphasized the role habituation plays in the moral growth of students. Aristotle is credited as the first person to classify knowledge by dividing and subdividing areas of inquiry—for example, biology, physics, chemistry. He is noted for developing deductive or syllogistic logic. For example:

> Premise: All fish can swim.
> Premise: This is a fish.
> Therefore, it (the fish) can swim.

Also, for centuries scholars adhered to Aristotle's belief that change is natural, that it happens through the natural order of events.

Aristotle was a strong supporter of education and believed that boys should receive a liberal education. He did not support women having the same political rights as men and he did not challenge slavery.

Far Eastern Philosophy

For generations, and often today in educational settings in the United States, kindergarten through college students are exposed primarily to Western philosophy. However, 21st-century technology, global commerce, and changing population demographics now demand that teachers have some understanding of philosophies from other countries. Students who are new immigrants from Asia probably live some of their daily life in accordance with non-Western philosophical beliefs. These beliefs may play a role in shaping students' classroom behavior. For example, an "apology" from a student who has recently arrived from China,

Japan, or another Asian culture may be perceived much differently than an apology from a student from a Western culture. "Some Chinese scholars suggest that the Western penchant for apologies grows out of the Judeo-Christian tradition, in which a simple confession brings prompt absolution. In contrast, an apology in China involves a much more formal and traumatic event."[6] Also, as PreK–12 students travel the Internet and communicate with their peers in different parts of the world, an understanding of different philosophical beliefs is necessary because they influence communication patterns, culture, and human interaction.

Eastern philosophy differs from Western philosophy in that it acknowledges and greatly respects the interdependency and unity of human beings and nature. It is also concerned with intrapersonal knowledge, peace and harmony, and the nature of society. In Eastern philosophy there is less of an attempt to control reality and more recognition that we are all part of reality.[7]

Confucianism   Confucianism and Taoism are two major strands of Far Eastern philosophy. Although they are different, they both start with the basic idea that nature and culture are interdependent.[8] **Confucianism** is concerned with ethics and morality, and it served as the foundation of Chinese civilization. It influences the social organization, the political structure, and the educational system. According to Confucianism, there are five key relationships: ruler and subject, father and son, husband and wife, elder brother and younger brother, friend and friend. Family is the most important relationship, and to be out of one's family is to forfeit a position in the social structure. Family is the foundation for economic welfare, and the head of the family has the responsibility to punish misdeeds to "save face."[9]

The importance of family, how it is constituted, the close relationship among relatives, and the respect for the elderly recognized in some Asian American students' homes will require teacher candidates to be more comprehensive and inclusive in their study of families, and in the selection of reading and social studies materials for discussion.

Confucius (or Kung Fu-tzu, 551–479 B.C.E.) was born into an era of great sociopolitical upheaval. He was a self-educated man who led a fascinating life. He served as a clerk, a magistrate, and a minister of justice, which included the duties of foreign relations. He began attracting students in his 20s. He traveled with his students for almost 13 years through nine states. Confucius' teachings influenced China, Korea, Japan, and Vietnam. Rulers considered him a threat, as he was charismatic and radical—a dangerous combination in a leader.

Confucianism has been characterized as a language of morals and laws. Confucius taught about literature, loyalty, and faithfulness. Also, he discussed history and the importance of ceremonial procedures with his students. Confucius taught from a humanist perspective and worked to redefine the traditional utilitarian and professionally oriented perspectives of Chinese education. He was concerned that China's ruling class was taking advantage of the people they governed by imposing heavy taxes to support their lifestyle. He proposed a new idea to the Chinese people: that those who were most capable of governing, whether they were born into influential rich families or not, should govern. Confucius believed that moral and ethical men make the best rulers and that virtue is one of the most important characteristics that a leader can have.[10]

Confucius believed that virtue can be attained by following proper ways of behaving, based on the principle of **li.** Li means behaving with courtesy and ceremony. Confucius believed that the Chinese practice of worshiping and paying respect to their family, especially their ancestors, should become a common practice that Chinese people extend to each other daily. For example, Confucius advocated that when people come to visit, you should treat them with the same respect that you would give them if they were to attend an important ceremony where you were presiding. This response is indicative of his dedication to both the self and society, as ceremonies were considered guidelines for proper social action.

According to the U.S. Census Bureau, a total of 2,271,562 Chinese Americans live in the United States.[11] Not all Chinese practice Confucianism, but many may hold cultural beliefs rooted in this belief.

Taoism   Taoism, or the Way, means oneness with nature: noninterference with natural events, leaving nothing undone, and simplicity of existence. Lao-Tzu (the "old master") introduced the philosophy of Taoism in the sixth century B.C.E. It became a religion when its teachings were adopted as a way to live. Various schools are believed to have emerged from the religious dimension of Taoism. These schools paid homage to the ancient philosophers. Philosophers of the Taoist school (Tao-Chia) formed small teaching circles composed of a master and a limited number of disciples.

Taoists contend that the less one worries, the happier he or she will be. Also, they believe that people who are able to live in harmony with nature and change will be happy and healthy, and live for a long time. In addition, Taoists believe that the natural forces of this world are the products of tension—namely, the ongoing tension between yin and yang.[12] Originally, yin–yang referred to the shady and sunny sides of mountaintops. Eventually, the two terms came to represent the feminine aspect and the masculine aspect. Yin and yang can be understood as relative categories, or in relation to one another. These two concepts were integral to all Chinese philosophical, religious, and scientific thought. The ancient Chinese conceived of the universe as an immense hierarchical whole constructed of parts, spaces, and times that correspond with one another. All of the entities included in this whole were fluid, momentary, and changing. Finding harmony with nature—which is a marriage of opposites of yin–yang, female–male—and the universe is the purpose of pondering the Tao. Additionally, Taoists believe that things are constantly shifting—for example, life is moving toward death.

Teachers should realize that students familiar with Taoist thinking may find Western schooling and its lecture style of teaching at odds with their beliefs. Fundamental to Taoism are personal freedom, self-knowledge, and contemplation.

Indian Philosophy

Philosophy in India is as old as ancient Greek philosophy, and continues to influence millions of people worldwide. For example the idea of **karma**—that what a person does influences what will happen to that person in the future—is a popular concept in today's society. Study, meditation, and yoga are central to Indian philosophy. Indian philosophy claims that through study, meditation, yoga, or a combination of the three, it is possible to transcend worldly cares and suffering that life brings. At some education in-service sessions, in order to get the participants motivated and in the right frame of mind to work, some staff developers will start the morning with yoga.

Buddha   Two Indian philosophers that some students may be familiar with are Buddha and Gandhi. Siddhartha Gautama, the historical Buddha, was born in the sixth century B.C.E. in what is today Nepal. Siddhartha came to be known as the Buddha, the "awakened one" or the "enlightened one," because of his discoveries about karma. Buddha began his work as a teacher at Sarnath in India. Many of his followers organized Buddhist communities and began the spread of Buddhism throughout Asia. Buddhism gained a great deal of popularity among the Chinese people and was taught in monasteries. Early Buddhist discourses were of a colloquial nature, often using metaphor and simile analogies. The emergence of the Abhidharma school of thought transformed this approach into "a method of textual exegesis combining scriptural citation and reasoned arguments."[13] The discussions centered on such issues as what social factors condition our recognition of reality and the various models for mental systems of reasoning such as inference and perception.

The Buddhist tradition is based on a belief that all suffering is caused by an inability to discern what things in the world are real and what things are fictitious. Buddhism largely vanished from India after the 12th century, after the invasion of the Muslims. Central to Buddhism is elimination of selfish desires, denial of worldly goods, and a life of meditation. Today, approximately 0.5% of the United States population, or just over 1 million people, practice Buddhism.[14]

Gandhi   Mohandas Karamchand Gandhi (1869–1948) was known as Mahatma (the Great Soul). Central to Gandhi's philosophy was nonviolence toward living things. He developed the concept of satyagraha (holding fast to the truth), which is the practice of nonviolent, noncooperative resistance to the authorities. His confrontations with racism in South Africa provided fertile ground for the emergence of this ideal. Gandhi is probably best known for bringing about Indian independence. When violence broke out between Hindus and Muslims in India in 1947, Gandhi would visit the trouble areas, fast, and conduct prayer vigils in an attempt to end India's religious strife. He argued for the unity of all people under one God and preached Muslim and Christian ethics along with his Hindu teachings. On January 30, in New Delhi, while on a prayer vigil he was assassinated by a Hindu extremist.

Nonviolence is used as a guiding framework for some conflict resolution and peer mediation programs in schools. And many of the events surrounding Martin Luther King Day in schools and across the United States involve dedication to peace, nonviolence, and harmony among humankind. Teachers can use Gandhi's model of nonviolence as a way to teach students how to disrupt circumstances that prevent them from achieving life opportunities in a manner that is consistent with democratic ideals.

Teachers may discover that a student's family believes in and practices Buddhism, Confucianism, and/or Taoism. All three philosophies work together. Buddhism offers optimism and hope, Confucianism offers harmony and strong family relationships, and Taoism offers ceremonies and rituals.[15] An awareness of Eastern discourses can help teachers to understand that people live by multiple philosophies. Consequently, some students in their class may not accept Western systems of reasoning. Nevertheless, these students have much to contribute to their classmates' understanding of the world and pluralism in the United States.

Different, but Much in Common

It is reasonable to assume that ancient civilizations such as those of China, Greece, and India all provided education for their children, though they may not have had a discipline or an independent, organized body of knowledge for guiding this education. Although Far Eastern and Indian philosophies differ, they all influence people's personal lives and behavior and the social, political, and religious institutions of their respective areas, and these influence are increasingly making their way into classrooms in the United States.

NEW AGE FOR PHILOSOPHICAL BELIEFS

In Western Europe, Aristotelian philosophy remained influential for almost 2,000 years. Around 1637, the age of modern philosophy arrived. It was at that time that the Frenchman René Descartes argued that beliefs, such as those advocated by Plato, Aristotle, the church, and others, need to be proven by scientific method. Also, Descartes argued that the responsibility for how people should behave was not completely up to the government and church. People should think for themselves about how they should behave. "Truth by authority" was losing its dominance. Instead, people were showing greater interest in political and secular issues. They marveled at the advances in science and wanted more books and education.

Along with new developments in **rationalism**—the practice of accepting reason as the only authority in determining opinions, courses of action, and knowledge without help from the senses—empirical science emerged. Philosophers saw these new developments in rationalism and in empirical science as providing a way for science to shed new light on political and moral philosophy. These new developments in science were seen as a way to influence how people thought and how society was structured. For example, people were changing their minds about church, authority, and aristocratic privilege. Some were arguing that political systems (law, politics, and government) needed to reflect the will of the people.

The currents of thought that started with Descartes facilitated the growth of the sciences of astronomy, biology, and physics and challenged traditional forms of government. These challenges, based on ideas about reason and natural rights, influenced the teaching of children.

The Influence of Philosophy on a Developing United States

During the 1700s, the colonists in America kept watch as people throughout Europe began to embrace these new enlightened ideas about inalienable rights and the importance of education to a government of the people, especially those ideas espoused by Francis Bacon in *The Advancement of Learning* and John Locke in *Some Thoughts Concerning Education.* Many appreciated what they were seeing. Although colonists had not yet received their independence, they wanted schools to prepare people to be able to manage their affairs to ensure life and liberty and allow for the pursuit of happiness. Colonists such as Benjamin Franklin, Alexander Hamilton, and Thomas Jefferson wanted a government in which the people's voice was the dominant political and social force and the people ruled. Thanks in part to the efforts of Jefferson, Franklin, and others, most colonists came to believe that educating the citizenry was essential in order for economic, political, and social systems to work. In his Philadelphia Academy, Franklin put into practice a 19th-century version of democratic opportunity in education. He started a school that would prepare citizens for the new social order, where students would learn to take advantage of opportunities for self-improvement and managing government. The academy stressed English, basic literacy skills, and vocational preparation for earning a living, instead of the classics like Latin and subjects that taught "ornamental knowledge."[16]

American schools and colleges, many colonists believed, should be secular instead of religious. They claimed that the purpose of education was social improvement and human happiness, not eternal salvation as was often stated in the Puritan educational credo.[17] Also, they believed that schools should be controlled by local authority. Local control of schools was included in Massachusetts's Old Deluder Satan Act of 1647, which stated that every township after reaching 50 households must appoint someone within the town to teach the children to read and write. The Act also stipulated that the salary must be paid by the parents or masters of the children. The local control of schools and the taxing of citizens to support schools that exist today were shaped by the philosophical beliefs of colonists centuries ago. Embedded in the philosophy driving the passage of the Old Deluder Satan Act was that education—for the children of free White landowners—was essential to the welfare of the colonies and that the emphasis in the curriculum should be on students' learning the basics.[18]

Educational Philosophy Is Shaped by Events and Conditions

These two ideas—an educated citizenry and local control—remain fundamental to public education in the United States today, but the philosophy directing those ideas is often a source of debate. For example, the question "What should be in the curriculum students receive to become educated?" will receive different responses depending on the educational philosophy of the responder. Philosophical questions and the responses they receive, whether from state governments, the federal government, professional organizations, citizens' groups, prominent citizens, or teachers, are energized by political and economic conditions, religious beliefs, scientific discoveries, social beliefs, and world events, as well as the background and experiences of those advocating a particular philosophical belief.

An example of how world events and social beliefs can shape the philosophy of education of a nation, and certain groups within that nation, can be seen in after the aftermath of World War II. The war gave new social and political hope and promises to women and people of color. As White women and women of color joined the workforce during the war, they enjoyed the benefits and privileges that come with working outside the home, including the privilege of having their "own" money. As a result, women increased their demands for equal social and employment opportunities. Men of color joined the army and fought and died for the freedom of people living in countries whose race and ethnic background were different from their own, and who at times showed limited respect for them; returning home, these soldiers of color demanded the elimination of racism and prejudice and an expansion of educational opportunities. In both cases—women and soldiers of color—the nation's philosophy regarding who should be educated, how they should be educated, and what should be included in the curriculum was being challenged. Teaching philosophies inspired by the dominant group's notions of who should be educated and receive the best employment opportunities were increasingly under attack. Female students and students of color came to school and college with a more militant attitude and exercised greater resistance toward traditional policies and procedures of educational institutions and instructors. These students began to tap into how "traditional" education worked and learned to use their own forms of power to inspire others and bring about change.

More recently, world events such as globalization, computer technology, and competitive market forces have pushed the national, state, and local governments and professional organizations to advocate an educational philosophy that prepares students to meet the demands of the market forces shaping the U.S. economy. The attention to curriculum standards, performance standards, and school and teacher accountability measures indicates a particular philosophy toward education. Although teacher candidates bring their own personhood to the development of their educational philosophy, the philosophy espoused by federal, state, and local governments will be the philosophy that is pressed upon teacher candidates as they are socialized into the role of teacher. It is important for teachers to realize that every movement or reform has a philosophy behind it, and to consider the source and think broadly about the ramifications of such movements and reforms for their many students.

EDUCATIONAL PHILOSOPHIES

There is "philosophy" and there is "philosophy of." Philosophy, we noted previously, is the search for "wisdom, truth, and knowledge" regarding the universe or humankind. Philosophy *of* science, philosophy *of* religion, and philosophy *of* education involve a search for wisdom, truth, and knowledge within a particular subject area or discipline. The concern of this text, philosophy of education, is thus a search for wisdom, truth, and knowledge about the domain of education, including teaching. A philosophy of education serves as an analytical tool to help teacher candidates explore questions of concern. A connection between philosophy and education, one could say, is that philosophy is a guide to educational practice, and education as a field of study yields certain information as a basis for philosophic judgments.[19] For example, as teacher candidates work with students, they construct notions about the nature of human beings, or more particularly the nature of children. They wonder if children are blank slates or curious individuals.

Many students of philosophy contend that philosophy of education is based in Greek philosophy, with Plato as its first architect. The writings of Confucius, Plato, and Aristotle show the importance of education to the state and the teacher's role in the educational process during ancient times. Ancient societies, like societies today, wanted to pass on their history and culture to the young. Religious institutions, the family, education, and especially teachers were seen as the way to make this happen.

Education and teachers have always been central to philosophical discussions. Philosophers across the ages have discussed such issues as the purpose of education, the education that males and females should receive, the state's role in education, the education of people of color, and the teacher's role in education. Exhibit 8.2 lists some past and contemporary male and female philosophers, along with some of their writings on education. Today, most education journals, many articles in the popular press, and numerous websites that discuss education similarly demonstrate the importance of education to the family, state, and nation.

EXHIBIT 8.2   PHILOSOPHERS AND THEIR WRITINGS

Philosophers	Educational Writings
Plato	*Apology, Meno, Republic*
Aristotle	*On Philosophy, On the Good*
Buddha	
Confucius	
St. Augustine	*Concerning the Teacher*
John Locke	*Some Thoughts Concerning Education* (1693)
Jean-Jacques Rousseau	*Emile* (1762)
Mary Wollstonecraft	*Thoughts on the Education of Daughters* (1787)
William James	*Talks to Teachers* (1899)
John Dewey	*My Pedagogic Creed* (1897)
	The School and Society (1900)
	The Child and the Curriculum (1902)
W. E. B. Du Bois	*The Soul of Black Folk* (1903)

(continued)

EXHIBIT 8.2   CONTINUED

Philosophers	Educational Writings
George S. Counts	*Dare the School Build a New Social Order?* (1932)
Michel Foucault	*Existential Encounters for Teachers* (1967)
	Madness and Civilization (1973)
	Power/Knowledge (1980)
Maxine Greene	*Teacher as Stranger: Educational Philosophy for a Modern Age* (1973)
Paulo Freire	*Pedagogy of the Oppressed* (1972)
	Education for Critical Consciousness (1974)
	Educational Practice of Freedom (1976)
Nel Noddings (with Paul Shore)	*A Feminine Approach to Ethics and Morals* (1984)
Judith Butler	*Gender Trouble* (1990)
Cornel West	*The American Evasion of Philosophy: A Genealogy of Pragmatism* (1989)
	Race Matters (1993)
Jane Roland Martin	*Changing the Educational Landscape: Philosophy, Women, and Curriculum* (1994)
bell hooks	*Teaching to Transgress: Education as the Practice of Freedom* (1994)

Why should teacher candidates be concerned at this point in their preparation about an educational philosophy when questions of discipline, classroom management, curriculum, and standards abound and seem more urgent? It is because a search for knowledge that takes into account the world we live in, teacher candidates' understanding of self, different notions of diversity, attention to religious differences, and the flow of power between and among groups can greatly assist teacher candidates' understanding about their role as a teacher. Also, because teachers deal with people, they are inevitably faced daily with philosophical problems and issues. They therefore need philosophical knowledge in order to recognize problems for what they are, as well as their historical context, and to be able to consider the alternatives available. For example, questions of the religious rights of students and the role of religion in the curriculum can become complex if the issues within debates are founded on differences between Western and Far Eastern philosophy. Additionally, by gaining an understanding of the history of philosophy, teacher candidates can learn how ways of thinking and power relations make it customary to overlook or ignore such issues as educational equity for women, the education of people of color, and the education of students with physical and mental disabilities.

In the United States, five philosophies of education have dominated or at least been a force on the educational landscape for decades: perennialism, essentialism, experimentalism, reconstructionism, and existentialism. Postmodernism, a philosophy that came into prominence in the 1950s, is added as a sixth philosophy. The visibility of these philosophies on the education landscape is often conditioned by global, national, or local conditions and events. Exhibit 8.3 lists six philosophies of education and notes their educational practice in such areas as curriculum, role of the teacher, and methods of teaching.

Perennialism

Perennialism is a belief that there are absolute truths and standards (moral principles) that are changeless and more real than the physical world. Perennialism as a philosophy of education is closely related to the classical philosophies of idealism and humanism. Idealism holds that our experiences are mental representations rather than representations of the world. In other words, your car only exists while it is being perceived. Classical humanism refers to Greek philosophers who were dedicated to discovering reason and truth for humankind. The connecting strand that links the educational philosophy of perennialism, idealism, and humanism is the search for "truth." Philosophers who influenced the development of perennialism include St. Thomas Aquinas, Robert Hutchins, and Mortimer Adler. Plato, Immanuel Kant, and Ralph Waldo Emerson are some of the philosophers who influenced the development of idealism.

Much of perennialist teachers' curriculum will come from the Great Books, classical literature, traditional history and biography, and the readings that are found in a traditional liberal arts sequence. The instructional methods in perennialist teachers' classes will be a good number of lectures, some discussion, and some small-group work. Essay examination will be the primary assessment tool, and the aim of schooling for both perennialists and idealists is to produce intellectual scholars. In the 1980s, a number of public schools in Chicago became "Paideia Schools." These schools were an outgrowth of the Paideia Proposal (1982) put forth by Mortimer Adler and the Paideia Group. The schools used Great Books as the source for curriculum and used the didactic method of instruction.

From the late 1960s through the 1980s, there was intense debate in PreK–12 education and on college campuses over cutting back on the perennialist curriculum that had dominated education in the United States for decades. People of color and women argued that the Great Books and much of the classical literature and traditional history that made up the curriculum excluded them and that teaching styles favored male students.

Essentialism

Essentialism is the belief that the primary purpose of schools is preserve the basic elements of human culture and transmit them to the young. Essentialists believed that classroom discipline must be emphasized because "genuine and lasting freedom is won and preserved by the systematic discipline of learning what needs to be learned for survival in a civilized society."[20] Essentialism in the United

EXHIBIT 8.3   PHILOSOPHIES OF EDUCATION

Educational Philosophy	Influence	Rationale	Curriculum	Teacher
Perennialism (Neo-Thomism)	St. Thomas Aquinas Jacques Maritain Robert M. Hutchins Stringfellow Barr Max Rafferty Mortimer Adler	Stresses intellectual attainment and the search for truth	The Great Books The classics Liberal arts	A taskmaster Philosophically oriented Knowledgeable about the Great Books
Idealism (Essentialism)	Plato Josiah Royce Immanuel Kant Ralph Waldo Emerson Herman Home	All material things are explainable	History Biography Humanities	Serves as the ideal A good role model
Realism (Essentialism)	Alfred N. Whitehead Aristotle John Amos Comenius Johann F. Herbert John Locke Harry Broudy	Propositions are true only if they correspond with known facts	Science Mathematics Quantitative subjects Foreign language	Presents subject in a highly organized and very exact manner
Pragmatism	Boyd Bode John Dewey William James Charles Peirce William Kilpatrick	Search for things that work Experimental Democratic	Core curriculum Student centered Revolves around the interest of the student	A guide One who can present meaningful knowledge with skill
Reconstructionism	Theodore Brameld George Counts Harold Rugg Ivan Illich John Holt Paul Goodman	Seeks to reconstruct society through education	Current events Social problems Futures research Sociology Political science	Social activist
Existentialism	John Paul Sartre Søren Kierkegaard Martin Buber Albert Camus Martin Heidegger A. S. Neill Carl Rogers	Importance of the individual Subjectivity Discover the inner nature of things and people	Individual preference Psychology Human relations	Very committed individual Person who is both teacher and learner One who provides a free environment to learn
Postmodernism	Michael Foucault Jacques Derrida Jean-Francois Lyotard Judith Butler	De-centers the subject		Flexible Sensitive Forms of multiple interpretation of what students are

Source: Developed by Timothy J. Bergen, Jr., University of South Carolina, and modified by Carl Grant, University of Wisconsin–Madison and Maureen Gillette.

Educational Philosophy	Methods of Teaching	Examinations	Preferred Architecture	Criticism
Perennialism (Neo-Thomism)	Lectures Discussions Seminars	Essay	Classical	Very elite and aristocratic Must be accepted on faith and absolute truth
Idealism (Essentialism)	Lectures Discussions Imitation	Essay	Traditional	Elite
Realism (Essentialism)	Lectures Demonstrations Sensory experiences Teaching machines	Objectives	Efficient Functional	Often fails to deal with social change
Pragmatism	Discussions Projects	Gauge how well people can problem-solve	Flexible Natural	Permissive Very democratic Replace history with social studies
Reconstructionism	Real-life projects	Student select, administer, and evaluate Gauge ability as an activist	Non-school setting "Schools without walls"	Very utopian Very impatient
Existentialism	Learner is encouraged to discover the best method for him/ herself		Individual preference	Unsystematic Rejects all authority
Postmodernism	Praxis integrations Open Anti-representational Erases differences	Objectivity narratives		Messy and often leaky

States got underway in the 1930s. The movement was started to counteract the ideas on pragmatism proposed by John Dewey and others, and the ideas on social reconstruction proposed by George Counts and others. The essentialist movement was led by William C. Bagley, a professor of education at Teachers College, Columbia University. He and other essentialists were concerned about how poorly U.S. students were performing in comparison to students in Europe, and students' lack of attention to basic skills. The essentialists were critical of educational policies and procedures that included social promotion and curriculum experimentation, such as team teaching. Also, they complained about the quality of the teaching force, arguing that many teachers were poorly prepared.

According to essentialism, the curriculum should be organized systematically and sequentially. Assessment of curriculum knowledge is by measurable objectives predetermined and written by the teachers or other education authorities. Teachers, according to this philosophy, are the central authority in the classroom, and the textbook is the primary source of curriculum. Instruction stresses rote learning and memorization of facts and concepts learned by way of logical, chronological, and causal relationships. Michael Demiashkevich, who is credited with coining the term *essentialism*, stated this view as a question:

> Should not our public schools prepare boys and girls for adult responsibility through systematic training in such subjects as reading, writing, and arithmetic, history, and English, requiring mastery of such subjects, and when necessary, stressing discipline and obedience?[21]

Essentialism is always a major actor on the educational landscape, but its presence is particularly visible during times when the United States is having political and economic difficulties. For example, during the 1950s, especially after the Russians launched *Sputnik*, which exacerbated the Cold War between the United States and the Soviet Union, the public schools were harshly criticized. Critics such as Arthur Bestor, Max Rafferty, and Hyman Rickover claimed that the U.S. public school system was academically inferior to the school systems in Europe. Bestor claimed that professional educators have undermined public confidence in schools by arguing for educational aims that "forfeit the respect of thoughtful men, by deliberately divorcing the schools from the disciplines of science and scholarship."[22]

Similarly, in the 1980s, when the United States was experiencing difficulty in the international economic marketplace because Japanese and European products were in greater demand, essentialism reappeared. As we have noted in previous chapters, the report *A Nation at Risk: The Imperative for Educational Reform*, released in 1983 by the National Commission on Excellence in Education, did not hold back on its criticism of the educational system. The Commission's criticism is reflected in the following statement:

> If an unfriendly foreign power had attempted to impose on America the mediocre educational performance that exists today, we might well have viewed it as an act of war. As it stands, we have allowed this to happen to ourselves. We have even squandered the gains in student achievement made in the wake of the Sputnik challenge. Moreover, we have dismantled essential support systems which helped

to make those gains possible. We have, in effect, committed an act of unthinking, unilateral educational disarmament.[23]

At the beginning of the 21st century, an essentialist educational philosophy continues to be a major force, carrying on the efforts started in the 1980s, with such efforts as the standards movement and the reinforcement of traditional ways of thinking echoed in the publication of E. D. Hirsch's *Cultural Literacy: What Every American Needs to Know* (1987).

The essentialist philosophy is one that is going to be hard for most teacher candidates to avoid, as the use of standards to assess both students and teacher candidates is widespread. You may be using standards within your own teacher education program to organize a portfolio or some other tool to show that you are making progress toward becoming a professional within teaching. Within an essentialist classroom, the use of standards for assessment will be evident. There will be standardized tests given at each grade level. Textbooks and a fixed curriculum will be used throughout the school, with every teacher expecting every other teacher to use that curriculum. Some of the same practices mentioned within the perennialist classroom will be used in the essentialist classroom, focusing on the rigorous use of Great Books and science and math texts that urge all students to master a cumulative, growing body of knowledge that will help them show this mastery on standardized tests. One thing that some fear within essentialist classrooms is a constant "teaching to the test," especially if there is great pressure for students to achieve at high levels on standardized forms of assessment. Some argue that teaching this way teaches children not to think and draw conclusions from data, but instead to memorize disconnected bits of information, and that it does not encourage any type of reasoning or overlap of skills in other areas.

Experimentalism

Experimentalism is the belief that the primary purpose of schools is to teach students to think effectively. In other words, experimentalist philosophy teaches students to analyze, criticize, select between alternatives, and propose solutions based on analysis and selection. Experimentalism is sometimes referred to as progressivism, which is often associated with **pragmatism.** The relationship to pragmatism is in part because John Dewey's philosophical beliefs were grounded in both pragmatism and experimentalism. Dewey believed that ideas should be tested by experiments, and Charles Peirce and William James were also interested in the relationship between thought and action. They believed that an idea must be tested. An idea was true when it worked—that was James's pragmatic way of thinking. Charles Peirce is often called the father of pragmatism, and pragmatism is usually referred to as an American philosophy because, unlike many of the other philosophies, it has its roots in the United States. Cornel West, whose writings (e.g., *American Evasion of Philosophy,* 1989) engage the tradition of American pragmatism, especially the work of John Dewey, is equally noted, if not more so, for his efforts to transform linguistic, social, cultural, and political tradition in order to increase individual development and democratic action. West believes that as schools teach students to think effectively, fundamental to this way of thinking are considerations of race, justice, and democracy. West's book *Race Matters* is a significant contribution to the national conversation on race, justice, and democracy.[24]

In a classroom guided by an experimentalist's philosophy, the curriculum is based on student interest and a good deal of time is devoted to "learning by doing" through discovery and experimentation. Democratic principles guide classroom management and discipline. Individual and class projects and discussion make up a good deal of the instructional method. Assessment is based on how well students' projects meet instructional goals.

Social Reconstructionism

Social reconstructionism is an educational philosophy that seeks to reconstruct society through education. Social reconstructionists believe that students should be educated to change society. They should be taught to build a more just social order that better meets the needs of all people, and thereby achieves greater democratic effectiveness. George Counts and Theodore Brameld were major contributors to the early work on social reconstructionism. Counts was dissatisfied with events taking place in the United States during the 1920s and 1930s. The Roaring Twenties, Prohibition, and the stock market crash had the United States acting like a ship without a rudder. In response to national events and conditions, and motivated by Dewey's statement about the role of the teacher in "My Pedagogic Creed," Counts issued a challenge to schools and teachers in "Dare the School Build a New Social Order?" (1932):

> We are all, I think, growing increasingly weary of the brutalities, the stupidities, the hypocrisies, and the gross inanities of contemporary life. We have a haunting feeling that we were born for better things and that the nation itself is falling far short of its powers. The fact that other groups refuse to deal boldly and realistically with the present situation does not justify the teachers of the country in their customary policy of hesitation and equivocation. The times are literally crying for a new vision of American destiny. The teaching profession, or at least its progressive elements, should eagerly grasp the opportunity which the fates have placed in their hands. Such a vision of what America might become in the industrial age I would introduce into our schools as the supreme imposition, but one to which our children are entitled—a priceless legacy which it should be the first concern of our profession to fashion and bequeath.[25]

Brameld claims that social reconstructionism offers a "critique of modern culture."[26] It holds that "magnificent as their services to society [may] have been in the past, the major institutions and the corresponding social, economic and other practices that developed during the preceding centuries of the modern era are now incapable of adequately performing those services."[27] Therefore, schools and other societal institutions need to be reconstructed to meet present-day needs.

Scholars of color and women have been major contributors to efforts to reconstruct societal instruction. One example is Judith Butler, whose work examines the way race, gender, sexual orientation, and other markers of identity conflict and support each other. Butler's *Gender Trouble* (1990) and *Bodies That Matter* (1993) are credited with laying the foundation for what has become known as "queer theory." Sarah Margaret Fuller's work, which is considered to be in the transcendentalist and idealism camp, is credited with writing America's first major feminist manifesto, *Women of the Nineteenth Century*.[28] Fuller argued that women should be self-reliant and optimist and should see themselves as unique individuals. Many educators currently use bell hooks's *Teaching to Transgress* to shape their way of teaching. In her writings, hooks argues that education is a practice of freedom. She argues in *Teaching to Transgress* that "teaching is a performative act . . . that offers the space for change, intervention, spontaneous shifts, that can serve as a catalyst drawing out the unique elements in each classroom."[29] The teaching and writings of Hypatia of Alexandria, virtually ignored by historians of philosophy for 1,500 years, are found mainly on a website (www.geocities.com/Athens/Forum/9947/old.html). According to some sources, Hypatia, who lived in the 4th century C.E., was the greatest philosopher of her day and headed up the neo-Platonic school of Polotinus. W. E. B. Du Bois's life and work were dedicated to changing White Americans' and some Black Americans' thoughts about the Negro. He possessed a keen concern for his race and assertively attacked racial injustice and defended the freedom of African Americans. His book *The Philadelphia Negro* "revealed the Negro group as a symptom, not a cause; as a striving, palpitating group, and not an inert, sick body of crime; as a long historic development and not a transient occurrence."[30] Du Bois's *The Souls of Black Folk,* published in 1903, continues to be must reading for many present-day educators. At the launching of the book Du Bois stated, "Herein lie buried many things which if read with patience may show the strange meaning of being black here in the dawning of the Twentieth Century. This meaning is not without interest to you, Gentle Reader; for the problem of the Twentieth Century is the color-line."[31] Mary Wollstonecraft fought to change how women were trained to be subordinate to men. Viewed as a radical, she worked to help women achieve a better life, not only for themselves and for their children but for their husbands. Her book *Thoughts on the Education of Daughters* (1787) argued that women were as capable of intellectual achievement as men. Also, in *Vindication of the Rights of Woman* (1792) Wollstonecraft attacked the double standard between men and women. She argued that the imbalance of power between the sexes corrupts both the oppressed and the oppressor. Wollstonecraft sought an education for women and men that would lead to individuals with knowledge, reason, and virtue.

Current events and social problems, especially those that explore economic, political, and social issues, make up a good deal of the curriculum in a social reconstructionist class. Teachers guided by a social reconstructionist philosophy are socially conscious about issues facing the students in their classrooms as well as broader societal issues that affect those with less privilege. The teaching of the basics in part occurs through working on social issues.

The work of Paulo Freire, especially *Pedagogy of the Oppressed*, is an example of a social reconstructionist instructional approach. Through a process called "conscientization," Freire believes that people should learn to question society, see through versions of "truth" that teach people to accept unfairness and inhumanity, and become empowered to envision, define, and work toward a more humane society. The reconstructionist philosophy in teaching has been put into practice actively over the last two decades in such instructional models as emancipatory pedagogy (Gordon),[32] critical teaching (Shor),[33] transformational education (Giroux),[34] education that is multicultural and social reconstructionist (Grant and Sleeter),[35] multicultural education (Suzuki),[36] antiracist teaching (Carby,[37] Mullard[38]), social feminism (Jaggar and Struhl),[39] culturally responsive teaching (Irvine),[40] and decision making and social action (Banks).[41] Although educators using these different terms do not advocate exactly the same things (one main difference being that some focus primarily on race, others on gender, still others on social class), their theoretical assumptions are based on social reconstructionist ideas.

We use the theme of education that is multicultural and social reconstructionist (MCSR) within this text to emphasize the issues that became important with the movement of social reconstructionism. We believe this theme helps us help readers to understand the multiple perspectives that exist, and that it can help teachers and students to construct education toward social justice issues that make schooling relevant and enriching for all students.

Existentialism

Existentialism is a philosophy that seeks to understand what it is like to be an individual living in the world. It challenges traditional Western European philosophy that seeks to find truth and reason based upon empiricism and rationalism. Instead, existentialists believe that the search for universal truth has blinded philosophers to being able to deal with human existence.[42] They believe that philosophy should be a passionate encounter with the problems of life and the inevitability of death. Existentialism developed in Europe in response to the economic hardships and military uncertainties of the 20th century.[43] Kierkegaard, Nietzsche, Heidegger, Sartre, Camus, Buber, and Simone de Beauvoir are proponents of existentialism. Simone de Beauvoir's *Irrational Man: A Study in Existential Philosophy* is considered to offer the finest definition of existentialist philosophy. Simone de Beauvoir's book is recognized for introducing existentialism to the United States in 1958.

In life, existentialists argue, individuals constantly make important decisions with only limited knowledge and a short time in which to decide. Also, human beings are constantly having to decide what is right and what is wrong, what is true and what is false, which beliefs to accept and which to reject. Therefore, it is up to the individual to decide what to accept and what to reject. This freedom to choose brings with it responsibility for the choices made. Also, it brings with it anxiety about having to make the choices. The anxiety over the responsibility for making choices, existentialists argue, causes humans to ignore or deny their freedom of choice and responsibility. This leads to self-deception. Existentialists contend that if humans are to live meaningful and authentic lives, they must gain an awareness of the human condition and learn to accept it. Additionally, because existentialists are attempting to learn about humans within the context of the total human experience, they often write about death and the shadow it casts on life, and the struggles that individuals face in getting along with one another.[44]

Students play a major role in determining what they will study in an existentialist teacher's classes. Teachers see their role as providing a caring classroom that stimulates individuality, where learners can pursue knowledge at their own pace and in ways that best meet their learning styles.

Postmodernism

The concept of **postmodernism** has its roots in the 1950s world of art. Today, postmodern analyses are applied in many different areas. Ray Linn, in *A Teacher's Introduction to Postmodernism*, one of the many books on the market to help teachers apply postmodern ideas to their work, argues that postmodernism is a widespread cultural development that has been taking shape during the last few decades and that it is important because of its treatment of several interrelated themes. These themes include truth, language and its relation to thought and to the world, reason, science and technology, human nature and the self, the Other (an individual or group considered as different), power and oppression, and creativity and the aesthetic.[45] Although some teacher candidates have concerns about all of these themes, for some the focus on postmodernism is to question the relationship between knowledge and power as it applies to U.S. society and particularly as it affects schools.

Traditionally, assumptions have been made about how the social world is constructed. Many of these assumptions are taken-for-granted beliefs about the way things are, based on science or common culture. Postmodernism argues that such assumptions must be examined because they are often grounded in relations that favor some and not others. For example, in the past and still too often today, some students are seen as less capable than others of achieving academically because they have been raised in a "second-class" culture: a single-parent home, a home where people speak nonstandard English, or a home where caregivers are not providing materials and experiences that promote readiness to learn traditional school knowledge. Also science such as genetics, for example, has been used to present arguments such as the one in *The Bell Curve: Intelligence and Class Structure in American Life* by Richard Herrnstein and Charles Murray. Herrnstein and Murray argue that heredity has a greater influence than environment on intelligence and that White people, as a group, are intellectually superior to Blacks.[46] Proponents of postmodernism, such as Judith Butler, discussed previously, argue that how we think about race and gender, for example, is socially constructed and has its roots in power relationships. For example, up until passage of Title IX of the Education Amendments of 1972, girls were denied many athletic privileges and opportunities that boys took for granted, solely because they were male. Postmodernists argue this separation of what is considered male and female is artificially created. The belief that women are not as capable of performing such jobs as CEOs of *Fortune* 500 companies, bus drivers, telephone line stringers, and professional basketball players is based on ideas disseminated as "truths" by systems of ideas that make some things acceptable and others less so. Often these systems are so ingrained in society that the "why" of how things work is invisible to the forces of dissemination. Society often accepts many of these things without question until someone points out the way these systems work to favor some and not others. Often there is an initial backlash against this position by those wishing to maintain the status quo because they feel threatened by the changes that may take away some unearned privileges they have enjoyed for decades or even centuries.

Teachers who advocate postmodernist philosophy approach educational issues, problems, and traditions with the question "What kind of power is embedded in educational issues, problems, and traditions?" They will also ask, "What kind of power is embedded in the ways teachers are asked to teach and reformers advocate to change schools?" In other words, postmodernist teachers examine their teaching to see how it is politically, legally, culturally, institutionally, artistically, and/or intellectually benefiting some groups of students more than others.[47] They expose their students to multiple interpretations and communities of knowledge. Also, their curriculum comes in part from local narratives of everyday life events, and is considered partial, fluid, and messy. Additionally, they seek to make certain that students can integrate what they are learning with what they want to do.

French philosopher Michel Foucault, often described as a historian of systems of ideas, is one of the postmodern thinkers that many educators are reading to learn about postmodernism. Foucault uses history to study human interactions and practices that are social and economic, and that occur in institutions such as hospitals, universities, and prisons. In carrying out his studies, Foucault examined what he refers to as discourses. A discourse is a regulated system of statements that can be analyzed not solely in terms of internal rules of information, but also as a set of practices within a social milieu.[48] A discourse does not have to be a set of *true* statements. But in defining what can be said, thought, and accepted, a discourse promotes the assessment as true.

Cleo Cherryholmes, drawing upon Foucault's work, explains the relation between discourse and power. Cherryholmes argues that the dominant discourse in a historical period and geographical location determines what counts as true, important, or relevant, what gets spoken, and what remains unsaid.[49] For example, during Galileo's time the teachings of the Church were the dominant discourse. After writing *A Dialogue on the Two Principal Systems of the World* in 1632,[50] a paper that went against the teachings of the Church, Galileo was called to the Holy Office to face an Inquisition. After a lengthy trial, he was forced to repudiate the ideas published in the manuscript. The teachings of the Church, the dominant discourse of the time, were generated and governed by rules and power, and were products of history, culture, politics, economics, and language. Galileo, as well as most Christians and clergy, had been socialized by the Church's systems of reason.

It is postmodern theories that encouraged us to write this text with power as one of its twin themes. Looking at schooling situations with power in mind helps us to more fully understand the complexity of schools. We hope it helps readers to understand the complexity as well.

With this information about different philosophies of education, teacher candidates can know the social and historical moorings of the philosophies to which they are drawn when they review the educational philosophy survey in Exhibit 8.1. The survey will place teacher candidates closer to one or possibly two educational philosophies than others. With that information in hand, teacher candidates can move toward developing their own educational philosophy.

REASONS FOR DEVELOPING A PHILOSOPHY OF EDUCATION

"What is your philosophy of education?" is a question that teachers are asked throughout their teaching careers. So far, our discussion has tended to focus more on professional reasons for developing a philosophy of education. In other words, the focus has been on how a philosophy of education will help once the teacher candidate begins teaching. However, there are some reasons for teacher candidates to develop a philosophy of education *before* receiving their teaching license. First, student teachers who do not develop a philosophy of education may have difficulty establishing or attaining well-defined goals and objectives for their students' education. Second, "What is your philosophy of education?" is frequently asked during the interview for a teaching job. Your answer gives a hiring committee a snapshot about the way you will teach, and your beliefs about the aims of education. Also, it gives the committee some indication as to whether your thoughts on teaching are compatible with those of other staff members at the school. Third, because the educational philosophy question is often asked in job interviews, developing your answer now will give your professors more time to assist in that development. Having assistance in the selections of resources and activities is very helpful when starting in a new area of study. Fourth, questions about your educational philosophy are also posed to teacher candidates by cooperating teachers with whom they are assigned to work during their student teaching and during other school and community placements. Your response gives an indication about the compatibility between you and your cooperating teacher within the teaching relationship. Your philosophy, even if unstated, will guide your beliefs during your teacher education program. Thus, it is important to be consciously aware of these beliefs.

No matter what motivates teacher candidates to develop a philosophy of education, most educators will argue that it is essential that candidates undertake the challenge to develop their educational philosophy. A teacher's philosophy is inseparable from daily experience; it is a way of viewing the world. Its presence is constant, helping to shape, and being shaped by, the tangible means (e.g., laws, policies, codes of conduct) through which teachers carry out their day-to-day responsibilities. In every phase of life—material, spiritual, secular, professional, social—teacher candidates believe certain things about the activities they perform. These beliefs, usually to a far greater extent than is realized, not only reflect one's day-to-day activities but in turn mold and direct these activities and interactions with others.

Questions to Guide the Development of Your Philosophy of Education

Some who study philosophy say that a philosophy of education must answer three questions: "What is education? What ought it to accomplish? How can these aims be realized?" The philosophy of education that teacher candidates develop will change somewhat, but for the most part it will stay with them and guide them when course content and student teaching have faded into the recesses of their mind. It will help them to gain deeper insights into why they are teaching, what they are teaching, and how these purposes relate to their school, the local community, and society at large. They will learn with a philosophy of education what they are doing and why they are doing it. In order for teacher candidates to consider their philosophy of education, it is suggested that they keep in mind the following four questions:

1. What is the nature of the learner? (What are your thoughts about the students you will teach?)
2. What is the nature of subject matter?
3. What is the nature of the learning process? (How is the teacher using subject matter and other experiences to guide students toward meaningful learning activities?)
4. What behaviors (disposition and attitude) should the teacher exhibit in order to carry out his or her philosophical position?

These questions, and the information about them that follows, can be used as teacher candidates compose their philosophies of education.

The Nature of the Learner   The nature of the learner is usually contrasted along a continuum from (a) students are curious, willing, and eager to learn, to (b) students are blank slates, disinterested learners, or reluctant to engage in learning. If students are seen as curious, willing, and eager, teachers expect them to be active contributors to classroom activities and to delve into learning because of their intrinsic motivation rather than external motivation or coercion. If students are seen as reluctant learners, blank slates, or empty vessels, teachers do not expect student input in making classroom decisions and use extrinsic motivation to spark students toward academic learning.

The Nature of Subject Matter   The nature of subject matter refers to whether knowledge is presented as discrete bits of information or broad concepts. For example, if subject matter is seen as a collection of bits of knowledge, students may be required to memorize the Gettysburg Address, for example, without learning its cultural, historical, and social context, or to learn the capitals of the 50 states only for the sake of being able to write them on a test. If subject matter is viewed as broad concepts, students learning the Gettysburg Address will also learn about the pros and cons of the Civil War and how cultural legacies from that war, such as the debate over the display of the Confederate flag in South Carolina, remain today. The nature of subject matter also refers to the extent to which students' experiences as well as the content in books count as knowledge.

For example, history can be taught as facts and concepts about recorded events of the past. However, history also can be taught as the personal narratives of class members and the oral histories passed down within families. Students can learn that the history of an event has many stories and interpretations.

The Nature of the Learning Process   The nature of the learning process refers to the extent to which one believes that learning takes place through cognitive, affective, or psychomotor experience. Some people believe that all students learn best through reading and hearing knowledge. Others believe students learn best when feelings and attitudes are incorporated into the teaching/learning process. Some believe that students need to be physically involved in learning. Finally, many people believe that different people learn best in different ways, and that teaching needs to be targeted toward the variety of ways students learn.

Behaviors to Carry Out a Philosophy

The behaviors teachers use to carry out their philosophical position are usually described as authoritarian, democratic, or laissez-faire. Teachers operating from an *authoritarian* position most of the time present students with a single point of view and expect students to learn that point of view without exploring alternatives. They let the students know that any decisions made in the classroom are under the teacher's control. Teachers operating from a *democratic* position will offer students different perspectives on an issue and encourage them to seek different points of view, thereby helping students to think divergently rather than convergently. Many classroom decisions will be made according to democratic principles. Teachers operating from a *laissez-faire* position will often sit back and observe, letting students initiate much of their own classroom learning. They will provide students with little structure in the curriculum and instruction and will not establish any standard procedure for making classroom decisions.

Some teacher candidates may never have thought about how they would answer these questions about the nature of learners, subject matter, learning processes, and the teacher's role in all of these. Beginning to answer these questions now can guide teacher candidates in the constant questioning and articulation of what they think are the purposes of education, and their roles within it, throughout their teacher education sequence and their teaching careers. The next section, "Finding a Voice," will help readers envision how a philosophy of education can guide teacher candidates' actions within the practices of schooling.

FINDING A VOICE

Maria, Jean, and Mark are three teacher candidates who are concerned about what is happening at Woodrow Wilson Elementary School, where they are student teaching. The school, they told their university supervisor Joan, was pushing the three Rs at the expense of art, physical education, and music. Jean said, "It looks like we are getting a firsthand look at essentialism in action." Teachers at the school who usually taught the art, physical education, and music classes were now required to teach reading, math, and science during that scheduled time. The principal, Ms. Lucas, told the faculty that this was not an idea that she liked or planned to continue to enforce. She said that the school would return to the regular schedule of teaching art, physical education, and music as soon as the students' reading and math scores improved.

Maria, Jean, and Mark were empathetic about the pressure on the principal to raise the achievement levels at the school. They had heard of reports that some principals had lost positions at their schools because of low test scores. However, they did not like the idea of the students' being penalized and held solely responsible for their low scores. Woodrow Wilson, they knew, had been neglected for decades by the local board of education. A social reconstructionist approach that one principal had tried to bring to the school had been resisted. Teacher turnover and community apathy were two of the reasons. Of the school's teaching staff, 30% were long-term substitutes and 50% had taught for less than four years. The other 20% had taught for more than six years, but some of these were secondary teachers who had been reclassified after high school enrollment had dropped. Teachers were still adjusting to the change. Some were annoyed because they had to teach at a lower grade level. Some had not yet developed the sensitivities helpful in working with younger elementary school students. Records indicated that teachers who took their first assignment at Woodrow Wilson usually stayed at the school for about three years, or until they received tenure. They would then transfer to a more affluent school. The school has had five new principals in the last seven years, and this is Ms. Lucas's first assignment as a principal.

Maria, Jean, and Mark asked Joan if she would look at an interdisciplinary unit they had developed that took into account the three Rs and also art, physical education, and music. They wanted to present the unit and other ideas to Ms. Lucas and their cooperating teachers as a way to teach the three Rs while incorporating art, physical education, and music. Joan said, "Given the tension at Wilson and the difficulties the principal and staff are facing, maybe the best way for you to help is just to do an outstanding job in the class and to do volunteer work with the students after school. Anything else may be considered disruptive by the cooperating teachers and the principal."

Maria, Jean, and Mark understood the significance of Joan's statement, but they were not satisfied with it. Mark said to Joan, "Change and new ideas are often considered disruptive. However, we believe that we need to interrupt this 'no art and music' policy before students' morale goes out the window. Also, there are very few data in the educational literature that support such a plan."

Joan said, "OK. I will look over your unit and go with you when you present your idea, but take it easy and don't get upset if you are turned down."

Grateful for the support, Maria said, "Maybe we can finish the unit before the faculty meeting next week. If we do, we can ask to be placed on the agenda."

After the three presented their unit to the faculty, Ms. Lucas thanked them and said, "This is a good idea and we appreciate all the hard work that you have put into it. But now, I think that it is best to leave things as they are." Although disappointed at Ms. Lucas's response, Maria, Jean, and Mark showed no emotion as they returned to their seats.

At the close of the school day, the three teacher candidates heard a request over the PA system for them to report to the principal's office. Jean said, "Now we are going to get it. At least she did not put us down in front of the faculty."

When the three arrived, Ms. Lucas said, "I have been thinking. Why don't we implement your interdisciplinary unit in two of your classes? We can track the effects on the students. Then one of you, whose class is not involved, can help to collect data on what's happening and serve as a resource. Think about it and let's talk on Monday."

As the three headed out of Wilson to start their weekend, Mark said, "Life is full of surprises."

Jean replied, laughingly, "Well, Maria and I decided that we will teach the unit and you will be the resource. See, there is another surprise for you!"

SUMMING UP

Philosophy, a "love of wisdom," in a more practical sense is a way of thinking logically about questions that concern humankind. Since the early history of civilization, societies worldwide have had an appreciation for philosophy. Philosophical thinking over the centuries has assisted humankind in efforts to better understand the universe and to make life more fulfilling.

Socrates, Plato, and Aristotle were ancient Greek philosophers who are still noted for their contributions to Western civilization. Socrates shifted philosophical thinking away from a search for the "unity of things" to understanding morality and discovering truth and good. Plato is credited with starting the first university, the Academy, and writing several distinguished works including *The Republic,* which laid out a plan for a "perfect" society ruled by wise philosopher-kings. Aristotle, a student of Plato, is credited with Aristotelian logic, or deductive logic. It deals with the relations between propositions in terms of their form instead of their content. Aristotle advocated the first classification system.

The philosophy of India is believed to be as old as Greek philosophy. Buddha began his work as a teacher at Sarnath in India. Many of his followers organized Buddhist communities, which spread throughout Asia. Buddhism largely vanished from India after the 12th century and the invasion of the Muslims. The concept of karma—that what a person does influences what will happen to that person in the future—is an idea that is popular in many Eastern societies. Indian philosophy includes the belief that through study, meditation, yoga, or a combination of the three, it is possible to transcend worldly cares and the suffering that life brings.

Eastern philosophy differs from Western philosophy in that it respects the interdependency and unity of human beings and nature; it is concerned with interpersonal knowledge, peace and harmony, and the nature of society. Confucianism and Taoism are two major strands of Far Eastern philosophy. Li and Taoism are two important concepts in Far Eastern philosophy. Li means behaving with courtesy and ceremony; Taoism means "the way" and being one with nature.

The demographics in classrooms in the United States are becoming increasingly like a global village. Teachers are teaching students from all parts of the world. Understanding the philosophies that direct the social and cultural behavior of students can be a vital key to successful teaching.

The political and philosophical writings of Francis Bacon and John Locke affected the thinking of the English colonists in America. Benjamin Franklin and Thomas Jefferson were especially influenced by Locke's discussion of inalienable rights of citizens and the connection of an educated citizenry to a government run by the people for the people. These philosophical ideas became the foundation of the educational system of the United States.

Over the decades, six educational philosophies have influenced the U.S. educational landscape: perennialism, essentialism, experimentalism (pragmatism), reconstructionism, existentialism, and postmodernism.

Perennialism is a belief in absolute truths and standards. The Great Books, classical literature, traditional history, and biographies make up a good deal of the curriculum. Lectures dominate as an instructional practice, and essay exams are a way of assessing student learning.

Essentialism is the belief that the primary purpose of school is to preserve the basic elements of human culture and transmit them to the young. Essentialists become very vocal after a perceived national crisis, such as when the Russians sent *Sputnik* into space in 1957 or when there is a downturn in the national economy caused by greater technological efficiency on the part of other countries. Essentialists argue that schools should stress the basics and eliminate curriculum frills. The teacher is the dominant actor in the classroom, and the textbook is the chief instructional tool. Essentialism in the United States started in the 1930s as a reaction against the pragmatism and reconstructionism that were popular at the time.

Experimentalist philosophy teaches students to analyze and critique, and to make decisions based on their analysis. Charles Peirce is considered the father of pragmatism, which is considered an American philosophy. A teacher who adheres to the experimentalist philosophy will organize the curriculum according to students' interests, and "learning by doing" through discovery and experimentation will be the focus of the instruction. The classroom will be a community, with classroom management and discipline adhering to democratic principles. Individual and class projects and discussion make up a good deal of the instructional methods, and assessment is based upon student projects.

Social reconstructionism is an educational philosophy in which the school, including teachers and students, are encouraged to change society for the betterment of those who are marginalized. Social reconstructionists believe that students should be prepared to build a more just social order, one that better meets the needs of all people, thereby achieving greater democratic effectiveness. Current events and social problems make up a good deal of the curriculum, and the basics are taught through students' working on problems facing them or their communities. It may seem that scholars of color and women are contributors to the reconstructionist philosophy more than to other philosophies. This is perhaps so, because scholars of color and women are more likely to argue for changes in the status quo, especially changes related to race, class, gender, disability, and sexual orientation.

Existentialists believe that philosophy should be a passionate encounter with the problems of life and the inevitability of death. In an existentialist classroom, students play a major role in determining what they will study. Learners may pursue knowledge at their own pace and in ways that best meet their needs. Teachers see their role as providing a caring classroom that stimulates individual learning styles.

Postmodernism has its roots in the 1950s world of art. Postmodernism argues that multiple interpretations of events and issues should be presented to students, the curriculum should include locally based narratives of everyday life and events, and knowledge should be presented as partial. The role of the teacher is to expose students to multiple communities of knowledge. The themes of postmodernism include notions of constructed truth, language, reason, science and technology, human nature and self, power and oppression, and creativity and aesthetics. Postmodernists argue that how we think about race and gender, for example, is socially constructed and has roots in power relationships.

The twin themes of this book are power and education that is multicultural and social reconstructionist. We use these themes to evoke ideas that come from different philosophical movements, including social reconstructionism and postmodernism. We use them to inform our choices in this book and to explain the multiple perspectives and power relationships that are embedded within schooling practices.

The importance of developing a philosophy of education early in teacher training is that it frames how you think and learn about teaching. It can be used to assess the fit between your own teaching beliefs and those of a particular school and its staff. The following four questions provide a framework for teacher candidates to develop their philosophies of education: (1) What is the nature of the learner? (2) What is the nature of subject matter? (3) What is the nature of the learning process? (4) What behaviors (disposition and attitude) should teachers exhibit in order to carry out their philosophical position?

KEY TERMS

Confucianism	pragmatism
essentialism	postmodernism
experimentalism	rationalism
existentialism	social reconstructionism
karma	Socratic dialogue
li	Taoism
perennialism	

QUESTIONS FOR REFLECTION

1. The ideas about the role of teachers in John Dewey's *My Pedagogic Creed* are said to have been a source of inspiration for George Counts's book *Dare the School Build a New Social Order?* What political or social writing have

you read lately that is a source of inspiration for your actions as a teacher candidate? Please identify and explain.

2. Philosophers are considered very wise people. Yet they can also be considered xenophobic and biased about social background and gender (calling for little or no education for women and none for those who were servants or slaves). Is "wisdom" conditioned by historical, cultural, and geographical context?

3. Are there social and academic benefits for students who one year have a teacher with one educational philosophy and the next year have a teacher with a different educational philosophy? If so, what are the benefits? Or would it be better for students to have teachers who share the same philosophy?

4. In a class in which some students are influenced by Far Eastern philosophy, others live according to Indian philosophy, and still others are influenced by Western philosophy, should the teacher have classroom discussions about the impact of these philosophies on the lives of the students?

5. Should teachers transfer from a school if the philosophy of the school undergoes a 180-degree change because of the hiring of a new principal and other key staff members? Or should the teachers change their philosophy of education to be compatible with that of the new principal?

ACTIVITIES

1. Compare and contrast William James's and James Baldwin's "A Talk With Teachers." What are the similarities between the two essays and what are the differences?

2. The ideas in Benjamin Franklin's "Proposals Relating to the Education of Youth in Pennsylvania" are said to have contributed a good deal to education in the United States as we now know it. Read the "Proposals" and identify the features that are common in schooling today. Also identify the features that are not common and suggest why they are not.

3. Ask your professor/advisor what his or her educational philosophy is, and how it influences teaching. Record the comments that address the four guiding questions provided in this chapter. Then assess the extent to which you see that educational philosophy enacted in his or her teaching.

4. Ask your cooperating teacher the extent to which current educational policy, such as standards, vouchers, and IEPs affect teaching according to his or her educational philosophy.

GETTING CONNECTED

www.askasia.org/frclasm/readings   ASKASIA provides information, including articles on Asian philosophy and religion.

www.geocities.com/Tokyo/Place1757   This website provides numerous articles and references on Asian philosophy and religion.

www.freedomforum.org

First Amendment Center provides materials for educators and community members about such issues as teaching and religion, character education and religion, Supreme Court and religion.

SUGGESTED RESOURCES

Marshall, Brenda K. *Teaching the Postmodern: Faction and Theory.* New York: Routledge, 1992.

This book offers an introductory discussion of postmodernism that is accessible to college students. It includes key concepts and terminology such as structuralism, poststructuralism, critiques of rationality, representation, and several other concepts.

Reed, Ronald F., and Tony W. Johnson, eds. *Philosophical Documents in Education.* New York: Longman, 2000.

This is an edited anthology of 15 essays on different philosophical traditions written by historical and contemporary Western scholars. The essays include the work of such scholars as Plato, Aristotle, Rousseau, Dewey, and Counts.

Rosenau, Pauline Marie. *Post-Modernism and the Social Sciences.* Princeton, NJ: Princeton University Press, 1992.

This book is a discussion of how postmodernism challenges rationality in the liberal arts and social science academic areas. It explains why and how different elements within the postmodern approach question modern science and the idea of objective truth. The text is both comprehensive and accessible.

Seager, Richard Hughes. *Buddhism in America.* New York: Columbia University Press, 1999.

This book explains how the Buddhist community has grown over the past few decades in the United States. An Asian immigrant population, Asian Americans who have converted to Buddhism, and old-line Asian American Buddhists make up this population. The experiences of these groups of Buddhists in the United States are discussed.

Wollstonecraft, Mary. *A Vindication of the Rights of Women.* New York: Prometheus, 1989.

Originally published in the late 18th century, this book argues for the rights of women in every area of social life. It discusses the social forces that resisted women's rights and attempted to keep them inferior to men. The author argues that such social forces as prevailing attitudes and customs prevent women from realizing their potential.

Wong, Eva, trans. *Seven Taoist Masters: A Folk Novel of China.* Boston: Shambala, 1990.

This is a story about six men and one woman who overcome tremendous hardships on the journey to self-mastery. The novel illuminates the essentials of Taoist philosophy and practice as it relates to overcoming the four obstacles of anger, greed, lust, and drunkenness.

NOTES

1. Anthony Kenny, "History of Philosophy: Historical and Rational Reconstruction," in *Methods of Philosophy and the History of Philosophy,* Proceedings of the Institut International de Philosophie, Helsinki, ed. Simo Knuuttila and Ilkka Niniluoto, Vol. 61 (1995), 67.
2. F. W. Garforth, *The Scope of Philosophy* (London: Longman, 1971).

3. Cornel West, *The American Evasion of Philosophy: A Genealogy of Pragmatism* (Madison: University of Wisconsin Press, 1989), 5.

4. Ibid., 5.

5. http://www.geocities.com/Athens/Forum/9974/old.html

6. Elisabeth Rosenthal, "For a Fee, This Chinese Company Will Beg Pardon for Anyone," *New York Times,* 3 January 2001, A4.

7. Jay Stevenson, *Philosophy* (New York: Simon and Schuster, 1998).

8. Ibid.

9. Karen Lurie, *Global Studies* (New York: Random House, 1998).

10. Paul Frankenstein, "The Origins of Chinese Civilization" (2001), http://asterius.com/china/chinal.asp

11. U.S. Census Bureau, *Census 2000* (Washington, DC: U.S. Government Printing Office, 2000), 4.

12. Steven Zenith, "Taoism" (2001), http://www.thetemple.com/alt.philosophy.taoism/taofaq.htm

13. O. B. Duane, *Zen Buddhism* (London: Brockhampton Press, 1997), 51.

14. The Graduate Center, City University of New York, Faculty Books and Research, "American Religious Identification Survey," http://www.gc.cunt.edu/studies/key

15. Zenith, "Taoism."

16. Edward Power, *Educational Philosophy: A History From the Ancient World to Modern America* (New York: Garland, 1996), 104.

17. Ibid., 13.

18. Ibid., 13.

19. Ibid., 48.

20. Ibid., 103.

21. Quoted in Donald J. Butler, *Four Philosophies* (New York: Harper and Brothers, 1951), 10.

22. Arthur E. Bestor, *The Restoration of Learning* (New York: Knopf, 1956), 4.

23. National Commission on Excellence in Education, *A Nation at Risk: The Imperative for Educational Reform* (Washington, DC: U.S. Department of Education, 1983).

24. Cornell West, *Race Matters* (Boston: Beacon Press, 1993).

25. S. George Counts, *Dare the School Build a New Social Order?* (Carbondale: Illinois University Press, 1932), 16–18.

26. Theodore Brameld, *Pattern of Educational Philosophy of Education: A Democratic Interpretation* (New York: World Book Company, 1950), 31.

27. Theodore Brameld, *Toward a Reconstructed Philosophy of Education* (New York: Holt, Rinehart and Winston, 1956), 37–38.

28. Sarah Margaret Fuller, *Women in the Nineteenth Century* (New York: Greeley and McElrath, 1845).

29. bell hooks, *Teaching to Transgress: Education as the Practice of Freedom* (New York: Routledge, 1994), 11.

30. Gerald Haynes, "A Biographical Sketch of Du Bois," http://www.duboislc.org/html/DuBoisBio.html

31. W. E. B. Du Bois, *The Soul of Black Folks* (1903; Penguin Books Reprint Edition, 1996).

32. Beverly Gordon, "Toward Emancipation in Citizenship Education: The Case of African American Cultural Knowledge," *Theory and Research in Social Education* 12 (1985): 1–23.

33. Ivor Shor, *Critical Teaching and Everyday Life* (Boston: South End Press, 1980).

34. Henry A. Giroux, "Theories of Reproduction and Resistance in the New Sociology of Education: A Critical Analysis," *Harvard Educational Review* 53 (1983): 257–293.

35. Carl A. Grant and Christine E. Sleeter, "Race, Class, Gender in Educational Research: An Argument for Integrative Analysis," *Review of Educational Research* 56 (1986): 195–211.

36. B. H. Suzuki, "Curriculum Transformation for Multicultural Education," *Education and Urban Society* 16 (1984): 294–322.

37. H. Carby, "Schooling in Babylon," in *The Empire Strikes Back: Race and Racism in 70's Britain,* ed. Centre for Contemporary Cultural Studies (Wolfeboro, NH: Longwood, 1982), 183–211.

38. C. Mullard, "Racism in Society and Schools: History, Policy, and Practice," Occasional Paper No. 1, Centre for Multicultural Education of London, Institute of Education, 1980.

39. A. M. Jaggar and P. R. Struhl, eds., *Feminist Framework,* 3rd ed. (New York: McGraw-Hill, 1993).

40. J. J. Irvine, "Culturally Response Pedagogy: Myth and Misperception" (paper presented at the annual conference of the American Association of Colleges of Teacher Education, San Antonio, TX, February 1991).

41. James A. Banks, *Multiethnic Education: Theory and Prac*tice (Boston: Allyn and Bacon, 1981).

42. Ivan Soll, "What Is Existentialism?" *The World Book* (Chicago: Field Enterprises Educational Corporation, 1970), 338.

43. Lloyd Duck, *Teaching With Charisma* (Boston: Allyn and Bacon, 1981).

44. Soll, "What Is Existentialism?"

45. Ray Linn, *A Teacher's Introduction to Postmodernism* (Urbana, IL: National Council of Teachers of English, 1996), xiii.

46. Richard Herrnstein and Charles Murray, *The Bell Curve: Intelligence and Class Structure in American Life* (New York: Free Press, 1984).

47. Thomas S. Popkewitz, Lynn Fuller, and James E. Browne, "Postmodernism," in *Dictionary of Multicultural Education,* ed. Carl A. Grant and Gloria Ladson-Billings (Phoenix, AZ: Oryx Press, 1997), 219.

48. Grant and Ladson-Billings, *Dictionary of Multicultural Education,* 222.

49. C. H. Cherryholmes, *Power and Criticism: Poststructural Investigations in Education* (New York: Teachers College Press, 1988), 35.

50. Carl Chase, "Galileo," *The World Book* (Chicago: Field Enterprises Educational Corporation, 1970), 9–11.

GOVERNANCE OF EDUCATION: WHO CONTROLS EDUCATION?

FOCUS QUESTIONS

1. How have presidents over the years used moral suasion and the bully pulpit to pursue their educational agendas?
2. Whose voice is most influential in the governance of education in the United States: the federal government, state government, or local government?
3. How and why is the co-sponsored educational summit that President G. H. W. Bush and Governor Clinton held during the fall of 1989 still influencing education today?
4. Why does each state have its own educational system?
5. How effective is local governance in running the schools in its district when it feels the pressure of the federal and state governments?
6. Within this hierarchical system of governance, how do different interest groups become involved in educational governance?

VIGNETTE

ALLY AND REGINA: WHO CONTROLS EDUCATION?

Ally and Regina are two students in an Introduction to Education class. One of their assignments is attending a school board meeting. We meet Ally and Regina as they are walking back to their dorm from the meeting.

REGINA: *Ally, what did you think about the school board meeting?*

ALLY: *Parts of it were boring, but I liked the discussion of standards and per-*
formance evaluation and the school district's take on the new testing program
that the state is planning to legislate. Standards and performance evaluation
will affect us when we start teaching in a couple of years.
REGINA: *Yes, there are some concerns about the state pushing a testing*
program that the school district doesn't believe it needs. Who controls
education, anyway? Does the local district or the state?
ALLY: *I believe both of them control education. As I listen to members of*
the school board, I also hear concerns about the control exercised by the
federal government.
REGINA: *I wonder what our other class members got out of this meeting*
and who they think controls education.

This chapter focuses on governance of, or control and influence over, education at the federal, state, and local levels. Although we focus on government, this
is not to imply that other organizations and groups do not participate in the governance of education in the United States. For example, teachers' unions and professional associations can exert great influence on the governance of education. In
Chapter 10, "Teachers' and Students' Rights and Responsibilities," you will see
how legal mandates and court decisions also govern education.

The point to remember is that power circulates through all governing actions.
There is always a push and pull between organizations and groups to gain influence, and this influence impacts on teachers' work. For example, the pressure by
political leaders for each school to have a report card that shows students' achievement scores, and the propensity to compare schools and districts based on report
cards, has come about through the effects of power. Consequently, many organizations and associations, along with the federal, state, and local governments, compete for control and influence over education in the United States. In reading this
chapter, keep in mind that governance of education operates in a broader context
than is described in any one chapter. In this chapter, we focus on the federal, state,
and local levels of government to highlight the official voices in educational decision making.

FEDERAL GOVERNANCE OF EDUCATION

The federal government has a long and active history of influencing U.S. education. Presidents, the Department of Education, and the legislative branch are all
major actors in making certain that a federal voice is present. We begin this section with a discussion of the history of the federal government's role in education.
This will be followed by a discussion of the president's role, the Department of
Education, and the legislative branch.

The History of the Federal Government's Role in Education

Are you, like Ally and Regina, somewhat unclear about the federal government's role in education? Some believe that this is a moot question, because everyday life teaches that the federal government is actively involved in education. From watching television reports or reading about educational issues in the print media, it is easy to become convinced that the federal government plays a major role in education. The voices of the president, the 100 senators, and the 235 congressional representatives are influential, and at times very persuasive, especially when federal dollars are connected to the voices. From the time that the U.S. Constitution was written to the present day, the relationship between the federal government and education can be described as a work in progress. The Constitution does not directly address education, and any powers not explicitly assigned, as the Tenth Amendment states, are reserved to the states. Many people believe in minimizing federal involvement in state affairs. They would argue that the federal government should let each state take care of its own educational business. However, others support the federal government's having a strong voice in state affairs. For example, during the 1960s civil rights organizations took numerous actions to bring about increased federal involvement in education, especially concerning issues of equity and equality.

Given that the Tenth Amendment reserves unassigned powers to the states, constitutional scholars and educators have had to identify amendments and clauses in the Constitution that would give the federal government a voice in educational matters. The Tenth Amendment, the "general welfare" clause (Article I, Section 8), and the preamble are the sections of the Constitution that give the federal government a right to become involved in educational matters. The general welfare clause states, "The Congress shall have power to lay and collect taxes . . . and provide for the common defense and general welfare of the United States." This clause is interpreted as giving Congress the power to tax for social purposes and to act in educational areas. The preamble to the Constitution states, "We the people of the United States, in order to form a more perfect Union, . . . provide for the common defense, promote the general Welfare and secure the Blessing of Liberty . . . do ordain and establish this Constitution." Scholars have argued that this sentence gives the federal government the right to be a major player in education because education promotes the general welfare. Many, including the nation's founding fathers, have believed that a democracy needs a literate citizenry to survive and thrive.

The federal government has influenced education by providing services, such as granting land and money for schools to states, distributing surplus goods (e.g., food to support school lunch programs), and establishing educational agencies (e.g., Department of Education). The federal government has also established criteria for the receipt of federal dollars to be used in education. The Title IX guidelines that ensure compliance with gender equity mandates in public schooling are one example. In addition to these more traditional roles played by the federal government, the Department of Education also influences education by funding colleges and universities to conduct educational research and by providing technical assistance to school districts. For example, the federal government has supported the study of innovative programs, including the Eisenhower National Math and Science Project, the National Institute on Early Childhood Development and Education, the National Institute on Educational Governance, Finance, and Policy Making, and Project Head Start.

Another major source of federal influence is **moral suasion**—the promotion of ideas and goals by top government officials through reports, speeches, and publications. It is most readily observed in the actions of the president, the secretary of education, and state governors. Rather than legislation that mandates action, such as the No Child Left Behind Act, some elected officials prefer to use influence. When President George H. W. Bush called an educational summit that was led by then Governor Bill Clinton of Arkansas, the result of the meeting was a report titled *America 2000*. This report was widely disseminated throughout the educational community and individual governors used it to make changes within their states, but the report was not translated into law. Rather, it was used to influence and give shape to educational policy and practice.

The Executive Branch: The President's "Bully Pulpit"

The Oval Office is the office of arguably the most powerful person in the world, the president of the United States, and many have chosen to use it as a **bully pulpit.** This means that the president uses the power and prestige of the office to initiate educational programs and policies, and to influence Congress and the general public to accept and implement educational ideas and programs that come out of that office. Many of these programs are recommended to the president by professional organizations and prominent individuals and groups. As you read about the presidents of the past half-century, think about the different groups that influenced their decisions about education.

The Influence of Presidents Kennedy, Johnson, and Nixon   The influence of numerous civil rights organizations and reports of serious problems with social justice led President Kennedy to charge the federal government to become more responsive to the needs of all citizens. After the assassination of President Kennedy, President Johnson, in a like-minded spirit, initiated and sustained a War on Poverty. Believing that poverty is passed from generation to generation through a lack of education and job training, Johnson initiated a major federal effort to change the so-called "culture of the lower class." The War on Poverty was designed to change the living patterns of poor families. Project Head Start, for example, freed up a mother or father to work by establishing day care centers and involving their young children in school-related activities at an earlier age. President Johnson used moral suasion and his office as a bully pulpit to promote passage of the Elementary and Secondary Education Act (ESEA) of 1965, which was the educational centerpiece of the War on Poverty. ESEA, perhaps the most significant and sweeping educational legislation in effect today, included nine "titles." The titles, specific areas identified for funding, included assistance to local educational agencies for the education of low-income families; for school libraries

and the purchase of textbooks and other instructional materials; for guidance, counseling, and testing services; for educational research and training; for the education of all handicapped children; for bilingual programs; and for implementing prohibitions against sex discrimination toward students and employees of federally funded education programs and activities.

The major campaign of the War on Poverty lasted until the 1970s, when Richard Nixon became president. Nixon was not dedicated to dealing with poverty as a focus of his administration. His aim was to reduce the amount of federal involvement in education. Nixon was plagued by the Vietnam War, which had citizens in the United States verbally and physically fighting one another, and by domestic issues such as school desegregation. These domestic issues were also causing heated debates and some violence between Blacks and Whites. Nixon cut back on several educational programs started during Johnson's War on Poverty. Others, such as Head Start and bilingual education, are still around today.

The Influence of President Carter

Jimmy Carter was the first president to be endorsed by the National Education Association (NEA), in 1976. Carter showed his appreciation for that endorsement when he established the Department of Education and reestablished increased federal involvement in education, including greater federal monies allocated to education.

The Influence of Presidents Reagan and Bush

Ronald Reagan vowed, during his 1980 campaign, that he would eliminate the Department of Education instituted by Jimmy Carter. However, once Reagan became president, he did not act on that promise. *A Nation at Risk* was published in 1983, pointing out serious problems in the U.S. educational system. This report influenced Reagan to maintain the Department of Education so that a strong federal voice remained. However, he did use his presidency to increase state governance over education decisions. By using the power of his office and moral suasion, he helped states and local school districts find a greater voice in educational governance. For example, because of his actions, states had a choice of which bilingual model to adopt, the transitional or the structured immersion approach. He reduced the amount of monies that the federal government contributed to education and signed the Education Consolidation and Improvement Act (ECIA). This legislation changed the name and structure of Title I of ESEA, which provided funds to assist schools in the education of low-income students, to Chapter 1 of ECIA. This change was consistent with Reagan's goal to give the states more control over education decisions. It not only reduced the amount of monies that the federal government contributed to educational programs but also reduced the number of students eligible for such funds.

Chapter 1 is often described as the federal program that provided schools with extra funding to buy materials and hire staff to help with the reading and math of underachieving students. In your elementary and middle school, you may recall students who were having difficulty with their reading leaving the classrooms for about an hour several days during the week to work with a reading specialist. Money to hire these teachers usually came from ECIA.

President George H. W. Bush purposefully set out to have a major impact on educational policies and procedures. He followed Reagan in working to reduce the amount of federal governance in education and return it to the states. Bush declared in the 1988 presidential campaign that, if elected, he would be the "education president" and would use his bully pulpit to lead the charge to improve the condition of American education described in *A Nation at Risk*. Although Bush made this claim, his major contribution to education grew out of the Education Summit Conference that he held with the nation's governors in 1989. This conference resulted in a report titled *America 2000. America 2000*, as we noted previously, contained six national education goals that he and the 50 governors announced should be achieved by the year 2000.

The Influence of President Clinton   President Clinton's national influence on education began when, as governor of Arkansas, he chaired the National Governors' Association educational conference. He co-hosted this educational summit conference with President Bush, and participated in writing *America 2000* goals. During his presidency, Clinton drew upon the ideas of both conservative and moderate groups and used his bully pulpit to initiate the Goals 2000: Educate America Act. The Clinton administration broadened Bush's six goals in *America 2000* and added two additional goals. Goals 2000 promotes the attainment of these eight goals through the use of categorical aid—monies appropriated by the federal government for specific goals. You will learn more about categorical aid and other types of aid in the chapter on funding.

In his 1997 State of the Union Address, President Clinton claimed, "My number one priority as president over the next four years is to ensure that Americans have the best education in the world." To accomplish this goal, he laid out a 10-point plan in *Call to Action for American Education*:

1. National curriculum standards to guide state standards, and *voluntary* national assessments in reading and mathematics
2. Funding to help the National Board for Professional Teaching Standards certify 100,000 experienced teachers
3. An "America Reads" program to teach literacy skills to young children using 1 million volunteer tutors
4. Expansion of Project Head Start to reach 1 million students
5. The creation of 3,000 charter schools to test innovative ideas and promote competition among public schools
6. Character education, school uniforms, truancy laws, curfews, and zero tolerance of guns and drugs, all to promote safe, well-disciplined schools
7. Funding to help states and school districts pay for school renovations and construction
8. Federal tax credits and deductions, expanded IRAs, and increased Pell Grants to promote postsecondary education and make 14 years of schooling universal
9. A GI Bill for workers to encourage skills training
10. Internet connections to bring the world into every classroom and library[1]

Points 1, 2, and 4 have received attention, in part because the states and local school districts see points 1 and 2 as important to the education accountability effort that they are trying to put in place. For the most part, states have adopted curriculum and assessment standards that are fundamental to their education evaluation framework. Many states, acting on the belief that receipt of the state teaching license should only be the beginning in a teacher's professional preparation, are providing some funds to assist teachers with the National Board for Professional Teaching Certification Program. Point 4, Head Start, a major program in Johnson's War on Poverty, has over the years gained credibility and support from the American people. It does not necessarily need strong advocacy by the president. Point 5, creating charter schools, has had great influence as the number of charter schools has increased to approximately 800 since Minnesota passed the first charter law in 1991. The extent to which charter schools compete with other public schools is not clear, but if the number of charter schools continues to grow, their competition with traditional public schools will become much more public. Action on the other six points (3, 6, 7, 8, 9, 10) is proceeding, but at an uneven pace.

The Influence of President George W. Bush President George W. Bush vowed that "no child would be left behind" and proposed legislation that soon came to be known by the slogan. The No Child Left Behind (NCLB) Act of 2001 included a number of significant changes to the federal role in education. Central to President Bush's changes were an emphasis on doing "what works based on scientific research," expanded parental options, expanded local control, and increased testing and accountability. President Bush proposed that states test all students in mathematics and reading, annually in grades 3 through 8 and once in grades 10 through 12, as a condition for receiving federal Title I aid. Title I aid provides funds to schools serving the neediest students in order to help close the achievement gap.[2] Schools and districts must report the test scores, disaggregated by race, gender, and ability. School vouchers are to play a significant role in encouraging accountability. President Bush recommends that students in schools that fail to make satisfactory progress each year for three consecutive years should be able to use Title I funds, matched by state dollars, to transfer to a higher-performing school. States and schools that make the most progress in narrowing the achievement gap would be rewarded financially.

The Department of Education

Before education was given cabinet status, it was located in the Department of Health, Education, and Welfare (now renamed the Department of Health and Human Services) as the U.S. Office of Education. In 1867 Congress passed legislation that gave education a federal office. Initially designated as the Federal Department of Education, its main purpose was to provide technical assistance (e.g., consultant services in agriculture) and minimal education funding. In 1869 the office was transferred to the Department of the Interior, where its name was changed from "office" to "bureau" and back to "office" again. It remained in the Department of the Interior until 1939, when it became part of the Federal Security Agency.

In 1953, Education became one of the agencies in the newly created Department of Health, Education, and Welfare. This agency began to play a major role in shaping the administration, organization, and direction of education in the United States. During the 1976 presidential campaign, Jimmy Carter argued for a separate department for federal governance of education, and he promised to initiate its creation if elected. The Department of Education was created in 1979, becoming the 13th cabinet level agency.

The Department of Education serves the country in three major areas: research, publication, and dissemination of information on education in the United States. For example, each year the department issues RFPs (respond to federal proposal) inviting institutions and school systems to apply for monies to conduct educational research. The department disseminates information through the publication of many educational monographs and reports. The *Condition of Education*, published annually, provides information on the status and progress of education in the United States. Many of these publications are free to the public. (See "Getting Connected" at the end of this chapter for the Department of Education website address to view its many services and publications.)

Finally, as you'll remember from the chapter opening, Ally had asked about the local school board's concerns about the power of the federal government. We wonder how Ally, keeping in mind that educational governance is reserved to the states, would compare the influence of the Department of Education with that of other departments in the federal government—for example, the Department of State and the Department of Defense. Such a comparison may indicate to teachers how the current administration is addressing educational problems and issues, in comparison to issues in defense and foreign affairs.

The Legislative Branch

Since the early days of this country, Congress has passed legislation to provide financial assistance and to give direction to education. Legislation has provided land and the means to establish colleges, universities, and military academies. This section begins with a discussion of the history of the influence of early land ordinances.

History of Ordinances   In 1785 the Congress of the Confederation passed the Land Ordinance. This ordinance called for public lands in the Northwest Territory to be laid out into six-mile-square townships. Each township was to be subdivided into 36 lots, or sections, one square mile each, with one section of land being reserved for the maintenance and endowment of schools. Stating that one section of land was to be reserved for a school made this ordinance the first legislation to establish a policy of governmental support for education. Two years later, in 1787, the government further affirmed its commitment to education with passage of the Northwest Ordinance. This ordinance declared that "religion, morality, and knowledge being necessary to good government and the happiness of mankind, schools and the means of education shall forever be encouraged." This statement is considered by some to be "the charter of public education."[3]

By the beginning of the 19th century, Congress was aware that just providing land grants for elementary and secondary education was not sufficient to meet the needs of a rapidly growing country. A college education was becoming increasingly necessary, as was an education in military tactics. Thus, Congress provided funds and lands to create special schools and land-grant colleges. In 1802 the first special school and, for that matter, the first federal institution of higher education, the U.S. Military Academy at West Point, was established to provide for the nation's defense needs by training army officers. In 1845, the U.S. Naval Academy was built at Annapolis, Maryland, to train naval officers. The emphasis in these early schools was on national defense, but Congress soon broadened its involvement in education with the Morrill Act of 1862.

Land-Grant Colleges In the second half of the 19th century, Congress took action to provide greater educational opportunities, demonstrating a broader commitment to citizens' receiving a general college education. Three acts were passed: the Morrill Act of 1862, the Hatch Act of 1887, and the Second Morrill Act of 1890.

The Morrill Act of 1862 gave each state 30,000 acres of land or land scrip for each of their senators and representatives. The states sold the land or the scrip to obtain funds to establish a college. These colleges, Congress declared, were to be concerned with practical subjects such as agriculture and mechanical arts. In addition to courses on agriculture, engineering, and natural science, the land-grant colleges were required to implement a course on military science such as the Reserve Officer Training Corps (ROTC) program.

The Hatch Act was the first federal legislation to provide funds to states for practical research. Much of this research was directed toward various agricultural experiments. The Second Morrill Act provided federal funds to land-grant colleges to continue instruction in agriculture and mechanical arts. Together, these three pieces of legislation expanded the agricultural and mechanical benefits the United States received from higher education and provided increased opportunities for people to attend school. Also, the establishment of state colleges greatly increased the popular appeal of attending a college.[4]

Not every student dreamed of going to college. Some students wanted to learn a trade. In 1917, Congress passed the Smith Hughes Act, which provided monies for vocational education, home economics, and agriculture subjects. This act was the first of the federal government's annual appropriations for public secondary education. Over the years the act has been extended; it now provides benefits to people with disabilities, single parents, homemakers, and those in prison.[5]

Many land-grant colleges evolved into state universities. Nineteen states established more than one land-grant college; specifically, southern states established two colleges—one for Black students and the other for White students.[6] Many historically Black colleges and universities (HBCUs) continue to operate today. However, with the passage of civil rights legislation, the HBCU campuses, like the predominantly White campuses, were integrated. A typical HBCU may have a student population that is approximately 88% African American, 10% White, and 2% Asian American, Latino, and Native American.[7]

Congress became more active in the nation's educational affairs during the 1930s Depression Era. Between 1787 and 1937, Congress had passed only 14 major educational laws. However, over the past 50 years Congress has passed more than 125 major laws.[8] These laws bring with them federal dollars *and* guidelines for receiving and spending these funds. Such guidelines give Congress a major influence in educational matters in states receiving the monies.

As we have seen, the federal government influences education, particularly through the president's use of the Oval Office as a bully pulpit and the use of moral suasion. The secretary of education and other officials of the executive branch use their position and the revenues they control to influence the direction of educational policy, research, and practice. Congress, because it passes educational laws and financial appropriations to accompany them, is also a major player in the country's educational affairs.

Federal involvement in education has come to be viewed as a mixed blessing: States want the money, but do not want any strings attached to the money they receive. The "strings" have caused some teachers to resent the money for academic results proposed by the Bush administration. However, money without strings and accountability, as anyone who deals with the federal government quickly learns, is not how things operate. Thus, states will continue to ask, "Does increased federal involvement in education strengthen local school programs, or does it just extend bureaucratic control over local programs?"

While states examine the question of federal control, people who are marginalized because of state actions need to consider how they are affected by federal involvement. Educational issues such as school desegregation, gender equity, and inclusion of students with disabilities were not major concerns of many state schools until the federal government stepped in and provided leadership and direction and demanded accountability. Many educational reformers are pleased with the provisions in the No Child Left Behind Act that require school districts to report their test scores by race, gender, and ability. This prevents diverse districts from hiding the fact that poor students, students of color, and students with disabilities have traditionally had lower test scores than their wealthier White counterparts. One factor in this trend is that poor students, students of color, and students with disabilities are not encouraged to take academically rigorous coursework. In many districts and states, once test scores were disaggregated and inequities made public, money was provided for teacher training and academic support to increase the achievement of those groups of students.

STATE GOVERNANCE OF EDUCATION

Although responsibility for public education is vested in state legislatures, the day-to-day operation of the schools is usually controlled by the state board of education, the state department of education, and the chief state school officer. The nature and function of these administrative offices will be discussed, starting with colonial times.

When and How Did State Governance Start?

The development of state school systems can be traced to early colonial times. Some colonists with a vision toward the future realized that educating only the privileged and the elite with a religion-based curriculum was not smart if the colonies were to survive and grow. In Massachusetts the idea of educating all the colonists gained enough support that in 1642 the General Court passed an education act that required parents to ensure that their children could "read and understand the principles of religion and the capital laws of the country."[9] This law was soon followed by passage of the **Old Deluder Satan Act** in 1647, a law that ordered towns of 50 or more households to hire a teacher and towns of 100 or more to set up a school. These laws set in motion the establishment of public schools.

Although these laws were relatively ineffective, the concept of public education had been strongly planted in the American psyche, and the idea grew as local citizens became increasingly involved in educational decision making. Nevertheless, it still took individuals of stature to shape the role and the future of education in the early days of the country. Thomas Jefferson, one of the early influential advocates of public education, equated education with virtue and self-control. Jefferson, along with Horace Mann, is most frequently mentioned as the person who argued that there is a direct connection between an educated citizenry and fulfillment of the democratic way of life. In 1779, before the Virginia Assembly, he proposed a plan for a state school system, "A Bill for the More General Diffusion of Knowledge." Under this plan each county was to be divided into "hundreds" of such size that all children living in these subdivisions could conveniently attend the school that was to be established in each. All free children, girls as well as boys, were to attend school for three years without paying tuition and longer at private expense if their parents, guardians, or friends thought proper.[10]

Jefferson's plan was not accepted, but the idea of a state system of public education was created and continued to grow. Ten years later, Alexander Hamilton helped to organize the first New York citizens' group at the state level to administer public education.[11]

By the mid-1800s, changes were needed in the educational system to accommodate the growing and increasingly urbanized population. By 1846, one-eighth of the entire U.S. population consisted of first-generation immigrants who were new to Anglo-American traditions. Many U.S. leaders and citizens argued that the new arrivals needed to be "Americanized" to prepare them to become productive members of society and to prevent social unrest. The public schools, it was agreed, were where Americanization would take place. Many public school facilities, however, were in poor condition. Many teachers had only a basic education and were largely untrained to lead such a major educational effort. Instructional materials were few, if available at all, and the curriculum had not been designed with Americanization as a goal. During this time many Americans were migrating from rural to urban areas and from the east to the west, and schools needed to consider how best to educate them. An articulate vision, clear leadership, and direction in education were desperately needed.

A lawyer and former member of the Massachusetts legislature, Horace Mann became the person for the job. Mann became the secretary of the newly created State Board of Education of Massachusetts in 1837. A tireless advocate for education for the masses, Mann knew that the U.S. educational system was in shambles. For 12 years, he worked tirelessly to educate the people of Massachusetts about the necessity for education and conditions of education within the state. Mann argued that education could become the "balance wheel of the social machinery"[12] and that the development of "common schools," as they were called in Massachusetts, could result in a "free school system." Mann often described his dream for the educational system as follows: "It knows no distinction, of rich and poor, of bond and free, or between those who, in the imperfect light of this world are seeking through different avenues, to reach the gate of heaven."[13] During his tenure as secretary of the state board of education, Mann's efforts resulted in several key educational developments, including the establishment of the first "normal," or teacher training, school. Normal schools played a major role in encouraging women to become teachers. Mann's educational legacy also includes establishing the purpose and function of the state board of education.

State Boards of Education

Forty-nine states have **state boards of education,** whose primary purpose is to supervise elementary and secondary education within the state. Wisconsin is the only state that does not have a state board. Although the history of the state board of education dates back to New York in 1784, it was not until 1837, during the tenure of Horace Mann in Massachusetts, that a state board of education similar to the model in use today was established. Today the function and responsibilities of the state board of education include the following:

- Set curriculum standards for the state
- Determine qualifications and appoint personnel to the state department of education
- Establish standards for issuance and revocation of teacher and administrative certificates
- Establish standards for classifying, approving, and accrediting schools, both public and nonpublic
- Prescribe a uniform system for gathering and reporting educational data, for keeping adequate educational and finance records, and for evaluating educational progress
- Interpret its own rules and regulations and, upon appeal, hear all controversies and disputes arising therefrom
- Provide, through the state department of education, supervisory and consultative services and issue materials that would be helpful in the development of educational programs
- Advise the governor or legislature on educational matters
- Accept and distribute in accord with law any monies, commodities, goods, and services that may be made available from the state or federal government or from other sources[14]

The commissioner or superintendent of education and the state board of education are sources of power in governance of education at the state level. However, control of education at the state level mostly resides with the governor. In most states, it is the governor who has the authority to decide or greatly influence educational legislation, as well as who serves as state superintendent and who serves on the state board of education. The procedure for selecting state board members varies from state to state, but in 35 states they are appointed by the governor. Approval by the state senate or state assembly is necessary in some states. In 14 states and the District of Columbia, members are elected by the people or representatives of the people (state legislature or members of local school boards).[15]

The Chief State School Officer

The chief state school officer (CSSO), sometimes referred to as state superintendent or commissioner of public instruction, is responsible for the general supervision of the state public school system. In 37 of the 50 states, as well as the District of Columbia and outlying territories, the chief state school officer is appointed. In 26 of these states and the District of Columbia, the appointment is made by the state board of education, and the CSSO serves as its executive officer; in 5 states, the governor appoints the chief state school officer. In 8 of the remaining states, the chief state school officer is elected.[16]

Whether the chief state school officer is appointed or elected, the role includes counseling the governor on educational issues, serving as executive officer of the state board of education, apprising the board and the public about the operation of the public schools, and working with local school boards and other educational institutions within the state to improve education. The role also involves ensuring compliance with state education statutes and regulations, explaining and interpreting the state's school laws, rendering decisions concerning the administration of schools within the state, organizing committees and task forces to study educational problems and offering recommendations, and preparing a budget for the state education program.[17]

CSSOs are carrying on the tradition of Horace Mann. The CCSO is the point person for the state's educational programs, giving public voice to educational needs. CSSOs inform citizens about educational innovations that are good for the children of the state; encourage citizens to express their ideas about educational issues, recommend courses of action to the state board of education, and offer suggestions and recommendations to the state legislature.[18] President Bush and Governor Clinton's educational summit in1989 resulted in a national education plan, *America 2000*, and a power shift in education at the state level. The Bush–Clinton conference inspired the governors to take a more active role in state education.

This idea was further encouraged because governors wanted more control over the education dollars coming from the federal government. The governors wanted more say about educational choice (e.g., tuition tax credits and vouchers), the direction of educational curriculum in the state (e.g., content and performance standards), and how colleges and universities prepare teachers. Before the publication of *A Nation at Risk* and the Bush–Clinton conference, both governors and state boards of education left a good deal of the public expression of educational needs and ideas up to the chief state school officer. Now, many governors are vying for the lead in voicing the big educational ideas for their states. You will hear governors argue that federal education dollars should go directly to the state (i.e., the governor) instead of going to a state agency selected by the federal government.

The chief state school officers, especially those who are appointed, are told to get behind the governor and to follow his or her lead. The power flow from the CSSO's office to the governor's office has shifted to a flow that runs from the governor's office to the CSSO's office. This shift has led to some tension in educational governance at the state level. In some cases, the flow of power is more connected to politics than to education.

Teacher candidates starting their professional education have often thought that education was "neutral," not political. Many teacher candidates have not been overly concerned with the viewpoints being expressed as long as they seem consistent with the democratic way of life. This was due in part to a lack of immediate access to the range of debates and discussions on educational issues. Now, with increasing media access to heated educational debates among politicians, interest groups, and professional organizations, teacher candidates can more readily observe that neutrality in education is a myth. The ideas of those in dominant positions (e.g., governor, president, interest group chair) are usually presented as neutral, not favoring one group over another, or favoring those who have been left behind. Sometimes, in actuality the ideas being proposed keep life conditions much the way they have always been and do not help those who have "been left behind." It is also important to look at other social conditions that disadvantage people so proposals can be assessed through many avenues, not just through educational reform, which surely cannot solve all of society's ills on its own. For example, it is insufficient to reform education if funds are not simultaneously directed at health care, family support, housing, and wages. If a family cannot support itself, provide for the physical well-being of the children (i.e., medical and dental care), and keep food on the table, no matter how excellent the educational system is, the child will face an uphill battle to achieve academic success.

The State Department of Education

The state department of education (or the Department of Children, Families and Learning as it is called in the state of Minnesota), with the chief state school officer as its elected or appointed leader, is responsible for the operation of school systems at the state level. These responsibilities, somewhat expanded over the last five decades, include the following seven areas: (1) accrediting schools, or making certain that schools meet the educational standards imposed by the state; (2) certifying teachers; (3) apportioning funds; (4) overseeing student transportation and safety; (5) monitoring state regulation; (6) conducting research, evaluating programs, and issuing reports; and (7) monitoring federally funded programs to ensure compliance with regulations.[19]

For years, teachers' direct contact with their state departments of education was limited to applying for a teaching license. Now that states are committed to standards, the influence of the state department is increasing. For example, data on standards that states collect are being used to drive the curriculum in some of those states. State departments of education are playing a major role in the development of state standards in all subject areas, and are coordinating efforts with subject matter specialists working on standards at the national level to make certain that results of the two efforts are compatible. An increasing number of teachers are reaching out to their state departments, especially in the area of school improvement, to discover how the departments' services can help them to become more effective teachers.

The Governor

Some argue that changes in state constitutions that increase the governor's term of office to four years, along with the opportunity to serve more than one consecutive term, have enhanced gubernatorial power, including the governor's influence in educational matters.[20] As we discussed earlier in this chapter, because the U.S. Constitution does not refer directly to education or delegate power over education to the federal government, each state is responsible for its own educational system. Consequently, the governor of a state is the educational leader.

Much like the president of the United Sates at the national level, the governor influences education at the state level through his or her own "bully pulpit." The power and prestige of the governor's office enables the individual serving as governor to influence education. For example, the amount of monies the governor's budget appropriates to education, and the educational areas that the monies are directed to, provides a signal to the state about the governor's commitment to education. A governor can influence education at the state level by vetoing or signing educational legislation. If a state's statutes allow the governor to appoint the chief state school officer and members of the state board of education, the governor can influence educational policies and practices through appointment.

Over the past several decades, a number of governors have visibly exerted their influence in education. During the 1960s, several southern governors opposed school desegregation. You may remember or have seen video images of former Alabama Governor George Wallace blocking the doors to the University of Alabama to prevent African American students from entering. In the 1980s, after publication of *A Nation at Risk*, governors realized that they could gain political points by actively promoting educational excellence. For example, the governors of Florida and Georgia argued that students graduating from high school had to meet a minimum competency requirement. Other governors have entered the national spotlight by arguing for merit pay plans for teachers, a longer school year, tougher graduation requirements, math and science academies, and higher standards for teacher certification.[21]

Governors, however, do not work in a vacuum; sometimes their actions are aimed at pleasing their political constituencies. Interest groups and political groups are continually trying to influence a governor to consider their position on education issues. During gubernatorial elections, candidates' positions on educational issues are presented to persuade voters to vote for or against a candidate. Such issues as reform programs, voucher plans, charter schools, and bilingual education can influence the outcome of a governor's race. Teachers for the most part have a history of being apolitical as a group, sometimes arguing that they are "above" politics or that they should not have a political voice. This is a naïve stance because teaching is a political act. What is taught or not taught influences students in a political way. To say that teachers are above politics is just to say that they do not care about how politics unfairly disadvantages their students. It means that these teachers do not recognize that their voices will not be heard if a candidate is proposing counter-educational strategies. This position, however, has been changing over the past decades as teacher organizations have given support to political candidates.

The political position of teachers is not the issue here. Our concern is that teacher candidates understand how their job is shaped by federal, state, and local politics. They should take an active interest in the educational policies and programs that come out of the governor's office. For example, on a visit to an elementary school in Madison where Carl's grandson Gavin was receiving his screening for kindergarten, he asked, "What will the teacher–pupil ratio be in the kindergarten classes?" Alicia, Gavin's mother and an education student, and Carl were told that depended on whether the governor funded the SAGE (Student Achievement Guaranteed in Education) program. SAGE has the goal of achieving a student–teacher ratio of 15:1 in a full-day kindergarten program. Do you think that, as both an education student and a mother, Alicia is interested in the governor's decision?

Ally and Regina may also find it informative to learn their governor's position on educational issues, especially those affecting beginning teachers and the students in the area where they would like to teach. Listening to the governor's State of the State address in January of each year and examining his or her record in comparison to pre-election statements are two ways to begin to understand where the governor stands on education and whether some interests are being served more than others. Also discerning which groups influence the governor's educational agenda is necessary to understanding the reasons behind his or her actions.

LOCAL GOVERNANCE OF EDUCATION

As noted before, local governance of education had its origin in the early days of the country's history. Over the decades, the meaning of local governance has been challenged and reinterpreted by different groups in response to changing times, contested issues, and needs. However, for the most part local governance of education is a valued tradition in the United States.

Teachers are more concerned about local educational issues in part because of local governance. Teachers and teacher candidates will find this level of governance more accessible in that they can go to board meetings and hear and see the superintendent speak. They have more opportunity to interact with and learn about what is driving the major players to respond as they do. Teachers should be aware of which groups are promoting which educational ideas and for what reasons. They should also be aware of which groups' voices are muted, or if some groups claim to be acting on behalf of a marginalized group when in fact they have duped some in the marginalized group to let them represent them, in order to make it appear that they have the group's interest at heart. Power expressed through governance, or who controls education, has a long history in the United States; however, it is only recently that teachers have actively joined in the power struggle and, as when joining any new activity, they need a score card that tells them who the players are and how they play.

Central to the twin themes of this book, power and education that is multicultural and social reconstructionist (EMCSR), is the notion that different education stakeholders influence teachers and their work. Those that affect the work of teachers and the local educational scene the most are the school district, the board of education, and the superintendent of schools.

The Local School District

One way that states tried to make education more responsive to the local needs of an area (e.g., city, town, rural community) was to create basic structural units or subdivisions, designated as school districts, to administer the educational program at the local level. The local school district is a unique U.S. institution. Its distinguishing characteristic is the close relationship between the schools, the teachers, and the community served. In one sense, the local school district is a state corporation, carrying out the state's educational program. Yet in another sense, it receives its vitality and ways of thinking from the local community. It is to the local school district that teachers apply for a job.

During colonial times, the township was the earliest administrative unit for public education. Colonists soon discovered, however, that it was wiser to situate the governance of schools within a smaller area. School districts were formed that took into account the wide scattering of populations and limitations of transportation and communication. Therefore school districts were established within a geographical area that allowed most students to walk to school.

As the idea of school districts came into favor, it was implemented by the colonists wherever they moved. Today, most local school districts are subdivided into **school attendance areas.** A school attendance area is defined as an area that serves a single school. Although a school district may have only one school, usually it has more.

The fact that school districts were not being run by professional educators became a growing concern during the early years of the country as the population grew and the need for an educated citizenry increased. Some civic leaders began to argue that schools should be placed under the control of professional educators. This idea grew in popularity, as teachers too argued that professional leadership in education was necessary. Throughout the United States, governance of education was increasingly put into the hands of professional educators, where it remains for the most part today.

Population growth also brought increased diversity to cities and towns. This demographic diversity caused parents and others to seek changes in school districts' policies and practices. Such changes were as broad as the establishment of so-called "separate but equal" education facilities within a school district, and as narrow as encouraging teachers to have high expectations for students of color and to engage them actively in learning.

A school attendance area or a school district and the schools therein have often been regarded by local residents as a representation of their ways of thinking and life. Issues of power and control over curriculum and teaching staff sometimes became a problem when new residents moved into the school district. The problems often centered on all students' receiving equal opportunity and achieving equitable outcomes. One such problem with a lasting legacy is school desegregation.

In the 1950s through the 1970s, people of color demanded greater access to better educational opportunities. Often to comply with court decrees, local school boards bused students of color from a school district whose population was mostly or completely students of color to a school district or attendance area that was mostly or completely White. Frightened and annoyed White parents, using their greater influence, often organized to prevent their children from being bused to another attendance area or from having students of color bused into *their* school attendance area. White parents argued that the school attendance area, for years a representation of their way of life, was being compromised. Parents of color became angry and frustrated because of the rejection of their children. Also, they argued that it was usually their children who were being bused into the White school districts or attendance areas, rather than the other way around.

Arguing that the decision-making processes ignored their children's academic needs, some parents of color began to demand their own schools. In the 1980s, the notion of Afrocentric schools and curriculum became increasingly popular and touched off another round of issues for local school districts—especially school districts that have several attendance areas, some of which enroll predominantly students of color or predominantly White students. Conservative scholars such as Diane Ravitch, E. D. Hirsch, and Arthur Schlesinger, Jr., argued that school districts that are predominantly African American or Latino/Latina could allow a school's curriculum to reflect multiculturalism but not particularism, or centrism, focusing on one group. Ravitch explains, "The real issue on campus and in the classroom is not whether there will be multiculturalism, but what kind of multiculturalism will there be."[22] In other words, Ravitch and the others oppose having schools that are Afrocentric, Arab American–centric, or Latino-centric. Of course, they do not address the fact that most "traditional" education is Eurocentric or North American centered.

To illustrate a part of these debates, we will show how two teacher education candidates, Katie and Margaret, might discuss these issues. Katie, a White student, and Margaret, a biracial Korean–African American student, make the following arguments in a report on "The Local School District and School Desegregation":

KATIE: *The idea of a local school district or school attendance area is not the real problem of school desegregation. The problem is racist and elitist attitudes on the part of some parents and members of society in general, and the attitudes gained from living in oppression and poverty by the other parents. Parents of color and White parents believe that they are losing power. They believe that power and control reside in the court decision or the administrative decision made by the local school board that orders the school desegregation. The judges and school administrators who execute desegregation policies argued that school desegregation is the law of the land, thus they too are only following orders. They too believe that they have little power.*

MARGARET: *What Katie and I kept asking each other as we were preparing this report was, did the parents of color and the White parents ever try to sit down together and work things out? We wonder about this because of what happened when we started working together. I did not know too much about Katie and she did not know too much about me. I guess we were suspicious of each other. We had a hard time beginning our conversation, especially with issues like race and poverty in education. However, once we started working together, we learned that we had things in common and our inhibitions gradually went away. I cannot say that we will ever be best friends, but we have gained respect for and acceptance of one another.*

KATIE: *I guess what we are saying is that a number of the problems and issues that school districts have—for example, trying to pass school bonds to raise money, or the adoption of certain curriculum materials—is often more about the attitudes and ways of thinking of the school administrators, community people, and parents than about an education that will prepare students to live in a pluralist country and a global society.*

The Local Board of Education

The governing body of a school district is the **local school board.** The flow of power between individuals and among interest groups can be witnessed at a local school board meeting, especially as board members debate issues of multicultural education. Here the teacher candidate can get a firsthand view of how the effects of power dictate what will happen to students in their classrooms and policy decisions that affect the total school. The school board, acting in accordance with state statutes on education, institutes the school district's educational policies and practices.

The local school board got its start during colonial times. The first school board was the committee of citizens who were charged with the responsibility of executing the decisions made at New England town meetings. The functions of school boards may vary somewhat from school district to school district, but common duties and responsibilities include:

- Selecting the superintendent of schools
- Establishing policies and procedures for schools to follow
- Adopting the budget and enacting provisions for financing the schools and acquiring and developing property and supplies
- The hiring and firing of teachers, administrators, and district offices staff
- Overseeing students' rights and responsibilities, promotion and graduation requirements, attendance, and extracurricular activities

- Establishing and developing community relations with parents and other members of the school community
- Establishing intergovernment relations with state and federal agencies to make certain that mandates are carried out and monies are properly spent
- Appraising the work of teachers and schools and adopting plans for improvement and expansion[23]

Perhaps the single most significant and sometimes most difficult function of the school board is to select a superintendent of schools. Unfortunately, this duty has to be conducted approximately every four years in many school districts. For several reasons, including differences of opinion with board members, inability to increase students' achievement, and career advancement to larger school districts, superintendents do not last long in one place.

As the legal education agent of the state, the board is responsible for carrying out the state's education plan. On the other hand, politically, the board represents parents, students, and the ways of thinking of the majority in the school district. In some school districts that are made up of different political factions or interest groups, the local board membership composition is often representative of these different groups. Thus, school board meetings sometimes become the place where different points of view on education are hotly debated. Controversial issues (e.g., sex education) and challenging problems (e.g., increasing teachers' salaries, getting monies to put ample technology in the school) face every school district.

Community leaders, politicians, and parents continually evaluate the performance of the school board to ascertain how well it is doing its job. These groups do not hesitate to let the school board know when they do not like the job the board is doing. At local school board meetings, teachers, parents, and representatives from different interest groups will ask to address the board. These groups use this opportunity to make their views on the school board's performance known to the board and other members of the community. Citizens are usually allowed three to five minutes to state their case before the local school board, providing they have informed the secretary of the board beforehand that they wish to speak.

The work of the local school board can influence the community much as the work of the chamber of commerce does. One of the primary reasons given by parents for moving into a community is the quality of the school. Parents searching for a new home ask, "What are the schools like? How are the teachers? What kind of curriculum is offered?" These educational questions are often shaped by the work of the local school board. Also, as more and more people of color join the middle class, searching for a life outside urban areas, they look for communities where the schools will be culturally responsive to their children. Parents of color often ask the same questions about the local schools, but they look for answers that are both academically appropriate and sensitive to their cultural and language background. Local school boards have to keep up with demographic and economic changes in their district and make certain their work meets the needs of all the students in the school district.

In small towns and rural areas, those who seek membership on the school board are typically White, male, 41 to 50 years old, married, and with children in school. The typical school board member is a college graduate, holds a professional or managerial position, has a middle-class income, is Republican and conservative on education, and serves in the position about four years.[24] In some large urban school districts, the face of the school board is more racially heterogeneous. Twenty percent of the board members are African American or Latino and 45% are female.[25] School board members are elected for a specified term by residents of the school district.

Another example of local control is the **local school council,** or **site-based council,** as it is sometimes called. The purpose of the local school council is to give parents and other community members more voice in the policies and procedures of the local school. Local councils have a voice in the hiring of the school's principal, other staff members, and textbook adoption. Also, they have a voice in the school's budgetary decisions. Typical council composition is six parents of students who attend the local school, two community leaders (for example, a business and a religious leader), two teachers elected by the teaching staff, and the school principal.

One example of a school with a local school council, or site-based council, is La Escuela Fratney in Milwaukee, Wisconsin. Fratney is a school that grew out of parents' and teachers' efforts to control the mission, curriculum, and decision-making process of the school. Over the past decade, the site-based council at the school has continued to maintain the rights of parents and teachers to be the major decision makers. An example of both local and national school governance is Central Park East Secondary School, jointly directed by Community School Board #4, the New York City Board of Education Alternative High School Division, and the Coalition of Essential Schools.[26]

In sum, the local board of education is an expression of democracy at the grass-roots level. Attending a board meeting will enable a teacher candidate to observe the ebb and flow of power among board members over educational issues. The political makeup of a board (e.g., liberal and conservative) frequently gives direction to its decision making. Issues of equity (e.g., financial, cultural) are often at the center of school board meetings, especially in urban school districts. Increasingly, school board members over the past few decades have come to understand that their tenure on the board is often shaped by how they cast their vote. Power, they learn, flows to or away from them depending on their views of diversity and other educational issues.

Ally asked Regina, "Who do you think has the final word about education, the local school council or the local school board?" Regina replied, "I believe the overall responsibility for education in a school district lies with the local board of education." What do you think?

The Superintendent of Schools

The position of superintendent of schools has evolved from a minor position to one with great responsibility. Ronald Campbell describes the development of this position from its creation more than 100 years ago to the present day in terms of four stages. In the first stage, or formative years, the duties of the superintendent were primarily clerical. In the second stage, as a result of the increased bureaucracy in the educational system, a professional educator was sought to fill this position, ideally a scholar with a reputation. In the third stage, a dual plan was implemented in which the superintendent was hired for both educational and business reasons. Although this plan did not take hold, superintendents since that time have become more skillful in business management. Today, during the fourth stage, which is still evolving, the superintendent of schools is described as the "chief executive and the chief professional advisor" in the school system.[27]

The superintendency now requires an extensive background in education and is considered to be the highest professional education position in the school district. However, this increase in status has not been accompanied by protection in terms of tenure in office. The position of superintendent of schools remains tenuous, particularly in relation to social issues. It could be likened to that of a college or professional coach: If you are not achieving, you are dismissed. Local boards of education and the general public are very quick to vent their displeasure toward the superintendent if the local educational system is not running smoothly, according to their perceptions. March and March report that the average term of a superintendent is about four years.[28] This is not a great deal of time to learn about the school district, its citizens and students, and to put a quality education program in place and assess the results. As a result, there is a nationwide shortage of superintendents and many non-educators are moving into the superintendency. There is some sentiment that running a school district is akin to running a corporation, especially when many school districts have multimillion-dollar budgets. Thus, several districts have turned to former businesspeople or former military officers to run the district.

The high turnover rate of school superintendents has caused some teachers to be hesitant about changing their ways of teaching. Teachers are heard to say, "Why change? I have seen them (superintendents) come and go. Many come with good ideas, but if the school board or community does not like the superintendent, they are gone, and the teachers who have made the changes they suggested are left holding the bag."

The superintendent, as the executive officer of the local school board, is responsible for executing educational policy as formulated by the local board of education. With the exception of a few large cities where statutes define the duties of the superintendent, the school board determines the superintendent's duties. Typically, the responsibilities of the superintendent include the following: to serve as chief executive officer of the board of education and thus to be responsible for all phases of the work; to provide leadership in planning and evaluation of all phases of the instructional program; to recommend and appoint all personnel; to guide the in-service growth for staff members; to prepare a budget for submission to the board and to administer it after its adoption; to determine building needs and administer building programs' construction, operation, and maintenance; and to serve as leader of the board, the staff, and the community in the improvement of the educational system.[29]

The superintendent in concert with the school board holds a great deal of power in determining how the news media, interest groups, parents, the business community, and students see their school district. The superintendent is also the school district point person for the implementation of educational ideas.

For example, the extent to which school districts embrace diversity or whether they adopt a new math and science program depends a great deal on the superintendent's support of the idea. Although the average period of employment is only four years, it should not be assumed that the superintendency is a weak position. Many superintendents learn how to work with the different interest groups and establish excellent working relationships with school board members.

FINDING A VOICE

John Salter turned his Lexus into the parking lot of the board of education and started searching for *his* space. Next to the entrance hung the sign he was looking for: "Reserved for the President of the Board of Education." As John pulled in, his mind raced back three weeks to April 5th. That day he and four others had won seats on the school board, and at the first meeting of the board he was elected board president. He thought, "A year ago very few people in this area knew of my existence." Now, thanks to Nell, his daughter's teacher, and Julie, another teacher at Edison School, that was no longer the case.

A tapping noise brought John back to the here and now. As he looked up, he saw Nell Greenfield tapping on his window. A third-grade teacher, Nell, who had started him on his civic journey to become president of the school board, said, "Come on out, Mr. President." As John opened the door, Nell continued, "You know, I have to be here! I have to witness your first meeting as president of the local school board. I don't know who is happier about your presidency, you or me."

It was a year ago that John met Nell. He had come up to school to protest the use of a book, *Nappy Hair*, that Nell was reading to her third-grade students. John's daughter Sharon, who was in Nell's class, and some of her girlfriends were teasing one another as they discussed the book during a sleepover at John's home. John overheard one girl, brushing his daughter's hair, say, "You have nappy hair like the girl in the book our teacher read."

John and his wife Maryland had several concerns about Edison School's attention to diversity, and this *Nappy Hair* incident was exacerbating the situation. The Salters had moved to Crossfield six years ago because of job opportunities for Maryland. Crossfield was a thriving community only a short drive down the freeway to the third largest city in the United States. Over the past six years Crossfield was showing signs of change. Several of the restaurants had closed and two small malls with specialty stores were closing down because a large super mall was constructed about 10 miles away. The number of students of color attending the school was steadily increasing as families of color fled the inner city. At the same time, the number of White students was rapidly decreasing because children of White families in the community had completed school and moved on and other Whites were no longer moving into the community. There were also some changes on the predominately White teaching staff, mostly younger White teachers taking the place of older White teachers. Teachers for the most part enjoyed working in the Crossfield district. Although some teaching jobs were available in other suburban school districts that were still predominantly White, many teachers were concerned they would not better themselves by changing school districts. In the Edison district, the salary, the opportunity to work during the summer, and the health package, which included dental insurance, were excellent.

More than 50% of the teachers in the Crossfield school district were in their late 40s, approximately 25% were 20 to 40, and the other 25% were in their mid- to late 50s. Only a few teachers retired each year. According to the school district's human resource office, teachers were not taking early retirement, and were also working much later in life. Nell was one of the few teachers of color the school district was able to recruit and hire for one of the few teaching positions it had available.

The Salters had first experienced the lack of cultural sensitivity at the school when they enrolled Sharon. They saw the school as almost totally White in its students and personnel, curriculum, and environment. They sensed a paternalistic attitude toward them when the assistant principal discussed Sharon's room assignment. He did not even mention that there was a program for gifted students. Instead, he placed Sharon in Mrs. Michael's room, which had most of the average and slower learners. They had similar experiences when they attended PTA meetings and other school events. Maryland said to John one evening after attending a PTA meeting, "It's like taking a time travel back to the 1950s, when Black people were seen as second-class citizens." The Salters were concerned about the Eurocentric school curriculum and the overall lack of culturally relevant teaching. They wondered what the lack of cultural sensitivity was doing to Sharon's cultural identity. They had rationalized by saying they would give Sharon extra academic and social attention at home to make up for what she was not receiving in school. However, this idea was still more promise than action, since both John and Maryland's jobs kept them very busy.

"This *Nappy Hair* thing," John said to Maryland, "is the last straw. This is unfair to Sharon and us. I am going up to Edison first thing Monday morning to find out what's going on." John paused for a minute and then with less passion in his voice said, "Maybe better you should go, Maryland. You are usually more diplomatic than I am, and we don't want to do anything that will have lasting repercussions for Sharon."

"Oh, no," said Maryland, "Did you forget that I told you I have to go to New York Monday morning? We are starting our ad campaign for that new product I have been telling you about." Maryland continued, "I'm always the one who goes up to school to see about Sharon. I go to the PTA meetings and all the other little meetings. You have been to only two PTA meetings since Sharon started school. *Nappy Hair* is your thing. Besides, have you read the book?"

Knowing that he was in a no-win situation, John relented and agreed to go on Monday. "That movie you want to see, *Shakespeare in Love,* is about ready to come on. Why don't I make some popcorn and fix some drinks. We can enjoy the movie together."

On Monday when John arrived at school with Sharon, he was shocked to see that Sharon's teacher, Nell, was an African American. He was also surprised that she knew him. Nell said, "Hello, Mr. Salter, it's good to see you." Quickly, however, he went from being speechless to being angry and confused. He thought to himself, "How can this sister read my daughter a book titled *Nappy Hair*? They have really brainwashed this younger generation of people of color."

Then he could hear Sharon say, "Miss Greenfield, I believe my dad wants to talk to you about *Nappy Hair*." Upon hearing that, Nell jubilantly exclaimed, "Isn't that the greatest book! I wish we had many more culturally relevant materials. Julie and I are working on how to raise funds to purchase other materials like this for the students. We could really use the help of the parents."

It was as if someone had pressed Nell's fast forward button. John felt caught up in a whirlwind. No longer was this his meeting, this was Nell's meeting. It was as if she had happened upon a long-awaited opportunity and was not going to let it get away.

Over the next few minutes several events happened quickly. The PE teacher came to pick up Nell's class and the class across the hall, which John soon learned was Julie's class. John met Julie, a teacher who had joined Edison's faculty three years before Nell. Nell and Julie prepared a cup of coffee for John, seated him between them at a table, and began to explore his willingness to be a supportive parent. Nell and Julie cited changing demographics to help make their case. Enrollment of students of color at Edison was up to 31% and the enrollment of students of color at other district schools was a bit higher and increasing. Suspension rates had increased 40% over the past four years. Referrals of students of color to special education programs were growing, and their academic achievement levels were falling. The teachers, Nell and Julie told John, did not know how to handle the change in student diversity and were not receiving much help from their principal nor from the central office. The school superintendent for the past six years had adopted educational standards as the centerpiece of his administrative program. However, the rumor mill, Nell claimed, "is saying that he is searching for a new superintendency. The challenge of the changing community demographics is not something he wants to undertake."

John was astounded on two accounts. One, he wondered why two young teachers would talk like this to a parent they didn't know. Two, he had no idea that Crossfield's schools were experiencing these problems to the depth that Nell and Julie were explaining. Nell's use of the book *Nappy Hair*, the reason that had brought him up to school, now confused him even more. Why, John thought, did two conscientious teachers promote the use of a book with a title like *Nappy Hair*? John, who lacked Maryland's diplomatic approach, asked directly, "Why are you telling me all this? If what you are saying is true, and I am not disputing you, why aren't these issues being addressed by the board of education and the district's teachers and administrators?"

Julie looked John directly in the eyes and said, "We did not know you were coming up this morning. But we know about you. I told Nell that you were chairperson of the Black Students Solidarity at State U. for two years. I heard you speak at a campus rally when I was in high school and came up to the campus to visit my sister Christina. Christina was a spokesperson for the Committee on Gay and Lesbian Rights. I learned so much that week observing several campus groups challenge the university administration's treatment of them. You were everywhere, speaking eloquently about the different problems and issues. You seemed to understand all the different groups' concerns, not only the African Americans. Also, I learned about my sister's sexual orientation. Wow, was that a week!"

Julie continued, "When I was on door duty one morning, I saw you drop Sharon off. I told Nell about you. We both wanted to call you, but were afraid you were too busy establishing your CPA firm. When we saw you this morning, we saw it as an opportunity to tell you how the school, better yet the district, needs your help, your knowledge, activism, and energy. The teachers here are not mean, and they care about all the kids, but increasingly the students of color, let me speak plainly, are being screwed. Since I am White, I hear things that they don't say in front of Nell about the kids of color—things like "This school and the other schools in the district are going downhill, losing their reputation for hard work and excellence. These kids' parents just don't seem to care. These kids are so low."

As Julie paused, John said, "I am concerned and I am not afraid of a fight, but what do you specifically want me to do?"

Nell said, "What did you do when you were in college? You know more about this than we do. Maybe you could start by finding out what's going on at the other schools in the district."

John said, "Yes, I guess I do know. The setting is different. Here it's a school district, not the university, but the music's the same. I'll start by getting a few parents together. Then we will see where it goes from there."

John heard his name being called and his thoughts of the past quickly came to the present when he turned and saw Julie. He smiled at her and offered his hand, but she hugged him, and said, "I think people who have known each other for over a year are entitled to more than a handshake." They proceeded to enter the board of education building where John would chair his first meeting.

The board meeting was perfunctory, much quieter than the past several meetings had been. The new board had put in place an in-service plan for all teachers. A new superintendent search was underway, and three excellent candidates were on the short list. As soon as John brought the gavel down to close the meeting, he saw Maryland and Sharon walking toward him. Maryland said to Sharon, "You should be proud of your father. He is a great role model."

"Mr. President," Maryland said, "To celebrate your first meeting as president you may take your wife, daughter, and Sharon's two favorite teachers out to dinner."

As Sharon, Maryland, Julie, and Nell headed toward the cars in the parking lot, Nell said, "You know, Mr. Salter, there is something I have meant to ask you for months. Why did you come up to school with Sharon that morning? What was it you wanted to know about *Nappy Hair*?" Nell continued, "Isn't that the greatest book?"

John sidestepped the question and said, "Sharon, ride with your mother, please. I will meet all of you at the restaurant, Charlie's, right?"

About two blocks from the restaurant, Maryland saw John's car turn into the Barnes and Nobles parking lot. She smiled and said to Sharon, "It looks like your dad is going to find out about *Nappy Hair* tonight."

SUMMING UP

The public schools are governed by a hierarchical system that includes executive and legislative responsibilities at the national, state, and local levels. The bulk of the responsibility for providing and administering a public education system resides with the state, although over the past five decades the federal government has greatly increased its role in education. The launching of *Sputnik I* by the Soviets can be cited as one of the major reasons that spurred greater federal government involvement in education. Americans believed that in order for the United States to win the space race, changes in the educational system were needed.

U.S. presidents have made education a personal and political issue. Presidents Kennedy and Johnson tried to use education to eliminate poverty; President Nixon worked to return educational decision making to the states and made cutbacks on educational programs from the Johnson administration; President Carter established the Department of Education. President Reagan vowed to eliminate the Department of Education but did not do so; his administration produced *A Nation at Risk*, which set off the ongoing educational reform movement. President G. H. W. Bush introduced national standards in *America 2000*, and President Clinton added to the educational goals, calling his program *Goals 2000*. President George W. Bush has proposed greater accountability in the form of testing student achievement and rewarding schools that show progress. School vouchers are proposed as another way to achieve greater academic progress. Students may receive a voucher along with matching state funds to attend another public school or a private school if their school performs poorly for three consecutive years.

Each state has the primary responsibility for its educational system. State governance in education can be traced back to local towns' movements to educate their citizens, beginning with the Old Deluder Satan Act of 1647. Thomas Jefferson argued for public education, and Horace Mann worked to make it a reality at the state level by helping to set up state boards of education. The state board of education is a key governing body in making decisions, along with the state department of education and the chief state school officer, about the education that takes place within the state. Education has increasingly become more connected to politics at the governor level, as interest groups strive to influence educational decisions. For example, debates over whole language and phonetics have been inspired by interest groups more than by classroom teachers, who argue that students need the instruction that will help them to achieve. Also, governors are demanding a more influential role in order to have a greater say in how education revenue is distributed.

Local governance of education is an American staple, historically reflecting the way of thinking of the community. However, with many communities becoming culturally diverse, local governance has become an expression of who has the political muscle. Local governance is never long without some democratic expressions, such as debate and controversy. The local board of education takes very seriously its role in shaping education for the school district. However, its decisions affect not only the community, but also how the community and school district are perceived on the state or national level. The vitality of the local system of education depends on the school district, the agent responsible for the state educational program; the local school board, the governing body that formulates educational policy; and the superintendent of schools, who executes the board's policies. The vitality of the local system of education also depends on individuals who are civic minded and recognize the value of participating in educational policy and practice at the local level. Finally, the vitality of the local system of education depends on all the agencies, boards, and individuals responsible for education. They can use their influence and power to ensure that education is equitable for all students.

In recent years in some school districts, local school councils have become a part of the local governance decision-making process. The movement to local school councils occurred in part to locate educational decisions as close to the people who are affected by them as possible. Finally, the job of superintendent has become more tenuous and complex as the school district chief executive faces a broad array of educational, social, and budgetary issues.

Although this chapter has outlined the system of education in the United States as hierarchical, many educational decisions are contested and some are rejected by those who are affected. The flow of power and influence is not unidirectional, coming down from above, as individuals and groups within these hierarchies are continually advocating making education work the way they believe it should. Who controls education will always be open to debate. Perhaps given the importance of education to a democracy, no single person or groups should control education. The question that should be asked is, "When will all students be the recipients of educational equity?"

KEY TERMS

moral suasion   Old Deluder Satan Act
bully pulpit   school attendance area
local school board   state board of education
local school council (site-based
  council)

QUESTIONS FOR REFLECTION

1. Over the past two decades, what has been the role of the president of the United States in shaping educational policy?
2. Why are some state boards of education and chief state school officers arguing that their role in educational decision making is dissipating?
3. How have parents and local citizens' groups worked to have greater control of their schools?

4. How does the role and purpose of the local school board differ from the superintendent's job?
5. What are some reasons that local boards of education are faced with social controversy?
6. Why and how do interest groups and organizations become involved in education at the federal, state, and local level?

ACTIVITIES

1. Review the history of your institution to determine if it was originally started from a land grant given to the state by the federal government.
2. Ask your professors if they have ever received federal funding to do educational research or to direct a program. If so, ask them to explain their responsibilities and obligations for using the federal funds.
3. Attend several local school board meetings over a school year and compare and contrast the discussion in the chapter with what you observe.
4. Visit the website of your department of public instruction to ascertain the services they list and the materials they provide.
5. Examine several issues of *The Conditions of Education* to review the types of useful information the Department of Education makes available free of charge.
6. Katie and Margaret prepared a report on the school district and school desegregation. They concluded that parents and others groups with seemingly different attitudes need to focus on what they have in common, the children. Interview some officials working in the school district office to ascertain how school desegregation or other hot issues are dealt with.

GETTING CONNECTED

United States Department of Education
http://www.ed.gov

The Department of Education website offers many different publications dealing with a range of educational topics, such as the conditions of education, innovative programs, and school demographics.

No Child Left Behind
U.S. Department of Education
http://www.nclb.gov

This website provides teachers, administrators, and parents with specific documents related to the 2001 No Child Left Behind Act.

National Association of State Boards of Education
http://www.nasbe.org

NASBE provides publications for educators, parents, and community members on various educational issues, including accountability and standards.

SUGGESTED RESOURCES

Apple, Michael, and James A. Beane, eds. *Democratic Schools.* Alexandria, VA: Association for Supervision and Curriculum Development, 1995.

Bailey, William J. *Organizing Schools.* Lancaster, PA: Technomic, 1997.

Hodgkinson, Christopher. *Educational Leadership: The Moral Art.* Albany: State University of New York Press, 1991.

Sarason, Seymour B. *How Schools Might Be Governed and Why.* New York: Teachers College Press, 1997.

Short, Paula M., and John T. Greer. *Leadership in Empowered Schools: Themes From Innovative Efforts.* Upper Saddle River, NJ: Merrill, 1997.

NOTES

1. "Clinton's 'Call to Action,'" *Education Week,* 12 February 1997, 32.
2. Washington State School Directors' Association, "President Bush to Request Title I Increase," 2003, http://www.wssda.org
3. Arthur Mochlman, *School Administration: Its Development, Principles, and Function in the United States* (Boston: Houghton Mifflin, 1951), 24.
4. Francesco Cordasco, *A Brief History of Education* (Totowa, NJ: A Little Field, Adams, 1970).
5. Fred C. Lunenburg and Allan C. Ornstein, *Educational Administration,* 2nd ed. (Belmont, CA: Wadsworth, 1996), 241.
6. Charles Judd, Glenn Holmes, and Ward Reeder, "History of Education," in *The Lincoln Library of Essential Information*, ed. Clyde Park (Buffalo, NY: Frontier Press, 1963), 1615–1698.
7. Harry Ploski and James Williams, eds., *The Negro Almanac: A Reference Work on African Americans,* 5th ed. (Detroit: Gale Research, 1989), 763.
8. Lunenburg and Ornstein, *Educational Administration,* 240.
9. Act of 1642, General Court of Massachusetts Bay Colony, as cited in *An Overview of American Education,* Joseph Cresmbent and Raymond Mammarella (Dubuque, IA: Wm. C. Brown, 1963), 65.
10. Ronald Campbell, Luvern L. Cunningham, Ralph O. Nystrand, and Michael Usdan, *The Organization and Control of American Schools*, 6th ed. (Columbus, OH: Merrill, 1990), 31.
11. National Association of State Boards of Education, *Boardsmanship Review* (Alexandria, VA: Author, January 1996), 4.
12. J. Messerli, *Horace Mann: Biography* (New York: Knoops, 1972).
13. Ibid., 167.
14. Lunenburg and Ornstein, *Educational Administration*, 267; Stephen J. Knezevich, *Administration of Public Education,* 4th ed. (New York: Harper and Row, 1984), 249–253.
15. National Association of State Board of Education, *State Education Governance at a Glance* (Alexandria, VA: Author, 1998), 1–5.
16. Campbell et al., *Organization and Control of American Schools*; Lunenburg and Ornstein, *Educational Administration*, 268; Knezevich, *Administration of Public Education*, 212–213.

17. Ibid.

18. Campbell et al., *Organization and Control of American Schools*, 56; Knezevich, *Administration of Public Education*, 214.

19. Lunenburg and Ornstein, *Educational Administration*, 268.

20. Thomas J. Sergiovanni, Martin Burlingame, Fred S. Coombs, and Paul W. Thurston, *Educational Governance and Administration*, 4th ed. (Boston: Allyn and Bacon, 1999), 287.

21. Ibid.

22. Diane Ravitch, "Multiculturalism Yes, Particularism No," *Chronicle of Higher Education*, 24 October 1990, A44; E. D. Hirsch, *Cultural Literacy* (New York: Houghton Mifflin, 1987), 18; Arthur Schlesinger, Jr., *The Disuniting of America* (Whittle Direct Books, 1991).

23. Lunenburg and Ornstein, *Educational Administration*, 294–295; Edgar Morphet, Johns Roe, and Theodore Reller, *Educational Administration* (Englewood Cliffs, NJ: Prentice-Hall, 1959), 216.

24. Lunenburg and Ornstein, *Educational Administration*, 254; Campbell et al., *Organization and Control of American Schools*, 215–216.

25. Fredrick Hess, *School Board at the Dawn of the 21st Century: Conditions and Challenges of District Governance* (Alexandria, VA: National School Board Association, 2002).

26. Michael W. Apple and James A. Beane, eds., *Democratic Schools* (Alexandria, VA: Association for Supervision and Curriculum Development, 1995).

27. Campbell et al., *Organization and Control of American Schools*, 238.

28. James C. March and James G. March, "Almost Random Careers: The Wisconsin Superintendency, 1940–1972," *Administrative Science Quarterly* 22 (September 1977): 377–409.

29. Campbell et al., *Organization and Control of American Education*, 251; Sergiovanni et al., *Educational Governance and Administration*, 214–221; Morphet et al., *Educational Administration*, 238.

TEACHERS' AND STUDENTS' RIGHTS AND RESPONSIBILITIES

FOCUS QUESTIONS

1. How is power played out in discussions of teachers' and students' rights and responsibilities?
2. Although most teachers are in favor of tenure, why do some believe that tenure hurts the profession?
3. Why is due process such an important concept in teachers' and students' rights?
4. Why does academic freedom for K–12 teachers differ from academic freedom for college teachers?
5. Can acting in loco parentis (acting in place of a parent) save a teacher from being sued if the teacher has been negligent?
6. How are students' rights and responsibilities affected by growing violence in the media and in society? Are students as a group achieving more rights and having to assume more responsibilities, or are they losing rights they originally had?

WHAT ARE MY RIGHTS ANYWAY?

Graduation day, the day when Jennifer will receive her teacher license, is only three weeks away. Jennifer has mailed her resume to more than 15 school districts seeking a job. She has told her family that she wants to teach close to home, but secretly she wants to find a job out of her home state. She thinks a large urban community would be a good place for her. Jennifer is lesbian and has told a few close friends, but not her parents. She believes that if she were to get a teaching job in a small town like the one she grew up in, she might be fired if the school district discovered her sexual orientation. In an urban setting, she hopes there will be more acceptance as well as anonymity. She hopes that in a more progressive area the school board and community members will not penalize her for being lesbian.

For years, Jennifer has been afraid to discuss her sexual orientation with anyone besides a few close friends. She promised herself that once she graduated, she would be open to people about her sexual orientation. In anticipation of this she has wanted to find out more about the rights of gay teachers, but was unsure of where she could go to get this information. Also, she was afraid that someone would discover why she wanted the information.

Jennifer's roommate Maggie is just beginning the teacher education program. She too is interested in teachers' rights but for a different reason. Maggie's 12-year-old brother Brian was suspended from school because his teacher found a six-inch pocket knife in his locker during an unscheduled locker search. Maggie's parents are upset over the incident because they believe Brian has been treated unfairly. He was not allowed to explain why the knife was in his locker nor whom the knife belonged to before he was suspended. He was immediately sent home. Maggie's parents asked her to find out about the rights of teachers and students from her professors.

Teachers' and students' rights and responsibilities are enactments of power. What happens to Jennifer and Brian will indicate how power is enacted among teachers, students, and the local school board. This chapter looks at the rights and responsibilities of teachers and students in K–12 education. Essential to understanding these rights and responsibilities is understanding that there are no neutral actions within these enactments of power. Also in this chapter, the tenets of education that is multicultural and social reconstructiontist (EMCSR) are more often played out in the context of power. By that we mean that the characteristics of EMCSR, such as race, class, gender, sexuality, language, religion, and ability, are embedded in the power enactments of teachers' and students' rights and responsibilities. Teacher candidates should ask whether some teachers' and students' rights give power to some more than others, and whether these "rights" are justified based on deeds or are privileges that only some students and teachers receive. If you read this chapter with these ideas in mind, it will help you to gain a deeper appreciation of the social context of teaching and educational settings.

TEACHERS' RIGHTS

Over the past 45 years, teachers' rights have commanded the attention of school officials, the courts, and society in general. Here we can often see the effects of power—for example, as teachers negotiate their concerns with the school board.

During the 1960s and 1970s, when many groups in the United States (e.g., African Americans, Native Americans, Asian Americans, women) were fighting for their civil rights, teachers began to fight for their rights too. Teachers demanded that they be treated as professionals. Their demands included improvements in working conditions, such as more control over the curriculum, reduced class size, and increased salaries. As the demands intensified, the period became known as one of teacher militancy.[1] Corwin notes that this militancy was manifested in several ways: teacher strikes, the amassing of a political base as teachers joined the National Education Association (NEA) or the American Federation of Teachers (AFT), the use of collective bargaining, and engagement in political activity. This new militancy was particularly visible to the general public in the form of teacher strikes. For example, during the beginning weeks of school in 1979, nearly 33,000 teachers went on strike in 14 states.[2] Many in the public were angry with teachers for striking. They argued that teachers, like firefighters and police officers, have a duty and responsibility to the broader community, and they should not strike.

In 1983, with the publication of *A Nation at Risk*, attention moved away from teachers' rights to a focus on teachers' responsibilities regarding students' poor academic achievement. Schools, it was argued, were not doing a good job of preparing youth to be tomorrow's leaders. Instead, schools were plagued with drugs and violence, as well as bickering over contracts and other collective bargaining issues. Drugs and violence no longer stopped at the school boundaries, but instead were in regular attendance on many campuses to varying degrees. Teachers' out-of-school behavior was becoming a topic of debate, along with issues of academic freedom and negligence of responsibility for student achievement. With growing concern over issues such as violence, drugs, and academic freedom, teachers increasingly wanted to know the legal rights available to them in dealing with these and other causes of disruption. The courts, as they often have to do when teachers' rights are in question, offered an observation: "Maintaining order . . . has never been easy, but in recent years, school disorder has often taken particularly ugly forms: drugs and violent crimes in the school have become major social problems."[3] Court decrees and other legal and administrative mandates not only inform teachers about their legal rights and responsibilities, but also put them on notice that it is necessary to know and to act on these rights.

The following sections discuss issues that are of concern to teachers. These issues, involving teachers' rights and how and where to verify what they are, include licensing and certification, contracts, tenure, due process, collective bargaining, academic freedom, tort liability, and behavior outside of school. These are areas in which teachers' responsibilities also need to be considered. As teachers, it is essential to remember that rights and responsibilities are intertwined. Consideration of one should introduce consideration of the other.

Licensing and Certification

Maggie entered Carl's office and said, "Professor Grant, I am currently in the 1–6 licensure programs. Do you think it would be smarter to apply for a change to the 1–8 licensure programs?" When Carl asked why she wanted to change, Maggie responded, "I want to move to a more urban setting when I graduate. The 1–8 licensures will increase my chances of getting a job. It will give me greater employment flexibility."

Maggie's remarks told Carl that she was pretty clear about how licensure works. She knows a teacher needs the approval of the state in order to teach, and that George W. Bush's No Child Left Behind Act (NCLB) mandates that elementary teachers have a teacher licensure in grades K–5 and be "highly qualified" in every subject area in grades 6–8. However, Carl was unsure whether Maggie was keeping up with the direction in which teacher certification and licensing are moving.

Some educators and concerned citizens are suggesting that teacher licensure should be organized around a **national career ladder**—a system of granting incentive pay to teachers in steps, from initial to advanced levels, so that teachers achieve professional growth with increased experience and training. The idea of a national career ladder for teachers was inspired by arguments to reform teacher education in *A Nation at Risk*. The Carnegie Forum on Education and the Economy picked up on this idea and recommended that a National Board for Professional Teaching Standards (NBPTS) be created. Established in 1987, the board's purpose was to establish uniform standards for high professional teaching competence and to issue national certification to people who meet these standards.[4]

According to the NBPTS, teachers' preparation would include three steps. The first step would be achieved when teachers receive their initial license from the state after meeting state standards (usually graduation from a four-year college) to teach a subject or grade level covered by the license. To reach the second and third steps, a teacher would need to earn two certificates: a Teacher's Certificate, and an Advanced Teacher's Certificate. "The first would establish a high entry level standard for teachers. The second would be an advanced standard, signifying the highest level of competence as a teacher and possession of the qualities needed for leadership in the schools. Certificates at both levels would be specific to subjects taught and grade ranges and could be endorsed on examination for other areas of specialization."[5] The Carnegie Forum's plan parallels the medical model of licensing and certification. After doctors receive their medical license, they must then take and pass board exams to be certified for their area of specialty.

Maggie is correct if she concludes, as we noted in Chapter 9, that the state legislature or the state board of education enacts the laws governing certification. However, it will be necessary for her to revisit changes in teacher certification and licensing proposed by the NBPTS approximately every five years. Her teaching license may be earned from the state, but her certification from the National Board denotes mastery beyond state licensure.

Finally, teacher candidates often wonder how they are permitted to student teach, because there are strict guidelines for receiving a teacher license. A teacher candidate can student teach without a license because state statutes or board of education rules permit student teaching to take place when properly supervised by certified teachers with two or more years of teaching experience.

Contracts

The teacher's contract is the beginning point for ascertaining the rights, duties, and responsibilities of the teacher and the school district. The contract is a work agreement that results from power enactment through negotiations between the teacher and the board of education. The board of education is vested with its power to negotiate contracts with teachers by the state statutes. Regardless of its complexity, every contract must contain five elements:

1. The parties to the contract must be competent.
2. The contract must be based on the mutual assent of the contracting parties.
3. The contract must include valid and adequate consideration.
4. The contract must be sufficiently clear and definite.
5. The subject matter of the contract must be lawful and in a form required by law.[6]

During this nation's early years, the first contracts negotiated between village schoolmasters or schoolmistresses and town officials were probably oral agreements, because at that time oral contracts linked people and businesses more than paper contracts. These oral agreements gave way to written employment contracts as the boundaries of the country expanded, decreasing personal contact between people. No longer would a handshake cement a business arrangement. Early contracts were usually a list of duties and obligations covering both in-school and out-of-school behavior to which a teacher had to adhere to receive a salary. Two examples, one from 1872 and the other from 1930, are listed in Exhibit 10.1.

EXHIBIT 10.1 **RULES FOR TEACHERS**

1872

Teachers each day will fill lamps, clean chimneys.

Each teacher will bring a bucket of water and a scuttle of coal for the day's session.

Make your pens carefully. You may whittle nibs to the individual taste of the pupils.

Men teachers may take one evening each week for courting purposes, or two evenings a week if they go to church regularly.

After ten hours in school, the teachers may spend the remaining time reading the Bible or other good books.

Women teachers who marry or engage in unseemly conduct will be dismissed.

Every teacher should lay aside from each pay a goodly sum of his earnings for the benefit during his declining years so that he will not become a burden on society.

Any teacher who smokes, uses liquor in any form, frequents pool or public halls, or gets shaved in a barber shop will give good reason to suspect his worth, intention, integrity and honesty.

The teacher who performs his labor faithfully and without fault for five years will be given an increase of twenty-five cents per week in his pay, providing the Board of Education approves.

(continued)

EXHIBIT **10.1** **CONTINUED**

1930

In 1930, the duties were more directed toward female teachers, as more women were joining the teaching force.

I promise to take a vital interest in all phases of Sunday school work, donating of my time, service, and money without stint for the uplift and benefit of the community.

I promise to abstain from all dancing, immodest dressing, and any other conduct unbecoming a teacher and a lady.

I promise not to go out with any young men except insofar as it may be necessary to stimulate Sunday-school work.

I promise not to fall in love, to become engaged or secretly married.

I promise to remain in the dormitory or on the school grounds when not actively engaged in school or church work elsewhere.

I promise not to encourage or tolerate the least familiarity on the part of any of my boy pupils.

I promise to sleep at least eight hours a night, to eat carefully, and to take every precaution to keep in the best of health and spirits, in order that I may be better able to render efficient service to my pupils.

I promise to remember that I owe a duty to the townspeople who are paying my wages, that I owe respect to the school board and the superintendent that hired me, and that I shall consider myself at all times the willing servant of the school board and the townspeople.

Source: Poster published by Student National Education Association.

Although these contracts may seem amusing today, they illustrate how the school boards enacted the power they had to control teachers. School boards could dictate the standards they deemed appropriate for teachers to follow. A shift in the power balance between teachers and school boards was not achieved until after World War II. After the war, teachers became politically active. They worked to reduce school board control over their private and professional lives. They pushed for tenure laws, they encouraged other teachers to join their professional organizations and associations, and they demanded collective bargaining rights. Also, teachers no longer wanted to negotiate their contract with the school board individually. Instead they sought to have the National Education Association (NEA) or the American Federation of Teachers (AFT) represent their interests.[7]

Today, teacher employment contracts define the rights and responsibilities of the teacher and the school board in the employment relationship. Besides the five basic elements of (1) competent parties, (2) offer and acceptance, (3) consideration, (4) legal subject matter, and (5) proper form, a teacher contract must meet any requirements specified in state law and administrative regulations.[8] The authority to negotiate a contract with teachers is an exclusive right of the school board. The contract a school board may offer a teacher includes (1) salary, (2) duration of position, and (3) duties and responsibilities. A teacher's acceptance of the agreement creates a binding contract.[9]

Because teachers are employed under different guidelines and arrangements, two types of contracts are issued to them: term contracts and tenure contracts.

Term contracts are given for a fixed period of time, one or two years. At the end of the term, renewal is up to the local school board, and nonrenewal requires no explanation unless mandated by statute. Teachers are granted tenure after they pass a probationary period, usually three years, and are favorably assessed, usually by the principal of the school. **Tenure contracts,** created through state legislative action, assure teachers their employment will be terminated only for a good and just reason and that they will be entitled to due process. In interpreting tenure laws, courts attempt to protect teachers' rights while simultaneously preserving school administrators' flexibility in personnel management.[10] Court rulings have by and large kept the balance of power between teacher unions and boards of education fairly equal. Once teachers or their representatives and a school board agree to the terms of a contract, the teachers are obligated to honor their commitments as stated in the document. Failure to honor the contractual commitment is a breach of contract, and the wronged party is usually entitled to recover damages.[11] (We had more to say about this in Chapter 6, "Teaching: The Profession.")

Finally, at the close of a school year, or weeks before the opening of a new school year in several school districts across the nation, it is fairly common to see media reports of contract disputes between teachers and boards of education. Whereas these contract disputes are often regarded as two parties struggling over issues such as salary, class size, benefits, and working conditions, they are also power contests to determine who has the "juice," or whose argument will be more favorably received by the community. Whose position do the newspaper and television editorials support? Media support may sway public opinion to support one side over the other. How each side is portrayed influences how the public perceives the issues and the people involved. Is the community willing to both give the teachers a 6% salary raise and reduce class size, even though the local board may be suggesting only a 3% raise and a reduction in class size only in the primary grades? Or is the community firmly behind the school board, believing that teachers are paid too much, especially when the national reports are saying that students' achievement is low?

Although contract debates are often presented as debates over money between two parties, teacher candidates will discover that they are much more than that, and that there are no neutral actions. Sometimes they are expressions of political and ideological positions and values, and not necessarily with a primary focus on student interest. For example, part of the contract debates might include whether to give health benefits to domestic partners of teachers. Debates about this issue often ignite discussion about gay and lesbian rights and raise questions about much more than whether teachers' pay should increase. Similarly, debates over whether math and science teachers should receive more money, or whether a recruitment bonus should be paid to attract beginning teachers to an area, are usually about more than the budget. Concern about traditional ways of doing things and some teachers' being upset with the opportunities of other teachers are also central to the problem.

Tenure

After an observation visit to an elementary school, Maggie, who is in Carl's class, said, "During our school observations, I observed several teachers who seemed lazy and are not really teaching. I saw an overuse of worksheets, and a good deal of busywork. What can be done about teachers who stop teaching?" Before Carl could respond, Maggie said, "That's one of the problems with tenure—you cannot get rid of teachers who are not really teaching! Right, Professor Grant? You are going to tell us about how this tenure thing works in class, right?"

What Carl told his class includes much of the following. But did he give his class enough information to answer Maggie's question?

As we noted in the previous section, teacher employment is usually granted under two types of contracts: term contracts and tenure contracts. **Tenure** is the equivalent of civil service for teachers, and its history has paralleled the development of civil service in this country. In the 1800s, use of the spoils system in appointing government officials led to the hiring of a number of poorly qualified and inept individuals. Therefore, in 1883, the first civil service act was passed, setting the terms for hiring and continued employment of government officials. Two years later, a teachers' union, the National Educational Association (NEA), studied the possibility of applying the principles of civil service to the teaching profession. The NEA believed that "for the good of the schools and the general public the profession should be made independent of personal or political influence and made free from the malignant power of spoils and patronage."[12]

In 1886, the state of Massachusetts passed a law extending tenure to teachers, allowing school districts to make contracts with teachers for more than a year. Three years later, the Boston School Committee suggested a tenure law that is similar to that of many school districts today.[13] Today, to receive tenure in most school districts, teachers work a probationary period of approximately three consecutive years and if an assessment, usually made by the school principal, is favorable, the teacher is awarded tenure.

Most teachers' organizations and associations support tenure in order to protect good teachers from arbitrary and unwarranted release, especially during a period of so-called teacher surplus.

Maggie thought to herself, "What happens when tenure protects the jobs of lazy teachers? It does not seem that tenure is the real problem. The real problem, I believe, is that when teachers burn out they should leave teaching, instead of hanging on and doing just enough to get by. Maybe we need to examine what it takes to get rid of a teacher."

Due Process in Relation to Discharge

Tenure laws usually prescribe procedures for the discharge of a teacher. A key aspect of the discharge procedure is **due process**. Due process rights are embodied in the Fourteenth Amendment, which guarantees that no state shall "deprive any person of life, liberty, or property without due process of law." In accordance with due process, the teacher being discharged has to receive written notice of the charges and the right to an administrative hearing. The notice should include the date and place of the hearing and clearly articulate the charge against the teacher. At the hearing, the teacher is entitled to have legal counsel and to present witnesses. Also, the hearing is subject to judicial review.

From examining state statutes and court decisions, Thomas, Sperry, and Wasden (1991) have identified four types of teacher discharge:

Dismissal: The permanent discharge of a nontenured teacher during a contract period or of a tenured teacher at any time is classed "dismissal," although "termination" is also sometimes used.

Suspension: The temporary discharge of a teacher is called "suspension" because the teacher may return to employment once the reason for the suspension is resolved. However, a suspension may be a preliminary step to one of the other types of discharge.

Nonrenewal: Failure to renew an employment contract after it expires; applies only to contracts of nontenured teachers.

Reduction in Force: Often called "furlough" and sometimes "suspension," a reduction in force (RIF) action is taken when a school district must discharge teachers because of financial limitations, declining enrollments, or reorganization of curriculum or school structure.[14]

The history of public schools shows that teachers have been discharged from their positions for many reasons, some valid and some arbitrary and capricious.[15] Before the enactment of tenure statutes, teachers had very little protection from unreasonable discharge. It was not until after World War II that tenure laws, court decisions, and collective bargaining agreements prevented teachers from losing their jobs for arbitrary and capricious reasons and gave them recourse when they believed they had been discharged in violation of their rights to employment.[16] Although teachers now have these legal protections, the school board holds the right to determine the fitness of teachers to maintain the integrity of the school. According to the U.S. Supreme Court, the school board has a *duty* as well as a *right* to see to the fitness of a teacher. In *Adler v. Board of Education of the City of New York,* the Supreme Court declared:

> A teacher works in a sensitive area in a schoolroom. There he shapes the attitude of young minds towards the society in which they live. In this, the state has a vital concern. It must preserve the integrity of the schools. That the school authorities have the right and the duty to screen the officials, teachers, and employees as to their fitness to maintain the integrity of the schools as a part of ordered society, cannot be doubted.[17]

To date, the fitness of teachers has been called into question most often when they are incompetent, immoral, or insubordinate, or neglect their duty and conduct themselves unprofessionally.[18] However, given current thinking on what makes a teacher unfit, unless a school administrator can prove that the teacher's teaching methods and procedures meet one or more of the statutory reasons for teacher dismissal or suspension, the teacher is protected by tenure laws. Some states feel powerless against tenure laws; therefore, to maintain power, some states (e.g., Georgia) no longer tenure teachers.

Tenure is in place to support dedicated, hardworking professional teachers and to protect them from losing their jobs as a result of changes in the schools such as changing administrators. Unfortunately, some teachers do not work the way they should and are not always encouraged to change their ineffective practices. They, too, are protected by tenure laws. Power here is enacted through the rights that teachers' unions have negotiated with school boards. These rights have vested power equally in all teachers who gain tenure. The challenge to the students in Carl's class is to make certain that a few years from now, some teacher candidates are not observing them and questioning their professionalism. The students will have to ask themselves whether having tenure laws is more beneficial than having some ineffective teachers protected by these laws.

Collective Bargaining

Collective bargaining, the obligation of representatives of an employer to meet with representatives of employees to discuss and agree on questions and problems concerning work conditions, is relatively new to teachers. If your grandparents taught before the 1950s, they probably did not have collective bargaining. In the late 1950s, when tenure laws were being passed and courts were starting to recognize teachers' constitutional rights, enrollment in teacher organizations grew.[19] Teachers realized that they were better able to take advantage of their power and use it effectively if they united and worked together. Currently, more than three-fourths of all teachers belong to national organizations that negotiate labor relations for them with their employing school boards. However, the labor laws and statutes that provide the climate for the establishment of collective bargaining are not uniform across the states; therefore, collective bargaining also is not uniform. Some states prohibit collective bargaining laws by court order. Yet Thomas, Sperry, and Wasden offer a definition of collective bargaining that can for the most part be generalized across the states:

> Collective bargaining occurs when a municipal employer, through its officers and agents, and the representatives of its employees, meet and confer at reasonable times, in good faith, with respect to wages, hours and conditions of employment with the intention of reaching an agreement, or to resolve questions arising under such an agreement.[20]

Before the school year is over, many teacher candidates will read about a city or town where the local school board and the local teacher association are in contract negotiations. Collective bargaining normally takes place over salaries, benefits, and working conditions.

Usually, both the local board and the teacher association strive for agreement because a strike is a no-no as far as parents and caregivers are concerned. The state statutes limit what public employees can do against the school board. A strike by teachers interrupts a public service and is harmful to a third party—the public—that is in need of that service. Those hurt by teachers' strikes are not the members of the school board or the school administrators, but the public, particularly the students.[21]

A strike in the private sector, for example, or a baseball or basketball work stoppage, is seen differently than a strike in the public sector. This is because the public for the most part are not directly involved. Although the vendors at the ballpark or basketball stadium cannot work because there are no customers, the general public is not affected. In the private sector, negotiations between labor and management are usually over money and working conditions. Although these are the same factors that teachers negotiate, unlike a teacher strike, in the private sector labor and management are the major parties who are hurt by the strike.

Collective bargaining, most teachers would argue, has been good for both teachers and the boards of education. Because of collective bargaining, power is more evenly distributed between the two parties. However, school boards do maintain their managerial prerogative to make educational policy, a right that cannot be delegated or bargained away, and teachers have collective bargaining rights over their salaries and working conditions.

Academic Freedom

The concept of **academic freedom**—the right to pursue an argument, idea, or discussion wherever it may lead—dates back to the time of Plato. However, some scholars (such as Newton, discussed in Chapter 3) have been penalized for their pursuit of intellectual discoveries, and some scholars, philosophers, and others have died in their quest to have the freedom to think, to learn, and to teach. Scholars demand the right to analyze, critique, and question prevailing theories, practices, and values. They argue that such investigations are vital to human progress. In the United States, Thomas Jefferson comes quickly to mind as a person who advocated intellectual freedom.[22]

Academic freedom historically has been more often associated with institutions of higher education than with PreK–12 public schools. At institutions of higher education, professors are charged with discovering and expanding knowledge and truth, as well as investigating how knowledge is socially constructed, meaning that knowledge develops within social conditions of time, place, and movements of people. Also, college students are legal adults who have made a personal decision to attend the college of their choice to learn and explore how to implement what they learn for their own personal and professional interests.

Teachers in public schools are taught that their major responsibility is to transmit knowledge. PreK–12 students are not usually encouraged to construct knowledge based on their experiences and learning. For example, when Asian American students see themselves stereotyped in textbooks and other media either as a model minority or as habitual foreigners in the United States, they are not often asked to see themselves as a range of kinds of people. Up until the time PreK–12 students leave high school, society is very controlling of them. PreK–12 educators design curricula to ensure that accepted state and local school board–approved concepts are taught and students are not indoctrinated with ideas antithetical to the interest of the dominant group in society.[23]

When teachers demand academic freedom, their source of reference is usually the First Amendment to the Constitution. The First Amendment gives teachers the right to speak freely about the subjects they teach. It also protects teachers against special or individual interests that would force them to instruct in a particular manner, using particular materials. The following are examples of cases that have addressed the question of academic freedom for teachers.

Cases of Academic Freedom and Curriculum Materials   The first three cases involve academic freedom and curriculum materials.

Rarducci v. Rutland involved an English teacher who was dismissed for using Kurt Vonnegut, Jr.'s *Welcome to the Monkey House*. The principal argued that the story was "literary garbage" because it condoned free sex and the killing of elderly people. The federal court in 1970 supported the teacher's actions and ordered that she be reinstated and her record expunged of the dismissal charge. The court stated:

> Although academic freedom is not one of the enumerated rights of the First Amendment, the Supreme Court has on numerous occasions emphasized that the right to teach, to inquire, to evaluate, and to study is fundamental to a democratic society. . . . Since the [board has] failed to show either that the assignment was inappropriate reading for high school juniors, or that it created a significant disruption to the educational processes of this school, this Court concludes that [the teacher's] dismissal constituted an unwarranted invasion of her First Amendment right to academic freedom.[24]

In the 1976 case of *Harris v. Mechanicsville Central School District,* a high school English teacher was dismissed for using *Catcher in the Rye* by J. D. Salinger. The teacher decided to use the book even after it had been taken off the approved curriculum list. Although parents and the school board protested the teacher's actions, the teacher continued to use the book. The school board charged the teacher with insubordination. The court disagreed with the local school board and ruled in the teacher's favor, declaring that it would not support censorship.

In *Boring v. Buncombe County Board of Education,* a tenured high school teacher argued that her First Amendment rights were violated by the school board and concerned parents in connection with her selection of a play for a statewide competition. This play involved a single-parent family: a divorced mother, a lesbian daughter, and an unmarried pregnant daughter. The U.S. Court of Appeals for the Fourth Circuit ruled in 1998 that academic freedom in curriculum development should be left up to the local school authorities rather than to teachers.[25]

Cases of Academic Freedom and Teaching Methods   The next three cases consider academic freedom and teaching methods. Here academic freedom permits teachers to speak freely and not be denied a choice of teaching methods.

In the *Mailloux v. Kiley* case in 1971, a teacher was dismissed because during a talk-and-chalk session on taboo words, he wrote the four-letter word meaning to have sexual intercourse on the board. Although the court admitted that the teaching method was probably not appropriate, it stated that the teacher had used the method in good faith and had never been warned not to use it.[26]

The 1980 case of *Kingville Independent School District v. Cooper* in Texas involved the dismissal of a teacher by the local board because she had been instructed not to use materials that roused strong feelings among students on racial issues. She had been told not to discuss the role of African Americans in U.S. history, or anything controversial. She refused such instructions. The U.S. Court of Appeals, Fifth Court, overruled her dismissal.[27]

Finally, in *Memphis Community School District v. Stachura,* 1986, the court ruled that a teacher was wrongly dismissed because parents protested his instructional methods for teaching a unit on human reproduction in a life science class. The teacher had obtained approval to teach the unit, and the textbooks that he used had been approved by the school board. Nevertheless, parents claimed that he was a "sex maniac." The court found the charge to be false and ordered him reinstated.[28]

The use of these examples is not intended to imply that teachers may say anything they wish. The academic freedom of a teacher has to be balanced against the competing rights or demands of school administrators, boards of education, and parents. Also, academic freedom in some cases gives way to previously negotiated settlements. For example, in *Carey v. Board of Education of Adams–Arapahoe*, high school teachers brought civil rights actions against the local school board, claiming that it improperly restricted the use of the following books in contemporary literature classes:

- *A Clockwork Orange* by Anthony Burgess
- *The Exorcist* by William P. Blatty
- *The Reincarnation of Peter Proud* by Max Ehrlich
- *New American Poetry* by Donald Allen
- *Starting From San Francisco* by Lawrence Ferlinghetti
- *The Yagé Letters* by William Burroughs and Allen Ginsberg
- *A Coney Island of the Mind* by Lawrence Ferlinghetti
- *Kaddish and Other Poems* by Allen Ginsberg
- *Lunch Poems* by Frank O'Hara
- *Rosemary's Baby* by Ira Levin[29]

The teachers claimed that their rights had been violated under the First and Fourteenth amendments to the Constitution. The school board pointed out to the teachers that they had a contractual agreement with the teacher association, of which the plaintiffs were members, that gave the school board the right to make these curriculum decisions. The local school board won the case because, as we stated above, once teachers or their agent and a school board agree to the terms of a contract, they are obligated to honor the commitment made to each other as stated in the document.[30]

Much of what we have discussed about academic freedom connects it to higher education and secondary education, rather than PreK–8. There is greater disagreement among individuals, organizations, interest groups, and governing structures as to what younger PreK–8 students should study. Should there be more allowance for materials about body image, sexuality, violence, and identity? In order to engage students and present alternative points of view, some teachers will choose materials that some groups believe do not belong in schools. When teachers use these materials in class, these groups may go to school officials to protest. In order to continue to use the materials they select, teachers sometimes claim academic freedom.

We believe that over the next decade PreK–8 teachers will become much more involved in academic freedom controversies. This is so because an increasing number of current teacher candidates' coursework includes multicultural education along with concepts about culturally relevant teaching. Multicultural education is preparing these teacher candidates to more closely evaluate the instructional materials they use for diversity. In the first chapter, we talked about providing education that is multicultural and social reconstructionist (EMCSR). This particular approach will not only encourage teachers, with their students, to examine and evaluate the materials available to them in their classrooms, but will also encourage them to question what is not there, or what is censored from schools. As teachers begin to use the multicultural concepts and practices in their teaching, school boards, parents, and interest groups may challenge them. They will have to claim their academic freedom privilege.

Tort Liability

Maggie asked Carl, during his Introduction to Education class, "Can a teacher be sued?" Carl answered, "Yes, teachers can be sued. The liability brought against a teacher is called a tort. But suing a teacher is not an easy matter." Teachers, like everyone else, are accountable for their on-the-job behavior. However, there is a difference between teachers and other professionals because most teachers work with students who are not adults. Because teachers work with minors, they are given the legal right to stand in for the parent, **in loco parentis.** In loco parentis is a relationship that carries both special privileges and responsibilities. For example, if a teacher imposes reasonable disciplinary action on a student, the court will not usually impose liability because disciplining a youngster is a parental responsibility that the teacher is legally granted during school hours.

Teachers are responsible for ensuring the safety of their students. For example, teachers are expected to alert students to the risks involved in school-related activities, such as using machinery and participating in sports. They must also enforce safety rules regulating the use of equipment that could potentially cause harm to students. Additionally, teachers are obligated to intervene in playground disturbances, such as fights. If teachers do not properly supervise their students and a student is injured, the teacher may be held liable. This is one reason teachers are told to never leave their students unsupervised.

The liability that a teacher faces is called a **tort.** A tort is generally defined as a civil wrong, independent of breach of contract, for which a court will provide relief in the form of damages.[31] "Tort cases primarily fall under state laws and are grounded in the fundamental premise that individuals are liable for the consequences of their conduct that result in injury to others."[32] Torts are a part of old English common law. They came about as a result of written law that provided no remedy for the victim of an injurious intentional or negligent action by another person. Torts that occur most often in school are of two kinds: negligence and intentional torts.

Negligence Tort   A negligence tort occurs when teachers do not carry out their duty to protect students from unreasonable risks of harm—for example, when a teacher fails to intervene in the case of an improper action that results in injury or loss to students. However, for a teacher to be considered negligent, an injury must be avoidable by the exercise of reasonable care. Also, the following four conditions must exist to support a successful claim: "(1) the defendant had a duty to protect the plaintiff from unreasonable risks, (2) the duty was breached by the failure to exercise an appropriate standard of care, (3) there was a casual connection between the negligent conduct and the resulting injury (i.e., proximate or legal cause), and (4) an actual injury resulted.[33] In simpler language, Ms. Blanchard, the shop teacher, has a duty to give her students instructions on how to use the equipment they are about to operate. Similarly, Ms. Rico has a duty to supervise the students' activities on the playground, including making certain that the students do not play on any defective equipment. However, if one of Ms. Blanchard's students accidentally cuts himself with the power saw and one of Ms. Rico's students falls off a swing that is in good working condition and breaks her arm, most courts would not find these teachers liable. In such cases, teachers are not negligent in their duty.

Intentional Tort　A person who carries out an action with the full knowledge and intent to harm another person is undertaking an intentional tort. Since it is rare for teachers to intentionally or maliciously engage in actions that would cause injury to students, few teachers have been charged with intentional torts. Assault, battery, slander, libel, false imprisonment, and trespassing are examples of intentional torts.[34]

Corporal punishment, the spanking or whipping of students, is the one area where teachers have been charged with the intentional torts of assault and battery. Education law literature since World War II is replete with court cases involving corporal punishment. After World War II, many in society began to consider that other methods of disciplining children were more psychologically and socially effective and better for children than whipping or spanking. Parents became angry if their children were spanked or whipped in school, and some turned to the court for redress. Over the years, the courts in most cases have sided with the school over issues of corporal punishment.

The concept of in loco parentis has provided teachers with the right to discipline students when teachers deemed punishment appropriate. However, an increasing number of court cases against teachers for assault and battery in disciplining students has led some school districts to abandon paddling. Where paddling is still permitted, it requires written parental consent, and some school districts have a policy that only principals may paddle students with a witness in the room.

Finally, in another form of tort, **intentional inference,** intent refers to the consequence of an act rather than the act itself. In addition to cases of serious injury to students, intentional tort extends to actions causing emotional harm to a child such as practical jokes.[35]

In summary, most teachers will probably teach their entire professional career without any claim of negligence or intentional torts being brought against them. Nevertheless, because injuries and harm can befall a person in seconds, teachers need to always be alert to this possibility.

Freedom to Be Yourself Outside of School

Teachers have always been expected to be their community's pillars of dignity and respect. The story in the box "Miss Jones: Pillar of the Community?" was reported by a teacher in a high school in the early 1900s and vividly captures society's expectations of that time.

Miss Jones: Pillar of the Community?

During the summer when Mr. Blank, our superintendent, was on vacation, Miss Jones came to apply for a position. Miss Jones was a very good looking young lady, 19 years of age, and just graduated from a small sectarian university. She herself belonged to the sect. The school board had one fellow sectarian and, as the principal remarked, two others who were susceptible to good-looking young women. Miss Jones was hired. Mr. Blank had intended to fill her place with a young man. Miss Jones, being the only member of the high school faculty belonging to this sect, chose to room alone. From the first it was noticeable that young men frequented Miss Jones' room in the mornings and noon before school had taken up and after school evenings. That started talk. The story was passed around that Mr. Blank hadn't wanted her in the first place and that she had better be careful.

Several of the teachers talked to her in order to get her to confide in them. Then the rest of the teachers were informed of what had occurred. She remarked that there wasn't a single man in town that she hadn't dated. Several times she had accepted rides with high school boys. If she walked up the street with one of the boys at noon, this was further cause for gossip. One teacher was reported to have said that she had better leave her gentleman friend alone or she would scratch her eyes out. Every move Miss Jones made was watched and catalogued. A teacher told the others that at one of the class parties some boys had come up to her and politely inquired as to how she had enjoyed the party, then turned to Miss Jones and asked her to go riding with a group of them after the party. By established custom, public dancing was not allowed among the teachers. Miss Jones was seen numerous times at public dances. Once she told a group of teachers that she was not cut out to be a teacher and that she was not coming back. The school teachers, principal, and superintendent were all brought forcefully to the attention of the public through this unfortunate affair. The town took sides on the question, which disturbed the entire school and the entire community.

Source: Document submitted by a school, in Willard Waller, *The Sociology of Teaching* (New York: Wiley, 1932), 45–46.

Teachers are still expected to lead exemplary lives because they are role models for young people. However, standards by which teachers are judged today are not as puritanical as in the case of Miss Jones. Reasons for these changes in standards include teachers' more skillfully using enactments of power expressed in the U.S. Constitution and other documents. For example, the concept of personal liberty found in the Fourteenth Amendment gives teachers privacy rights not only in terms of what they do but where they do it. Teachers use this knowledge of their constitutional rights to challenge school officials' authority to control their personal lifestyle choices.

Courts try to balance teachers' privacy interests against the school board's legitimate interests in safeguarding the welfare of students and effectively managing the school.[36] Teachers cannot be discharged solely because school officials disapprove of their personal and private conduct, but restrictions can be placed on unconventional behavior that is detrimental to job performance or harmful to students. For example, some state laws put prohibitions on certain sexual acts and relationships. However, the courts have protected teachers who have engaged in consenting sexual relationships out of wedlock, noting that this is not a basis for dismissal unless teaching effectiveness is impaired.[37]

Another area of outside school behavior concerns actions teachers may take toward the school system they work for and toward their employer. Up until 1968, teachers were subject to severe repercussions if they took a stand against the policies and practices of their local board. However, all of this changed when Marvin Pickering, a teacher, wrote a letter to the local newspaper, which was printed, criticizing the board of education's plans. The board's plans included spending money to sod a football field instead of paying the teachers and purchasing needed supplies. As a result of the letter, the board fired Pickering. It claimed the letter contained "false statements" that would damage the reputation of the school board members and the administration. Mr. Pickering took the case to court, claiming he was protected by the First and Fourteenth amendments. The case ultimately reached the Supreme Court, where the decision was reversed. In delivering the court's verdict, Justice Marshall made the following statement, which remains relevant for teachers today:

> Teachers are, as a class, the members of a community most likely to have informed and definite opinions as to how funds allotted to the operation of the school should be spent. Accordingly, it is essential that they be able to speak out freely on such questions without fear of retaliatory dismissal.[38]

The *Pickering* case established the right of teachers to talk out without fear of reprisal. Teachers can write letters to newspaper editors, send e-mails, or talk on the radio or television about employment conditions without threat of dismissal. The *Pickering* case also serves as the legal basis for protecting teachers who, after unsuccessfully going through proper channels, have taken their problem to a higher official outside the school or school district, such as their congressional representative. Teachers can also march in demonstrations; they are protected in carrying out this activity by the U.S. Constitution. Over the years, teachers have gained more control over their out-of-school behavior. Currently, teachers for the most part are free to live and behave like other citizens.

In conclusion, Marvin Pickering's court case set a precedent for teacher candidates like Jennifer, whose situation we discussed at the beginning of the chapter. She will be happy to know that in most states she cannot be legally discharged because of her sexual orientation. Jennifer and any other teachers should keep in mind that if they believe their rights have been violated, they should look to the Constitution and state statutes for their rights to due process and personal freedoms.

Along with discussing teachers' rights, some attention needs to be given to teacher responsibilities. Rights usually bring with them responsibilities, and teachers have important ones to students—especially the responsibility to provide equity in the classroom.

TEACHERS' RESPONSIBILITIES: EQUITY IN CLASSROOMS AND SCHOOLS

Ever since *Brown v. Board of Education* in 1954 held that segregated schools were unconstitutional, striking down the "separate but equal" doctrine of *Plessy* v. *Ferguson* (1896), schools and teachers have had a definitive legal and social responsibility to ensure that students experience racial equality. Congressional and state legislation and court decisions have been instrumental in giving teachers rights to exercise such responsibility. Teacher candidates have probably already experienced or been influenced by some of these responsibilities during their PreK–college education (e.g., school desegregation, gender equity, inclusive classrooms). The discussion here will address several of the equity and equal opportunity issues for which classroom teachers are responsible. These include the responsibility to treat students fairly based on race, gender, language, and ability.

Racial Integration

Teachers have a responsibility to make certain that no student is segregated because of his or her race or ethnic group. *Brown* put a stop to de jure segregation, or segregation of races that occurs by law. However, *Brown* has not been able to put a stop to de facto segregation, or segregation that takes place for other reasons such as segregated living patterns. De facto segregation also occurs in schools when students of color are denied access to certain classrooms, such as upper-level math and science courses. It occurs, too, when such students are not given the opportunity to have the lead role in school plays, are allowed only token representation on the cheering squad, or are suspended disproportionably. To eliminate de facto segregation, teachers have a responsibility to make certain that racial prejudice does not influence classroom decisions.

Some teachers are heard saying, "I am color-blind." Whereas this statement may seem to support equity and equal opportunity, it can signal to students of color that their race and color are less important in a society that boasts White history and culture.

Teachers have a responsibility to deal with racism. This term includes racial prejudice that is evident in statements made between teacher and students, or between student and student, and in grouping patterns that place students of the same racial group together most of the time, especially when core academic subjects are being taught. Racial segregation has a way of reinventing itself even as teachers and students work to eliminate it; therefore, teachers have a responsibility to always be on guard and always work to help students recognize it and eliminate it.

Gender Equity

Since 1972, Title IX of the Education Amendments has prohibited sex discrimination in any educational program or activity receiving federal funds. Title IX called attention to the lack of gender equity in all schooling, set guidelines for equal spending for both genders, and made it possible for students to attend school if they are married or pregnant. Title IX put in place the idea that gender inequities need to be corrected, and that teachers have a responsibility to participate actively in this process. Since Title IX, teachers have been more conscious of gender equity in their classroom; for example, do they call on girls as often as they call on boys, do they assign girls and boys equally to leadership positions, and do they give girls and boys equal wait time when asking questions? Also, teachers are taking more responsibility to provide both White girls and girls of color with role models and welcome them to participate in all of the school's programs and activities. Additionally, teachers are increasingly concerned to see that curriculum includes women's history and culture and that instructional materials are gender fair. Finally, teachers have a responsibility to disrupt gender stereotyping, or any thinking that suggests that female students are expected to be passive and conforming whereas male students are supposed to be independent, assertive, and challenging.

Elimination of Sexual Harassment

Teachers have a responsibility to make sure that students are not sexually harassed. **Sexual harassment** is the request for or requirement of sexual relations in a relationship where power between the parties is unequal.[39] Because the student–teacher relationship is one of unequal power, a teacher must see that students are not penalized for not submitting to any sexual demands. Alexander and Alexander describe two types of sexual harassment. The first type is quid pro quo, or bargain harassment, in which "the person in power (e.g., teacher, administrator) attempts to compel submission to sexual demands by conditioning rewards or punishment upon the student's acquiescence or lack thereof."[40] The second type is hostile environment harassment, in which "the teacher or administrator makes the educational environment hostile, offensive, or intimidating to the student."[41]

Teacher candidates probably remember being taught how to safeguard themselves from sexual harassment during their early childhood years. For example, they may have learned "No, go, tell" (say no, go to someone you trust, and tell what happened). Sexual harassment instruction should be periodically revisited and modified when necessary to meet the needs of the students at different ages. Teacher candidates have a responsibility to help students understand how to identify and avoid sexual harassment.

Schools have taking steps to avoid peer sexual harassment since the U.S. Supreme Court's 1999 decision in *Davis v. Monroe County Board of Education* declared that educational institutions that show deliberate indifference to known sexual harassment between students may be liable for the resultant damages under Title IX. A teacher can no longer ignore complaints of student sexual harassment, insisting it is "normal behavior." The Court confirmed that schools must change their disposition and investigate reasonable complaints within schools and classrooms.[42]

Language Equity

In 1968 Congress, as part of President Johnson's War on Poverty, passed the Bilingual Education Act. This legislation appropriated funds to local educational agencies for the development and implementation of programs to meet the needs of students with limited English-speaking abilities. The Bilingual Education Act placed upon schools and teachers the responsibility to provide language equity and an equal opportunity for learning for students whose first language was not English. Since its passage, there has been much political and educational debate over the need for schools and teachers to provide instruction in the language of students whose native language is not English. Although this language debate may continue for years and different states have their own mandates about language instruction, teachers still have a responsibility to students whose first language is not English regardless of the state's mandate. This responsibility includes respecting languages other than English, encouraging curiosity about different languages, and not relying solely or mostly on an oral method of instruction.

Disability Equity

Teachers have a responsibility to ensure that disabled students have an equal opportunity to learn. Since 1975, when Congress passed Public Law 94-142 ensuring the right of all handicapped students to a public school education, teachers and other educators have been held responsible for the education of students with physical and mental disabilities. Over the years state and federal courts have had to interpret the meaning of PL 94-142 to clarify teachers' responsibilities to students with disabilities. Much of the debate is over who (federal, state, local government) should pay for the services needed to educate students. Teacher candidates will need to find out how PL 94-142 is being applied in their school districts.

With regard to how and where students labeled as handicapped are to be educated, PL 94-142 provides that

> to the maximum extent appropriate, handicapped children, including those children in public and private institutions or other care facilities, are educated with children who are not handicapped, and that special classes, separate schooling, or other removal of handicapped children from the regular educational environment occurs only when the nature or severity of the handicap is such that education in regular classes with the use of supplementary aids and services cannot be achieved satisfactorily (PL 94-142, Section 1412 [5] [5]).[43]

Initially, teachers interpreted the law to mean they were responsible for teaching students in the least restricted environment. In other words, students with disabilities who could benefit were to be mainstreamed, or integrated into the rest of the traditional class. Mainstreaming, however, often resulted in students' being integrated into a class only part-time. Also, it often required that students with disabilities achieve a certain academic level before they would be accepted in a traditional classroom. In other words, the traditional classroom teacher had only a part-time responsibility for educating students with disabilities, and these students did not receive their full share of benefit from being in a traditional classroom.

A push from parents and concerned educators in 1986 led the U.S. Department of Education to issue the Regular Education Initiative. This initiative placed a responsibility on both the traditional teaching staff and special educators to work more closely together to teach students with disabilities in a regular classroom. As a result of this effort, the traditional teaching staff and special educators developed strategies for including students with disabilities in the classroom. This concept, which became known as **inclusive education,** put in place a way of thinking about educating students with disabilities. It addressed the traditional classroom teacher's responsibility in this undertaking, saying that they were to be actively involved in educating or helping to educate students with disabilities.

In sum, as teachers seek to discern their rights, they also need to discover their responsibilities to the students they are teaching. Responsibilities for addressing equity, which have not always been fulfilled, sometimes have to be pointed out to teachers. The courts and government mandates are often the reason many teachers become involved. These same mandates often provide guidelines for teachers regarding their responsibility to make education equitable for all students. Teacher candidates' success in the job market and as beginning teachers depends on knowing and understanding their responsibility to all the students who enter the schoolhouse door.

STUDENTS' RIGHTS

Students gained more rights during the 1960s as African Americans and other groups working within the civil rights movement inspired many others to work in similar ways to improve their life and work conditions. The increase in students' rights did not come about as part of a movement with a vision and organization like that of civil rights groups. However, since the 1960s students have become much more sophisticated about their rights and have come to understand that enactments of power assigned by the Constitution to U.S. citizens are in many cases assigned to them. For example, students are aware of legal entitlements such as due process, and will remind school administrators of their rights when necessary.

Many administrators and teachers discuss school discipline and control of students. These discussions are often void of the notion of power vested in students' rights. All students have power. For example, students can resist by boycotting the food in the cafeteria or by standing up for a teacher who has been reprimanded by the administration. However, power and privilege may be vested with some groups of students more than others. For example, students who do not speak English as their first language will find their native language less respected than English. The power to speak their native language will have meanings not associated with school achievement. The idea of social justice and a critical examination of social structures within the EMCSR approach will help teacher candidates understand how power circulates differentially among groups of students.

Keep the notion of power and the EMCSR approach in mind while reading the following sections on students' rights. They offer a deeper understanding of the policies and practices affecting students. The section begins with a student right that students may question as a "right"—school attendance.

School Attendance

Some students may not perceive it as a "right," but students have the right to attend school. The legal basis for attendance in school is the common law doctrine of parens patriae, which means that the state has the authority to enact reasonable laws for the welfare of its citizens and the state.[44] In most states, parents are obligated to make certain that their school-age children attend school up to the age of 16. The exception to attending school is being educated at home. Over the past two decades, a small but increasing number of parents have decided on a home school program. Although the guidelines for a home school program are different across the states, many states require home tutors to have a teacher license or to hold a baccalaureate degree. Also, most states require that students schooled at home be tested to make sure they have the basic skills.[45]

"School attendance is a funny kind of students' right," some middle school students told us. We agreed, and were about to join in the frivolity when Nam Jou, a refugee from Southeast Asia, said, "In the camp where we lived for three years, the one glimmer of hope that helped our parents was that we [the children] were able to attend school some of the time." Nam Jou's comment about his sometime opportunity to attend school made everyone understand that the right to attend school needs to be seen as the privilege that it really is.

Freedom From Arbitrary Suspension

Suspension, an action taken by the school to punish students for violating school rules and regulations, is a short-term denial of school attendance. However, a suspension cannot be an arbitrary act. In *Goss v. Lopez*, the Supreme Court ruled that a student must receive due process before being suspended. Since the Goss ruling in 1975, most state boards of education have instituted suspension guidelines that take into account a student's constitutional rights. These guidelines state that, prior to a suspension, a student must receive the following:

- Oral or written notification of the nature of the violation and the intended punishment
- An opportunity to refute the charges before an objective decision maker
- An explanation of the evidence on which the disciplinarian is relying

Suspension became a cause célèbre in the *Tinker v. Des Moines Independent Community School District* case in 1969. This was during the time of the Vietnam

War, when emotions and behaviors in the United States were governed by strong beliefs and short fuses. In the *Tinker* case, three students attending a public high school in Des Moines, Iowa, were suspended because they wore black armbands to protest U.S. participation in the Vietnam War. They had been informed a few days earlier that the school had adopted a rule that any student wearing an armband to school would be requested to remove it. If the student refused, he or she would be suspended until the rule was complied with. The suspended students filed a class action suit in the U.S. District Court and lost. However, the U.S. Supreme Court heard the case and reversed the decision in favor of the students. The statements by Justice Fortas, shown in the box "Justice Abe Fortas on Student Rights," are often used to influence the decisions in other student rights cases brought before the courts.

The *Tinker* case has served as the model for a number of actions related to students' rights. The ruling in this case is clear with such statements about student rights as "It can hardly be argued that either students or teachers shed their constitutional rights to freedom or expression at the schoolhouse gate" and "Students in school as well as out of school are 'persons' under our Constitution." These statements helped to make visible students' power expressed in the students' rights discourse. Students' rights that have drawn attention include the right of students to exercise free speech and distribute literature, to wear certain clothes, to remain in school when pregnant or married, to be free from unreasonable search and seizure, and to have no requirements to participate in religious activities in a public school setting. Let us examine these rights.

Freedom of Speech and Distribution of Literature

Increasingly since the mid-20th century, the Supreme Court has argued that K–12 students do not give up their rights when they attend school and that schools are the appropriate educational setting for students to learn about and gain respect for First Amendment freedoms. The notions of schools being a "marketplace for ideas" and the "robust exchange of ideas" are grounded in the writings of the Supreme Court.[46] For example, students have the right to distribute leaflets, pamphlets, or other literature even if these materials criticize school policy. Also, students have the right to organize and attend peaceful assemblies or to picket the school.

However, the Supreme Court has also held that although students have a right to free speech, "the constitutional rights of students in public school are not automatically coextensive with the rights of adults in other settings."[47] In other words, freedom of speech must be considered within the context of the special circumstances of an educational environment. For example, courts have upheld school authorities' banning of libelous, defamatory expressions in the content of publications to be distributed at school. Also, the courts have argued that First Amendment rights do not protect the use of obscene, vulgar, or inflammatory expression. For example, the court said that a student was not permitted to wear a Confederate flag sleeve patch in a racially tense, newly integrated school in Tennessee.[48] Additionally, the courts have argued that school officials can censor student speech and writing in school publications and other school-related activities as long as the censorship is

Justice Abe Fortas on Student Rights

The wearing of arm bands in the circumstances of this case was entirely divorced from actually or potentially disruptive conduct by those participating in it. It was closely akin to "pure speech" which we have repeatedly held is entitled to comprehensive protection under the First Amendment. . . . First Amendment rights, applied in light of the special characteristics of the school environment, are available to teacher and students. It can hardly be argued that either students or teachers shed their constitutional rights to freedom of speech or expression at the schoolhouse gate. . . .

In our system, undifferentiated fear or apprehension of disturbance is not enough to overcome the right to freedom of expression. Any departure from absolute regimentation may cause trouble. Any variation from the majority's opinion may inspire fear. Any word spoken, in class, in the lunchroom, or on the campus, that deviates from the views of another may start an argument or cause a disturbance. But our Constitution says we must take this risk, . . . and our history says that it is this sort of hazardous freedom—this kind of openness— that is the basis of our national strength and of the independence and vigor of the Americans who grow up and live in this relatively permissive, often disputatious, society. . . .

In our system, state-operated schools may not be enclaves of totalitarianism. School officials do not possess absolute authority over their students. Students in school as well as out of school are "persons" under our Constitution. They are possessed of fundamental rights which the State must respect, just as they themselves must respect their obligations to the State. In

our system, students may not be regarded as closed-circuit recipients of only that which the State chooses to communicate. They may not be confined to the expression of those sentiments that are officially approved. In the absence of a specific showing of constitutionally valid reasons to regulate their speech, students are entitled to freedom of expression of their views. . . .

The principal use to which the schools are dedicated is to accommodate students during prescribed hours for the purpose of certain types of activities. Among those activities is personal intercommunication among the students. This is not only an inevitable part of the process of attending school; it is also an important part of the education process. A student's rights, therefore, do not embrace merely the classroom hours. When he is in the cafeteria, or on the playing field, or on the campus during the authorized hours, he may express his opinions, even on controversial subjects like the conflict in Vietnam, if he does so [without] materially and substantially interfering with the requirements of appropriate discipline in the operation of the school and without colliding with the rights of others. . . . But conduct by the student, in class or out of it, which for any reason—whether it stems from time, place, or type of behavior—materially disrupts class work or involves substantial disorder or invasion of the rights of others is, of course, not immunized by the constitutional guarantee of freedom of speech.

Source: *Tinker v. Des Moines Independent School District (Ia.), 393 U.S. 503; 89 S. Ct. 733 (1969).*

based on legitimate pedagogical reasons. For example, in *Hazel School District v. Kuhlmeier*, the court upheld the principal's decision to delete two pages from the school newspaper because the principal feared that the individuals discussed in the articles on divorce and teenage pregnancy would be recognized.[49]

The courts acknowledge and support students' rights consistent with the Constitution. Nevertheless, the courts remind students that along with the enactment of power they receive from the Constitution go responsibilities.

Dress and Grooming

Dress and grooming are often contested areas for students and school officials, in which there can be a very visible clash between student power and school power. Clothing worn to school by girls, such as pants, shorts, or miniskirts, has been the subject of heated debate, leading to the establishment of policies prohibiting the wearing of certain clothes to school.

Boys' wearing of long hair or facial hair to school has been the subject of debate and several court cases. In some instances, the cases have been won by the students and in others, by the local board. So far the Supreme Court has declined to consider grooming cases and to resolve this conflict, thereby leaving the rulings of local or regional courts in place.[50] In such debates, is there a right or wrong, or does one group seeking to have its way succeed simply because it is using power more effectively than the other group? One could argue that in those cases in which the students won, they used their power more effectively to get their way; in cases where the local board won, the reverse was true.

Considering what "proper attire" is seems to generate enough controversy to require U.S. courts to become involved. In 1970s, the wearing of jeans was seen as a reason to send a student back home to change. For example, in 1970, school officials in New Hampshire argued that the wearing of jeans contributed to students becoming "lax and indifferent." The court disagreed, holding, "The school board's power must be limited to that required by its function of administering public education."[51] However, schools have received greater authority from the courts to restrict students' attire since the rise of street gangs and school violence. For example, in 1993 in *Jeglin v. San Jacinto* the court sustained a ban against attire featuring certain sports teams or colleges at a high school, on the ground that the banned attire was emblematic of school gangs and had the effect of intimidating other students.[52] Certain colors, jewelry, and T-shirts with gang symbols are other items banned from being worn in school.

Some schools are requiring students to wear uniforms because of gang problems associated with students' attire and concerns that as more schools become racially and socioeconomically diverse, the problem of students' dress will worsen. For example, school officials believe that uniforms will reduce separation of students because, for example, some wear Wal-Mart clothes and other wear clothes from the Gap. Also, the wearing of clothes that represent a particular ethnic group is kept to a minimum.

In some schools where gang colors are not at issue and finances are not a major concern, the clothes students wear have become how the students and the school battle over power. Such clashes of power between students and administrators has led to students' having a day, often Friday, on which regulations regarding dress are relaxed. As a teachers, what do you believe your role should be in teaching students about how the effects of power operate when it comes to a goal they are pursuing that may go against the school?

Pregnancy and Marriage

It was a hectic day. "There are times when these eighth-grade students are out of this world," Catherine Frazier mumbles to herself as she gathers up her things to head home. "What's for dinner? Tonight, I need more than just a salad and a roll." As Catherine continues to consider dinner possibilities, Joyce, one of her favorite students, enters the room. Joyce's body language, although unnoticed by Catherine, shows a person uncomfortable about being here. As Joyce walks closer, Catherine looks up. Her thoughts are, "I hope whatever the person wants, it is something that can be taken care of quickly on my way out of the room."

"Oh, hi, Joyce, did you forget something?" Catherine asks. Joyce, with tears now streaming down her face, says, "Ms. Frazier, I need your help and some information. You're the only teacher that I feel comfortable talking with about this." She blurted out, "I am ten weeks pregnant. I have decided to have the baby, and I want to know if I can continue school during pregnancy and after the baby comes. What rights do I have?"

Joyce may attend school during her pregnancy and after she has the baby. Since the 1960s, the courts have ruled, given the Fourteenth Amendment and Title IX, that students must be protected from unjustified classifications that limit their educational opportunities. This means that discrimination based on pregnancy, false pregnancy, termination of pregnancy, or childbirth is prohibited. A student also cannot be prohibited from attending school once he or she gets married.

As Catherine tells Joyce about her student rights, Joyce began to feel a bit better. Her future does not seem so bleak now. However, she knows that a major hurdle lies ahead. Telling her mother she fears in the worst way. But now that she has learned that she can continue to go to school, she has something to say that may make this whole situation go down a bit easier.

Freedom From Unreasonable Search and Seizure

A principal hears from several reliable students that another student has brought a gun to school and the gun is in his locker. Since the principal has the master key to all students' lockers, can he search this particular student's locker?

The Fourth Amendment that protects against unreasonable search and seizure is largely silent in upholding this right for students in school. Whenever action against such a search has been taken to court, the courts have usually rejected the argument on the following grounds. First, a school locker is not the student's property in the same way that property in a home or apartment belongs to the student. The school actually owns the locker and therefore has greater license to search it.

Second, the courts have held that if the teacher has reasonable grounds for suspicion and if the scope of the search is reasonable, then it is legal. Most teachers' suspicions and searches have been considered reasonable to this point.

Purses, book bags, and other student property are also subject to search if the school has reasonable grounds for suspicion. For example, in a case brought before the Supreme Court, a teacher reported that a student was smoking in the restroom. When the assistant principal questioned the student, the student denied smoking and furthermore claimed that she was not a smoker. Nevertheless, the assistant principal opened the student's purse to search for evidence to support the suspicion that she did smoke. He found a package of cigarettes in the girl's purse and, upon removing them, also noticed paper used for rolling cigarettes, some marijuana, and other evidence that suggested that the girl was dealing drugs. The court supported the school's position that a reasonable search had been conducted because it noted that the assistant principal had reasonable grounds for suspicion that the girl smoked based on the information received from the teacher who reported the incident.

Presently, as a nation, we are increasingly accepting the idea that a search, although an inconvenience, is a good thing. It provides safety and peace of mind in a world that is becoming evermore concerned with terrorism and other forms of violence. Many public buildings, including schools, are accepting the use of metal detectors as a way of life that will probably not change in the near future, but instead become more a part of world culture. In 1998, 15% of schools overall used metal detectors, including 39% of urban school, 10% of suburban schools, and 6% of rural schools.[53]

Student Records

Over the years, parents have been concerned about what school records say about their children and who has access to the information in these records. Before 1974, a number of court cases challenged the material placed in school records.[54] These cases led Congress in 1974 to enact the Family Educational Rights and Privacy Act (FERPA). This act is an example of how the effects of power displayed by the federal government influences school policy. FERPA states that federal funds can be withdrawn from any educational agency or institution that fails to provide parents access to their child's educational records or that disseminates such information, with certain exceptions, to third parties without parental permission. Because the federal government contributes approximately 6.8% to public school budgets[55] and supports such school services as the free lunch program, the threat of withdrawing funds has induced school districts to comply with FERPA. FERPA also states that upon reviewing their son or daughter's file, parents can "request that the information be amended if it is believed to be inaccurate, misleading, or in violation of the student's protected rights."[56] Additionally, this act stipulated that upon reaching 18, students may exercise the rights guaranteed to parents under this law.[57] If you were a member of Congress, would you have voted for the FERPA? Do you think that the FERPA is a good exercise of power by the federal government? Or do you think the federal government is abusing its power?

Student records have become an issue with some divorced parents. Teachers wondered, for example, if they could give a student's report card to a father who was not living in the home with the student, but who had been awarded joint custody by the court. Several court cases led to the conclusion that joint custodial parents have equal access to education information about their child.[58]

Finally, school records, because they document students' successes, failures, health, family, and other demographics, are central in discussions of students' rights. Teacher candidates need to remember that student records are to be kept confidential.

Church, State, and Students

Proponents of including religion in the public school and those for keeping religion out of public schools are constantly at odds. Proponents of religion in the school argue that since the United States relates so much of what it does to God—for example, "In God We Trust" is inscribed on the penny—teachers should be able to talk about God in the classroom. However, proponents of not having religion in public school contend that public schools should be religiously neutral. These proponents argue that the Supreme Court in 1879 established a wall of separation between church and state. This wall influences the material resources that students in private schools have a right to receive from the federal and state governments, and it influences instruction that students in public schools can receive. Over the years, despite countless attempts to tear it down or to put a major hole in it, the wall of separation between church and state for the most part has remained intact. However, students in religious private schools have won the rights to receive:

- State-prepared standardized tests and scoring services
- Speech, hearing, and psychological services, whether offered at the parochial school or a neutral place
- Cash reimbursement for costs associated with state-mandated testing and reporting requirements in connection with tests prepared by the state but scored by parochial school personnel
- State income tax deductions available to both public and private school parents for expenses incurred for tuition, textbooks, and transportation to school
- Federal grants for care and prevention services regarding teenage pregnancy provided by religious and nonreligious organizations[59]

The rights of public school students not to engage in religious activities is covered in the First Amendment to the Constitution, which states in part, "Congress shall make no law respecting an establishment of religion, or prohibiting the free exercise thereof." Within this statement are the two religious clauses that protect public school students' religious liberty rights: the **establishment clause** and the **free exercise clause.** There is, however, some tension between the two. The establishment clause was intended to prohibit the federal government from declaring and financially supporting a national religion. The free exercise clause was intended to prevent the federal government from exerting any restraint on the free exercise of religion. It secure an individual's religious liberty by prohibiting any invasion of that liberty by the civil authority. An example used to show both the tension and common values in the clauses is: "Some people might suggest that providing a military chaplain for troops stationed overseas violates the Establishment Clause, while other might suggest that *failing to provide* a chaplain violates the Free Exercise Clause rights of the same troops."[60]

In public schools, the debate revolves mostly around "school prayer." Students do not have to read the Bible or recite the Lord's Prayer; the U.S. Supreme Court has found the requirement to read or recite biblical material unconstitutional.[61] The debate over separation of church and state shows no signs of winding down. The rights of students attending public schools and the rights of students attending private schools will continue to be tested. For example, a group of Roman Catholic parents brought suit against the Westchester County School District in the state of New York to prevent teachers from incorporating religious practices into their lessons. Judge Brieant of the Third Federal District Court ruled that the school district was violating its students' First Amendment right to religious freedom by permitting schools to engage in religious-oriented activities. These activities included the construction of a Hindu god's likeness by students in third grade and New Age prayer recitals at a high school Earth Day celebration.[62]

The effect of power, as illustrated by some candidates running for public office, is to promise to their constituents a greater or lesser inclusion of religion in the public schools. Some educators claim that the effect of power—that is, to include more religion in the public schools—is being demonstrated in President Bush's ideas to make character education a part of the school curriculum and to give public funds to faith-based institutions for use in helping the needy. They argue that the school already influences the character of students in both the overt and hidden curriculum. Proponents argue that given school violence and other teenage problems, such as drugs, smoking, and pregnancy, more attention needs to be given to character development. What do you think? What ideas do the politicians running for public office in your area have in their platforms about religion and education? How will these ideas affect the schools? A good way for teacher candidates to begin to understand the school district's view on separation of church and state is to review the district's guidelines concerning the celebration of holiday days such as Christmas.

In sum, students are learning their rights at an increasingly early age. They demonstrate their understanding of these rights in the actions that they take. Some examples include suing parents, and two lesbian students attending a prom together. Acting upon these rights, educators hope, will also inform students about the responsibilities they have to themselves and others.

STUDENTS' RESPONSIBILITIES

Students' rights are a prominent topic in the educational literature. They are addressed throughout teacher candidate programs. Students' responsibilities, on the other hand, are not as clearly addressed. Much of the discussion of students' responsibilities concerns academic achievement. However, with acts of violence in schools on the rise, student responsibility is receiving major attention. School and public officials are demanding that students be more responsible for their actions. A no-nonsense attitude is being adopted toward students concerning their help in eliminating school violence, and schools are taking a proactive stance against all forms of violence. For example, following the message on signs at airport security stations that prohibit joking about security issues, schools are forbidding loose talk or joking about school violence and are dealing with it seriously.

Other ways schools are working to prevent school violence include getting students to learn and use conflict resolution skills and to know the school's student handbook. Students in some states have a responsibility to learn conflict resolution skills to handle arguments and disagreements between themselves and other students. They are also expected to be able to assist disputing parties in working out their differences. In some schools, students are provided with folders that include all school policies, such as graduation requirements, dress codes, attendance policy, and zero tolerance policies.

School violence can occur in any area—urban, suburban, or rural. School violence has everyone in the United States worried and searching for answers on how to eliminate it. One common answer is that there is no magic solution that will put an end to school violence. Teacher candidates will have to stay cognizant of the potential sources of school violence and appropriately remind students of their roles in eliminating it. Teachers must remain approachable so that students who may know someone is thinking of committing a violent act feel comfortable speaking up. Also, teachers must get to know their students in order to encourage them to "talk out" problems instead of resorting to violence.

FINDING A VOICE

As Catherine starts to drive home, she realizes that her hectic day is nothing compared to the day Joyce is having. She does not envy Joyce having to tell her mother about her pregnancy. "Wow," thought Catherine, "Joyce is handling this much better than I could. My mother and father would have disowned me!"

As Catherine looked at her watch, which read 3:45, she got a flash. She decided to head for the central office instead of going directly home. She thought that at the central office she could pick up some information about students' rights regarding pregnancy and child care that Joyce could show to her mother. She would also inquire about any other services available to help Joyce.

As Catherine was heading into the central office building, she got another flash. She wondered about her rights as a teacher to help Joyce. Would she be able to stop by Joyce's home and help her with her schoolwork if she had difficulty keeping up, or if she had a difficult pregnancy and needed to remain at home? While I am here, thought Catherine, I will find out my rights as a teacher.

An hour later, Catherine was heading back to her car with both her head and her hands filled with information. She was pleased that she had come to the central office. She had brochures and other material that included the excerpts from the state statutes regarding students' rights about pregnancy and child care services. She had spoken to a very kind staff person who had even encouraged her to help Joyce and who had given her names of people working in city and state agencies that would help Joyce.

Sometimes, Catherine said to herself, my father would say, "When you think life has given you lemons, you take them and make lemonade." Now, thought Catherine, "I really know what Dad means. This looks like one of those times, and I will have to help Joyce make the lemonade. And maybe if I had been in Joyce's situation, Dad and Mom would not have disowned me. I hope they would have reached out to help me, the way I am helping Joyce, and the way I hope her mother will."

SUMMING UP

This chapter has noted that both teachers' and students' rights are written in and interpreted from the same sources: the U.S. Constitution, congressional legislation, and state statutes. These sources are enactments of power that give expression to "rights."

Over the years, states have become more understanding of the rights of teachers and students. Documents that address K–12 legislation and statutes are continuously examined to see where and how power is vested and how it can be interpreted. Tenure, collective bargaining, academic freedom, and control of one's behavior outside of school, for example, are not rights originally bestowed on teachers, but rights that teachers have achieved by demanding examination and interpretation of the Constitution and other legal documents. Activism for students' rights, as for teachers' rights, received a wake-up call during the civil rights movement and Vietnam War era. Students today, because of the actions of students and concerned citizens in past decades, are now treated with a good deal more respect and dignity.

The United States was founded on the belief that no one is above the law and every one has a right to due process. If so inclined, a person may take legal action against others. Teachers and students are often at the center of legal activity. This legal activity is an example of enactments of power and power struggles, and is debated in the teachers' and students' rights discourses.

As teachers and students have acquired rights, they have also acquired responsibilities. Teachers' and students' rights bring responsibilities that demand that they be fair and responsive to one another and to themselves. For example, teachers have a major responsibility in making inclusive schooling work, and similarly, students need to be respectful of all their classmates. The responsibilities discourse, however, does not receive the explicit attention in the education literature that the rights discourse does because the rights discourse is often explicitly or implicitly connected to major court decisions or to federal and state mandates. By contrast, teachers' and students' responsibilities are connected to students' achievement, attitudes, and behavior in school.

Also relevant are discussions about the rights of groups of teachers and/or students—for example, gay and lesbian teachers and students of different abilities.

The EMCSR approach will help students understand that the playing field is not level and that different people's rights are vested with power differently. The EMCSR approach, with its attention to analyzing social inequality, using multiple perspectives, and practicing democracy, can help better prepare teacher education candidates to work in diverse educational settings and to understand, achieve, and use their rights in these settings.

KEY TERMS

academic freedom
collective bargaining
corporal punishment
due process
establishment clause
free exercise clause
in loco parentis
inclusive education

intentional inference
national career ladder
sexual harassment
suspension
tenure
tenure contract
term contract
tort

QUESTIONS FOR REFLECTION

1. What are the many different ways that you and your students can achieve power in school and classroom settings?
2. Does a Southeast Asian student have a right to demand that his/her language and culture be included in the curriculum? Does a teacher have a responsibility to include the language in the curriculum?
3. Does a gay student, even in a predominantly fundamentalist Christian community, have the right to ask for literature by and about gay, lesbian, bisexual, and transgendered people? What are a teacher's responsibilities to gay, lesbian, bisexual, or transgendered students?
4. Some argue that if students were required to wear uniforms, it would help to resolve the dress and grooming problems in school. Would it be a violation of students' rights to require them to wear uniforms to school?

ACTIVITIES

1. Interview a teacher or professor who acknowledges gay and lesbian people and who uses literature by and about gay and lesbian people.
2. Interview students from a History or Literature department about any debates on academic freedom involving speech codes, censorship, or selection of curriculum materials.
3. Interview K–12 students about rules in their school for dress and conduct. Do they agree with them? Have complaints? What are their rights, in their opinion?

4. Review Justice Fortas's opinion in the *Tinker* decision about students' rights. On your next visit to a school, observe students to see how they are making use of rights resulting from the *Tinker* decision.

GETTING CONNECTED

http://hkptu.org.hk/engptu/services/rights	An introduction to teachers' rights surrounding issues of employment and termination
http://www.Fac.org/religion/haynescol/haynes18.htm	Discussion of religious rights of teachers
http://www.abanet.org/irr/hr/yared.html	Discussion of civil rights for gay teachers
http://www.aclu.org/isues/student/ires.html	A list of websites relating to ACLU work on student rights
http://www.abacon.com/books/ab_0205166768.html	A discussion of public school law and teachers' and students' rights

SUGGESTED RESOURCES

Alexander, Kern, and M. David Alexander. *American Public School Law,* 5th ed. St. Paul, MN: West, 2001.
Johnson, John W. *History U.S. Court Cases: An Encyclopedia,* 2nd ed. New York: Routledge, 2001.
Johnson, John W. *The Struggle for Student Rights: Tinker v. Des Moines and the 1960s.* Lawrence: University Press of Kansas, 1997.
Morris, Arval A. *The Constitution and American Education.* St. Paul, MN: West, 1980.
Rapport, Doreen. *Tinker v. Des Moines: Student Rights on Trial.* New York: HarperCollins, 1993.

NOTES

1. Ronald G. Corwin, "The New Teaching Profession," in *Teacher Education*, ed. Kevin Ryan (Chicago: University of Chicago Press, 1974), 230–264.
2. "Teachers' Strikes Affect 650,000 Pupils in 14 States," *New York Times,* 7 September 1979, A12.
3. *New Jersey v. T. L. O.,* 469 U.S. 325 (1985).
4. Carnegie Forum on Education and the Economy, *A Nation Prepared: Teachers for the 21st Century* (Washington, DC: Author, 1986).
5. Ibid., 22.

6. Gloria J. Thomas, David J. Sperry, and Del F. Wasden, *The Law and Teacher Employment* (St. Paul, MN: West, 1991), 1.

7. Willard Waller, *The Sociology of Teaching* (New York: Wiley, 1932), 43.

8. Martha M. McCarthy, Nelda H. Cambron-McCabe, and Stephen B. Thomas, *Public School Law: Teachers' and Students' Rights*, 4th ed. (Boston: Allyn and Bacon, 1998), 251.

9. Ibid., 253.

10. McCarthy, Cambron-McCabe, and Thomas, *Public School Law*, 253.

11. Thomas, Sperry, and Wasden, *Law and Teacher Employment*, 17 .

12. Arval A. Morris, *The Constitution and American Education* (St. Paul, MN: West), 497–498.

13. Ibid.

14. Thomas, Sperry, and Wasden, *Law and Teacher Employment*, 81.

15. Ibid.

16. Ibid.

17. *Adler v. Board of Education, City of New York*, 342 U.S. 485, 493 (1952).

18. Thomas, Sperry, and Wasden, *Law and Teacher Employment*, 91.

19. Ibid., 203.

20. Ibid., 21.

21. Ibid., 232.

22. Ibid., 153.

23. Ibid., 153.

24. *Rarducci v. Rutland*, 316 F. Supp. 352 (M.D. Ala. 1970).

25. *Boring v. Buncombe County Board of Education*, 136 F. 3d 364; U.S. App. (1998).

26. *Mailloux v. Kiley*, 323 F. Supp. 1387 (D. Mass. 1971).

27. *Kingville Independent School District v. Cooper*, 611 F. 2d 1109 (5th Cir. Tex. 1980).

28. *Memphis Community School District v. Stachura*, 477 U.S. 299, 307 (1986).

29. *Carey v. Board of Education of Adams-Arapahoe*, 427 F. Supp. 945–956 (1996).

30. Thomas, Sperry, and Wasden, *Law and Teacher Employment*, 17.

31. McCarthy, Cambron-McCabe, and Thomas, *Public School Law*, 435.

32. Ibid., 435.

33. Ibid., 436.

34. Thomas, Sperry, and Wasden, *Law and Teacher Employment*, 240.

35. Kern Alexander and M. David Alexander, *American Public School Law*, 5th ed. (Belmont, CA: West/Wadsworth, 2001), 549.

36. McCarthy, Cambron-McCabe, and Thomas, *Public School Law*, 306.

37. Ibid.

38. *Pickering v. Board of Education*, 391 U.S. 571–572; 88 S. Ct. 1731 (1968).

39. C. MacKinnon, *Sexual Harassment of Working Women*, as cited in Alexander and Alexander, *American Public School Law*, 4th ed. (Belmont, CA : West/Wadsworth, 1999), 335.

40. Alexander and Alexander, *American Public School Law*, 4th ed. (Belmont, CA: West/Wadsworth, 1999), 335.

41. Ibid.

42. *Davis v. Monroe County Board of Education*, 526 U.S. 629; 119 S. Ct. 1661 (1999).

43. Quoted in M. A. Falvey, C. C. Givner, and C. Kimm, "What Is an Inclusive School?" in *Creating an Inclusive School*, ed. R. A. Villa and J. S. Thousand (Alexandria, VA: Association for Supervision and Curriculum Development, 1995), 5.

44. Ibid., 73.

45. Ibid., 77.

46. *Keyishian v. Board of Regents*, 385 U.S. 589, 603 (1967).

47. *Bethel Sch. Dist. No. 403 v. Fraser*, 478 U.S. 675, 682 (1986); see also *Tinker v. Des Moines Independent School District*, in McCarthy, Cambron-McCabe, Thomas, *Public School Law*, 114.

48. *Melton v. Young*, 465 F. 2d 1332 (6th Cir. 1972); cert. denied, 411 U.S. 951 (1973).

49. *Hazelwood School District v. Kuhlmeier*, 484 U.S. 267.

50. William D. Valente, *Law in the Schools*, 4th ed. (Upper Saddle River, NJ: Merrill, 1998), 177.

51. *Bannister v. Paradis*, 316 F. Supp. 185 (D.N.H. 1970).

52. *Jeglin v. San Jacinto Unified School Dist.*, 827 F. Supp. 1459 (Cal. 1993).

53. Kathy Davis, John Kelsey, Dia Langellier, Misty Mapes, and Jeff Rosendahl, "Surveillance in Schools: Safety vs. Personal Privacy," retrieved 1 September 2004 from http://students.ed.uiuc.edu/jkelsey/surveillance/detectors.htm

54. *Griswold v. Connecticut*, 381 U.S. 479 (1965).

55. U.S. Department of Education, National Center for Education Statistics, *Digest of Education Statistics, 1996* (Washington, DC: U.S. Government Printing Office, 1996), 151.

56. McCarthy, Cambron-McCabe, and Thomas, *Public School Law*, 104.

57. Thomas J. Flygare, *The Legal Rights of Students* (Bloomington, IN: Phi Delta Kappan Educational Foundation), 45.

58. *Page v. Rotterdam-Mohonasen Cent. Sch. Dist.*, 441 N.Y.S. 2d 323 (Sup. Ct. 1981); *Fay v. South Colonies Cent. Sch. Dist.*, 802 F. 2d 21 (2d Cir. 1986).

59. Michael Imber and Tyll van Geel, *Education Law* (New York: McGraw-Hill, 1993), 70.

60. "Introduction to the Establishment Clause," http://www.law.umkc.edu/faculty/projects/ftrials/conlaw/estabinto.htm, p. 1.

61. *Engel v. Vitale*, 370 U.S. 421 (1962); *S. D. of Abington Twp., Pa. v. Schempp*, 374 U.S. 203 (1963); *Lemon v. Kurtzman*, 403 U.S. 602 (1971).

62. Paul Zielbauer, "Judge Rules That School Curriculum Crossed Church–State Line," *New York Times*, 22 May 1999, A15.

EDUCATIONAL FINANCE: WHO PAYS?

© Peter Ciresa/Index Stock Imagery

FOCUS QUESTIONS

1. Why do we have a "free" educational system in the United States?
2. Why does the federal government contribute the least amount of money to education but still have a major voice in educational matters?
3. What are the history and nature of state support of education?
4. What determines a state's willingness or ability to finance education?
5. Why has the cost of education risen in recent years?
6. How and why have courts played a major role in how education is financed?

VIGNETTE ## IT TAKES *YOUR* MONEY TO RUN THE EDUCATIONAL SYSTEM

JACQUELINE: *Did you ask your parents if they would help you out with the plane fare to Florida for spring break?*

ROSALINE: *No, the timing was not right. Since I arrived at home on Friday, my mom and dad have been carrying on about our property tax bill. Dad says that it has increased 5% over last year, and last year's bill was outrageous. Mom, who usually tries to keep Dad calm on such matters, joined in on the harangue. She started talking about an article she read in the newspaper that said the mayor is considering proposing a sales tax to the city council to raise needed school revenue. The school board says that the town needs to engage in a major school construction and remodeling effort, and the mayor believes that a 1% city sales tax is the way to go. With that statement from Mom, Dad jumped back in, pointing out that he believes in paying his fair share because he remembers how his father used to carry on about how the federal government supported his education when he came home from World War II. He said he also remembered the importance of federal government support to special education that started in 1975 with the passage of PL 94-142 because it helped my Aunt Miriam, who has Down syndrome, to receive an education. But my father said that now it is to the point where he is paying more than his fair share.*

JACQUELINE: *What are you going to do? You are already working all the hours you can work while attending classes.*

ROSALINE: *I don't know. When they asked me about what I was doing in school, stupid me mentioned that I was learning about how education is financed. I mentioned how important it is that this country have a free education system. Wow! Why did I say that?! It got my father started again. He screamed, "What free education system? Haven't you been hearing Mom and me?! We pay big bucks each year to support the education in this town." My mom chipped in too. She said, "If the mayor has her way, not only will we pay a 5% sales tax to the state, most of which goes to education, but we will also pay an additional 1% sales tax, which will go to the town for education." Since then, and because I do listen to my folks, I have become confused about why we call it a "free" educational system.*

JACQUELINE: *I hear you. But nothing is really free. Remember that book by Jonathan Kozol, Savage Inequalities? You and I grew up with a good education because of where we lived, and because our parents could pay. Our schools, unlike many of those schools in Kozol's book, received money to get us books, good teachers, and programs. Kozol talked about how poor many schools in the United States are. It looks like money is really necessary for making a good school. But all of this is confusing. I don't know what to make of your parents' comments, Kozol's argument, and the idea that our educational system is "free"? We should ask Dr. Hill to clarify these issues.*

ROSALINE: *That's a good idea. Now, do you have a good idea about how I can get the additional $100 I need for my plane fare?*

EDUCATION IS A BIG FINANCIAL ENTERPRISE

Education in the United States is a multi-billion-dollar enterprise. Clichés associated with education expenditures are "Education in the United States is big business" and "Education is a major user of the nation's economic resources."[1] During the 2000–2001 school year, close to $420 billion was raised to support public education pre-kindergarten through grade 12. Current expenditures, excluding construction, equipment, and debt financing, exceeded \$368 billion.[2] Most states and local governments spend the major portion of their budget on education, including postsecondary education. Monies are spent for administration of schools, instruction, plant operations and maintenance, fixed charges, and other school services. Other costs to consider are those associated with summer school, adult education, community colleges, and interest on school debt. Exhibit 11.1 shows how such expenditures have increased from 1919 to 1996 and how much of the total is spent on each service. Exhibit 11.2 is a pie graph of current expenditures by function for the 2001–2002 school year.

Because parents and child care providers who send children to public school do not take the money directly out of their pockets to pay for education, the United States is said to have a "free" public education system. But is education really free in the United States? And how did we come to declare that we have a free educational system?

The Development of the Free Public Education Idea

Money for Jacqueline and Rosaline's public school education is not paid directly to the school by their parents. So, because no tuition is paid directly for public education, some argue that education is free. But as these two prospective teachers have discussed, citizens do pay property tax, sales tax, and state income tax, and these taxes are used to support the educational system. In reality, education is not free. Any U.S. student, regardless of whether his or her parents pay or do not pay property tax or any other tax, is entitled to attend school without having to pay. Children who are refugees from another country and children of migrant workers are entitled to a free public education. For example, the Office of Migrant Education (OME) in the U.S. Department of Education has as its purpose the improvement of teaching and learning for children of migrant workers. Its mission is based on the premise that children of migrant workers "although affected by poverty and the migrant lifestyle, can and should have the opportunity to realize their full academic potential."[3] This office works to ensure that children of migrant workers take advantage of our educational system.

The concept of a free public education system began during the early days of this country. During colonial times, providing an education was the responsibility of parents and the church. Through the early part of the 19th century, education in the United States was considered very much a private and religious undertaking. The responsibility of the local community to finance schools is an idea that members of the 13 colonies brought with them from Europe. As discussed in Chapter 9, "Governance of Education", in 1647 the general court of Massachusetts passed the Old Deluder Satan Act, which required every town to set up a school or pay a sum of money to a larger town to support education. This act required

EXHIBIT **11.1** **EXPENDITURES FOR ELEMENTARY AND SECONDARY EDUCATION, BY PURPOSE: 1919–1920 TO 1995–1996**

Purpose of Expenditures	1919–20	1929–30	1939–40	1949–50	1959–60	1969–70	1979–80	1989–90	1994–95[a]	1995–96
					Amounts in Thousands of Dollars					
Total expenditures	$1,036,151	$2,316,790	$2,344,049	$5,837,643	$15,613,255	$40,683,429	$95,961,561	$212,763,564	$279,000,318	$293,610,849
Current expenditures	864,396	1,853,377	1,955,166	4,722,887	12,461,955	34,853,578	87,581,727	191,205,902	249,026,087	259,804,398
Public elementary and secondary education	861,120	1,843,552	1,941,799	4,687,274	12,329,389	34,217,773	86,984,142	188,223,359	243,877,582	255,079,736
Administration	36,752	78,680	91,571	220,050	528,408	1,606,646	4,263,757	16,346,991[b]	19,877,848[b]	20,697,641[b]
Instruction	632,556	1,317,727	1,403,285	3,112,340	8,350,738	23,270,158	53,257,937	113,550,405[b]	150,556,118[b]	157,480,290[b]
Plant operation	115,707	216,072	194,365	427,587	1,085,036	2,537,257	9,744,785[c]	20,261,415[b]	24,542,922[b]	25,725,984[b]
Plant maintenance	30,432	78,810	73,321	214,164	422,586	974,941	—	—[c]	—[c]	—[c]
Fixed charges	9,286	50,270	50,116	261,469	909,323	3,266,920	11,793,934	—	—	—
Other school services[d]	36,387	101,993	129,141	451,663	1,033,297	2,561,856	7,923,729	38,064,548[b]	48,900,694[b]	51,175,821[b]
Other current expenditures										
Summer schools	—[e]	—[e]	—[e]	—[e]	13,263	106,481	24,753	2,982,543	5,148,505	4,724,662
Adult education[e]	3,277	9,825	13,367	35,614	26,858	128,778	—	—[f]	—[f]	—[f]
Community colleges	—[e]	—[e]	—[e]	—[e]	34,492	138,813	—	—[f]	—[f]	—[f]
Community services	—[d]	—[d]	—[d]	—[d]	57,953	261,731	572,832	—[f]	—[f]	—[f]
Capital outlay[g]	153,543	370,878	257,974	1,014,176	2,661,786	4,659,072	6,506,167	17,781,342	24,456,100	27,547,918
Interest on school debt	18,212	92,536	130,909	100,578	489,514	1,170,782	1,873,666	3,776,321	5,518,131	6,258,534

[a]Revised from previously published data.
[b]Data not comparable to figures prior to 1989–90.
[c]Plant operation also includes plant maintenance.
[d]Prior to 1959–60, items included under "other school services" were listed under "auxiliary services," a more comprehensive classification that also included community services.
[e]Prior to 1959–60, data shown for adult education represent combined expenditures for adult education, summer schools, and community colleges.
[f]Included under summer schools.
[g]Prior to 1969–70, excludes capital outlay by state and local schoolhousing authorities.
[i]Less than 0.05 percent.
— Data not available.

Purpose of Expenditures	1919–20	1929–30	1939–40	1949–50	1959–60	1969–70	1979–80	1989–90	1994–95[a]	1995–96
					Percentage Distribution					
Total expenditures	100.0	100.0	100.0	100.0	100.0	100.0	100.0	100.0	100.0	100.0
Current expenditures	83.4	80.0	83.4	80.9	79.8	85.7	91.2	89.9	89.3	88.5
Public elementary and secondary education	83.1	79.6	82.8	80.3	79.0	84.1	90.6	88.5	87.4	86.9
Administration	3.5	3.4	3.9	3.8	3.4	3.9	4.4	7.7[b]	7.1	7.0[b]
Instruction	61.0	56.9	59.9	53.3	53.5	57.2	55.5	53.4[b]	54.0	53.6[b]
Plant operation	11.2	9.3	8.3	7.3	6.9	6.2	10.2[c]	9.5[b]	8.8	8.8[b]
Plant maintenance	2.9	3.4	3.1	3.7	2.7	2.4	—[c]	—[c]	—[c]	—[c]
Fixed charges	0.9	2.2	2.1	4.5	5.8	8.0	12.3	—	—	—
Other school services[d]	3.5	4.4	5.5	7.7	6.6	6.3	8.3	17.9	17.5	17.4
Other current expenditures										
Summer schools	—[e]	—[e]	—[e]	—[e]	0.1	0.3	—[h]	1.4	1.8	1.6
Adult education[e]	0.3	0.4	0.6	0.6	0.2	0.3	—	—[f]	—[f]	—[f]
Community colleges	—[e]	—[e]	—[e]	—[e]	0.2	0.3	—	—[f]	—[f]	—[f]
Community services	—[d]	—[d]	—[d]	—[d]	0.4	0.6	0.6	—[f]	—[f]	—[f]
Capital outlay[f]	14.8	16.0	11.0	17.4	17.0	11.5	6.8	8.4	8.8	9.4
Interest on school debt	1.8	4.0	5.6	1.7	3.1	2.9	2.0	1.8	2.0	2.1

Note: Beginning in 1959–60, includes Alaska and Hawaii. Beginning in 1980–81, state administration expenditures were excluded from both "total" and "current" expenditures. Beginning in 1988–89, extensive changes were made in the data collection procedures. Because of rounding, details may not add to totals.

Source: U.S. Department of Education, National Center for Education Statistics, Statistics of State School Systems; and Common Core of Data surveys. (This table was prepared June 1998.)

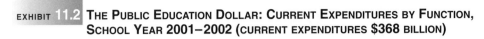

EXHIBIT **11.2** THE PUBLIC EDUCATION DOLLAR: CURRENT EXPENDITURES BY FUNCTION, SCHOOL YEAR 2001–2002 (CURRENT EXPENDITURES $368 BILLION)

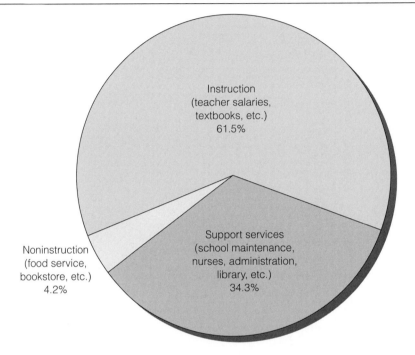

Source: U.S. Department of Education, National Center for Education Statistics, Common Core of Data (CCD), "National Public Education Financial Survey," 2001–02.

that masters, parents, and the people living in the town pay for schooling. Colonies raised money to pay for schools by charging tuition or selling and renting land. The idea of taxing people in the town, described in the Old Deluder Satan Act, put into place taxation as an idea to finance schools.

Massachusetts and Connecticut were in the forefront in recognizing the importance of education to the development of the United States and began taxing property as a way to support schools. Other states began putting in place a taxing scheme to support public education.[4] The popularity of a property tax to support schools grew, and by 1890, all states in the union had a tax-supported system of public education. However, each state interpreted its financial responsibility to education differently, a characteristic that continues today. Now, all states have constitutional provisions related to free public education.[5]

The creation of free common schools moved major control of education away from the church and parents and placed the responsibility with the state. Because financial commitment is often connected to influence, states, by assuming financial responsibility, established a strong voice in educational matters. Some citizens were reluctant to give up local control of education to the state, and this concern

EXHIBIT **11.3** THE PUBLIC EDUCATION DOLLAR: REVENUES BY SOURCE, SCHOOL YEAR
2001–2002 (TOTAL REVENUES $420 BILLION)

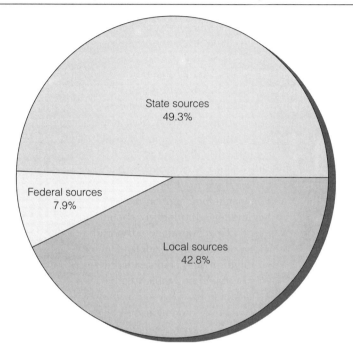

State sources
49.3%

Federal sources
7.9%

Local sources
42.8%

Source: Data reported by states to the U.S. Department of Education, National Center for Education Statistics, Common Core of Data
(CCD), "National Public Education Financial Survey," 2001–02.

led to the creation of local boards of education. The local board of education, it
was argued, was to function in the place of parents and the church.[6]

The opening vignette illustrated that although monies come from the state to
support public education, some monies also come from the local town and the
federal government. Exhibit 11.3 is a pie graph that shows sources of funding for
public education. Exhibit 11.4 gives you an idea of how much money the federal,
state, and local governments provide to each state and U.S. territory.

FEDERAL SUPPORT OF EDUCATION

Federal governance in education is often a contested issue. The amount of money
the federal government should contribute to education, the method used to fund
education, and the degree of influence that the federal government has over state
and local policies are issues of debate. This section begins with an overview of
how federal dollars are generally used in education and outlines when in our history federal financial support began.

EXHIBIT 11.4 REVENUES FOR PUBLIC ELEMENTARY AND SECONDARY SCHOOLS, BY SOURCE AND STATE, 1999–2000

State or other area	Total, in thousands	Federal			State		Local and intermediate		Private [a]	
		Amount, in thousands	Per student	Percent of total	Amount, in thousands	Percent of total	Amount, in thousands	Percent of total	Amount, in thousands	Percent of total
United States	**$372,864,603**	**$27,097,866**	**$578**	**7.3**	**$184,613,352**	**49.5**	**$152,368,480**	**40.9**	**$8,784,905**	**2.4**
Alabama	4,832,135	438,526	592	9.1	3,003,809	62.2	1,150,210	23.8	239,590	5.0
Alaska	1,359,764	209,975	1,562	15.4	801,151	58.9	312,174	23.0	36,464	2.7
Arizona	5,503,272	591,915	694	10.8	2,397,670	43.6	2,371,453	43.1	142,234	2.6
Arkansas	2,730,722	240,942	534	8.8	1,644,700	60.2	793,186	29.0	51,895	1.9
California	45,058,305	3,934,645	652	8.7	27,162,573	60.3	13,474,124	29.9	486,964	1.1
Colorado	5,044,275	271,353	383	5.4	2,083,173	41.3	2,458,683	48.7	231,066	4.6
Connecticut	6,065,482	251,564	454	4.1	2,437,888	40.2	3,220,255	53.1	155,774	2.6
Delaware	1,072,494	80,475	713	7.5	703,331	65.6	275,434	25.7	13,254	1.2
District of Columbia	875,619	179,021	2,319	20.4	†	†	688,396	78.6	8,202	0.9
Florida	16,946,014	1,429,395	600	8.4	8,381,170	49.5	6,528,299	38.5	607,150	3.6
Georgia	11,076,955	732,555	515	6.6	5,302,674	47.9	4,853,886	43.8	187,840	1.7
Hawaii	1,404,897	127,044	684	9.0	1,247,257	88.8	7,649	0.5	22,947	1.6
Idaho	1,472,070	113,611	463	7.7	899,725	61.1	433,034	29.4	25,700	1.7
Illinois	16,590,948	1,276,444	630	7.7	5,114,557	30.8	9,848,371	59.4	351,576	2.1
Indiana	8,427,757	443,820	449	5.3	4,407,729	52.3	3,334,419	39.6	241,789	2.9
Iowa	3,714,861	225,622	454	6.1	1,879,143	50.6	1,413,128	38.0	196,968	5.3
Kansas	3,408,634	213,344	452	6.3	2,127,046	62.4	977,081	28.7	91,163	2.7
Kentucky	4,330,619	433,290	668	10.0	2,628,338	60.7	1,172,764	27.1	96,227	2.2
Louisiana	4,907,761	562,977	744	11.5	2,427,118	49.5	1,810,617	36.9	107,049	2.2
Maine	1,811,965	144,465	690	8.0	807,656	44.6	819,576	45.2	40,269	2.2
Maryland	7,242,344	408,613	483	5.6	2,821,796	39.0	3,771,826	52.1	240,109	3.3
Massachusetts	9,260,130	488,986	503	5.3	4,048,287	43.7	4,580,966	49.5	141,891	1.5
Michigan	15,385,152	1,051,747	609	6.8	9,935,347	64.6	4,057,262	26.4	340,796	2.2
Minnesota	7,188,407	346,396	406	4.8	4,311,209	60.0	2,305,012	32.1	225,790	3.1
Mississippi	2,778,506	380,949	761	13.7	1,561,897	56.2	746,447	26.9	89,213	3.2
Missouri	6,665,304	439,526	481	6.6	2,507,804	37.6	3,456,589	51.9	261,384	3.9
Montana	1,101,615	134,315	852	12.2	491,890	44.7	428,637	38.9	46,773	4.2
Nebraska	2,216,656	152,084	528	6.9	812,386	36.6	1,132,316	51.1	119,870	5.4
Nevada	2,262,002	113,706	349	5.0	658,889	29.1	1,406,829	62.2	82,577	3.7
New Hampshire	1,559,653	68,391	331	4.4	869,992	55.8	584,283	37.5	36,988	2.4
New Jersey	14,882,015	582,043	451	3.9	6,124,074	41.2	7,884,738	53.0	291,160	2.0
New Mexico	2,240,777	315,325	972	14.1	1,602,483	71.5	275,360	12.3	47,609	2.1
New York	32,403,066	1,881,476	652	5.8	14,503,218	44.8	15,732,342	48.6	286,029	0.9

State or other area	Total, in thousands	Federal			State		Local and intermediate		Private [a]	
		Amount, in thousands	Per student	Percent of total	Amount, in thousands	Percent of total	Amount, in thousands	Percent of total	Amount, in thousands	Percent of total
North Carolina	8,797,269	625,846	491	7.1	5,949,172	67.6	2,004,692	22.8	217,559	2.5
North Dakota	749,936	96,945	860	12.9	301,279	40.2	311,972	41.6	39,741	5.3
Ohio	15,231,086	888,673	484	5.8	6,473,138	42.5	7,290,288	47.9	578,986	3.8
Oklahoma	3,705,393	368,669	588	9.9	2,164,236	58.4	977,794	26.4	194,695	5.3
Oregon	4,333,956	293,463	538	6.8	2,473,350	57.1	1,444,365	33.3	122,778	2.8
Pennsylvania	16,224,853	1,044,167	575	6.4	6,136,158	37.8	8,740,103	53.9	304,425	1.9
Rhode Island	1,448,205	83,799	536	5.8	597,832	41.3	747,026	51.6	19,548	1.3
South Carolina	4,917,485	412,054	618	8.4	2,595,941	52.8	1,719,083	35.0	190,408	3.9
South Dakota	865,041	108,264	826	12.5	298,364	34.5	433,361	50.1	25,051	2.9
Tennessee	5,378,527	485,024	529	9.0	2,463,997	45.8	2,275,894	42.3	153,612	2.9
Texas	28,657,019	2,469,744	619	8.6	12,654,437	44.2	12,855,259	44.9	677,579	2.4
Utah	2,579,092	192,462	401	7.5	1,527,108	59.2	796,260	30.9	63,262	2.5
Vermont	966,128	65,152	623	6.7	711,262	73.6	174,328	18.0	15,386	1.6
Virginia	8,749,757	494,794	436	5.7	3,723,104	42.6	4,368,072	49.9	163,787	1.9
Washington	7,573,768	550,202	548	7.3	4,812,763	63.5	1,958,804	25.9	251,999	3.3
West Virginia	2,294,744	217,540	745	9.5	1,415,246	61.7	631,257	27.5	30,701	1.3
Wisconsin	7,785,586	370,452	422	4.8	4,201,630	54.0	3,035,625	39.0	177,879	2.3
Wyoming	786,582	66,077	717	8.4	408,356	51.9	298,951	38.0	13,198	1.7
Outlying areas										
American Samoa	58,640	44,436	2,871	75.8	10,920	18.6	3,196	5.5	88	0.1
Guam	—	—	—	—	—	—	—	—	—	—
Northern Marianas	53,895	17,239	1,771	32.0	36,280	67.3	299	0.6	76	0.1
Puerto Rico	2,222,824	627,035	1,023	28.2	1,595,389	71.8	151	#	250	#
Virgin Islands	150,060	27,567	1,321	18.4	—	—	122,244	81.5	249	0.2

† Not applicable.
# Less than .05 percent
— Not available.
[a] Includes revenues from gifts, and tuition and fees from patrons.
Note: Excludes revenues for state education agencies. Detail may not sum to totals due to rounding.
Source: U.S. Department of Education, National Center for Education Statistics, Common Core of Data survey (This table was prepared April 2002.)

Where Do Federal Dollars Go?

Historically, the federal government's role in education has been threefold. First, it provides money to support educational research and, in the early years, it provided land for educational purposes. Second, the federal government disseminates information and provide advisory assistance to state and local governments. Finally, it distributes free surplus goods for school breakfast and lunch programs.

The federal government's financial support of education has waxed and waned over the years. In 1919–1920, the federal government contributed 0.3% of the total amount spent on education; in 1979–1980, the federal government contributed 9.8%, the highest percentage in the past 80 years; but in 1995–1996, the federal government's portion of the education dollar fell to 6.8%. Similarly, perhaps because of its increasing financial contribution, the federal government's role in education has become more influential over the decades. In 2003, federal spending for K–12 education was $49.9 billion; in 2004, it increased 6.4% to $53.1 billion.[7]

The passage of various pieces of legislation contributes to conceptions of the federal role in education. The **Northwest Ordinance** provided land grants to the states for education, the **Morrill Acts** provided land to establish colleges and money for agricultural experiments, the **G.I. Bill** provided monies to World War II veterans for education, and **Project Head Start** provides funds to support the education of preschool children. These are all examples of indirect but influential ways the federal government has supported and continues to support education. More recent examples include providing monies to conduct research for professional development, bilingual education, reading, science, and math. Results from these research efforts are often used to make educational policy decisions and to inform educational practice from Pre-K through college. Research data collected by the federal government are used to inform the general public and professionals in the field about the status of education in the United States, about effective research-based practices, and about how U.S. students compare to other students around the world. Much of the statistical and demographic information in educational publications and textbooks, such as the one you are now reading, come from government publications. If you are doing any type of educational research, you will most likely come across the federally funded National Center for Education Statistics (NCES). NCES publishes many reports, such as *The Condition of Education*, a publication of the U.S. Department of Education. You can find the website for NCES in the "Getting Connected" section of this chapter.

Periods of Federal Support

The many reasons for federal support of education may be more easily understood if viewed as periods of dual federalism, national federalism, and new federalism.[8] **Dual federalism** is when the state and federal governments share responsibility for much of education, including finances. During the first 150 years of the United States, the federal government took a passive and uncoordinated role in education, relying on states to fulfill their constitutional role of being in charge and financially supportive of their educational programs.

National federalism in education has been evident during times of national crisis, such as after the Great Depression, after *Sputnik*, and during the War on Poverty. During these times, the federal government has recognized that national action and national coordination of programs and activities are necessary to respond to and resolve national problems—problems that extend beyond the boundaries of state and local governments. Also, it is understood that federal dollars are needed to support these efforts.

New federalism has as its purpose reducing federal involvement in education, including reduction of educational funding. It was introduced during the presidency of Ronald Reagan in the 1980s and continued by President George H. W. Bush, who followed him. New federalism, according to Clark and Amiot, can be characterized as follows:

1. Diminution—reduction of federal expenditures in education
2. Deregulation—revocation of federal enforcement of rules and regulations
3. Decentralization—the belief that the ills of education are related to federal intrusion into what should be a state or local responsibility
4. Disestablishment—limiting the powers of the Department of Education and other federal agencies
5. Deemphasis—the sum of the preceding aspects, or the narrowing of the focus and scope of the federal role in education[9]

President Clinton moved away from the Reagan–Bush policy of "hands off" for the executive branch. In keeping with his declaration of being the "Education President," Clinton saw the need for federal involvement in the areas of finance and policy. President George W. Bush, in turn, heavily involved the executive branch in educational matters. His approach was to work in partnership with the states through his testing and accountability movement in education. Although Clark and Amiot would probably still place the Clinton and G. W. Bush presidencies within the period of new federalism, they would have to admit that the actions of these two presidents are not as clear examples of new federalism as were those of Reagan and G. H. W. Bush.

Need for Federal Dollars

Many school districts argue that receiving federal dollars is a must because the cost of education is constantly rising. For example, between 1977 and 1994, the number of students with disabilities attending public school increased 46%.[10] Federal dollars are continually necessary to help states and local districts comply with the Individuals with Disabilities Education Act (IDEA). This act mandates that all children have available to them a free and appropriate education designed to meet their needs in the least restrictive environment. Another example can be taken from *The Condition of Education 2003*, which reported that 16% of children in the United States live below the poverty level. Because children living in poverty may not come to school ready to learn, monies are needed to provide additional services (e.g., medical, dental, educational).[11]

The history and significance of the federal government's providing monies to states and local districts to support education are part of the American social fabric. A good deal of the money the federal government has provided over the years has been targeted to address equity issues. PL 94-142 focused on special education programs; Title IX dealt with gender equity; Head Start was aimed at helping preschoolers living in poverty "catch up" to their suburban counterparts; and the No Child Left Behind Act was to provide each student with a "level playing field" along with the resources (materials, schools, teachers, supplies, personnel) to achieve. The federal government has taken action to target issues dealing with equity in a very deliberate manner. The correction of historical injustices such as school segregation has often taken federal legislation or a Supreme Court decision. These decisions or pieces of legislation have come with implementation dollars attached. At the state and local level, the focus is on local issues, and there has always been the danger of focusing on the most advantaged so that they remain that way. Civil rights leaders tend to believe that the federal government will more actively and judiciously pursue issues of equity than will state and local officials. Because local officials have to deal with pressure from regional economic and political interests, they are often more susceptible to pressure from majority groups when making decisions that affect minority populations or interests.

Power, which is invested in the actions and interests of people who historically have had influence, becomes a motivation for resistance. Those in the majority can sometimes see change as a way of undercutting a way of life that places their needs first. Consequently, change disrupts or interrupts power that is invested in the actions and interests of people like themselves.

Methods of Federal Support

You will often hear people debate how the federal government should respond financially to equity issues as well as other educational issues. For example, providing federal funds to address the persistent achievement test score gap between urban students and their suburban counterparts has been the subject of intense discussion. Some believe that low achievement and equity issues are concerns of the residents of a state. The state is in a better position to know best how to help its people deal with the problem, and the state is also in a better position to know how to distribute federal dollars. Others believe that if low achievement and equity issues are left up to the states, these issues may not receive the attention they deserve. Those who favor this side of the argument reason that the federal government needs to provide guidelines for the money it gives to states. The federal government typically uses one of three ways to distribute money to state and local districts: general aid, categorical aid, and block grants.[12]

General Aid   **General aid** consists of unrestricted monies that are not earmarked for specific educational purposes but are available for general education purposes. For example, broadly improving elementary and secondary education is one use for such aid. General aid gives the state or local districts greater flexibility in the use of federal dollars. General aid also demands less accountability, reporting and evaluation. Many educators believe that general aid is needed to equalize funding because (1) states differ greatly in their ability to finance education,

(2) quality education programs should be available nationwide, and (3) quality education programs are necessary for the general welfare of the nation.

Categorical Aid **Categorical** aid is money that is designated for specific programs. Congress uses categorical aid to earmark federal dollars for programs such as safety education, career education, vocational education, and improved library resources. Critics of categorical aid claim that this method of funding provides Congress with a way to exercise control over education.

Block Grants **Block grants** are similar to categorical aid in that a block of federal money is given to a state or local school district. Although this money is usually designated for certain programs, states are given greater discretion regarding how the funds can be spent.

These three ways to distribute federal education money to the state and local level are sometimes used more by one political party than the other. The Democratic Party is often associated with categorical aid, and the Republican Party is more often associated with general aid and block grants. In Chapter 9, we discussed some of the educational programs of Democratic presidents Kennedy, Johnson, Carter, and Clinton. A good deal of their proposed legislation was in the form of categorical aid, more so than the proposed legislation of Republican presidents Reagan, G. H. W. Bush, and G. W. Bush, who believed more in block grants. For example, when President Carter was in office, he signed legislation to give categorical aid for bilingual education. Earmarking bilingual funds is in keeping with the idea of people with a particular interest appealing to the federal government for help. Earmarking funds for bilingual education would ensure that there would be funding to continue dual language programs for non–native English speakers who want to maintain their first language while learning English. President Reagan, upon taking office, had the money previously earmarked for bilingual education sent to the states in the form of block grants, meaning that the states were allowed to spend the money on bilingual education or another educational program that they deemed more important. As a result, the use of federal funds for bilingual education was stopped in several states; in others, bilingual education was continued but the allocation was greatly reduced. Advocates of bilingual education saw this reallocation as unfair. Citizens who supported the "English Only" movement saw it as a positive move that kept English as the primary and only language in United States.

Burrup, Brimley, and Garfield believe that although both categorical aid and block grants contribute significantly to education, the goals of education in the United States require the distribution of general aid from the federal government.[13] The method of distribution, however, is usually a secondary concern to the amount of money contributed by the federal government.

Jacqueline and Rosaline may come to agree with Rosaline's parents about the idea of a free education not being free, when they examine their payroll stubs. Their payroll stubs will show that they provide the federal government with money to support education and other federal programs. Every two weeks, they each have gross earnings of $474 as servers at La Casa Grande Restaurant. They pay a percentage of their earnings to both the federal and the state government. These payments, commonly known as withholding tax, are the ways the government collects income tax. Federal income tax is the primary source of federal government revenue, which is where much of the money comes from that the federal government sends to the states and local districts as general aid, categorical aid, or block grants.

STATE SUPPORT OF EDUCATION

Over the years, many states have struggled with how to come up with adequate funds to support their educational system and how to fund schools. This section will discuss the methods states use to fund the educational system, what affects a state's ability and willingness to finance education, how states fund local school districts, and where state educational dollars go. A brief history of when and how states began to support education opens the section.

When and How State Support Began

States' financial support of education dates back to the early history of the country. During those early days, much of the cost of operating schools was defrayed through services provided by town leaders to the schools and the teachers. Teachers often received room and board and fuel to heat the school in lieu of salary and other benefits.[14] It took many years for states to develop a system of financing schools as we know it today.

As each state was responsible for its own system of education, many different systems were used to finance education. A major source of finance was land, or the revenues received from the sale or renting of land—every 16th section—that many states received when the Northwest Ordinances of 1785 and 1787 were implemented. Gifts, tuition fees, and lotteries were other means of financing schools. As the population across the nation multiplied and the idea developed that education was necessary for democracy, states sought more reliable means of supporting education. Gifts, tuition, and lotteries did not provide enough funding and were not consistent, dependable sources of revenue. Taxation gradually became the preferred way of supporting schools. By 1890, all states had a tax-supported system of public education. At that time, state support ranged from 15% to 50% of the cost of public education.[15] Today, state support is approximately 50%.

Forms of Taxation and Lottery

In the United States, several different forms of taxation are used to collect monies to pay for education. The two largest sources of tax revenue used to support public education are the sales tax (approximately 33%) and the state income tax (approximately 32%). These two methods of taxation provide about two-thirds of state tax revenue. Other forms of taxation include corporate income taxes (about

7%) and excise taxes (about 16%). Some states also use revenue from state-run lotteries to support education.[16]

Sales Tax   The sales tax is a popular means of raising revenue because it is believed to be fair and impartial to all state residents. The state sales tax is usually applied to all items purchased except food and medicine, so that everyone pays the same amount of tax (a percentage of the purchase) regardless of income. Also, the sales tax is *elastic,* which means that the revenue derived from it tends to parallel economic conditions. The downside of using the sales tax is that state revenue is reduced when the state falls on hard times because people buy fewer items.[17]

Personal Income Tax   The second largest means of securing revenue for most states is the personal income tax. Only 10 states do not have a personal income tax. The personal income tax, like the sales tax, is considered a fair means of collecting revenue. It is elastic, in that it allows the state government to vary rates according to the economy, and is designed to consider both the taxpayer's income and ability to pay. Also, it takes into account the special circumstances of the taxpayer—such as number of dependents and medical expenses—and allows taxpayers to take tax deductions or credits. The personal income tax concept of fairness breaks down when taxpayers exploit the tax deduction process by falsely claiming benefits.[18]

Corporate Income Tax   A corporate income tax is a tax on companies, or on incorporated entities. A corporation is an organization that is considered to have its own legal identity separate from that of its legal owners, the shareholders. The corporate income tax has been a matter of controversy as some consider it a form of double taxation, taxing the corporation once and then taxing the shareholders who receive the dividends that are paid when there are profits. States often offer corporations various tax preferences as an inducement to do business in the state. Giving such breaks to companies is said to be a good idea because the revenue not earned from taxing, it is hoped, will be spent or invested within the state to encourage local development and create more jobs.[19] Most states get only a small percentage of their revenue for schooling from a corporate income tax.

Excise Tax   An **excise tax** is not like a personal or corporate income tax. It is called an expenditure tax and is based on the idea that consumption (purchases or expenditures) is "an index of a person's ability to pay."[20] The assumption is that those who have a greater ability to pay for things (more income) will in fact buy more. An excise tax is a selective sales tax levied on designated types of purchases such as motor fuels, tobacco, and alcoholic beverages. They are designed to raise revenues, though some are also used to discourage the consumption of certain goods. Excise taxes are often used for specific education mandates, whereas sales and other taxes go into general funds.[21]

State Lotteries and Gaming   Twenty states have earmarked a portion of state lottery proceeds for the support of education, and several states now have some type of casino or other gaming whose revenues provide support for education.[22] Many states instituted the lottery system based on the argument that the monies accrued would be for the purpose of education. This reasoning has not been found to be valid for the majority of states. Revenue from the lottery is being diverted to other social concerns, such as health care, social welfare, and road construction. In many states that have a lottery, the contribution to education is less than 2% of the total education budget.[23]

Critics of lotteries argue that it is not a fair means of raising educational revenue. They believe that lotteries and other forms of gaming prey on the poor, who are misled by lottery ads and the attention paid to winners into thinking that the odds of winning are better than they actually are. Researchers have found a higher percentage of lottery billboards and other ads in poor areas, inducing the poor to spend money on gambling rather than on basic necessities. In fact, a higher proportion of poor people spend a larger percentage of their annual income on gambling in those areas where it is legal.[24] Such actions divert monies from important areas of health and welfare, which can cause harm to people who need help the most and in the long run, critics argue, will cost taxpayers more.

Supporters of lotteries and gaming consider them a painless tax because people are not forced to gamble and they have fun while contributing to education and other civic projects. Supporters argue that numbers games and other forms of gambling have historically occurred illegally in our communities and the state might as well make some profit from people who choose to gamble. They add that to prevent people from gambling would be paternalistic and elitist.

What Factors Affect States' Ability or Willingness to Pay for Schooling?

How does the personal wealth of the citizens living in a state affect their ability to pay for education? How do the attitudes of a state's inhabitants toward education affect their willingness to pay? These two fundamental questions demand a response when discussing a state's ability and willingness to finance education.

Ability to Finance Schooling   States differ in the amount of money they provide to local school districts. The amount of money that a state contributes has a great deal to do with the personal wealth of the people living in the state. People with more money will usually pay a higher personal income tax and contribute more to sales tax revenue because they are better able and more inclined to purchase more, including expensive items. In addition, over the years, some states have tended to spend more per student (based on average daily attendance) than others (see Exhibit 11.5). In 2001–2002, per-pupil expenditures in Massachusetts, Connecticut, New York, New Jersey, and the District of Columbia were $10,232, $10,577, $11,218, $11,793, and $12,102, respectively. In the same year, Alabama, Idaho, Arizona, Mississippi, and Utah spent $6,029, $6,011, $5,964, $5,354, and $4,900 respectively.

Educational economists argue that it is misleading to use the amount of money that a state contributes to education as a yardstick to judge the state's commitment to education. Instead, educational economists argue that examining the percentage of total revenue that a state collects that is given to education is a better indicator. Although Utah spends less than $5,000 per student, it devotes 37.6% of state revenue to education. Although Alaska spends more than $9,500 per student, it devotes only 23.5% of its revenue to education.

EXHIBIT **11.5** STUDENT MEMBERSHIP AND CURRENT EXPENDITURES PER PUPIL IN MEMBERSHIP FOR PUBLIC ELEMENTARY AND SECONDARY SCHOOLS, BY FUNCTION AND STATE, SCHOOL YEAR 2001–2002

State	Fall 2001 student membership	Current expenditures per pupil in membership			
		Total	Instruction	Support services	Noninstruction
United States	47,647,972[a]	$7,734[a]	$4,755[a]	$2,657[a]	$322[a]
Alabama	737,190[a]	6,029[a]	3,692[a]	1,920[a]	417[a]
Alaska	134,358	9,563	5,617	3,627	319
Arizona	922,180	5,964	3,387	2,201	375
Arkansas	449,805	6,276	3,867	2,088	321
California	6,223,821[a]	7,434[a]	4,590[a]	2,564[a]	279[a]
Colorado	742,145	6,941	4,010	2,683	247
Connecticut	570,228	10,577	6,772	3,425	380
Delaware	115,560	9,284	5,719	3,132	433
District of Columbia	75,392	12,102	6,007	5,726	369
Florida	2,500,478	6,213	3,664	2,240	309
Georgia	1,470,634	7,380	4,714	2,287	380
Hawaii	184,546	7,306	4,417	2,481	409
Idaho	246,521	6,011	3,672	2,079	259
Illinois	2,071,391	7,956	4,733	2,964	259
Indiana	996,133	7,734	4,707	2,710	317
Iowa	485,932	7,338	4,373	2,432	533
Kansas	470,205	7,339	4,290	2,707	342
Kentucky	654,363	6,523	4,003	2,160	360
Louisiana	731,328	6,567	4,014	2,136	417
Maine	205,586	8,818	5,877	2,646	295
Maryland	860,640	8,692	5,408	2,872	413
Massachusetts	973,140	10,232	6,515	3,399	318
Michigan	1,730,668[a]	8,653[a]	4,968[a]	3,419[a]	266[a]
Minnesota	851,384	7,736	4,924	2,482	331
Mississippi	493,507	5,354	3,224	1,781	349
Missouri	909,792	7,135[b]	4,346[b]	2,472	317
Montana	151,947	7,062	4,374	2,393	295
Nebraska	285,095	7,741	4,879	2,313	549
Nevada	356,814	6,079	3,794	2,086	199
New Hampshire	206,847	7,935	5,148	2,534	253
New Jersey	1,341,656	11,793	6,975	4,454	364
New Mexico	320,260	6,882	3,848	2,716	318
New York	2,872,132	11,218	7,660	3,256	302
North Carolina	1,315,363	6,501	4,115	2,010	376
North Dakota	106,047	6,709	4,117	2,073	519
Ohio	1,830,985	8,069	4,683	3,109	277
Oklahoma	622,139	6,229	3,600	2,223	407
Oregon	551,480	7,642	4,490	2,896	256
Pennsylvania	1,821,627	8,537	5,318	2,894	325
Rhode Island	158,046	9,703	6,260	3,186	257
South Carolina	676,198	7,017	4,225	2,411	381
South Dakota	127,542	6,424	3,803	2,273	348
Tennessee	924,899[a]	5,959[a]	3,878[a]	1,789[a]	291[a]
Texas	4,163,447	6,771	4,089	2,343	339
Utah	484,677	4,900	3,197	1,435	268

(continued)

EXHIBIT **11.5** **Continued**

State	Fall 2001 student membership	Current expenditures per pupil in membership			
		Total	Instruction	Support services	Noninstruction
Vermont	101,179	9,806	6,314	3,217	275
Virginia	1,163,091	7,496	4,620	2,583	293
Washington	1,009,200	7,039[b]	4,189[b]	2,508	342
West Virginia	282,885	7,844	4,838	2,549	457
Wisconsin	879,361	8,634	5,351	3,005	277
Wyoming	88,128	8,645	5,263	3,096	285
Outlying areas					
American Samoa	15,897	2,906	1,377	845	683
Guam	31,992	—	—	—	—
Northern Marianas	10,479	4,438	3,692	501	245
Puerto Rico	604,177	3,563	2,506	694	363
Virgin Islands	18,780	5,716	3,620	1,870	226

—Not available.
[a]Prekindergarten students were imputed, affecting total student count and per pupil expenditure calculation. Prekindergarten students and tuition expenditures (included in Instruction) were imputed in Tennessee.
[b]Value affected by redistribution of reported expenditure values to correct for missing data items.
Note: Detail may not sum to totals because of rounding. National totals do not include outlying areas.
Source: Data reported by states to the U.S. Department of Education, National Center for Education Statistics, Common Core of Data (CCD), "National Public Education Financial Survey," 2001–02.

Willingness to Support Education. A state's commitment to education is also affected by its inhabitants' attitudes toward education. For example, a number of the states in the Southeast and Southwest are more politically conservative and spend less money on human services than the Northeast states. In 2001–2002, 11 of the 12 states in the Southeast, and all 4 states in the Southwest, spent less money on education per student than the national average ($7,734). In contrast, in the Northeast, all 11 states spent more money per student than the national average.

Willingness and ability to provide revenue to schools can work for or against educational equity. Providing revenue to teach the "three Rs," most state governments believe, is consistent with their constitutional obligation to provide education, and they are forthcoming with funding. However, providing revenue to make learning culturally relevant, inclusive, and gender fair in some cases tests the willingness of state officials to support educational equity. For example, the Education of All Handicapped Children Act (PL 94-142), passed in 1975 during the Ford administration, was initiated and came to fruition because local parent groups strongly lobbied their elected officials at the state and federal levels. Their actions have paid off, as federal funding for special education has increased from $100 million in 1975 to $4.99 billion in 2000.[25] This example of parent groups' advocating for PL 94-142 helps to show how citizen groups' exercise of power can affect state officials' attitudes toward providing education revenue.

How Do States Fund Local School Districts?

States commonly use one of five methods to finance public education: (1) the flat grant plan, (2) the foundation plan, (3) the power-equalizing plan, (4) the guaranteed tax base plan, and (5) the weighted-student plan. As you review these five plans, determine which one you would prefer to support and why. Ask a friend who is not in education which one he or she prefers and why.

Flat Grant Plan   The **flat grant plan** gives a fixed amount of money to a local district in accordance with the number of students who are in attendance. For example, the state may appropriate $3,000 for each of the 42,000 students in attendance ($126 million). The flat grant plan, the oldest way of funding local school districts, is also the most unequal because it gives very little consideration to students' special needs. For example, special education or bilingual students may require more money for additional teachers, supplies, and staff. Nor does the flat grant plan consider that some school districts may need more money because they are less wealthy than other school districts.[26]

Foundation Plan   The purpose of the **foundation plan** is to provide each school district with a level of finance necessary to guarantee each student access to a minimum level of educational services in terms of dollars per pupil as prescribed by the state. Each school district in the state receives this minimum funding regardless of its wealth or lack of wealth. The foundation plan is the most common approach found in school districts.[27]

Power-Equalizing Plan   In the **power-equalizing plan,** the state pays a percentage of the local school district's expenditures in inverse proportion to the wealth of the district. That is, wealthier districts receive less funding than poorer districts with this plan. School districts still maintain the right to establish their own expenditure levels. However, wealthier districts usually receive fewer matching state dollars. The power-equalizing plan is relatively new, and an increasing number of states are considering it.[28]

Guaranteed Tax Base Plan   In the **guaranteed tax base plan,** an assessed valuation, or amount a state wants to spend per student, is guaranteed to the local school district by the state. The money the state gives to each district is then determined by the difference between what the district raises per student and what the state guarantees per student. This plan is similar to the power-equalizing plan.[29]

Weighted Student Plan   In the **weighted student plan,** students' needs are weighted in accordance with their special characteristics (e.g., disabled, non–native English speaker) or special programs (e.g., vocational) to determine the cost of instruction per student. For example, a state may appropriate $5,000 for each student in the basic program but provide 1.3 times that amount ($6,500) for students in the vocational program and 1.5 times the basic amount ($7,500) for special education students.[30]

The decision about how to fund education is not as easy as it might sound, and state courts have had to get involved in educational funding in many communities. A specific example can illustrate the difficulty of funding decisions and the relationship between money, power, and diversity. The ongoing implementation of a 1985 New Jersey Supreme Court decision in the case of *Abbott v. Burke* provides such an example. The New Jersey Supreme Court ruled in 1973 that funding schools through property taxes discriminated against poor school districts. In response, the New Jersey Public School Education Act was passed in 1975. This act created a new formula for funding schools, but the legislature did not pass a tax increase to fund the act, so nothing changed. In 1976, the New Jersey Supreme Court ordered that all public schools be shut down for eight days until the legislature could come up with a funding plan. As a result, the first New Jersey state income tax was put into place. Still, not much changed in terms of equal access to a quality education and equal outcomes for students in New Jersey's poor school districts. Fed up with the continued underfunding of poor urban school districts in New Jersey, the Education Law Center filed a suit (*Abbott v. Burke*) in 1981 challenging the Public Schools Act as an inadequate solution to the issue of equitable funding. The suit came to a close in 1985 with the New Jersey Supreme Court ruling that to satisfy the state constitution, New Jersey must ensure that all children in poor districts receive an education that enables them to compete with their suburban counterparts.

Two governors have attempted to develop plans to provide equity for the 33 poorest school districts in New Jersey, but political fighting, money, and power have come into play in each attempt. Democratic Governor Florio introduced the Quality Education Act (1990), which included a $2.8 billion tax increase to pay for education and fund a budget deficit. He later amended the act to offer tax relief but was voted out of office over high taxes. Republican Governor Christie Todd Whitman (1996) developed a plan that would cap spending in suburban districts at a minimum level but ended up signing into law a plan without the caps. By 1997, the New Jersey Supreme Court agreed with the Education Law Center that the state seemed unable or unwilling to come up with an equity plan and ordered state officials to increase funding to equalize funding between urban and suburban districts. This was the beginning of a serious financial commitment to the 33 poorest school districts in the state. To date the Education Law Center has obtained seven *Abbott* follow-up rulings seeking compliance with the original court mandate.

Many positive changes have been made in New Jersey's *Abbott* districts as a result of increased revenue. For example, free preschool is now available for all young children in the *Abbott* communities, and there has been a significant budget commitment for new school building and refurbishing of outdated facilities. But not much has changed in traditional markers of quality such as standardized test scores and dropout rates. You may wonder why. It should not come as a surprise that New Jersey is a state with one of the largest gaps between rich and poor. Despite extra funding, persistent problems such as high student mobility, secondary schools with more than 1,500 students, and crumbling facilities cannot be rectified overnight. Additionally, the parents in wealthier school districts began to supplement their state allocations by raising private funds. Most disturbing is a growing resentment in districts populated by working poor that are not economically disadvantaged enough to be among the poorest 33 whose schools receive funding under the *Abbott* rulings. This resentment stems from the fact that in today's difficult economy, the working poor feel neglected by the state. As the economy tightens, there appears to be very little collective concern for everybody's children. The wealthy are supplementing their state allocation to ensure a quality education for their children, the politicians are concerned about constituencies who vote (often not those in the poorest areas), and the working poor are struggling to meet their basic needs. It is incumbent upon state and local leaders to unite people to coalesce around the common good and provide an excellent education for all children.

Where Do State Funds Go?

The money states appropriate to local school districts is spent in three major areas: instruction (e.g., teacher salaries, curriculum materials); support services (e.g., teacher aides to meet the needs of special education students); and capital outlay (e.g. computers, new school construction, facilities renovation). The decisions that local school districts make about how money is spent are influenced by such factors as organizational structure of the district, the number of administrators and district office personnel, salaries, and state goals. For example, the push toward curriculum standards has required that school districts devote significant amounts of money to professional development.

The goal of school funding plans is to provide financial equity for all students. However, the amount of money appropriated to instruction, support services, and capital is influenced by the income of the people living in the district.

Jacqueline and Rosaline will come to realize that states finance education in many ways and that being a citizen of a state requires paying for education in a variety of ways. They can look at their pay stubs or at their shopping receipts to see the different taxes they are paying to contribute to education. They can also attend to the ways that education is discussed in the newspapers and even within their own families, and to people's opinions on what they are willing or able to pay. During their student teaching semester, they will experience the result of educational finances at the local level, and we now turn our discussion to local support of education.

LOCAL SUPPORT OF EDUCATION

Local school districts are responsible for paying their share of the cost of schooling. Generally, local school districts are second to the state in the financial contribution made to education. We learned from Rosaline's father in the opening vignette that property taxes are a source of revenue for local school districts. Another source of revenue for local school districts is the money received from user fees. These funding sources are described in this section.

Property Tax

The **property tax** is the major source of money for most school districts (95%).[31] Property taxes are determined by the *market value* of the property—the price for which the property could probably be sold. The property is given an *assessed value* based on a predetermined index or ratio, such as one-fourth or one-third of the market value. For example, a property with a market value of $200,000 might have an assessed value of $50,000. The assessed value is always less than the market value. The local tax rate, expressed in *mills* (one-thousandths of a dollar), is then applied to the assessed value. Thus, a tax rate of 25 mills amounts to $25 for each $1000 of assessed value.

In spite of the extent to which property taxes are used for educational funding, there are several problems with using it as a way to raise revenue for schools. First, people with very similar types of property may pay different taxes because assessment practices and valuation procedures are not standardized. Second, the taxes assessed may not be affordable for everyone. Especially as people retire and start to live on fixed incomes, they sometimes have difficulty keeping up with property tax increases. In some instances, people have to sell their homes because they cannot afford the property taxes. Third, the property tax is not as elastic as some of the other taxes, such as the sales tax, because it is not as responsive to changing economic conditions. Assessments or reassessments of property may not take place often enough to keep up with economic changes. In some local school districts, property may be reassessed every two years; in others, it may be only every three or four years. If the property value has risen since the last reassessment, the local district will lose money. If the property value has gone down since the last reassessment, the property owner may be paying too much.

User Fees

Fees charged to people who use a school facility (e.g., gymnasium, classroom) or services (e.g., bus service) are called **user fees.** School districts find it financially rewarding to rent out school building space to organizations for events. These fees are additionally important because they may serve to bring into the school community people who do not normally visit the school.

Funding Concepts

Two funding concepts govern educational finances: educational needs and ability to pay. In combination, these two concepts determine local **fiscal capacity.** Usually, fiscal capacity is expressed as a district's monetary resources or tax base divided by a measure of the district's educational need for those resources.[32]

Educational need can be defined as the demand placed upon a district's resources available to finance education. This demand is related to the number of students within a district (usually weighted for differences in student characteristics), the cost of educating different groups of students, and other educational cost factors that are beyond the control of the district.[33] As students have different characteristics, some need more educational services and therefore require more of the district's education dollars. Most states, therefore, use a weighting procedure to account for differences in the cost of educating different groups of students. Weighting procedures, as noted previously, adjust the student count to provide a better reflection of a school district's educational needs. Most weighting procedures consider differences in grade level and student ability.

Ability to pay, according to the American Education Finance Association, is directly related to the fiscal resources available to the local school district. As most local school districts use property taxes to finance education, the measure of a district's wealth is monies that can be assessed in property valuation. Thus, most states take into account the local district's ability to finance education when appropriating funds.

It may seem like a relatively simple idea that a family's wealth influences the ability to fund schools at the local level, but another New Jersey example will demonstrate how complicated the issue is in some areas where communities are small and have to share resources. Again, you will see how power, diversity, and money play an important role in educational decisions.

New Jersey has both urban and rural areas, some highly populated and others containing fewer families. In communities where the number of students is small, it is common to share a high school in order to reduce costs to individual towns. In 1960, Manchester Regional High School was opened to accommodate students from three communities: Haledon, North Haledon, and Prospect Park. At this time, each community paid a fixed amount per student for the cost of running the regional high school. You may recall, from our earlier discussion of New Jersey's attempt to equalize educational outcomes through increased funding for the poorest districts, that in 1975 the formula for funding schools was redesigned and based upon property values and per capita income. By this time, the three communities that shared a high school were becoming demographically different. North Haledon, the wealthiest, ended up contributing the most to the regional high school. The ethnicity and income levels of the three communities continued to change. As the 2004 school year approached, North Haledon was to pay 43.8% of the high school's budget although the number of students it sent to Manchester made up only 25% of the student body. Prospect Park, the poorest of the three districts, sent the most students but paid only 19.8% of the school budget.

A group of citizens in North Haledon decided that they had paid enough and rallied support for leaving the regional high school. With them would go their state dollars. They filed an appeal, which eventually turned into a lawsuit, asking permission to leave Manchester Regional High School and send their children to a high school in another, less diverse community where they would not be required to carry such a large percentage of the tax burden. Many heated community meetings took place, at which the pro-secession citizens of North Haledon were accused of racism. Public comments were made that caused many to believe that the real reason some in North Haledon wanted to leave was because they did not want their children to go to school with students of color from Prospect Park. A group of citizens formed to support keeping North Haledon in Manchester Regional, arguing that if North Haledon students left, the diversity balance would be upset and all of the students would suffer from an education that lacked diverse ideas and perspectives. The New Jersey Supreme Court agreed with the diversity argument and ruled to prevent North Haledon from leaving Manchester Regional High School. However, the court ordered the New Jersey Commissioner of Education to work with the mayors and school boards in the three communities to come up with an equitable funding formula for the three districts.

INCREASING COST OF EDUCATION

Rosaline's parents are angry not because they have to contribute to paying for the cost of education in their community, but because the cost of education keeps increasing. As a result, they have to pay a higher property tax. The major reason why the cost of education has gone up, many would say to Rosaline's parents, is to meet a national goal of significantly upgrading the quality of education students receive.

In 1983, with the publication of *A Nation at Risk,* a national movement was set off to improve the quality of education. Federal, state, and local governments argued that education from Pre-K through college levels needed to be improved. Political and business leaders claimed that education was the key to state and national economic well-being, and essential to the U.S. position in the world marketplace. The nation became galvanized over the notion that its educational system, as described in *A Nation at Risk,* was a "rising tide of mediocrity." Thus, education became more of a policy issue, and as the voices of business leaders and politicians gained influence, the voices of educators lost influence, including teachers who waited anxiously to see what the reforms would include and how the reforms would affect them.

In order to improve education, states shifted their concern from issues of educational equity, such as providing revenue for students with special needs, to allocating more money to improve curriculum, instruction, and student achievement. State support of education rose to 50% of the total cost, making states the largest of the three levels of government financing education. However, with these increases in funding, business and political leaders expected that education would be reformed. Educational reform came to be symbolized by increased accountability and higher student achievement. Mandatory standardized testing at regular intervals, such as 3rd, 8th, and 11th grades, became commonplace. Exit exams for high school graduation were implemented in most states. Tests and test taking received additional dollars.

The passage of PL 94-142 (the Education for All Handicapped Children Act) in 1975 and its reauthorization in 1997 as the Individuals with Disabilities Education Act increased attention to educating all students with special needs. The current Individual with Disabilities Education Improvement Act (IDEIA) governs the education of students with a variety of disabilities, including metal retardation; serious emotional disturbances; autism; brain injuries; speech, hearing, and visual impairments; and physical handicaps. Exhibit 11.6 gives the percentage distribution of disabled persons 6 to 21 receiving education services. As noted previously, inclusion has increased the cost of schooling.

EXHIBIT **11.6** PERCENTAGE DISTRIBUTION OF DISABLED PERSONS 6 TO 21 YEARS OLD RECEIVING EDUCATION SERVICES FOR THE DISABLED, BY EDUCATIONAL ENVIRONMENT AND TYPE OF DISABILITY: UNITED STATES AND OUTLYING AREAS, 1999–2000 AND 2000–2001

Type of disability	All environments	Regular school, outside regular class			Separate public school facility	Separate private school facility	Public residential facility	Private residential facility	Homebound/ hospital placement
		Less than 21 percent	21–60 percent	More than 60 percent					
					1999–2000				
All persons, 6 to 21 years old	100	47.3	28.3	20.3	1.9	1	0.4	0.3	0.5
Specific learning disabilities	100	45.3	37.9	15.8	0.4	0.3	0.1	0.1	0.2
Speech or language impairments	100	87.5	6.7	5.3	0.2	0.2	#	#	0.1
Mental retardation	100	14.1	29.5	50.5	4.1	0.9	0.4	0.2	0.4
Emotional disturbance	100	25.8	23.4	32.8	7.5	5.5	1.5	2	1.5
Hearing impairments	100	40.3	19.3	24.5	5.4	1.6	8	0.6	0.2
Orthopedic impairments	100	44.4	21.9	27.7	3.5	0.7	0.1	0.1	1.6
Other health impairments	100	44.9	33.2	17.2	0.9	0.7	0.1	0.2	2.7
Visual impairments	100	49.1	19.5	17.7	4.6	1.1	6.5	0.9	0.6
Multiple disabilities	100	11.2	18.8	43	15	6.8	1.3	1.4	2.5
Deaf-blindness	100	14.8	10.1	39.7	13.8	3.4	12.2	4.2	1.7
Autism	100	20.7	14.5	49.9	7.9	5.4	0.2	1.1	0.5
Traumatic brain injury	100	31	26.6	31.6	2.6	4.6	0.4	0.9	2.3
Developmental delay	100	44.7	29.7	24.2	0.8	0.2	#	#	0.3
					2000–2001				
All persons, 6 to 21 years old	100	6.5	9.8	19.5	1.9	1.1	0.4	0.3	0.5
Specific learning disabilities	100	44.3	40.3	14.4	0.3	0.3	0.1	0.1	0.2
Speech or language impairments	100	85.6	8.4	5.1	0.2	0.6	#	#	0.1
Mental retardation	100	13.2	29.1	51.7	4.2	0.9	0.3	0.2	0.4
Emotional disturbance	100	26.8	23.4	31.8	7.7	5.4	1.6	2	1.3
Hearing impairments	100	42.3	20	22.5	4.4	1.9	8.3	0.6	0.2
Orthopedic impairments	100	46.4	23.4	24.3	3.5	0.7	0.1	0.1	1.6
Other health impairments	100	45.1	33.9	16.7	0.8	0.8	0.2	0.2	2.4
Visual impairments	100	50.5	20.1	16	4.7	1.2	5.9	0.9	0.7
Multiple disabilities	100	12.1	16	45.5	14.6	6.9	1.3	1.3	2.3
Deaf-blindness	100	18.1	9.9	34.2	14.5	4.5	12.5	4.4	1.9
Autism	100	24.3	15.3	46.4	7.2	5.2	0.3	0.9	0.4
Traumatic brain injury	100	32.3	27.9	29.4	2.8	4.2	0.3	0.9	2.2
Developmental delay	100	46.4	29.9	22.3	0.6	0.4	#	0.1	0.2

Rounds to zero.

Note: Data by disability condition are only reported for 6- to 21-year-old students. Detail may not sum to totals due to rounding.

Source: U.S. Department of Education, Office of Special Education and Rehabilitative Services, *Annual Report to Congress on the Implementation of The Individuals with Disabilities Education Act*, and unpublished tabulations. (This table was prepared July 2003.)

The cost of schooling, as of most other things in life, will continue to increase. The U.S. economy and our place in the world order are influenced by global forces that demand schools do a better job of educating our young people. Business leaders require this so that our economic markets remain strong and competitive. Advocates for global peace require this so that our citizens recognize that we live in a world characterized by diverse people, viewpoints, and ways of living and working. These dual requirements of competition and cooperation in a global society will necessitate that the U.S. educational system continue to better itself—and this requires money.

COURTS AND EDUCATIONAL FINANCES

In Chapter 10, "Teachers' and Students' Rights and Responsibilities," we discussed court cases as a major influence on curriculum, instruction, and teacher and student behavior. Court decisions have also had a significant impact on educational finances. The series of influential court cases that are still having an impact on educational finance today began with the *Kalamazoo*[34] case in 1874. The outcome of this case put in place a legal system of taxation to finance secondary education.

In 1954, the Supreme Court in *Brown v. Board of Education*[35] decided that two separate systems of education, one for Blacks and one for Whites, should not be financed. Thus, the financing of a dual education system in the South was stopped. *Serrano v. Priest*[36] in 1971 corrected the funding inequities based on property tax between school districts in California. The California Supreme Court discovered that students who lived in school districts where property values were low received less educational funding. The court held that because education of students is "a fundamental interest" of the state, a system of educational finance that works against that interest is unconstitutional. This ruling was a landmark decision because it was the first time a higher court ruled against a state's use of a particular system for funding education.

San Antonio Independent School District v. Rodriguez[37] in 1973 had the entire educational community buzzing because the U.S. Supreme Court ruled in a 5-to-4 decision that education is not a fundamental interest because it is not a right "explicitly or implicitly guaranteed by the Constitution." The Court held that although some school districts received a lower-quality education than others, that was not a constitutional issue. Thus, the Supreme Court ruled against the concept of wealth-based inequalities and returned the financial problem to the states to decide.

In *Serrano II,* however, the California Supreme Court asserted "independent vitality," or the state's right to make its own decision (thereby disagreeing with the results in the *Rodriguez* case). The California Supreme Court thus became the first state supreme court to hold that unequal educational opportunities among school districts are unconstitutional under the equal protection provisions of a *state* constitution, unaided by the Fourteenth Amendment of the U.S. Constitution.[38]

In 2000, the Supreme Court let stand the rule that special education services could be provided to students in religious schools, by not hearing the appeal in *Board of Education of Central Community School District 301 v. Scionti.* In this case, an Oregon family challenged the state rule barring the provision of special education services on the premises of religious schools. The family, along with religious liberty groups, argued that the state's action was violating its First Amendment right to free exercise of religion.[39]

We have told you about the ongoing battles in New Jersey to equalize educational outcomes through funding in the seven *Abbott v. Burke* decisions handed down by the New Jersey Supreme Court. The final landmark decision that is extremely important for you to know about was handed down in 2001 by New York Supreme Court Judge Leland DeGrasse in the case *Campaign for Fiscal Equity v. State of New York.* In this decision, Judge DeGrasse declared the state of New York school-funding system unconstitutional for failing to provide the students of New York City with a "sound basic education." What is especially interesting about this case and its appeal is that the courts took it upon themselves to define what constitutes a "sound basic education." Judge DeGrasse ruled that high school graduates "must be able to evaluate complex issues that may arise in jury service or voting and they must also be able to obtain and hold competitive employment."[40] Many people across the county applauded Judge DeGrasse's emphasis on employment and citizenship.

The case got complicated when, on appeal, a court determined that a sound basic education consisted of "the basic literacy, calculating, and verbal skills necessary to enable children to eventually function productively as civic participants capable of voting and serving on a jury."[41] The appellate court noted that for a child to *eventually* function productively, skills equivalent to an eighth-grade education were all that was required. However, this appellate court decision was overturned in a 4-to-1 decision in which Judge Judith Kaye wrote that "students require more than an eighth grade education to function productively as citizens."[42]

Judge DeGrasse's original decision was upheld, but by the end of 2004, no equitable funding solution for the New York City public schools had been reached by the state of New York. Again, politics, money, and power caused legislators and Governor George Pataki to engage in stall tactics, delays, and outright opposition to the idea of providing the New York City public schools with enough money to offer students an education for "employment and citizenship." The lawsuit was brought by the Campaign for Fiscal Equity, a group dedicated to ensuring that all children in New York receive a quality education. Grass-roots groups made up of teachers, parents, community leaders, labor union officials, and businesspeople such as the Alliance for Quality Education supported the lawsuit and Judge DeGrasse's ruling. Despite all this, a collective concern for the education of New York City children on the part of many politicians and citizens was absent from the discussion.

FINDING A VOICE

The school needs more money, Alberto thought to himself as he headed for the school board meeting. The board secretary had scheduled 30 minutes on the agenda for him to discuss the results of a needs assessment survey. Alberto was chair of the committee to assess teachers' needs at his school. The district had been losing a number of teachers to surrounding school districts, so the board had established several district and school-based committees to identify the causes of teachers' leaving and to offer recommendations to eliminate the problem. The local board of education had requested that each school have the teachers identify their three top instructional needs as part of the district's "Support the Teacher" program that they had put in place to demonstrate their high regard for the teachers in the district and their willingness to help them.

Results of the needs assessment survey conducted by Alberto's committee identified the teachers' three top priorities as (1) up-to-date computers and software for each class at all grade levels; (2) renovation of the teachers' workroom, including new furniture; and (3) an upgrade in science education across the board, including the installation of three science labs, the hiring of three teachers with certification in science, and new science materials and equipment.

When the secretary of the school board called his name, Alberto somewhat nervously moved toward the microphone, introduced himself, identified the members of his committee, and began the report. He told the board about the three needs that the teachers had identified and then added, "The reason teachers are leaving this district is that over the years we have had very little involvement in the decision-making process, especially concerning curriculum and instructional practices. Teachers realize that the national and state governments, along with professional organizations, are pushing hard for better schools. Many argue that standards and accountability will lead to a better education for our students and thus increase their success in the job market. However, this district has gone overboard, not just in their demand that teachers follow this philosophy, but in their authoritative manner of making certain that teachers adhere."

Alberto continued, "Teachers want excellent schools too, and they take pride in the U.S. position in the world. But we are equals in this effort, not servants to this cause. One teacher captured the feeling of the other teachers when she made the point that there is a need for power to circulate more equally among teachers, administrators, the local board, and parents. For many years, teachers have only known a top-down form of school governance. In many teachers' opinion, the local board is not assertive in requesting additional revenue from the town to support increasing educational needs and in seeking additional state and federal educational dollars."

Alberto continued, "Teachers are aware that additional revenue from the town will mean an increase in property tax, but they also know, as the *Conditions of Education* note, 'No one can deny the importance of money to build schools, hire teachers, buy textbooks, and otherwise acquire the resources needed to create a safe and supportive learning environment.'" As Alberto spoke, the passion and concern that a number of the teachers had voiced to his committee during the interviews was coming out in his presentation. This passion, along with what he was saying, caused all of the seven board members to focus intensely on him. This board was not used to hearing that they were not doing their job, and they grew increasingly uncomfortable as Alberto spoke.

Upon the completion of the report, the chair of the board said, "Mr. Rodriguez, the board wishes to thank you and your committee for such a fine report. Do you have any further comments?" Alberto had not prepared himself for such a general question from the chair. He hesitated a minute and then heard himself saying, "When should the teachers expect some action on the needs we have identified? You identified the problem you want information on, put in place a committee structure, and scheduled a time for the committees to report to you. May the teachers suggest a time when they would like to hear from the board on their report?"

The faces of the board members reflected surprise and some board members nonverbally communicated a degree of annoyance with Alberto's statement. However, they kept calm, observing that the news reporters welcomed this spirited moment. The chair of the board, looking toward the other members for agreement with his reply, said, "Mr. Rodriguez, if you and the chairs of the committees from the other schools come to the board meeting next month, this board will be prepared to give you our agenda for action. It will include priorities and expected start-up dates, along with a plan for more teacher involvement." Alberto replied, "Mr. Chair, we will be here, and I believe that many, many teachers will come out to hear this good news. Thank you!"

Who pays for education? Everyone does, in one way or another—maybe through federal and state income taxes, sales and property taxes, the purchase of a lottery ticket, or some other form of tax, and maybe through a combination of several taxes, but we all pay. Important to paying is working out a fair way to assess what people need and ought to pay, and making certain that those schools and students who may need a little more financial assistance receive it. After all, it benefits everyone in the community.

Summing Up

The cost of education in the United States runs into the hundreds of billions of dollars. Teachers' salaries, instructional materials and equipment, school building construction, and the expanded use of technology make education a big budget item.

The idea of free public education started in early colonial times. It is a concept, like freedom and liberty, that came with the colonists from Europe. Early ordinances such as the Old Deluder Satan Act established the belief in financial support to schools. All three levels of government—federal, state, and local—financially support public education. The federal government provides about 7% of the educational dollars in the United States. From colonial times when land scrip was used to support education, to later times with the establishment of West Point and Annapolis, to current monies to fund numerous programs from PreK through college, the federal government has supported education in the United States.

Education is the responsibility of the state, and historically states have been active in financing education. During the early years of the country, states experimented with various ways to fund education such as charging tuition and selling or renting land. Early methods did not prove successful, so states gradually moved to using a sales tax. Presently, much of the money that states use to support education comes from state sales taxes. In some states, money from lotteries and personal income taxes are also used to support education. A state's willing-ness to support education is not always connected to its ability to pay. In some states, the attitude of the citizens toward education influences the amount of money appropriated to schools. The state contribution to the education dollar has increased over the years. States currently provide 50% of the educa-tional dollars.

The money from property tax assessed in a local town is used to pay the local district portion of the education bill. The nation's courts have played an influential role in determining how the educational dollars will be spent. Cases such as *Serrano v. Priest*, which corrected funding inequities based on property tax, and *San Antonio Independent School District v. Rodriguez*, which ruled that educa-tion is not a right "explicitly or implicitly guaranteed by the Constitution," still influence how educational dollars are spent today.

KEY TERMS

block grants	Morrill Acts
categorical aid	national federalism
dual federalism	new federalism
excise tax	Northwest Ordinance
fiscal capacity	power-equalizing plan
flat grant plan	Project Head Start
foundation plan	property tax
general aid	user fees
G.I. Bill	weighted student plan
guaranteed tax base plan	

QUESTIONS FOR REFLECTION

1. If you had 10 minutes to speak to Rosaline's parents on behalf of the federal, state, or local government about their sentiments toward paying more money to support education, what would you say to them?
2. Do you believe that the federal government should contribute more money to education? If so, should it also have more control over how the educa-tional dollars are spent?
3. Do you support the establishment of a lottery system to help finance educa-tion? Why or why not?
4. Which decision, *Serrano v. Priest* or *San Antonio Independent School Dis-trict v. Rodriguez*, do you believe should direct how education is funded? Why?
5. To what extent do you believe that citizens' liberal or conservative attitudes should influence the way a state supports education?

ACTIVITIES

1. Using recent issues of *The Condition of Education*, prepare a report that considers the relationship between cost and quality of education.
2. Working with at least three other students, examine the property tax bills of several homeowners and prepare a 10-minute argument to support an increase or decrease in their bill.
3. Interview a member of the local school board or a member of the town finance committee on education to ascertain that person's opinion on how education is funded at the federal, state, or local level.
4. Interview administrators responsible for directing one or more of the school district's special needs programs and inquire about the adequacy of financial support.
5. Determine historically, or in present conditions, how inequities in education for some lead to society's paying a higher cost later.
6. Create a chart that compares the per pupil spending of five demographically different school districts in your state. How do you account for those differences? Now look at the standardized test scores of those districts. Do you seen any difference in test score results? Why or why not?

GETTING CONNECTED

National Center for Education Statistics http://www.nces.ed.gov	Describes developments in school finance and focuses on the estimates of disparities and analysis of their causes.
Alliance for Quality Education http://www.allianceforqualityeducation.org	The AQE is a nonprofit group of parents, child advocates, teachers, clergy, labor leaders, business leaders, and others who believe in "fair funding and smarter spending" to support better schools in New York. The AQE mission is to see that every child gets a quality education from preschool through high school.
http://welfareinfo.org/school.htm	A review of key cases about school finance litigation.
Campaign for Fiscal Equity http://www.cfequity.org	The CFE is an organization dedicated to fighting unequal educational policies and procedures in the New York City area, especially as they relate to funding.
Education Law Center http://www.edlawcenter.org	The ELC advocates on behalf of New Jersey public school children for access

to an equal and adequate education under federal and state laws. The ELC uses the courts when necessary to ensure equitable funding for New Jersey's low-income students.

http://www.ncrel.org   A call for and look at reform of school finance including site-based management.

SUGGESTED RESOURCES

Alexander, Kern, and Richard Salmon. *Public School Finance.* Needham Heights, MA: Pearson Education, 1995.
Jones, T. *Introduction to School Finance.* New York: Macmillan, 1996.
Kozol, J. *Savage Inequalities: Children in America's Schools.* New York: Crown Publishers, 1991.

NOTES

1. Percy E. Burrup, Vern Brimley, Jr., and Rulon R. Garfield, *Financing Education in a Climate of Change,* 6th ed. (Needham Heights, MA: Allyn and Bacon, 1996), 33.
2. U.S. Department of Education, National Center for Education Statistics, *Revenue and Expenditures for Public Elementary and Secondary Education: School Year 2001–2002* (Washington, DC: U.S. Government Printing Office, 2004).
3. Office of Migrant Education, www.ed.gov/offices/OESE/MEP/aboutus.html, p. 1.
4. Burrup, Brimley, and Garfield, *Financing Education,* 175.
5. Allen R. Odden and Lawrence O. Picus, *School Finance: A Policy Perspective* (New York: McGraw-Hill, 1992), 8.
6. Ibid., 9.
7. U.S. Department of Education, "2003 Budget Release," retrieved 3 February 2003 from http://www.ed.gov/news/pressreleases/2003/02/02032003.html
8. Fred C. Lunenburg and Allan C. Ornstein, *Educational Administration: Concepts and Practices,* 2nd ed. (Belmont, CA: Wadsworth, 1996), 233.
9. David Clark and Mary A. Amiot, "The Reagan Administration and Federal Education Policy," cited in Lunenburg and Ornstein, *Educational Administration,* 234.
10. U.S. Department of Education, National Center for Education Statistics, *The Condition of Education 1996* (Washington, DC: U.S. Government Printing Office, 1996), 140.
11. U.S. Department of Education, National Center for Education Statistics, *The Condition of Education 2003* (Washington, DC: U.S. Government Printing Office, 2003), iv.
12. Burrup, Brimley, and Garfield, *Financing Education,* 205–211; Lunenburg and Ornstein, *Educational Administration,* 246–250.
13. Burrup, Brimley, and Garfield, *Financing Education,* 211.
14. Ibid., 171.
15. Ibid., 174.
16. American Education Finance Association, *Public School Finance Programs of the United States and Canada 1993–1994,* vol. 1, ed. Steven D. Gold, David Smith,

Stephen B. Lawton, and Andrea C. Hyary (Albany: State University of New York, Nelson A. Rockefeller Institute of Government, 1995), 11.

17. Lunenburg and Ornstein, *Educational Administration*, 336.

18. Ibid.

19. R. J. Hy and W. L. Waugh, Jr., *State and Local Tax Policies: A Comparative Handbook* (Westport, CT: Greenwood Press, 1995), 56.

20. Ibid., 111.

21. Ibid., 111–112.

22. K. K. Manzo, "Study Offers New Insights on State Lotteries," *Education Week* 20, no. 9 (1 November 2000): 21.

23. Hy and Waugh, *State and Local Tax Policies*, 337.

24. Ibid.

25. Ibid.

26. Joetta L. Sack, "Schools Grapple With Reality of Ambitious Law," *Education Week* 20, no. 14 (6 December 2000): 1, 27, 28.

27. Hy and Waugh, *State and Local Tax Policies*, 340.

28. Ibid.

29. Ibid.

30. Ibid.

31. U.S. Department of Education, *Condition of Education 2003*, 77.

32. Hy and Waugh, *State and Local Tax Policies*.

33. Ibid., 16.

34. *Stuart v. School District No. 1 of the Village of Kalamazoo*, 30 Mich. 69 (1874).

35. *Brown v. Board of Education*, 347 U.S. 483 (1954).

36. *Serrano v. Priest*, 5 Cal. 32 584, 96 Cal. Rpt 601 P.J. 1241, 1244 (1971).

37. *San Antonio Independent School District v. Rodriguez*, 411 U.S. (1973).

38. *Serrano v. Priest*, 20 Cal.3d 25 (1977) .

39. *Board of Education of Central Community School District 301 v. Scionti*, 00-406 (2000).

40. *Campaign for Fiscal Equity v. State of New York*, 86 N.Y.2d 307, 655 N.E.2d 661, 631 N.Y.S2d 565 (1995).

41. *Campaign for Fiscal Equity v. State of New York*, 100 N.Y.2d 293; 801 N.E.2d 326; 769 N.Y.S2d 106; 203 N.Y. LEXIS 1678 (2000).

42. Ibid.

WE'RE ALL IN THIS TOGETHER: MEANINGFUL FAMILY AND COMMUNITY INVOLVEMENT IN SCHOOLS

FOCUS QUESTIONS

1. What are some ways that parents are currently involved in schools? Do you think that these are effective?
2. Why is it important to involve the community (non-parents) in the school and classroom?
3. How does the economy affect family involvement in the schools?
4. What implications does changing family demographics have for your teaching?
5. What community-based organizations can assist you in your teaching?
6. What do you think will be the most difficult aspect of working effectively with parents and other caregivers when you are teaching?

VIGNETTE

PARENTS JUST DON'T CARE

What the best and wisest parent wants for his own child, that must the community want for all its children. Any other ideal for our schools is narrow and unloving; acted upon, it destroys our democracy.

—John Dewey[1]

The purpose of this chapter is to help you reconsider traditional ways of looking at parent and community involvement in schools. We will focus on deconstructing myths about how and why parents and others are involved (or not involved) in schools and turn the spotlight on what schools and communities might do to foster more meaningful involvement of caring and interested adults in schools today. We begin with a vignette that occurred in a school where Maureen taught for several years.

It was early October and the faculty meeting agenda turned to the annual fall parent–teacher conferences that were to take place in a few weeks at Rosa Parks Elementary, a K–8 school in a midsize industrial city in the Midwest. As the principal raised the issue, teachers began to complain about having to do conferences. Conferences had traditionally taken place the final week of October. Early dismissal was usually scheduled for three days during the week; teachers scheduled parent conferences from 1:00 to 5:00 P.M. on two days and from 1:00 to 9:00 P.M. on the third day. Class sizes generally ranged from 22 to 28 students, so the schedule was set up with enough 10-minute time slots for each family to speak to each child's teacher.

The discussion started off with the eighth-grade teachers complaining that the parents did not even care enough to show up. They stated that the days were a waste and could be better spent with the kids in their classes. "It's always the same parents, and those are the ones I usually don't need to speak to," complained Mr. Torrez. "Yes, " chimed in Ms. Freeman, the second-grade teacher. "The ones I really need to see don't show up, and half the time when I try to call, their phone is disconnected. I send notes home with the children, but who knows what happens to them." Mr. Brown, the sixth-grade teacher, complained that it is always the mothers who come. "It's nice to see the moms, but I sure would like to see the fathers once in a while. Out of 26 kids, I might get two or three dads in here to discuss a student's progress."

The lamenting went on until Mrs. Lott, the principal, had heard enough. "Every year we complain about the lack of parent participation, and I guess I'd like to see what we can do about it rather than continue with the same old thing year after year. Let me think about this and we'll take it up next week."

Mrs. Lott thought about her own experience as a single mother. She had not been able to take time from her day to get to her daughter's school for parent conferences last year, and she wondered if the teachers at her daughter's school complained about her. She went on the Internet and began to look up the research on parent involvement. What she found surprised her and, armed with some data, she began to plan next week's faculty meeting. When the teachers sat down, she asked them to brainstorm a list of all the reasons they could think of for a lack of parent participation in school conferences and other events. At first the teachers were stymied—stuck on the "they don't care" reason. Finally, Mrs. Lott got the ball rolling. She told them about how she was unable to make her parent–teacher conference at her daughter's school because an emergency had come up at Rosa Parks. As a single mother, she had no backup plan and her daughter's father did not live close enough to make the appointment. "So," she began, "the inability to take time from work for a 10-minute conference might be one reason more parents cannot come." Soon the teachers were throwing out ideas. Mrs. Lott was pleased because she could see that the teachers had really keyed into the idea that many of the Rosa Parks families could be classified as "working poor"—that is, the parents working at low-paying jobs. Additionally, Rosa Parks served a community of recent immigrants and the teachers took that into account. Mrs. Lott recorded all of the possibilities on chart paper:

- Lack of babysitting
- Lack of transportation

- Inability to take time from the job(s)
- Inability to speak and/or understand English
- Belief that the school knows best, so no reason to come
- Little education, intimidated by the teacher
- Disability or illness, reducing ease of mobility

The staff then began to brainstorm ways to overcome these obstacles and get the parents to come to conferences and other school events. Mrs. Lott asked the faculty to think about the times when family involvement was the greatest. The teachers made another list:

- When food was served
- When there was some type of active involvement, such as the school carnival or book fair
- When the event occurred on the weekend

Mrs. Lott watched as the "lightbulb" went on in the heads of some of the teachers. Finally, Mrs. Z., the sixth-grade teacher, spoke. "We've been going about parent conferences all wrong! We want parents to come and discuss their child's progress, but we have not set up the times or the setting in a way that is inviting to most of our working parents. And really, although we say we give them options if they cannot come at their assigned time, my options are always at 3:15 other days of the week. If a parent can't take off work on Monday, she probably can't take off work on Wednesday! We need to rethink this whole thing." Mrs. Lott said, "Well, how do we begin the rethinking? We've got a month to reorganize."

You will read about the outcome of this real-life vignette at the end of this chapter. However, it is a good example of how, given some time for reflection, teachers can get beyond the idea that parents "don't care" and begin to explore some of the underlying reasons that some parents do not act in ways that the teacher views as being involved in the school. This chapter explores the issues of family and community involvement from multiple perspectives and considers how power relationships between different constituencies are played out in ways that can be beneficial to students but oftentimes end up creating misunderstanding between parents and teachers.

We would like to begin this chapter with a discussion of the changing nature of families in the United States. In this chapter, we will use the word *parents* to stand for all of the people who care for students today. We do this to make your reading easier, but we know that we run the risk that you will forget the myriad people who nurture and support today's students. We ask you to pay close attention to the first section, "The Changing Nature of Families," because we want you to be ever mindful in the classroom that you cannot make assumptions about who is raising the students who sit before you each day. We want you to apply Dewey's concept of "open-mindedness" to the idea that you will need to observe and investigate the home situations of all of your students in order to be sure that you can work effectively with all of a student's caretakers.

THE CHANGING NATURE OF FAMILIES

Statistics tell us that households in which children are being raised by two parents constitute 69% of families in the United States.[2] This may seem like a large percentage, but demographers are not able to break this number down. It includes children who live with two biological parents, those who live with a stepparent, and those who live with an adoptive parent. Today's family patterns are as diverse as our nation. According to the American Association of Retired Persons (AARP), about 2.4 million grandparents are taking on primary responsibility for raising their grandchildren.[3] **Kinship caregivers**—grandparents or other relatives other than parents who are raising children—sometimes do not get the benefit of the full range of support services available because they may be unaware of policies and services that can support their task. The prevalence of kinship caregivers constitutes a very large shift in child rearing from a time when grandparents and other relatives served as supports to parents.

The increased number of children being raised in a foster care situation also affects the children and the schools. More than half a million children in the year 2000 were being raised in foster care. The Pew Commission on Children in Foster Care reports that 47% of children in foster care live in a home setting with a non-relative, 10% live in institutions, and 8% are in group homes. About 25% of children in foster care live with a biological relative, but most do not. [4] The number of African American and Native American children in foster care is grossly disproportionate to their numbers in the population. African American children represent 14% of the population in the United States, yet they comprise 41% of the children in foster care. Similarly, 2% of Native American children are in the system though they comprise only 1% of the total population. This has severe implications for future success in life. Children who grow up in foster care may exhibit intense insecurities, experience a fragmented education, and feel stigmatized long into their adult years.[5]

The number of children being raised by gay and lesbian parents has been steadily rising. Statistics are difficult to capture because of the fear on the part of some gay and lesbian parents that reporting their status will result in harassment of their children. The ACLU reported in 1999 that anywhere from 6 to 14 million children are being raised by at least one gay or lesbian parent.[6]

Recent statistics indicate that more than 2 million children under the age of 18 have a parent who is incarcerated.[7] Children of parents in jail or prison may suffer from separation anxiety, anger, confusion, shame, and stigmatization. These feelings may manifest themselves in the classroom as developmental delays, aggression, withdrawal, and problems paying attention. It is obviously difficult for children of incarcerated parents to build family relationships. It is even more difficult for a teacher. When a parent goes to jail, he or she is no less concerned about the children. The teacher should work with social services and the student's caregiver to determine the best way to support the student.

Maureen's experience with a student whose father was jailed demonstrated the importance of showing understanding and patience in helping the student through the difficulties of such a situation. One of her third graders, Mike, entered the classroom one morning with a note from his mother indicating that "Mike's father made headlines in the wrong way." Mike's father had robbed a bank in a nearby town and was caught after a wild chase through the streets of several local communities. Maureen's heart sank thinking about how this might affect Mike, but also because she was worried about Mike's mom. When Mike's mom had not shown up previously for parent–teacher conferences, Maureen had called the home and arranged to meet Mike's mom on Saturday morning in a diner. The mother had confided that Mike's parents were divorced and with three children, she was working two jobs while the oldest, a seventh grader, watched Mike and his 5-year-old sister. Things would be even more difficult now because there would be no more child support.

The bank robbery story had made the evening news the previous night and the front page of the morning paper. Mike's peers entered the classroom making comments such as, "Hey, Mike, I saw your dad on the news last night." Mike denied that the man arrested was his father and told the class that he did not know the robber. He became sullen and withdrawn, saying nothing about his situation for several weeks. Maureen heard through the district grapevine that Mike's older brother had been suspended for fighting after he beat up another student who had teased him about the situation. Mike refused to admit to the school social worker that his father was in jail and eventually would not see the social worker. Through communication with Mike's mom, Maureen learned that Mike had weekly visits with his father in the local jail, where he was awaiting trial. One day during a lesson on letter-writing format, the students were assigned to write a friendly letter that would be mailed the next day. Mike called Maureen over and whispered in her hear, "Can I write to my dad? You know he's in jail but I have his address." Thus began a weekly ritual in which Mike and Maureen wrote to Mike's dad. Mike wrote about his week and Maureen included some information about his school progress.

The rising divorce rate in the United States has brought with it a steady increase in the number of children being raised by single parents as well as an increase in the number of **blended families**—families formed when two single parents remarry. You may teach children who have two sets of parents and four sets of grandparents as the number of blended and gay and lesbian families increases.

Finally, we want to comment on the importance of understanding the way religion affects families and individual students. Religious institutions, along with the family, are considered to be major socializing factors in a student's life. About 80% of Americans report that they are connected to a particular religion, and about two-thirds say that they are formally affiliated with a religious organization.[8] At the same time, a growing number of families reject organized religion altogether. Religious diversity affects the curriculum, extracurricular activities, the school calendar, and student behavior. You will hear faculty, administration, parents, and school boards discussing questions such as the following:

- Should we teach about religions in social studies, or should we leave religion out completely?
- Should we plan celebrations for various days, or should all celebrations be banned?

- What days will school be open and closed based on religious holidays?
- If school is open, how does the teacher help students whose families keep them home from school for religious observance?
- Muslim students will fast during Ramadan. What modifications or arrangements, if any, will assist students during this time?
- Will the cafeteria serve only fish on Fridays during Lent?
- How do I help students understand that a classmate from a family whose faith is based in the Church of the Latter Day Saints will not stand for the Pledge of Allegiance or attend class parties?

Teachers will need to work with parents, community members, and perhaps local clergy to understand how religious beliefs and practices may affect teaching, learning, and parental relationships.

Family demographics are just one way that families have changed in the past few decades. The economy has affected families in several ways. Many upper- and middle-class families have increased their wealth in good economic times. This, as well as some degree of career dissatisfaction and a reevaluation of priorities after September 11, 2001, has led to an increase in the number of stay-at-home parents. Unfortunately, most families have not had this luxury as our economy has waxed and waned over the past 30 years. More and more parents are being forced to work longer hours and in more than one job. Eighty-eight percent of children live in households in which at least one parent works outside the home.[9] The fact that the minimum wage in our country is not enough to support children adds to the stress of families. This has affected the type of school participation in which parents are able to engage. It also has an impact on other factors that most teachers believe contribute to a child's ability to learn: the type of home support available, health issues, and the general welfare of children. For example, approximately 8 million students between the ages of 5 and 14 spend time without adult supervision on a regular basis.[10] The time differential between school dismissal and parents' arrival home from work can total 20–25 hours per week.[11] As you can imagine, children left alone can experience loneliness, fear, and worry. Additionally, they risk injury or victimization and are susceptible to gang recruitment. Some older students may argue for being left home alone, but it is important to note that the reason many children are alone after school and into the evening is that their parents cannot afford child care.

We have discussed the influx of new immigrants to the United States. Recent estimates indicate that more 14 million children live with at least one foreign-born parent, representing almost 20% of the total number of school-age children in our nation.[12] Immigrants to the United States, regardless of the level of education attained in their home country, are typically forced to work in low-wage jobs in order to offer their children a promising future. As a result, "children of foreign-born parents are more likely to live in families with income below $30,000 per year" than their peers.[13] As you can see, the number of children in families living at or below the poverty level is also increasing. This causes a ripple effect in a number of ways that manifest themselves in the classroom. Student learning opportunities may be affected if their families cannot afford classroom supplies or cannot pay the fees to attend school field trips.

Adequate housing is an issue that faces thousands of American families. You read in Chapter 7 about the rising number of families who do not have a stable home. What you may not know about is the increasing number of families that live in inadequate housing. For example, families who live at or below the poverty line may have enough income or support to obtain an apartment. However, as Jonathan Kozol documented in *Rachel and Her Children*[14] and *Ordinary Resurrections: Children in the Years of Hope*,[15] they often end up living in rat-infested buildings where heat and plumbing may not function. Children may be left alone for long periods of time if their parent(s), working long hours for little pay, cannot provide a babysitter. Children living under such conditions often suffer from asthma, anxiety, and sleeplessness.

Finally, family health is an issue that is taking center stage in all income levels. There is much concern about our nation's unwillingness to provide adequate, minimum health care for all citizens, but especially for children. Today, approximately 12% of all children in the United States have no health care coverage.[16] It is not possible to maximize one's school experience if a student has tooth decay or a chronic illness or if family time is spent sitting in the emergency room, a setting that for many has replaced the family physician's office. Included in any discussion of health care should be a mention of the importance of mental health issues. In Chapter 3 we discussed the rise of school violence, noting that many perpetrators of extreme violence in our schools have come from families with adequate financial resources. Issues of divorce, abuse, and neglect plague families in all income brackets, and the importance of mental health assistance is often overlooked. Some families do not have the means to ensure adequate mental health; others lack the support to seek help when a family member is in need.

You may be wondering why we would spend time discussing the economy, housing, and health care under a section about changing families. It is important that you consider the ways that our nation's economy, and the way that those in power opt to address issues that support families, affects what happens in schools. Teachers often blame parents for not being involved in school, for not seeing that their children complete their homework, and for myriad other ways in which parents appear to neglect their children's education. Parents, as you will read below, often feel the same way about teachers! We want to point out that when these two groups point the finger of "not caring" at each other, they miss the big picture. Lost in all the blaming is the notion that how schools function, and how parents and teachers come to view each other, is based on what is happening outside of schools in the larger society—in particular, the economy. When joblessness reaches epidemic proportions, when the minimum wage does not support children, and when workers have insufficient or no benefits, families suffer. James Comer has pointed out, that to survive and thrive as a democracy, a society must attend to three areas:

- It must develop a sound and growing economy that permits the participation of all citizens.
- It must maintain sound community and family functioning so that critical tasks, particularly child rearing, can be well performed.
- It must have a culture that values both and facilitates the critical interaction between the two.

They are linked. When the economy works, heads of households can earn the resources to promote adequate family functioning. When families function well, children are more likely to grow up prepared for success in schools, as citizens, and at work.[17]

Comer suggests that the degree to which parents can support their children's education depends on their ability to be gainfully employed in a job that pays a living wage and provides benefits that support a family. Many young men and women who end up in jail are there because they have reached the legal school leaving age (16, 17, or 18) and do not have the skill level to graduate from high school, go on to college, or get a well-paying job. In many cases, crime provides a living income. Currently, we are building prisons faster than we are building schools. What does it say about our society when more than 100,000 young women and men under the age of 18 are incarcerated and most are functionally illiterate, reading at or below a fifth-grade level?[18] How can young men and women be gainfully employed and expect to raise a family when they cannot read, write, or calculate? How do the jobless statistics in our nation change if one considers incarcerated individuals as jobless?

Teachers and administrators often do not connect their work to the current economy, current social conditions, and the success of future generations. The work that we do to ensure that all children get a high-quality education—one that promotes a love of learning and prepares students with the skills and knowledge to be successful, contributing members of society—will affect our future.

Teachers often devote their time and energy to what happens inside of the school and classroom. Of course, this is of prime importance. But we have centered this text around the notion that a teacher must be culturally responsive and use the authority bestowed upon the position of "teacher" to make a positive impact. This requires a teacher to be aware of how the political, social, and economic realms beyond education affect the ability to teach, as well as educational outcomes, because of how they affect children and families. It requires a teacher to be involved in the community, to know where community resources are, and to be willing to advocate for the inclusion of a wide array of community involvement in the classroom and the school.

PARENTS AND TEACHERS: THE IMPORTANCE OF LISTENING TO EACH OTHER

Corbett, Wilson, and Williams[19] conducted a very interesting research study about the ways in which parents and teachers view each other. These researchers consistently heard from teachers in low-income areas that families were not involved in the children's education. Teachers believed that they cared more about the students than did the parents, that the parents did not value education, that the parents had negative school experiences, and that they were unwilling to work with teachers. Many teachers that Corbett, Wilson, and Williams talked to actually believed that the parents impeded a student's academic progress. Unfortunately, you may hear attitudes such as this from some teachers when you are in the schools, as similar studies indicate that teachers often express the "parents don't care" belief.

Corbett, Wilson, and Williams wanted to find out what parents thought, so they embarked on a survey of parents and received more than 900 responses to their questionnaire.[20] They found that "parents mistrusted teachers' concerns for their children's educational needs just as teachers mistrusted the parents."[21] Corbett, Wilson, and Williams used six categories of parent involvement partnerships based on work by another researcher, Joyce Epstein.[22] Think about these six categories, because they may stretch your conception of what constitutes parent involvement. Also consider how often the schools with which you are most familiar partner with parents at these levels:

1. *Parenting.* Includes sharing and collaborating on parenting skills, ideas about child and adolescent development and the types of home settings that encourage and support learning.
2. *Learning at Home.* Involves families in learning activities, including homework, games, reading to children, and other strategies that are tied to curriculum.
3. *Communicating.* Establishing two-way communication; notes, e-mails, websites.
4. *Volunteering in the School.* Recruitment, training, scheduling, and task analysis that involves families and other community members in school and school-related activities.
5. *Decision Making and Advocacy.* Includes parents in governance, policy making, and important decisions through PTA/PTO, Principal's Council, and other such bodies and organizations.
6. *Community Collaboration.* Integrating community resources and services into the school to enhance student achievement and support families.

Corbett, Wilson, and Williams found that parents believed that they were intimately involved in their children's education, especially in the areas of parenting and learning at home. Interestingly, parents said that they were not involved in decision making and advocacy or in volunteering because the school did not encourage them in these areas. In other words, parents are typically left out of positions of power and influence. They are continually relegated to more passive roles that involve one-way communication in which the teacher talks, or sends notes, and the parents listen.[23]

And what about upper-class or wealthy parents? There is often the same kind of mistrust between parents and teachers. Teachers sometimes view wealthy parents as "too involved," seeking to micromanage their child's education or rendering the child blameless when serious behavior problems are evident. The report *Playing Their Parts: Parents and Teachers Talk About Parental Involvement in Public Schools*[24] summarizes survey data in which teachers reported that "overprotective" parents and those who "refuse to hold their children accountable" were seen as problems. Parents may feel that teachers are "picking on" or neglecting their child if the student does not achieve the results they expect or the student does not get into the college that the parents have decided is best. Dan Kindlon, author of *Too Much of a Good Thing: Raising Children of Character in an Indulgent Age*,[25] suggests that wealthy parents, those who have access to power roles in districts based on their resources, also need assistance in knowing how

What Parents Want

1. *Don't Give Up on Students.* Parents want teachers to devise ways to offer extra help for students who need more time or who just do not "get it." They suggested that teachers could offer help sessions during school hours, before and after school help times, and summer programs for students who may not be failing but who need extra assistance. As you will read below, it is possible for community agencies to assist in this endeavor.
2. *Maintain High Expectations.* Parents expressed concern that the curriculum be demanding and that the teacher never lower his or her high expectation for student success. These parents wanted their children to be successful and knew that inflated grades and easy assignments do not help students to achieve.
3. *Enhance Lines of Communication.* Parents report that they often do not know that their child is in trouble, academically or behaviorally, until it is too late. For the parents in this study, there was no such thing as too much communication.
4. *Put Variety in the Instructional Day.* Parents stressed the importance of active learning and were critical of teachers who lectured or offered too many worksheets.
5. *Build Strong Relationships With Students.* All parents want their child to have a teacher who cares.

Source: D. Corbett, B. Wilson, and B. Williams, *Effort and Excellence in Urban Classrooms: Expecting and Getting Success With All Students* (New York: Teachers College Press, 2002), 40–41.

best to help their children. Although parents with many resources often provide many "extras" for the school, they may also attempt to leverage their way into shortcuts for their children rather than listening to teachers and administrators about what is best for students. It may also be the case that parents who are accustomed to being "in charge" dominate committees or power positions to the exclusion of others. You may hear teachers and administrators complain that some parents are always involved and always appear to get into positions of power.

Corbett, Wilson, and Williams's survey results indicated strongly that what the parents believed they did most, parenting, received the least support from the school! The researchers point out that there is a "mismatch between what parents and teachers are looking for in each other, a mismatch bred of ignorance about one another's intentions and actions—that led to counterproductive finger pointing."[26] Unfortunately, this research supports research that is decades old that found that although teachers and administrators said they wanted more parent involvement, they did not attempt to involve parents on more than a superficial level.

The parents in Corbett, Wilson, and Williams's study provided advice to teachers that we would like to share with you (see the box "What Parents Want"). We then offer some ideas on how to begin to follow this advice.

We have worked for a long time with all types of parents. Although we acknowledge that there are stories of parents from all income brackets who abuse and neglect their children, we believe that the vast majority of parents want their children to be successful. Some parents may not know how to assist their children in this endeavor. If parents were not born and raised in this country, they may not know how the "system" works here. If parents did not attend college, they may not know how to help their child select courses in middle and high school so that they gain the knowledge they need to do well on required exams such as the SAT or the ACT. Parents may have substance abuse or immigration issues and may be unwilling to engage with teachers for fear that their children will be taken away. There are a host of issues that parents face. But if you really listen to parents, in addition to talking to them, you will find that they have modest but clear goals: that their child does well in school, gets help when he or she needs it, and leads a happy life. It may seem simplistic but most parents are interested in helping you help their child.

Parents, teachers, administrators, and community members must begin to talk to each other if we are to get beyond traditional misconceptions and mistrust. The onus is on you, the teacher, to reach out to parents in order to bridge the gap between home, school, and community. Luis Moll, a researcher who focuses on effective educational strategies for Latino youth, recommends that teachers investigate and tap into the "funds of knowledge" that families hold and use that information to teach for high academic achievement.[27] Moll and his team of researchers have discovered that Latino families pass on to their children a deep knowledge base and a broad set of skills by teaching them tasks that require complex thinking and expecting results. Latino students may underperform on traditional school tasks because they are simplistic and rote. Hands-on learning takes place in the family and community, where students are taught and expected to master a variety of tasks in such fields as agriculture, electrical wiring, construction, and culinary arts. Knowledge and skills are not hoarded, but shared between members of the community. We recommend that you use a personal touch to tap into the "funds of knowledge" held by the families with whom you work and design ways to use students' home knowledge to help them achieve in the classroom. You can do this, as Moll recommends, through home visits or other group forums such as coffees at school or in a local community center. As difficult as it may be, A. Lin Goodwin and Sabrina Hope King, researchers who have written about culturally responsive parent involvement,[28] suggest that you begin by listening, centering the conversation around such questions as

- What would like me to know about your child?
- What is working well for you and your child in this class/school?
- What concerns do you have about your child's academic progress, this class, or this school?
- What do you need me to know more about?
- How do you think the educational experience could be more meaningful for everyone?
- What are ways that you would like your child's culture to be affirmed in school?

- What are examples of the ways that your child's culture has been negated in school?
- What should we do differently?
- What kinds of experiences or instructional materials would you like to be a part of your child's experiences at school?[29]

We begin the next section with a discussion of the community school movement. We use the notion of a community school to help you understand how schools can build a foundation for student success by meeting the needs of families. We then offer some ways that districts and teachers can begin to reach out to parents if their area has not adopted the idea of the community school.

COMPREHENSIVE COMMUNITY INVOLVEMENT IN SCHOOLS: THE COMMUNITY SCHOOLS CONCEPT

We have enumerated the issues that can face caregivers as they strive to be involved in their children's education. The concept of a **community school** arose as one means to help families get the services they need while simultaneously meeting the needs of the community. The Coalition for Community Schools defines a community school as "both a place and a set of partnerships between the school and other community resources. Its integrated focus on academics, services, supports and opportunities leads to improved student learning, stronger families, and healthier communities."[30] A community school uses the local school as a center not solely for PreK–12 education, but for lifelong learning and community activism.

You have learned throughout this text that districts and schools are primarily local entities, although they are loosely coupled with the state and federal government. The idea that the community and its schools are responsible for and to each other is not new. Jane Addams, a pioneer in progressive, activist, and community-based social reform, demonstrated this concept with the 1889 founding of Hull House in Chicago. Addams saw the need to consolidate community services if immigrants, working-class families, and the poor were to achieve "the American dream." Hull House exemplified the ideals of a community school because it combined multiple facilities into a "one-stop shopping" center for students and community members. Hull House, now a historic site in Chicago, combined such facilities as a school, a day care center, an art gallery, a library, public baths, a drama club, citizenship preparation courses, an employment bureau, and several other community service agencies in one place where community members could have their needs met. Hull House served as a center for community activism yet, as an entity run by women, it was characterized by its family atmosphere. Addams never lost focus on social reform, and she served as a role model for civic participation. She believed that people would take up the cause of collective participation in reform when their own basic needs for food, clothing, shelter, health and safety, and education were met. Hull House, the precursor to the community school idea, was designed to assist in that endeavor. Thus, the philosophy and ideals underpinning community schools have been around for more than 100 years. The movement got a boost in the 1970s when Congress passed PL 93-381, the Community Schools Act. Since that time, the network of community schools has been growing. The Coalition of Community Schools reports that today, there are community school networks across the country.

How might a community school look today? The structure of a community school can take several forms but basically, a community school is a local school that is characterized by a set of specific and deliberate partnerships between the school, its agencies (e.g., the PTA), outside community agencies (e.g., social service agencies, a local university, local family support agencies), and individual community members. The goal of such a partnership web is "to create the conditions necessary for all children to learn at their best."[31] The Coalition for Community Schools states that the partners work to achieve the following goals:

- Children are ready to learn when they enter school and every day thereafter.
- All students learn and achieve to high standards.
- Young people are well prepared for adult roles in the workplace, as parents, and citizens.
- Families and neighborhoods are safe, supported, and engaged.
- Parents and community members are involved with the school and their own lifelong learning.[32]

The philosophy of the community school movement is that all families have strengths and all families have ways in which they can participate in the life of the school. They also recognize that many families have needs that must be met in order for them to become full partners in the school experience. As you may have guessed based on the goals, the school is open not only during the day but also evenings and summers so that families and community members can attend classes and use the facilities in myriad ways.

We have been in community schools with a dentist office where local dentists take turns volunteering a few hours a week in the schools. Children who come from families without dental insurance are able to have their teeth cared for by a professional at no charge. Evenings may find parents and other community members participating in computer courses, book clubs, GED or ESL classes, seminars on home buying, or even swimming lessons! Local agencies may set up a food bank or a clothing distribution center in the school, and a local university may run an evening "homework help group" every night of the week.

The community school movement acknowledges the importance of integrating community members without children currently in the system into the life of the school. Schools are currently funded by taxes paid by community members, many of whom do not have a child in the school system. It is important that these community members learn about and understand what their taxes pay for and how they benefit from this expenditure. The idea that we are all responsible for the success of our students and we all reap the benefits of an excellent school is an important lesson for all schools and communities to consider. The design of each community school is different and tailored to meet the needs of the local community. However, the Coalition for Community Schools lists six shared key principles:

- Foster strong partnerships.
- Share accountability for results.
- Set high expectations for all.
- Build on the community's strengths.
- Embrace diversity.
- Avoid cookie cutter solutions.[33]

Finally, and most important, the tradition of family and community activism is upheld in excellent community schools. Parents and community members understand the political process and work to make changes that benefit the K–12 students. You may be thinking that not all parents are politically savvy, and you would be right. The partnership aspect of a community school means that there is a wealth of resources from which to draw in helping provide workshops, retreats, and other means to educate families and community members about how to bring about change. The best examples we can offer to illustrate the idea of social activism integrated into the community schools concept are the schools sponsored by Association of Community Organizations for Reform Now, or ACORN. ACORN is a grass-roots community organization that takes as its priority building organizational structures for "bottom-up" change in low-income areas. ACORN works on a variety of issues such as voter registration, home ownership for low-income community members, fair lending practices, and civil rights violations, to name just a few. ACORN has sponsored three community high schools in New York City: Bread and Roses Integrated Arts High School in West Harlem, ACORN Community High School in Prospect Heights, and the ACORN High School for Social Justice in Brooklyn. Each of these schools is build on a philosophy and around a curriculum of social reform that hearkens back to the work of Jane Addams more than 100 years ago.

We encourage you to check out the ACORN website for details, as well as the website of the Coalition of Community Schools, both of which appear in the "Getting Connected" section of this chapter.

STRATEGIES FOR WORKING EFFECTIVELY WITH FAMILIES AND COMMUNITIES

We have given you a brief glimpse at the diversity of families that populate today's schools as well as how a community school can begin to meet the needs of students, teachers, families, and community members. But what if your community or the school leadership has not even considered the idea of a community school? Although the community school movement is growing, most districts and schools still operate as isolated units, often disconnected from families and the community. In providing you with the following list of ideas about involving caring adults in the life of the school and classroom, our goal is to get you to really think about the myriad ways that not only parents but the entire community can be involved in the school. This is an important step in supporting children as they strive to meet your high expectations, and it is key to building the support you need as a teacher in doing your job.

Who is everyone? We think that your first priority is to ensure that the people who are direct caregivers for students are involved in the school. Next, we believe it is important for you to involve a wide array of community members and others in your classroom and school because volunteering in the schools is a "win-win" situation. It provides community members with a firsthand view of the wonderful things going on in local classrooms, and it provides the students with a diversity of community members as role models and mentors. For example, the National Association for the Education of Young Children (NAEYC) has published a wonderful pamphlet on the importance of involving men in the lives of children. Currently, more than 16.5 million children live with a single mother.[34] Additionally, many children are growing up away from extended family. Many of the suggestions listed below are adopted or adapted from the NAEYC brochure. The emphasis of NAEYC is on young children, but the organization stresses that all children "need to spend time in the company of both men and women to form healthy, realistic images of adults."[35] Because so many children today grow up without a male figure in the home, it is especially important that schools reach out to men in the community.

What Schools and Districts Can Do

- Establish a district and school website. Collect family e-mail addresses and send information regularly. Post important news and provide incentives for families to "click on" to see what is happening in the district.
- Post events where the parents are active in the community. Grocery stores, houses of worship, pharmacies, eating and drinking establishments, dry cleaners, coin laundries, barber shops, and beauty salons are all places where schools can post notices about upcoming events. That way, if the student fails to bring the notice home, the parent will see it elsewhere!
- Establish a Family Resource Center. Keep a pot of coffee and some tea ready for parents who drop in for support, resources, or information. Develop a Community Cultural Resources binder that helps parents locate resources when needed. Establish a Family Lending Library that includes books (in multiple languages), learning games, software, and laptops. Post a calendar with the dates of school events. Be sure that volunteer opportunities, a family events calendar, and a list of needed supplies or other items that families can donate are posted and updated regularly. Publicize the Center!
- Examine school policies and organizations to ensure that parents from all subgroups of the school community are included at all levels. Monitor participation of parents to ensure that no group of parents is excluded from decision making and active participation.
- Have each family complete a family inventory, and analyze the results to begin planning events and strategize about how to reach out to parents who are rarely involved. Goodwin and Hope King[36] suggest questions such as:
  What languages are spoken in the home?
  What are the family's cultural practices and traditions?

What are the parents' previous experiences with schools, schooling, teachers?
What are the parents' hobbies, skills, interests, talents?
Do parents have scheduling issues or transportation needs?
What are parents' working hours?
What culturally rich materials and resources that can be shared with the school?
What do parents see lacking in terms of diversity in their child's schoolwork?

- Provide all school notes and notices in multiple languages. Provide adults who can translate (including sign language) for conferences and family events. Be sure you have a bank of community resource people who can assist with many different languages.

- Establish a family liaison system (some districts refer to them as parent liaisons). Many school districts, including one as big as New York City, have established a parent liaison system. A **family liaison** is a person in the school (usually paid) who is responsible for ensuring that parents are informed, involved, and connected to the school. The liaison is the go-between for the teacher and the parents in appropriate situations. The liaison advocates on behalf of parents, teachers, and community members, depending on the issue.

- Hold monthly Family Activities, some with an academic focus, some with a community service focus, and some with a social focus. Family Literacy Night and Family Math Night have proved to be successful in schools in urban, rural, and suburban areas. Teachers and teacher candidates from local universities teach parents and students games and other educational activities that can be done at home. If a game requires materials, they are provided and the parents and students make the game together. At the junior high and high school level, an academically oriented Family Night can focus on problem-solving strategies, course selection for college, or the relationship between careers and the curriculum (with parents and teachers as co-presenters). Research by the Center for Research on Education, Diversity, and Excellence (CREDE) has shown Family Night to be a great success.

- The school can arrange a community service activity such as cleaning up an area around the school or in the community, painting the school or local area, planting a community garden, or helping senior citizens with home repairs. In these types of activities, it is usually the parent who teaches the student some new skills, but the goal is for the school staff and the families to undertake an activity together. Social activities are times when school staff and families come together to get to know each other. It may be as simple as a pot-luck dinner or as involved as a school carnival. All of these activities typically involve food, fun, and fellowship for families. If the school budget allows (or if the teachers and administrators prioritize), families are provided with T-shirts, mugs, or some other type of remembrance that helps build community and school spirit.

- Parent nights are also important events because sometimes parents need time away from the students to discuss topics of interest to the parents. The community has vast resources to provide advice, information, and discussion facilitation for parents. We have found that when the topic is of interest to the parents (e.g., How can I get my child to do homework without a battle? How can I prepare my child for college? How does our curriculum meet state standards?), and time is set aside for socializing and snacks, parent participation is high.

- Be sure all forms include all significant people in the family. Given the diversity of families today, the school might be unaware of an adult who is supposed to receive school information. Be sure that emergency forms, parent contact sheets, phone trees, and other communication lists include all appropriate adults.

- Organize an "adopt a senior buddy" program. Here, students in the early grades adopt senior citizens as their "adopted grandparent or buddy." Despite the growing number of children being raised by grandparents, many children today do not interact with seniors on a regular basis. Seniors have a wealth of history and local community knowledge stored in their memories and love to share their knowledge and expertise with young people. These "senior buddies" follow the students as they progress through the grades. They visit school for special events and parties and at times are the only adult who is there for a child on special days. We have seen schools where this program provides yet another "win-win" situation. Young people gain a new respect for seniors, and the seniors have a young person to mentor. We have also seen that in these situations, a senior citizen may pass away. This has provided the teacher with an opportunity to discuss life, death, and the importance of each person with the class. It also happens that students move away. Seniors adapt quickly and almost always are ready to take on a new student.
- Be sure school and district events and projects are inclusive. Sometimes titles can exclude certain students. For example, rather than the Father–Daughter Dance, the school could title the event in a way that includes granddads, uncles, stepfathers, big brothers, or other significant adults.
- Reach out to many community agencies (e.g., 100 Black Men, Police Athletic League) to garner a diverse group of school volunteers. Often firefighters and police officers have variable schedules that might allow them to volunteer one day a week in a classroom or read to students who need a reading buddy. Be prepared to offer workshops and orientations for volunteers so that they are fully aware of rules, policies, and schedules in the school. It is also important to incorporate "volunteer appreciation" activities into the school year that involve teachers, students, and parents.

What Teachers Can Do

You may find yourself in a school or district where there is little enthusiasm for community involvement. This is an unfortunate situation, but it does not mean that you cannot involve the community in your classroom. What can you do?

- Get to know the community and its resources. It is important that you know the history and current status of the community where you teach. Teachers need to become familiar with community leaders, community organizations, and religious institutions. Just knowing about such entities is often not enough. You should join local organizations such as the National Association for the Advancement of Colored People (NAACP), ACORN, the League of United Latin American Citizens (LULAC), or the League of Women Voters and find out what issues are of concern to parents and other community members. Not only can these issues be used as part of the curriculum to engage students in community study, they will help you understand the perspectives and viewpoints of community members. Read community newspapers. Visit and volunteer at youth clubs and community agencies. If possible, hold curricular and other school events at various places in the community. For example, we know one middle school teacher who developed a unit on community history. She had the students do traditional research and then conduct oral history interviews to gather information from community members. The unit culminated in a presentation at the local history museum, where many parents, community members, and local dignitaries came to see and hear about the students' work.

- Establish a classroom website on which you post homework, important information, and general classroom news.
- Go where the parents are, and get involved. Oftentimes the only conversation that teachers and parents have is in regard to academic or behavioral issues. Social conversation in an informal setting such as a sporting event, restaurant, or house of worship can go a long way to building positive communication. When we know people on a more personal level, it becomes easier to discuss difficult situations should those arise.
- Survey children on the first day of school regarding family members, pets, and favorites (hobbies, etc). That will be useful information for you to use in the curriculum and during the year. It will also give you a point of comparison with significant adults on the child's official school record so that all caregivers who have a legal right to information about the child can be included. Be sure to ask if the student has a mentor or tutor whom you can contact. Learn the names of all the important people in children's lives, invite them to the classroom, and greet them by name.
- Home visits are the single most important thing you can do to help you understand the students and families with whom you will work. It is important to note that you are making a home visit to gain information, not to give it! Your goals should be to find out what the parents want for their child during the academic year, to explore any concerns they might have, and to open lines of communication on the parents' "turf." The questions provided by Goodwin and Hope King in the previous section are a great place to start. Unfortunately, we know of some districts that will not allow home visits. An administrator might worry about liability issues if a teacher gets hurt in a neighborhood that is prone to violence. In cases such as this, we have met parents at the local McDonald's or Burger King for coffee and talk. We have found that even the most economically disadvantaged parents will offer to buy the coffee as a token of their appreciation for a teacher who really goes out of his or her way to make a connection with the family.
- Participate in the life of the community. Live in the community if possible. If living in the community is not possible, worship, shop, and regularly attend events in the community. Tell your students about events that you are attending and encourage them to meet you there. For example, if the local library is having a lecture, story hour, or other event, let students know you will be there and then be sure to appear!
- Be sure the overt curriculum (e.g., textbooks, classroom library materials) includes and addresses all types of family structures.
- Be sure the "hidden" curriculum includes and addresses all types of family structures, including men as well as women. Room environment, guest speakers, classroom volunteers, and even the music and snacks you might have on special occasions should be diverse and representative of the community and the nation.
- Encourage multiple forms of communication. Use e-mail, regular mail, phone, fax, and any other means to begin and maintain contact with significant adults.

BACK TO THE VIGNETTE: IMPLEMENTING SIMPLE SOLUTIONS TO THE PROBLEM

You may recall that we left the faculty of Rosa Parks Elementary (K–8) in a brainstorming session about why parents were not coming to parent–teacher conferences. The teachers were trying to figure out how to increase parental involvement at conferences. They felt it was important to have a face-to-face meeting with parents more than once a year and were perplexed by the large number of "no shows" at parent–teacher conferences. They had listed several reasons why parents might not be coming for the traditional 10- to 15-minute parent conference. As the next meeting opened, a veteran teacher, Mrs. Tavares, spoke first.

"I think that several of the issues that we identified as preventing more parents from coming are things we could easily address. The lack of babysitting can be taken care of by having the seventh and eighth graders volunteer to watch children in the gym, cafeteria, or library. We would only need one or two adults to supervise the babysitters. The inability to speak or understand English can be addressed by getting some community members into the school as translators. The lack of transportation can be quickly fixed if the district would run the bus schedule on conference days so parents could catch the same bus their children catch for school. But I am very concerned about the fact that some parents cannot take time off from work and that we may intimidate them based on their own school experiences or their cultural beliefs about the authority of the teacher, or based on our body language or use of certain educational vocabulary."

Ms. Martinez, a teacher with five years of experience and a community member, chimed in. "I think your initial ideas are great and I'd be willing to head a committee to get the babysitting organized. I've given this a lot of thought and I have a pretty radical suggestion to put on the table. I think we should increase the time we conference and hold parent–teacher conferences on Saturday. We could still do another day of the week, afternoon and evening, for parents who can come then. On both days, we would have the cafeteria set up with coffee and donuts in the morning, a basic lunch like soup and sandwiches at noon, and some cookies in the afternoon. We'll put tablecloths on the cafeteria tables and have student work samples on display. That way, any teacher who has a free conference slot can come into the lunchroom and chat with parents more informally. It would certainly help us get more working parents in here, and we can begin to build positive relationships with reluctant parents over a donut. We could speak with the union about arranging a comp day for working on Saturday."

As soon as Ms. Martinez finished, the discussion heated up. Most teachers were willing to entertain the idea of Saturday conferences, but two very vocal seventh-grade teachers immediately objected. "I'm not working on Saturday," began Ms. Mitchell, "no way." Her colleague agreed, "The union will never make us do this."

Mrs. Lott, the principal, sought to calm the waters. "I can really see some merit in the idea of Saturday conferences, but it is clear that we need to think this through and involve the teachers union and the upper-level administration. We may be able to develop a plan whereby those who want to hold conferences on Saturday can do that and those that do not can make other arrangements. Let's explore this. In the meantime, let's keep the fall schedule as is and see if we can begin to improve parental attendance through a pilot implementation of some of the ideas generated today. I'll do some budget work and get the money for snacks, coffee, and some ambiance in the cafeteria during conferences. You all should begin to gather student projects for display there. Ms. Martinez has volunteered to organize the babysitting. I'll speak to the superintendent about the bus idea, which I think is great. We do have to find a way to cover the cost of running extra routes. Is anyone willing to work on translators from the community? We will probably need at least two volunteers per conference day because we would want one posted in the cafeteria for the entire session." Mrs. Tavares volunteered to organize translators because she sat on the board of the local Latino Community Resource Center and the primary language spoken at home in the district was Spanish.

Mrs. Lott continued by speaking to the building union representative, Ms. Colburn. "How about inviting the union executive committee to our next meeting. If our goal is to increase parent involvement, a concept that is cited in all of the educational research as a key to student success, we should be able to work out a plan. In the meantime, I am also going to develop a survey to ascertain the extent to which parents have circumstances such as illness, disability, or financial constraints that we could address in other ways."

Mrs. Lott publicized the new efforts through flyers that were sent home with the students, posted in community sites, and put on the home page of the school website. She asked key parents, three of whom were bilingual, to begin making phone calls to encourage parents to come to the fall conferences.

The pilot changes generated much enthusiasm from the parents but only slightly increased the number of parents who showed up for conferences. Mrs. Lott and the faculty agreed to continue the babysitting, cafeteria food, transportation, and translators for the spring. She found out through her survey and informal conversations with parents that most parents worked so far from school that they would have to take a half-day from work to attend conferences. The parents told Mrs. Lott that they simply could not afford to take a half-day to attend a 10- to 15-minute conference. They did not feel that the short conference was enough time to really understand how their son or daughter was doing, and it just was not worth it to come. This issue of conference scheduling was clearly an impediment to parent participation.

Over the course of the fall and winter, the teachers worked out an agreement with the union so that any teacher who wanted to hold conferences on Saturday would be eligible for a floating personal day during the year. This caused a few ripples throughout the district as other teachers had the same mixed reaction to the idea as the Rosa Parks staff. Mrs. Lott's informal conversations with parents during the fall conference days, in addition to information gathered by a family survey, led her to believe that parents had much more interest in speaking to teachers than even she realized. She began to hold focus groups for parents, meeting with between four and eight parents at a time to listen to their ideas and concerns. She reached out to the most uninvolved parents through personal phone calls and home visits. She began monthly Saturday morning focus groups at the local McDonalds. She regularly shared the results of her conversations with the teachers.

The idea of Saturday conferences was implemented in the spring. Parent attendance at conferences rose by 48%, with more fathers showing up on Saturday than anyone ever expected. The teachers were pleasantly surprised. As the faculty discussed the results of their experiment, even the two teachers who refused to conference on Saturday were coming around. Not only was there a bit of peer pressure to join everyone else, there was also a degree of parental pressure. The families, especially the males in the household, could not say enough about how much they appreciated the Saturday conference day. The teachers could no longer complain that the parents didn't care—it was clear that the results of altering the conference schedule to meet the needs of the parents indicated that they cared very much about finding out how their child was performing.

As the year came to a close, the staff was pleased with the increased parental interest in what was going on their child's classroom and in attending parent–teacher conferences. Mrs. Lott told the teachers that there would be a midsummer family picnic for the school community so that they did not lose the connections that had been established. She indicated that attendance at the picnic was voluntary, but the teachers enthusiastically jotted down the date. Plans were already underway to continue those things that they had begun during the year and to begin experimenting with new ways to involve parents in the life of the school.

It may be easy for you to see how this story relates to our chapter theme, but you may be wondering what it has to do with power and multicultural education in schools. The faculty with whom Maureen worked addressed tough teaching dilemmas with one question in mind: What is best for kids? Mrs. Lott was a principal who used her power to make those around her more effective: the teachers and the parents. She treated teachers as professionals and listened to the parents. She held the same high expectations for them as she expected them to hold for the students. She could have dictated changes, chastised teachers for not doing more to involve parents, or blamed parents for not being involved. Mrs. Lott, a parent herself, simply would not accept the idea that parents just did not care. Instead, she facilitated a process that resulted, over time, in the inclusion of almost all parents in some aspect of the school. But she did it in a way that enhanced teacher professionalism: she presented them with a dilemma, periodically slipped them some research, and supported the ideas that came from their discussions. The most exciting change was that formerly uninvolved and quiet parents, especially those who were not totally fluent in English, began appearing at school more and more.

Sometimes the road to multicultural education begins with baby steps. The tenets of multicultural education support the creation of a school community, beyond just bringing in translators for students or parents who are not fluent English speakers. The goal of an education that is multicultural is an excellent education for all students, and that is difficult to achieve without family involvement. The discussion that began with parent–teacher conferences mushroomed over the next five years. A faculty member developed a Family Resource Center, writing a grant to buy books and materials. Mrs. Lott established a Community Relations Committee comprised of teachers, parents, and community members. The faculty worked with the community to establish a "senior buddies" program. A group of seventh- and eighth-grade babysitters came up with the idea of using their lunch period to work with kindergarten and first-grade students on reading and math skills. Mrs. Lott provided a steady stream of reading material on parent and community involvement. Based on their reading, the teachers began holding Family Activity Nights four times a year. Nothing changes overnight. But nothing will ever change if teachers and administrators continue to blame others without searching for solutions, refuse to look to themselves for answers and try new ideas, and wield the power invested in them by virtue of their position in ways that alienate all but a few parents.

FINDING A VOICE

Nadine and Patsy Cordova are sisters who taught in the Vaughn, New Mexico, school system until they were fired in 1997. Vaughn is a small school district with approximately 70 students in Nadine and Patsy's school. Because the district is so small, the superintendent approves the teachers' lesson plans and curriculum decisions, and writes the teachers' annual evaluations. We want to tell you this true story because it involves the two teachers, the school board, the community, and the students. Intertwined in the firing and subsequent lawsuit filed by the Cordova sisters are issues of power, multicultural education, teachers' rights, and community involvement.

The story begins in 1996 when Nadine, who had been teaching seventh- and eighth-grade language arts, drama, and "Skills for Living" for 12 years, offered to sponsor a student club called Movimiento Estudiantil Chicano de Aztlan (MEChA). The club, already organized by the students, had 23 members but no sponsor and had not been recognized as an official school club. Patsy, who had been teaching New Mexico history to high school students for 17 years, agreed to support her sister in working with the students. MEChA is a national organization with local chapters in schools, communities, and universities. MEChA has had a reputation for activism and radical politics, but the stated goal of the Vaughn club was "to promote and understand through knowledge, awareness of and sensitivity to culture, tradition, history and issues of the Chicano people and our communities."[37]

The Vaughn superintendent officially approved the club for the 1996–1997 year. In an opening assembly, a student in the audience raised her fist and shouted, "Viva la Raza" in response to a pitch for new members by MEChA club leaders. Word of this "radical" response to the club got out into the community and the president of the school board complained to the superintendent. Two weeks later, Nadine was told that MEChA would not be given any school funds, could not use any school facilities, and could not even post announcements in the school. When she questioned the principal about why an approved club was not allowed the privileges accorded to other clubs and organizations, he told Nadine that he would not go against the wishes of the board president.[38] It was at this time that the superintendent began to inform Patsy and Nadine that there were concerns about their teaching.

Supporting and teaching about the history of the Chicano people, the relationship between the United States and Mexico, and current issues in the community were not new to Patsy and Nadine Cordova. Both teachers, who had consistently received high marks in their annual evaluations, had been supplementing the required textbook with books and materials about (and by) Chicano people and their history. The teachers had submitted their curriculum outlines and lesson plans (aligned with New Mexico's Content Standards) to the superintendent, who approved them. For example, prior to the formation of MEChA, Nadine had used a video of the PBS show *Chicano! History of the Mexican-American Civil Rights Movement*. Of course, when you use materials written from multiple perspectives, not everyone will agree with the varied perspectives. This is especially true when using materials written by oppressed people. Patsy and Nadine drew upon materials by Chicanos who presented history and current issues from the Chicano perspective. By the fall of 1996, the sisters were receiving written warnings accusing them of teaching with a MEChA philosophy and requiring them to cease any type of teaching that promoted "racial intolerance, a biased political agenda, and a militant attitude."[39] The debate in the school and community became so heated that the students could not continue and the MEChA club disbanded.

One might assume that the school board and community members who objected to a multicultural curriculum were White. In fact, Vaughn is a town comprised of Latinos who describe their ethnicity in different ways. Some people refer to themselves as Chicano, others as Mexican Americans, others as Spanish. Another group, the most vocal critics of Patsy and Nadine, refer to themselves as American. You can see that one's view of self, in part, determines where one stands on how the curriculum should be taught. Mexicans, who may view Spaniards and people from the United States as colonizers and oppressors, would certainly view historical events differently from people who affiliate themselves with Spain or consider themselves as simply "Americans." This second group affiliated with a "Manifest Destiny" point of view. You can see that they might be threatened by a curriculum that included people and ideas that were fighting against oppressive structures in society, such as Cesar Chavez, Dolores Huerta, and La Causa. The community was embroiled in a very important debate over who gets to choose the curriculum and methodology used to teach the New Mexico Curriculum Standards. Most state curriculum standards are broad enough that teachers can justify complex, in-depth curriculum. We have never seen a set of standards so narrow as to allow only one perspective or dictate that one text must be used in a course. Patsy and Nadine justified their selection of materials based on the New Mexico Standards. The president of the school board accused them of "making the students forget that they are Americans first"[40] and justified his objections based on the same Standards. Although the board president was a cousin of the Cordova sisters, his understanding of what it means to be an American differed significantly from that of Patsy and Nadine.

In October of 1996, Patsy and Nadine contacted the American Civil Liberties Union, which agreed to represent them in litigation based on what they considered to be a violation of the sisters' First Amendment rights. The formation and sponsorship of MEChA was almost forgotten as the case zeroed in on the curriculum being used by Nadine and Patsy. On July 7, 1997, the board voted to fire Patsy and Nadine Cordova and the sisters proceeded with litigation.

Patsy and Nadine won a court-approved settlement with the Vaughn School District in November of 1998. The agreement states that Nadine will receive $450,000, and all derogatory references to Patsy and Nadine were removed from their records. The attorney for the Vaughn school board was required to pay the sisters $70,000 in damages related to their firing. Unfortunately, the students of Vaughn ended up losing the opportunity to have two gifted teachers in their school experience. After the settlement, Patsy decided to teach in another city and Nadine went to graduate school to further her studies.

We hope that the story of Patsy and Nadine Cordova has inspired to you be a "boat rocker" in the classroom, a teacher who is not afraid to speak up and act in the best interests of the students. We have faith that excellent teachers will never be without a classroom. But we know that, as beginning teachers, what happened to the Cordova sisters may scare you a bit. We hope it makes you think about how community values affect classroom practice and about the type of community in which you would like to teach. Community values, like individual community members, play an important role in what you will and will not be able to do in the classroom and, like Patsy and Nadine, you have to be prepared to justify your actions based on sound principles of curriculum design, instructional practice, and reflective thinking. Are you willing to teach in a community whose norms and values conflict with your own? Some teachers are so desperate to get a job that they will teach anywhere, even if it means having to teach curriculum or use methodologies to which they are philosophically opposed. Are you willing to search for a community whose values match yours? How will you prepare yourself to face a parent or community member who is opposed to your choice of curriculum or your instructional strategies? Now is the time to begin to consider these questions.

Patsy and Nadine Cordova have been recognized for their willingness to stand up for what they believe in, for their commitment to teach multiple perspectives and to connect the curriculum to their students, and for their willingness to speak out. In 1998 they were awarded the Multicultural Educator award by the National Association for Multicultural Education, and in 1999 they received the National Council for the Social Studies/SIRS Academic Freedom Award. The story of Patsy and Nadine Cordova received a lot of press, including a cover story in the August–September 1997 issue of *Teacher.* You can find that story on the Web.

SUMMING UP

We think you know by now that it is not enough to simply go into your classroom, shut the door, and teach the students who sit before you. The goal of this chapter was to review and reinforce the importance of involving families and community members in your school and classroom. We discussed the impact of changing family demographics and the economy on parent participation. It is interesting to look around at a variety of schools to ascertain their philosophy of parent involvement. So many schools and districts continue the same traditional means to involve parents that were used 40 years ago! Many of them did not work then, and most of them do not work now. If teachers and administrators really want parent and community involvement, they will have to look at the research, talk to successful colleagues, and experiment with ideas that meet the needs of the population served by their school.

This chapter also addressed the notion of a "community school." It is true that the community school concept was initially implemented in low-income communities where families often lack the resources to access the services and resources provided by a community school. Today, community schools can be found in communities of all income levels because, given the economy, the fact that schools are still funded primarily through taxes, and shifting demographics that result in some community members being detached from the local schools, it is recognized that community support is essential to every school district.

Finally, we gave you a list of ideas for involving families and community members in your district, school, and classroom. Whenever you hear your colleagues complain that the parents don't care, we hope you will look around and evaluate the ways that the school staff welcomes parents into the school and involves them in meaningful ways. We also hope that you will examine the way that community members are invited to participate in the life of the school. You may find that it is up to you to take the first step to break down the stereotypes and misunderstandings that parents and teachers hold about each other.

KEY TERMS

blended families   family liaison
community school   kinship caregivers

QUESTIONS FOR REFLECTION

1. Why is it important to analyze parent involvement and develop a plan to ensure that all parents are involved in the classroom or school?
2. Define different types of parent involvement and give examples of each. Which ones do you value the most and why?
3. What strategies for parent involvement do you feel comfortable implementing now? How will you work to gain more experience listening to parents?
4. What do you know about the local communities where you would like to teach? List five things that you could do to learn more and five ways that you could become involved in the community.
5. What types of family structures are you most comfortable with, and what types do you need to learn more about? What will your first steps be in educating yourself about the possible needs and issues of students living in family situations with which you are least familiar?

ACTIVITIES

1. Conduct a community study of a community in which you would like to teach. Develop a community resource handbook that can burned onto a CD for distribution to teachers in the community.
2. Interview several different types of people with children in PreK–12 education (e.g., divorced parents, adoptive parents, gay or lesbian parents, grandparents raising grandchildren). Use the questions developed by Lin Goodwin and Sabrina Hope King in this chapter to explore what parents expect from schools and teachers. Write a reflective paper about what you learned and how you could apply it to your role as a teacher.
3. Select two districts in your state, one in a wealthy community and one in a low socioeconomic area. Find the state school report cards on the Web and compare/contrast the data provided (e.g., per pupil expenditure, average SAT scores, percentage of students going to college). Then find the web page for each city and investigate the economic resources available to the city and school district. Visit a school in each area and find out the level of parent and community involvement. What strategies have been used to involve parents and community members? What hypotheses can you suggest?
4. Look on the website of the Coalition for Community Schools and find a community school in your area. Go for a visit. Have a prepared set of questions that you would like answered based on your understanding of community schools. Report your findings to the class.
5. Investigate various community agencies in an area where you might like to teach. Develop a resource list that includes the purpose and goals of the agency, the way in which one joins, and the schedule of meetings or events.

GETTING CONNECTED

Stepfamily Association of America
650 J Street, Suite 205
Lincoln, NE 68508
http://www.stepfam.org

A nonprofit organization the provides resources, guidance, and support for families with children from previous relationships.

Center for Research on Education, Diversity, and Excellence (CREDE)
University of California
1156 High Street
Santa Cruz, CA 95064
http://www.crede.ucsc.edu

Among many other resources, CREDE provides research and recommendations for effective parent involvement in schools.

National Parent Teacher Association
330 N. Wabash Avenue,
Suite 2100
Chicago, IL 60611
http://www.pta.org

The PTA provides information and support for parents on educational policy, practice, and resource building. It also helps to establish local affiliates and encourage parental involvement in the schools.

Parents and Friends of Lesbians and Gays (PFLAG)
1726 M Street NW, Suite 400
Washington, DC 20036
http://www.pflag.org

PFLAG provides support and resources to parents and educators on a wide array of gay and lesbian issues, including those issues that relate to education.

Coalition for Community Schools
c/o Institute for Educational Leadership
1011 Connecticut Avenue NW, Suite 310
Washington, DC 20036
(202) 822-8405
http://www. communityschools.org

Provides information, tools, publications, and a wealth of resources for creating and sustaining community schools.

AARP
601 E. Street NW
Washington, DC 20049
http://www.aarp.org

AARP serves the interests of persons 50 years and older. They address issues relating to grandparents raising and supporting grandchildren.

Children of Lesbians and Gays Everywhere (COLAGE)
3543 18th Street #1
San Francisco, CA 94110
http://www.colage.org

COLAGE works to empower the children of lesbian, gay, bisexual, and transgendered parents and families.

Parents Without Partners
1650 South Dixie Highway, Suite 510
Boca Raton, FL 33432
www.parentswithoutpartners.org

PWP provides single parents and their children with support and resources to enhance personal growth, self-confidence, and sensitivity toward others.

The Fatherhood Project
www.familiesandwork.org/fatherhood

The Fatherhood Project is a national research and education project that supports men's involvement in child rearing. It provides resources, seminars, training, and practical strategies for parenting.

National Center for Fathers and Families (NCFF)
Dr. Vivian Gadsen, Director
University of Pennsylvania
3440 Market Street, Suite 450
Philadelphia, PA 19104
http://www.ncoff.gse.upenn.edu

This policy research center has as its primary goals to expand the knowledge base on father involvement, strengthen practice through discussion and collaborative activities, and contribute to policy discussions at the local, state, and federal levels.

ACORN (National)
88 3rd Avenue
Brooklyn, NY 11217
718-246-7900
http://www.acorn.org

The Association of Community Organizations for Reform Now is the largest grassroots organization of low- and moderate-income people in the United States. ACORN strives for "bottom-up" change and works on all equity issues.

ASPIRA National Office
1444 I Street NW,
Suite 800
Washington, DC 20005
(202) 835-3600
http://www.aspira.org

ASPIRA is the only national nonprofit organization devoted solely to the education and leadership development of Puerto Rican and other Latino youth. The address here is for the national office, but there are local affiliates in communities and schools and on college campuses.

SUGGESTED RESOURCES

Godwin, L. A., and S. Hope King. *Culturally Responsive Parent Involvement: Concrete Understandings and Basic Strategies.* Washington, DC: AACTE Publications, 2002. Out of print but available as a free download at http://www.aacte.org

Women's Educational Media *It's Elementary: Talking About Gay Issues in School.* Debra Chasnoff and Helen Cohen, producers. 1997. http://www.womedia.org

This video assists teacher candidates in understanding how to teach about gay and lesbian issues in the PreK–12 classroom.

Women's Educational Media. *That's a Family.* Debra Chasnoff and Helen Cohen, producers. 2000. http://www.womedia.org

This video helps elementary children (and their teachers) understand various family structures.

NOTES

1. J. Dewey, *The School and Society* (Chicago: University of Chicago Press, 1902), 3.
2. J. Fields, *Children's Living Arrangements and Characteristics: March 2002* (Washington, DC: U.S. Census Bureau, 2003).
3. American Association for Retired Persons, *Kinship Care State Facts Sheets: A Resource for Grandparents and Other Relatives Raising Children* (2004), http://research.aarp.org
4. A. Perez, K. O'Neil, and S. Gesiriech, *Demographics of Children in Foster Care* (Washington, DC: Pew Charitable Trust, 2004).
5. Pew Commission on Children in Foster Care, *Voices From the Inside* (Washington, DC: Author, 2004).
6. American Civil Liberties Union, *ACLU Fact Sheet: Overview of Lesbian and Gay Parenting, Adoption, and Foster Care* (New York: Author, April 1999).
7. North Carolina Division of Social Services, *Practice Notes for North Carolina Child Welfare Workers* 7, no. 1 (2002).
8. Barry A. Kosmin and Ariela Keysar, *Religion in a Free Market* (Ithaca, NY: Paramount Market Publishing, 2001).
9. Fields, *Children's Living Arrangements.*
10. National Institute on Out of School Time, *Fact Sheet on School-Age Children's Out-of-School Time* (Boston: Wellesley College, March 2001).
11. D. W. James and S. Jurich, *More Things to Do That Make a Difference for Youth: A*

Compendium of Evaluations of Youth Programs and Practice, vol. 2 (Washington, DC: American Youth Policy Forum, 1999).

12. Ibid., 15.

13. Ibid.

14. J. Kozol, *Rachel and Her Children* (New York: Fawcett Columbine, 1988).

15. J. Kozol, *Ordinary Resurrections: Children in the Years of Hope* (New York: Crown, 2000).

16. U.S. Census Bureau, *Statistical Abstract of the United States: 2003* (Washington, DC: Author, 2003).

17. J. Comer, *Waiting for a Miracle: Why Schools Can't Solve Our Problems—And How We Can* (New York: Putnam Penguin, 1998), 10–11.

18. J. Hodges, N. Giuliotti, and F. M. Porpotage, "Improving the Literacy Skills of Juvenile Detainees," *Juvenile Justice Bulletin* (U.S. Department of Justice, Office of Justice Programs), October 1994.

19. D. Corbett, B. Wilson, and B. Williams, *Effort and Excellence in Urban Classrooms: Expecting and Getting Success With All Students* (New York: Teachers College Press, 2002).

20. Ibid.

21. Ibid., 34.

22. J. L. Epstein, "School/Family/Community Partnerships: Caring for the Children We Share," *Phi Delta Kappan* 76 (1995): 701–712.

23. D. B. Reed and D. E. Mitchell, "The Structure of Citizen Participation: Public Decisions for Public Schools," in *Public Testimony on Public Schools,* ed. D. B. Reed and D. E. Mitchell (Berkeley, CA: McCutchan, 1975).

24. Public Agenda, *Playing Their Parts: Parents and Teachers Talk About Parental Involvement in Public Schools* (1999), cited in K. Murfitt, *Addressing the State of Parent–Teacher Relations* (22 May 2001), Washingtonpost.com

25. D. Kindlon, *Too Much of a Good Thing: Raising Children of Character in an Indulgent Age* (New York: Miramax, 2003).

26. Corbett, Wilson, and Williams, *Effort and Excellence,* 37–39.

27. L. C. Moll, C. Amanti, D. Neff, and N. Gonzalez, "Funds of Knowledge for Teaching: Using a Qualitative Approach to Connect Homes and Classrooms," *Theory Into Practice* 31, no. 2 (1992): 132–141.

28. A. L. Goodwin and S. Hope King, *Culturally Responsive Parent Involvement* (Washington, DC: AACTE, 2002).

29. Ibid., 12.

30. Coalition for Community Schools, *Making the Difference: Research and Practice in Community Schools* (Author, 2003), 2.

31. O. Heifets and M. Blank, "Community Schools: Engaging Parents and Families," *Our Children* (The National PTA Magazine) 29, no. 4 (January–February 2004).

32. Coalition for Community Schools, *What Is a Community School?* (2004), www.communityschools.org

33. Ibid.

34. Fields, *Children's Living Arrangements,* 5.

35. National Association for the Education of Young Children, *Involving Men in the Lives of Children* (Washington, DC: Author, 1999).

36. Goodwin and Hope King, *Culturally Responsive Parental Involvement,* 12

37. D. Hill, "Sisters in Arms," *Teacher,* August–September 1997, 28–34.

38. Ibid., 31.

39. Ibid.

40. Ibid.

EPILOGUE:
TEN THINGS YOU CAN DO *NOW*
TO BEGIN YOUR PROFESSIONAL JOURNEY

> *Stop your moaning and groaning and tell me what you are going to DO!*
> —Asagai to Beneatha in *A Raisin in the Sun*

We have been described by those who read our words and hear us speak as being passionate about what we do. Once, in the middle of a presentation to some high school teachers, Maureen asked if there were any questions related to what she had presented about the relationship between teacher expectations and student achievement. A White male gym teacher raised his hand and said, "You seem so passionate. Why do you do this?" Underlying this question is the one the teacher really wanted to ask: Why would a White woman care so much about the education of poor students in a community where she did not even live? The answer is the same for both of us. We care because we believe that the future of our democracy is at stake. We care because we value equity and justice. We care because we want everybody's children to be valued in society. We have our own children, grandchildren, nieces, nephews, grandnieces, and grandnephews. Our family members come in many different shades and colors. They don't all worship in the same way; they don't all learn in the same way; they don't all behave in the same way. Some can speak more than one language; some have been labeled as "gifted" and some have been referred for special education; some are males and some are females. We love them all and we want them to develop into happy, productive, active people who try, in their unique ways, to make the world a better place. We see them in each child we meet as we visit schools around the country.

Many of the teacher candidates we have in class feel somewhat overwhelmed at the end of the semester and at the end of this book. They wonder if they will ever be the type of teacher we describe in class. They know we expect them to be teachers who are able to prepare all children to participate fully in our democracy.

We want them to prepare exciting lessons that teach children to think critically and get them excited about learning more. We want to see lessons that are multicultural being used for all learners and we expect them to be able to articulate why that is important. We expect them to be aware of all the aspects of school and society that have been discussed in this text and to create caring, equitable, and just classrooms. Sometimes they come back from their field and clinical experiences and tell us that they as individuals will be powerless to make changes. They are ready to give up, to drop out of teaching, and to believe that they cannot make a difference. We think they can make a difference and we think that you can too. We do not want you to give up. In fact, we want you to ACT! That is why we wrote this book. What makes us think that things can be different? We believe it because we have seen it and we have lived it. Here are two small pieces of evidence that a committed person, working with others of like mind, can make a world of difference. Here are our stories.

MAUREEN'S STORY

I attended a large midwestern urban public high school of about 1,600 students where I began my sophomore year in 1969. As you know, this was a time of great unrest in our nation. The war in Vietnam was generating massive protests at home, the civil rights movement was reeling from the assassination of Dr. Martin Luther King, Jr., and advocates for students with special needs were making inroads in the courts. My high school was unusual in several respects. It was 14 years after *Brown v. Board of Education* and many communities were refusing to comply with or struggling with desegregation mandates. In my school, things were different. Students from all ethnic groups got along well, interracial dating was not uncommon, and interracial friendships were taken for granted. There was an African American on the school board, there were African American teachers on the faculty, and there were African American, Asian American, and Latino students in almost every club, organization, and group. These included concert choir, band, orchestra, student council, plays, and library club.

More changes were needed, though, and they came about through student activism. For example, in 1969 when I entered the high school, a dress code required females to wear skirts or dresses to school every day. Females from all ethnic groups banded together and organized a major protest. Male students and the faculty supported us as we walked between classes and removed our skirts, unrolling the legs of the pants we had hidden underneath. Most faculty refused to turn us in for punishment and the boys hid us from the watchful eyes of administrators whose job it was to catch us breaking the rules. By the fall of 1970, the entire dress code was rewritten and females were allowed to wear pants.

At the end of my sophomore year, no African American female was selected for the cheerleading squad (those selected were all White) although the sports teams were dominated by African American males. The African American students, supported by many other students, walked out in a mass protest. They demanded that the cheerleading tryouts be done again with results that reflected the ethnic makeup of the sports teams. The point was clearly made that the African American females who were trying out for cheerleading had been passed over based on race, not based on being less athletically talented than their White counterparts. The teachers who sponsored cheerleading were in full support of the protest. The try-outs were re-held and an African American was selected for the squad. When it was time for tryouts for the pom-pom squad three weeks later, there was no doubt that the team would include African Americans and Latinas.

Many areas of our school needed improvement, such as the number of African Americans and Latinos in college preparatory courses, yet in 1969 my high school was much farther ahead in its efforts to equalize the entire school experience than many school districts. Our neighborhoods were still fairly segregated but there was no busing. The student body was desegregated because our community was diverse. However, one area was woefully lacking, even at the time I graduated in 1971.

I graduated from high school before Title IX was passed in 1972. That means that when I went to school there were very few opportunities for females to play sports. The main role of female students was to cheer for the boys' teams. When I entered as a sophomore, there were no sports teams for females. By the time I graduated, we had one sport, tennis, in which females could participate. This team was formed in my senior year after several years of a club called G.A.A., or the Girls Athletic Association, an organization designed to teach females how to play sports properly. G.A.A. was formed by our female gym teachers in anticipation of allowing females to compete in interscholastic sports. These teachers were instrumental in getting females involved in sports and working to establish teams in our school. The tennis team that was formed in my senior year was the first team to play other schools in our conference. Although we won only one game, it was the beginning.

Title IX, the legislation that denied federal funds to any public school that did not provide equal opportunity for females in a variety of venues, was passed in 1972. By the time I began my teaching career in 1973, middle school girls all over my town were forming basketball teams and beginning to play against girls from other schools. This change required federal action at the highest level that was spurred on by local, state, and national activists. Because our female gym teachers were involved in this movement, they were ready to begin implementing female interscholastic sports in my high school as soon as Title IX was passed.

I learned directly from my school experience that change could happen both "top-down" and "bottom up." The key is that students, teachers, and administrators must be willing to examine school policies and practices, to speak up for what is right, and to act to rectify unfair or inequitable situations.

CARL'S STORY

I wish to share two stories, the first a very recent one. This story involves an opportunity to make a difference by holding firm to an idea and not being swayed when you know that you are doing the right thing. This story begins in 2001 when I was asked to serve as the faculty director for the first "multicultural learning community" at the University of Wisconsin–Madison. The idea was in the conceptualization stage, with the suggestion that space on one or two floors in one of the dormitories on campus be the initial site. Those in on the planning stages of the MLC thought that it might begin with approximately 60 first-year students. A steering committee was organized to discuss the idea and to work out plans for the start-up. The vision for the MLC was that it would be a space where a culturally, ethnically, linguistically diverse group of students, including students who were straight and gay, could come together to have a multicultural experience. Such an experience, it was argued, would enrich not only the students' personal lives, but the collegiate experience as well. The hope was that the impact of the MLC would remain with the students long after college and into their professional lives.

Soon detractors began voicing dissenting views. Some called the MLC a ghetto, asking, "Why should we encourage freshmen to live in a ghetto?" Imagine the underlying assumptions in that sentence! Coupled with this resistance was the fact that only a small number of students were signing up to live in the MLC. Only seven students listed the MLC as their first choice for a living space; another four students listed it as their second choice and five as their third choice. In sum, not enough incoming first-year students requested to live in the MLC and a good number of people outside of the steering committee were arguing it was a bad idea. These difficulties were compounded by arguments within the MLC steering committee where members wanted the MLC to emphasize "race."

After many meetings filled with rigorous debate, the "go" or "no go" decision was placed in my lap. As faculty director, "the buck" was to stop with me. It is certain that my plate was already filled. I was chair of a large department at the university; I held several book contracts with rapidly approaching deadlines; I was committed to write several journal articles; and I was responsible for mentoring 10 or more graduate students. In other words, did I really need to engage in one more thing, especially something that was becoming so clearly controversial?

What did I do? I said yes! The MLC was a go. I argued that the initial idea, which had come from students, was now supported by a critical mass of faculty, staff, and students. These supporters had labored for more than a year to get the MLC started and I believed that we should not be deterred after one failed attempt or by an uninformed rhetoric that termed the MLC a "ghetto." As a multicultural educator who knows that change takes time, who trusts in the idea that in a democracy we should be about the creation of multicultural learning communities, and who understands that every good idea has its detractors, I was determined to see the MLC succeed!

The MLC is now in its second year, with more than 60 students as members, including several returning students from the first year. The first year of operation ended up being very successful. I often visit, have dinner with the students, and discuss multicultural issues (as well as some others!) with them. They teach me as much as I teach them, and I have been reinforced in my belief that if given the opportunity to do something that I know is right, even in the face of adversity, I should persevere!

The second story took place during my first year of teaching during the 1960s. The 1960s was a time when civil rights movements—the fights for racial equality, gender equality, gay/lesbian equality, and equity for people with disabilities— were very active. It is important to note that at the same time, a movement to maintain the status quo, or "business as usual," was also underway. Many members of dominant groups resisted these civil rights movements and attempted to maintain traditional routines of power and privilege.

I began my teaching career with four sections of junior high science. All of my students were African American. I observed that none of the instructional materials I received included suggestions about how to relate science concepts to ideas that came out of the students' life spaces (e.g., local, community, ethnic background). None of the instructional material included illustrations or any other kind of marker (e.g., pictures of African American scientists, or any other scientists of color) that would suggest to the students that that their group had contributed to the field of science. None of the materials I was given were written in a way that suggested to students that science was a field that they might wish to pursue professionally. The civil rights ideology, which included greater academic achievement for African American students, had not influenced the beliefs of many at my school.

I brought these observations to the principal and asked if I could purchase other materials or seek other materials from the District Science Center. My principal became very patronizing. He contended that I had the skills and ability to adapt the material to the background of my students. He claimed that there was no need for me to order new textbooks or trouble the District Science Center for different materials. Perhaps because I was a new teacher, I was caught off guard by his statement. First, the principal seemed to be complimenting me by telling me that I "had the skill and ability." But more careful reflection made me see the statement for what it was worth. It was patronizing. I realized that my principal held very little regard for the present and future academic and social success of the students.

I reassessed the "problem" and realized that first I should have consulted with the other two science teachers, as one had been teaching at the school for six years and the other had been at the school for many years. I should have shared my observations and tried to get their perspective. I did this, and both found my observations insightful. Unfortunately, they were not immediately motivated to do anything. So, I became a good-natured pest. I raised the issue in a positive way whenever possible. Finally, after a good deal of ongoing discussion, they decided that they would quietly contact the District Science Center because one of my colleagues was a good friend of its director.

I know that my colleagues decided to help, in part, to shut me up but I didn't care because we received different science materials! I cannot say this material, which was much more relevant to the students' backgrounds, made a major difference in their achievement. It did enable me to make better connections to my students' life experiences and to local community residents. It gave them the opportunity to see themselves as future scientists. The most gratifying thing for me was to see my students a-buzz over reading about the contributions of African Americans to the field of science. I learned that I should never be afraid to ask for what I think is best, especially when I know that I have the students' academic well-being at heart. I also learned, though, that there are ways to go about getting what you want and maybe heading straight for the building principal wasn't the best way to begin!

In sum, opportunities to make a difference come at all different times and in all different forms; when you are the new kid on the block and when you are the wise old owl. Entering into such an engagement, becoming an agent of resistance or change, is both challenging and fulfilling, and at the end of the day significantly helpful to students who sometimes have a very small voice in the conversation.

We hope our stories point out to you in a small way that change can occur and that many changes, like those described here, occur from the "ground up" when people speak up and act out. As we hope you have learned from reading this text and discussing educational issues with your professors and colleagues, many positive changes have occurred since the inception of public schooling in the United States to make that schooling more equitable. Yet serious inequities continue to exist. You may be wondering what you, a teacher candidate, can do when you are in your teacher preparation program and in your first few years of teaching. This is a time of great vulnerability for you, and many candidates are told by practicing teachers that there is nothing that they can or should do until they get tenure. We disagree strongly. We are not blind to the realities of life in schools. We know that you have to pay attention to school culture but we are encouraged every year when we see student teachers, interns, and beginning teachers making a positive impact on their school by using their words and deeds to make changes.

CARL AND MAUREEN'S TOP TEN LIST

We want to end this text with 10 things that you can do now to put yourself on the path to becoming an excellent teacher, one who is an activist and an advocate for students and colleagues now and in the future.

1. Get experience with all types of learners and their families. We have repeated this suggestion several times throughout the text. You will need to learn to strike a balance between the importance of recognizing students as individuals regardless of race, ethnicity, gender, ability, language proficiency, social class, or sexual orientation and affirming their group affiliations as a integral part of their multiple identities. Finding this balance will help you maximize educational opportunities for all learners. We build such understandings by listening to and learning from a wide variety of students and their families. The teacher who accepts less than the best from a student who comes from a background of poverty because the student is economically disadvantaged is committing an injustice and perpetuating unequal education. That teacher might be more apt to hold that student to high expectations if the teacher understands that the parents, like all parents regardless of income level, want what is best for the child.

2. Get political. We are not necessarily suggesting that you join any specific political party, although that is one way of becoming politically astute. You could join a professional organization such as NEA, AFT, or the specialty professional organization in your area of teaching such as CEC, NAEYC, NCSS, NSTA, NCTE, or NCTM. You might join a broader educational group such as NAME, GLSEN or Rethinking Schools. There are also community-based organizations such as the NAACP, ACORN, and LULAC that welcome teacher candidates. All of these organizations will help you understand the ways in which local, state, and national issues affect education and your community. They will help you keep abreast of where your local, state, and national legislators stand on issues that are important to teaching, schools, and communities. It may take you a while to get the courage to act, but the impetus for action is an understanding of the issues from multiple perspectives and support from a peer group.

3. Take your education seriously. When you read this point, your thoughts probably went immediately to your current grade point average and your most recent exams. Of course, we want to you to take your formal studies very seriously. We have already explained why content and pedagogical knowledge, skills, and dispositions are so important. But we are speaking of education in the broadest sense of the word. We are always surprised by how few of the teacher candidates with whom we work read a reputable newspaper on a daily basis. After the United States was attacked on 9/11/01, many teacher candidates could not locate Afghanistan on a map and knew almost nothing about the Muslim religion or the Middle East. You will not be able to develop curriculum that is accurate, multicultural, and tied into students' prior knowledge if you are not well versed in your content. You will need to know how to find accurate information and develop habits of inquiry so that you can pull information from a variety of sources.

4. Become aware that you are a role model and act accordingly. Read a diversity of material, for fun and for information. Write, write, and write some more. You cannot help students write across the curriculum if you are not a writer. Regardless of your subject matter, you are a teacher of writing. Continue refining your educational philosophy and practice ways to blend theory and practice. Expect the best from yourself. We have a rule that we do not ask teacher candidates to do anything we have not done. Students must see you modeling the types of behaviors that you expect of them.

5. Become active in your community. Get involved in coaching, volunteer with senior citizens, register voters, deliver "meals on wheels" to people with AIDS, attend local school board and city council meetings, or find some other activity that helps you get to know the community and its resources. You will meet people who can serve as classroom resources, you will get to know your community and its resources, and you will come to understand that the success of a community lies in its people. Our democracy depends on our involvement and will die with complacency.

6. Volunteer in or join an organization or get involved with a group that is comprised of people who are significantly different from you. You may be thinking that this suggestion is the same as the previous one, but the goal of this

suggestion is to gain intimate knowledge of a group in which you are the minority. Being in this position should teach you to listen and to learn from others, a skill that is vital to excellent teaching. It may also help you gain a unique understanding of what it feels like to be a student who is "different" from the majority of students in some way. For example, if you join a group such as LULAC in which the majority of the people may be conversing in Spanish much of the time and you do not speak Spanish, it will be uncomfortable. But you will gain so much. You will come to appreciate how difficult it is for students who are not fluent in English to understand the teacher. You will gain an understanding of issues important to the League of United Latin American Citizens, you will see the diversity of people that come under the umbrella of "Latin American Citizens," and you will most likely be spurred on to begin to learn Spanish. It may be intimidating if you have never been the minority in a group before, but it is a learning experience like no other. As you gain comfort in the group, you will begin to feel confident in your new environment and learn to transfer that experience to the educational setting as an advocate for children and families.

7. Develop ways to "recharge your battery." There will be days when you do want to quit. You will work with colleagues who are not as committed as you. You may be tired of fighting bureaucratic rules that are not in the best interest of children or of fighting parents who may seem not to care. You may have a day or a week when it seems that you worked as hard as you can possibly work and the students did not learn what you were trying to teach. You may feel burned out. You have to have hobbies, activities, or a place to "get away" to help you relax, refocus, and remember why you love teaching.

8. Practice democratic principles. Look for opportunities in your daily life to speak up for equity and diversity. If you are in a group of people who are talking, perhaps in the college classroom, check out the group dynamics. If you notice that certain people are dominating the discussion while others get their remarks cut off or never get to speak, practice saying things such as, "Excuse me, I would like to hear what Safira had to say and she did not get to finish her thought." This type of interjection is polite but sends the message to all discussants that the power of taking the floor in a discussion should be shared. If you are in a group and someone makes a racist or homophobic remark, practice saying, "I'm sorry, I don't think I understand what you meant by that. Could you explain?" This may be uncomfortable because it places the speaker who made the remark on the spot, but it is a way to bring attention to the issue without having tempers flair. If you are part of a group that is electing officers or developing rules, you can seek to ensure that attention is paid to equity and diversity. If speaking up is new to you, it may be uncomfortable at first. You will find your voice. Start slowly— but start.

9. Learn to identify allies. Allies are like-minded and committed peers who can reinforce the notion that you are on the "right track" when others may criticize you. They provide support, perspective, and collegiality when you need it. They will provide you with an honest response to your ideas and your work, and they will expect you to do the same for them.

10. Study effective teachers. You will need to become a student of pedagogy if you are to be your best. This means that you should ask parents and administrators to recommend teachers whom you can observe when you have the time. Be sure to ask those who make recommendations to describe why they think a particular teacher is excellent. Once you get permission to observe in the classrooms of those teachers, take notes and ask questions. Use the chapters in this text as the basis for developing questions: Why did the teacher choose the room organizational pattern? How were family and community relationships developed? How does the teacher foster independence and self-discipline? Your observations, notes, and reflections will provide you with a repertoire of strategies that are underpinned by expert knowledge, and the breadth of your experience will help you solidify your own philosophy of education with ideas for practice.

SEEING YOUR STUDENTS AS THE FUTURE

Many African American researchers have studied the costs and benefits of segregated schooling for African American students. One benefit that is often discussed is that the African American teachers of African American children understood that teaching was a political act. They recognized the power they had to positively influence the children's belief in themselves, to rigorously educate them in a way that helped them achieve their dreams, and to uplift the entire race by uplifting each child. These teachers accepted the responsibility to educate all children as if each one was their biological child. This is our vision of the power inherent in becoming a teacher who is multicultural. You must see the children who sit before you, as well as those in someone else's classroom, as belonging to you because their future is inextricably tied to yours. In his 2004 address to the Democratic National Convention, then Senate candidate Barack Obama said, "If there's a child on the south side of Chicago who can't read, it matters to me, even if it's not my child. If there's a senior citizen somewhere who can't pay for their prescription and has to choose between medicine and the rent, that makes my life poorer even if it's not my grandparent. If there's an Arab-American family being rounded up without benefit of an attorney or due process, that threatens my civil liberties. It is that fundamental belief that I am my brother's keeper, I am my sister's keeper, that makes this country work."[1]

We know that you will continue in teaching because you want to make a difference. The time to begin to make that difference is now.

NOTE

1. "Transcript: Illinois Senate Candidate Barack Obama," *Washington Post,* 27 July 2004, FDCH E-Media, washingtonpost.com

Name Index

Abadal-Haqq, Ismat, 161
Addams, Jane, 454
Adler, Mortimer, 319
Albert, Linda, 112
Alexander, Kern, 391
Alexander, M. David, 391
Alexander, William, 166, 274
Amiot, Mary A., 419
Andrade, Ana Maria, 181
Apple, Michael, 153, 154, 157
Aquinas, Saint Thomas, 319
Aristotle, 24, 310, 317, 333
Armento, Beverly, 56
Aronowitz, S., 146, 158
Augustine, Saint, 317

Bacon, Francis, 315, 334
Bagley, William C., 322
Baldwin, James, 336
Banks, James A., 12, 326
Barton, James, 198
Beauvoir, Simone de, 326
Bell, Andrew, 175
Bent, Richard, 192
Bestor, Arthur, 322
Biklen, D., 6
Brameld, Theodore, 324
Brimley, Vern, Jr., 421
Bruner, Jerome, 156
Bryan, William Jennings, 149
Buddha, 313, 317, 333
Burrup, Percy E., 421
Bush, George H. W., 26, 153, 157, 185,
    344, 345–346, 353, 419
Bush, George W., 63, 89, 153, 256, 287,
    347, 419
Butler, Judith, 318, 324–325, 327

Campbell, Ronald, 361
Canter, Lee, 110, 111, 112–114
Canter, Marlene, 110, 111, 112–114
Carby, H., 326
Carey, Janice, 159, 160
Carter, Jimmy, 256, 345, 348, 421

Chasnoff, Debra, 18
Cherryholmes, Cleo, 22–23, 328
Chester, David T., 213
Chimerine, C. B., 190
Christian, Donna, 265–266
Clandinin, J. D., 64
Clark, David, 419
Clinton, Bill, 26, 153, 185, 344,
    346–347, 353
Cohen, Helen, 18
Collins, Angelo, 198
Collins, Catherine, 5–6
Collins, Marva, 27–28
Collopy, Rachel, 182
Coloroso, Barbara, 111
Comer, James, 449–450
Confucius, 311, 317
Connelly, M., 64
Corbett, D., 450–452
Cordova, Nadine, 464–466
Cordova, Patsy, 464–466
Corwin, Miles, 80
Counts, George S., 318, 322, 324,
    335
Cremin, Lawrence A., 156–157
Crockett, Davy, 189
Cronbach, L. J., 153
Cuban, Larry, 202
Cubberly, Ellwood, 104
Curwin, Richard, 111

Darrow, Clarence, 149
DeGrasse, Leland, 435
Delpit, Lisa, 58, 272
Demiashkevich, Michael, 322
Densmore, Kathleen, 38–40
Descartes, René, 314
Dewey, John, 38, 62, 66, 77–78,
    107–108, 115, 183, 241, 317, 322,
    323, 335, 443
Diggins, John Patrick, 150
Dodd, Anne, 180
Doyle, Arthur Conan, 308
Du Bois, W. E. B., 317, 325

Emerson, Ralph Waldo, 319
Emilia, Reggio, 271–272
Enrique de la Pena, José, 189
Epstein, Joyce, 451

Faltz, C. J., 261
Feistritzer, C. Emily, 213
Finkelstein, Barbara, 176
Foster, Sherian, 196
Foucault, Michel, 22, 318, 328
Franklin, Benjamin, 104, 144, 274,
    315, 334, 336
Frantz, Douglas, 5–6
Freire, Paulo, 318, 325–326
Froebel, Friedrich, 270
Frost, Robert, 177
Fuller, Sarah Margaret, 325

Gadsen, Vivian, 469
Galileo, 27, 328
Gandhi, Mohandas K., 313
Garfield, Rulon R., 421
Gay, Geneva, 56, 178
Gilligan, Carol, 69
Ginott, Haim, 111
Ginsberg, M. B., 179, 180
Giroux, Henry A., 146, 158, 326
Glassner, William, 111
Gluck, Carol, 150
Goodlad, John, 152
Goodwin, A. Lin, 453
Gordon, Beverly, 326
Gordon, Thomas, 111
Grant, Carl A., 32, 178, 326
Graue, Claire, 191
Green, Theresa, 182
Greene, Maxine, 318
Grossman, P. L., 72

Haberman, Martin, 57, 60–61, 77, 121
Hakim, Delia, 181
Hamilton, Alexander, 315, 351
He, M. F., 64
Henry, Jules, 145, 146, 158

Subject Index